THE IMPACT OF THE GLOBAL FINANCIAL CRISIS ON EMERGING FINANCIAL MARKETS

CONTEMPORARY STUDIES IN ECONOMIC AND FINANCIAL ANALYSIS

Series Editors: Robert J. Thornton and J. Richard Aronson

Recent Volumes:

Volume 83: Foreign Direct Investment in the United States, Edited by W. L. Casey

Volume 84: Colombia: An Opening Economy? Edited by C. M. Callahan and F. R. Gunter

Volume 85: The Irish Economy in Transition: Success, Problems and Prospects, Edited by J. R. Aronson, V. Munley and R. J. Thornton

Volume 86: Asia Pacific Financial Markets in Comparative Perspective: Issues and Implications for the 21st Century, Edited by Jonathan A. Batten and Thomas A. Fetherston

Volume 87: Developments in Litigation Economics, Edited by P. A. Gaughan and R. J. Thornton

Volume 88: European Responses to Globalization: Resistance, Adaptation and Alternatives, Edited by Janet Laible and Henri J. Barkey

Volume 89: Globalization: Perspectives from Central and Eastern Europe, Edited by Katalin E. Fabian

Volume 90: Privatization in Transition Economies: The Ongoing Story, Edited by Ira W. Lieberman and Daniel J. Kopf

Volume 91: Personal Injury and Wrongful Death Damages Calculations: Transatlantic Dialogue, Edited by John O. Ward and Robert J. Thornton

Volume 92: Moving Beyond Storytelling: Emerging Research in Microfinance, Edited by Todd A. Watkins and Karen Hicks

CONTEMPORARY STUDIES IN ECONOMIC AND FINANCIAL ANALYSIS VOLUME 93

THE IMPACT OF THE GLOBAL FINANCIAL CRISIS ON EMERGING FINANCIAL MARKETS

EDITED BY

JONATHAN A. BATTEN

Hong Kong University of Science & Technology, Hong Kong

PETER G. SZILAGYI

University of Cambridge, United Kingdom

Emerald

United Kingdom – North America – Japan
India – Malaysia – China

Emerald Group Publishing Limited
Howard House, Wagon Lane, Bingley BD16 1WA, UK

First edition 2011

Reprints and permission service
Contact: booksandseries@emeraldinsight.com

British Library Cataloguing in Publication Data
A catalogue record for this book is available from the British Library

ISBN: 978-0-85724-753-7
ISSN: 1569-3759 (Series)

CONTENTS

PART II: POLICY IMPLICATIONS OF THE FINANCIAL CRISIS FOR EMERGING MARKETS

PART III: REGIONAL STUDIES

LIST OF CONTRIBUTORS

Ilan Alon	The China Center at Rollins College, Rollins College, Winter Park, FL, USA
John Ammer	Division of International Finance, Board of Governors of the Federal Reserve System, Washington, DC, USA
Jonathan A. Batten	Department of Finance, Hong Kong University of Science and Technology, N.T., Hong Kong
Renaud Beaupain	IESEG School of Management, Lille Catholic University, Lille, France
Paul Bennett	Rutgers Business School, Rutgers University, Newark, NJ, USA
Jenny Berrill	Business School, Trinity College, Dublin, Ireland
Josep García Blandón	Facultat d'Economia IQS, Universitat Ramon Llull, Barcelona, Spain
Irina Bunda	Singapore Regional Training Institute, IMF, Singapore
Fang Cai	Division of International Finance, Board of Governors of the Federal Reserve System, Washington, DC, USA
Csaba Csavas	Magyar Nemzeti Bank (Central Bank of Hungary), Budapest, Hungary
Kevin Daly	College of Business, University of Western Sydney, NSW, Australia
Ali M. El-Agraa	Faculty of Commerce, Fukuoka University, Fukuoka, Japan

Craig Ellis	College of Business and Law, University of Western Sydney, NSW, Australia
Oral Erdogan	Department of International Finance, Istanbul Bilgi University, Istanbul, Turkey
Szilard Erhart	Magyar Nemzeti Bank (Central Bank of Hungary), Budapest, Hungary
Luiz Paulo Lopes Fávero	School of Economics, Business Administration and Accountancy, University of São Paulo, SP, Brazil
Xiaobing Feng	Shangai Institute of Foreign Trade, Shanghai Songjiang University Town, Shanghai, China
Renée Fry	Centre for Applied Macroeconomic Analysis, Research School of Economics, Australian National University, Canberra, Australia
Sergey Gelman	International College of Economics and Finance, Higher School of Economics, Moscow, Russia
Aleksandr V. Gevorkyan	New York University and Capco, New York, NY, USA
Carlo Gola	Bank of Italy, Specialized Intermediaries Supervision Department; Risk Analysis and Financial Innovation Division, Roma, Italy
Martín Grandes	Centro de Investigaciones Aplicadas, School of Business, Pontifical Catholic University of Argentina, Buenos Aires, Argentina
Ki C. Han	School of Management, Suffolk University, Boston, MA, USA
Colm Kearney	Business School and Institute for International Integration Studies, Trinity College, Dublin, Ireland

Subir Lall	International Monetary Fund, Washington, DC, USA
Sukhun Lee	School of Business Administration, Loyola University Chicago, Chicago, IL, USA
Faysal Mansouri	Institut des Hautes Etudes Commerciales de Sousse, Sousse, Tunisia
Marie Marticou	IESEG School of Management, Lille Catholic University, Lille, France
Lei Meng	ESEG School of Management, Lille Catholic University, Lille, France
Khaled Mokni	Institut Supérieur de Gestion de Sousse, Sousse, Tunisia
Anna Naszodi	Magyar Nemzeti Bank (Central Bank of Hungary), Budapest, Hungary
Marcel Peter	Swiss National Bank, Zurich, Switzerland
Nicolas Pinaud	OECD Development Centre, Paris
Klara Pinter	Magyar Nemzeti Bank (Central Bank of Hungary), Budapest, Hungary
Olga Saldakeeva	VTB Capital, Moscow, Russia
Chiara Scotti	Division of International Finance, Board of Governors of the Federal Reserve System, Washington, DC, USA
Willi Semmler	The New School, New York, NY, USA
Sunil Sharma	Singapore Regional Training Institute, IMF, Singapore
Samer Shousha	Department of Economics, Columbia University, NY, USA
Douglas Sikorski	Laguna Beach, CA, USA
Galina Smirnova	Sberbank, Moscow, Russia

Elvira Sojli	Finance Group, Rotterdam School of Management, Erasmus University, Rotterdam, The Netherlands
Fernando Barreira Sotelino	School of International and Public Affairs, Columbia University, NY, USA
Francesco Spadafora	Bank of Italy, Rome, Italy and International Monetary Fund, Washington, DC, USA
David Y. Suk	College of Business Administration, Rider University, Lawrenceville, NJ, USA
Maike Sundmacher	College of Business and Law, University of Western Sydney, NSW, Australia
Peter G. Szilagyi	Judge Business School, University of Cambridge, Cambridge, UK
Chanikarn Teresa Tosompark	Assumption University, Bangkok, Thailand
Gyorgy Varga	FCE Consulting, Praia do Flamengo, Rio de Janeiro, Brazil
Dimitrios I. Vortelinos	Department of Economics, School of Management and Economics, University of Peloponnese, Greece
Maxim Wengert	Quantumfundos, Rio de Janeiro, Brazil

PART I
AN OVERVIEW OF THE FINANCIAL CRISIS AND ITS IMPACT ON EMERGING MARKETS

THE IMPACT OF THE GLOBAL FINANCIAL CRISIS ON EMERGING FINANCIAL MARKETS: AN INTRODUCTION

Jonathan A. Batten and Peter G. Szilagyi

ABSTRACT

Emerging financial markets have largely proven resilient to the consequences of the Global Financial Crisis. While this owes much to the bitter experience and economic strategies developed and implemented following the Asian Financial Crisis of 1997–1998, providence also played a hand in that relatively few of its financial institutions were exposed to the complex structured products that underpinned the demise of many financial intermediaries in the United States and Europe. The objective of this volume is to investigate and assess the impact and response to the crisis in emerging markets from a number of perspectives. These include asset pricing, contagion, financial intermediation, market structure and regulation. Our hope is that the assembled chapters offer clear insights into the complex financial arrangements that now link emerging and developed financial markets in the current economic environment. The volume spans four dimensions: first, a series of background studies offer explanations of the causes and impacts of the crisis on emerging markets

The Impact of the Global Financial Crisis on Emerging Financial Markets
Contemporary Studies in Economic and Financial Analysis, Volume 93, 3–16

ISSN: 1569-3759/doi:10.1108/S1569-3759(2011)0000093003

more generally; then, implications are considered. The third and final sections provide insights from regional and country-specific perspectives.

Keywords: Banking reform; credit crisis; financial crisis; economic crisis; financial regulatory reform; emerging economies; 1997 Asian Crisis.

JEL Classifications: E44; E65; F3; G01.

PART I: AN OVERVIEW OF THE FINANCIAL CRISIS AND ITS IMPACT ON EMERGING MARKETS

The ongoing trend of financial market deregulation, undertaken in earnest over the past 20–30 years and facilitated by technological innovation, has enabled the development of a complex, financial market architecture, comprising interconnected but increasingly disintermediated domestic financial systems, many at different stages of economic development. In this setting, global corporations and increasingly global financial intermediaries – many of these now from emerging markets – trade a host of financial products and services and reallocate capital worldwide.

As the new century unfolds, we witness further integration of both developed and emerging financial markets. One critical lesson from the recent Global Financial Crisis is how connected all of these markets have become, and as a consequence how difficult it is now to diversify the risks that arise in both the national and international context. In fact, there is now almost instantaneous price adjustment and volatility transmission across a host of asset classes and markets, irrespective of location, or degree of integration with the more dominant financial markets of the major economies.

In an environment where the world economy continues to suffer the consequences of the Global Financial Crisis, the role of emerging markets has reached unprecedented importance. While much attention has focused on the better growth prospects of these nations, the continued build-up of their foreign reserves, and the form and method chosen for their allocation – especially those from the Asia-Pacific region[1] – the situation is more complex and anomalous than it would first seem. For example, many emerging nations domiciled in some of the poorest regions of the world, including Africa, the Middle East and South America, are now capital exporters to the developed world, not only in the traditional form of portfolio investment, but increasingly as Foreign Direct Investment (FDI). The latter brings with it a host of geopolitical issues and concerns. Nonetheless, one thing is now clear: the economic and financial landscape of this century will be shaped not just by the saving and consumption patterns of countries in the developed world but also by the manner and direction of allocation of the wealth that has now been accumulated in many emerging nations. These flows, given their scale and scope, now appear unstoppable.

Many questions arise as a consequence of these developments. First, how well do we understand the phenomenon and role that emerging markets now play in broader financial markets, especially developments over the past decade? Overall, it appears that emerging market finance remains little understood in the academic literature, which as it now stands is dominated by studies and analyses of the institutional structure and features of the major developed economies, especially those in the United States. Second, what new insights can be gleaned from the application of the standard models of finance and economics to the often limited and difficult data sourced from emerging nations? Or, third, can researchers develop new models to accommodate the new and often unique institutional features of the financial markets that are present?

The primary objective of this volume is to add to this exciting and relatively limited literature investigating those financial markets and economic systems present in emerging markets. The focus is on the investigation of the impact and response to the crisis in emerging markets from a number of perspectives including asset pricing, financial intermediation, contagion, market microstructure and regulation. Our hope is that the assembled chapters will offer clear insights into the complex financial arrangements that link emerging and developed financial markets in the current post-crisis environment. The volume spans four dimensions: first, a series of background studies offer explanations of the causes and impacts of the crisis on emerging markets more generally; then, implications are considered. The third and final sections provide insights from regional and country-specific perspectives. These will be discussed in turn.

The first part of the volume provides a general overview of the Global Financial Crisis and its impact on emerging markets. There are four chapters in this section with the first chapter by Douglas Sikorski providing a detailed discussion of causes and events that led to the crisis and the evolving solutions that followed including the worldwide Keynesian style stimulus, the subsequent and unprecedented bailout of non-bank financial intermediaries, followed by efforts in the United States to assist homeowners and the car industry. He then considers the global regulatory response and proposals to improve the risk governance of the financial sector. The fact that the regulatory response evolved in response to a changing political agenda – especially in the United States – and now is at best a patchwork of reforms, mostly with indefinite outcomes is clearly established. Finally, two important questions are considered: first, what lessons arise from this crisis for markets and economies, including the critical issue of compensation in financial institutions; and second and perhaps most important, what are the immediate fiscal and monetary issues that must be resolved going forward.

The next chapter by Ali M. El-Agraa focuses on the international nature of the causes of the global financial crisis, especially the build-up of external surpluses, and emphasizes the role of capital adequacy as a longer term solution. This chapter follows on from the future role of fiscal and monetary policy considered by Sikorski and asks what measures should be undertaken to insure against the recurrence of another crisis? While it is acknowledged 'financial crises' are inherent to an economic system, it should be possible to mitigate potential consequences. His discussion ends with a number of recommendations including: the need for the financial community to add intuition when applying sophisticated mathematical tools for evaluating its risky investments; strict rules must be applied to ensure that the banking community has sufficient capital to sustain it during the bad times and this requires further reform of the Basle Capital Adequacy Guidelines; capital pro-cyclicality must be catered for and counter-cyclicality promoted; and finally, improvement is required in the international regime for the control of cross-border financial activities.

The third chapter is by Irina Bunda, Subir Lall and Sunil Sharma and provides a detailed analysis of the impact of the global financial crisis on the emerging and newly industrialized countries of Asia. This region is of particular interest given the strong economic recovery that has been experienced since 2007. Their analysis of the movement of capital in financial markets and economic activity shows that the degree of openness of a country to trade and finance and the degree of integration into international financial markets are important determinants of the swings in economic activity and capital flows during both the reversal and recovery phases of the crisis. Their study highlights those factors that determine which Asian countries were most affected by the deleveraging and the flight to quality in the recent crisis and also explains why capital inflows and economic growth resumed fairly rapidly.

The fourth and final chapter in this section by Willi Semmler and Aleksandr V. Gevorkyan extends the analysis of Bunda, Lall and Sharma by focusing on the blend of fiscal-monetary rules, nominal targets and debt dynamics policies that contributed to the rapid recovery of emerging markets. Their investigation of the role these policies played in the Commonwealth of Independent States (CIS) provides an alternate perspective to those experiences of emerging nations based in the Asia pacific region, which formed the basis for analysis in earlier chapters. Their chapter proposes three possible post-crisis scenarios, each with a unique solution for reserves, exchange rate, sustainable debt and output levels. Their theoretical framework of the monetary control problem accounts for changes in reserves and the effects on foreign currency denominated debt. Categorizing between net exporters and net importers based on a countries' external position enables group-specific results to be derived. While both of these groups are shown to be susceptible to exchange rate risk affected by a multitude of shocks due to their fragility of the local financial system, net importers risk high inflation, but net exporters risk over-borrowing. Their chapter offers a number of conclusions, although the critical role played by a combined fiscal and monetary policy in the development process and regulation of crisis-prone foreign currency denominated transactions cannot be underestimated.

PART II: POLICY IMPLICATIONS OF THE FINANCIAL CRISIS FOR EMERGING MARKETS

The second part of the volume comprises four chapters that focus on the implications of recent events for emerging markets. The section begins with the expansive chapter by Ki C. Han, Sukhun Lee and David Y. Suk that investigates the bargaining game that may arise as part of the restructuring of commercial bank debt owed by emerging nations. While their empirical analysis focuses on the experience of commercial bank debt restructurings from 1980 to 1989, the potential debt restructuring of European bank exposures to Greece, Italy and Spain is also discussed in light of their empirical findings.

It is well established in the international finance literature that default of sovereign debt is common when issued in the form of bonds (examples include Russia in 1998 and Argentina in 2001). However, sovereign bank debt, typically syndicated, is rarely defaulted: nations would rather renegotiate their debt service obligations. One important reason why there is a willingness by both borrowers' and creditors' to restructure is to preserve international trade ties. The authors' question whether the benefit associated with maintaining international trade ties is shared equally between the borrower and creditor banks or is the outcome dependent on a so-called bargaining game between the borrower and creditor banks? Their analysis suggests that as a borrower's trade ties with developed countries strengthen, the borrower's (and/or creditor's) bargaining power diminishes (strengthens), which may result in restructuring at less favourable terms. Nonetheless, despite variation in the type and extent of the trade ties, major borrowers are able to extract more concessions from the lenders.

The next chapter by John Ammer, Fang Cai and Chiara Scotti considers the important question of the extent that international financial co-movement has changed as a consequence of the global financial crisis. Recall that much of the capital flows from developed markets to emerging markets in the lead up to the current crisis were driven by investors chasing the higher yields on offer in emerging market stock and bond markets, and the prospect of the risk diversification available from holding these assets in an international portfolio. These flows occurred despite the historic vulnerability of emerging markets to external shocks as witnessed in the Asian Crisis of 1997–1998.

In the Ammer, Cai and Scotti chapter, the authors examine the links between the stock and the bond markets present in both emerging and developed countries over the past two decades, with a focus on how these relationships played out during the global financial crisis of 2007–2009. They find that the long-term trend is for both emerging and developed markets to move in the same direction and that this co-movement has persisted. However, consistent with an increase in the degree of global market integration, emerging market sensitivity to external shocks and emerging market-specific volatility appears to have decreased over time. This is also consistent with improved fundamental stability of emerging market economies and likely reflects their reduced vulnerability to external shocks in general. This is consistent with considerable improvements in the underlying fundamentals of emerging market economies over the decade preceding the onset of the global financial crisis.

The third chapter by Carlo Gola and Francesco Spadafora examines the process by which the international monetary fund (IMF) has increasingly deepened its involvement in financial sector surveillance (FSS). It is noteworthy that emerging market and developing economies constitute the majority of the IMF's 186 members, and currently receive over 50 programs of financial support totaling over $150 billion. The authors note that the FSS process began in the 1980s and early 1990s where it was mainly directed to the research and technical assistance activities related to monetary and financial deregulation being undertaken by several member countries at that time. The background to these activities was the rapid pace of financial market deregulation that was occurring worldwide aided by improvements in information and communication technology and the simultaneous efforts by the Bank for International Settlements (BIS) to introduce a uniform capital adequacy framework.

Gola and Spadafora note that the first 'official' phase of the Fund's involvement in FSS started in the aftermath of the Mexican crisis, and the perceived need to include financial sector issues among the core areas of Fund surveillance. The second phase focused on recent attempts to integrate financial analysis into the Fund's analytical macroeconomic framework, which may signal the beginning of a new phase of FSS. The authors argue that the IMF's FSS is of paramount importance for both emerging market and developing countries, since they are vulnerable to the spill-over effects from crises originated in advanced economies.

The final work in this section is by Ali M. El-Agraa, who asks the question of what can East and Northeast Asia learn from the European Union (EU)? The context of his chapter lies in empirical work that highlights the development of an Asian economic and currency bloc, integrated with China and Japan. The author begins by drawing attention to ongoing efforts by former Japanese Prime Minister Yukio Hatoyama to promote an East Asian Community (EAC), an initiative especially relevant given the economic significance of the Asia-Pacific region and its role in assisting the global economy emerge from the recent financial crisis. He specifically focuses on what the EAC can learn from the experience of the EU and argues that the current best option is for a 'preferential trade and investment arrangement', between China, together with Hong Kong and Taiwan, Japan, both the Koreas and the United States, although 'this is a hope which reality suggests is beyond reach'.

PART III: REGIONAL STUDIES

The third part of the volume provides a number of studies that take international or regional perspectives. This part begins with the chapter by Berrill and Kearney that investigates the impact of the global financial crisis on those multinational corporations (MNCs) based in emerging markets. The background to their analysis is the contribution that MNCs make to international economic and financial systems and the relative neglect of research on the behaviour, operations and performance of developing and emerging market MNCs.

Berrill and Kearney begin by categorising firms from every country in the world according to their degree of multinationality and then investigate a group of the world's largest firms, the Global Fortune 500 (henceforth GF500). The authors show that the number of GF500 firms from emerging markets has increased significantly over the past decade and that the international financial crisis of 2007–2010 has further enhanced this trend. Importantly, a comparison of these firms based on their relative risk-adjusted performance shows that although the GF500 firms from developed markets tended to be more multinational, those from emerging markets outperformed the former over the past decade – both before and after the recent international financial crisis.

The next chapter by Csaba Csavas, Szilard Erhart, Anna Naszodi and Klara Pinter, investigates the changes to central bank transparency in Central and Eastern Europe during the financial crisis. The argument in favour of central bank transparency is well known: improved transparency should reduce the uncertainty surrounding future monetary policy decisions and thereby help agents make better investment and saving decisions. Their chapter analyses the degree of transparency of central banks in Central and Eastern Europe and the changes that arose during recent periods of financial stress. The findings show that during the recent financial crisis central banks became less transparent, and this resulted in greater variation in the degree of disagreement by professional forecasters of the future short-term and long-term interest rates.

The chapter by Josep García Blandón investigates several well-known calendar anomalies: day of the week, turn of the month, turn of the year and holiday periods in four of the most important stock markets in Latin America: Argentina, Brazil, Mexico and Chile. His results indicate that these markets generally display these calendar anomalies: a day of the week effect is reported for all the stock markets but the Mexican; the turn of the year effect is observed only in Argentina; and moderate holiday and turn of the month effects are reported in the Brazilian and the Mexican markets, respectively. The authors' results also demonstrate that the effect of the global financial crisis on the various calendar anomalies has been limited.

Emerging stock markets are also investigated by Khaled Mokni and Faysal Mansouri, who focus on how long memory in volatility affected market risk estimation during the recent global financial crisis period. The authors apply short (GJR-GARCH) and long (FIAPARCH) memory volatility models to compute in-sample and out-of-sample one-day-ahead VaR. They investigate the returns of six emerging stock markets – Hang

Seng Index (HSI) of Hong Kong, IPC of Mexico, Jakarta Composite (JKSE) of Indonesia, KLSE of Malaysia, Seoul Composite (KS11) of Korea and Strait Times (STI) of Singapore – and show that by taking into account the long memory property enables more accurate VaR estimation and prediction. Thus conservative risk managers may adopt these long memory models to better assess emerging market risks.

The next chapter by Craig Ellis and Maike Sundmacher extends the long memory theme by investigating long-term dependence and return distributions in seven emerging Asian stock markets during the Asian Crisis (1997–1998) and recent global financial crisis periods: China (Shanghai A 30); India (S&P CNX 500); Indonesia (Jakarta SE Composite); Korea (KOSPI); Sri Lanka (Colombo SE All); Taiwan (Taiwan SE Weighted); Thailand (Bangkok S.E.T.). The authors begin by considering the extent that the return series display the properties of normality and independence and then determine the extent that these statistical properties changed during the crisis period. Importantly, the authors demonstrate positive evidence of non-periodic cycles, which confirms the non-Gaussian and non-independent nature of emerging Asian stock market returns. These results question the applicability of standardized models of financial asset pricing and risk analysis to those in emerging markets.

Luiz Paulo Lopes Fávero and Fernando Barreira Sotelino continue the theme of studies investigating stock market returns in emerging markets by investigating the elasticity of stock prices using a panel data approach. Their extensive sample includes 5,167 stocks of companies from 38 emerging countries. The benefit of using panel models is that they allow the testing of the relationship between some performance variable (like the evolution of stock prices) and some predictive variables. Such an approach allows the determination of the influences of temporal and regional differences on price evolution. Their results highlight the impact that stock quantity and total volume traded per month influences closing price behaviour over time, with more efficient estimators for the fixed effect model, and the variations that exist among countries.

The next chapter in this section, by Elvira Sojlia and Renee Fry, compares the impact of the global financial crisis on Russia and Turkey. The authors begin by discussing the hypothesis that the level of economic development of a country may exacerbate the impact of contagion during times of crises, thereby providing a motivation for emerging markets to develop quickly. In their chapter, they examine the impact of the Russian and Turkish crises across several South Eastern European exchange rate markets of differing levels of development, thereby clarifying the relative importance of contagion in currency markets compared to common and own shocks. Contagion is defined as the unanticipated transmission of a shock across national currency markets during a crisis period and is a critical issue given potential enlargement of the European Monetary Union and the adoption of inflation targeting frameworks. Their results demonstrate that Albania has relatively isolated financial markets compared to others in the sample and was not affected by contagion, while Croatia was most affected.

The final chapter in this section by Galina Smirnova, Olga Saldakeeva and Sergey Gelman investigates how the global financial crisis has affected the autocorrelation structure of the BRIC's (Brazil, Russia, India and China) stock markets. Short-term autocorrelation – both negative and positive – is a well-known feature of the returns of many stock markets and offers the potential for economic profit-taking using trend following trading systems. The literature in this area suggests that during periods of increased volatility, feedback traders change trading strategies and become 'trend-chasers', thereby providing an explanation for the observed changes in the autocorrelation structure of returns. The objective of their chapter is to use the global financial crisis as a natural experiment to first test the impact of the financial crises on the markets of other emerging countries and then endogenously estimate the changing points (i.e., time periods with different autocorrelation), to allow for other factors to cause autocorrelation shifts.

Smirnova, Saldakeeva and Gelman identify structural breaks in the parameters of an ARMA-GARCH-model with the standard endogenous search procedure. Their results yield no statistically significant evidence of changes in the autocorrelation structure due to the effects of crisis. The key exception was India where the decline in autocorrelation in 1998 seems to be economically relevant, but was not significant statistically. Of importance for regulators was the fact that significant shifts appear related to microstructural changes, such as abolishment of price change limits by China and the removal of a leading player in India's market in 1992. In conclusion the authors suggest that even though extreme negative events on financial markets may induce changes in feedback trading strategies, their influence on autocorrelation is clear, thereby highlighting the importance of regulatory factors in improving the market dynamics

PART IV: EMERGING MARKET COUNTRY STUDIES

The final part of the volume provides evidence of the effect of the Global Financial Crisis on specific countries. There are eight chapters in this section and begins with Samer Shousa's investigation of the term structure of interest rates in Brazil. The main contribution of Shousa's chapter is establishing whether macro variables help explain the dynamics of the yield curve in an emerging economy. The novelty lies in the inclusion of a number of external sector variables to understand their impact on interest rates in the small open economy of Brazil. The period chosen for investigation is from September 1999 to July 2008, which allows for consolidation of the inflation targeting regime.

Shousa finds that macro variables help explain the dynamics of the yield curve in emerging markets, specifically in periods of high volatility. The macro variables investigated include the output gap, inflation and the change in the nominal exchange rate change, which collectively explain up to 53% of the forecast errors. The extent that emerging markets are vulnerable to external shocks is confirmed by the strong role of the nominal exchange rate change, which explains up to 37% of the variation in yields in Brazil. However, the model does a poor job in forecasting yields during the financial crisis of 2008. The author argues that this was likely due to decline in international commodity and industrial goods prices (in dollar terms) during the crisis period, which limited the pass through from the strong depreciation of the exchange rate to inflation.

The second chapter in this section, by Gyorgy Varga and Maxim Wengert, maps out the impact of the crisis on the Brazilian mutual fund industry. Brazil in recent times has been subject to significant flows of inbound capital, which has put pressure on the exchange rate. This study focuses on the evolution of the Brazilian investment fund industry, the impact of domestic and international crises on investors, managers and the main types of funds offered in Brazil. Varga and Wengert explore the effect of the subprime crisis and show that the first wave of this crisis had very little impact, but the second wave which began with the collapse of Lehman Brothers had a greater impact on risk, returns and flows of the mutual fund industry in Brazil. They attribute this finding to the more far reaching impact of the second phase of the crisis on international market liquidity.

The third chapter in this section by Xiaobing Feng and Ilan Alon discusses the exchange rate regime in China. This topic is of particular relevance in the post-crisis period given the structural imbalance between China and the United States. The Chinese currency the renminbi (RMB), was effectively pegged to the US Dollar from 1997 to 2005, when the government switched from a dollar-fixed regime to a managed floating regime that referenced a basket of currencies. However, the authors note that although China has claimed that it will move towards a more market-oriented system of managing its foreign exchange, it has remained in part a managed economic system.

The key innovation in their chapter is the examination of the RMB exchange rate relationships from a number of perspectives including both linear and nonlinear artificial intelligence models. These latter models capture non-linearity in the system but unlike linear models are unable to measure the magnitude of the contribution of each variable in the system. Importantly, the authors find that the emphasis on the US dollar as a reference currency has declined, while the genetic programming approach is among the best performing in minimizing forecasting error. Overall, the authors argue that China is gradually moving its currency system from the single dollar peg and moving towards a basket peg, which is, in fact, a much more flexible regime.

The next chapter by Renaud Beaupain, Lei Meng and Marie Marticou is also a China based study, although their focus is on stock market investment and long-term commonality in three low-frequency liquidity estimators in the Shanghai Stock Exchange (SSE). The SSE market has one unique institutional feature compared with stock markets from developed economies: the trading volume is dominated by individual investors rather than institutional investors. The long-term behaviour of commonality in liquidity is estimated using principal component analyses and panel regressions. The findings provide strong evidence of liquidity co-movement on the SSE from its inception until the present day, although the degree of commonality is time varying. The authors conclude that their results inform asset pricing in the face of potential systematic liquidity risk while also providing insights to regulators regarding the liquidity implications of the participation of a large number of individual investors.

The chapter by Dimitrios I. Vortelinos investigates the properties of realized correlation in intraday data from the Greek stock market. Four realized correlation estimators are considered: (i) the simple realized correlation estimator, (ii) the simple realized covariance divided by the square roots of the realized bipower variations of the two assets, (iii) the simple realized covariance divided by the square roots of the realized Parkinson estimators of the two assets and (iv) the realized optimal correlation estimator, with modelling undertaken for the presence of correlation jumps. The correlations are between the three main indices of the Athens Stock Exchange (ASE), with the estimators used to test normality, long-memory, asymmetries and jumps. The heterogeneity in realized correlations is shown to be highly significant with meaningful coefficients for all correlations and realized correlation estimators. Overall the results reveal the lack of normality and the presence of long-memory, asymmetries and jumps in realized correlations.

Martín Grandes, Marcel Peter and Nicolas Pinaud investigate the pricing of the currency premium under the flexible exchange rate regime of South Africa, a market with highly liquid spot and forward markets. Interest rate parity establishes the exchange rate difference between the spot and forward exchange rates as representing the interest rate differential between the local and foreign interest rate. The total interest rate differential can in turn be decomposed into the currency premium, the credit spread and the jurisdiction premium. When the borrower in question is the government itself, the credit spread is often called sovereign spread and reflects mostly sovereign risk. The sum of the sovereign spread and the jurisdiction premium is often called the country premium or simply country risk.

The Grandes, Peter and Pinaud investigation of the South African rand–U.S. dollar currency premium uses monthly data over the period 1997–2008. Their findings show that the currency premia are largely driven by long-run movements in the expected inflation differential between South Africa and the United States, risk aversion as a proxy for the price of rand exchange risk and the volatility of the rand exchange rate as an indicator of the quantity of that risk. Therefore their results confirm the important role played by monetary policy in determining the currency premium and, hence, the level of domestic interest rates in South Africa. Thus monetary policy oriented towards producing low inflation and stable exchange rates should significantly reduce the currency premium component of domestic interest rates.

The penultimate chapter by Kevin Daly and Chanikarn Teresa Tosompark analyses the determinants of FDI inflows to Thailand. The authors note that before the 1997 Asian Financial Crisis, Thailand had the fastest growing level of FDI inflows among the Asian economies and was the least affected during the current crisis. Their empirical investigation of the determinants of Thailand's FDI reveals that FDI has a positive relationship with real wages and a negative relationship with imports. The remaining variables over the sample period were not statistically significant.

The final chapter in the volume is the study by Paul Bennett and Oral Erdogan who compare the financial robustness of the United States and Turkey during the crisis period 2007–2010. Their comparison is undertaken to demonstrate how a more conservative and supervised, but supported, banking system can be an advantage during a crisis period. Turkey's experience is impressive: although Turkey's real economy was affected like many other emerging economies during the global financial crisis, the Turkish banking system withstood the stress better than its experience of their 2000–2002 banking and currency crisis. Importantly, no major Turkish banks failed in 2007–2010.

Similar to emerging economies in the Asia-Pacific region after the Asian Crisis, Turkey implemented reforms after 2002 to strengthen its banking system, improve government finances and reduce inflation through inflation targeting. Turkish banks were conservative and limited credit risk and were not dependent on short-term money markets for funding their asset portfolios. These experiences offer a simple but effective road-map that many other emerging nations could observe as they undertake reform of their financial markets to maintain the pace of economic development.

NOTE

1. As noted by International Monetary Fund (2010), 'Asia is set to become the largest economic region in the world over the next two decades. According to IMF forecasts, by 2030, Asian gross domestic product (GDP) could exceed that of the Group of Seven (G-7) major industrial economies'. The contributions made by Korea, China, India and Singapore to support the IMF's lending capacity is also noteworthy, especially given its timing- these commitments followed the US$100 billion extended by Japan. The Central Bank of India later also purchased 200 metric tons of gold from the IMF.

REFERENCE

International Monetary Fund. (2010). Asia and the IMF. *International Monetary Fund Factsheet*, July 9, pp. 1–3.

THE GLOBAL FINANCIAL CRISIS: EXPLANATIONS AND IMPLICATIONS

Douglas Sikorski

ABSTRACT

This chapter analyses the causes and effects of the financial crisis that commenced in 2008, and it examines the dramatic government rescues and reforms. The outcomes of this, the most severe collapse to befall the United States and the global economy for three-quarters of a century, are still unfolding. Banks, homeowners and industries stood to benefit from government intervention, particularly the huge infusion of taxpayer funds, but their future is uncertain. Instead of extending vital credit, banks simply kept the capital to cover other firm needs (including bonuses for executives). Industry in the prevailing slack economy was not actively seeking investment opportunities and credit expansion. The property and job markets languished behind securities market recovery. It all has been disheartening and scary – rage against those in charge fuelled gloom and cynicism. Immense private debt was a precursor, but public debt is the legacy we must resolve in the future.

Keywords: Credit crisis; financial crisis; economic crisis; toxic assets; stimulus; bailout; financial regulatory reform; emerging economies; 1997 Asian Crisis.

The Impact of the Global Financial Crisis on Emerging Financial Markets
Contemporary Studies in Economic and Financial Analysis, Volume 93, 17–90

ISSN: 1569-3759/doi:10.1108/S1569-3759(2011)0000093004

JEL Codes: E44; E65; G01.

1. INITIAL CAUSES AND EFFECTS OF FINANCIAL TURMOIL

In early autumn 2008, credit markets froze on Wall Street.[1] Following on to the credit crunch was a crisis in confidence – that ephemeral commodity that is everything in financial markets. A wider financial crisis rapidly escalated, just as the June–July 1997 currency crisis had escalated in Asia, exacerbated by governmental paralysis. Politicians in America dithered, then took several iterations to come up with a plan, but still the damage accumulated faster than governments could come up with fixes. The contagion evolved into a global crisis initially reflected in a number of European bank failures, emerging economies' currency declines and crashes in stock indices worldwide.

As *The Economist* magazine put it, the panic choked the arteries of credit and we faced the danger of a global heart attack. Financial firms get preferential treatment to be rescued by governments because they constitute these arteries, extending vital credit to each other and the larger economy. (A major controversy was that bank executives and investors became primary beneficiaries of the bailout.) Banks used government-provided liquidity to strengthen their capital positions and were reluctant to make loans despite government guarantees. Well into 2009, 'the arteries of credit' remained blocked.[2]

The Wall Street model had been a financial machine of globally mobile capital and highly leveraged, lightly regulated players with high-tech market instruments and instantaneous transactions, which displaced the 'traditional banking' model from about the 1980s. Its hallmark was securitization: the pooling and repackaging of debt assets by lenders into bond-like instruments, with differing risk tiers and other features, and these sophisticated securities were then marketed globally. With the lender's balance sheet thus unburdened, the lender can lend again, with the original risk increasingly untraceable. The unregulated hedge funds,[3] with 30% of equity trades, added to the credit volume and market activity. Derivative products aided by computer[4] applications created a dazzling array of instruments, which led to a complex and opaque derivative market with a volume in 2007 surpassing global output by 11 times. Few financial institutions could calculate their own credit risk and fully comprehend the nature of their own assets and financing now. Such was the case of the world's largest insurance company AIG (American International Group) with its mind-boggling array of financial ploys including synthetic 'collateralized debt obligations' (CDOs), 'finite insurance' policies and 'special purpose entities' to hold underperforming assets; all contributed to the crash of AIG. (See note[5] on the AIG case.)

Perhaps the most prominent example, the CDS (credit default swap) was one financial innovation that served ostensibly as insurance and freed up capital that would otherwise be tied up as collateral for loans. Arguably, the swaps market creates liquidity and mitigation of risk; but neither buyers nor sellers completely understood the new risks they were creating, and much of the private deal-making was cloaked in secrecy and beyond the scrutiny of regulators. (See note[6] for how a CDS deal works.)

Basically, the panic froze credit because no financial institution knew how much bad debt was out there and owed by/to whom. Credit and asset inflation had grown to many multiples of the basic underlying, say, mortgage, as loans were securitized, repackaged and resold at discount again and again, including pyramids of derivative instruments. In the aftermath of the panic, credit was so totally withdrawn that even viable business could not get a loan. The real risk became a great depression where economies approach ground zero and many venerable business institutions disappear.

Asset markets collapsed: Household net worth fell by $11 trillion in 2008. Total household debt fell in the 4th quarter of 2008 for the first time since World War II. De-leveraging the hedge funds and others in the 'shadow banking system' was most traumatic, as withdrawal of credit forced a massive offloading of assets. Restrictions to stem the meltdown eliminated some arbitrage activities (especially short selling), and hedge funds further wound down their long positions. Many American investment banks, that quintessential Wall Street animal that relied on high leverage and wholesale (interbank) funding, disappeared; and those institutions that survived reverted to normal, conservative commercial banking. (The two survivors, Morgan Stanley and Goldman Sachs, became bank holding companies in September 2008, increasing their dependence on retail depositors that had suddenly become more stable than wholesale funding.[7])

LIBOR, a rate that represents what banks pay to borrow from each other, hit record highs; but when the rates subsided after massive interventions by central banks, still loans were not made. Money market funds also declined to take commercial paper from corporations for their working capital. The Federal Reserve created major new commercial paper programmes to facilitate purchase of mutual fund assets and short-term notes from companies, but with only limited success in freeing up these markets.

One measure of the GDP (gross domestic product) is defined as equal to money supply (MS) x(times) velocity which is its turnover. (Irving Fisher's 'quantity theory of money' held this equal to the price level times economic output.) Velocity approached zero in the crisis, so GDP was falling whatever the money supply. This is the 'liquidity trap', where the Federal Reserve increases MS (buying T-bills or other securities such as T-bonds, Fannie Mae securities, corporate or state bonds), but there is no growth. Thus, monetary policy fails. The government then pursues its alternative option, fiscal policy – spending money and/or reducing taxes – where net government outlays increase velocity of the liquidity. (The 'right wing' argues for tax cuts instead of spending, but taxpayers can save the money – not spend it – which is especially likely in a bad economy.)

In such an economic climate, how do we get bankers to lend, businesses to invest and consumers to spend? Potential returns, no matter how high, are perceived as too risky, despite almost zero cost of capital.[8]

2. EVOLVING SOLUTIONS

The solutions to the crisis in America have been varied, often complex, and continually evolving. Of course, there are implicit questions of equity: Who should get priority in any rescue attempt by government – Wall Street? Lenders, or alternatively borrowers? Homeowners facing foreclosure? States and municipalities needing to fund essential services? Or the American businesses suffering the knock-on effect of the original credit crisis – not to mention the subsequent economic crisis – that now threatened their previously viable enterprises?

There is certainly considerable doubt that government bailouts should be provided at all. If free-market initiatives were to be relied upon to resolve the crisis, would private bailouts occur without too much damage incurred as investors await the 'right market opportunity'? Do government bailouts tend to be misdirected or ineffectual? The amounts of taxpayer money committed – with questionable impact – were immense. Although conventional economists generally agree that governments should help its citizens contend with a market collapse, there is considerable disagreement on how and to what extent.

2.1. Rescuing the Economy: Keynesian Stimulus

The Obama administration's fiscal stimulus plan, despite the political wrangling, should be less controversial in principle than bailouts because deficit finance is a standard anti-recessionary tool for governments. As established by John Maynard Keynes, public expenditure counters recession by offsetting declining private outlays, and the economic downturn is thus abated. It is a case of government intervention in response to market failure. (However, fiscal policy may be less effective if credit markets remain frozen.)

The devil is in the details.[9] Partisan debate raged around particular expenditure items ('pork', long delays in actual cash outlays or misguided projects – 'building a bridge to nowhere'). Of course, it is quite unreasonable to expect stimulus money to be appropriated, allocated and finally spent in a way that precisely matches needs of the economy[10] – especially given the American political imbroglio.

The size of the fiscal package was a serious bone of contention because it dramatically escalated the already acute budget deficit, but it seemed to necessarily be immense because of the severity of the economic decline. The amount signed into law by the president on 17th February 2009 was $789 billion – $507 billion in spending and $282 billion tax relief.[11]

Cutting tax is the alternative to fiscal spending, favoured by those who distrust government designs and prefer to put the money directly into the hands of consumers and businesses. However, tax rebates may be saved – especially likely in such a bad economy. Taiwan and China issued coupons[12] to poor people for Chinese New Year shopping, instead of tax cuts, which guaranteed most of the amount would actually be spent; but the US Congress took no action in 2008, awaiting the first steps of the new administration.

Fiscal expenditure is amplified by a multiplier effect to the extent the cash infusion is spent again by whatever contractor or other recipient gets the money, and the process continues as long as the cash is recycled. Estimates were that the multiplier effect of the Obama stimulus would be 1.57 for the fiscal expenditure but only 0.99 for the tax cut (*Los Angeles Times*, 17th January 2009, p. C3). Tax cuts would increase the MS much sooner than government projects implemented after the tax rebates paid in 2009, but the multiplier effect only works for what the taxpayer actually spends – temporary tax cuts are less likely to be calculated into budgetary expenditure plans of recipients.

The official stated purpose for the stimulus was threefold: new investment to put citizens to work, increase productivity with improved industries and infrastructure, and create confidence in the economy. Confidence was eventually restored, as reflected in strong stock market performance, the Dow index breaking 10,000 during October 2009. The recession was officially declared ended when the economy expanded by over 3% in the 3rd quarter of 2009.[13] However, by 2010, there was considerable doubt that stimulus bills had provided value added in terms of quality infrastructure and industrial development.

By late 2010, the greatest criticism of stimulus expenditures was that the outlays had accumulated to a multi-trillion-dollar fund transfer from taxpayers that was not perceived as doing the job. Politically, it had become increasingly difficult to justify any more fiscal spending, whereas the Federal Reserve had no such political constraints for its alternative to fiscal policy: monetary policy. Short-term rates were held at near-zero but without sufficient impact on credit creation. Long-term rates emerged as the major policy focus, whereby the Fed buys long-term bonds with newly created money.

This so-called 'quantitative easing' of the Fed[14] contributed a much larger infusion of cash, going to even further extremes to stimulate demand than the grandest dreams of the Obama administration. Arguably, the loose monetary policy had potentially more dramatic knock-on effects than the fiscal deficits, since monetary policy was less direct and depended on the market response of the financial community to put the cash infusions to work.

Quantitative easing could result in economic growth by spurring borrowing and investment, boosting the value of market investments as well as other asset values and making the currency less appealing due to its low real interest return. The latter effect had the most controversial international impact. The first channel for economic growth did not open effectively because investment was not forthcoming – neither in property nor in industry. The primary assets to appreciate were in the securities markets rather than the 'real economy'. Ultimately, of course, 'printing' more money creates more federal debt, which might be unsustainable in the long term. A strongly negative market reaction could lead to a severe decline of the dollar and even to another global financial panic.

The greatest disappointment as it turned out was lagging job creation. The White House claimed that it created or saved one million jobs by the 3rd quarter of 2009, based on compiled reports from recipients of $160 billion of the stimulus money. The reports showed employers created or saved 640,000 jobs, rising to one million from indirect benefits as when a recipient of stimulus funds spends the money, and on track to reach 3.5 million jobs in 2010. However, the figures were very controversial. Certainly, 'saved' jobs were not clearly measurable, that is, whether stimulus money legitimately saved a job about to be eliminated. Also, jobs were being lost much faster than they were saved or created, as job losses in one month alone often exceeded the touted 640,000 figure. The unemployment rate climbed relentlessly, exceeding 10% by October 2009.

If the new investment by government leads to further nationalization of industry or otherwise an enlarged management role for government, then the stimulus becomes something new; it goes beyond the traditional fiscal policy – rather like the 'bailout'.

2.2. Rescuing Financial Institutions: The Bailout

2.2.1. The Government's Evolving Rescue Strategy

The major bailout fund coming from the Treasury was the $700-billion Troubled Asset Relief Program (TARP), proposed on 19th September 2008 and passed by Congress on 3rd October. (This early instance of political delays was costly in terms of the spreading contagion and market volatility caused by uncertainty, but such 'political risk' was of course encountered for every plan that had to pass Congressional scrutiny.)

Half the funds were released in 2008, the largest component being $250 billion channelled to selected banks to encourage them to lend. Stronger banks were selected, to shore up their balance sheets and instil confidence in the national financial system for the purpose of thawing the credit freeze. By year end, 209 banks had received $162 billion.

The Obama administration renamed TARP the Financial Stability Plan. Including the huge infusions from the Federal Reserve for a combination of loans to banks and incentives for private capital participation to rescue the financial system, by autumn 2009, new commitments made the bailout effectively over $2.5 trillion. Total government expenditure including the stimulus and omnibus bills, and other costs, was estimated to reach potentially as much as $11 trillion (BBC, 6th March 2009).[15]

The Federal Reserve designed dozens of new programmes to facilitate credit markets, most inconceivable before the crisis. In November 2008, the Fed bought $600 billion in mortgage-related securities, with $850 billion more in March 2009, to push down interest rates. Numerous individually tailored programmes were introduced – for example, the Fed's secured lending services for AIG and for buyers of securities backed by consumer loans. Thus, the Fed had created incentives to over-borrow reminiscent of the excessive lending that begot the crisis in the first place. (As economic conditions improved, the Fed scaled back the plethora of programmes it had initiated when the financial crisis began to emerge in late 2007.[16] Unwinding the emergency liquidity facilities would become the priority, to remove government props to the economy. The Fed announced on 16th

December 2009 that it would end 'most' emergency programmes early in 2010.)

The Fed's one-year, $1.25-trillion programme to prop up the housing market by purchasing mortgages (ended 31st March 2010) made it the world's largest single holder of mortgages. Going forward, if private institutions did not step in to pick up the slack, mortgage rates could move up dramatically. It could be challenging for the Fed to perform its main job of managing interest rates. Also, major defaults would hurt the Fed's balance sheet.

The Fed's easy-money policy could not be sustained indefinitely. Interest rates began going back up in the spring of 2009, despite continued intervention by the Fed in long-term bond markets. As the supply of the Fed bonds kept ballooning to fund deficit spending and melt the frozen debt markets, potential inflation was a concern. Purchasers of treasuries were balking at the low coupons at new bond auctions, which forced yields up. Nevertheless, the Fed was determined to keep interest rates at 'exceptionally low levels ... for an extended period'. The Fed bought mortgage-backed securities in an effort to keep home loan rates down; and in March 2009, the Fed committed to buying $300 billion in its own treasury securities over six months, hoping to restrain bond yields.[17] Still, bond yields were expected eventually to rise, presuming at least modest economic recovery.

2.2.2. Strategies for Dispensing TARP Funds

Initially, TARP funds were contemplated to be used for direct purchases of non-performing assets (mostly mortgage related); but valuation was problematic, not to mention the question of which debtors to rescue. Instead, the favoured bailout tactic employed (announced ex post facto by Treasury Secretary Paulson) was to provide capital directly to financial institutions.

Banks can generally expect to get paid back on their loans, presuming borrowers want to be creditworthy. This idea has always been a bulwark of financial systems; and it became the *modus operandi* of TARP that taxpayers would save the lenders rather than the borrowers. This central principle may come into question if municipalities, homeowners and businesses (not to mention entire countries, as in Europe) come to reasonably expect creditors to share the costs of financial ruin. However, any widespread debt write-off would be severely deflationary.[18]

TARP funds were provided in the form of preferred non-voting stock. It was contemplated that more capital would enhance credit creation on the basis of capital adequacy – presumably going further than the government taking over bad debts. Preferred stock offered the government and taxpayers more security than common equity, but it did not significantly boost the banks' lending. Unlike with common stock, preferred dividends (and interest on debt) accumulate and to breach payment would risk default. Therefore, long-term capacity to absorb losses was unchanged. Conceivably, preferred stock can be required to bear losses along with common stock, but taxpayers are unlikely to tolerate high exposure to losses especially with limited scope for gains.

To allow taxpayers to share in potential improvement in the banks' prospects, banks receiving TARP funds were required to supply warrants to allow the government to buy stock at an amount, price and deadline set by contract. If TARP funds were repaid, the banks could make an offer to buy back the warrants. A problem that emerged later was determination of the price for the warrants. Public auctions were one possibility, but most warrants were not publicly traded.

The preferred stock can carry interest coupons to compensate taxpayers as well as other provisions such as veto power over management deals. Convertible features could allow conversion to common stock at an agreed price, thus increasing both the risk and the reward to the investor and providing the bank more 'tier 1' capital to be used for new loans or for paying off bad debts. The government investment was designed to be relatively short term and also put some political pressure on firms to perform according to expectations. However, few reporting and other oversight requirements were stipulated (which caused strong criticism of the initial TARP commitments), and the funds were not utilized for loans as the government had hoped.

New lending awaited a better market. A vicious cycle had emerged of more bank losses, reluctant private investors and new bank appeals for federal help. The stock price of banks in the TARP scheme continued to decline, reflecting investor uncertainty about the future of banks still carrying bad debts in their accounts. Also, investors might not buy stock if their interests could potentially be pushed aside by government stockholders.

2.2.3. Strategies for Ridding the Banks of 'Toxic Assets'

As the Obama administration took over, the design of rescue policies remained in flux due to the great complexities in the policy options and their impacts. One idea was a federal entity similar to the Resolution Trust Corporation,[19] which had disposed of assets of failed savings and loan banks two decades earlier. However, pricing the debts purchased ran the risk of either hurting the banks by pricing too low or hurting taxpayers by pricing too high, which had deterred the government from this approach originally. Government can pay more for the bad assets because its cost of capital is less relevant than for private investors, and it can hold the assets until maturity; but private investment was preferred.

Another tactic was to take an immediate write-off against market value of 'toxic assets' and put them into a 'bad bank', giving a clean break for the remaining 'good bank'. Co-investment by private investors (especially the banks themselves) can be stipulated. Private equity provides profit incentive to get the price right, plus to negotiate workouts with debtors. Government guarantees and insurance can cover the healthy assets that remain plus future loans. This keeps the assets in the hands of experienced bank managers instead of the government; yet the government may not be able to compel credit expansion by private institutions. Forced lending anyway was seen by the government as undesirable, and it instead only required the banks to submit plans explaining how they intended to improve lending.

Government had a great responsibility to get the price right, which held true for purchasing either bad debts or equity. The Congressional Oversight Panel for the TARP bailout released an estimate on 5th February 2009 that the Treasury Department had paid $78 billion too much for its investment in stock and other bank assets. The panel also estimated the value of assets initially transferred from AIG to the government at only $14.8 billion, but AIG received $40 billion for them. In July 2009, the panel reported that 11 smaller banks had repurchased their warrants held by the government for a total payment of $18.7 billion, but the panel estimated that the warrants were worth $28.2 billion.

In the event, Timothy Geithner's Treasury chose a hybrid approach to bailouts, announcing on 23rd March 2009 a public–private partnership to back purchases of 'toxic assets' by private investors. Various federal agencies would provide very cheap loans or other resources to buy up as much as $1 trillion in bad debts.

The stock market responded with apparent approval at this stage with a major uptick, but critics raised many objections not least of which were doubts that $1 trillion was enough – bad debts were still soaring, estimated at $2 trillion by July 2009. Congress was not in the mood to provide more funds, so the Treasury had to continue to tap TARP.

Implicitly, the government was relying on the money managers and insurers to become active investors in a bad market and start borrowing again just when they had been cutting back on leverage. Also, the government was depending on the banks to accept the current, very low market price to get rid of their 'toxic assets'. Under accrual accounting, banks were booking losses over several years and were unwilling to take a larger loss all at once and thus reduce their capital dramatically.[20] Also, banks that had already written down their debts hoped to recover some of their losses – possibly enhancing their chances to get out from under TARP obligations.[21]

Through a complicated formula, taxpayers were committed to cover most of the losses but only get half the profits. Geithner regarded this as a necessary price to pay to remove the bad debts from banks' balance sheets, as the Resolution Trust Corporation had resolved the savings and loan crisis decades earlier. Political objections to giving hedge funds and other speculators a taxpayer-subsidized opportunity to profit from delinquent mortgages and other loans – by modifying terms, or selling them to debt collectors, etc. – were negated by the common sense that the banks were not handling the problem themselves. Reworking a defaulting or delinquent mortgage is a labour-intensive process, not always well managed by bank officers with a large file of loan contracts.

One motivation to encourage the banks to sell their toxic assets was the 'stress tests' commencing on 25th February 2009. The Treasury audited the 19 largest banks to judge potential insolvency in mock scenarios, with a 'worse case' given as a two-year recession with rising unemployment[22] and declining house prices. The banks needed to demonstrate capital adequacy, determined by rather indefinite means to measure the worth of bank assets and the quality of capital. Any bank that was seen as needing more capital would be given six months to raise it from private sources but, if unsuccessful, would be proffered more bailout funds (preferred, dividend-paying stock). Thus, the banks would be compelled to fix values on toxic assets, both to satisfy regulators and also presumably satisfy potential buyers of these assets,[23] as well as justify potential new capital infusions from the government.

Stress tests took several weeks, and the whole drawn-out process allowed market players to anticipate results – not enhancing awareness but rather creating uncertainty.[24] One fear was that the government would compel banks to accept only emergency capital to stay afloat but not restore financial health enough to encourage robust lending to resume. Furthermore, there were doubts that TARP funds were available in sufficient quantity.

The Obama administration needed a strategy to communicate the results of the stress tests. The timing of any announcement and the extent of detail could destabilize markets. Market players eagerly sought this information and were prone to seize on any uncertainty. The market could anticipate which institutions got high marks as the banks either tried to raise capital or reported no need for additional capital. The government planned to reveal all results simultaneously; the banks were told not to disclose their performance on the tests during upcoming earnings announcements. If one banker bragged about receiving high marks, other banks could be punished by investors for keeping quiet. Unless all banks were dealt with at once, compelling one bank deemed insolvent to accept more capital could start a market sell-off of many others. Uncertainty about such hesitant steps was costly and a self-fulfilling prophecy towards more bailouts for the financial sector. Borrowing costs were rising as bondholders anticipated they would be affected by government-compelled restructuring, which further pushed stock prices down and credit costs up and exacerbated the need for more government bailouts. (This was also true for the auto industry – see later. Auto purchases were deferred or going to foreign brands while consumers awaited 'final' deliberations by the Obama administration on the rescue of the US auto companies.)

The Treasury declined to endorse the idea of separating assets between two institutions, 'bad' and 'good' banks. Instead of a 'bad bank', there would be the 'public–private partnership' to take over the toxic assets. How this is not nationalization is indeed subtle: Despite the massive government financing, private investors would be doing the whole exercise, with easy credit and co-investment by the government.

The British approach, to leave the assets with the banks and insure them for a fee, was also eschewed. The Treasury did that for Citigroup[25] but did not adopt the idea for the banking system as a whole.

The issue was to determine the best way to rid the financial system of the 'toxic assets'. Taxpayers provide 'patient' capital because the government is able to wait until maturity of any assets acquired to hopefully collect maximum interest plus principal. Private investors should be better at finding the right price for bad debts, will have incentive to chase after debtors or rework contractual terms to achieve the best market value of the asset, and sell the worst assets to 'vulture investors'.

Although the government denied takeover intentions, it seemed to some pundits that 'creeping nationalization' of insolvent banks was in the cards, either as the outcome of the 'stress tests' or even by stealth – by surprise takeover, say, over a long weekend and forcing a restructuring exercise. However, probably it would be illegal for the government to takeover banks without agreed compensation. It would take a new law, and that seemed a daunting legislative challenge in the short term. (A 'resolution authority' to takeover failing institutions was enacted into law on 21st July 2010.)

The bad assets for the most part were destined to remain with the banks even after they began paying back bailout funds to the government. Most banks elected to work out their own weak balance sheets by conservatively building up capital through stock issues and converting preferred stock into common stock. The market for 'toxic assets' improved after March 2009, enhancing banks' ability to raise capital again.

In the end, the Treasury downsized its programme to buy toxic mortgage-backed securities. It was finally launched on 8th July 2009 with the naming of nine investment companies to purchase the assets. Fund managers would raise up to $10 billion and tap up to $30 billion from the government. The original plan, called the Legacy Loan Program, also called for federal debt guarantees to attract investors into directly buying assets from banks. However, the initiative never became more than a pilot project under the Federal Deposit Insurance Corporation (FDIC).

The TARP programme formally ended on 3rd October 2010, with mixed reviews of its success. Of the total $700 billion authorized by Congress, only $475 billion was used ($205 billion for banks). Thus, $225 billion was never paid out, a considerably smaller bailout than anticipated. Of the $475 billion, $290 billion was paid back with interest, leaving $185 billion still owed. Despite early concerns that much of the bailout would never be recovered, the Congressional Budget Office projected a final loss of only $66 billion.

The programme had little success settling toxic assets and therefore had not helped the mortgage market and housing values. The $75-billion mortgage modification programme under TARP had not stemmed foreclosures. Certainly, under TARP, taxpayer money transferred to Wall Street had not rescued 'Main Street' – the most glaring failure. Also, using TARP for purposes beyond the bank bailout, including funding the bankruptcy plans for the Big 3 auto firms, was technically illegal because the law stipulated any repayments be used to pay down the federal debt.

2.2.4. The Issue of Nationalization

Outright nationalization of troubled banks is the most controversial alternative. The government restructures the bank, revaluing its assets and sorting any loss between investors and taxpayers. Valuation is still a problem but the government is on both sides of the deal. The government can influence lending policies, but with the real danger of non-market failure – all the politicization and bureaucratization this entails. Another ideological difficulty is the timeframe: When the takeover will be reversed.

Nationalization would work in several steps:

1. Determine which banks are not going to survive without restructuring.
2. Take them over, simultaneously suspending market trading.

3. Restructure the balance sheet to cordon off non-performing assets and devise a means to liquidate them. Now unencumbered, the bank would be sold on the market or to a strategic buyer, hopefully fit to lend and otherwise function normally.

Presuming a takeover is with compensation to stockholders and bondholders, the difference between what the government pays and what it gets for the liquidation of assets will be net loss or gain to taxpayers. The government does not have the authority to take over private property like banks without compensation, so there would have to be a valuation process to put a price on the assets. This process takes time, and it is not precise.

Bondholders generally would have priority in liquidation before the government's preferred stock. If bondholders were forced to share the losses incurred by stockholders, they may need incentive in terms of sharing potential gain by debt-for-equity swaps. One difficulty in this arrangement is that many bondholders are foreign governments which then become owners of banks, perhaps unacceptable to American politicians.

Nationalization has a major advantage: breaking up the largest finance houses, which had become 'too big to fail'. With the financial sector thus restructured in future, markets and bankruptcy courts could be left to sort out insolvent institutions instead of there being a need for a government rescue to save the overall economy.

Opponents called the whole rescue scheme 'socialism'; indeed, the government role in the economy was greatly enlarged, at least for the moment. Such large investments as have been made in the private sector would take some time to divest and return a profit to taxpayers. Nevertheless, Britain used the same formula for its earlier bank bailout (announced 8th October 2008), and the British staunchly avoided repeating their mistake of the nationalized industries in the post-war era when the government took over the 'commanding heights' of the economy. The purpose of governments' investments was limited this time to the rescue effort. However, the political debate only intensified over any government role in the private sector. It would seem that leaders on all sides should agree: It was time to put dogma and politics aside and concentrate on pragmatic solutions.

There was also a need to support consumer financing and other evolving issues,[26] which became part of the financial reform law (see later). Perhaps the fundamental quandary for policymakers was how to mitigate mortgage foreclosures, which we now address.

2.3. Rescuing Homeowners

2.3.1. Origins of the Mortgage Crisis

The current crisis has roots in the 'sub-prime mortgage crisis'. Some bloggers (e.g. *Muth's Truths*, 29-9-08) attribute the origins of the sub-prime mortgage market to President Carter's 1977 Community Reinvestment Act and President Clinton's National Homeownership Strategy initiated in 1994.[27] These policies encouraged measures to make home financing more accessible to the poor – what the 1977 Act referred to as 'communities of color'. The Department of Housing and Urban Development (HUD) complied with this political imperative and compelled Fannie Mae and Freddie Mac[28] to purchase such 'affordable loans'. As late as 2006, this allowed Fannie and Freddie to classify 'billions of dollars they invested in sub-prime loans as a public good that would foster affordable housing' (*Washington Post*, June 10, 2008).

Fannie and Freddie had repurchased about 40% of all US mortgages – a figure that rose significantly after takeover of 80% ownership by the federal government in September 2008. Until the government conservatorship in 2008, Fannie and Freddie were owned by private shareholders but chartered by Congress. They are effectively subsidized because implicit government backing means they can borrow more cheaply than other investors. In return, they are expected to serve public purposes including the policies to make home buying more affordable. These institutions were also motivated to maximize private shareholder wealth by participating in the new opportunities that emerged in recent decades.

Fannie and Freddie effectively were recipients of a federal bailout, like Wall Street banks, through their takeover (not funded through TARP) and thus were part of the debate about their own institutional failings and even misbehaviours. For 2009 and 2010, their chief executives were set to earn as much as $6 million, which provoked public outrage given the perceived blame of these institutions for the lax mortgage standards that led to the housing boom and subsequent financial crisis.

Compensation packages in the financial community were supported not by turning down imprudent business but by seeing how much business could be done. This epitomized the 'moral hazard' of government interference in the mortgage market. Given federal guarantees, it would seem that bankers had turned a blind eye to credit risk, and all the while Fannie and Freddie operated under the theoretical assumption that bankers would exercise prudence. As long as house prices continued to climb upward, it was a boondoggle for borrowers as well as lenders including Fannie and Freddie.

As the share of Americans who owned homes rose, the value of homes also rose, and loans thus became even less affordable to the poor. The sub-prime crisis emerged in this environment, along with securitization of existing loans and creating new ones. The housing boom exposed deficiencies in the underwriting and credit-rating practices by banks and investment houses, which underpriced risk and allowed excessive leverage, and was compounded by the creation and proliferation of complex and opaque financial products. Financiers failed to adjust to the shakier asset portfolios caused by lending to borrowers with weak credit histories. Boosted also by credit card debt, low inflation, Asian financing of the perennial current account deficit, all this contributed to a seemingly unending expansion of financing for American profligacy.

A ban on sub-prime mortgages might seem appropriate but that is simply one category. 'Alt-A' mortgages emerged in the space between prime and sub-prime categories, with features such as negative amortization where borrowers pay less than the accrued interest and add the difference to the balance due.

The Congressional Budget Office estimated in March 2009 that the total cost to taxpayers of the takeover of the agencies would accumulate to $389 billion.[29] As Fannie and Freddie's operating losses mounted, the Obama administration in December 2009 lifted a $400-billion federal commitment through 2012, to support Fannie and Freddie's role in the vast majority of all new residential mortgages. During the crisis and through 2010 at least, the two companies almost single-handedly kept housing finance operating since private investors had fled the market.

2.3.2. Incipient Reform Measures[30]

During March 2009, the US Federal Reserve and Treasury began disclosing some 'architecture' for a new housing finance system. The government had pledged more than $1.5 trillion to keep the mortgage market working but removing the risk from Fannie and Freddie. Fannie Mae and Freddie Mac already held over half of the $10-trillion US mortgage market and, with private investors sidelined by the crisis, were now issuing or guaranteeing nine out of ten new residential mortgages. Although Fannie and Freddie had raised their fees and tightened underwriting criteria, mortgages originated in 2006 and 2007 accounted for two-thirds of ongoing credit losses. The cost of any liquidation of damages would be high.

Options for policymakers to overhaul housing finance might include maintaining the existing hybrid public–private model, consolidating Fannie and Freddie into a single government agency, or else they might be completely broken up and a separate system of rules established to leave mortgage financing completely to private banks. New rules will evolve gradually, in fits and starts, striving to have successful funding and securitization of mortgages but without posing systemic risks to financial markets and the economy. Some federal role seems inevitable to facilitate and back up the mortgage market, but pricing of loan guarantees must be designed to recoup potential losses.

By August 2009, the concept of a 'good bank, bad bank' structure was being mooted, with the good bank attracting private investment in support of mortgage financing and the bad bank trying to settle past due 'toxic' loans. Among other policy measures on-the-table to promote loan refinancing were short-term moratoriums on foreclosures, tax credits for home purchases, allowing bankruptcy judges to order banks to reduce principal (in cases where foreclosure would yield less than loan modification), using TARP funds to pay down second mortgages that may be hindering a workout on the first mortgage, various schemes for mortgage refinancing and other ideas. (See note[31] for details of the programme for federally sponsored mortgage refinancing.)

Reducing principal on mortgages by judges – 'cramdowns' – was already allowed for commercial property and second/vacation homes. In a bankruptcy proceeding, the mortgage would be split into two: a secured claim equal to the current appraised value of the property and another claim for the remainder of the full loan amount. The borrower would pay on the secured portion, but the incremental claim for the additional unpaid balance would be treated like any unsecured debt. Lenders would in effect receive payment on the amount they should receive on a foreclosure, that is, the market value of the loan collateral. Cramdowns had been adopted for agricultural loans when farming incomes declined precipitously in the early 1980s – Chapter 12 of the Bankruptcy Code was established by Congress to keep farmers from losing their homes.

Lenders dislike being at the mercy of a judge who may be more sympathetic with a troubled borrower than a rich bank. Bankers also argued that allowing cramdowns on home mortgages would cause financing costs to go up to compensate for the risk of bankruptcy court revisions, and investment in the mortgage market would decline. However, one study found that Chapter 12 'did not change the cost and availability of farm credit dramatically' (Fitzpatrick & Thomson, 2010).

On 5th March 2009, the House passed legislation approving cramdowns for primary residences, targeting abusive loan practices. The mortgage industry lobbyists[32] won their argument in the Senate as the measure was voted down on 30th April.

The main government programmes for homeowner relief through 2009 primarily reduced interest payments, usually leaving the principal intact. Cramdowns were seen as problematic: They would only go to selected homeowners – or opportunistic borrowers – causing more moral hazard. Losses must be covered, whether by taxpayers or banks. Also, owners of mortgage-backed securities could sue if mass write-downs were attempted. Still, there was always an undercurrent of opinion that outright forgiveness of mortgage debt was more equitable than the bailouts – rescue the borrowers, not the lenders. The concept ranged from government refinancing for 'underwater' mortgages to turning part of the loan into an equity stake for the lender. A Fannie Mae loan could take over the amount of the mortgage that covered the market value of the house, with the Treasury taking over the excess debt over equity with some provisions for leniency. However, this policy option never progressed, as taxpayers could not be coaxed to pay the bill.

Furthermore, it was never contemplated that every foreclosure should be stopped. Besides the moral hazard issue, the fact was that it would not be equitable (especially since borrowers often deserved their own fate). Also, it would be too expensive and probably would not succeed since many people had gotten into homes they simply could not afford.

Although government and private lender attempts to stem the home foreclosure crisis mostly focused on loan modification and refinancing, loan modification was seldom the first recourse. Certainly, loan modification programmes were holding foreclosure rates below where they otherwise might be; but unemployment was still high and home prices still weak, making it more futile to achieve any refinancing, from both the lender's and the borrower's perspectives. The government and lenders might have to revisit some ideas that had so far proved untenable such as reduction of the principal.

The Home Affordability Modification Program (HAMP) compelled banks and other mortgage servicers to modify rather than foreclose loans. However, the vast majority of borrowers entering the programme failed to provide required documentation (especially proof of income) to last beyond the three-month trial period. Foreclosure sales had initially been relatively low as lenders awaited details of the loan modification plans, but as it became clear the new programmes would not save many borrowers in default, banks became anxious to clear up their large backlog of mortgages in default.[33] Many foreclosure moratoriums were expiring, and unemployment was disqualifying more borrowers from loan modifications. In 2009, over a million trial plans were offered to borrowers, but less than 10% of the loans were permanently converted. Also, the number of defaults greatly exceeded the number of homeowners in the programme. Nearly 3 million properties filed for foreclosure in 2009 (though only 871,086 were actually repossessed during that period).

Housing finance in America had to address some particularities: For example, for primary mortgages in default, bankruptcy judges were not allowed to change the terms or reduce principal, which was standard procedure for credit card, car and other loans under court-ordered debt restructuring. Another difficulty was 'no recourse' mortgages in some American states, which limited the bank's recourse in defaults to the home and other collateral alone. Banks recover insufficient costs and owners are more likely to allow foreclosure, both of which augment the overall downturn. Banks might be wise to write down the mortgage to keep owners in the home, but securitized mortgages may prevent any one bank from agreeing a deal to forgive debt. (Nor could banks easily foreclose on loans that had been securitized.) There seems a need for a formula whereby governments step in to change the terms of securitized loans when neighbourhood housing prices decline significantly, or for government low-cost loans to supplement the outstanding debt. Larger schemes were afoot for the government to directly provide home loans (through Fannie and Freddie) at interest rates only slightly above government bonds.

The Federal Reserve 'quantitative easing' announced on 18th March 2009 targeted long-term rates to ease the credit crunch affecting mortgages and corporate bonds.[34] Rejuvenating the market for mortgage securities was a fundamental concern. To protect taxpayers from defaulting issuers, the Fed invests in high-quality bonds, strengthening the market for investment-grade debt. The price of mortgage and Treasury bonds in the marketplace would be forced up, lowering yields for new bond issues and hence reducing borrowing costs. This translates to support for equity markets, steering investment to firms with less risk of default, and it encourages new bond issues by these firms; but it might also be expected to exclude new or risky firms. Alternatively, pushing down long-term yields can chase investors into riskier investments for higher returns.

Quantitative easing directly reduces interest rates for targeted bonds only. It might not be effective at lowering costs and risks for individual borrowers and lenders. At best, there must be a significant time lag before any impact is felt in the broader market. Also, despite the gigantic size of the Fed's market interventions, it was always possible that market forces would overwhelm the programme. Bond traders might decide to liquidate holdings to take advantage of Fed demand, pushing borrowing costs up instead of down. If the power of the Fed's printing press does not prevail, that could damage the Fed's credibility and raise borrowing costs broadly (or even cause another market panic).

The effect of the government intervention was hampered by the complexity of the new housing regime. Mortgage rates and house prices were down, but tightened rules for underwriting, appraisal, etc. required adjustments by borrowers and loan officers. For example, Fannie and Freddie imposed extra fees for loans purchased after 1st April 2009, based on the type of property being bought or refinanced, credit scores and the amount of down payment. Fannie and Freddie also required appraisals to conform to the new Home Valuation Code of Conduct, which incurred more fees. Banks added their own new rules.

By year end 2009, it was clear that HAMP was not resolving the financial crisis for homeowners. HAMP had targeted helping 3 to 4 million homeowners avoid foreclosure through 2012. Foreclosures had been filed on 2.8 million homes, projected to reach 10–20 million by 2012. Over a million three-month trial modifications had been started but less than 170,000 mortgages had been permanently modified; half of these defaulted again after nine months. During 2009, a key measure of mortgage loan delinquencies – the percent of foreclosures plus 90-day past due payments – had reached the highest peak since tracking began in 1972 (*Los Angeles Times*, August 21, 2009). Delinquencies (90-day) continued to rise to 1.6 million by year end. In 2010, finally the number of loans going into delinquency was abating, but home foreclosures kept climbing as mortgage servicers worked through the backlog of troubled loans. Although home prices were stabilizing, the property market seemed unlikely to recover substantially until the bulk of foreclosures was worked out.

2.4. Rescuing the Car Industry

The first major pleas for government assistance of a national industry came from the so-called Big 3 automobile manufacturers: General Motors (GM), Ford and Chrysler. (Ford excluded itself but was implicitly part of the overall debate[35] – hereinafter by 'Big 3', we refer to only Chrysler and GM.) At Congressional hearings on November 18–19, 2008, the Big 3 asked for only an emergency loan, testifying that their businesses were viable once the car market recovered in 2010 or 2011. Considerable progress had been made to restructure the companies already, stripping out 2 million units of capacity, converting to manufacture more fuel-efficient cars and featuring a 2007 deal with the United Auto Workers (UAW) union to cut costs per car by $1,000 starting in 2009.

The UAW had to reduce so-called 'legacy costs' for pensions, healthcare, severance pay (the 'jobs bank' that paid nearly full wages to workers laid off), and allow more flexible work rules regulating what a unionized worker can be asked to do. However, the cost comparison was not straightforward. The US car market was more open than many foreign markets, giving the US domestic producers a disadvantage *vis-à-vis* foreign producers. Foreign carmakers in the United States were not unionized and anyway had smaller legacy costs because of their briefer history, and they often benefited from large incentives offered for foreign investment by state and municipal governments.

The initial formula for federal 'bailout' was in the form of loans with warrants attached and other conditions stipulated. The warrants allowed the Obama administration options for preferred stock investment, possibly attaching punitive dividends that would take the place of interest on a loan. Although this would presumably be non-voting stock, it was still equity and a recallable loan, allowing the government to maintain an ongoing influence on management. This approach would also deter other industries from requesting aid, to avoid government meddling. Potentially, the Obama administration could guide management towards the major industrial-policy goals that were being contemplated to combat global warming, reduce oil imports, etc.

Besides contributing to national plans for a future transportation system, a multi-billion dollar bailout investment might be much cheaper than the knock-on costs of bankruptcy. However, despite any bailout, much depends on the whims of American consumers – consumers might refuse to buy in to the trends desired by government and instead demand large, gas-guzzling cars as they have in the past.

2.4.1. The Issue of Bankruptcy in the Auto Industry

The alternative to government bailout was Chapter 11 bankruptcy whereby a company effectively operates under bankruptcy court 'protection' against lawsuits by creditors. The company remains in possession of its assets, operating the business under the supervision of a federal judge and for the benefit of creditors, but deferring payments to pre-bankruptcy claimants so as to fix its businesses as deemed necessary. Ostensibly, the difference with a bailout would be the supervisor: a court instead of the government. Also, the court would primarily be responsible to the firm's creditors, whereas the government would be concerned with implications for the larger industry and economy.

'Creditors' to be satisfied included bondholders and other account holders of legal liabilities, and also employees – both past and present – who had union-negotiated pay, pension and healthcare contracts. Under Chapter 11, some contracts may be rejected if cancelling them would be financially favourable to the company and its creditors.[36]

The Big 3 had argued that the industry's future was bright and they required only a bridging loan, but there had been little confidence that total taxpayer support could be limited to the amount requested. Initially, the bailout was planned at $25 billion, later reduced to $17.4 billion, then increased to as much as $50 billion for GM alone by June 2009 (although only a small part of these funds was initially utilized). Indeed, if bailouts were insufficient, bankruptcy was inevitable. Even higher costs might be incurred from the economic fallout of bankruptcy, impacting all businesses and individuals whose fortunes are tied to the auto industry.[37] In February 2009, GM estimated full-scale bankruptcy would cost taxpayers $100 billion, three times the total bailout to that point.

The supplier market would collapse along with the domestic automakers, which would affect even foreign-invested firms. On 19th March 2009, $5 billion was made available to auto suppliers, but it was funnelled through the US automakers to give them the power to decide which suppliers would receive aid. This signalled the government's intention to keep the Big 3 in business by helping only their supplier base.

President Obama pledged support to the automakers unequivocally in a speech to Congress on 24th February: 'Millions of jobs depend on it. Scores of communities depend on it. And I believe the nation that invented the automobile cannot walk away from it'. A month later, he observed, 'We cannot, we must not, and we will not let our auto industry simply vanish'. Nevertheless, the dismal prospects of the American auto industry were leading consumers to abandon Big-3 products apparently because of uncertainties about warranties being honoured, spare parts and components being manufactured and kept on hand, dealer availability and resale markets drying up. A survey released in March 2009 by polling firm Rasmussen Reports found 63% of Americans would prefer not to buy a car from a bankrupt company. Worse, 88% preferred not to buy a car from an automaker receiving government aid. Consumers were reflecting perhaps the emotional response to long drawn-out appeals by the automakers for more government loans and the pressure from politicians for drastic reforms. To counter this consumer uncertainty, the Obama administration instituted a $650-million programme in March 2009 to back up the warranties. Rationally, now with its warranties explicitly guaranteed and the supplier industry on government life support, the Big 3 seemed a safer bet than consumers perceived.

It is unusual for the management of a company in Chapter 11 to be fired, as it may be reasonably assumed that the present management team knows far more about the firm and its customers than would new management. As GM faltered towards bankruptcy, the Obama administration replaced its CEO upon passing a second deadline on 30th March without satisfactory restructuring plans being received from his executive team. To many observers, the CEO had failed to muster the stomach for the drastic restructuring that ultimately was necessary. To many others, this government intervention into a usual prerogative of the board of directors was inappropriate in the United States, and it signified a politicization that had intensified in the private sector since the onset of the crisis.

Stockholders inevitably are displaced in the event of a bankruptcy. If the business' debts exceed its assets, then at the completion of bankruptcy the company's owners all end up without anything. The Chapter 11 plan, when confirmed, terminates the stock of the company rendering the stock valueless. Holders of unsecured debt might similarly be wiped out, but their legal rights were no different from the union. Secured debt holders, as in the case of Chrysler, had legal rights superior to the union. Thus, although equity and unsecured debt might be sacrificed, senior debt holders could benefit from bankruptcy.

A Chapter 11 plan of reorganization is confirmed only upon the affirmative votes of the creditors. If a plan cannot be confirmed, the court may convert the case into liquidation under Chapter 7. Chrysler's secured creditors hoped for better treatment under Chapter 7. Other (presumably foreign) auto firms would cherry-pick the assets and keep them going, settling with holders of collateralized debt but shedding the cost burdens of expensive employee pensions, union contracts and healthcare. Chapter 7 is an unlikely option for viable enterprises; but Chrysler at least was saddled with out-of-date factories and brands, and the firm lacked sufficient economies of scale and scope.

2.4.2. Chrysler Files for Bankruptcy

On 30th March, the government set a 30-day deadline for Chrysler to form a merger with Fiat (*Fabbrica Italiana Automobili Torino*), and on 30th April a complex deal was announced. However, not all Chrysler stakeholders had agreed (about 40 banks and hedge funds, some holding senior Chrysler debt obligations), so the deal needed to be settled in Chapter 11 bankruptcy court. President Obama was not disposed to consider these 'holdouts' as deserving of return on their investments when the workers and the communities were so severely impacted by the plight of Chrysler. Obama said:

> In particular, a group of investment firms and hedge funds decided to hold out for the prospect of an unjustified taxpayer-funded bailout. They were hoping that everybody else would make sacrifices, and they would have to make none. Some demanded twice the return that other lenders were getting. I don't stand with them.

Debt holders responded that they had a responsibility to their investors to recover more of what they were owed and complained of being treated worse than other creditors. However, pressure mounted on the creditor outliers after the bankruptcy court judge blocked their request to have their names kept anonymous because of death threats they said they had received after President Obama bashed the group publicly by calling them 'speculators' only interested in money. On 1st May, their resistance to the deal collapsed.

Chrysler was judged too small and weak to survive on its own; its only option, according to Mr Obama, was to complete the deal to merge with Fiat. In exchange for a 35% stake, Fiat had offered such assets as fuel-efficient engines, small-car platforms and distribution channels outside North America, but no capital injection. Fiat's initial stake was reduced to 20% after discussions with the president's auto task force, rising to 35% after fulfilling criteria set by the Treasury, and ultimately limited to 49% until Chrysler repaid American taxpayers for their bailouts. Fiat would not finance Chrysler until the full benefits of the partnership were evident, which Fiat estimated as two years.

The UAWs' healthcare trust fund for retirees would swap its $10.5-billion unsecured debt for a $4.5-billion note and a 55% equity stake, becoming the new majority owner. Four major banks with 70% of the firm's debt would cut their nearly $5-billion debt down to $2 billion, but 42 other debt holders did not accept the Treasury's offer of $2.2 billion on their $6.9-billion debt.[38] The Supreme Court on 8th June decided to release the asset sale to the bankruptcy court.

Chrysler would get as much as $8 billion in working capital from the Treasury, on top of $4 billion lent to Chrysler in January; the government anticipated losing all that investment. The US government would get an 8%

stake and the Canadian government 2%. The US Treasury would select four independent members of the board of directors.

2.4.3. GM also Steers towards Bankruptcy

Before he was ousted by the Treasury's auto task force, GM's chief executive said bankruptcy was not an option, fearing the company might be left in limbo for years and customers would abandon GM products. The president had implicitly promised that GM would not be liquidated, but he expressly allowed Chapter 11 as an option for both GM and Chrysler, to be done 'quickly'. Such an accelerated bankruptcy had been termed a 'prepackaged bankruptcy' during early debate in Congress. Negotiations with the union and other concerned parties would be accomplished in advance, in this instance along with a loan advanced by the government. The government loan made it a creditor, giving the Obama administration a role in the court deliberations. The Bush administration had initially granted a $17.4-billion loan because it could still be called in if the industry failed to impress the new administration, leading to bankruptcy in the end.

A 'quick rinse' bankruptcy was increasingly the accepted concept. GM was to be reorganized into two firms: a new GM with the most competitive assets, immediately ready to offer the best products on the market; and an old GM[39] with old factories, weak brands, etc. to be slowly liquidated, as well as over $50 billion in legacy liabilities to bondholders and employees. The 'new' GM would have the brands, technologies, and seemed to have the economies of scale and scope to compete in the global marketplace.

On 27th April, the new CEO of GM put forward a restructuring plan to be negotiated by the various stakeholders and potentially a bankruptcy judge. The company proposed giving the government a 50% stake for half of $15.4 billion of bailout funds GM had already received and $11.6 billion more to be received at the new deadline of 30th May if GM's plan was approved. The UAW would get 39% plus a $10.2-billion cash settlement for $20.4 billion owed to the retiree healthcare trust. Bondholders were offered a 10% equity stake in exchange for $24 of their $27 billion in debt, a price one-fourth of UAW's and less than 8 cents on the dollar. About $6 billion worth of the debt was unsecured debt in the hands of tens of thousands of retail investors – typically small investors and often former employees who had put much of their savings in company bonds upon retirement. Among the hundreds of banks and hedge funds that held the rest, some were protected from bankruptcy by CDSs which provide insurance against default.

Just prior to entering bankruptcy, the GM deal had been renegotiated in favour of the bondholders (but still with some debtors not signing on). The government would provide $30 billion in additional cash, converting most of the $50 billion total it had lent to 60.8% of the stock. The Canadian government got 11.7% in exchange for $9.5 billion in financing. The retiree healthcare trust of the UAW would own 17.5% plus warrants for an additional 2.5% (which seemed about half the previous offer) in exchange for forgiving about $10 billion in debt. The offer to bondholders was 10%, giving the bondholders a much lesser equity/debt exchange than the UAW and the government. This last agreement gave the bankruptcy judge fewer contentious issues to handle, so was more quickly settled by the court. GM exited the bankruptcy court even faster than Chrysler – remarkably fast compared to major instances of bankruptcy in the United States.[40]

2.4.4. The Contentious Relationship with the Dealers

GM was closing many plants and dealerships. Without bankruptcy, it was unlikely GM could so easily implement such restructuring given the legal and political protection dealers enjoyed – onerous state franchise laws had long frustrated the Big 3 in their efforts to modernize their dealer systems. For example, GM had spent over a billion dollars to buy out retailers affected by its decision to eliminate its Oldsmobile brand in 2001. Bankruptcy allowed the Big 3 to overcome political resistance – car dealers, supported by umbrella organizations such as the National Automobile Dealers Association (NADA), were among the country's most effective lobbyists, with close ties to the local communities. During May 2009, with Chrysler already in bankruptcy and GM on the verge, both firms announced a restructuring of their dealer networks. NADA estimated that nearly 200,000 jobs would be lost as a result of the closures.

The auto companies argued that too many dealers were a legacy of earlier decades when the Big 3 had dominated the American market. Chrysler said in a bankruptcy filing that Toyota, with about 1,400 US dealers, sold an average of 1,292 vehicles per showroom, whereas Chrysler, with 3,280 dealers, sold only 303 vehicles per showroom. This so-called over-dealered status hurt profits and prevented upgrades of old showrooms. A dealer countered, 'Dealerships don't cost the automakers one cent, and cutting them doesn't save them any money'. Chrysler was asking the bankruptcy judge to cancel the franchises of 789 of its 3,200 dealers representing only 14% of sales; GM planned to cut 18% of its dealer network by the end of 2010, which accounted for only 7% of its sales.

The automakers said they had far too many dealerships for a market that had shrunk over 40% and that too many dealers caused individual showrooms to be unprofitable and uncompetitive. They claimed that too many dealers were financially weak and therefore inclined to slash prices to move inventory fast. Weak dealers also could not hold up their end on promotions or customer service. Thus, the automakers and administration task force argued that the overgrown dealer networks and weak dealers reduced both brand equity and profitability. Certainly, a bad dealer could hurt its carmaker.

Dealers contended that cutting franchises would simply cut sales. NADA argued that dealers' costs were not shared by the automakers; in fact, they buy the cars from the factory, pay for their transport and pay for local advertising. Historically, the carmakers took advantage of their monopoly supplier position, forcing dealers to take unwanted inventory, even cutting off franchisees in favour of more compliant local merchants.

The one advantage the dealers had was local political clout. Since the 1950s, local businessmen had pressed their legislators to protect their franchises, giving them special rights versus the manufacturers that more than levelled the playing field. It became very difficult to terminate dealers or impose inventories or expenses on them. Indeed, the obvious way carmakers could overcome these constraints was through bankruptcy proceedings, where a judge's authority trumped state franchise laws.

Now dealers (and their communities[41]) would suffer considerable hardship, and many dealers had been in business for decades. NADA estimated the average dealer had around 50 employees and contributed $16.5 million into their local economy. Dealers also could be stuck with ending inventories, so Chrysler, for example, was asking surviving dealers to buy the 44,000 excess vehicles leftover on lots of terminated dealers.

2.4.5. Future Prospects for American Industry Bailouts[42]

Difficulties of government ownership were manifest in persistent political pressures. For example, lawmakers complained that GM should build a small, fuel-efficient car at factories in their districts, and there was also criticism about dealership cuts. The House Appropriations Committee prepared legislation that required both GM and Chrysler to restore cancelled dealer franchises. Another bill in Congress would require post-bankruptcy carmakers to cover legal claims that had been cancelled in bankruptcy court for accidents due to defective vehicles.[43]

The ideological issue remains unanswered: Should government intervention be used to return major industries to profitability, or should 'free markets' be relied upon to run their course? The Big 3 initially favoured a bailout, arguing that bankruptcy would be disruptive. The industry clearly perceived a better future allied with the government.

Few other national industries were considered to merit a similar rescue. Unless the overall economy was at risk, 'free markets' should presumably work to clear the recessionary imbalance between supply and demand at appropriate price levels.

An exception was made in June 2009 when the Federal Reserve's Term Asset-Backed Securities Loan Facility (TALF) programme[44] was extended to commercial real estate, offering credit for investors buying commercial mortgage-backed securities. Commercial property loans accounted for over 20% of American banks' loans at that point, and commercial real estate prices had dropped by one-third.

3. THE GLOBAL RESPONSE

3.1. Prospective Regime Change

3.1.1. Global Economic Governance

A global fix is needed, one that accommodates all major national regimes. A rescue and reform programme that is internationally coordinated will establish common principles – such as open markets – but especially be more potent than isolated national efforts. There were some early negotiations among world political leaders, national ministers of finance and central bank directors – for example, there was a coordinated cut in interest rates on 8th October 2008, but the rate only matters if a loan actually is made.

Reforms are being mooted to address issues for supranational regulation, even far-fetched notions of a 'Breton Woods II' conference. A meeting on 14–15 November 2008 of the G-20 (20 leading economies) addressed some issues, particularly coordinated fiscal and monetary stimulus, but reform mostly awaited crucial deliberations at meetings in April 2009, again in September, and ongoing follow-up. The dual considerations of capital adequacy and global regulatory frameworks were mostly relegated to international bodies – individual countries agreed on little. The global response inevitably encountered conflicts with parochial interests in constructing a worldwide reform agenda.

Approaching the April 2009 meeting, the United States called for the G-20 to do more to stimulate demand, but there are intrinsic regional factors that led to differences in opinion. Europe has more automatic stabilizers such as social welfare and unemployment payments that may compensate for smaller fiscal initiatives, and anyway the European Union has rules limiting deficits. Europeans also have their own difficulties overcoming internal divisions to achieve a common economic policy, and the euro area generally needed a cohesive approach to keep its currency zone stable. Germany disagreed with applying the American approach worldwide, stressing a quick return to balanced budgets.

Europe's reluctance to spend more on stimulus efforts portended slower recovery than in America but also less debt burden[45] (except countries with long-standing deficits, e.g. Greece). Fiscal stimulus in East Asia as percentage of GDP was even higher than in America, helping Asia bounce back from the recession strongly. Asian banking systems were in much better shape and sovereign debt dynamics supported economic expansion.

Possible ideas for future discussion, at least at a conceptual level, might be quite far reaching. The post-war Breton Woods arrangement would be renegotiated to create a new financial system less reliant on the US dollar as well as addressing concerns about America's de facto veto power in global institutions. Although these notions will probably remain 'academic' for the foreseeable future, there must be ways to correct the huge imbalances – for example, Asian saving and Western consumption – that fuelled the boom.

According to *The Economist* (16-5-09, p. 80), 'the next monetary order is more likely to be made in Beijing than in New Hampshire'. As the major creditor to the United States, China[46] may be calling the shots. Pointing out that the global imbalances are due in large part to the reserve status of the dollar, the governor of the People's Bank of China (Zhou, 2009) called for the dollar to be replaced as the main reserve currency by the SDR. (The Special Drawing Right is an artificial currency created by the International Monetary Fund (IMF) in 1969, now mainly used for IMF accounting with member countries. The value of the SDR currently is a weighted average of the dollar, euro, yen and pound.)

Surplus countries such as China had little choice but to put their savings into dollars due to the dollar's central role in world trade and finance. China's concern was that the Federal Reserve's response to the crisis would be inflationary and ultimately lead to devaluation of the dollar; China's huge reserve assets were held around two-thirds in dollars.

The governor suggested a substitution account at the IMF where countries could deposit their dollars for SDRs, avoiding the market exchange rate and the adverse consequences of a dollar decline for the United States, euro area and China itself. However, the SDR's potential is limited by the fact that only governments use them.

With the Federal Reserve leading the bank rescue effort by such huge expansion of credit, central bankers have risen to a prominence as never before; and they will ultimately have the added responsibility to help their countries (notably the United States) meet the claims of foreign creditors on their debts. A new system, perhaps more to the liking of China with its capital controls and managed currency, must allow settlements to clear without sky-high interest rates or too much depreciation of the dollar.

3.1.2. Risk Governance in Banks

Fixing financial management in the banks entails new emphasis by boards of directors and chief executives on the monitoring of risk itself, as opposed to the emphasis on the opportunities presented by high-tech trading mechanisms and investments. Financial engineering had advanced to such a high level of quantitative risk analysis that banks were lulled into complacency by their own sophisticated probability models, all figures indicating huge potential returns, and small risks estimated with great precision.

The 'new paradigm' that had led to crisis was that risk seemed to have been permanently reduced. Low perceived risk combined with macroeconomic policy errors such as low-interest rates, promotion of home-ownership, etc. lead to the huge growth in leverage, derivatives, and the securitization phenomenon for decomposition and distribution of credit risk throughout the financial system. Although financial engineers – the 'quants' – could demonstrate low risk of particular investment strategies, they failed to foretell the consequence of broader market asymmetries and overruns that especially occur when every market participant mimics the successful risk-taking of everyone else.

Extremely unlikely but catastrophic events, called 'black swans', have become much more likely and greatly amplified in global financial markets, far more than the usual probability models indicate. The new strategy for managers must be to discount the precision mathematics and reawaken the old spirit of conservative fiduciary responsibility.

There seem to be no new tools for top management, only a return to cautious stress tests, scenario planning and the like, with a shift in the balance of power in organizations from risk-takers to those who police them. Risk managers, rather than traders, became (for awhile) the hottest recruitment area in finance.

3.2. The Evolving Regulatory Approach

Is re-regulation the answer? The problem of unintended consequences argues against tight regulatory regimes. Technological and other innovation will focus on avoiding the strictures of rules, and the innovators will be smarter and have more incentive than the regulators. Regulatory improvements are obviously needed, but sometimes they should be modest to avoid chasing financiers offshore or interfering with new enterprising ideas. For example, short selling[47] was a big problem in the 1997 Asian Crisis; and the regulatory approach was to ban it in some instances where it was perceived as actually or potentially harmful but, in most cases, simply impose new rules for transparency. When selling got too wild, market-makers were called in for discussions with a government minister and warned they could be in danger of losing their licence – they tended to be sensitive to 'moral suasion' in their host country.

The Asian Crisis resulted in very little reform of global banking. In contrast to the way Asia was treated by the 'Washington Consensus',[48] a decade later the United States Federal Government agreed to infuse huge amounts of cash to bail out banks and other American interests. Finally, regulation of American and global banking was considered very seriously – to avoid another bailout.

In the 2008–2009 crisis, Asian countries at least had huge dollar reserves and well-capitalized, profitable banks. The region's banks (except in South Korea) could finance their loans with deposits, which made them less reliant on strained money markets. Banks in Western countries even sought bailout by turning to such Asian savings (Yueh, 2008).

Global reform was primarily a project for international institutions, not national governments. The central bank for the world's central banks is the Bank for International Settlements (BIS), in Basel, Switzerland (established 1930). The so-called Basel Accords provide guidelines for capital adequacy; but these accords gave responsibility for assessing risks to credit-rating agencies[49] and the banks themselves, which assessments have obviously been discredited. The riskiness of bank assets that brought on the credit crisis was quite impossible to measure. 'Basel 2' was partially in effect for the crisis; now there is an emergent Basel 3 (see later), even suggestions that other disciplines such as computer science need to be incorporated to address the complications of modern finance. Basically, risk management and appropriate levels of capital are at issue.

The Financial Stability Forum (FSF) brought together financial regulators, central banks and treasuries from major Western economies, initially in advance of the G-20 summit in April 2009. Deep divisions among participants prevailed, for example, how to handle the failure of giants. The FSF was examining the issues of systemic risk, proper international leverage ratios and off-balance-sheet exposures. The off-balance-sheet vehicles, which had allowed capital ratios to be manipulated and assets' risks to be understated, were ruled out. Also forbidden were over-reliance on wholesale funding and excessive compensation policies. Simple ratios of equity to capital would be monitored, and banks would be required to build up capital during good times. Amounts of capital are addressed by Basel 3. Exact mechanisms and many other specific questions have yet to be decided. In April 2009, the FSF charged that the enforcement of rules needed to be less permissive. Those practices forbidden or ruled out were still very much in.

The US Federal Reserve was grappling with these and more regulatory issues. Regulators needed to scrutinize the risk of the system overall, not just individual lenders. However, relying upon a single global regulatory authority seemed unlikely. A nominal global watchdog was embodied in the FSF, in collaboration with the IMF, but it seemed unlikely that their warnings or (heaven forbid) directives would get much attention. Certainly, Americans would not have permitted a global regulator to disallow their sub-prime mortgages; nor would banks – for the sake of counter-cyclical provisioning – have set aside capital that was being loaned out so profitably during the credit boom. Appeals for limits on leverage would also fall on deaf ears (although fewer loans may do more to cap bankers' bonuses than explicit regulations or any attempt at better corporate governance).

Obviously, no new regulations were binding and anyway many future reforms are less obvious now. American tax policy might be reformed in the longer term to remove tax incentive for leverage, but tax reform will not overcome political hurdles soon. Ideas include revising corporate tax codes that favour debt over equity, disallowing mortgage interest to be tax deductible on personal tax returns, a counter-cyclical tax on mortgages that rises during property booms and falls during busts,[50] and other structural changes.

3.3. Schemes for National and Global Financial Reform

Governments already provide extensive protection against crisis, including liquidity support from central banks, deposit insurance and (explicit and implicit in the latest crisis) credit guarantees. Arguably, this has created moral hazard and allowed banks to relax their own fiduciary vigilance. Since 1988, global capital levels have been set by the Basel Committee at 4% of risk-adjusted assets; before that, when banks did not rely on government backing, they often carried much bigger buffers to protect themselves.

3.3.1. The American Legislative Process Identifies Priorities and Scope

The US Congress endeavoured to establish new regulatory frameworks to provide oversight of the banking industry for

- insuring capital adequacy and liquidity,
- policing threats to the economy (systemic risk) and
- monitoring consumer banking (the job of the new Consumer Financial Protection Agency – CFPA – see below).

New agencies would strip powers from the Federal Reserve and other existing agencies, but in a political compromise, the new consumer protection bureau (CFPA) became an autonomous division within the Fed. The Fed was denigrated for historically not treating consumer protection as a central part of its mission.[51] Still, consumer protection arguably should remain a responsibility of bank regulators – primarily the Fed.

To police systemic risk, the government wanted authority to seize and dismantle large firms that appeared near collapse and to regulate hedge funds and derivative markets. Supervision of institutions 'too big to fail' would be consolidated under the Fed (or else a new agency). The Fed would, in turn, be advised by a council of regulators that would scan the horizon for emerging risks. The priority was to create a mechanism to wind down financial giants – an alternative to either bailout or bankruptcy.

Creating a 'resolution authority' to move a failing firm's assets and liabilities to newly created bridge financial companies implies a new insolvency regime beyond the existing bankruptcy code. Also, any special bank tax to fund such an operation (based arbitrarily on an institution's size), plus the new regulatory agencies, could make the United States an unattractive jurisdiction for financial companies. Certainly, creditors would lose access to assets taken over by the FDIC, the Fed or other authority.

Moreover, Congress wanted to establish oversight for 'shadow banking' – the vast market for derivatives that were 'off-balance-sheet' transactions as contingent liabilities or assets. Banks' dealing and trading on their own account would also be restricted, to remove risky proprietary activities from access to the Fed's discount window, FDIC insurance and taxpayer guarantee. Although banks might engage in derivatives and other securities business on behalf of clients, the types of derivatives dealt by banks would be limited to specific instruments – allowing interest rate, currency and other hedging devices for clients but disallowing CDOs, for example. The intent was to prevent banks from making excessive speculative investments with their own capital and to compel transparency – to preclude banks from operating in 'shadow banking' arenas.

Of course, Wall Street banking goes far beyond simply taking deposits and lending to customers.[52] Indeed, the vast majority of banks' trading transactions are in the interbank market, that is, within the financial community. So-called 'proprietary trading' is not easily separated from market-making and necessary hedging against clients' trades. Balancing fiduciary roles as adviser, financier and market-maker for clients, plus 'enlightened positioning' of the bank's own account, became more problematic as finance got more complex and as Wall Street thrived on the new opportunities.

Those who package loans for securitization would increase disclosure plus retain a small ownership in any deal to encourage better underwriting. (However, instead of tying up capital in this way, requiring securitizers to sign warrantees and agree to buy back bad loans could have the same effect.) Arrangers' fees would be paid over time and reduced if loans fail. Derivatives not cleared centrally or traded on an exchange would face higher charges. A new CFPA would protect the public from rapacious lending practices, usurping a domain of the Fed.

Despite widespread agreement that regulation of financial institutions had been remiss, the banking industry opposed the proposals for a CFPA. The American Bankers Association said the new agency would have 'powers to mandate loans and services that go well beyond consumer protection'. The Consumer Bankers Association said the proposed agency 'would create a maze of regulations suppressing creativity and product innovation'. Arguably, the CFPA could even push banks to accommodate consumers at the expense of the banks' financial soundness. Presuming competitive and transparent financial markets, financial services should compete and succeed by treating customers with integrity. But that had certainly not happened with mortgages and credit cards. In a speech on 17th June 2009, Obama observed that 'a culture of irresponsibility' had taken root on Wall Street and elsewhere, that 'there were millions of Americans who signed contracts [for loans, credit cards, etc.] they didn't always understand offered by lenders who didn't always tell the truth. … Companies compete not by offering better products but more complicated ones, with more fine print and more hidden terms'.

The administration's 'concept plan' intended to rationalize multiple regulating agencies.[53] The advantage of multiple regulators was more oversight, but interagency conflict was problematic and banks tended to shop around for the easier regulators. This 'concept' was at odds, of course, with the legislative intent to create even more agencies.

All this (and more – see next section) required Congressional action,[54] where jurisdictional and ideological disputes raged. There was also a need for a global strategy.

3.3.2. Extending Oversight to All Major Financial Activities

Regulating global finance might best be by function. Extending oversight to the unregulated frontiers of finance such as hedge and investment funds is necessary; also on the agenda are valuation and disclosure standards for the exotic new financial assets.[55]

There is thus a need to formulate national and international accounting standards covering particular new financial instruments, as well as the need to address capital adequacy against failure in the wide range of new securities. Prevailing accounting standards (IAS37) did not require provision for contingent liabilities and assets where the future value, timing and possibility of actual need for settlement were so indefinite in each instance. This allowed banks to hold the items off their balance sheets, and it created huge unknown potential losses. One improvement was the routing of some instruments such as CDSs through clearing houses rather than being settled privately.

Clearing houses, or central counterparties (CCPs), act as buyer to every seller in a market and vice versa, collecting margins on every trade. A reserve fund is set up by members; thus traders only have to worry about the viability of one entity with which they can net their trades. The failure of one big trader is less likely to bring down the whole financial system. However, derivative products might be too specialized to be marketable beyond the originator and the buyer, so traders tend to deal directly with each other. Arguably, traders may take on risky positions if losses are ultimately borne by the CCP. Also, the CCP may not monitor the complex derivative positions of particular traders. Finally, CCPs become just one more institution 'too big to fail', as the big trading banks that act as CCPs are already.

Certainly, the huge financial institutions that had become 'too big to fail' and the accumulating off-balance-sheet positions needed to be regulated. Until April 2009, in the United States, only banks were supervised by federal regulatory authorities, while non-bank institutions were supervised on a state-by-state basis. The nature of liabilities of insurers,[56] for example, was less volatile because long-term policyholders were less inclined to cash in than nervous depositors in banks. Life insurers traditionally had lower gearing, and they balanced liabilities to holders of insurance policies by investing in long-term assets such as corporate bonds and commercial real estate. However, the reality of AIG's misadventures with derivatives changed that perception. Along with the hedge funds, mutual funds, etc. clustered in the financial centres of London and New York, these global financiers had become a major destabilizing factor. Nevertheless, insurers differed from banks in one important respect: They were not holding depositors' money and counter-party positions so were less essential to bail out.

US Treasury Secretary Geithner on 26th March 2009 had proposed subjecting the entire US financial system including the non-bank sector to federal supervision. A single regulatory authority was contemplated for oversight of the 10–20 institutions that were so large and interconnected that potential failure represented 'systemic risk' for the entire economy. There were two schools of thought: either place tighter constraints on risk-taking of specific institutions or take measures to reduce their financial influence. The first approach could require them to maintain higher capital balances and submit to other special rules – implicitly promising bailout if these institutions got in trouble. The effect might be to discourage certain firms from growing, or alternatively attract investors and depositors towards these large institutions with implicit government subsidy – which would further enlarge the most ponderous firms. The alternative to de-concentrate financial influence could be accomplished by limiting mergers or restoring some of the previous (Glass–Steagall Act) boundaries between commercial and investment banking.

The Obama administration proposed a new rendition of the Glass–Steagall Act of the Great Depression, repealed in 1999, that had separated commercial and investment banking (the Volker Rule). The purpose was to both limit risky investments by banks and control their size and scope. Access to low-interest loans from the Fed and the FDIC-insured deposits were a special advantage of commercial bank status, and the major investment banks had sought bank charters amid the crisis in late 2008 to protect themselves from the turmoil and avail themselves to the cost advantage. In the wake of the new policy approach, Goldman Sachs and Morgan Stanley might have to choose between their bank status exclusively or revert back to investment banking (if prevented from doing both).

The administration wanted to cap the size of banks, and also to ban or limit 'proprietary' trading and involvement in hedge funds and private equity that had incurred risky investments with bank capital. The plan was much more liberal than the old Glass–Steagall Act, allowing banks to continue some investment-banking activities such as underwriting and other market-making. The purpose was to stop Wall Street from gambling with subsidized deposits. At least, entities with access to the Fed discount window (i.e. banks) would have to spin off the more speculative activities to non-bank subsidiaries; at most, there could be an outright ban. This would represent a huge loss of profits. Ultimately, the unintended outcome might be that the newly regulated activities migrate to the large, independent hedge funds, increasing the unregulated financial sector. Then banks, being the biggest lenders to private equity and hedge funds, incur risky asset portfolios all over again. Worse: New rules could drive such trading offshore.

The new legislation comprised many other measures, including a non-binding vote by stockholders on executive pay and retirement packages. It seemed that nothing – neither contractual obligations the banks had undertaken in return for a bailout, nor moral suasion through public censure, nor repentance by the banks for past mis-investment – nothing had stemmed the tide of bonuses awarded to executives. In January 2010, Obama proposed a fee to be assessed against big banks' liabilities (excluding domestic deposits), with accompanying rhetoric implying the measure was punitive. By the end of 2009, the big banks were awarding more high bonuses to executives even while bank lending continued to languish. Arguably, however, the fee was a legitimate way to offset the lower cost of capital for big banks that were implicitly guaranteed by the government: a systemic-risk tax. European governments were also proposing levies on their banks, with IMF and European Commission support, at significant potential cost to banks.

Regulatory unpredictability could raise perceived risk and hence the cost of debt. Furthermore, a global patchwork of ideas was emerging, with possible overlapping rules or inconsistencies. For example, regulatory reform in America to control institutions 'too big to fail' might not be well coordinated with global reform efforts spurred by the G-20. The G-20 agenda (and Basel 3 – see next section) was emphasizing capital adequacy, having concluded that breaking up banks would be difficult and of uncertain benefit.

A new 'macro-prudential' regulatory approach is necessary that accounts for the health of individual institutions as well as systemic vulnerabilities. Even strong firms, acting prudently in times of crisis, can fail and undermine the system. It also would be appropriate to have different capital adequacy measures at different stages of the economic cycle. A possible mechanism is 'dynamic provisioning' for banks, setting aside profits in boom times as a reserve to offset bad loans in a future crisis; but such provisions potentially create opportunities for banks to manipulate earnings reports.

3.3.3. A Patchwork of Global Reforms, Mostly with Indefinite Outcomes

Proposals dubbed 'Basel 3' were published in December 2009 by the Basel club of bank supervisors. They addressed the issue of capital adequacy (rather than the issue of the size of institutions that is an American reform priority). Two capital components were contemplated: a coverage ratio of high-quality liquid assets and a funding ratio requiring a higher level of longer term financing of assets.

The new proposals defined capital more strictly so that essentially only pure equity counted as core ('tier 1') capital, disallowing equity-like instruments that might really be debt such as preferred stock. Core capital would be increased to maintain confidence of depositors, creditors and counterparties, and further enhanced to withstand a market meltdown. On 12th September 2010, the Basel Committee agreed to the new rules (Basel 3), requiring global banks to keep common equity equal to at least 4.5% of risk-weighted assets, compared to 2% now. This rule would not go into effect until 2015, with an additional 2.5% counter-cyclical buffer not due to take effect until 2019. The long lead times would soften the impact of bigger capital buffers on growth of banks. With reserves thus totalling 7%, capital for risky operations could be over three times larger.

The second component, augmenting quasi-capital or 'tier 2' securities, imposes losses on creditors rather than only on equity (sparing taxpayers, in the event of government rescue). One such instrument is 'contingent convertible' (Coco) capital, which is debt that converts to equity in the event of crisis. An unresolved issue is that Coco investors can insure against their Coco risk and thereby pass the risk onto counterparties like AIG, ultimately recreating the need for bailouts. An alternative to Cocos is partial bankruptcy, for example, government guarantees only for deposit-taking parts of banks and allowing the rest to face bankruptcy, thereby avoiding depositor-runs on banks in crisis and also making banks – not taxpayers – pay for bank failures.

The Institute of International Finance, a bank lobbying body, argued that the cost of big new capital and liquidity safety 'buffers' would be excessive. Although banks had not experienced the erosion of capital earlier forecast by the Federal Reserve's stress tests, reducing their structural reliance on short-term funding would require raising trillions in customer deposits or bonds to achieve a 'net stable funding ratio'. Still, banks may be pre-empting imminent regulatory regimes by shifting towards stronger safety measures already. Risk adjustment of bank assets should also be more stringent and less dependent on credit ratings. There are many more ideas on the drawing board, and many criticisms.

Financial regulation will be approached differently for countries that value financial stability over innovation, directed credit and state banks to avoid financial market failures (especially in developing countries), etc. It seems unlikely a single global regulatory agency with, say, a binding code of international conduct, would displace distinctive national approaches. By allowing a variety of national regulatory models to flourish, the best global regulatory regime can emerge (though with the possible overlap and inconsistencies mentioned above). The European Union mooted an idea for 'colleges' of national regulators to approach regulation with more sensitivity. Cross-border supervisory colleges could share information about global banks – but not to sacrifice national regulatory sovereignty to international agencies.

The IMF remains the global institution best suited to attend to a dysfunctional international payments situation. Besides quotas and standing arrangements to borrow from members, the IMF has the ability sometimes to elicit funds from reserve-rich member countries willing to provide extra funds beyond their 'tranche' such as Japan, China, the Middle East or the Nordic countries. The IMF had been responsible to deal with the Asian Currency Crisis, but the conditions it applied to its loans were controversial. IMF 'conditionality', plus the stigma of an IMF bailout, makes some countries reluctant to take the IMF route. There were also doubts that the stand-by arrangement, designed for short-term balance of payments difficulties, is appropriate for the problems that exist today. Thus, on 29th October 2008, the IMF announced a new short-term liquidity facility for three-month loans awarded to countries without the previous conditionality, which in turn was replaced in 2009 by the Flexible Credit Line (FCL).

The intent was to have a less strict, more accessible IMF. At the April 2009 G-20 London summit, it was decided that the IMF would require additional financial resources to meet prospective needs of its member countries resulting from the global crisis. IMF resources were tripled to $750 billion. At the height of the crisis from November 2008 to March 2009, nine countries (all lower-income) were awarded IMF loans, with Mexico first in line for the FCL in April. (East Asian countries that felt abused by the IMF a decade earlier – Korea and Indonesia – demurred.) By 2010 the IMF was mounting rescue efforts in the euro zone, starting with a record bailout for Greece (110 billion euros) in May 2010, to prevent a new financial crisis starting in the European Union.

This crisis has required massive, globally coordinated mobilization of capital – with the ultimate goal of establishing global financial stability and balance of payments equilibrium. The United States is the only country immune from balance of payments difficulties because, the dollar being the world's main reserve currency, the United States simply 'prints' more dollars, which are accumulated by its creditors such as China and Japan. The limit to this 'Faustian bargain' is unknowable, but it seems we are destined to find out, as the US government deficits, current account outflows and national debt soar to new heights.

4. LESSONS OF RECENT HISTORY

4.1. The American Current Account Deficit

For decades, the American consumer seemed immune to the usual laws of economics in the sense they could spend and borrow with seeming impunity, and the US dollar would hold its value despite persistent deficits. Classical theory of international economics purports that foreign exporters would redeem their surplus dollars for gold or other reserves from the US central bank, the dollar would devalue (due to less reserve backing and/or increased supply of dollars in the economy), and Americans would be prevented from importing so much. However, exporters to America were willing to save their surplus dollars and invest them back in America, in the form of debt (Treasury Bills or other loans to Americans) or capital (foreign direct investment in new business or other equity such as property investments). From 2000 to 2007, America received nearly $6 trillion from overseas, counterbalancing a persistent current account deficit that peaked at 6% of GDP in 2006. (A level of 4% is considered dangerous, portending devaluation.)

The problem, it seemed to many economists, was not that Americans spent too much but foreigners saved too much.[57] Savings in America declined from around 10% of disposable income in the 1970s to 1% after 2005. In contrast, high saving was a key element of the Asian economic 'miracle', along with export-oriented industrialization. Asians were willing to invest at low interest the dollars they earned by selling to America, effectively underwriting American consumption. The American economy conformed to the normal case scenario of individual utility maximization, an economy that aimed for maximum benefit to consumers; whereas Japan was 'different'. Lester Thurow (then dean of MIT's Sloan School of Management) famously dubbed Japan's system 'producer economics' because they seemed to prefer producing rather than consuming.

It would take many decades for America's colossal deficit spending to finally come home to roost, as China, for example, willingly accumulated $2 trillion in reserves. (Such high reserves were deemed useless by many economists.) If China were to liquidate their dollars, it would have a devastating effect on both China and the United States. China's dollar reserves would be devalued, and their own currency would revalue upwards and kill their export industries; and for America, its long consumption and investment boondoggle would end. China had witnessed the same imbalance between the United States and Japan in the 1980s, which finally resulted in a revaluation of Japan's currency and a halt to Japan's rapid growth in the post-war era. China, keeping its part of the 'Faustian bargain', invested trillions of dollars earned mostly from manufactured exports into American government bonds and government-backed mortgage debt. This kept interest rates low and fuelled America's consumption binge and housing bubble. Both countries were happy: America got cheap imports, low inflation and low-cost foreign financing for economic growth, and China industrialized rapidly with financial stability and a strong export platform. Not unlike Britain's financing of American railroads and other infrastructure in the 19th century, it was mutually beneficial. Economists were cognizant of the danger from the tremendous trade and financial imbalances, but there seemed no solution without better international cooperation.

Clearly, the global imbalances that were the contributing cause to the crisis should be corrected, but the status quo is imperative for the moment. China's fortunes remain tied to America's and vice versa.[58] The US Treasury needs China to finance its trillion-dollar bailout to banks and Obama's stimulus plan and upcoming programmes. China needs the US market to keep its trade from collapsing and causing social unrest. The American proclivity to overspend now must be the initial solution to America's own dilemma – indeed, saving is not helpful and politicians entreat Americans to shop as a patriotic duty.

The government's initiatives to stimulate spending have been huge – with doubtful success. Transition to global economic balance will be a much greater challenge.

4.2. The Role of Market Speculators

Do speculators deliberately promote runs on markets and cheer as currencies, stocks and other target markets plummet – and economies collapse? It seemed, as always, that the only participants in the market turmoil to be actually savouring uncertainty and the misfortunes of others were the traders.

The eternal issue is who to blame for capitalist abuses and how to reform.

Hedge funds have been important, even dominant, investors worldwide and often have more funds available (through leverage) than individual governments. The multi-billion dollar hedge funds certainly thrive on market volatility, and it matters not which way the market is moving, only that they can get on the bandwagon. With hedged positions, they are on both sides of the markets and benefit from the volume. With unhedged positions, if they bet wrong they can still win. The strategy is simple: Well before they mount an assault on a particular asset, the hedge funds borrow huge amounts of the very asset they want to bring down. They might borrow many multiples of the amount they intend to sell. When they start selling, interest rates spike up as a result. Lending at, say, 20% what you borrowed at 5% is indeed lucrative; it yields huge profits when you are lending in the billions. Even if the central bank succeeds in defending its markets and inflicts losses on speculators, the hedge funds would have made many times more in the lending market. What if the central bank buckles and allows its assets to fall? Then the funds hit a double jackpot. When the Thai baht was attacked in this way in June 1997 – said to be led by George Soros – the major funds walked away with profits of billions of dollars. A few months later, it was the turn of the Indonesian rupiah, then the Hongkong dollar. When interest rates exploded with the force witnessed in the Asian markets, the first to plunge were the stock markets. The next to come under pressure were the real estate markets. And if interest rates stay high, the whole economy slows down. As they launch their attack, the hedge funds short-sell the stock market, knowing that other, less agile, market players will have to sell their stocks to maintain liquidity. This stock sell-off frightens genuine long-term investors into selling out too; that is how it all snowballs.

Given the tremendous size and scope of the US government role in 2008–2009, it is sad in retrospect that the Washington Consensus disparaged any financial rescue during the 1997–1998 Asian Crisis, preferring to 'let the markets decide their fate'.[59] Now this amorphous alliance of dictators is less reverent about market discipline.

Job losses in America in September and October 2008 totalled 723,000, increasing to nearly 600,000 monthly November through January 2009, and approaching 700,000 in both February and March.[60] Since the recession officially began in December 2007 until then, the economy had lost over 5 million jobs.[61] A later *Economist* survey ('The Long Climb', October 3, 2009, p. 5) estimated that before the crisis is over, 25 million may lose their jobs in the 30 rich OECD countries. Indonesia saw 25 million become unemployed in the early days of its crisis in 1997, and they hit the streets looting and raping.

The lesson of history is that early, decisive government action can stem the panic and the costs. However, this crisis was so much more complicated, affecting more types of markets in many more countries than any past crisis. Comprehensive solutions seemed sensible enough but had to overcome global political hurdles. The world blamed this on America, McCain blamed greed and corruption (though legal 'intent' in the disclosure and valuation shortcomings would be impossible for prosecutors to prove), but some wonder if this simply reflects the need to change our entire lifestyle. Nevertheless, boom and bust is an ancient story – just worse in today's globalized markets. Emerging countries share some blame for financing the boom by continuing to loan to America.

The banking system was stricken by what *The Economist* on 11th October 2008 (p. 93) identified as a three-headed monster: solvency, funding and liquidity. Thus, there were three related developments associated with the collapse of the asset and credit bubble: bank insolvency, requiring capital injection; the inability of banks to borrow longer term to finance the share of their assets not covered by deposits; and the need of still-solvent banks for liquidity to compensate for the inability to access money market funds for short- and medium-term needs. Then there was a need to keep any available funds from walking out the door in the form of withdrawals by customers, distributions to owners, mergers and acquisitions, etc., or simply held for liquidity needs to offset the reduction in capital from the massive charges taken for bad debts. Ultimately, there was the severe impact on the 'real economy' as well as the impact on public financial burdens. Means of governance over the 'three-headed monster' were extremely inadequate.

5. WHERE FROM HERE?

Deregulation had been the value orientation of the 'Washington Consensus' since at least 1981. Complex, potentially dangerous financial instruments came into vogue, and the new academic field of 'financial engineering' provided legitimacy – and new graduates – for the boom in finance. It became possible for banks to simultaneously float risky loans and minimize their exposure to default by passing on the debt as marketable securities that were highly lucrative and seemed risk free. CDSs even made it possible to both market unreliable securities and profit from their failure. Innocents abounded to take part in the boom in property values, sub-prime mortgages, derivative trading and other speculations.

The burst of the property bubble created credit losses, financial institutions lost capital, but illiquidity was a problem even for strong businesses and banks. Most banks could still lend, but uncertainty about their own and their customers' access to funds made them hold their money. Government priorities were to unblock credit, using central banks for adding liquidity and other actions such as selling guarantees for private sector loans, buying commercial paper, interest rate cuts, etc. Providing capital to enable banks to expand credit seemed a sensible solution, but banks kept new capital infusions simply to cover ongoing losses or other firm needs (including bonuses for executives). So none of this quickly and completely worked through the system, and global stock markets[62] reflected the uncertainty over the outcome or that enough had been done.

This begs the question: How much capital is needed worldwide to stop the rot, and how should it be raised: from taxpayers, or will the private sector finally come forward? Nobody knows the answer, and figures tended to keep going up, awaiting the contagion to stop spreading and business to resume investing. But many central banks had lots of cash, especially in Asia. It seems there are no limits to what can be done, all the way to financing and operating entire economies. When global finance stops, only governments can get it started again. Although the private sector in the United States could afford to recapitalize the banking industry, it could not have been expected to step forward on its own.[63]

5.1. Issues for the Medium to Long Term

5.1.1. Unwinding Government Intervention

Some of this runs the risk of 'moral hazard' (incentive for banks to behave recklessly and depend on government bailouts). The government may also politicize the allocation of funds or disregard the ultimate purpose of maximizing the profit for their taxpayers' reluctant investment in the bailout. Governments resolve blithely to eschew these temptations and also not reward managers and shareholders of rescued institutions.

Moral hazard is only a theoretical concern, though it was compelling enough to overrule American participation to bail out Asia in 1997–1998. Today, the ideologues must take a back seat, as even the American right wing should allow (with sensible exceptions) that government funds and government intervention must lead the rebuilding of balance sheets, and ultimately the whole economy will need rebuilding. Capitalism, freedom and the American way are not under threat, but governments are responsible to help their countries withstand the biggest asset and credit collapse in history. The free market system without government support, constraints and oversight can become unsustainable, harmful to the players themselves and even harmful to society.

Another 'theoretical' concern is the efficacy of industrial policy. The government rescued both old, struggling sectors such as car manufacturing and new, dynamic sectors (mostly through the stimulus) such as high-speed rail, green technologies, etc.; but it is widely believed that these business ventures will mostly become 'white elephants'. Of course, the US government has long helped business – for example, the Small Business Administration (SBA) was established in 1953, but the Obama administration is finally funding the SBA better and setting up a national network of business incubators. The government even bailed out Chrysler before (1979), but this time around Obama observed (2009) that the government must make 'strategic decisions about strategic industries'. The size and scope of industrial policy has greatly expanded, in contrast to earlier administrations (since Reagan) that tried to eliminate industrial policy wherever possible. 'Today the US federal government is the world's biggest venture capitalist by far' (Rodrik, 2010).

The loans and equity investments by governments cannot be reimbursed soon, as such huge amounts of capital cannot be liquidated without depressing markets further. This raises two very important questions: What effect might a longer term government stake have on the banks, car companies, etc.? In the modern era, there is less inclination for socialist-style management as there once was, for example, in the era of the nationalized industries in post-war Britain. Nevertheless, taxpayers and politicians will certainly speak out and expect to be heard by managers of national industries. There must then be some confusion added to the corporate objective function.

This impact can be positive, as it was in some instances of Asian industrial policies, for example, if government capital develops infrastructure and institutions for more sustainable future industry. However, in the United States, the experience may be chaotic with such extreme politicization of business decision-making.

5.1.2. Taming Deficits

The second question is the sustainability of such deficit spending, the impact on the national debt and the need for eventual debt reduction. The

US government cannot hope to reduce its burden soon, with important implications for interest rates and the value of the US dollar. At the onset of the credit crisis, the US dollar rose significantly, due to its safe-haven status and also due to the widespread need to purchase US dollars for funding international debt obligations. If this dollar strength had prevailed (ending a six-year decline), it would have hampered recovery of US industry, because any new demand resulting from fiscal stimulus or general market recovery would be dissipated on cheaper imports. Thus, the United States could be stimulating other countries' industrial recovery, not its own.[64]

The dollar continued to appreciate until March 2009 despite poor economic growth and low short-term interest rates in the United States, for a complex of reasons. Because of the deflationary conditions, real yields on Treasury bonds were relatively high, attracting capital flows into the United States. The global slowdown along with a falling oil price caused the US current account deficit to shrink, further boosting the dollar. American investors were also repatriating investments from overseas, so the dollar benefited from stock market sell-offs. Some emerging economies were impacted worse from the severe decline in exports. Finally, American economic policy was perceived as more credible than the cautious Europeans, and also the euro zone happened to have more scope for interest rate cuts. (From March 2009, the dollar began a new, but gradual and irregular, decline.)

In the longer term, the huge increases to the federal deficit, current account deficit and national debt will tend to be inflationary, and the US dollar might decline precipitously. Certainly, the US dollar has been most compromised since the United States was at the epicentre of the crisis. The dollar's reserve status will be questioned in some quarters if it declines significantly. Currencies worldwide might decline as they did in the 1970s, except some emerging-market currencies (especially as the Chinese yuan appreciates). Commodities considered a store of value, such as gold and eventually property, increase in value and should once more become hedges for inflation.

The task for the US government is fundamental tax and spending reform to control inflation and interest rates in the long term, especially addressing the federal budget outflows for 'entitlements' (Social Security, Medicare, etc.), which are way more expensive than all stimulus and bailout costs.[65] Inflation and the value of the dollar are very much a result of market expectations after all, and 'the markets' are watching how America will correct the immense expansion in all its deficits in the long term.

Deflation may be a greater threat than inflation, both short term as a result of the severe recession and long term in a world where jobs are disappearing, massive wealth has been lost in the stock and housing markets' crashes, and manufacturing overcapacity is prolonged. In this bleak future of permanently reduced demand but increasing global competition for production opportunities, low growth and deflation may be endemic.

These dismal projections for the future consequences of the global financial mess are alarming, but the huge debt and expenditure on bailouts, stimulus plans, and job creation and unemployment benefits were essential at least in the near term. Without the bank bailouts the financial crash would have been far worse, and without stimulus spending the recession would have been deeper and longer. A prolonged downturn does much greater damage to public finances. However, the present fiscal policies are not sustainable, and world governments must eventually deal with immense debt burdens.[66]

Obviously, America needs to drastically cut national spending. This argument is generally associated with an emphasis by conservative proponents on getting the government out of the economy – and cutting taxes, instead of the need to raise tax revenues to fund the spending. Leaving aside the conservative argument, let us address the deficit directly, by examining means to cut spending and increase revenue-raising potential. Finally, we question the real impact of the primary means for financing of the net fiscal imbalance between outflows and inflows, which may make the whole debate moot: US Treasury Bills.

Taxes in America are already low as a ratio to GDP compared to other OECD countries – though corporate tax is 2nd highest. Flying in the face of our penchant for cutting taxes, government expenditure persistently exceeds tax revenue (augmented by the need to finance the added costs of American 'exceptionalism' – especially the inordinate expenditures incurred for national defence, policing foreign conflicts, rescuing disaster areas and other fairly unique priorities). Indeed, public debt seems to be the only part of the economy that can be relied upon for growth. Ideas put forward to cut costs often advocate stopping our involvement in wars or eliminating superfluous weapon systems, shrinking government services and payrolls, and programmes for the poor, or questioning items in the stimulus, jobs bills or other purportedly misguided policies. However, cost cutting efforts in the most essential areas have seldom been sufficient, especially America seems unable to avoid spending increasing amounts on core entitlement programmes such as Medicare.

Fundamental tax reform is unfortunately not yet on the agenda despite growing advocacy.[67] Politicians stymie progress by pouncing on any mention of 'the T word'. Most economists favour a greatly simplified, progressive tax with few loopholes, and reducing some marginal taxes such as the corporate tax rate to improve competitiveness and retain jobs. Other sensible but unlikely changes in the basic structure might include a national sales tax – a 'value-added tax', to tax consumption rather than income and saving. A better tax system must reduce consumption, which is a central problem with the American economy that has not abated, and instead encourage investment and innovation – and of course boost revenues.

The concept of 'fiscal subsidiarity' may be attractive to both Republicans and Democrats. The idea is to pass federal revenues down to states and municipalities for solving problems at the grassroots, relying less on direction from Washington. Taxes collected by the federal government would be transferred to where the programmes have local design and backing, whether for infrastructure, healthcare, clean energy, etc.

A broad principle should be to rely upon private initiative whenever possible. This implies, for example, that private insurers and providers in the healthcare industry not be eliminated, only regulated better, as we do with public utilities. Minimal tinkering with the market would be preferred, such as a simple carbon tax rather than an unwieldy cap-and-trade system to move us towards a low-carbon energy system.

The other facet of the tax-and-spend conundrum, financing the difference, is actually a simpler issue than we tend to assume. As explained earlier, the Fed is the only central bank that can print money (expand credit) almost with impunity – the 'Faustian bargain'. The Chinese, and even the global investment community (that puts prime value on liquidity and safety), seem willing to accumulate US Treasury Bills indefinitely, which allows the Fed to finance deficit spending at a very low interest cost. Concerns for rising interest rates, inflation, and taxes, dollar devaluation, and an intergenerational debt burden that seems too big to be paid off in the foreseeable future, all these are more emotional than real issues for the present. Interest rates remain low, so the pain of repayment of debt is not currently felt. Even if investors someday demand higher yields on government securities, in America, more expensive government borrowing still just pumps more money into the economy to spur growth and encourage private lending. US treasuries are still snapped up at auction at whatever interest, and bond traders still want treasuries more than any other instrument for liquidity and safety. The global financial community has no alternative to the US Treasury market.

Also, they can see no currency alternative to the US dollar – certainly neither the euro nor the yen can replace the dollar. If US deficit spending does spark a crisis and currency devaluation, as long as it does not turn into a dollar rout, American private assets will still have their intrinsic value and money will flow back.

The argument that we are passing an insurmountable debt burden to future generations may also be countered by pointing out a need to spend more, not less: Sacrificing education, job creation, healthcare and other spending priorities is really the way to burden the next generation with an insurmountable disadvantage.

America's huge debt burden is certainly a matter of grave concern, but for the federal government, unemployment now trumps deficit worries. High permanent debt reduces growth potential at some point (once the original benefit of leverage is served) – a figure of 2% reduction in GDP growth was found where national debt in developed economies exceeds 90% of GDP (Reinhart & Rogoff, 2009). Reduced growth of course impacts the ability to pay off debt, a vicious cycle of economic decline. For many other countries, sovereign default has ultimately occurred; but not the United States – at least, not yet.

Governments must commit themselves to fiscal prudence for the long term and establish principles for how to proceed. The concept of a binding framework of fiscal rules, perhaps enforced by an independent 'fiscal council' (as in Hungary), might embrace various approaches; but even if one administration complied, there would be no guarantee that the next administration would commit to the same restraints. Procedural rules are conceivable, such as a cap on growth of public debt, public sector pay or spending. Budget-balancing targets could be consistent with a stable or falling debt burden, allowing politicians to make tax and spend decisions only within those limits (similar to set-ups in Chile and Sweden). Fiscal projections that address when and how deficits will be controlled would reduce uncertainty. The pay as you go (PAYGO) plan proposed by the Obama administration on 9th June 2009 and signed into law on 13th February 2010 obliges Congress to pay for new spending either by raising taxes or cutting outlays.

Budgetary restraint will thus be an essential priority. Defence and discretionary spending might shrink, and farm support and other programmes trimmed or decentralized. Other conceivable fiscal strategies include lifting the age ceiling on retirement, means testing or other tinkering with benefits, to boost tax revenues (as people work longer) and cut future pension costs. Another target for reform is healthcare costs, especially in America that allegedly has the most wasteful system in the world (disregarding here the 2010 legislation). Another is efficiency-enhancing tax reform such as the deductibility of employer-provided healthcare and mortgage interest. Essentially, economists believe tax reform should be biased in favour of taxing consumption and perhaps property instead of income and payroll taxes (which penalizes work and encourages borrowing and consumption). Certainly, less complexity is desirable – tax exemptions, credits and miscellaneous loopholes cost trillions of dollars in revenues.

5.1.3. Future Shock

There has long been an undercurrent of dissatisfaction with 'maximizing' principles – profit maximization in particular, to instead emphasize social values, for example. The banks were especially criticized for pursuing short-term profit rather than serving their community. Such rethinking seems especially relevant in the current era.

Ultimately, the more idealistic wing of the Obama administration hopes to seize the opportunity of the great investment of national wealth and energy the United States is putting into resolving the huge financial and economic malaise. The new administration thus seemed well placed to help address wider problems in the global environment; but political opposition became inexorable. Presuming someday there is a national and international political consensus (unlikely now), a sort of New World Economy might gradually emerge – a new financial regime will certainly be essential, but also we might look forward to global trends emphasizing cross-border co-ordination for eco-system conservation, sustainable industries, 'green hubs', nature reserves, options and future trading for pollutants and depleting resources, and the like.

In early 2009, the World Social Forum, expected to be too radical for practical policy ideas, suggested the United Nations be charged with preventing large trade imbalances from accumulating, controls on exchange rates and international movement of capital, reform of credit-rating agencies, bank risk-taking and pay incentive reform, and the elimination of 'shadow banking' institutions such as hedge funds and private equity firms and their instruments such as over-the-counter derivatives (OTCs) and CDOs. A 'speculator pays' principle should apply to systemic losses. The Forum recommended a global stimulus plan in the form of a green New Deal. Bits of this platform may some day become reality.

5.2. Rethinking Established Orthodoxy

5.2.1. Austerity versus Stimulus

Government stimulus spending under the administration of Franklin Delano Roosevelt (FDR) is touted as the precedent that proved the Keynesian theory. When FDR took office in 1932, unemployment was almost 25%. The Civilian Conservation Corps was created to put men to work in national parks and forests, but with limited success. Then the Federal Emergency Relief Administration was charged with feeding and sheltering the poor, which put 2 million people to work by the fall of 1933. The next effort, during the winter of 1933–1934, was the Civil Works Administration, which put 4 million more people to work mostly repairing roads and public works. (It expired, as planned, after five months.) The Works Progress Administration addressed a wide range of infrastructure needs starting in 1935, taking 3.5 million on its payroll by the fall of 1936. By the spring of 1937, the unemployment rate had dropped to 14%, and the infrastructural improvements provided necessary and lasting benefits to the country.

Several major contrasts with today's stimulus can be drawn. Deficit spending and the national debt incurred by the FDR administration were relatively new, though alarming concerns. Obama instigated deficit spending at a time when a growing national debt had been institutionalized for three decades already – yet suddenly the opposition Republican Party resisted more spending (as happened in FDR's Congress also). FDR had a much stronger majority in Congress that overcame weaker political resistance and passed his bold stimulus programmes. Another contrast is that current stimulus and other programmes may not have been sufficiently well designed – the jury is out on that verdict. The ultimate contrast was that FDR's debt was paid off by the economic boom of the post-war era, whereas today there is real concern that economic growth in the future might be modest, at best.

A debate prevailed amongst economists (and politicians) as to which was the most appropriate policy for emerging from recession today: Keynesian stimulus, or austerity. Government stimulus supports short-term demand; whereas government austerity can be considered a supply-side means to foster growth, implying need for boosting longer term availability of factors of production supplied from the private sector. This still might imply a need for government policies, for example, to facilitate labour mobility and training, enhance market confidence and availability of capital, etc.

Those who favour more stimulus to revive the US economy emphasized the need for urgent action to rescue the economy, and the risk to the recovery of withdrawing budgetary liquidity. Advocates of this strategy posited several arguments:

- Government debt was relatively cheap at prevailing interest rates, and any resulting weakness in the dollar should also benefit exporters.

- The 'crowding-out effect' of government spending and borrowing was minimal because in the prevailing slack economy the private sector was not actively seeking investment opportunities and credit expansion.
- If government spending leads to inflation, interest rates must rise, but nominal GDP will also expand, keeping the GDP/debt ratio steady.
- There is no operational limit to US government debt because of its monetary sovereignty – it prints money as needed.
- The equity purpose of government taxing and spending must also be considered, that is, it redistributes wealth – though sometimes with adverse effects such as the overspending on least productive members of society.

Of course, the downside of government deficits is the debt burden and interest cost that must ultimately be borne by taxpayers. The real danger is that financial markets may judge that the debt is unsustainable and will detract too much from future growth, and the US currency and financial markets may then come under sustained selling pressure. The austerity school of thought posits further arguments:

- Government deficit spending had already transferred funds to the private sector, so the real problem was that the private sector was not investing it sufficiently. The market was awaiting more certainty, not more deficits.
- Low prevailing interest rates and other direct or indirect government subsidies can cause the economy to misallocate resources.
- Low rates also subsidize borrowers at the expense of savers.
- The government was repeating Japan's mistake of the 1990s of creating 'zombie' borrowers, as a result of cheap debt and the failure to resolve the problem of 'toxic' loans where defaulting mortgages and companies' unpaid debt were not compelled into liquidation. Bad loans clogged the banks' books and capital was not being reallocated for new investment.
- The austerity school is strengthened by the concept of 'generational accounting', which attempts to measure not only current deficits but also future anticipated tax and spend figures. The gap grows larger with adverse population trends, that is, the aging of societies results in senior citizens paying less tax but becoming costly for the younger generation to support. (Kotlikoff & Fehr, 1997.)

In the heated political debate, it seemed that both austerity and stimulus schools of thought existed obliviously side by side. Governments must have coherent strategies to boost both demand and supply. Of course, the direct cause of the economic crisis – as well as the weakness of the subsequent recovery – was the dramatic withdrawal of the private sector. The argument that governments have no role to play in such circumstances seems spurious.

5.2.2. Re-evaluation of Financial Management Theory

The four-decade long creed that 'the free market' would be rational, efficient and far-sighted has been exposed as false. The intellectual edifice of this belief, the Efficient Market Hypothesis (EMH), led us to a misguided trust in 'market forces' and a false sense of security that resulted in financial and economic disaster.

The EMH came to prominence from about the 1970s, holding that the price of a financial asset reflects all market information accurately and completely, with estimations of future relevant information discounted to the present value. Asset prices are thus driven by economic fundamentals.

Sceptics and revisionists have relied more on behavioural economics (although there was always considerable credence given to such 'perfect market' theory as the EMH). One behaviourist practitioner, George Soros, ironically was making his fortune by exploiting market imperfections as a hedge-fund trader.[68] Soros (1987) suggested a 'reflexive' theory of markets. Reflexivity meant that traders acted not on economic fundamentals but rather on how they expected other market participants to act. The point was to exploit market movements faster than other traders, thus to ride market trends to their advantage. According to the EMH, market trends do not exist because future trends should be discounted into current market prices.

One implication of behavioural aspects of financial markets is that bankers become overconfident with prolonged success of a particular strategy and then extrapolate prevailing trends into the future, a tendency that contributes to market bubbles. On the other hand, losses can create irrational risk aversion, causing market panic despite what the economic fundamentals might indicate.

The belief that an existing market price is kept in correct equilibrium has taken a serious hit. Economists now see a more legitimate role for government to oppose market forces when there is an impending bubble or crash – 'leaning against the wind' to reduce market volatility. Another priority is to have improved information on what all players are doing to better monitor situations when too many players were leaning in one direction, to anticipate systemic risk. Furthermore, there is a need to manage 'moral hazard' if government regulation or implied guarantees encourages market players to take bigger risks than they might undertake without any reliance on government safety nets.

The pre-Keynesian mode of thought held that full employment would prevail because supply created its own demand (Say's law). In a classical economy, whatever people earn is either spent or saved, and savings is invested.[69] The classical assumption was that when market demand faltered, asset prices would fall until markets cleared at a lower price level, leaving no unsold goods or unemployed workers; and efforts by governments would do more harm than good. This lack of faith in government prevails today.

The pragmatic Keynesian view was that wages and prices might fail to adjust and policymakers must step in. Modern economists accepted the necessity for government intervention to support the prices of goods and services, but they had too much faith that financial markets would get asset prices right. Asset prices were deemed to be determined by economic fundamentals, not panics or other market irrationality, so policy should address these fundamentals. A corollary assumption was that prices exist for everything at any time so that market players could always borrow money or sell assets at the going rate. By this logic, mortgages or other debts could always have a market. When funds dried up and markets thinned out in late 2008, the Credit Crisis was upon us.

Economists need to better understand why liquidity suddenly dries up. Economic theory still relies on Keynes' 'liquidity preference' notion. In the face of uncertainty, savers might decline to invest or spend, and therefore government must intervene to cut interest rates or create public works to restore market demand.

5.2.3. The Compensation Issue in Financial Institutions

Thus, there is a need for more understanding of bankers' behaviour and the inner workings of the financial system. In modelling the economy, financial intermediaries like banks might never be mentioned and insolvencies cannot occur. In recent decades, theorists have been paying more attention to institutional questions, including the controversial issue of pay and bonuses for executives. Arguably, the finance profession is human-capital intensive, like law and medicine, with individual talent wresting relatively more of the economic rents away from stockholders (which is why partnership–ownership structure was preferred in traditional banks, like law and medical practices).

Although executive-pay decisions thus have behavioural aspects, competitive enterprises should structure incentives based on long-term economic performance. At least, bonuses for making new loans should be deferred until the borrower establishes a reliable payback record. Incentive in the form of long-term stock options rather than cash aligns management incentive with ownership, which is theoretically the best approach.

Pay and bonuses cannot be regulated easily, and managers arguably should be rewarded for their contribution to firms. However, compensation practices have allowed great disparities in income and strongly encouraged risk-taking over prudence. Even the banks subject to conditions for bailout funds still dished out lavish bonuses. Despite rules enacted in February 2009, for the first half of 2009, nine banks gave out more than $32 billion in bonuses, even as the banks took $175 billion in taxpayer dollars. Nearly 5,000 people received $1 million or more. At year end 2009, large bonuses were awarded again.

The administration proposed new rules on 4th February 2009, and again on 10th June. A 'pay czar' would oversee pay packages to the highest paid employees of the largest institutions that received bailout funds, including limits on bonus and severance packages. He could ban pay packages at large institutions that would encourage 'inappropriate' risk-taking, but it was unclear how to judge when a pay plan could fuel 'inappropriate' risks. The criteria were arbitrary, for example, oversight applied to only the top 100 executives of seven selected firms. During October 2009, the 'pay czar' cut the pay of the top five executives and 20 highest paid employees at the seven banks; in December, a $500,000 pay cap was imposed (with exceptions), at least half total pay deferred three years (including stock options), and cash limited to 45% of bonuses. The 'czar' decreed that bonuses be based on 'real performance measures' and be taken back if results they were based on 'prove illusory'. However, he resisted suggestions of a broader authority over more banks or to require corporate-governance changes.

The Treasury secretary said government would not meddle in the details of compensation packages, and it would not impose restrictions such as caps on pay on other companies outside the bailout scheme; but companies should adopt a series of broad principles and improve stockholder oversight. The principles might include to avoid rewarding short-term risk-taking and 'golden parachutes', and to ensure compensation committees are independent of management. Consultants who advise such committees sometimes work for bigger firms that are concerned with keeping other businesses with bosses under scrutiny; so their independence is also in question. The Sarbanes–Oxley Act, which restricted auditors' ability to cross-sell other services, might apply to compensation consultants who should be similarly restricted to bolster their independence. Any such rules would certainly be tested for loopholes by the job market – all affected firms and employees would look for an escape.

One proposal was to let stockholders vote on executive compensation – a 'say on pay' resolution (passed in July 2010). However, the vote would not be binding. Another voluntary measure was a 'brake provision' to withhold such payments in a financial crisis. The Obama administration also proposed legislation to give the Securities and Exchange Commission (SEC) power to ensure that compensation committees are independent in ways similar to corporate audit committees and can hire independent consultants.

The traditional argument against modifying bonus systems has been that each institution had to reward talent handsomely or competitors would poach its people, but after the crisis any bank failing to reduce its bonuses tended to be publicly challenged by the media, politicians and be scrutinized by regulators.

Banks need to use risk-adjusted measures in calculating the size of the bonus pool and allocating it. Economic-capital models designed to allocate capital based on expected losses are being studied by firms and may be used increasingly in the future ('Special Report on International Banking', *The Economist*, 16-5-09, p. 15). Cost of capital for investment in talent as well as new assets must properly reflect risk.

However, such theoretical strictures are impractical. Perhaps our best hope is for widespread public disapprobation to compel some change in the culture of firms – pay for top executives in the United States was estimated to be 400x the pay of workers, whereas the difference is only 12x in Japan and 11x in Germany (BBC World Service, 29-10-08).

In American society, the capitalist culture has long considered it legitimate, even desirable, to embrace the reality of a growing income gap between the rich and the poor, management and labour, etc. – that is, the legitimacy of the notion that star performers should collect inordinately greater rewards for their efforts than average. However, the economic reality of a wide income gap – between salaries of executives versus average workers at least – is relatively recent. Almost all income gains in America since 1975 have been among the richest 20% of households. The richest 1% of Americans accounts for 24% of national income; yet that share of national income was only about 18% in 1915, the era of worsening class warfare and relatively wide sympathy for Marxism (CIA World Factbook).

5.2.4. Unemployment as the New Normal

While a few employees were thus getting bonuses, vastly more workers lost their jobs or were having their pay reduced – a payroll tug-of-war between the rich and the poor being won by the rich. Job scarcity, not to mention scant pay raises, further depressed consumption that was needed to spur job-creating investment. Existing businesses used the opportunity to reduce the labour burden that was perennially a major business cost.

Never had business shed so many workers so fast, and unemployment totalled so many workers looking for work or dropping out of the labour force, creating a serious national (and international) dilemma. As with the issue of the eternal rich–poor gap, there were no long-term policy solutions agreeable to mainstream economics. At the Forum on Jobs and Economic Growth in early December 2009, the president challenged the participants to come up with 'fresh perspectives' and 'new ideas'. However, the proposals were primarily short-term spending initiatives revolving around Obama's stated priorities of bolstering small business growth, providing emergency aid to people and places, advancing the energy efficiency of homes, and expanding investments in transportation and communications infrastructure. Practical solutions for more stimulus-created jobs, especially infrastructural projects, seem attractive but are economically problematic. Worse, nations resort to beggar-thy-neighbour job protectionism.

According to the concept of 'hysteresis', employment capacity may suffer lasting decline due to deleterious effects on the workforce and other causes. (Blanchard and Summers (1987) developed the concept to contest Milton Friedman's 1968 argument for a 'natural' rate of unemployment equilibrium.) Hysteresis is poorly understood in practice. Essentially, the unemployed workers' skills atrophy or become outdated; also, existing workers demand wages that create barriers to new hiring. Governments of course agree that rising unemployment justifies urgent policy actions. Solutions have included wage and hiring subsidies, early retirements, retraining or other services for job seekers, enlarging the public sector, or even taking an opposite tack to minimize the moral hazard of their own benefits for unemployment insurance and welfare. Such policies persist worldwide, with mixed results and no widely accepted long-term policy solutions.

Employment is inevitably a lagging indicator of economic recovery from recession, but in this case the problem did not appear to be abating. There are exotic ideas out there involving 'job sharing'.[70] However, government-designed schemes and subsidies may only delay job losses and inevitable closure of unviable firms.

A great question loomed as a threat to labour relations (and political stability) in the future: Could high unemployment become the new normality? Many American businesses had little incentive to start hiring or to raise pay and benefits, simply because labour remained in surplus supply worldwide. Economic revisionists are coming to believe that putting America's army of jobless back to work will require a deep reduction in labour costs – to become competitive with overseas workers who have reached high productivity at lower wages. The decline of the US dollar had slowly been achieving a cost adjustment since 2001, but a faster adjustment was indicated for the desperate jobless. A steep pay cut is a terrifying idea, a nightmare scenario that could compel a downward spiral in pay expectations – a 'race to the bottom'. Even if American workers improved their relative competitiveness, the global workforce surplus might remain unacceptably high. American consumers cannot resume indefinitely buying the products of global producers because this would recreate the imbalance that was largely to blame for the current economic demise. Ultimately, a future sustainable world economy may feature an abundance of production capacity and job seekers, chasing inadequate consumers.

5.2.5. Re-evaluation of Management Performance

Perhaps the central lesson of the entire economic fiasco is the failure of leadership in American business. What we have witnessed is a clear case of market failure, despite recriminations from the right wing about the risk of non-market failure (political and bureaucratic consequences of government intervention, government demand for funds crowding out private investment, etc.). It is free markets that have wrecked havoc, not governments. Bankers went on a high leverage binge of proprietary risk-taking and executive self-aggrandizement, and the car industry experienced decades of mismanagement and union intransigence.[71] Free-market capitalism itself has been discredited, and we can only hope a new model of business and financial management will emerge from the ruins. Asians had a sad lesson in 1997 about the fallacy of free capital markets – this was the mantra of the Washington Consensus and it disallowed government rescue as country after country experienced devastating financial turbulence. Those few voices that appealed for reasonable help for the East Asian countries were denigrated as 'economic revisionists'. Now that calamity has come to Americans, economic revisionism might proceed with less opposition.

Economic revisionists may conclude that banks needed to be temporarily nationalized to compel them to do what was needed at the height of the financial crisis: to provide vital loans and to purge bad debts from their portfolios. However, one obstacle to pragmatic action was the fear that public perceptions would interpret this course as 'creeping socialism'. American politics continues to impede rational policy-making and implementation. The great Jeffersonian legacy of government of the people and by the people must make way for the Hamiltonian politics of governmental empowerment for the collective purpose of nation building. Such arguments have increasing urgency.

5.3. Recap: The Aftermath

The final quarter of 2009 ended with the fastest pace of economic growth in six years (5.6% APR) and a surge of 8% in corporate profits, which was the biggest year-on-year gain in 25 years. Although corporate profits might be attributed to restructuring and cost cutting, some companies claimed to be experiencing stronger consumer purchasing, climbing exports and more business investment (e.g. Caterpillar Inc. and Boeing Co.) (*Los Angeles Times*,25-3-2010, p. B5). Still, unemployment and home foreclosures continued to increase.

The world economy did seem safer from immediate crisis in 2010, but recovery was hesitant. The economy was expected to perhaps encounter a 'double-dip' of recovering, then waning, growth as stimulus spending wound down and private business was not yet confident enough to take up the slack. Another crash could be on the horizon if the massive government 'debt bomb' sparked a crisis of confidence. Paradoxically, bank bailouts by governments led to a need for banks to support governments, but the herd-like behaviour in financial markets was prone to panic.

Worldwide, though some economies faced possible new debt crises, the global system would hopefully be anchored by resilient economies elsewhere. Many of the most dynamic 'emerging markets' – Brazil, Singapore, South Korea, Taiwan – had contracted in the last quarter of 2008 twice as badly as rich countries, but by the end of 2009 had recouped their losses generally better than the rich economies. Emerging economies had suffered disproportionately because of their trade and financial links with the West, and indeed exports had plunged and capital flows dried up; but many had instituted policy measures that led to quick turnaround. East Asia had learned a healthy scepticism towards American free-market financial theory, having taken painful medicine prescribed for their own crisis a decade earlier; and they have seen that their own model for market development – with less freedom and more control – was quite a legitimate formula.

The American economic and political establishment had lost some credibility just as it needed renewed energy to deal with many unresolved problems: establishing the new mechanisms for monitoring systemic risk and disposition of financial firms 'to big to fail', handling trading in fragile markets, winding down the government's huge stakes in banks, autos, housing (Fannie Mae and Freddie Mac) and overspending generally.

What really changed was social spending. Although some countries had to turn to the IMF and tighten fiscal policy, others (notably China) instituted stimulus programmes bigger as a share of GDP than most rich economies. China's spending arguably did more to combat global recession than the West; and their people and infrastructure benefited. China's policies forestalled the looming disaster of migrant-labour unemployment.

American business (especially smaller enterprises) awaited a more certain environment for investment. The job market continued to lag securities market recoveries. Consumers cut down personal debt rather than spend. Changes in the financial, healthcare, energy and other industries would take years to resolve. In the long term, the feeling in the air seemed to be that a new type of economy had to emerge, but would producers be stifled by regulation or seize new opportunities; would consumers be ebullient or was the future more bleak for the next generation? These unknowns created a cloud of doubt over corporate boardrooms, government offices, and kitchen tables all over the world.

NOTES

1. A timeline of failure might identify the precipitating event on Wall Street as the bankruptcy of Lehman Brothers (and the acquisition of Merrill Lynch by Bank of America) on 10th September 2008. The government announced a $85-billion rescue of American International Group on 16th September, and on 19th September the US Treasury and Federal Reserve approached Congress with a $700-billion plan to buy 'toxic assets', which passed two weeks later. On 25th September, Washington Mutual became the largest US bank failure. (The 2008 credit crisis had first emerged as severely tightened liquidity in August 2007, with the financial storm striking markets dramatically one year later.)
2. By the autumn of 2009, the crisis appeared to be abating as stock markets rebounded and credit flows resumed at a modest pace. However, few economists believed that there would be a return to business as usual. Wall Street will struggle to regain its swagger, and regulators and reformers are poised for a major revamping of financial capitalism, as this chapter will explain. Arguably, Wall Street's muted resurgence reflected primarily immense government liquidity infusions and guarantees for systemically important banks, artificially cheap borrowed funds and temporary tax incentives – the 'invisible wallet' of taxpayers.
3. A hedge fund invests money contributed by wealthy individuals, pension funds and others willing to undertake big-ticket investments. Unlike mutual funds, hedge funds were not open to the public or required to register with the Securities and Exchange Commission (SEC) (although the financial reform legislation signed in July 2010 mandated hedge fund reporting to the SEC). Of course, funds typically provided audited information to contributors, but such voluntary disclosures only gave regulators limited scrutiny.
4. Computers themselves may have contributed to the financial uncertainty. Globally fragmented information technology (IT) systems can obfuscate rather than clarify risk. (*The Economist*,12/5/2009, pp. 83–84).

5. The potential for a collapse of AIG to bring down other financial giants worldwide, because of what the insurer owed them, was the major justification the government cited for its biggest single bailout of one firm, totalling $182.5 billion. (Initial funding consisted of $85 billion from the Federal Reserve using its emergency lending power, with additional Fed money later, and Treasury bailout funds of $70 billion – TARP.) The government's initial payment to AIG in September 2008 was deliberately calculated as also a bailout of major Wall Street banks that were owed money by the insurance giant. As a result of the rescue, the government owned 80% of AIG, which AIG was paying back largely by selling off its profitable business units. There was considerable doubt that taxpayers would get all their money back.

6. Holders of debt instruments buy credit default insurance from dealers. The dealer, in turn, hedges its position by selling the insurance contract at discount. Traders of swaps need not own the underlying debt and may simply be speculators. The swap market can become quite frenzied and volatile, and not necessarily economically rational. (For California debt, adverse speculation in swaps implied a real default risk, which may make state bond issues more costly.) In the event of a missed loan payment, the actual obligation to pay the contract is determined by auctions run by a trade association of swap dealers.

7. Becoming a bank holding company provided Goldman Sachs and Morgan Stanley a strong competitive advantage. Their customer deposits were protected by the Federal Deposit Insurance Corporation (FDIC) as with any depositor-based bank, and they had access to the Federal Reserve's 'discount window' and other facilities only open to commercial banks. Thus, their risk was smaller because of explicit and implicit government support, thereby making even private borrowing cheaper. While still engaged in much of their old investment banking business, these two institutions could 'have their cake and eat it too', with a cost-of-capital advantage and the opportunity just as before to participate in market-making as a major player.

However, the risk to the overall economy could be considered to have worsened – the market concentration of investment banking was now much greater, with only two institutions in the market.

8. If interest rates on T-bills become negative, the government gets paid for borrowing rather than paying investors–an absurdity. Investors would thus prefer to buy the T-bills rather than hold cash. Implicitly, investors trust the US government more than its money. Theoretically, this cannot happen – reflecting risk of cash itself, yet the T-bills are paid off with cash.

9. Implementation of the stimulus also became an issue. It was necessary for the package to go through the appropriations process and allocated over time. Through the height of the crisis (the end of the first half of 2009), only $56 billion had been spent, with $158 made available, and only about one-fourth of the package would be spent by the end of 2009. Also, some was not spent as intended. Money going to the states was applied to fill budget gaps (90% going to Medicaid) instead of being invested in job-creating projects.

10. In this instance, the worst of the credit crisis was already past before any spending bill passed by Congress; tax cuts and other financial incentives were largely hoarded by banks, businesses and consumers, adding to savings but not investment; and the stimulus was dissipating just when more economic impetus was needed in

2010. The most visible impact was on the deficit, which further deflated market confidence.

11. By mid-year 2010, another stimulus bill was being debated. Republicans in Congress disallowed more spending, but renewal of the 'Bush tax cuts' signed into law on 17th December 2010 constituted an $858-billion stimulus – by ballooning the deficit.

12. The concept of alternative currencies that compel consumption is not new. Irving Fisher (1933) wrote a pamphlet 'Stamp Script' about a type of currency that, if hoarded, would be taxed with a stamp. In Bavaria today, a script called *chiembauer* is used alongside the euro for some purchases. The notes have an expiry date after which they require renewal with a sticker costing 2% of their value.

13. The Dow ended 2009 up 11%, and was up 19% in 2010; other securities markets did even better. In 2010, Standard & Poor's 500 (a benchmark for retirement accounts) increased by 12.8% and the Russell 2000 (small-company stocks) by 25.3%, indicating that investors were betting on economic recovery.

14. The Federal Reserve from early 2009 to early 2010 bought $1.75 trillion in debt, targeting long-term rates to ease the credit crunch affecting mortgages and corporate bonds.

Despite the Fed's political neutrality, it chose the day after the November 2010 congressional elections to announce a new $600 billion programme of quantitative easing; and even more was anticipated. The impact on global markets was also destabilizing, with global cash flows swamping the more attractive emerging markets, giving them appreciating currencies and falling exports, as well as frothy asset markets. Ultimately, it was argued that this would force some rebalancing in world trade, which was essential in the long run to solve the problem of America's longstanding current account deficit, and it would compel many major surplus countries to consume more. (see Section 4.1).

15. According to a later report ('Need to Know', *PBS*, Sept 3, 2010), federal bailout money lent, spent or guaranteed to Wall Street was $12.8 trillion. Estimated figures varied widely.

16. For example, by summer 2009, the Fed had reduced the amount of money available to its Term Auction Facility, decreased the amounts lent by the Commercial Paper Funds Facility and let the Money Market Investor Funding Facility expire – because it had never been used.

17. The corporate bond market benefited, as investors were more optimistic about private debt and equity markets and putting their money there instead of buying treasuries. Potentially, declining demand for treasuries may be tantamount to an indictment of US monetary and fiscal policy and rejection of the dollar.

18. Major sovereign defaults have occurred before (e.g. the Latin American debt crisis of the 1980s, Argentina's bonds in 2001, Russian bonds after the communist revolution and again in 1998), and also bankruptcy compels bondholders to accept restructured debt (e.g. General Motors in 2009).

Certainly the Treasury must pay back its bonds or the global monetary system will collapse. As long as the Fed can print more dollars the US government will meet its immense debt obligations.

19. A 'resolution authority' was included in the July 2010 reform law for future takeover of assets.

20. On 2nd April 2009, the Financial Accounting Standards Board (FASB), which oversees US accounting rules, changed the so-called mark-to-market accounting convention on mortgage-backed securities in effect since November 2007. The FASB now gave banks more leeway to revalue many 'toxic assets' depending on prices that might be realized in 'an orderly transaction' rather than at prevailing distressed prices. This potentially allowed banks to boost the asset values on their balance sheets and hence augment their lending capacity. Critics observed that banks could now understate potential losses to bolster their capital positions and that the FASB had acted under political pressure. Bankers responded that their current valuation practices would not be significantly altered since they would continue to exercise prudential valuation.

21. Banks seemed to be deciding that there was no free lunch to be gained from government bailout. By April 2009, five banks had repaid a total of $353 million in TARP bailout funds to escape the tough restrictions placed on participants in the rescue programme. (In addition, they paid $5.4 million in dividends.)

The Treasury was chary to allow repayment until the safety of the financial system was assured. Regulators gave 10 banks permission in June to repay their bailout funds in full. On 17th June, $68 billion was repaid; the Treasury still had about $129 billion invested in about 580 financial institutions. By December 2009, of TARP outlays totalling over $200 billion, more than half had been repaid including $10 billion in dividends and interest. (However, some loans were more problematic – for example, AIG and the Big 3 auto firms; and unutilized TARP funds were being channeled for other government stimulus priorities.)

22. Unemployment reached 10.2% in October 2009, already nearly equaling the Treasury's worst-case 'adverse' scenario of 10.3% in 2010, which made it clear that the forecasts had not anticipated such a weak recovery in employment. (In February 2009, the same month that the 'baseline' and 'adverse' scenarios were announced, unemployment in California reached 10.5% – soaring to 13% by 2010.)

23. The issue of 'asymmetric information', identified by Nobel prize-winning economist George Akerlof (1970), may come into play here. Buyers need the same information and the same capacity to judge value as sellers. It was difficult for either side to be confident about the value of such a tangled web of derivatives, sub-prime-mortgage-backed securities, etc. The liquidity crisis would be rekindled for the same reasons it occurred in the first place: neither borrowers nor lenders would step forward.

24. The actual results of the tests were announced on 7th May and were not as bad as some had feared – bank executives and the stock market welcomed the news. Ten of the 19 banks were told to develop detailed plans by 8th June to boost their capital by a combined total of $75 billion through stock offerings, selling business units or other assets, merging with competitors, converting government preferred stock into ownership stakes, or other means, with the government providing more bailouts as the last resort. (Already $216 billion had been provided to the 19 banks from TARP.) The tests found that the 19 banks would have needed $185 billion at the end of 2008 but had trimmed their losses; and they would face total losses of $600 billion in 2009 and 2010 in the specified 'worse-case scenario' and thus needed to raise more capital.

25. The government reached tentative agreement with Citigroup on February 27, 2009 (contingent upon agreement by the other preferred stockholders), to convert

some of its preferred stock to common stock at a premium of 32% over the previous market close. Becoming Citigroup's biggest owner, the government came closer to nationalizing a bank since the takeover of failed Continental Illinois in 1984. Existing common stockholders responded with a market sell-off, pushing the price down 117% below the conversion price and topping the record trading volume set by WorldCom in 2002. A congressman remarked: 'The only thing worse than nationalizing a bank is to pay for the entire bank and only get a third of it!'

26. The Credit Cardholders' Bill of Rights was signed into law on 22nd May 2009, designed to curb industry practices such as raising interest rates on existing balances without notice, sudden and unexplained fees, and marketing cards to people under 21. The bill had strong political support but was opposed by issuers who argued it might have the unintended consequence of constraining credit. By the time the bill went into force on 20th August, banks had taken steps to try to ensure that their credit card operations, historically one of their most lucrative businesses, remained that way. Banks had raised fees, interest rates, tightened lending standards and credit limits, and taken other measures, effectively revising their business model.

27. The broader origins of the crisis are attributed by some to the Reagan era. The Depository Institutions Act of 1982 ended restrictions on mortgage lending in effect since the 1930s. The ballooning of both public and private debt following Reagan deregulation culminated in the near-zero savings rate that prevailed on the eve of today's great crisis. Household debt was only 60% of income when Reagan took office, about the same as it was during the Kennedy administration. By 2007, it was up to 119% .

28. Fannie Mae is the nickname for the Federal National Mortgage Association, established in 1938 as part of President Roosevelt's New Deal. Freddie Mac is the Federal Home Loan Mortgage Corporation, established in 1970 to compete with Fannie Mae. The two provide a secondary market for mortgages by buying mortgages from lenders, securitizing them and reselling them as guaranteed investments. (A third government-sponsored enterprise, Ginnie Mae – Government National Mortgage Association, would keep its explicit government support and continue to back loans to low-income families.)

29. However, this estimate seemed high. Later estimates by Federal Housing Finance Agency (FHFA) ranged from $238 to $363 billion. The FHFA was suing for repayment by banks that sold bad loans to Fannie and Freddie, on the basis that the loans did not meet underwriting standards. Most bad loans had been incurred before the government intervention that had compelled Fannie and Freddie to reform lending practices.

(The FDIC also was initiating claims against officers and directors of banks it had shut down since 2008. As federal receiver for failed banks, the agency sells bank assets and backs up the liquidation process with its deposit insurance fund. The FDIC has three years from the date of the failure to file lawsuits for compensation for wrongdoing; thus the claims were just beginning – as was the case for FHFA lawsuits.)

30. Legislative stalemates and the difficulties of reform delayed the administration from issuing a complete overhaul proposal for the housing-finance system (to include Fannie and Freddie) until 2011.

31. A $75-billion Homeowner Affordability and Stability Plan announced on 4th March 2009 was a two-part programme: First, loans held or securitized by Fannie and Freddie would qualify for refinancing to prevailing lower interest rates. The programme was available to borrowers current on their payments where the mortgage balance due exceeded the value of the home by less than 105%. Such loans were otherwise likely to end in foreclosure. For those mortgages not qualified, a second part of the anti-foreclosure programme provided a subsidy for mortgage-servicing companies to modify loans to lower payments to 31% of the borrower's income. A series of actions were possible: reducing the interest rate to as low as 2%, extending the repayment period to 40 years, skipping interest payments or forgiving a portion of the debt. The plan was controversial because many loans exceeded the 105% loan-to-value limit and also were beyond the price limit for Fannie and Freddie financing – notably in California where property values were much higher.

Due to the complexities of the programme, eligible homeowners often failed to take advantage of their opportunity to refinance. Also, the voluntary nature of the programme meant banks failed to initiate loan refinancing despite the subsidies offered. Foreclosures did not quickly subside as hoped.

On 14th May, the plan was expanded to allow lenders incentive payments of as much as $1,000 even if a loan modification was not possible, by allowing the borrower a short sale in which the lender accepts less than the value of the mortgage, transferring ownership to the lender without a foreclosure. This constituted an acknowledgement by the government that not all distressed borrowers would be able to save their homes. Lenders had been initiating foreclosures despite the government programme. To that point, the government announced that more than 50,000 homeowners had been offered lower cost mortgages, and lenders representing 75% of the US mortgages had agreed to participate; but implementation was uneven.

On 26th March 2010, the administration proposed further adjustments: to give jobless homeowners a break on payments, give lenders more incentives to reduce principal and other steps. Bank of America had proposed its new mortgage modification programme a day earlier to cut the principal for some borrowers, an estimated debt forgiveness of $3 billion. Banks were desperate to keep borrowers from simply walking away from their properties, since 24% of mortgages exceeded their property value at the end of 2009.

32. Despite President Obama's efforts to block influence on his government by special interests, the legion of Washington lobbyists was growing, evidently to take advantage of stimulus funding opportunities. The number of registrations filed with the Senate Office of Public Records during the first quarter of 2009 was up from the year before. Mr Obama had barred lobbyists from speaking with administration officials about stimulus projects, and any written communication had to be posted online. However, lobbyists could try to influence senators and representatives to carry clients' messages to the White House.

33. Mortgage banks were accused of abuses, such as the infamous 'robo-signing' scandal that uncovered banks' approvals of improper foreclosures. Indeed, banks were quite overwhelmed by the wave of mortgage defaults, foreclosures, and modifications the crisis unleashed. Misguided incentive systems were also evident. For example, where mortgage servicers charged fees based on loan principle, banks were averse to reducing principle through modification and instead preferred

foreclosure to gain full reimbursement for servicers' fees and costs. This also constituted incentive for simply stretching out delinquent loans without either foreclosure or modification.

34. The Fed boosted its program to buy mortgage-backed securities from Fannie and Freddie to $1.25 trillion from a previous commitment of $500 billion, and it also said it would spend $300 billion to purchase longer-term T-bills and up to $200 billion on other agency debt. Rates were held low successfully.

On 29th April 2009, the Fed opted not to buy long-term Treasury bonds despite rising yields (declining prices), thus 'staring down' bond traders. Traders reacted by dumping treasuries, driving yields sharply higher. On the same date, the Treasury announced plans to boost sales of long-term bonds, to fund Treasury borrowing that had reached unprecedented levels. The Treasury seemed willing to get lower prices on its bond issues because mortgage rates were still low and investors were buying corporate bonds and stock.

35. Ford lost $14.7 billion in 2008 but it was soldiering on, without much government help. While GM and Chrysler were rationalizing their union and dealer obligations, rebuilding their balance sheets – all using bankruptcy protection and $62 billion in bailout funds from the Treasury, Ford was less able to overcome its own heavy debt and contractual obligations. On the plus side for Ford, its customer relations definitely benefited from its decision to eschew government help. Ford's market share in America leaped by over 2% during 2009 mostly at the expense of Chrysler and GM.

36. It seemed unlikely that the Big 3 hoped to abnegate their obligations for all pension plans, labour union agreements, healthcare insurance, and supply or operating contracts, unless eventually it becomes management's intention to forsake US operations as the mainstay of the company.

However, it was conceivable that management (though not the employee 'creditors') would be happy to further curtail their efforts in their home market where they had been uncompetitive for decades. The Big 3 had some remaining strong businesses and popular brands in Europe and in emerging markets with vast potential including China. With global markets likely to account for nearly all market growth in the future, North American operations had already been significantly reduced. Car sales in the so-called BRIC economies – Brazil, Russia, India, China – surpassed the American market in 2008 and was 10 million cars bigger than the size of the American market by 2010, after being 10 million cars smaller as recently as 2005 (*Financial Times*, 16/8/10; *The Economist*, 15/11/08). Nevertheless, some Big 3 operations overseas had been losing money for years and were earmarked for divestment (e.g. GM in Europe).

37. Bankruptcy would hurt advertising, impacting TV stations, newspapers and magazines that already were suffering from the recession. The multi-million dollar sponsorships for professional teams and other sports franchises had to be cut back. GM, Ford and Chrysler were, respectively, the 2nd, 6th and 10th largest advertisers in the US in 2008, but firms trying to emerge from bankruptcy cannot afford such big budgets. The Obama administration had asked Chrysler to halve its proposed marketing budget.

38. Ultimately, it was a small group of investors, referred to as Indiana pension funds, who appealed their case to the nation's top court. They argued that their

senior and secured investment status should be paid in full before lower priority creditors receive anything (and also arguing that use of TARP funds was illegal).

39. GM ceased to be a publicly traded company, with stock in the former GM tied to a new entity, Motors Liquidation Co., which remained in bankruptcy court along with the bad assets.

40. Lengths of Notable Bankruptcies (Data Source: *Los Angeles Times*, July 11, 2009, p. A12).

Company	Year	Number of Days
General Motors	2009	39
Chrysler	2009	41
Delta Air Lines	2005	593
Northwest Airlines	2005	624
Worldcom	2002	669
UAL	2002	1,150
Manville	1982	2,286
Dow Corning	1995	3,305

41. The federal and state governments scrambled to channel aid from existing programmes and find ways to help communities impacted most by all the business closures resulting from the bankruptcies. The Obama administration extended unemployment benefits, research grants for clean diesel engines, enlarged credit lines for small business, retraining and diversification support for clean-energy jobs, money to hire police officers, and used the bankruptcy process to facilitate the sale of closed plants. Although the bailout may have prevented liquidations that would have been even more destructive to the economy, some critics (e.g. Reich, 2009) believed that the huge cash injections for GM and Chrysler were misdirected; instead the bailout should have been allocated more towards communities in the states hardest-hit, such as tax breaks for relocating companies or seed capital for start-ups.

42. Unexpectedly, good news began to emerge in 2010 about the financial performance of the Big 3 (including Ford), bolstering the government's case for its various interventions. The Obama administration argued that its rescue operations had saved over a million auto-industry jobs. Then on 18th August 2010, GM filed for an initial public offering to sell part of the stock owned by the US and Canadian governments, UAW and former creditors. The timing of the IPO seemed driven by political, not market, considerations.

Banks also recovered (though they were not lending), and even AIG was promising to repay the government for its bailout (though it was not paying dividends on the 80% of its stock – largely preferred – owned by the government). What had been considered sunk costs for taxpayers had significantly declined.

43. Liability was eliminated for accidents that occurred prior to bankruptcy filing for both companies, although GM is liable for future accidents involving cars built before bankruptcy. Bankruptcy thus lifted a burden from lawsuits that cost the industry dearly, though obligation to victims of accidents due to alleged defects

would seem to be morally justified. Arguably, industry in America (notably healthcare) faced inordinate legal costs compared to foreign competition because of the litigious nature of American society.

44. TALF had been implemented in March 2009 to revitalize securitization and stimulate lending to small businesses and consumers. The Fed committed up to $1 trillion to investors in top-rated securities backed by auto and student loans, credit cards and other debts. The idea was that the programme could finance not only new asset-backed debt but also be part of the public–private programme to purchase toxic assets from banks' balance sheets. However, the $200-billion consumer-lending part of TALF was poorly utilized, with only $6.4 billion in loan requests during March–April. One reason for lack of demand was the bureaucratization and politicization of the lending process; participants were afraid of interference by Congress including executive-pay curbs, possible constraints on excessive profits or marketing budgets, and restrictions on hiring foreigners or investing overseas.

45. Moody's projected American government debt (including states) to hit 100% of GDP in 2010, higher than other AAA-rated nations – though greatly exceeded by Japan's debt at over 200%. Japan was downgraded to AA in 1998 after its prolonged banking crisis, low growth and numerous stimulus plans.

46. China's surplus seemed likely to continue indefinitely despite the problems caused by global financial imbalances. The Chinese government was intent on maintaining high employment in export industries. To keep its economy growing faster than any other major country in 2009, the central government invested heavily in infrastructure – placing restrictions on exports of key raw materials to support the investment, but raising tax rebates on exports of manufactured goods. The central government also ordered local governments to use only Chinese goods and services when spending money tied to the national stimulus plan. The restrictions on imports of foreign goods were partly in response to 'Buy American' provisions in the US stimulus package.

47. Short-selling, or selling securities by borrowing them with the idea of buying them back later at a lower price, is generally viewed as beneficial to market liquidity; but it can contribute to market collapse in a 'bear' market. The 'uptick rule', a Depression-era law, had prohibited short sales of stock unless the prior trade was at or above the previous price, to hamper relentless downward pressure on prices. Seen as ineffectual in modern liquid markets, the rule was eliminated in 2007. From 19th September to 8th October 2008, the Securities and Exchange Commission reinstated the ban on shorting to nearly 1,000 financial stocks, to counter widespread panic and concern that the financial industry was being trashed.

On 24th February 2010, the SEC imposed fresh curbs on short-selling when a stock fell by 10% in a day. At that point, short-selling would be allowed only if the sale price is above the market bid price. This was less strict than the former uptick rule, triggered only for stocks under severe pressure. Critics argued that such restrictions could sacrifice market integrity and efficiency.

48. Asian leaders were blamed by western bankers, politicians and media for causing their own crisis with misguided policies, government involvement in their businesses and banks, and profligate spending. Only the IMF would offer funding, but that institution insisted on economic orthodoxy that was inappropriate and

worsened the crisis in Asia. Americans believed that Asian companies and banks should go under, and governments should liberalize their capital markets to allow money to leave, which it promptly did. Today, American bailouts for their own institutions seem an unfair 'double standard'.

49. Credit rating had emerged as something of a scam. The three major bond raters: Standard & Poors, Moody's and Fitch were of doubtful veracity. As a ludicrous example, AIG and Citigroup enjoyed AAA ratings – far better than the state of California that has never defaulted and seems unlikely to do so. California is constitutionally obligated to make debt payments before paying almost anything else. After the state's credit was downgraded in late March 2009 to the lowest rating of any state, California had its largest and most successful bond issue in history according to the state treasurer's office. Evidently, investors disregarded the credit rating. It seems that a credit rating can be realistically irrelevant.

Yet the rating agencies are deeply embedded in the financial system. The Federal Reserve only accepts AAA-rated securities for collateral purposes. The Securities and Exchange Commission disallows money market funds to invest in paper below a certain rating. Pension funds are required to buy only bonds above a certain rating. For corporate issuers, a top credit rating means lower borrowing costs.

The rating agencies earn fees from issuers for rating their securities because that allows them to make all their ratings public without charging a subscription. However, the fees create a clear conflict of interest. Testimony before the Senate Permanent Subcommittee on Investigations indicated that executives at credit-rating agencies felt pressure to 'give Wall Street what it wanted' (*Los Angeles Times*, April 24, 2010, p. B4).

The obvious option to replace these agencies is to eliminate the agencies' official 'nationally recognized' status and open the business to competition. Ideally, the market itself should gauge credit risk, and the onus should be on investors to conduct their own due diligence and diversify their portfolios.

50. An expanding mortgage market acts as 'financial accelerator', raising the value of the real estate collateral. Increasing property prices, in turn, augment capacity of the mortgage market. During a downturn, the accelerator acts in reverse. This market externality of borrowing imposes costs on others and therefore might justifiably be paid in the form of a tax on borrowers (Posen & Korinek, 2010).

51. For example, Congress authorized the Fed in 1994 to write rules protecting consumers from predatory lending, but it took 14 years for the Fed to write the rules. In the interim, the Fed was seemingly oblivious of the rise and fall of the sub-prime mortgage market.

52. Goldman Sachs, for example, in the 1st quarter of 2010 reported revenue as 80.2% trading and principal investments, 10.5% asset management and securities services, and 9.3% investment banking.

53. The Office of Thrift Supervision was merged into the Office of the Comptroller of the Currency.

54. On 17th June 2009, the Obama administration unveiled an 88-page 'white paper' to regulate finance, constituting ideas that resurfaced later in Congress and elsewhere.

The 10th November 2009 Senate (Dodd) bill proposed three new regulatory agencies, including the CFPA. The House bill passed on 11th December (besides addressing the CFPA) proposed a $150-billion fund collected from Wall Street, plus additional government loans as necessary, for a 'resolution authority' to take over and restructure large financial firms instead of bailing them out. The House bill contemplated the FDIC handle the task, but the FDIC had not managed non-bank rescue efforts before.

A revised Dodd bill was published on 15th March 2010 and passed on 21st May. A new Financial Stability Oversight Council (FSOC) would identify financial firms 'too big to fail'. An 'orderly liquidation' of a failing firm by the Fed (rather than by the FDIC) would impose losses on stockholders and unsecured creditors. A $50-billion resolution fund collected from big banks (the House had approved $150 billion) had been dropped. Republican political resistance was based on the argument that such a fund would encourage future bailouts; but without such a fund available, taxpayers would likely be the first recourse for funding some future government-led financial rescue. Instead, the bill required post-resolution assessments on the financial industry to recoup any losses. Also, the FSOC would have the authority to impose stringent standards – capital, liquidity, concentration limits and heightened disclosure requirements.

The CFPA idea was retained but disallowed authority over the smallest banks – even though these banks were sometimes guilty of egregious consumer exploitation. Although housed in the Fed, the CFPA would nevertheless be autonomous. The Fed also would not have authority over small banks (and consumer protection), but it would retain its authority over big banks as well as adding authority over non-bank financial firms traditionally regulated by the states. However, the Fed's independence was at issue, with added political appointments and added pressures to be more responsible for financial stability.

New restrictions would be imposed on credit rating agencies, and stockholders given a say in corporate affairs. (Other, less significant, provisions are disregarded here.) One controversial provision not voted on would force big banks to spin off the very lucrative derivatives business altogether into separately capitalized corporate entities. The alternative approach, the Volker rule, would only constrain such proprietary trading (though significantly reducing total profit potential for the banks): Banks' investment in hedge and private equity funds would be limited to 3% of tier-1 capital.

The legislation finally cleared a House–Senate conference committee and was signed by the president on 21st July 2010; but the actual rule-making would take years – involving complex negotiations between regulators, the financial industry and other interested parties. Most sides agreed that financial regulation was essential, but it was a global problem without easy solutions. Washington politics seemed to compel either too much government intervention, or too little.

55. On 13th May 2009, the Obama administration proposed a broad framework to regulate derivatives. There were an estimated $400 trillion in outstanding contracts at the end of 2008. The administration wanted standardized derivatives to be traded through regulated central counterparties, or middlemen. Major dealers would be subject to supervision and regulation including reporting requirements and minimum levels of capital. Trades in customized derivatives would have to be reported to regulated trade repositories that would publicize aggregated data such as volumes and open positions. The Securities and Exchange Commission and the Commodity Futures Trading Commission would have joint oversight with increased

powers to monitor the markets for fraud, abuses and signs of risk to the overall financial system.

56. Treasury officials announced on 8th April 2009 that applications from life insurers for TARP money were now being considered since they too had been affected by the downturn in market values for their conservative investments in real estate and long-term debt. Insurance companies also had to boost capital reserves to reflect increased risk from the lowering of credit ratings on their holdings of corporate bonds.

Insurers had applied for support in 2008, and the Treasury granted preliminary approval on 14th May 2009 for a half-dozen applicants to receive TARP funds. The legislation creating TARP suggested that insurers could participate, but qualifying for federal supervision required consultation with state regulators.

57. The perennial Asian current account surplus by definition equals savings minus investment, indicating either too-high savings or too-low investment. By achieving saving rates of around 35% over several decades and using their surplus to invest in infrastructure and new industry, Asians have indeed sacrificed consumption; but future output and consumption have been enhanced.

Of course, too-high investment can result in excess capacity and falling returns on capital. Other concerns include overvalued asset prices and excessive expansion of credit. However, we cannot infer such misallocation from high investment alone. Developing countries generally have much less capital stock than rich countries, so they are unlikely to be adding too much unless there are evident productivity problems (poor capital/output ratios or total factor productivity – TFP).

58. China also perceives its fortunes tied to the European Union, as evinced by large Chinese bond purchases in 2010 from the most troubled governments in the euro zone. Effectively, China is the 'lender of last resort' to both the United States and Europe, assuming a position of importance beyond the IMF and even the Fed.

59. Yet in the credit crisis, emerging markets like in South East Asia did not suffer so much (except when the crisis got so much worse). China especially was relatively resilient because their financial system is tightly controlled, but China could not sell their exports; nor could South East Asia despite depreciating currencies there. Singapore has a large container port, which suffers from any decline in trade. Singapore has supervised its banks well and had little bad debt initially, and it has relatively high capital reserves in the banks and government coffers including its sovereign wealth fund. Singapore, however, as a financial centre shared the pain of global financiers. Singapore also experienced the race out of emerging-market currencies and institutions to US dollars to cover US dollar debt obligations. (The Japanese yen also appreciated, due to unwinding of the so-called 'carry trade' in which investors borrowed money cheaply in Japan and invested it overseas. This made Japanese goods more expensive on world markets and precipitated a steep plunge in Tokyo stocks.) A strong US dollar seems counterproductive because any American economic stimulus may only bail out foreign exporters, but the upward swing of the dollar continued inexorably into 2009.

60. Monthly job loss totals started falling finally, with 539,000 in April and 345,000 in May. Total jobs lost in the 1st quarter of 2009 were 2.1 million, declining to 1.3 million in the 2nd quarter. Thus, although total unemployment was obviously still rising, the rate of job loss was subsiding.

61. From December 2007 to year end 2009, 7.2 million jobs were lost and the number was still increasing.

62. *The Economist* (October 18, 2008, p. 86) divided the investment cycles of the 20th century into six phases:

Bear markets: 1901–1921, 1929–1949 and 1965–1982
Bull markets: 1921–1929, 1949–1965 and 1982–2000

From December 1999 to March 2003, the new bear market was characterized as the bursting of the dotcom bubble. From March 2003 to June 2007, we had the last full-fledged bull market. Lately, a new era has emerged, with an 86% gain from March 2009 to yearend 2010. Both these recent bull markets were accompanied by low interest rates and growing corporate profits. (The latest boom may also be considered artificial, sustained by stimulus spending and other government manipulation such as extremely low interest rates.)

Within these bear/bull timeframes, there were of course many ups and downs. The Dow Jones passed 1,000 in 1972 but fell to 616 by the end of 1974. In 1975, it rallied to 852 but then gained only 23 points in the next six years. In the current timeframe, the Dow dropped below 9,000 on 15th October 2008, a level it had passed in 1997; so the decade seemed to have been a wash. The recent downturn (since mid-2007) persisted until March 2009 when the depressionary mood seemed to be dispelled.

Subsequent growth in industry and jobs lags by far any growth in market investment. Profits fall rapidly in recessions because firms are relatively slow to cut fixed costs by closing factories and laying off workers. Profits recovered in the current recession after significant corporate downsizing.

63. The new approach after the Republican victory in November 2010 was to stop government spending and rely on the private sector to step forward (see Section 5.2.1).

64. Even with a weak US dollar much of America's spending goes to imports. In the 2nd quarter 2010 America's economy grew at an annual pace of 1.7% but imports grew by 33.5%.

65. The present value of the fiscal cost of healthcare and pensions in the rich world by 2050 is 10 times the fiscal cost of the financial crisis. (*The Economist*, June 13, 2009, p. 13; IMF calculations.)

66. The Moment of Truth, a report released on 1st December 2010 by the Obama administration's National Commission of Fiscal Responsibility and Reform, became the starting point for congressional action to reduce the deficit. It included a cap on discretionary spending, overhaul of the tax system, reforms to entitlement spending, healthcare and other policy spending (such as agriculture support), and other very controversial measures. Other proposals such as Domenici–Rivlin are added to the policy options. However, most specific reforms on the table seemed distant future possibilities at best.

67. Inspired blueprints were being proposed, such as the Mirrlees Review released on 10th November 2010.

68. Soros himself, a respectable intellectual as well as market manipulator, decried his very own business model that profited so handsomely from big-ticket market

trades. In genuine intellectual honesty, he once observed, *I'm afraid that the prevailing view, which is one of extending the market mechanism to all domains, has the potential of destroying society.*

69. It is an economic truism that savings must equal investment, equalized via the level of interest rates.

70. There seems to be growing interest in innovative schemes and possible policy approaches to the 'job sharing' concept, for example, the German *Kurzarbeit* formula to subsidize workers on a shorter work week. British higher education also developed a model.

71. British Petroleum's 2010 oil spill in the Gulf of Mexico is beyond the scope of this chapter. However, certainly this event can be seen as another instance of management (and government) failure to fully comprehend their own technologies, exercise full control over risky operations, conduct careful contingency planning and indeed to plan for more than just the predictability of revenue streams.

REFERENCES

Akerlof, G. A. (1970). The market for lemons: Quality uncertainty and the market mechanism. *Quarterly Journal of Economics*, *84*, 488–500.

Blanchard, O. J., & Summers, L. H. (1987). Hysteresis and the european unemployment problem, NBER chapters. In: *NBER macroeconomics annual 1986* (Vol. 1, pp. 15–90). National Bureau of Economic Research, Inc.

CIA World Factbook. Available at https://www.cia.gov/library/publications/the-world-factbook/.

Fisher, I. (1933). *Stamp Script*. New York: Adelphi Co.

Fitzpatrick, T., & Thomson, J. (August 2010). *Stripdowns and bankruptcy: Lessons from agricultural bankruptcy reform*. Federal Reserve Bank of Cleveland, OH.

Kotlikoff, L. J., & Fehr, H. (May 1997). *Generational accounting in general eEquilibrium*. NBER Working Paper No. W5090.

Los Angeles Times (various editions).

Posen, A., & Korinek, A. (2010). *Managing credit booms and busts: A Pigouvian taxation approach*. Available at www.korinek.com

Reich, R. (April 1, 2009). The auto bailout is going off the road. *Robert Reich's Blog*. Available at http://robertreich.blogspot.com/2009_04_01_archive.html

Reinhart, C., & Rogoff, K. (2009). *This time it's different: Eight centuries of financial folly*. Princeton, NJ: Princeton University Press.

Rodrik, D. (2010). *The return of industrial policy*. Project Syndicate.

Soros, G. (1987). *The alchemy of finance*. Simon & Schuster.

The Economist (various editions).

Yueh, L. (October 23, 2008). The financial cloud's silver lining. *The Guardian*. Available at http://www.guardian.co.uk/commentisfree/2008/oct/23/creditcrunch-recession

Zhou, X. (March 23, 2009). Reform the international monetary system (speech posted at: *People's Bank of China* Website).

FURTHER READING

Bibow, J. (2009). *Keynes on monetary policy, finance and uncertainty: Liquidity preference theory and the global financial crisis*. Routledge.

Fama, E. (1965). The behavior of stock market prices. *Journal of Business*, *38*, 34–105.

Marron, D., & Swagel, P. (May 24, 2010). Whither Fannie and Freddie? A proposal for reforming the Housing GSEs. *Economic Policies for the 21st Century,* Commentary Series. e21, Washington, DC: New York. Available at http://www.economics21.org/

Sikorski, D. (Spring 1999). The financial crisis in Southeast Asia and South Korea: Issues of political economy. *Global Economic Review, 28*(1), 117–129.

Sikorski, D. (2004). Globalisation or deglobalisation. In: J. Turner & Y. C. Kim (Eds), *Globalisation and Korean foreign direct investment*. Aldershot, UK: Ashgate.

THE CAUSES OF THE GLOBAL FINANCIAL CRISIS: WITH EMPHASIS ON CAPITAL ADEQUACY AND PRO-CYCLICALITY

Ali M. El-Agraa

ABSTRACT

The world has been gripped by the severest global financial (and economic) crisis since the Great Depression of the 1930s. How did it come about, what is being done to alleviate its consequences and, vitally, what measures should be undertaken to ensure against its recurrence are therefore questions that must be satisfactorily addressed. Preventing 'financial crises' from ever happening again is of course completely out of the question, they being inherent to the economic system as we understand it; rather that of those of the 'severest' kind. Fortunately, a vast literature has been accumulating on these issues, so the intention here is not to add to it and reinforce the perception that economists will offer more opinions on a single issue than the total membership of any assembled group thereof for the purpose. Hence, this is confined to a consideration of the most convincing explanations. Owing to space limitations, I shall not examine the recommendations for future action in

The Impact of the Global Financial Crisis on Emerging Financial Markets
Contemporary Studies in Economic and Financial Analysis, Volume 93, 91–126

ISSN: 1569-3759/doi:10.1108/S1569-3759(2011)0000093005

all the mentioned areas but will do so for what is being offered to cater for the capital adequacy and pro-cyclicality since they are of the essence and involve many players.

Jel Classifications: G01; G2; E1-E6; F3.

Keywords: Financial and economic crises; capital adequacy and capital pro-cyclicality; European Central Bank; UK Financial Authority; Turner Review; de Larosière et al. Report; leverage; asset-backed securities; collateralised debt obligations; special purpose vehicles; structured investment vehicles; sub-prime mortgages; securitisation; credit rating agencies; value-at-risk.

1. CAUSES OF THE FINANCIAL CRISIS

1.1. The Comprehensive Analyses

As just mentioned, explanations for the financial crisis have been forthcoming from a growing number of analysts, with six noted experts providing summaries in the special issue of the *eJournal USA* (2009). Credit must however go to Turner (2009, January) for being the first to offer a comprehensive rationale for the financial crisis. Although he did so in a public lecture, the definitive and detailed exposition on the basis of which he built his argument as well as his recommendations for what should be done in the future was soon made available (in March) in two publications by the UK Financial Services Authority (FSA), of which he is chairman: the *Turner Review* (UK FSA, 2009a) and *Discussion Paper* (UK FSA, 2009b). Indeed, the excellent analysis by de Larosière et al. (2009), in their February report to the European Commission of the European Union (EU), acknowledges this by their explicit reference to Turner's lecture (p. 17). It therefore suffices to confine the exposition to only these two.

In both the lecture (p. 1) and the two FSA publications, Turner begins by cautioning that it is only with hindsight that a fairly compelling and broadly agreed explanation can be set out. He then states that the crisis arose from a combination of macro-imbalances that had grown rapidly in the past decade and financial market developments and innovations that have been in progress over three decades but that accelerated over the past 10–15 years, partly under the stimulus of macro-imbalances (UK FSA, 2009a, p. 11). And de Larosière et al. (2009) reinforce that by arguing that the crisis is the outcome of a 'complex interaction of market failures, global financial and monetary imbalances, inappropriate regulation, weak supervision and poor macro-prudential oversight (p. 13).

They earlier elaborate that ample liquidity and low interest rates have been the main culprits of the present crisis but that financial innovation intensified and accelerated the outcomes of excess liquidity and rapid credit expansion. Strong macro-economic growth since the mid-1990s created an illusion that permanent and sustainable high levels of growth were not only possible, but likely. Owing to both inflation and interest rates being low, the volume of credit accelerated, and central banks, especially the US's FED, did not see a need for tightening monetary policy. Instead of raising the prices of goods and services, excess liquidity led to soaring asset prices. Such monetary policies then led to increasing imbalances in global financial and commodity markets (de Larosière et al., 2009, p. 7).

It seems natural to surmise that the very low US interest rates must have contributed to the creation of the widespread housing bubble. Both Turner and de Larosière et al. are of the opinion that the bubble was fuelled by unregulated, or insufficiently regulated, mortgage lending and complex securitisation financing techniques. Insufficient oversight over US government-sponsored entities (such as Fannie Mae and Freddie Mac) and strong political pressure on them to promote home ownership for low-income households aggravated the situation. Both recognise that within Europe, where there are different housing finance models, a number of EU nations experienced unsustainable increases in house prices, but in some they grew more moderately and, in general, mortgage lending was more responsible.

de Larosière et al.[1] then provide statistical information, and Turner offers an array of charts, tables and diagrams in support of their explanations. These clearly indicate that in the US personal savings fell from 7% as a percentage of disposable income in 1990, to below zero in 2005 and 2006; hence it is not surprising that consumer credit and mortgages expanded rapidly. In particular, sub-prime mortgage lending in the US rose significantly from $180 billion in 2001 to $625 billion in 2005. This was accompanied by the accumulation of huge global imbalances. The credit expansion in the US, depicted by a current account deficit of above 5% of GDP (or $700 billion a year) over a number of years, was financed by massive capital inflows from the major emerging countries and oil producers with external surpluses, notably China and Saudi Arabia. By pegging their currencies to the dollar, these countries in practice imported loose US monetary policy, thus allowing global imbalances to build up. Turner stresses that since China and other surplus countries are committed to fixed or significantly managed exchange rates, their excess savings take the form of central bank reserves that are typically invested not in a wide array of equity, property or fixed income assets, but almost exclusively in apparently risk-free or close to risk-free government bonds or government guaranteed bonds.[2] Current account surpluses in these countries were therefore recycled into US government securities and other lower-risk assets, depressing their yields and encouraging other investors to search for higher yields from more risky assets.

Turner[3] and de Larosière et al. are also agreed that in this environment of plentiful liquidity and low returns, investors actively sought higher yields and went searching for opportunities. Consequently, risk became undervalued, enticing the originators of investment products to develop more and more innovative and complex instruments designed to offer improved yields, often combined with increased leverage:

> In particular, financial institutions converted their loans into mortgage or asset backed securities (ABS), subsequently turned into collateralised debt obligations (CDOs) often via off-balance special purpose vehicles (SPVs) and structured investment vehicles (SIVs), generating a dramatic expansion of leverage within the financial system as a whole.

For example, the issuance of US ABS increased from $337 billion in 2000 to over $1.25 trillion in 2006, about a fourfold increase. Also, non-agency US mortgage-backed securities (MBS) rose from about $100 billion in 2000 to $773 billion in 2006. de Larosière et al. argue that although securitisation is in principle a desirable economic model, it was accompanied by opacity which camouflaged the poor quality of the underlying assets, thus contributed to credit expansion and the belief that risks were spread (de Larosière et al., 2009, pp. 7–8).

In turn, this led to increases in leverage and even more risky financial products. Given the macro-economic conditions preceding the crisis just mentioned, high levels of liquidity resulted finally in risk premiums falling to historically low levels. Exceptionally low interest rates combined with fierce competition pushed most market participants (both banks and investors) to search for higher returns, whether through an increase in leverage or investment in more risky financial products. Greater risks were taken, but not properly priced as shown by the historically very low spreads. Financial institutions engaged in very high leverage (on and off balance sheet), with many financial institutions having a leverage ratio of beyond 30, sometimes as high as 60, making them exceedingly vulnerable to even a modest fall in asset values (de Larosière et al., 2009, p. 8).

They stress that these problems developed dynamically. The rapid recognition of profits which accounting rules allowed led both to a view that risks were falling and to increases in financial results. This combination, when accompanied by constant capital ratios, resulted in a fast expansion of balance sheets and made institutions vulnerable to changes in valuation as economic circumstances deteriorated.

This raises the question of why investors acted as just described when spreads were very low. El-Arian offers a very convincing answer:

> the biggest puzzle of all [centred] on the reaction of investors – particularly the ability *and* willingness of the financial system to overconsume and overproduce risky products in the context of such large systemic uncertainty. Like others, I was struck by how two phenomena that [one] would expect to be negatively correlated ended up being positively correlated for so long – namely ... the significant fall in the premiums [which] investors were paid to assume risk and ... the investors' desire to assume more risk.
>
> The dynamics behind this positive correlation ... were something like this: Some investors were hesitant to accept the lower expected returns associated with the generalized decline in risk premiums. Accordingly, they tried hard to squeeze out additional returns. Leverage served as the best way to do so: By borrowing, they could put more money to work in their best investment idea; and this seemingly made sense as long as the expected return was higher than the cost of borrowing. In turn, the leveraged positions pushed risk premiums even lower, encouraging another round of leverage. (El-Arian, 2008, pp. 20–21)

1.2. Risk Management

Since risk management lies at the very heart of the problem, it warrants special consideration. Here, again, there is complete agreement between Turner and de Larosière et al. that there have been quite fundamental failures in the assessment of risk, both by financial firms and by those who regulated and supervised them. They point out that there were many manifestations of this, with a misunderstanding of the interaction between credit and liquidity and a failure to verify fully the leverage of institutions being among the most important. The cumulative effect of these failures was an overestimation of the ability of financial firms as a whole to manage their risks, and a corresponding underestimation of the capital they should hold.

de Larosière et al. elaborate on this:

> The extreme complexity of structured financial products, sometimes involving several layers of CDOs, made proper risk assessment challenging for even the most sophisticated in the market. Moreover, model-based risk assessments underestimated the exposure to common shocks and tail risks and thereby the overall risk exposure. Stress-testing too often was based on mild or even wrong assumptions. Clearly, no bank expected a total freezing of the inter-bank or commercial paper markets. (de Larosière et al., 2009, p. 8)

They believe that this was aggravated further by a lack of transparency in important segments of the financial markets, even within financial institutions, and the build up of a 'shadow' banking system. There was little knowledge of either the size or location of credit risks. While securitised instruments were meant to spread risks more evenly across the financial system, the nature of the system made it impossible to verify whether risk had actually been spread or simply re-concentrated in less visible parts of the system. This contributed to uncertainty on the credit quality of counterparties, a breakdown in confidence and, in turn, the spreading of tensions to other parts of the financial sector.

They draw attention to two aspects that are important in this respect. The first is that the Basel 1 framework did not cater adequately for, in fact encouraged, pushing risk taking off balance-sheets. This has however been partly corrected by the Basel 2 framework. The second being the explosive growth of the 'over-the-counter' credit derivatives markets, which were supposed to mitigate risk, but in fact compounded it.

They add that as the originate-to-distribute model developed, it created perverse incentives. This is because it blurred the relationship between borrower and lender as well as diverted attention away from the ability of the borrower to pay towards lending, often without recourse, against collateral. Indeed, a mortgage lender who knows that (s)he would transfer (sell) her/his entire default risks through MBS or CDOs had no incentive to ensure high lending standards. The lack of regulation, especially on the US mortgage market worsened the situation. de Larosière et al. (2009, p. 9) believe that empirical evidence suggests that there was a drastic deterioration in mortgage lending standards in the US during 2005–2007 with default rates increasing.

They point out that this was compounded by financial institutions and supervisors substantially underestimating liquidity risk:

> Many financial institutions did not manage the maturity transformation process with sufficient care. What looked like an attractive business model in the context of liquid money markets and positively sloped yield curves (borrowing short and lending long), turned out to be a dangerous trap once liquidity in credit markets dried up and the yield curve flattened. (de Larosière et al., 2009, p. 9)

They are also certain that the credit rating agencies (CRAs) aggravated the problem by lowering the perception of credit risk by awarding AAA ratings to the senior tranches of structured financial products, such as CDOs, the same rating they extended to standard government and corporate bonds. The major underestimation by CRAs of the credit default risks of instruments collateralised by sub-prime mortgages resulted largely from flaws in their rating methodologies (see later in text). The lack of sufficient historical data relating to the US sub-prime market, the underestimation of correlations in the defaults that would occur during a downturn and the inability to take into account the severe weakening of underwriting standards by certain originators have contributed to poor rating performances of structured products between 2004 and 2007 (de Larosière et al., 2009, p. 9).

They add that the conflicts of interests in CRAs made matters worse. The issuer-pays model, as it has developed, has had particularly damaging effects in the area of structured finance. Since structured products are designed to take advantage of different investor risk appetites, they are structured for each tranche to achieve a particular rating. Conflicts of interests became more acute as the rating implications of different structures were discussed between the originator and the CRA. Issuers shopped around to ensure they could get an AAA rating for their products. Furthermore, the fact that regulators required certain regulated investors to only invest in AAA-rated products also increased demand for such financial assets.

Failures in risk assessment and risk management were aggravated by the fact that the checks and balances of corporate governance also failed. de Larosière et al. (2009, pp. 9–10) claim that many boards and senior managements of financial firms did not understand the characteristics of the new, highly complex financial products, they were dealing with. On top of that, they were oblivious to the aggregate exposure of their companies, thus seriously underestimating the risks they were running. They add that many board members did not provide the necessary oversight or control of management and that the shareholders, the owners, were complicit in this. Moreover, the remuneration and incentive schemes within financial institutions contributed to excessive risk-taking by rewarding short-term expansion of the volume of (risky) trades rather than the long-term profitability of investments. And, the pressure exerted by shareholders on management to deliver higher share prices and dividends meant that exceeding expected quarterly earnings became the benchmark for the performance of many companies.

1.3. Regulatory, Supervisory and Crisis Management Failures

There is also broad agreement between Turner and de Larosière et al. that these pressures were not contained by regulatory or supervisory policy or practice:

> Some long-standing policies such as the definition of capital requirements for banks placed too much reliance on both the risk management capabilities of the banks themselves and on the adequacy of ratings. In fact, it has been the regulated financial institutions that have turned out to be the largest source of problems. For instance, capital requirements were particularly light on proprietary trading transactions while (as events showed later) the risks involved in these transactions proved to be much higher than the internal models had expected. (de Larosière et al., 2009, p. 10)

Both Turner and de Larosière et al.[4] point out that one of the mistakes made was that insufficient attention was given to the liquidity of markets. In addition, too much attention was paid to each individual firm and too little to the impact of general developments on sectors or markets as a whole (more on this later in text):

> Regulators were too focused on the institution-by-institution supervision of idiosyncratic risk: central banks too focused on monetary policy tightly defined, meeting inflation targets. And reports which did look at the overall picture, for instance the IMF Global Financial Stability Report ..., sometimes simply got it wrong, and when they did get it right, for instance in their warnings about over rapid credit growth in the UK and the US, were largely ignored. (Turner, 2009, p. 10)

They stress that these problems occurred in very many markets and countries, and aggregated together contributed substantially to the developing problems. Once problems escalated into specific crises, there were real problems of information exchange and collective decision making involving central banks, supervisors and finance ministries.

Both Turner and de Larosière et al. add that derivatives markets rapidly expanded (especially credit derivatives markets) and off-balance sheet vehicles were allowed to proliferate, with credit derivatives playing a significant role triggering the crisis. While US supervisors should have been able to identify (and prevent) the marked deterioration in mortgage lending standards and intervene accordingly, EU supervisors had a more difficult task in assessing the extent to which exposure to sub-prime risk had seeped into EU-based financial institutions. Nevertheless, they failed to spot the degree to which a number of EU financial institutions had accumulated – often in off balance-sheet constructions – exceptionally high exposure to highly complex, later to become illiquid financial assets. Taken together, these developments led over time to opacity and a lack of transparency (de Larosière et al., 2009, p. 10).

de Larosière et al. conclude that:

> This points to serious limitations in the existing supervisory framework globally, both in a national and cross-border context. It suggests that financial supervisors frequently did not have and in some cases did not insist in getting, or received too late, all the relevant information on the global magnitude of the excess leveraging; that they did not fully understand or evaluate the size of the risks; and that they did not seem to share their information properly with their counterparts in other [EU] Member States or with the US. In fact, the business model of US-type investment banks and the way they expanded was not really challenged by supervisors and standard setters. Insufficient supervisory and regulatory resources combined with an inadequate mix of skills as well as different national systems of supervision made the situation worse.
>
> Regulators and supervisors focused on the micro-prudential supervision of individual financial institutions and not sufficiently on the macro-systemic risks of a contagion of correlated horizontal shocks. Strong international competition among financial centres also contributed to national regulators and supervisors being reluctant to take unilateral action.
>
> Whilst the building up of imbalances and risks was widely acknowledged and commented upon, there was little consensus among policy makers or regulators at the highest level on the seriousness of the problem, or on the measures to be taken. There was little impact of early warning in terms of action – and most early warnings were feeble anyway.
>
> Multilateral surveillance (IMF) did not function efficiently, as it did not lead to a timely correction of macroeconomic imbalances and exchange rate misalignments. Nor did concerns about the stability of the international financial system lead to sufficient coordinated action, for example through the IMF, FSF, G8 or anywhere else. (de Larosière et al., 2009, pp. 10–11)

2. CAPITAL REQUIREMENTS AND PRO-CYCLICALITY

Both Turner and de Larosière et al. claim that the increasing scale and complexity of the securitised credit market was obvious to individual participants, to regulators and to academic observers. One should hasten to add that the academics also bear a great deal of responsibility since 'many of the intellectual underpinnings of the causes of the current crisis – be it financial innovations, capital account convertibility, deregulation or stock options – come from the best and brightest in US academia, not bureaucrats in dead-beat third world countries' (Kapur, 2009). Turner and de Larosière et al. call attention to the realisation that:

> the predominant assumption was that increased complexity had been matched by the evolution of mathematically sophisticated and effective techniques for measuring and managing the resulting risks. Central to many of the techniques was the concept of Value-at-Risk (VAR), enabling inferences about forward-looking risk to be drawn from the observation of past patterns of price movement. This technique, developed in the early 1990s, was not only accepted as standard across the industry, but adopted by regulators as the basis for calculating trading risk and required capital (being incorporated for instance within the European Capital Adequacy Directive). (Turner in UK FSA, 2009a, p. 22)

However, both Turner and de Larosière et al. endorse the scepticism of many professionals that there are fundamental questions about the validity of VAR as a measure of risk. The doubt is attributed to the intellectual assumptions on which previous regulatory approaches have largely been built, at the core of which has been the theory of efficient and rational markets, popularly known as the 'efficient markets hypothesis'. From this, five propositions with implications for regulatory approach have ensued: (a) market prices are good indicators of rationally evaluated economic value; (b) the development of securitised credit, since based on the creation of new and more liquid markets, has improved both allocative efficiency and financial stability; (c) the risk characteristics of financial markets can be inferred from mathematical analysis, delivering robust quantitative measures of trading risk; (d) market discipline can be used as an effective tool in constraining harmful risk taking; and (e) financial innovation can be assumed to be beneficial since market competition would winnow out any innovations which did not deliver value added. They stress that each of these assumptions is now subject to extensive challenge on both theoretical and empirical grounds, with potential implications for the appropriate design of regulation and for the role of regulatory authorities.[5]

Moreover, the use of VAR measures based on relatively short periods of historical observation (e.g. 12 months) introduced dangerous pro-cyclicality into the assessment of trading book risk. A capital adequacy regime is pro-cyclical if its operation tends to encourage or necessitate business responses that exacerbate the strength of the economic cycle: if capital requirements tend to fall in periods of strong lending growth and low credit losses, this can tend to accentuate the boom with well-capitalised banks able to expand lending aggressively; conversely if capital requirements rise in recessions, banks facing capital constraints may cut back the lending, making the recession worse.[6]

There are several reasons for pro-cyclicality, but to explain the most important of which it is necessary to provide a sketch of the basics of the system. One begins by observing over a past period (say last year) the distribution of profits/loss resulting over a defined time period (say 1 day to 10 days) from a given gross position. Then hold capital sufficient to cover some multiple of this VAR. These short-term observation periods (e.g. one year) can result in significant pro-cyclicality. As depicted in Fig. 1, 'Observation 1' reflects low volatility and thus low apparent risk; hence capital is attracted to position taking, reinforcing market liquidity. 'Observation 2' reflects high volatility following fall in confidence; hence liquidity dries up, exacerbating increase in volatility.

Turner believes that this method fails to capture 'fat-tail' risks: short-term observation periods plus the assumption of normal distribution can lead to large underestimation of probability of extreme loss events. It also fails to capture systemic risk because: (a) the methodology assumes each institution is an individual agent whose actions do not themselves affect the market; and (b) interconnected market events ('network externalities') can produce self-reinforcing cycles, which models do not capture and systemic risk may be highest when measured risk is lowest, since low measured risk encourages behaviour that creates increased systemic risks.[7]

Add to this that the:

> Very complexity of the mathematics used to measure and manage risk, moreover, made it increasingly difficult for top management and boards to assess and exercise judgement over the risks being taken. Mathematical sophistication ended up not containing risk,

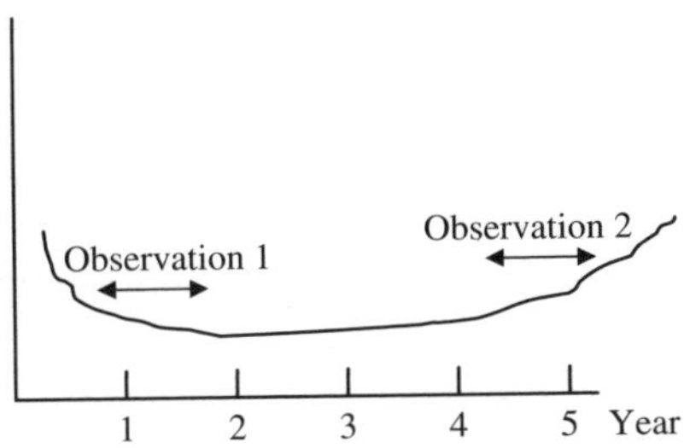

Fig. 1. Volatility in a Specific Market. *Source:* Adapted from Turner in UK Financial Services Authority (2009a, p. 23).

Box 1. Banking Book Capital Adequacy under Basel 1 and Basel 2 Internal Ratings.

Basel 1

Assets were grouped into buckets which have different average risk characteristics and then assigned weights, which determine different capital requirements as a percentage of assets.

	Asset Weight (%)		Required Capital to Weighted Assets (%)		Required Capital to Total Assets (%)
Corporate loans	100	*	8	=	8.0
Residential mortgages	50	*	8	=	4.0
Inter-bank	10	*	8	=	0.8

Basel 2: Internal rating-based approached

Guiding principle

- Banks should conduct detailed analysis of the relative riskiness of different classes of assets at a granular level (e.g. multiple different categories of corporate loans) and develop their own estimates of required economic capital, thus ensuring integration of capital adequacy conditions into bank risk management practices.
- Estimates should be subject to parameters and limits defined by the Basel 2 regulation and subject to agreement by national supervisors.
- Aggregate impact should leave total capital across banking system broadly unchanged, while changing significantly the weights against different loans to reflect their inherent riskiness.

Key calculations

- Banks analyse historic patterns of loan losses on different types of loans (e.g. corporate loans as categorised by the banks on internal credit scoring/ranking system) and determine estimates of:

Probability of default * Loss given default = Expected loss

- This is translated into Unexpected loss, the crucial driver of capital requirement, using defined methodologies.

Key parameters defined by regulation/supervisor guidance

- Floors on default possibilities
- Maturity adjustment on corporate exposures to ensure higher capital requirement on long-term commitments
- Correlation parameters within asset classes
- Multipliers to derive possible unexpected loss from estimates of expected loss
- Calibration factor (currently 1.06) to ensure that overall banking system capital is broadly unchanged from Basel 1

Source: UK Financial Services Authority (FSA) (2009a, p. 60).

> but providing false assurance that other prima facie indicators of increasing risk (e.g. rapid credit extension and balance sheet growth) could be safely ignored. (Turner in UK FSA, 2009a, p. 22)

2.1. The Recommendations

The analysis of the causes of the financial crisis thus implies the need for major changes in the approach adopted in several areas. As to what to do about them, Turner[8] offers recommendations on the regulation of capital adequacy of banks, management and regulation of liquidity as well as ensuring that financial activities in the future are always regulated according to their economic substance (shadow banks and near banks), as against their legal form, attaching equal importance to the first two. These are largely echoed by de Larosière et al., whose first of a total of 30 recommendations calls for a fundamental review of the Basel 2 rules (above), asking that the Basel Committee of Banking Supervisors be invited to urgently amend the rules with a view to: (a) gradually increase minimum capital requirements; (b) reduce pro-cyclicality, by for example encouraging dynamic provisioning or capital buffers; (c) introduce stricter rules for off-balance sheet items; (d) tighten norms on liquidity management and (e) strengthen the rules for bank's internal control and risk management, notably by reinforcing the 'fit and proper' criteria for management and board members. They add that it is furthermore '*essential that rules are complemented by more reliance on judgement*' (de Larosière et al., 2009, p. 19). Their second recommendation is

EU-specific calling for the adoption of a common definition of regulatory capital, clarifying whether, and if so which, hybrid instruments should be considered as Tier 1 capital (see later in text), with this definition to be confirmed by the Basel Committee.

Turner's recommendations are however relatively more specific, so the rest of this section is skewed towards them and limited to only the new approaches to the regulation of banks' capital adequacy and pro-cyclicality, they being our main focus. Turner stresses that these have of course been extensively revised by the introduction of Basel 2, which has aimed to achieve greater sensitivity of capital levels to the different risks which banks are running, and 'there are certainly benefits to the Basel 2 approach on which the future system should build' (Box 1). He stresses that one must realise that the crisis developed under the Basel 1 regime not Basel 2 and that Basel 2 would have addressed some of the problems which led to it, such as the failure to distinguish between the capital that is needed to support mortgages of different credit quality.[9]

This is reiterated by de Larosière et al.:

> It is wrong to blame the Basel 2 rules *per se* for being one of the major causes of the crisis. These rules entered into force only on 1 January 2008 in the EU and will only be applicable in the US on 1 April 2010. Furthermore, the Basel 2 framework contains several improvements which would have helped mitigate to some extent the emergence of the crisis had they been fully applied in the preceding years. For example, had the capital treatment for liquidity lines given to special purpose vehicles been in application then they might have mitigated some of the difficulties. In this regard Basel 2 is an improvement relative to the previous "leverage ratios" that failed to deal effectively with off-balance sheet operations. (de Larosière et al., 2009, pp. 15–16)

They are also agreed that, nevertheless, changes must be made to Basel 2, with Turner going for the need to adjust Basel 2 'in a number of ways'[10] and Larosière et al. for a 'fundamental review' of its framework (de Larosière et al., 2009, p. 16).

According to Turner,[11] the general drift will be towards higher levels of bank capital than had been required in the past, and 'in particular capital which moves more appropriately with the economic cycle and more capital required against trading books and the taking of market risk'. de Larosière et al. reiterate this by pointing out that because Basel 2 underestimated some important risks and overestimated banks' ability to handle them and due to the perceived wisdom that the distribution of risk through securitisation took risk away from the banks globally proving incorrect, 'too little capital' was required', so this 'must be changed' (de Larosière et al., 2009, p. 16).

Regarding the economic cycle, Turner refers to the considerable commentary on the pro-cyclical nature of Basel 2 risk-sensitive capital measures, adding that it is inevitable that any system which is risk sensitive, unless deliberate countervailing adjustments are made, will be to a degree pro-cyclical, that is capital requirements will rise as the economy heads into a recession and credit quality declines. But he stresses that:

> it is important to note that the degree to which Basel 2 is pro-cyclical in relation to the banking books – credit extension on balance sheet – depends crucially on how it is implemented and can be significantly reduced if banks use appropriate through-the-cycle approaches to estimation of probability of default and loss given default. It is therefore important to ensure that the detailed implementation of Basel 2 does not introduce unnecessary and unintended pro-cyclicality. (Turner, 2009, p. 9)

Turner draws attention to the fact that the FSA had indeed already issued a clarification of the approach designed to ensure this two days before Turner's lecture.

Looking forward, Turner however sees the need for going beyond the avoidance of unnecessary pro-cyclicality, to the creation of a system which introduces significant counter-cyclicality, requiring banks to build up substantial capital buffers in good economic times (ratios well above absolute minimum levels) so that they can run them down in bad. He argues that such an approach

> makes sense from a micro-prudential point of view, reducing the risk of bank failure. But it is also desirable from a macro-prudential and macro-economic perspective: it will tend to place at least some restraint on over-rapid expansion in the boom, and it will reduce the danger that impaired capital makes it more difficult for banks to lend in recessionary times, thus making the recession worse. (Turner, 2009, p. 9)[12]

Turner adds that, ideally, such a regime must be agreed at international level, and that the FSA is working closely within the Basel Committee on Banking Supervision and the Financial Stability Forum to design the details. He cautions that there are many details to be worked out on whether the buffer requirements will be defined in formulaic terms, as in the Spanish dynamic provisioning system, or by regulator discretion; and how to deal with the complexity of different economic cycles in the different countries in which a cross-border bank may operate. But he is certain that the principle is clear (Turner, 2009, p. 9).

He further argues that it is equally clear that in respect to the trading books of banks, one needs to remove pro-cyclicality and to increase capital requirements 'not just marginally but by several times'. This is due to the present system of capital regulation of trading books being 'from a prudential point of view' seriously deficient:

> Its reliance on [VAR] ... measures derived (usually) from the observation of the last year's movements in market prices is clearly pro-cyclical: if volatility goes down in a year, the measure tells banks that risks looking forward have reduced, and thus fails to allow for the fact that historically low volatility may actually be an indication of irrationally low risk aversion and therefore increased systemic risk. It fails to allow effectively for the low probability tail events which are crucial to extreme idiosyncratic and even more so to overall systemic risk. And, overall, the level of capital required against trading books has been simply too low relative to the risks being taken, given what we now understand about the systemic dangers of relying on liquidity through marketability, and about the susceptibility of securitised credit markets to irrational exuberance, sudden liquidity disappearance and rapid price collapse. Major banks with a large percentage of their balance sheets devoted to trading activity, have been required to hold only very thin slices of capital against it [see Table 1]. That will change radically given the proposals already issued by the Basel Committee, and these changes in themselves are likely to result in a significant contraction in the scale of future trading books. (Turner, 2009, pp. 9–10)

Given the mentioned linkage between risk and liquidity and looking forward, Turner adds that the FSA believes that a fundamental review is required of how trading books are defined and how risks in trading books are estimated. This is because VAR-based approaches were originally developed to model the risks in trading in markets likely to be continually and deeply liquid (e.g. government securities, major currency foreign exchange swaps and interest rates derivatives) and were adopted by regulators in the mid-1990s when a high proportion of bank trading was

Table 1. An Example of a BIS Estimate of Trading Book Assets and Capital in 2007.

	Capital Requirement as % of Trading Assets	Trading Assets as % of Total Assets	Trading/Market Risk Capital as % of Total Capital Requirements
Bank 1	0.4	34	11
Bank 2	0.4	28	7
Bank 3	0.1	57	4
Bank 4	1.1	27	7

Source: Adapted from Turner (2009), Exhibit 16.

concentrated in such highly liquid instruments. Over the last decade and a half, however:

> trading books have expanded rapidly to encompass the holding of many debt securities whose markets are imperfectly liquid even in normal times and which became suddenly illiquid when the downturn occurred; this booking of potentially illiquid assets in trading books was indeed in part driven by the lower capital charge there incurred. (Turner, 2009, p. 10)

He added that the FSA will therefore be proposing to the Basel Committee that a fundamental review of the division between the trading and banking books and of the appropriate use of VAR to measure risk is now required.

Since the most fundamental changes needed to create a sounder banking system for the future are those relating to capital adequacy,[13] accounting and liquidity policies, Turner offers seven required key measures: (a) increasing the quantity and quality of bank capital, (b) significant increases in trading book capital and the need for fundamental review, (c) avoiding pro-cyclicality in Basel 2 implementation, (d) creating counter-cyclical capital buffers, (e) offsetting pro-cyclicality in published accounts, (f) a gross leverage ratio backstop and (g) containing liquidity risks in individual banks and at the systemic level. Box 2 summarises the specific recommendations and their likely impact on the banking system and on financial stability.

Since what is in the box is self-explanatory, there is no need to elaborate except on a few cases. With regard to (a), the *Discussion Paper* (UK Financial Services Authority, 2009b, chap. 2) distinguishes two approaches to the definition of adequate capital. The first is a 'gone concern' approach in which what matters is the protection of senior creditors and depositors in the event of an individual bank failure within a stable overall system. Thus any capital claim which is ranked subordinate to senior creditors will protect them in terms of subordinated debt as much as common equity. The second is a 'going concern' approach in which regulators and macro-economic policymakers need to be concerned about the implications of bank capital structure for the behaviour of banks and the implications of that behaviour for the whole economy. Hence, it is essential that capital is available to absorb losses without banks being under excessive pressure to constrain lending to the real economy, and banks are not so highly leveraged relative to common equity as to create

Box 2. The Turner Recommendations for Capital, Accounting and Liquidity.

Recommendation	Detail	Impact
(a) Increase the quantity and quality of overall bank capital	• Focus on Tier 1 and Core Tier 1 capital for systemically important banks • Regulatory minima significantly increased from current Basel 2 regime	• Future banking system better able to absorb shocks • Will tend to mean lower return on equity but lower risk banking industry
(b) Major changes to trading book capital	• Major (e.g. more than 3 times) increases in capital required against key types of trading risk • Fundamental review of market risk capital regime (e.g. reliance on VaR, measures)	• Significant reduction in scale of proprietary risk taking • Will drive simplification and de-risking of securitised credit model
(c) Avoid pro-cyclicality in Basel 2 implementation	• FSA action already in hand to enable 'through the cycle' rather than 'point-in-time' estimates of credit risk	• Will reduce the extent to which lending capacity is impaired in economic downturn
(d) Create countercyclical capital buffers	• Capital levels to increase in booms and decrease in recessions • Variety of options: discretionary versus formula: in calculated capital or in reserves	• Dangers of banking system instability greatly reduced • Amplitude of economy cycles
(e) Offset pro-cyclicality in published accounts	• Countercyclical buffers to be defined in published accounts 'Economic Cycle Reserve'	• Remuneration and management behaviour less influenced by irrational exuberance

(f) Introduce a gross leverage ratio backstop	• Absolute limit on gross assets to some category of capital (e.g. Core Tier 1)	• Guards against under estimation of risks • Limits system-wide financial instability risks by limiting aggregate positions
(g) Major intensification of liquidity regulation and supervision	• Action already outlined in UK Financial Services Authority (2008) • Much more detailed information requirements on liquidity mismatches • Stress tests defined by regulators and covering systemic effects • Detailed mandatory individual liquidity guidance • Possible introduction of code funding ratio rule	• Reduced reliance on risky forms of 'liquidity through marketability' and risky levels of wholesale funding. • Reduced risks of liquidity strain driving financial instability • Will tend to constrain aggregate system maturity transformation and marginally change term structure of interest rates.

Source: Slightly adapted from UK Financial Services Authority (2009a, p. 54).

incentives for excessive risk taking (UK Financial Services Authority, 2009a, p. 53).

Turner stresses that the crisis has revealed the crucial importance of focusing on the second approach when determining bank capital adequacy rules for systemically important banks. He points out that the FSA therefore believes that required capital ratios for such banks should be expressed entirely in terms of high quality capital, broadly speaking the current Core Tier 1 and Tier 1 definitions, and should not count dated subordinated debt as providing relevant support. He adds that this is in line with the direction of Basel Committee deliberations.

For Turner, the crucial issue then becomes what minimum ratios should be set for Core Tier 1 and Tier 1 capital. He shows that the current international rules described in Box 3 effectively result in an absolute

Box 3. Minimum Quality and Quantity of Capital under Existing Rules.

Broad definitions*

Tier 2: subordinated debt
Tier 1 (not core): preferred stock
Core Tier 1 (CT1): common equity and retained earnings

Total and Tier 1 requirements (broadly unchanged between Basel 1 and Basel 2)

Total capital (Tier 1 + Tier 2) must be greater than 8% of weighted risk assets AND Higher quality Tier 1 capital must be at least 4% of WRA	Tier 1 capital must be at least 4% of WRA

Core Tier 1 requirements

Not formally defined within Basel 2 but BCBS guidelines suggest CT1 should be a predominant part of Tier 1. Many jurisdictions, including UK, treated this as implying CT1 at least half of Tier 1	Effective minimum Core Tier 1 of 2% of WRA (except for market risk)

Trading book/market risk variant

Basel 2 rules on quality of capital for market risk capital requirements are different from those for credit risk and more lenient.

As a result, a bank with significant trading book activity could face somewhat lower minimum CT1 than 2% and lower minimum Tier 1 than 4%.

*The precise definitions need to cover the complexity of hybrid instruments that have mixed characteristics of subordinated debt and preferred stock as well as complexities relating to what is included in retained earnings. An element of trading book/market risk capital can also be covered by 'Tier 3' capital.

Source: Slightly adapted from UK Financial Services Authority (2009a, p. 56).

minimum of 2% Core Tier 1 relative to Weighted Risk Assets (WRAs), 4% Tier 1 and 8% total capital (including dated subordinated debt). He is however quick to add that almost all major international banks already have ratios well above these levels, and that regulators already have discretion to require higher levels via Pillar 2 adjustments. This appears to be consistent with the conclusions of the *Supervisory Capital Assessment Program* (Board of Governors of the Federal Reserve System, 2009a–e; Geithner, 2009; US Department of the Treasury, 2009; Soros, 2009) (SCAP; see Section 2.3).

He also adds that these absolute minima were defined at the time of the Basel 1 accord which was implemented in the late 1980s. They were not based on any clear theory of optimal capital levels, but rather represented a pragmatic compromise between different objectives. There was a desire to achieve a level international playing field: a perception that some banks were very lightly capitalised, but there was no intention to drive a generalised increase in the capital requirements of all banks. This pragmatic approach to determining overall capital levels was carried over to the Basel 2 regime. While Basel 2 introduced a new approach to the definition of the relative capital requirements to be held against specific asset categories, it was deliberately 'calibrated' to ensure that the overall level of required capital across the banking system was broadly similar to that which the Basel 1 regime required (UK Financial Services Authority, 2009a, p. 55).

He then points out that the fundamental question which international debates on bank capital adequacy have therefore never answered and indeed hardly addressed is what overall level of bank capital is optimal. In theory he believes this should be based on a trade-off between benefits and costs. The former is about the economic benefits of higher bank capital in reducing financial instability, which arise both through reduced probability of bank defaults and through a reduced danger that bank capital strains will increase the amplitude of the economic cycle via the impact on lending capacity. The latter is concerned with the economic cost of higher capital, which arises because banks facing higher capital requirements will need to reflect that in higher intermediation margins (UK Financial Services Authority, 2009a, p. 55).

He stresses that estimating either of these effects is extremely difficult and so too is deciding what relative weight to attach to each effect.[14] But two arguments strongly support the proposition that the optimal level of capital is likely to be significantly higher than that which appeared appropriate in the past. The first is the massive scale of the economic losses now being suffered across the world as a result of banking system collapse. He argues that since any theory of optimal capital level must strike a balance between the increased costs of financial intermediation (which will result from higher capital requirements) and the benefits of the decreased probability of bank failure and economic harm which will be achieved, the crisis has forcibly reminded the world that the economic costs of bank system failures are extremely high. It therefore tips the balance in favour of setting higher requirements. The second is the fact that the increased economic costs resulting from higher capital requirements may be less than often supposed because

> simple calculations fail to allow for the insights of the Modigliani-Miller theorem relating to the cost of capital. This theorem (described in [(UK FSA, 2009b)]) identified that under certain assumptions higher leverage cannot in the absence of tax effects reduce a firm's cost of capital, since as leverage increases both the cost of debt and the cost of equity will increase to reflect heightened risk, offsetting the impact of a higher proportion of lower cost debt. In a tax-less world therefore the costs of regulator requirements on banks to hold more capital would be materially offset. Taxes on profits mean that, other things equal, there is a cost penalty ... But it remains the case that if regulators increase capital requirements, part of the cost impact will be offset by declining costs of both equity and debt to reflect lower risk. The future world of banking probably will and should be one of lower average return on equity but significantly lower risk to shareholders as well as to depositors. (UK FSA, 2009a, p. 57)

He draws attention to the fact that the FSA has commissioned analysis by the NIESR, using their NiGEM model, of the trade-off and during 2009 will publish a paper to stimulate public debate, in the UK and internationally, on the optimal level of bank capital. Yet he is adamant that there is a strong prima facie case that minimum bank capital requirements should in future be significantly above those which have applied in the past, pointing out that the FSA is already applying a set of guidelines, which imply a minimum Core Tier 1 capital of 4%. He suggests that a possible future regime might be one in which the minimum Core Tier 1 ratio throughout the cycle would be 4% and the Tier 1 ratio 8%. The dynamic capital mechanism is expected to generate an additional buffer equivalent to 2–3% of Core Tier 1 capital at the top of the cycle. It should remain open to supervisors to require a further discretionary buffer above this. He adds that it is however essential that the transition to higher capital requirements is phased, and takes account of the need to avoid pro-cyclical pressure on bank capital adequacy in the current economic downturn. Indeed, a whole chapter (4) is devoted to the appropriate design of the transition path (UK Financial Services Authority, 2009a, p. 57).

2.2. Creating Counter-Cyclical Capital Buffers

Turner warns that although these measures will significantly reduce the pro-cyclical impact of the Basel 2 risk-sensitive approach, they will not eliminate it. That, indeed, any approach to capital adequacy which is risk sensitive will produce somewhat higher capital requirements when economic conditions deteriorate since some risks truly will have increased.[15] Also, as already mentioned, there are many other features of the financial system which produce 'hard-wired' pro-cyclical effects which cannot easily be offset by specific policy interventions. He therefore believes that there is a very strong case for going further than reducing pro-cyclicality in capital requirements by introducing overt counter-cyclicality in order to offset the impact of unavoidable pro-cyclicality elsewhere. Under such a regime, required and actual capital would increase in good years when loan losses are below long run averages, creating capital buffers which would be drawn down in recession years as losses increase. Such a regime would: (a) decrease the probability of bank default or of public authorities having to take steps to prevent default, (b) decrease the probability of system-wide bank failures and (c) reduce the extent to which bank behaviour increases the amplitude of the economic cycle. A counter-cyclical capital regime would help constrain the growth of bank lending in the upswing, and in the downswing would reduce the extent to which banks need to cut back on lending to maintain capital ratios when capital is depleted by losses. He adds that the general principle of counter-cyclicality now has extensive support internationally, and both the FSA and Bank of England are arguing for it in international fora (UK Financial Services Authority, 2009a, section 2.6, pp. 83–86).

Turner then points out that there are two key choices that need making in designing the details of a countercyclical regime. The first is how the level of buffers is determined, the second how the impact is presented. The level of buffer can be defined in either a discretionary or a formula driven fashion. Under a discretionary system, bank regulators such as the FSA would need to judge the appropriate level of required capital ratios in the light of analysis of the macro-economic cycle and of macro-prudential concerns. The issue of how this analysis and these judgements would be shared between the Bank of England and the FSA is discussed in a full section (UK Financial Services Authority, 2009a, p. 61). He believes that such an approach could build on the Basel 2 Pillar 2 system, which already gives bank regulators the discretion to increase required bank capital above that indicated by Pillar 1 calculations, even though it was not originally designed to serve countercyclical purposes. The discretionary system would have the advantage of allowing a nuanced analysis of macro-economic and macro-prudential conditions to guide decisions, but it would depend crucially on the quality and independence of the judgements made. Under a formula-driven system, the required level of capital would vary according to some predetermined metric such as the growth of the balance sheet or estimates of average through-the-cycle loan. It would provide a preset discipline not dependent on judgement and not subject to the influence of lobbying (UK Financial Services Authority, 2009a, p. 61).

He adds that in both systems, complex issues would arise in relation to large cross-border banks operating in different national economies, and affected therefore by different economic cycles. And points out that the FSA believes that there is merit in making the regime at least to a significant extent formula driven. But this could be combined with regulatory discretion to add additional requirements on top of the formula-driven element if macro-prudential analysis suggested that this was appropriate.

The presentational choice is between a system in which the required capital ratio itself varies through the cycle, and one in which the buffer is present as a reserve but excluded from capital calculations. In the first system, either regulatory discretion or a formula would define a minimum required capital which would increase in periods of strong economic growth, for instance from a minimum required CT1 ratio of 4% to 7% at the peak. Banks would need to meet this rising ratio in the upswing, but would be permitted to run down the ratio towards the absolute minimum in an economic downturn. He believes that this would clearly communicate the intent of the policy, but has the danger that market expectations might constrain banks from reducing their ratios in the downturn given the apparently negative signal of a falling capital ratio. In the second system, the capital buffer would take the form of a reserve deducted from capital in periods of good economic performance, which would then be released in an economic downturn, but with the minimum capital rule kept constant throughout the cycle. He believes that the Spanish dynamic provisioning system (Box 4) combines this presentational approach with a formula driven approach to the calculation of the required buffer. He adds that this approach could allow for consistency between capital adequacy requirement rules and published account figures (UK Financial Services Authority, 2009a, p. 62).

Box 4. Dynamic Provisioning – Concepts and Spanish Application.

Dynamic provisioning uses a statistical method to allow for losses inherent within the portfolio which have not yet materialised.

- In economic upswing, it builds up a buffer by requiring provisions higher than recognised by standard 'incurred loss' accounting
- In economic downswing, it allows some losses to be met from the accumulated buffer.

Dynamic provisions can be either deducted from published profit and loss (P&L), or from regulatory capital, or both.

In June 2000 the Banco de España introduced a dynamic (also known as 'statistical') provision for Spanish banks and other credit institutions. It aims to ensure that aggregate annual provisioning – including the dynamic provision – equals average annual net losses suffered by the banking system in the last decade.

The current Spanish (post 2005) dynamic provision takes the form:

Dynamic provisioning change$_t$	$=\alpha * \Delta C_t + \beta * C_t$	$- \Delta$ specific provision
Inherent loss on new loans Growth	Average specific provisions over long-term	The provisions already deducted according to standard accounting

where C_t = stock of loans; α = inherent loss in each unit over the cycle and β = average specific provisioning rate over a long estimated period.

Source: UK Financial Services Authority (2009a, p. 63).

Turner stresses that the pros and cons of these alternative approaches need now to be debated and that the FSA would welcome responses to the *Discussion Paper* as an input to decisions on details. Also, that the FSA will be closely involved in international discussions with the aim of achieving an internationally agreed approach, pointing out that the Basel Committee is now committed to producing a proposal for a way forward by the end of 2009.

Nevertheless, Turner is adamant that *the position in principle is clear*:

> The capital adequacy regime, in addition to requiring more and better quality capital, should include the creation of countercyclical capital buffers which are built up in periods of strong economic growth and available for use in downturns. These are needed both to increase the resilience of the banking system and to reduce the potential impact of banking system cycles on the real economy. The appropriate size of the buffer requires detailed debate, but as a starting point proposal, the Discussion Paper suggests that buffers of the order of magnitude of 2–3% of WRAs might be appropriate at the peak of the cycle. (Turner in UK FSA, 2009a, p. 62)

2.3. The Supervisory Capital Assessment Program (SCAP)

It was stated earlier (p. 109) that Turner's claim that almost all major international banks already have capital ratios well above those dictated by the current international rules (described in Box 3), which effectively result in an absolute minimum of 2% Core Tier 1 relative to Weighted Risk Assets (WRAs), 4% Tier 1 and 8% total capital (including dated subordinated debt), seems to be consistent with the findings by SCAP (Board of the Governors of the Federal Reserve System, 2009a–e). This brief section provides information on this.

The SCAP process was conducted by the Federal Bank's regulatory agencies (the agencies) from 25 February through late April of 2009.[16] All 19 US 'holding bank companies' (BHCs) with year-end 2008 assets exceeding $100 billion were required to participate. The 19 collectively hold two-thirds of the assets and more than one-half of the loans in the US banking system and support a very significant portion of the credit intermediation done by the banking sector.

The 19 were asked to project their credit losses and revenues for the two years 2009 and 2010, including the level of reserves that would be needed at the end of 2010 to cover expected losses in 2011. They were given two alternative economic scenarios to consider. The *baseline scenario* reflected the consensus expectation in February 2009 among professional forecasters on the depth and duration of the recession, while the *more adverse scenario* was designed to characterise a recession that is longer and more severe than the consensus expectation (see Table 2). The firms were also asked to provide supporting documentation for their projected losses and resources,

Table 2. SCAP Economic Senarios.

	2009	2010
Real GDP		
Average baseline	−2.0	2.1
Consensus forecasts	−2.1	2.0
Blue Chip	−1.9	2.1
Survey of professional forecasters	−2.0	2.2
Alternative more adverse	−3.3	2.0
Civilian unemployment rate		
Average baseline	8.4	8.8
Consensus forecasts	8.4	9.0
Blue Chip	8.3	8.7
Survey of professional forecasters	8.4	8.8
Alternative more adverse	8.9	10.3
House prices		
Average baseline	−14.0	−4.0
Alternative more adverse	−22.0	−7.0

Source: Adapted from Table 1 in Board of Governors of the Federal Reserve System (2009d, p. 6).

including information on projected income and expenses by major category, domestic and international portfolio characteristics, forecast methods and important assumptions.

SCAP focused not only on the amount of capital but also on its composition as held by each of the 19. In other words, SCAP assessed the level of the Tier 1 risk-based capital ratio and the proportion of Tier 1 capital that is common equity.

The SCAP results indicated that if the economy were to track the more adverse scenario, losses at the 19 during 2009 and 2010 could be $600 billion, approximately $455 billion of which come from losses on the BHCs' accrual loan portfolios, particularly from residential mortgages and other consumer-related loans. The estimated two-year cumulative losses on total loans under this scenario would be 9.1% at the 19, which is in excess of that during the historical peak loss years of the 1930s. Estimated possible losses from trading-related exposures and securities held in investment portfolios came to $135 billion. In combination with the losses already recognised by these firms since mid-2007, largely from charge-offs and write-downs on the values of securities, the SCAP results suggested that financial crisis-related losses at the 19 could total nearly $950 billion by the end of 2010.

These losses were weighed against the potential resources available to the 19 to absorb those losses. At year-end 2008, capital ratios at all 19 exceeded minimum regulatory capital standards, in many cases by substantial margins, and most met supervisory expectations on the composition of capital. Tier 1 capital at the 19 came to about $835 billion in the fourth quarter of 2008. CSAP concludes that the practical implication of this capital is that many of the 19 already had substantial capital buffers in place to absorb their share of the estimated $600 billion of losses. In addition, banks will realise revenues from ongoing businesses to absorb losses, though at a lower level under the weak economic conditions of the stress scenario than in the baseline. However, CSAP believes that some of those revenues will need to go into building loan loss reserves against credit problems in 2011.

Taking into consideration the losses, revenues and reserve build requirements in all the 19 BHCs, SCAP found that these firms need to add $185 billion to capital buffers to reach the target SCAP capital buffer at the end of 2010 under the more adverse scenario. SCAP draws attention to two important matters concerning this estimate. The first is that the $185 billion accrues to 10 of the 19; thus 9 of the 19 firms already have capital buffers sufficient to get through the adverse scenario in excess of 6% Tier 1 capital and 4% Tier 1 Common capital. The second is that most of this $185 billion comes from a shortfall in Tier 1 Common capital in the more adverse scenario, with virtually no shortfall in overall Tier 1 capital. SCAP concludes that this result means that while nearly all the firms have sufficient Tier 1 capital to absorb the unusually high losses of the more adverse scenario and still end 2010 with a Tier 1 risk-based ratio in excess of 6%, 10 of the 19 BHCs had capital structures that are too strongly tilted towards capital other than common equity. Thus, each of the 10 needing to augment their capital as a result of this exercise must do so by increasing their Tier 1 Common capital.

The $185 billion estimated additional capital buffers correspond to the estimate that would have applied at the end of 2008. But a number of these firms have either completed or contracted for asset sales or restructured existing capital instruments since the end of 2008 in ways that increased their Tier 1 common capital. These actions substantially reduced the final SCAP buffer. In addition, the pre-provision net revenues of many of the firms exceeded what was assumed in the more adverse scenario by almost $20 billion, allowing them to build their capital bases. The effects of these transactions and revenues rendered the additional capital needed to establish the SCAP buffer equal to \$75 billion.

These results were met with a great deal of scepticism and cynicism (see, inter alia, Krugman, 2009), the former because even the more adverse scenario has been exceeded, the latter because many felt that the exercise was meant to assure the banking community. The cynicism is of course exaggerated since 10 of the 19 need assistance. Nevertheless, Turner is correct in claiming that almost all major international banks already have capital ratios well above those dictated by the current international rules.

3. SUPERVISORY CONTROL AND CROSS-BORDER CAPITAL ACTIVITIES

This may seem like a digression, but commenting on the demise of Lehman Brothers (in September 2008, following a loss of market confidence in the firm's solvency, arising from its overexposure to troubled asset classes, in particular, MBS and commercial real estate) and reflecting on the future approach to global wholesale banks, the FSA felt it vital to raise points on this issue. It points out that in the past the FSA's regulatory approach to large cross-border wholesale banks and investment banks, in line with that of most other regulators, assumed that primary responsibility for ensuring prudential soundness lies with the home country supervisor (though with extensive information sharing between home and host supervisors). It also assumed that it is appropriate for firms to gain efficiency benefits from global approaches to managing liquidity, allowing significant flexibility in the use of legal entities to book transactions across border, and to move liquidity between legal entities. The failure of Lehman Brothers demonstrated, however, that decisions about fiscal and central bank support for the rescue of a major bank are ultimately made by home country national authorities focusing on national rather than global considerations. It also illustrated that separate legal entities and nationally specific bankruptcy procedures have major implications for creditors.

In order to address these problems in the future, the FSA stresses that that would require some combination of:

- More international cooperation in ongoing supervision through, for instance, colleges of supervisors. And more intense international cooperation and coordination in crisis management.

- An increased use of host country powers to require strongly capitalised local subsidiaries, ring-fenced liquidity and restrictions on intra-group exposures and flows (UK FSA, 2009a, pp. 36–37).

In other words, dealing with the global crisis requires the taking of certain actions by countries other than the US, countries like the UK that are heavily subjected to the impact of the financial crisis.

Related to this and more to the point is the Icelandic banking crisis (Landsbanki) that affected the UK greatly, but swiftly dealt with by the British government. The FSA reminds us, after having set out the lessons arising from it (summarised in the Box 5) that:

- EU single market rules require that banks which are recognised by their home country supervisors as sound have a right to operate as branches in other member states; and
- that, as a result depositors in one country (or the government) can be vulnerable to the failure of banks in another country if the home country concerned lacks the supervisory resources to ensure bank solvency, or the fiscal resources to fund bank rescue, and if the deposit insurance cover is low and unfunded (UK FSA, 2009a, p. 37).

Then the FSA issues the warning that:

> These current rules and arrangements are untenable for the future and must be changed through some combination of:
>
> - more European coordination in regulation, supervision and deposit insurance; and
> - more host country national powers in regulating and supervising the branches of banks based in other member states. (UK FSA, 2009a, p. 37)

So what is the moral of this story? The UK is not in the eurozone and Iceland is neither in the eurozone nor is a member of the EU, but it enjoys all the privileges of the 'single market' because of its membership of the European Economic Area (EEA, see El-Agraa, 2007) which, with the exception of Switzerland, comprises all the EU and EFTA nations. Yet, as the FSA correctly argues, the financial problems occurring between two non-eurozone nations require action(s) by the entire EU. Thus, the 'one market' impinges on the 'one money' and is itself impinged upon by those not in the 'one money'. It is therefore essential to cater for cross-border capital activities and to involve a number of actors in dealing with them.

Box 5. Lessons from the Icelandic Banking Crisis.

The collapse of Landsbanki HF in October 2008 raises important issues relating to the appropriate regulation of bank branches within the European single market and appropriate approaches to deposit insurance.

Landsbanki operated in the UK as a branch, raising retail internet deposits under the Icesave brand. It had around £4.5 billion of retail deposits outstanding at the time of failure. These deposits were legally covered by the Icelandic deposit insurance scheme up to a value of €20,887. In addition, they were covered on a top-up basis by the UK Financial Services Compensation Scheme (FSCS), to which Landsbanki had chosen to opt in. As a top-up member, Landsbanki would have been liable to meet a share of the costs in the event of the default of another bank covered by the UK scheme.

The Icelandic government indicated that it would not be in a position to meet the liabilities of the Icelandic deposit insurance scheme immediately and is currently discussing the terms of a loan from the UK to allow it to meet those liabilities. In addition, there were £800 million of retail deposits which, because above £50,000, were covered neither by the Icelandic scheme nor by the FSCS top up. The UK government concluded that these deposits should be protected to underpin depositor confidence in the banking system. The total initial costs of retail depositor protection arising from the collapse of Landsbanki's UK branch have therefore been met by a combination of the UK government and the FSCS.

Landsbanki's UK branch was not subject to full prudential supervision by the FSA. This is because EU single market rules – which cover Iceland as a member of the European Economic Area (EEA) – allow banks in one country to operate as branches in another, with the supervision of solvency and of whole bank liquidity resting with the home country supervisor (this right is known as 'passporting'). The FSA, as host country supervisor, had only limited powers relating to the supervision of local liquidity.

The insolvency of Landsbanki therefore illustrates a weakness in the current European approach to a single market in retail banking. Depositors in one country (or their government) are vulnerable to the failure of banks in another country if the home country concerned lacks the supervisory resources to ensure bank solvency, or the fiscal resources or willingness to fund bank rescue, and if the deposit insurance cover is low and unfunded.

The approach to bank branch passporting rights, at least as they apply to branches conducting retail business, therefore requires review. Options for change could include:

Increased home country power:

- The restriction of branch passporting rights and the requirement that retail deposit gathering be conducted through fully capitalised subsidiaries supervised by the host country regulator.
- Host countries' supervisory powers to conduct a whole bank assessment and to refuse local branches the right to operate if not satisfied.

Increased European coordination:

- European-wide processes to assess the effectiveness of home country supervision of those banks wanting to conduct retail business in other member countries.
- Cross-European requirements for pre-funded and ring-fenced deposit insurance, combined with more overt warnings to customers of the limits of deposit insurance.

The relative merits of these different approaches are discussed in Section 2.10.

Source: UK Financial Services Authority (2009a, p. 38).

4. CONCLUSIONS

There are several conclusions, all but the first of which can be stated briefly.

First, it is an exaggeration to attribute the financial crisis to the US alone since China, Saudi Arabia and their ilk have contributed to it. Windler (2009) would however challenge this:

> The debate on whether regulatory failure or lax monetary policies, in particular in the United States, and/or global imbalances represent the fundamental causes of the crisis is still ongoing ... global imbalances are a symptom of the much deeper failure to provide the international financial system with an international [lender of last resort] and proper financial regulation and supervision. Thus, *global imbalances as such have not played a major role in causing the crisis.* (IMF, 2009a) (Windler, 2009, p. 25, emphasis added)

But what irrefutable proof does the IMF offer? Here is what it claims:

> we argued earlier that global imbalances were, at best, an indirect contributor to the build up of systemic risk. (IMF, 2009a, pp. 13–14)

Yet, this is what the IMF 'argued earlier':

> **The period was also characterized by large global imbalances, namely the large current account deficit of the United States matched by large current account surpluses in the rest of the world.** The roots of these imbalances were twofold: high saving in Asia (in particular China) and oil exporting countries and low saving in the United States; and a strong global preference for investment in [US] assets, considered both less risky and more liquid than most other assets. This geographical distribution of saving and portfolio preferences was reflected in large capital flows from surplus countries into the United States. (IMF, 2009b, p. 3)
>
> **One may still argue that low interest rates and capital flows into the United States created an environment favorable to the build up of systemic risk. The main culprit, however, must be seen as deficient regulation**. (IMF, 2009b, p. 4)

Really: is this a solid proof of their claim? I press this point because a very long time ago I dared to remind economists concerned with Japan's trade frictions that all one needs for this is basic macro-economics (El-Agraa, 1988). At a very elementary level, students are taught that a nations' trade account balance on goods and services (the difference between exports – X – and imports – M) is determined by the difference between the levels of national savings (S, for private savings and tax revenue – T – minus government expenditure – G – for public savings) and national investment (I). Using the basic national income accounting expenditure method, this means that $X - M = S + (T - G) - I$. Hence, nations with trade surpluses that also follow the US dollar, depositing their foreign exchange reserves with their central banks, and who prefer to invest in safe US financial instruments, are abetting in the sort of behaviour that has led to the risky investments so well described by Turner and de Larosière et al.

The second is that the financial community must learn to add intuition when applying its sophisticated mathematical tools for evaluating its risky investments. Its members must understand that their actions are interrelated; hence they need to see the 'wider picture'. They must also refrain from enticing financially poor customers into investments that are far beyond their means, especially those where inevitably higher future interest rates are not easily perceptible to those uninitiated desperate customers.

The third is that strict rules must be applied to ensure that the banking community has sufficient capital to sustain it during the bad times. Here, the recommendations by Turner and de Larosière et al., but especially Turner for the reform of Basel 2, cannot be improved upon and should be pursued without abandon.

The fourth is that capital pro-cyclicality must be catered for and counter-cyclicality promoted. Here, again, likewise for Turner and de Larosière et al.

Finally, the international regime for the control of cross-border financial activities must be improved. Since this depends heavily on international cooperation, all concerned must get together to device ways for doing so. Here, again, likewise for Turner and de Larosière et al.

NOTES

1. de Larosière et al. (2009, p. 7).
2. Turner in UK Financial Services Authority (2009a, p. 12).
3. Turner in UK Financial Services Authority (2009a, p. 14).
4. Turner (in UK Financial Services Authority, 2009a, pp. 22–23) and de Larosière et al. (2009, pp. 22–23).
5. Turner (in UK Financial Services Authority, 2009a, p. 39).
6. Turner in UK Financial Services Authority, 2009a, p. 59).
7. Turner in UK Financial Services Authority (2009a, p. 23).
8. Also in UK Financial Services Authority (2009a, Section 2.2., pp. 53–70).
9. Turner, 2009, p. 9 and in UK Financial Services Authority (2009a, p. 12).
10. Turner, 2009, p. 9 and in UK Financial Services Authority (2009a, p. 12).
11. Turner, 2009, p. 9 and in UK Financial Services Authority (2009a, pp. 53–54).
12. Also in UK Financial Services Authority (2009a, p. 59).
13. A banking institution holds capital to guard against uncertainty. 'Capital reassures an institution's depositors, creditors and counterparties – and the institution itself – that an event such as an unexpected surge in losses or an unanticipated deterioration in earnings will not impair its ability to engage in lending to creditworthy borrowers and protect the savings of its depositors' (Board of Governors of the Federal Reserve System, 2009a, p. 1).
14. 'To decide what weight to [be] attached to these two effects, requires that we know how relatively important to human welfare is (i) a slight increase in the long-term sustainable growth rate in GDP per capita rising from lower intermediation margins (ii) a decrease in the probability of significant economic volatility which, even if outweighed over the long term in terms of its impact on GDP per capita, will produce significant human welfare detriment during the period of instability, given the high welfare impact of sudden shifts in relative income or periods of unemployment' (UK Financial Services Authority, 2009a, p. 53).
15. Thus while 'through-the-cycle' estimates of the loss potential from long-term mortgage contracts can recognise that mortgages on the books in 2005 carried the risk of future credit losses even if arrears at that time were minimal, a one-year unsecured loan extended in 2005 truly was on average less risky than one extended today.

16. The federal bank regulatory agencies that participated in the SCAP are the Board of Governors of the Federal Reserve System, the Federal Reserve Banks, the Federal Deposit Insurance Corporation, and the Office of the Comptroller of the Currency.

REFERENCES

Board of governors of the federal reserve system. (2009a). *Agencies to begin forward-looking Economic Assessments*, Joint release, 25 February. Available at http://www.federalreserve.gov/newsevents/press/bcreg/20090225a.htm

Board of governors of the federal reserve system. (2009b). Joint statement by Secretary of the Treasury Timothy F. Geithner, Chairman of the Board of Governors of the Federal Reserve system Ben S. Bernanke, Chairman of the Federal Deposit Insurance Corporation Sheila Bair, and Comptroller of the Currency John C. Dungan, 6 May. Available at http://www.federalreserve.gov/newsevents/press/bcreg/20090506a.htm

Board of governors of the federal reserve system. (2009c). Statement by Chairman Ben S. Bernanke regarding the Supervisory Capital Assessment Program, 7 May. Available at http://www.federalreserve.gov/newsevents/press/bcreg/bernankescap20090507.htm

Board of governors of the federal reserve system. (2009d). The supervisory capital assessment program: Overall results, White Paper, Board of Governors, 24 April, Washington, DC. Available at http://www.federalreserve.gov/newsevents/press/bcreg/20090424a.htm

Board of governors of the federal reserve system. (2009e), The supervisory capital assessment program: Design and implementation, White Paper, Board of Governors, 24 April, Washington, DC. Available at http://www.federalreserve.gov/newsevents/press/bcreg/20090424a.htm

de Larosière, J., Balcerowicz, L., Issing, O., Masera, R., McCarthy, C., Nyberg, L., Pérez, J., Ruding, O. (2009), The high-level group on financial supervision in the EU, European Commission, Brussels, 25 February. Available at http://ec.europa.eu/internal_market/finances/docs/de_larosiere_report_en.pdf

eJournal USA. (2009). The global financial system, US Department of State, Bureau of International Information Program. Available at http://www.america.gov/publications/ejournalusa/0509.html

El-Agraa, A. M. (1988). *Japan's trade frictions: Realities or misconceptions?* (New York: St. Martins Press). London: Macmillan.

El-Agraa, A. M. (Ed.) (2007). *The european union: economics and policies*. Cambridge and New York: Cambridge University Press, 8th edition of the 1980 book; 9th edition forthcoming in 2011.

El-Arian, M. A. (2008). *When markets collide: Investment strategies for the age of global economic change*. New York: McGraw Hill.

Geithner, T. (2009). Testing the banks. *International Herald Tribune*, 8 May.

IMF. (2009a). Initial lessons of the crisis, 6 February, IMF, Washington, DC.

IMF. (2009b). Lessons of the global crisis for macroeconomic policy, 29 February, IMF, Washington, DC.

Kapur, D. (2009). Academia must also declare its material interest. *Financial Times*, 24 June.

Krugman, P. (2009). Stressing the positive. *International Herald Tribune*, 9–10 May.

Soros, G. (2009). My three steps to financial reform. *Financial Times*, 17 June.

Turner, A. (2009). The financial crisis and the future of financial regulation. The Economist's Inaugural City Lecture, 21 January. Available at http://www.fsa.gov.uk/pages/Library/Communications/Speeches/2009/0121_at.shtml

UK Financial Services Authority (FSA). (2008). *Strengthening liquidity standards*, December. Access from the FSA's website: http://www.fsa.gov.uk/

UK Financial Services Authority (FSA). (2009a). *The Turner review: A regulatory response to the global banking crisis*, March. Access from the FSA's website: http://www.fsa.gov.uk/

UK Financial Services Authority (FSA). (2009b). *A regulatory response to the global banking crisis*, a Discussion Paper, March. Access from the FSA's website: http://www.fsa.gov.uk/

US Department of the Treasury. (2009). Statement from the Treasury Secretary Tim Geithner regarding the treasury capital assistance program and the supervisory capital assessment program. May 7. Available at http://www.treasury.gov/press/releases/tg123.htm

Windler, A. (2009). The financial crisis – A wake-up call for strengthening regional monitoring of financial markets and regional coordination of financial sector policies? Paper presented at the Asian Development Bank Institute (ADBI), Tokyo, 21 July.

THE IMPACT OF THE GLOBAL FINANCIAL CRISIS ON EMERGING AND NEWLY INDUSTRIALIZED ASIA: CAPITAL FLOWS, FINANCIAL MARKETS AND ECONOMIC ACTIVITY

Irina Bunda, Subir Lall and Sunil Sharma

ABSTRACT

The paper analyzes the impact of the global financial crisis on capital flows, financial markets and economic activity in Asia and attempts to explain why Asian markets were hit hard despite relatively strong fundamentals, and why the subsequent recovery was relatively quick. The openness of a country to trade and finance and the degree of integration into international financial markets are shown to be important determinants of the swings in economic activity and capital flows during both the reversal and recovery phases. It also discusses the role played by macroeconomic and financial policies in the recovery and concludes with some lessons from Asia's experience.

The Impact of the Global Financial Crisis on Emerging Financial Markets
Contemporary Studies in Economic and Financial Analysis, Volume 93, 127–153

ISSN: 1569-3759/doi:10.1108/S1569-3759(2011)0000093006

Keywords: Global financial crisis 2007–2010; capital flows; financial markets; economic growth; Asia.

JEL Codes: G01; N15; N25.

1. INTRODUCTION

The worst global financial crisis since the Great Depression began in the sub-prime segment of the US mortgage market in the summer of 2007. Initially, as the stresses in this market spread, the impact remained largely limited to the financial systems of the United States and the major advanced economies of Western Europe until well into the summer of the following year. Indeed, with global trade relatively well supported and financial institutions in Asia having little direct exposure to the US sub-prime market, the key policy issue facing many Asian economies in the first half of 2008 related to high and rising commodity prices. Given the strengthening of corporate, financial and public sector balance sheets in the decade prior to 2008, the accumulation of foreign exchange reserves by some countries, and the current account surpluses or small deficits across much of Asia, the macroeconomic debate during much of the first half of 2008 centred around whether the region had "decoupled" from the advanced economies in the West. The strong fundamentals in emerging Asia and the growth of intra-regional trade notwithstanding, a number of studies (e.g., IMF, 2008) warned that the increasing extent of trade and financial integration over the last decade had made Asia's growth and finance more exposed to external demand shocks, and in particular, more synchronized with the US economic cycle.

After the demise of the investment bank Lehman Brothers in mid-September 2008, the global dimensions of the financial crisis became clear. The drying up of liquidity in financial markets and the abrupt deleveraging triggered by Lehman's collapse, coupled with a surge in global risk aversion, led to widespread selling of emerging market assets, including in Asia. Foreign portfolio investors withdrew from local bond and equity markets, and international banks cut credit lines with a number of Asian banks and repatriated funds from their branches in an effort to shore up liquidity. As a consequence, stock market prices across the region witnessed steep declines, spreads on emerging market bonds surged, and exchange rates depreciated sharply (Figs. 1a–b and 2a–b). The breadth of the sell-off, which affected economies with relatively sound macroeconomic fundamentals and healthy balance sheets, demonstrated that the crisis-related flight to safety was, at

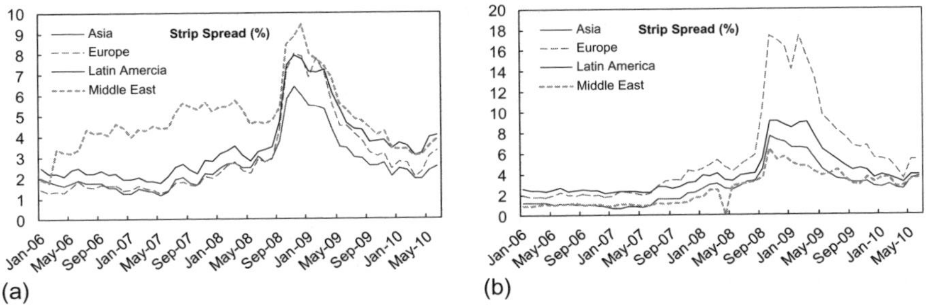

Fig. 1. (a) Evolution of Emerging Market Bond Global Index Regional Strip Spreads. (b) Evolution of Corporate Emerging Market Bond Index Regional Strip Spreads. Note the last observation refers to June 2010. *Source:* Morgan Markets.

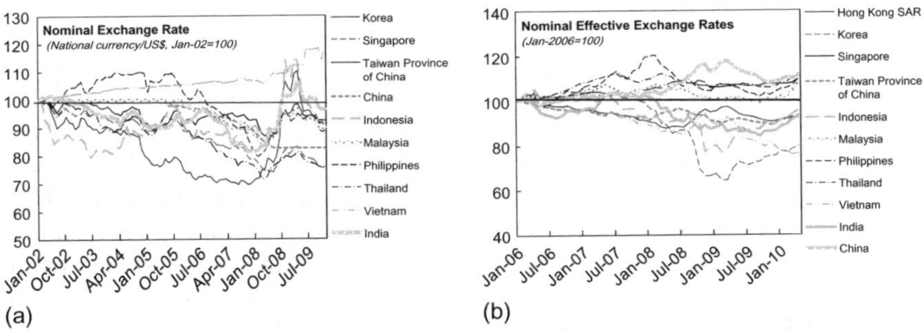

Fig. 2. (a) Evolution of the Nominal Exchange Rate, 2002–2009. (b) Evolution of the Nominal Effective Exchange Rate, 2006–2010. Note in Fig. 2b the last observation refers to April 2010. *Source:* International Financial Statistics, IMF.

least at that stage, largely indiscriminate and driven almost entirely by global factors.[1]

As the global dimensions of the crisis became evident, economic activity in Asia was not immune to the downturn underway in the United States and Western Europe, despite good fundamentals. Global trade collapsed in the last quarter of 2008, and, given the large export dependence of many Asian economies, overall economic activity fell along with exports (see Fig. 3a). As illustrated in Figs. 3b–c, compared to the Asian crisis of 1997–1998, the fall in exports was twice as large.

At the depth of the crisis, capital outflows from the Asian region and other emerging market economies were large by historical standards. In certain Asian countries, for some categories of flows, the outflows were even

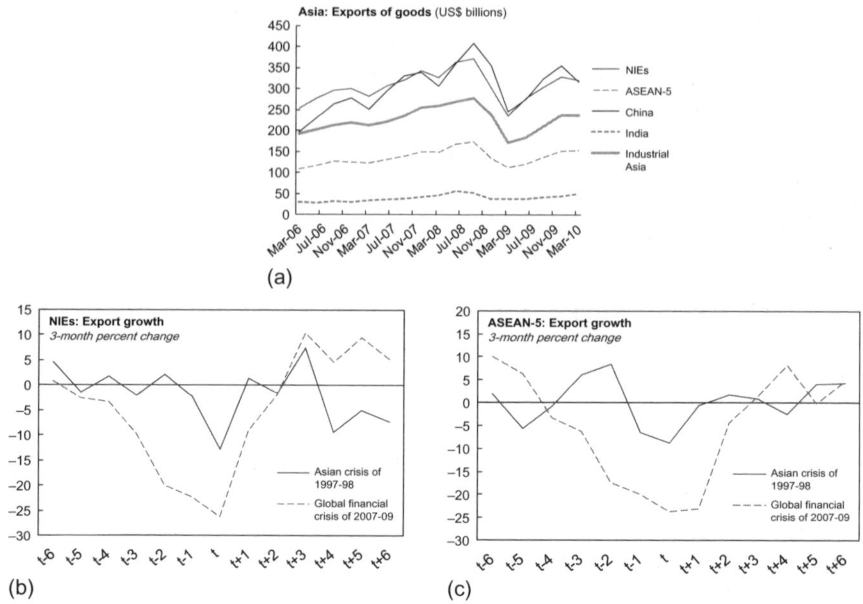

Fig. 3. (a) Evolution of Exports of Goods for Selected Asian Countries, in US $ Billion, 2006–2010. (b) Evolution of Export Growth during the Global Financial Crisis Compared with the 1997–1998 Asian Crisis. *Note:* The trough in exports growth (at time *t*) is January 1998 for the Asian Crisis and January 2009 for the Global Financial Crisis. (c) Evolution of Export Growth during the Global Financial Crisis Compared with the 1997–1998 Asian crisis. *Note:* The trough in exports growth (at time *t*) is June 1998 for the Asian Crisis and December 2008 for the Global Financial Crisis. *Source:* International Financial Statistics, IMF.

larger than during the Asian crisis of 1997–1998 (Singapore, Taiwan Province of China, and Thailand for portfolio flows, and Korea, for bank flows as a share of GDP).

In addition to the direct impact of the crisis on financial markets, Asian economies were also adversely affected by the collapse in trade following the slowdown in global demand. In the final quarter of 2008, GDP plunged across the world, in both advanced and developing countries. The widespread collapse of consumer and business confidence led to precautionary actions on many fronts, including curtailing investment spending, inventory accumulation, expenditures on consumer durables, and borrowing. Global trade contracted by 17 percent compared with the preceding quarter, as inventory accumulation effectively ceased in advanced countries. The downswing in Asian trade was larger than in other regions, including those at the epicentre of the global crisis.[2]

With policymakers acting promptly to stabilize the global economy and the financial system, activity in Asia bottomed out around the first quarter of 2009 and was followed by a relatively strong recovery. Capital flows to the region resumed quickly, helping local currency equity and bond markets to recover, spreads on external debt to narrow, and foreign currency liquidity to return to banks.

The chapter is organized as follows: after a presentation of the main stylized facts in Section 2, the chapter analyzes why Asian financial markets and economic activity were battered by the global crisis. Section 3 shows that factors not related to macroeconomic fundamentals may have been at play in determining which Asian countries were hit the hardest by the abrupt global deleveraging and the flight to quality in the recent crisis. Section 4 seeks to examine why capital inflows and economic growth resumed fairly rapidly in Asia after the peak of the crisis and discusses the role played by macroeconomic and financial policies. The last section contains some concluding remarks.

2. THE IMPACT OF THE GLOBAL FINANCIAL CRISIS ON CAPITAL FLOWS, FINANCIAL MARKETS AND ECONOMIC ACTIVITY

2.1. Capital Flows and Financial Markets

2.1.1. Run-up to the Crisis

In line with capital flows into most emerging markets during the period 2002–2007, Asian emerging markets were recipients of large volumes of capital flows, as investors took advantage of the robust economic performance of these economies against a backdrop of benign global financial and economic conditions:[3]

- During this period, average annual net capital flows into emerging Asia (including China)[4] were about $44 billion, with a peak of around $100 billion in 2007. On average, China was the destination for around $55 billion, while India and the Asean economies received some $9 billion. In contrast, the NIEs recorded average net outflows of around $20 billion.

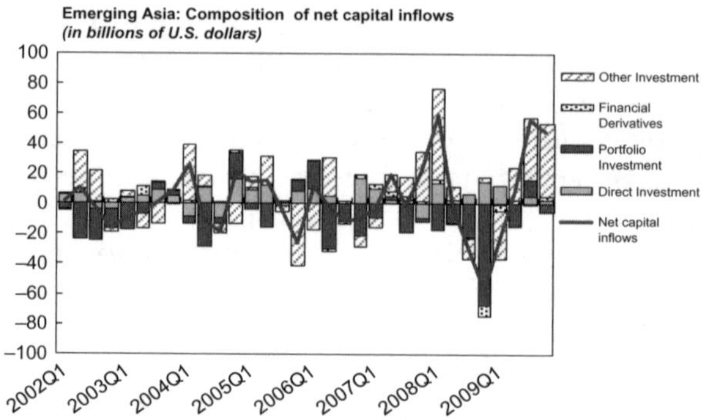

Fig. 4. Net Capital Inflows to Emerging Asia by Category of Flows, 2002–2009. Note that China was excluded from the sample. *Source:* Balance of Payments Database, IMF.

- The composition of capital inflows may be divided into three main categories: foreign direct investment (FDI), portfolio equity flows, and other investment flows – mainly bank loans and deposits. Fig. 4 depicts the evolution of these flows over 2002–2007. Net FDI for the region accounted for an annual average of $74 billion, led mainly by China. The net portfolio outflows of $39 billion on average over the same period reflect net capital inflows into India and the Asean-5 economies of around $6 billion and outflows from the NIEs and China of around $53 billion. As for other investment flows, they were around $7 billion per year on average over the period as inflows into the NIEs averaging about $20 billion were partially offset by outflows from India and the Asean-5 economies that averaged $7 billion. China also recorded outflows of about $5 billion in the "other flows" category. The geographic breakdown of different categories of capital flows is summarized in Figs. 5a–b.
- In response to these capital inflows, as well as the current account surpluses generated by many countries, nominal exchange rates appreciated steadily over this period across the region (see Fig. 2a–b in Section 1). In nominal effective terms, exchange rates appreciated by 6.5 percent on average for the countries included in the sample. Upward pressures on the currencies and the preference for stable exchange rates in the region progressively translated into massive increases in reserves, with the more managed exchange rate regimes accumulating the most. As an illustration, over this period, gross official reserves rose by $1,311 billion in China, $226 billion in India, $158 billion in Korea and $147 billion in Taiwan Province of China (see Table 1).

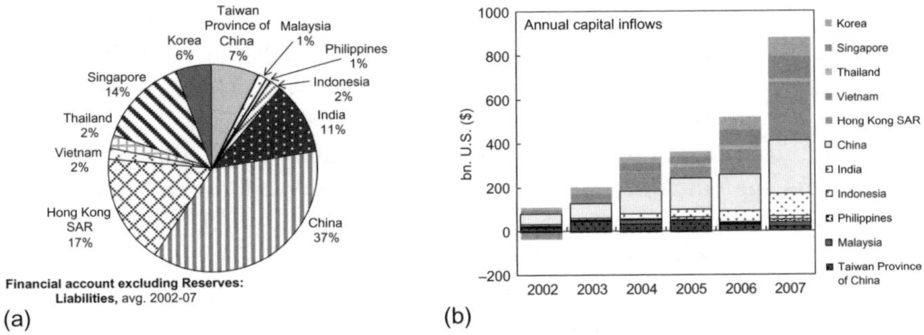

Fig. 5. (a) Country Breakdown of Average Capital Inflows to Emerging Asia, 2002–2007. (b) Annual Capital Inflows by Country, 2002–2007. *Source:* International Financial Statistics, IMF.

Table 1. International Reserve Accumulation in Emerging Asian Countries, 2002–2007.

Countries	Variation of Gross International Reserves (US$ Bn) 2002–2007	Countries	Variation of Gross International Reserves (US$ Bn) 2002–2007
Hong Kong SAR	41	Indonesia	29
Korea	158	Malaysia	71
Singapore	88	Philippines	20
Taiwan Province of China	147	Thailand	54
Total NIEs	*434*	Vietnam	18
India	226	*Total Asean-5*	*191*
China	1,311	*Total Emerging Asia*	*1,728*

Source: International Financial Statistics, IMF.

2.1.2. Impact of the Crisis

With the propagation of the global crisis to Asia after September 2008, there was an abrupt shift in the flow of capital to the region.

- With deleveraging in the global financial system, bank-intermediated flows into the region reversed sharply. The stock of cross-border bank loans for the Asean-5 economies, India and China, as reported by the BIS, was $430 billion in September 2008, but gradually fell during the following year to reach $310 billion in September 2009, a 28 percent year-on-year decline. In the case of the NIEs, the stock of cross-border bank loans dropped from $970 billion at end-2008 to $782 billion by the end of 2009, a 19 percent year-on-year fall. Countries that had been the largest recipients of cross-border bank flows (Singapore, Hong Kong SAR, China, Korea) witnessed the largest outflows (see Fig. 6).

- Turning to the "other" investment flows category in the balance of payments that includes transactions in currency and deposits, loans, as well as trade credits, the region received net inflows of $61 billion in the first quarter of 2008 but recorded net outflows of $14 billion in the third quarter of 2008, and a further outflow of $32 billion in the first quarter of 2009. The NIEs were the most affected, with outflows reaching $26 billion in the third quarter of 2008; for the rest of emerging Asia, overall outflows peaked at $17 billion in the first quarter of 2009. The economies that experienced the biggest outflows were Hong Kong SAR ($39 billion) in the third quarter of 2008, Korea ($36 billion) and Malaysia ($10 billion) in the final quarter of 2008, and India ($8 billion) in the Q2 of 2009 – see Fig. 7a.
- Portfolio equity and debt flows also saw a massive reversal in the flight to safety, affecting a much broader set of countries than those which had been large recipients of bank-intermediated flows. Following net inflows of $1.6 billion in aggregate to the NIEs in the Q2 of 2008, the outflows soared to $48 billion at year end. Net inflows into other Asian emerging markets (excluding China) also went into reverse, with a swing from net inflows of $12 billion during the first quarter of 2008 to net outflows of $14 billion in 2008 Q2 and $22 billion in 2008 Q3. The economies that saw the largest outflows were Hong Kong SAR ($50 billion in 2008 Q4), Malaysia ($16 billion in 2008 Q3), Singapore ($11 billion in 2009 Q3), Taiwan Province of China ($11 billion in 2008 Q3), and Korea ($9 billion in 2008 Q3). Thailand and India also experienced outflows, albeit to a lesser extent, and the magnitude of capital flow reversals was around $6 billion in both countries – see Fig. 7b.
- These flows, along with a reduction in risk appetite among domestic investors, led to dramatic declines in the local stock indices (see Table 2).
- The rapid outflows of capital also resulted in sharp depreciations of exchange rates against the US dollar. This was especially true, in nominal effective terms, for the Korean won, the Indian rupee and the Malaysian ringgit (see Table 3).

In many economies, policy makers responded to these sudden outflows by providing foreign currency liquidity to the banking system and/or trying to stabilize the exchange rates. For example, foreign exchange reserves in

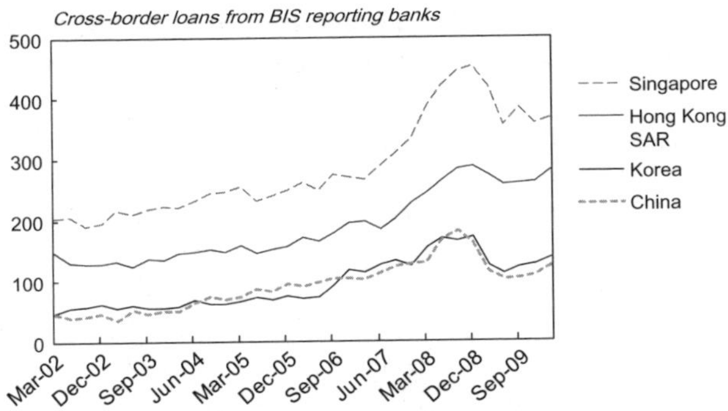

Fig. 6. Quarterly Cross-Border Loans from BIS Reporting Banks for the Top Four Emerging Asian Countries, 2002–2009. *Source:* Joint BIS-IMF-OECD-World Bank Statistics on External Debt.

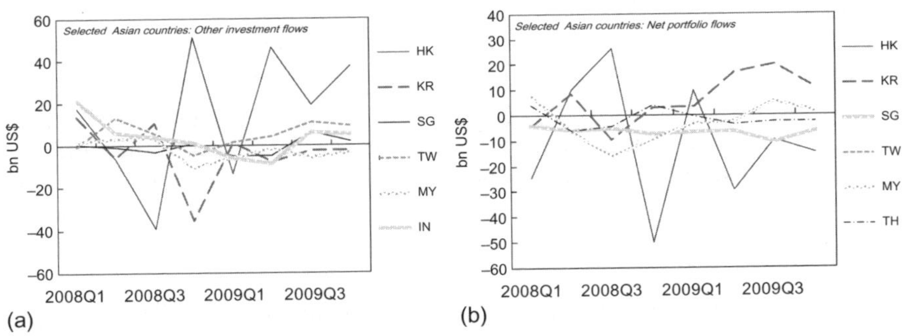

Fig. 7. (a) Quarterly Other Investment Flows for Selected Asian Countries, 2008–2009. (b) Quarterly Portfolio Debt and Equity Flows for Selected Asian Countries, 2008–2009. The following abbreviations are used: HK = Hong Kong SAR, IN = India, KR = Korea, MY = Malaysia, SG = Singapore, TW = Taiwan Province of China, TH = Thailand. *Source:* Balance of Payments Database, IMF.

Korea fell from a pre-crisis peak of $264 billion in March 2008 to $200 billion in November 2008, a drop of 24 percent. Malaysia's foreign exchange reserves dropped 30 percent from peak to trough, while India and Indonesia saw reserves decline by 21 percent and 17 percent, respectively. Some central banks in the region – notably the Bank of Korea and the Monetary Authority of Singapore – also set up bilateral currency arrangements (swaps) with the US Federal Reserve to gain access to foreign currency liquidity. Only the Bank of Korea accessed these lines during the crisis.

Table 2. Peak to Trough Percentage Fall in Stock Market Indexes across Asia during the Global Financial Crisis.

	Peak	Trough	Percentage
Industrial Asia			
Japan	Jun-07	Feb-09	−58
Australia	Sep-07	Feb-09	−50
New Zealand	Sep-07	Feb-09	−40
NIEs			
Hong Kong SAR	Oct-07	Feb-09	−59
Korea	Oct-07	Feb-09	−49
Singapore	Oct-07	Feb-09	−58
Taiwan Province of China	Oct-07	Feb-09	−53
Emerging Asia			
Indonesia	Dec-07	Feb-09	−53
Malaysia	Dec-07	Mar-09	−40
Philippines	Jun-07	Jan-09	−50
Thailand	Oct-07	Nov-08	−56
Vietnam	Feb-07	Feb-09	−78
India	Dec-07	Feb-09	−56
China	Sep-07	Oct-08	−69

Source: International Financial Statistics, IMF.

Table 3. Peak to Trough Variation of the Nominal Effective Exchange Rates in Emerging Asian Countries.

Country	Peak	Trough	Percentage
Hong Kong SAR	Feb-02	Apr-08	−22
Korea	Dec-06	Feb-09	−38
Taiwan Province of China	Feb-02	Mar-08	−9
India	Jun-02	Feb-09	−36
China	Jan-02	Sep-09	−22
Indonesia	Feb-02	Sep-09	−11
Malaysia	Feb-02	Dec-09	−39
Philippines	Jul-07	Dec-08	−7
Thailand	Jan-02	Nov-09	−13
Vietnam	Dec-07	Sep-09	−15

Source: International Financial Statistics, IMF.

2.2. Economic Activity

Asian emerging economies were adversely affected by the slowdown in global demand and the collapse of global trade in the last quarter of 2008. Merchandise exports from emerging Asia fell by 47 percent from 2008 Q3 to 2008 Q4. However, the extent of the export collapse varied by country. Taiwan Province of China, Singapore, Malaysia and India saw the biggest drops, of more than 60 percent. Slightly smaller but still dramatic declines in trade volumes, of between 50 percent and 60 percent,[5] were recorded in Korea, Indonesia, Philippines, Thailand and Vietnam. Hong Kong SAR and China saw quarter-on-quarter drops in goods exports of 17 percent and 33.5 percent, respectively.

Most affected were countries at the upper end of the value-added spectrum, that is, those that specialized in "advanced manufacturing" including electronics, automobiles and investment goods.[6] Demand for these goods is highly cyclical in nature, in part because it depends on the availability of finance in the importing countries. As credit dried up and consumer confidence weakened in the third quarter of 2008, expenditures on consumer durables and capital goods fell drastically. Within the region, the sharp slowdowns in Japan (16.6 percent annualized rate of decline in real GDP in the first quarter of 2009) and Korea (16.8 percent fall in the final quarter of 2008) manifested themselves most dramatically in the demand for advanced manufactures, with orders for heavy machinery, ships and factory equipment drying up almost completely. As new orders collapsed, firms cut back their production, leading to steep declines in inventories (see Figs. 8a–b).

The trade spillover effects seen in the global financial crisis were also caused by the international specialization and vertical trade integration in many Asian economies. Much of the intra-regional trade has come to reflect assembly operations at the industry level (with China playing a major role as the locus for final assembly), while the finished products continue to be shipped largely to the advanced economies. The fall in demand from the developed countries therefore propagated rapidly through the tightly integrated supply chain and had a negative impact on intra-regional trade.

Given the high export dependence of many Asian economies, especially when measured in value-added terms, overall economic activity contracted sharply in the region. Economic activity, expressed as quarterly seasonally adjusted real GDP, declined precipitously in many countries: Singapore (annualized rate of 12 percent, 2008 Q2), Taiwan Province of China,

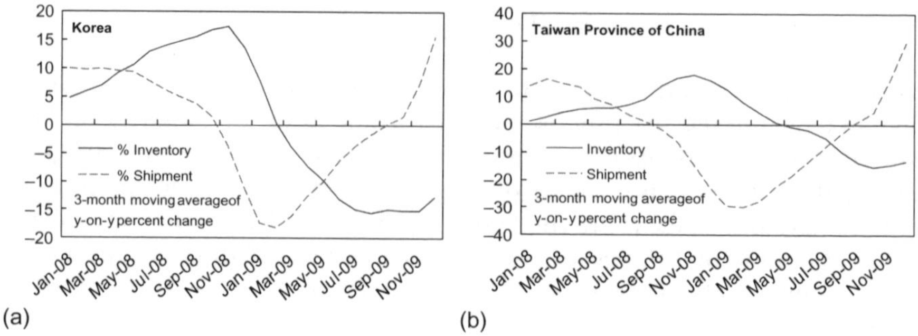

Fig. 8. (a–b) Evolution of Inventory and Shipments in Korea and Taiwan Province of China during the Global Financial Crisis. *Source:* International Financial Statistics, IMF.

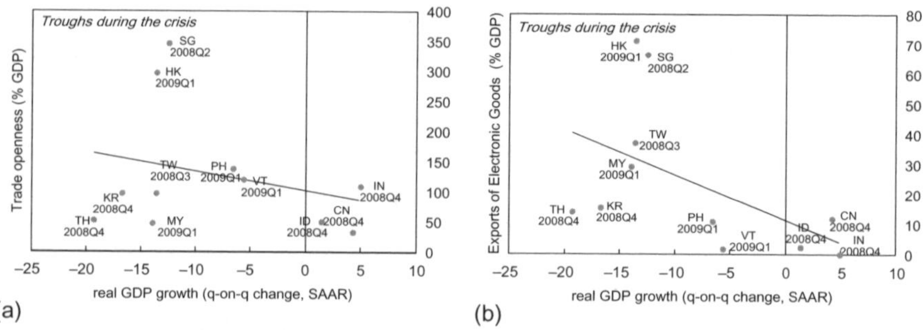

Fig. 9. (a) Troughs in Real GDP Growth Rates during the Global Financial Crisis and Countries' Degree of Openness to Trade. (b) Troughs in Real GDP Growth Rates and Countries' Exports of Electronic Goods. The following abbreviations are used: CN = China, HK = Hong Kong SAR, IN = India, ID = Indonesia, KR = Korea, MY = Malaysia, PH = Philippines, SG = Singapore, TW = Taiwan Province of China, TH = Thailand, VT = Vietnam. *Source:* Authors' calculations based on International Financial Statistics, IMF.

Hong Kong SAR, and Malaysia (around 14 percent, 2008 Q3), Thailand (18 percent, 2008 Q4) and Korea (17 percent, 2008 Q4). Fig. 9a shows that these economies which are relatively more open to trade than other Asian countries, experienced large quarterly declines in their real GDP.

It is worth noting that the magnitude of the peaks and troughs in quarter-on-quarter seasonally adjusted real GDP growth rates can also be associated with the share of durables in GDP (proxied by the share of electronic goods in Fig. 9b). Economies like Hong Kong SAR, Singapore, Taiwan Province of China and Malaysia are characterized by a large share of electronics exports relative to the rest of the sample and saw bigger drops in their quarterly GDPs. The explanation may lie, in part, with the role of China as the final assembly hub for the region. Economies such as Korea, Malaysia, Philippines and Taiwan Province of China that have substantial exports to China (more than 20 percent of their exports) were particularly affected by the collapse of global demand.

3. WHAT FACTORS DROVE THE REVERSAL IN CAPITAL FLOWS?

An important question, given the recent Asian experience, is why some economies were affected more than others by the decline in the risk appetite of global investors. The magnitudes of the swings in capital flows were large

Table 4. Macroeconomic and Financial Fundamentals in Asian Emerging Economies, End 2007.

Country	Current Account (% of GDP)	Short-term External Debt (% of Reserves)	Capital Adequacy Ratio	Non-Performing Loans/ Total Loans	Inflation Rate	Gross Public Debt (% of GDP)[a]	External Debt (% of GDP)
Hong Kong SAR	12.3	21	13	0.8	2.0	13	36
Korea	0.6	63	12	0.7	2.5	27	36
Singapore	26.7	6	13	1.5	2.1	88	15
Taiwan Province of China	8.4	31	–	–	1.8	29	24
Indonesia	2.4	53	19	4.1	6.3	31	33
Malaysia	15.9	24	13	6.5	2.0	42	33
Philippines	4.9	24	16	5.8	2.8	56	46
Thailand	6.3	28	15	7.9	2.2	38	25
Vietnam	−9.8	24	–	–	8.3	46	34
India	−0.8	16	12	12.3	4.8	59	17
China	10.6	15	8	0.8	4.8	17	11

Source: International Financial Statistics, IMF, and Economist Intelligence Unit.
[a]Note that for some countries, for example, Singapore, the ratio of gross public debt to GDP may not be an appropriate indicator of indebtedness since it does not account for assets held by the government.

Table 5. Reversals in Portfolio Flows-to-GDP and Other Investment Flows-to-GDP in Selected Emerging Asian Countries (in Percent).

Country	Portfolio Flows/GDP	Other Flows/GDP
Hong Kong SAR	−23.3 (2008 Q4)	−18.1 (2008 Q3)
Korea	−0.9 (2008 Q3)	−4 (2008 Q4)
Singapore	−5.9 (2009 Q3)	−2.5 (2009 Q1)
Taiwan Province of China	−2.7 (2008 Q3)	−1.1 (2008 Q4)
Malaysia	−7.1 (2008 Q3)	−4.7 (2008 Q4)
Thailand	−2.2 (2008 Q2)	−1.6 (2009 Q1)

Source: Balance of Payments Database, IMF.

in several countries as shown in Table 4. At the same time, macroeconomic fundamentals and financial soundness indicators in these countries were relatively strong based on a number of measures – the current account balance, short-term debt as a percentage of foreign exchange reserves, public and external debt, inflation, and capital-adequacy and non-performing loan ratios of the banking system.[7]

In Asia, the largest falls in net capital flows relative to annual GDP were seen in Malaysia (9 percent), Singapore (around 6 percent) and Korea (5 percent). By category of flows, the picture is more heterogeneous, as illustrated in Table 5. The biggest decrease in portfolio flows as a proportion of GDP was in Hong Kong SAR (23 percent), Malaysia (7 percent), Singapore (6 percent), Taiwan Province of China (3 percent) and Thailand (2 percent). As far as other investment flows (bank loans and deposits) are concerned, the largest decline took place in Hong Kong SAR (18 percent), Malaysia (5 percent), Korea (4 percent) and Singapore (2.5 percent).

The above suggests that large two-way movements of capital took place in countries that were more open and had relatively developed financial markets. This is illustrated in Figs. 10a–b and 11a–b using simple measures of openness and financial market development. These figures plot the troughs in portfolio flows and other investment flows as a ratio of GDP against (i) exports and imports as a ratio of GDP (a proxy for openness) and (ii) stock market capitalization as a ratio of GDP (a proxy for financial market development). Figs. 10c and 11c use the availability of foreign exchange reserves as a measure of the ease with which capital can be withdrawn by foreign investors. The charts show that the positive relationship between troughs in portfolio flows and stock of foreign

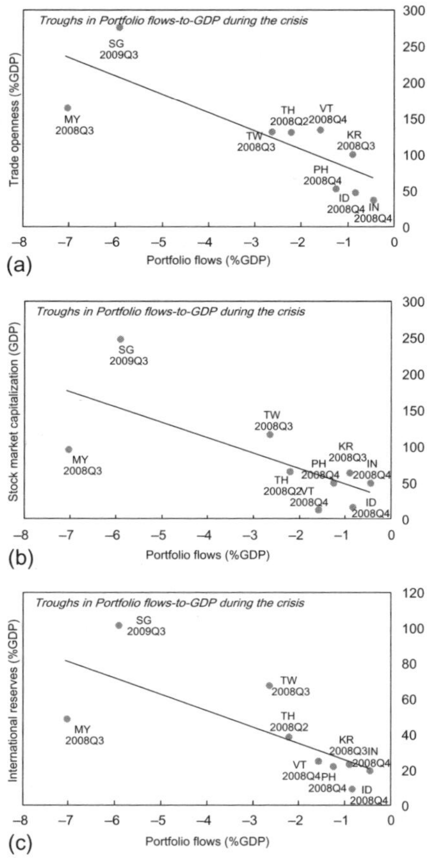

Fig. 10. (a–c) Troughs in Portfolio Flows-to-GDP during the Global Financial Crisis and Country Characteristics. *Note:* Capital Flows-to-GDP series are defined as the ratio of quarterly net capital flows (US$) to GDP of the last four quarters (US$). Troughs are defined as negative net capital flows that are local minima over the period 2008 Q1 to 2009 Q4. Trade Openness is the ratio of the sum of exports and imports (US$) to quarterly GDP (US$). International Reserves-to-GDP is the ratio of quarterly reserves (US$) to GDP of the last four quarters (US$). The following abbreviations are used: IN = India, ID = Indonesia, KR = Korea, MY = Malaysia, PH = Philippines, SG = Singapore, TW = Taiwan Province of China, TH = Thailand, VT = Vietnam. *Source:* Authors' calculations based on International Financial Statistics, IMF.

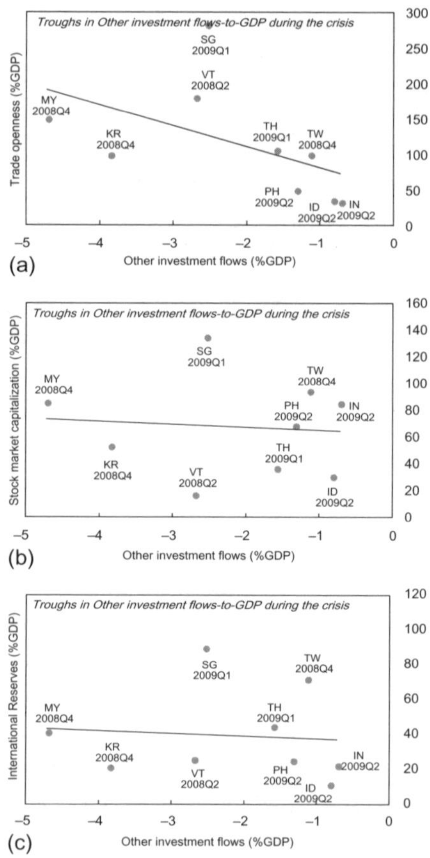

Fig. 11. (a–c) Troughs in Other Investment Flows-to-GDP during the Global Financial Crisis and Country Characteristics. *Note:* Capital Flows-to-GDP series are defined as the ratio of quarterly net capital flows (US$) to GDP of the last four quarters (US$). Troughs are defined as negative net capital flows that are local minima over the period 2008 Q1 to 2009 Q4. Trade Openness is the ratio of the sum of exports and imports (US$) to quarterly GDP (US$). International Reserves-to-GDP is the ratio of quarterly reserves (US$) to GDP of the last four quarters (US$). The following abbreviations are used: IN = India, ID = Indonesia, KR = Korea, MY = Malaysia, PH = Philippines, SG = Singapore, TW = Taiwan Province of China, TH = Thailand, VT = Vietnam. *Source:* Authors' calculations based on International Financial Statistics, IMF.

exchange reserves was much more pronounced than that between other investment flows and reserve stocks.[8]

What the experience illustrates is that international financial integration raises both prospects and vulnerabilities. On the positive side, countries may benefit from foreign capital through higher growth and consumption opportunities, but also indirectly through a facilitation of institutional development, better governance and macroeconomic discipline in the recipient countries. On the negative side, financial integration makes countries more vulnerable to external shocks and hence may lead to higher volatility in capital flows. In the long run, however, the benefits of having a relatively open and well-governed economy are likely to dominate.

A key difference of the recent experience as compared to earlier episodes is that previous bouts of capital outflows from EMEs were related to a combination of interest rate increases in developed countries, and weak growth prospects, unstable government finances, poor liquidity management, and weak corporations and financial institutions in recipient countries. In the recent case, the focus may have been less on recipient economy fundamentals and much more on the need to shore up liquidity and deleverage in countries supplying the capital. Hence, the withdrawal of capital from Asian countries probably depended on the ability of investors to reduce exposures and repatriate capital quickly at minimal costs.

4. WHAT EXPLAINS THE RAPID REBOUND IN CAPITAL FLOWS AND ECONOMIC ACTIVITY?

Following the sudden cessation in capital flows, the rebound of flows to Asia was quite remarkable. In the Q2 of 2009, total net capital inflows to the countries in our sample exceeded $8.7 billion. In many countries (Korea, Taiwan Province of China, Indonesia, Malaysia, Philippines, Thailand and India), portfolio flows recovered first, while other investment flows (bank loans and deposits) were still in negative territory. By contrast, for Hong Kong SAR, Singapore and Vietnam the recovery in capital flows was led by other investments, while net portfolio flows continued to lag. In the case of Hong Kong SAR, the currency board arrangement implied that capital inflows had to be accommodated without sterilization.

Inflows of capital to the region have clearly been driven not just by the abating of deleveraging pressures, but also by other push and pull factors that came into play as the region recovered. Risk appetite in global markets returned after the US and European markets rebounded in March 2009. In Asia, capital flows first returned to the relatively more liquid and financially developed economies in the region. This is illustrated in Figs. 12a–c and 13a–c, which plot "peak" inflows of portfolio and bank deposits as a ratio to GDP, against proxies for trade openness, development of financial markets and liquidity.

The rapid economic recovery in the region and better regional growth prospects relative to the rest of the world were driven largely by better fundamentals and a strong policy response in key Asian economies. In the aftermath of the crisis, economic activity recovered quickly in countries that had been most affected by the slowdown in global demand. Fig. 14a–b show that economies first to rebound (Singapore, Hong Kong SAR, Taiwan Province of China, Thailand and Malaysia) were those most open to trade, with a large share of durables in their total exports. These economies were also highly dependent on China which endured the financial crisis well.

In line with the global response to the crisis formulated at the G-20 Summit in April 2009, Asian countries responded by using monetary, fiscal and financial measures. First, central banks in the region used conventional monetary policy to stimulate the economy by cutting policy rates and reducing reserve requirements to help boost bank liquidity and prevent a rise in borrowing costs. All the emerging markets in our sample reduced policy interest rates from September 2008 to September 2009 – on average by 286 basis points. The biggest interest rate cuts took place in Vietnam, India and Korea, and the smallest in Malaysia, Singapore and China.

Given the limits of conventional monetary policy, central banks also undertook unconventional monetary policy measures. Liquidity management operations (LMOs) were explicitly used to target elements of the monetary transmission mechanism. Unlike traditional monetary policy instruments, LMOs can influence asset prices over and above the impact of policy rates and can be implemented regardless of the prevailing policy rate. LMOs became a substantive part of monetary policy during the crisis. They consisted of (i) influencing credit spreads by acquiring financial assets directly in the market (credit easing) and/or (ii) "quantitative easing" by injecting liquidity into the banking system by buying (usually government) securities.

At the same time, a number of measures were taken to support the banking sectors and safeguard financial stability. To limit currency volatility and alleviate funding pressures in foreign currencies, the authorities in a number of Asian countries stabilized the foreign exchange markets, or lent

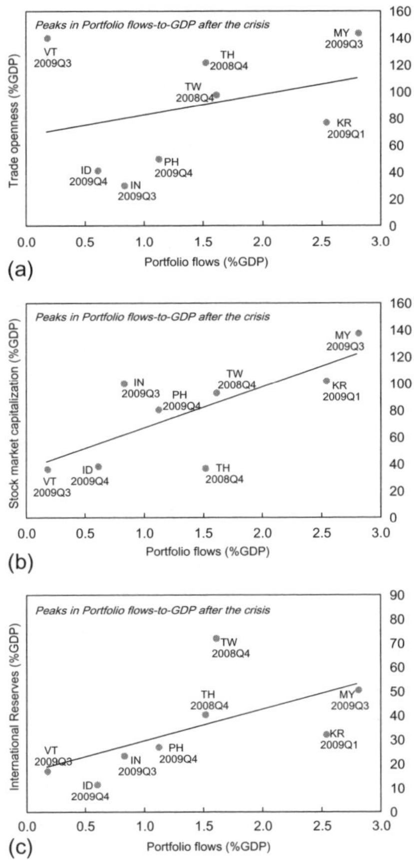

Fig. 12. (a–c) Peaks in Portfolio Flows-to-GDP after the Crisis and Country Characteristics. *Note:* Capital Flows-to-GDP series are defined as the ratio of quarterly net capital flows (US$) to GDP of the last four quarters (US$). Peaks are defined as positive net capital flows that are local maxima following the trough of the crisis. Trade Openness is the ratio of the sum of exports and imports (US$) to quarterly GDP (US$). International Reserves-to-GDP is the ratio of quarterly reserves (US$) to GDP of the last four quarters (US$). The following abbreviations are used: CN = China, IN = India, ID = Indonesia, KR = Korea, MY = Malaysia, PH = Philippines, SG = Singapore, TW = Taiwan Province of China, TH = Thailand, VT = Vietnam. *Source:* Authors' calculations based on International Financial Statistics, IMF.

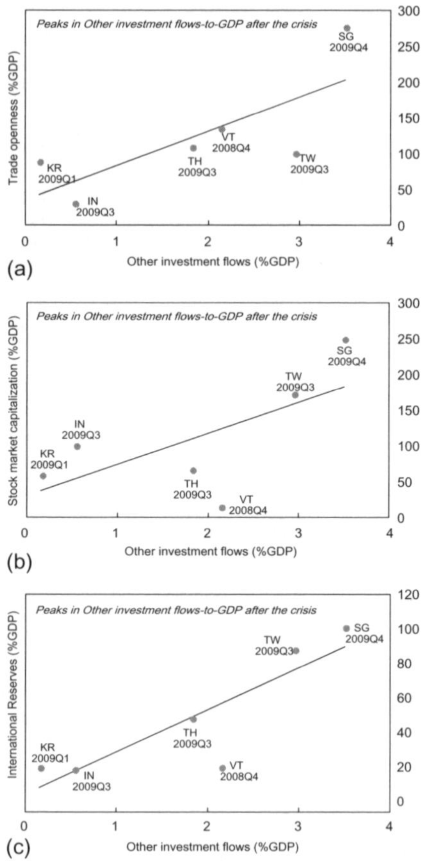

Fig. 13. (a–c) Peaks in other investment flows-to-GDP after the crisis and country characteristics. *Note:* Capital Flows-to-GDP series are defined as the ratio of quarterly net capital flows (US$) to GDP of the last four quarters (US$). Peaks are defined as positive net capital flows that are local maxima following the trough of the crisis. Trade Openness is the ratio of the sum of exports and imports (US$) to quarterly GDP (US$). International Reserves-to-GDP is the ratio of quarterly reserves (US$) to GDP of the last four quarters (US$). The following abbreviations are used: CN = China, IN = India, ID = Indonesia, KR = Korea, MY = Malaysia, PH = Philippines, SG = Singapore, TW = Taiwan Province of China, TH = Thailand, VT = Vietnam. *Source:* Authors' calculations based on International Financial Statistics, IMF.

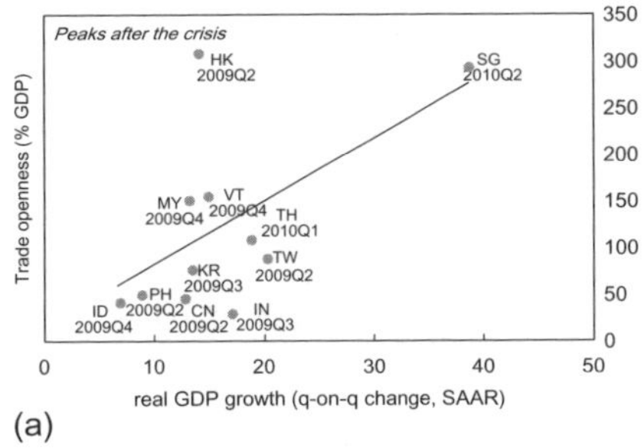

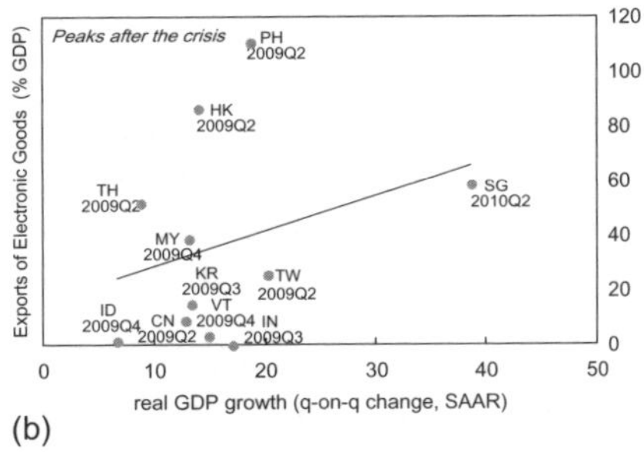

Fig. 14. (a) Peaks in Real GDP Growth Rates after the Crisis and Countries' Degree of Openness to Trade. (b) Peaks in Real GDP Growth Rates after the Crisis and Countries' Exports of Electronic Goods. *Note:* Trade Openness is the ratio of the sum of exports and imports (US$) to quarterly GDP (US$). The following abbreviations are used: CN = China, HK = Hong Kong SAR, IN = India, ID = Indonesia, KR = Korea, MY = Malaysia, PH = Philippines, SG = Singapore, TW = Taiwan Province of China, TH = Thailand, VT = Vietnam. *Source:* Authors' calculations based on International Financial Statistics, IMF.

directly to local banks either by using international reserves or by drawing on the swap lines set up with the US Federal Reserve.

Financial stability measures were aimed at improving bank liquidity and capital adequacy. Many central banks in emerging Asia put in place new facilities for providing liquidity support to credit markets. To avoid systemic stress and enable banks to lend to small and medium-sized enterprises, India, Indonesia and Korea supported banks through capital injections. The Hong Kong Monetary Authority created a temporary Contingent Bank Capital Facility to ensure that the banking system was well capitalized but did not need to activate it. The Korean Bank Reconstruction Fund was used to inject capital in local banks, especially systemically important ones, according to their capital adequacy ratio and their track record of lending to small enterprises. In India, authorities supported state-owned banks through share purchases, in order to help them maintain lending volumes.

The blanket provision of bank deposit insurance and/or the extension of guarantees for other liabilities were used to bolster confidence in the banking sector. In most Asian countries, these measures were limited to deposit guarantees. However, in some countries, Korea, for example, the government also provided guarantees on new foreign currency debt.

Regulatory forbearance was employed in many countries and a number of prudential rules were relaxed: for example, mark-to-market rules for the fair valuation of assets, and minimum liquidity ratios. The Philippines was the first country in the region to significantly loosen the mark-to-market rules to cushion the impact of plummeting asset prices on bank balance sheets. This measure implied that, for a period of time, banks were allowed to shift assets away from categories requiring mark-to-market accounting.

Regulatory measures were also introduced in the securities markets. A number of countries (Indonesia, Korea and Taiwan Province of China) introduced temporary bans on short-selling of assets, after the US stock market plunged in September 2008. In some other Asian emerging markets (e.g., China and Indonesia), state enterprises were encouraged to buy back their shares to put a floor on prices and boost activity in securities markets.

The fiscal policy response during the global financial crisis was substantial. The average stimulus in G-20 countries was about 2 percent of GDP in 2009 and slightly less in 2010. The fiscal stimulus was even larger in Asia. For instance in Korea, the government introduced crisis-related discretionary stimulus measures worth 3.6 percent of GDP, consisting of a broad range of measures on both the revenue and expenditure side, including multiyear cuts in income taxes, and policies to support employment, small and medium-size enterprises and infrastructure projects. In 2010, fiscal policy was still expansionary relative to the pre-crisis benchmark, but the government scaled back the stimulus measures significantly as the economy recovered and the fiscal impulse, consequently, turned negative.

Aggressive countercyclical monetary and fiscal policy played an important stabilization role in Asia. Fiscal packages in NIEs, China and India were considerably larger than the averages for the Asia-Pacific region or the G-20 countries.[9] Also the fiscal programs in Asia were implemented much faster, with spending programs focused on infrastructure and social safety nets – for example, rural pension reform and the provision of better public health, housing and schooling in China, and the expansion of employment guarantees and housing programs in India.

With growth prospects and inflation pressures remaining muted in the advanced economies, there has been some return of risk appetite for the high-growth economies. As a result, capital, led by portfolio flows, has returned to emerging markets and especially to Asia. However, bank loans to the region have not fully recovered to their pre-crisis levels, as international banks are still reluctant to expand their balance sheets given the pressures to conserve capital.

In some cases, recipient countries implemented macro-prudential measures to limit capital inflows and to prevent a buildup of vulnerabilities. Korea introduced measures to curb short-term foreign borrowing through ceilings on foreign exchange forward positions imposed on domestic banks and branches of foreign banks. Indonesia also announced a series of regulatory measures to contain short-term capital inflows. The maturity range of Bank Indonesia's debt instruments was extended (to 9 and 12 months from a previous maximum of 6 months) to encourage investors to keep their funds longer in *Sertifikat Bank Indonesia* (SBIs). At the same time, a minimum holding period of one month was imposed for all SBIs.

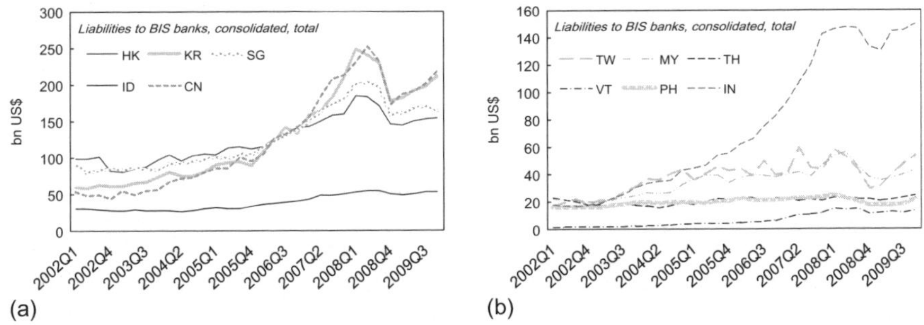

Fig. 15. (a–b) Evolution of Total Liabilities to BIS Banks, Consolidated, in US $ Billion, 2002–2009. The following abbreviations are used: CN = China, HK = Hong Kong SAR, IN = India, ID = Indonesia, KR = Korea, MY = Malaysia, PH = Philippines, SG = Singapore, TW = Taiwan Province of China, TH = Thailand, VT = Vietnam. *Source:* Joint BIS-IMF-OECD-World Bank Statistics on External Debt.

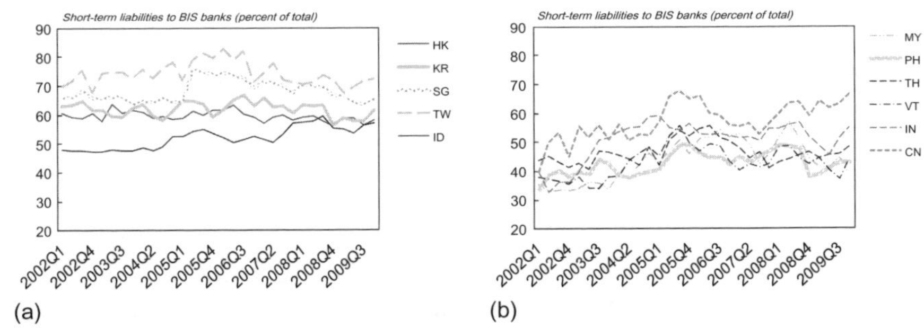

Fig. 16. (a–b) Evolution of Short-Term Liabilities to BIS Banks as a Share of Total Liabilities to BIS Banks, Consolidated, 2002–2009. The following abbreviations are used: CN = China, HK = Hong Kong SAR, IN = India, ID = Indonesia, KR = Korea, MY = Malaysia, PH = Philippines, SG = Singapore, TW = Taiwan Province of China, TH = Thailand, VT = Vietnam. *Source:* Authors' calculations based on Joint BIS-IMF-OECD-World Bank Statistics on External Debt.

Regulations were also introduced on net open foreign exchange positions of banks to restrain foreign currency borrowing.

For now, Asia continues to rely heavily on external financing. Figs. 15 and 16 show that for the vast majority of countries in our sample there has been a secular increase in total liabilities to BIS-reporting banks and an increase in the proportion of short-term liabilities to total liabilities. For debt issuance in international markets, Figs. 17 and 18 reveal that for most

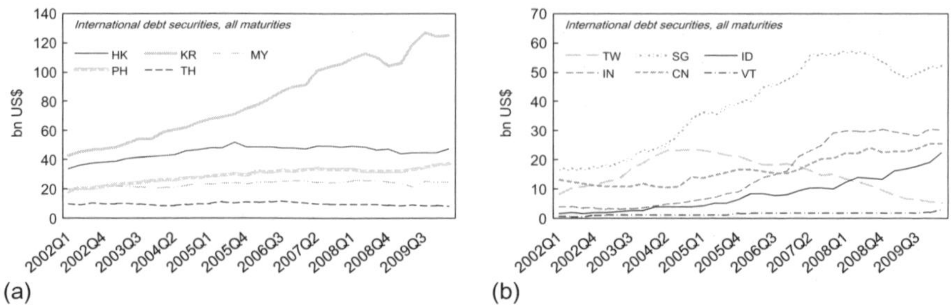

Fig. 17. (a–b) Evolution of International Debt Securities, All Maturities, in US $ Billion, 2002–2009. The following abbreviations are used: CN = China, HK = Hong Kong SAR, IN = India, ID = Indonesia, KR = Korea, MY = Malaysia, PH = Philippines, SG = Singapore, TW = Taiwan Province of China, TH = Thailand, VT = Vietnam. *Source:* Joint BIS-IMF-OECD-World Bank Statistics on External Debt.

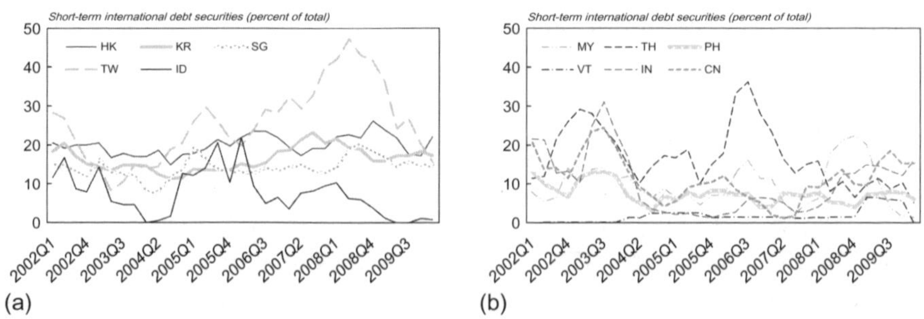

Fig. 18. (a–b) Evolution of Short-Term International Debt Securities as a Share of Total International Debt Securities, 2002–2009. The following abbreviations are used: CN = China, HK = Hong Kong SAR, IN = India, ID = Indonesia, KR = Korea, MY = Malaysia, PH = Philippines, SG = Singapore, TW = Taiwan Province of China, TH = Thailand, VT = Vietnam. *Source:* Authors' calculations based on Joint BIS-IMF-OECD-World Bank Statistics on External Debt.

of the countries there has been a secular increase, and the proportion of short-term debt has fluctuated between 0 percent and 30 percent.

5. CONCLUDING REMARKS

The chapter examined the nature and causes of swings in capital flows and economic activity in Asia during the global financial crisis. In the last few decades, emerging market crises and capital flow reversals were typically precipitated by domestic fragilities such as high indebtedness and balance sheet weaknesses. However, in the recent crisis, the shocks originated in the developed countries and were transmitted to the rest of the world. The analysis in this chapter suggests that the openness of a country to trade and the degree of integration into international financial markets were important determinants of the swings in economic activity and capital flows during both the reversal and recovery phases.

Regarding the trade channel, the chapter shows that Asian countries most affected by the slowdown in global demand were those relatively open to trade, with a high share of durables in total exports and a high trade exposure to China. Therefore, the recent crisis has emphasized the risks for the region of relying too heavily on external demand. Exchange rate flexibility acted as a shock absorber and depreciations paved the way for the subsequent recovery of exports in a number of affected countries. This ability of the exchange rate to act as a shock absorber was underpinned by relatively strong corporate and financial sector balance sheets in most countries, so that the depreciation of the exchange rate did not cause stresses of the type seen during the Asian crisis of 1997–1998.

As global growth prospects deteriorated, emerging markets were affected by the rise in risk aversion and the tightening of external financing conditions. Asian financial markets were drawn into the turmoil when US dollar liquidity dried up and financial institutions stopped lending to each other in the inter-bank market. Foreign exchange reserves did help to cushion some of the impact of capital outflows. Nonetheless, Asian economies still experienced a shortage of foreign currency financing. This raises the important question of assessing liquidity requirements for financial institutions and markets and how to provide the requisite support during a global liquidity and financial crisis.

NOTES

1. For an analysis of the transmission channels of the shock, see Carrasco, Hayashi, and Mukhopadhyay (2010) for South Asia, and Boorman (2009) for emerging market economies worldwide.

2. See Goldstein and Xie (2009) for a discussion of the macroeconomic effects of the crisis on Asia.

3. From a historical perspective, this is the third wave of capital flows to emerging market economies since the beginning of financial reforms in the late 1970s. The first wave started at the end of the 1970s and peaked in 1981 prior to the Latin American debt crisis. The second wave of capital inflows took place in the decade after 1985, peaking in 1996 in the run-up to the Asian crisis of 1997–1998.

4. The sample of Asian emerging markets includes India, the Asean-5 countries (Indonesia, Malaysia, Philippines, Thailand and Vietnam) and the Newly Industrialized Economies (NIEs: Hong Kong SAR, Korea, Singapore and Taiwan Province of China). Unless otherwise specified, China is not included in the sample due to data limitations.

5. Measured as the three-month percentage change of the three-month moving average, seasonally adjusted.

6. See, for example, IMF (2009).

7. See Bank for International Settlements (2009) for an elaboration on pre-crisis fundamentals. Kato (2009) addresses the issue of why Asia was not immune to global financial turmoil despite sound financial institutions and large reserve stocks.

8. Hong Kong SAR is an outlier and its inclusion only reinforces the results presented. For Hong Kong SAR, the trough in portfolio flows-to-GDP was −23 percent in 2008 Q4, and for other investment flows-to-GDP was −18 percent in 2008 Q3.

9. See IMF (2009).

ACKNOWLEDGMENTS

We are grateful to Mangal Goswami, Mico Loretan and Grant Spencer for helpful comments. The views expressed are those of the authors and do not necessarily represent those of the IMF or IMF policy.

REFERENCES

Bank for International Settlements. (2009). *The international financial crisis and the policy challenges in Asia and the Pacific*. Basel: BIS.

Boorman, J. (2009). The impact of the financial crisis on emerging market economies: The transmission mechanism, policy response and lessons. Emerging Markets Forum. Available at http://www.emergingmarketsforum.org/papers/

Carrasco, B., Hayashi, T., & Mukhopadhyay, H. (2010). *The impact of the global crisis on South Asia*. South Asia Working Paper Series No. 1, Asian Development Bank.

Goldstein, M., & Xie, A. (2009). The impact of the financial crisis on emerging Asia. Federal Reserve Bank of San Francisco Asia Economic Policy Conference. Available at http://www.frbsf.org/economics/conferences/aepc/2009/09_Goldstein.pdf

International Monetary Fund. (2008). *World Economic Outlook*. International Monetary Fund, Washington DC, April.

International Monetary Fund. (2009). *Regional Economic Outlook: Asia and Pacific*. International Monetary Fund, Washington DC, November.

Kato, T. (2009). Implications for Asia from the global financial crisis and policy perspectives. Harvard Asia Business Conference. Available at http://www.imf.org/external/np/speeches/2009/021409.htm

SAILING OUT OF CRISIS EMERGING MARKETS STYLE: BLENDING FISCAL–MONETARY RULES, NOMINAL TARGETS AND DEBT DYNAMICS IN SOME TRANSITION ECONOMIES☆

Willi Semmler and Aleksandr V. Gevorkyan

ABSTRACT

Emerging markets are said to have sustained relatively well in the recent global crisis. There are several factors that help explain this popular view, such as, for example, perceived separation from key international financial centres. Still a lot is to be digested in the crisis aftermath with immediate implications for financial markets and real economy. This chapter offers a unique insight into dynamics within transition economies via an extended blended fiscal–monetary policy rules model with possibility of foreign reserves targeting and foreign currency-denominated debt dynamics.

☆Views expressed in this chapter are solely those of the authors and do not represent the views of the institutions they are affiliated with.

The Impact of the Global Financial Crisis on Emerging Financial Markets
Contemporary Studies in Economic and Financial Analysis, Volume 93, 155–195

ISSN: 1569-3759/doi:10.1108/S1569-3759(2011)0000093007

Calibration is based on actual data and is done under various targets and financial risk conditions. Prudent monetary policy and fiscal policy initiatives within current context drive the choice of targets. That may help dampen negative impacts of the crisis and thwart potential currency run. This chapter advances three possible post-crisis scenarios, each with unique solution for reserves, exchange rate, sustainable debt and output levels. Categorizing between net exporters and net importers based on countries' external positions, group-specific results are derived. While both groups are susceptible to exchange-rate risk affected by a multitude of shocks due to their fragile financial system, net importers risk high inflation, but net exporters over-borrowing. This chapter contributes to the literature on global financial crisis, macroeconomic policy, and role of nominal targets and foreign reserves in emerging markets.

Keywords: International finance; global crisis; foreign reserves; macroeconomic policy; foreign currency-denominated debt; emerging markets.

JEL Classifications: C6; E5; F3; G1; P2.

1. INTRODUCTION

Most of recent economic downturns have followed similar pattern: instability spreads beyond the financial sector resulting in significant contraction. Some of the well-documented cases are the Mexican crisis of 1994, East Asian of 1997, Russian of 1998 and Argentinean of late 1990s early 2000s. Today as developed economies seem to be slowly pulling out of recession and chaos of the 2008–2009 global financial crisis, destiny of the financial systems and entire economies of the emerging and transition countries remains unclear, despite the optimism.

Attention is drawn to the problems of exchange rate, currency runs, foreign exchange reserves and foreign currency-denominated debt. Analytical attempts assessing relevant issues on a macro scale are diverse. In this chapter we extend the theoretical approach of Kato, Proano, and Semmler (2008) to the specific case of the economies of the Commonwealth of Independent States (CIS). Extending the basic model we add dynamics of sovereign, private, public and financial institutions' debt. Thus, this study offers a solid theoretical backing to the proposed policy actions in the context of the current financial crisis.

For the emerging markets in general, a key dimension is a potential run on domestic currency evolving into a self-fulfilling currency crisis (as discussed in Krugman, 1979, 2000; Flaschel & Semmler, 2003 and Kato et al., 2008). Somewhat of the sort was witnessed in the earlier mentioned cases and has occurred to varying degrees most recently. In the CIS, with implicit strong link between fiscal and monetary authorities that possibility then makes decisions of monetary control and budget policy interconnected. In fact, compounded with volatile financial markets and sporadic speculative capital flows the 12 economies have seen large unexpected exchange-rate fluctuations, exerting strong pressure on domestic currencies, interest rates and foreign currency debt.

Anticipation of currency depreciation may spur foreign capital outflow resulting in disastrous aftershocks to the economy. That is very relevant in the CIS and has been witnessed over late 2008 through early 2009. In this chapter, we amend a theoretical framework with monetary control problem to account for changes in reserves and effects on foreign currency-denominated debt. The latter matters given inherent instability of the CIS public, private sector's liabilities and foreign currency peg.

The rest of the chapter is structured as follows. We review some stylised facts from international experience in Section 2. In addition theoretical arguments from relevant literature are discussed. In Section 3, we gauge empirical discussion to the case of the CIS. Section 4 develops the two-country group monetary control theoretical framework. Section 5 discusses stabilisation effects of the model as well as reviews possible analytical scenarios of impacts on output, exchange rate and reserves in the background of ongoing crisis. The chapter concludes with discussion on policy implications and a references section.

2. SOME STYLISED FACTS ON FINANCIAL CRISIS FROM INTERNATIONAL EXPERIENCE

Elsewhere it has been noted that introduction of floating exchange rates and liberalisation of capital account, appear to be the key driving factors (e.g. Obstfeld, 1984; Kato et al., 2008; Flaschel & Semmler, 2003; Krugman, 2000; or Semmler, Greiner Diallo, Rezai, & Rajaram, 2007 for an added fiscal-policy dimension) in spreading the crisis across economic sectors. But a financial crisis is not just a monetary problem affecting exchange rates and interest rates. For increasing number of countries, a crisis comes in two dimensions: as credit crisis and as currency crisis.

By credit crisis we refer to (a) sudden drop in liquidity and (b) rapidly increasing large indebtedness of domestic agents (including corporate, banking and household debts). If debt liabilities are denominated in foreign currency, as is often for countries that cannot borrow in own currencies, that may negatively affect capital flows rushing currency depreciation. This pattern fits the transitional phase of the liberalisation reforms in emerging markets (Latin America) and in economies in transition.

The self-propagating mechanism leads to increasing interest rate, instability in the stock markets, further drop in cross-bank lending, and by extension real economy's contraction incited by lack of credit to sustain operations. Alternatively, Flaschel and Semmler (2003) note that such classical scenario and the strains on national balance sheets may be relaxed and instability may not be propagated. The problem is with the severity of the expected depreciation that causes foreign currency-denominated liabilities to suddenly increase and whether that can be controlled via some policy. Reserves play a crucial role in this.

The crises of the 1990s carry an important lesson for the current research. Specifically, there is a strong correlation between current account deficit and probability and severity of a crisis. Corsetti, Pesenti, and Roubini (1999) observe that among the East Asian countries that saw significant collapses in the currency regimes were primarily those with large current account to GDP ratios (e.g. Thailand, Malaysia and others). Across those economies, current account deficit ranged anywhere between 3 and 10 percent of GDP before and during the crisis. This was primarily due to trade balance and low net-factor payments to the world. Countries with better current account to GDP ratios escaped the worst impacts.

Kato et al. (2008) and other observers note that despite severe deterioration, currency depreciation led to competitiveness improvement as the economies were able to revert current account deficit to current account surplus. Country specifics are important. One must keep in mind the economic development process of East Asia preceding the crisis of 1997 and the export-oriented structure of those economies. East Asian goods competitiveness in quality was aided by additional competitiveness in price due to sharp deterioration.

Nevertheless, the crisis and with it the current account deficit soon reverted in growth. Fig. 1 helps illustrate the tendency by outlining the GDP growth and current account to GDP ratio across East Asian economies (e.g. see Amsden, 2001 for overview). The initial collapse due to crisis around 1997 and eventual pickup within a year or so right after are clearly seen, in particular for Korea and Indonesia. But it is this real economy's diversification and competitiveness that the economies of the CIS, and in fact transition countries

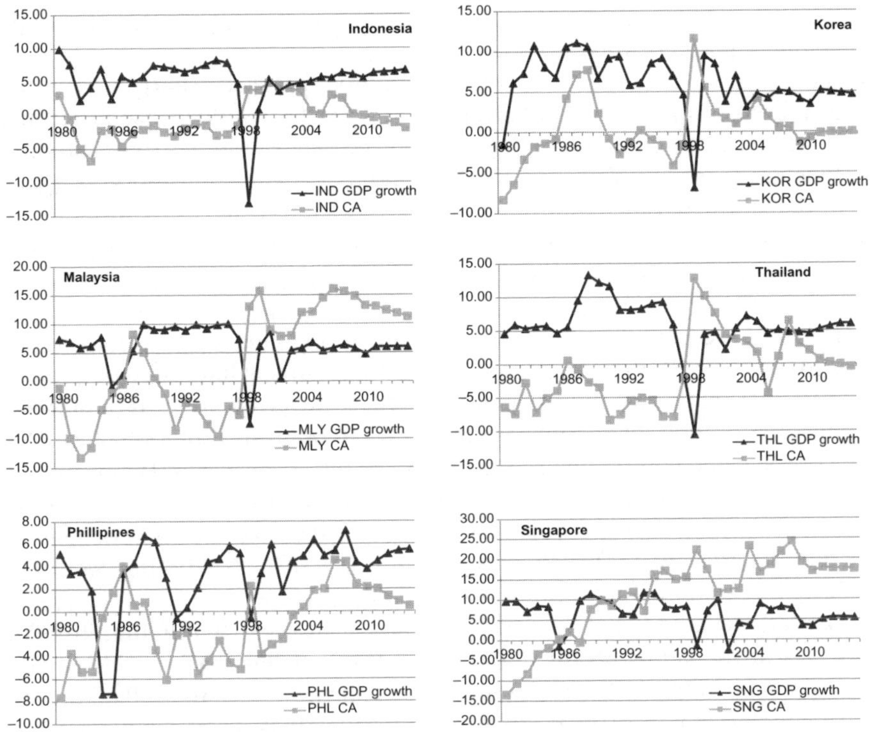

Fig. 1. Current Account (% of GDP) Change and GDP Growth in East Asia (%). *Source:* Authors' Calculations Based on International Monetary Fund (IMF) (2009a, 2009b) data. *Note:* Estimates beyond 2008 are from IMF based on 2007 actual data.

of the Central and Eastern Europe, and some other emerging markets, lack as we have pointed out numerous times across our research.

Based on the above, it is possible to derive a set of general characteristics of a typical financial crisis. These facts are inspired by discussions in Kamin (1999), Corsetti et al. (1999) and significantly by work of Flaschel and Semmler (2003):

- A currency crisis is preceded by current account deficit (increase in current account deficit to GDP ratio).
- There is an increase in overall indebtedness of economic agents. Often private debt of 'too-big-to fail' entities is guaranteed by the state.

- Reversal of capital flows, 'capital flight', puts pressure on domestic financial markets and currency.
- As foreign exchange leaves the economy, there is sharp and often unexpected currency depreciation. That leads to a sudden rise in foreign currency-denominated liabilities as debt becomes more costly to service.
- Increase in interest rates via monetary policy, possible abruption or panic in the stock markets and banking crises as lending activity contracts.
- Eventual deterioration in real economy as firms are unable to procure credit for operations and long-term investment.

It is striking how the above observations fit the current global economic environment. With varying degrees and perhaps somewhat different starting points, that is, not all have experienced sharp reversals in current account trends, the outflow of foreign capital from the peripheral markets has been one of the key common denominators. Since the crises of late 1990s, rapidly growing developing countries of East Asia and many CIS economies have accumulated significant foreign exchange reserves. Fig. 2 illustrates change in total reserves to GDP for selected countries. For generality, the *x*-axis reflects five years before and after the crisis.

Overall the trend in Fig. 2 shows a sharp increase in foreign currency reserves in the countries hit by crisis the most. It has been suggested that reserves serve a precautionary purpose helping economies defy any potential currency runs (e.g. Kato et al., 2008). This ultimately suggests a managed float

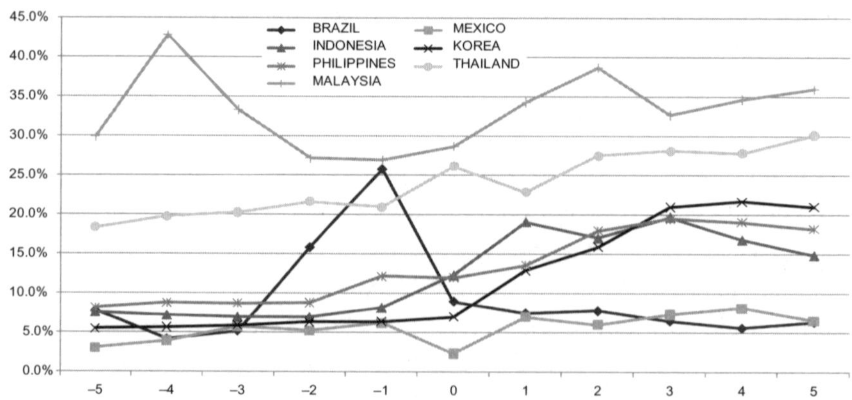

Fig. 2. Total Foreign Reserves (Less Gold) to GDP Ratio (%). *Source:* Authors' calculations based on the IMF (2009a, 2009b) Data. *Note:* Time period 0 indicates the year of the crisis in each economy.

exchange-rate policy. Aizenman and Turnovsky (2002) also argue, that sufficient reserves build-up acts as collateral to sovereign borrowing in the international capital market. By this logic, rising international reserves reduce default risk that lenders face.

Credibility then helps borrowing economies attract more in loans and potentially invest in productive sector. This and the implied guaranteed return potentially raise welfare in the borrowing and lending economies. Kato et al. (2008) offer clarification to an increase in international reserves in the emerging markets. The authors note that initial increase in reserves comes from the pickup in the economic growth. The second effect is the actual reserves build-up as part of the macroeconomic policy. In Section 3, we gauge this analysis to the specific case of the CIS in the current crisis environment.

3. HOW THE CIS FITS THE EMERGING MARKETS STORY

The CIS is a diverse group of economies with independent policy making and unique priorities. Nevertheless, it is possible to identify common characteristics that allow analytical comparison. Earlier, we advanced four channels of crisis propagation in the CIS (Gevorkyan, 2009). We have briefly touched on each in the above discussion. The key channels are:

- Strong dependence on primary commodities exports and immediate impact of international prices decline and drop in global demand for energy products.
- Currency pressures and capital flight.
- Increased foreign currency-denominated debt via banking system and in private sector.
- Dry out of foreign workers' remittances from host to home economies (see Gevorkyan & Gevorkyan, 2010 for more on labour migration in the CIS).

Helpful to our analysis is the analytical separation of the 12 CIS economies between net exporters and net importers based on each country's external trade position. A brief reference built on historical data is shown in Table 1. This classification is instrumental in understanding the specifics of each country's development and current crisis impacts.

As mentioned, CIS economies can be categorized in two country groups: *net exporters* and *net importers* (Republic of Georgia has recently opted out of the CIS but is kept in the sample for the purposes of this study). The latter group

Table 1. CIS Groups Based on Income Sources from International Transactions.

Group	Country	Main Export Commodity	Main Export Commodity, % of Total Exports (Average of 1995–2005)	Main Import Commodity	Main Import Commodity % of Total Import (Average of 1995–2005)	Average Share of Remittances to GDP (1998–2006)	Average Share of Official Aid Received to GDP (1998–2006)
Net exporters	Azerbaijan	Primary (fuels)	77.5%	Manufactured (machinery)	67.2%	2.37%	3.33%
	Belarus	Manufactured (machinery)	69.8%	Manufactured (machinery)	55.1%	1.27%	0.04%
	Kazakhstan	Primary (fuels)	48.8%	Manufactured (machinery)	72.8%	0.49%	0.79%
	Russia	Primary (fuels)	48.3%	Manufactured (machinery)	58.6%	0.47%	
	Turkmenistan	Primary (fuels)	79.2%	Manufactured (machinery)	80.3%		0.66%
	Uzbekistan	Raw materials (cotton)	41.7%	Manufactured (machinery)	81.2%	5.96%	1.00%
	Ukraine	Manufactured (misc)	67.5%	Primary (fuels)	53.0%	0.40%	0.12%
Net importers	Armenia	Manufactured (misc)	59.4%	Manufactured (machinery)	49.6%	12.13%	11.53%
	Georgia	Primary (food/ores/metal)	47.7%	Primary (food/fuels)	50.1%	7.58%	8.28%
	Kyrgyz Republic	Primary (agriculture/food)	43.1%	Manufactured (machinery)	54.9%	4.92%	17.11%
	Moldova	Primary (agriculture/food)	63.1%	Manufactured (misc)	56.3%	20.63%	5.96%
	Tajikistan	Primary (ores/metal)	44.1%	Primary (food/fuels)	52.7%	16.86%	12.78%

Source: Gevorkyan (2009).

presents a case of chronic current account deficit and strong reliance on imported consumer and capital goods, and, to a smaller degree, agricultural products. The countries in this group are highly dependant on cross border foreign currency flows and lack any particular core industry in terms of development model. The net exporters on the other hand exhibit current account surplus. This has been guaranteed by consistent improvement in net exporters' terms of trade, due to recently high international prices on basic commodities and energy products – the primary exports of the seven net exporters. A recent drop in global demand and sharp declines in raw materials prices under the ongoing global economic slowdown have negatively affected the large CIS economies. It may be a matter of time then for the net exporters' current account surplus reverting to a deficit. Hence, for the region, current account deficit may in time prolong the crisis.

Foreign currency-denominated debt poses another instability threat to highly dollarized CIS economies. As Curtis, Gardner, and Waller (2005) note in their analysis of Ukraine, for example, persistent dollarisation is due to domestic currency inflation, exchange-rate instability and remaining shadow economy. Much of the public, commercial banking, corporate and household debt then is either explicitly denominated in foreign currency or implicitly pegged to prevailing exchange rate. For example, the largest economy in the region, Russia, has accumulated foreign currency-denominated private debt of over USD 500 billion, just a notch below its October 2008 total reserves level (Mau, 2009). Latest available European Bank for Reconstruction and Development (EBRD) Transition Report (EBRD, 2009) alludes to an almost double increase in foreign currency-denominated debt in transition, in Russia specifically, from early 2000s up until 2007 when the first indications of the global spread of the crisis became evident.

It is clear that there is a strong reliance on international capital in the CIS, confirmed in Fig. 3 (panels (a) and (b)) shows external debt – foreign currency-denominated total debt – trend across CIS-country groups. The debt ratios to GDP and total exports have not been stable and peaked over 100 percent, in particular for net importers.

Krugman (2000) reviews these ratios as indicative of country's openness and possibility of default on its liabilities. There is an evident concern and for the net importer states primarily. Consider the current debt situation in Central and Eastern Europe. According to some recent estimates (e.g. FT, 2009a), increasing of credit to the region by the Western European banks since early 2000s is now holding entire economies hostage to capability of extending the credit lines. With up to USD 1.5 trillion total exposure by the Eurozone banks in 2008, both Europe's crippling financial system and shaky transition

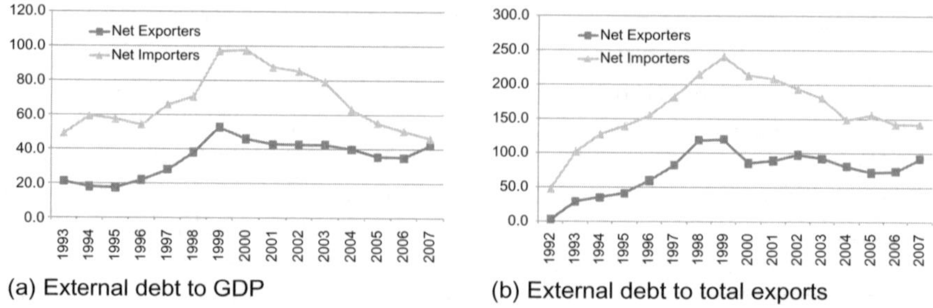

Fig. 3. External Debt Ratios in the CIS by Country Groups (%). (a) External Debt to GDP. (b) External Debt to Total Exports. *Source:* Authors' calculations based on the EBRD (2009) Data.

economies could suffer immensely if the credit lines break. In relation to GDP developed economies' banks' stakes range from 12 percent (Russia) to 146 percent (Estonia). Since January 2008, domestic currencies lost their value in relation to Euro up to 38 percent as in Ukraine for example. But the process is ongoing and events develop rapidly.

Total international reserves accumulation is another integral component shaping today's macroeconomic policy decisions in the transition economies. Here, the spread is again not even between two-country groups. Fig. 4 outlines the trend for the past 10 years.

Due to their advantageous endowments, net exporters have been more successful in building up significant reserves stockpiles. Russia – the largest in the CIS – reported up to USD 600 billion at its high times in mid-2008 (CBR, 2010). In relation to GDP, net exporters' total reserves range between 20 and 35 percent, significant considering their relative scales.

As the pressure intensified, authorities across all CIS countries significantly relied on the reserves to defend domestic currencies from dramatic depreciation. Russia is a vivid example, where within short span of three months of late 2008 and early 2009 official reserves were halved in an effort to avert a severe currency drop, liquidity pressure and decline in export revenues (the latter was due to sharp drop in energy prices worldwide). At the time, this combination of external events and fiscal and monetary authorities' combined reforms was seen as the 'perfect storm' hit on the CIS economies.

It should be noted that public funds have also been invested in various fiscal stimulus programs including private corporations and bank bail-outs, consumer credit programs and administrative measures for price controls on consumer staples. A strong de facto link between monetary and fiscal

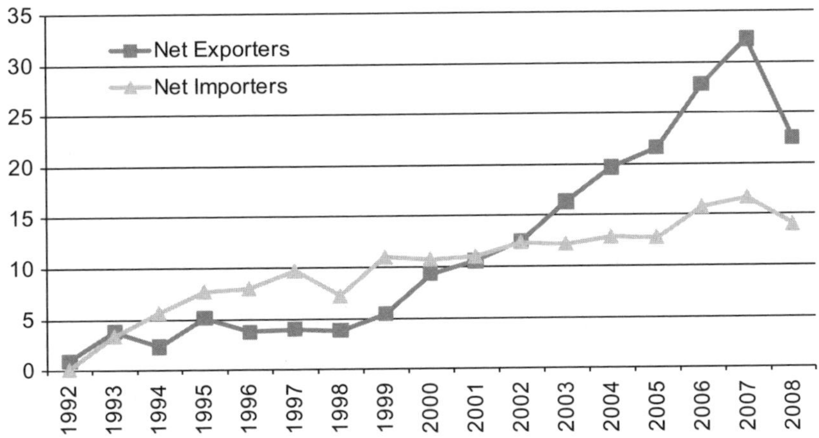

Fig. 4. Total International Reserves to GDP Ratio in the CIS by Country Groups. *Source:* Authors' calculations based on the EBRD (2009) Data.

authorities has solidified, since the earlier studies of banking independence in transition (e.g. Wagner, 1999, 2000; Loungani & Sheets, 1997 and others). This suggests joint management decisions and explains the sharp decline in reserves starting early-mid-2008 as in Fig. 4 for CIS and Fig. 5 for Russia only.

On yet another dimension is the interest rate. In the CIS, the average refinancing rate – analogous to the US Fed discount rate – has settled in the range of 5–14 percent. The standard argument suggests that a relatively high interest rate may be regarded as a positive aspect in terms of staving off inflation and in an open economy sustaining competitive currency value, assuming some type of interest parity condition holds. But a too high interest rate translates in more expensive loans by commercial banks adding to the overall economy's solvency worries (e.g. Russia described in FT, 2009b).

In the CIS, this standard view crumbles against rich political economy content. For politically vulnerable import-relying economies, preventing sharp depreciation of their domestic currencies then becomes a matter of social content as well. Similarly abrupt sustained increase in price levels poses a risk to destabilising economy and society. Such intermix of seemingly purely economical with social aspects in the CIS is key to the unique nature of those economies. In that sense technical models may shed additional light on specific country circumstances and prompt relevant policy solutions in the context of the current economic environment. We address this in Section 4.

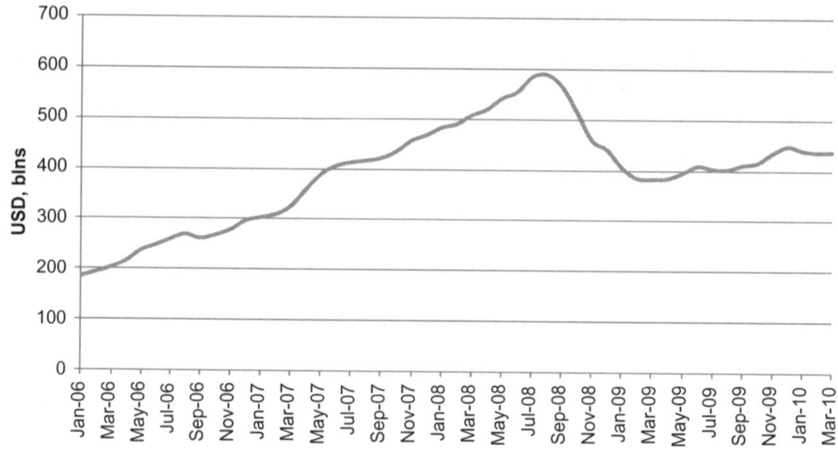

Fig. 5. Russia's International Reserves, Monthly Average (January 2006–March 2010). *Source:* Authors' calculations based on CBR (2010).

4. A TWO-COUNTRY GROUP THEORETICAL MODEL WITH FOREIGN RESERVES

Our analysis is built on the model introduced by Kato et al. (2008) and further extended in Gevorkyan (2009). This model is modified for considerations of the CIS specifics, debt and existence of two-country groups. Following Kato et al. (2008), we describe economy by the following relations:

$$y = \alpha - \beta(i - \pi^e) + X(e^e);\ X'(e^e) > 0 \tag{1}$$

$$\pi = \pi^e + \eta(y - y_n) \tag{2}$$

$$\dot{e} = i - i^f - \rho(i - i^f, R);\ \rho_{i-i^f} > 0,\ \rho_R < 0 \tag{3}$$

where Eq. (1) describes a standard open economy output y relation that depends negatively on real interest rate i and positively related to the net exports $X(e^e)$, which in turn react positively to expected exchange-rate e^e depreciation; α and β are positive constants. Eq. (2) describes domestic inflation rate π that depends on expected inflation rate π^e and a variation of actual output from the natural level y_n (NAIRU). Note that for convenience we assume policy target $y^* = y_n$.

Eq. (3) is a modified interest rate parity condition, where i is the domestic interest and i^f is the foreign interest rate (average one year LIBOR rate for convenience); and ρ is a country-specific risk premium to cover uncertainty. One of the risk factors is the exchange-rate volatility that causes high uncertainty. That is captured in ρ by $i - i^f$. The second risk factor relates to potential losses associated with financial instruments such as foreign exchange reserves, R. Since the reserves become a closely watched proxy for domestic currency's stability, per our earlier discussion, an abrupt drop in reserves may indicate high risk of keeping assets denominated in local currency for a potential investor. Within the model, reserves dynamics can be expressed as follows:

$$\dot{R} = X(e^e) + F(e^e, R); F_{e^e} < 0, F_R > 0 \tag{4}$$

where $F(e^e, R)$ is the net inflow of financial assets that also results in an increase in foreign exchange reserves and can be expressed as

$$F(e^e, R) = n(e^e) - z(e^e, R); n'(e^e) < 0, z_{e^e} > 0, z_R < 0 \tag{5}$$

where net inflow is the difference between inflow n and outflow z (for simplicity we subdue any interest rate and expected exchange-rate effects). Note that in Eq. (5), only z is a function of expected exchange rate, e^e, and reserves, R. This accounts for our earlier statement on investor's reaction to reserves depletion: as reserves decrease there is a potential risk for currency depreciation, hence, motivation for foreign investors to pull out.

As an extension to the main model by Kato et al. (2008), we introduce five new parameters each reflecting different types of debt and foreign currency-denominated assets dynamics in the transition economies. The new parameters are: b-ratio of total foreign currency-denominated sovereign debt to national income y, $b \equiv B/y$, where B is the total sovereign debt level; a generic term d, $d = D/y$, where D is the total foreign currency debt level (with later distinction between public and private debt); private household foreign currency debt or, also, demand for foreign currency, h, $h = H/y$, where H is the total level; and an efficient leverage as a ratio of financial institutions foreign currency debt K in relation to their earnings V, then $k = K/V$. We use the term d interchangeably and interpreted it depending on exact country grouping explained below.

For the net exporter economies d represents a ratio of total foreign currency-denominated private debt to national income y and for the net importers it is the ratio of total foreign currency-denominated public debt to income, y. Net exporters have seen increasing private (corporate, banking and households) indebtedness, D_{prv}. As has already been mentioned, Russia's private debt now exceeds the levels of the country's public debt at the time of the 1998 default. Current estimate of Russia's private debt of USD 500 billion also exceeds the total value of the country's foreign reserves (Mau, 2009). Since many large corporations and financial entities (principle borrowers) are implicitly supported by the state, debt increases in the background of the currency depreciation and loss of foreign reserves destabilises the economic situation significantly. For the net importers, aside from the regular sovereign debt B, a major factor in the economy is state borrowing. We refer to net importers' state debt as D_{pub} in our model. We are concerned with foreign currency-denominated debt that affects balance sheets via implied foreign currency peg described above.

For the fragile transition economies change in value of foreign currency-denominated debt has a strong impact on the economy and investors' decisions to stay or pull out of the country. Then in transition environment sustaining a competitive exchange rate may be a priority given high value of foreign currency-denominated (or pegged to exchange rate) debt. Expected exchange-rate depreciation then explodes the debt-to-be-repaid value.

Increasing liabilities and indebtedness may stir expectations of country's insolvency, default and spur capital flight. Without implication of specific causality of related effects there is a strong interconnection among all components in the transition economies. Therefore, all types of debt introduced above carry a risk premium that compensates for the underlying risks and uncertainty. In each case dynamics can be described as follows:

$$\dot{b} = \gamma b - \frac{X(e^e)}{y} - g_y b \tag{6}$$

$$\dot{d}_{\text{prv}} = \text{inv} - s(p - ud_{\text{prv}}) - g_y d_{\text{prv}} \tag{7}$$

$$\dot{d}_{\text{pub}} = g - t + zd_{\text{pub}} - g_y d_{\text{pub}} \tag{8}$$

$$\dot{h} = \theta h - \frac{c - w}{y} - g_y h \tag{9}$$

$$\dot{k} = \phi k + \frac{X^f}{V} - \zeta k - g_v k \tag{10}$$

The first term b net foreign assets (sovereign debt) to income ratio described by Eq. (6). Change in b is given by the difference in total interest payments γb and current account, or net exports, $(X(e^e))/y$ (all expressed as ratios to income) less the product of the real GDP growth rate and debt-to-income ratio: $g_y b$. Note that per our assumption current account to income ratio for net exporters reflects a surplus position and a deficit position in the net importers case. The interest rate on debt is $\gamma = i + \tau_1$, where i is the domestic real interest rate found in the model and τ_1 is a transition economy risk premium, equal to or greater than zero. For example, sovereign bonds issued to the Diaspora (as discussed in Gevorkyan, 2008) would carry a low τ_1 risk, and the yield is then mainly defined by domestic interest rate, i. A more conventional bond issuance on the other hand would require a value greater than zero on τ_1 as investors require higher returns given increased exchange-rate risk, country risk and risk of outbound growing debt in the transition economies. Eq. (6) applies in both net exporters and net importers cases in our model.

Next, change in private debt to income ratio d_{prv} in the net exporting economies, as in Eq. (7) above, is determined by a share of required investment to income ratio, inv, less the remaining balance of profits to income ratio p covering interest payments ud_{prv} income share, reduced by debt to income ratio growing proportionately to total income, $g_y d_{\text{prv}}$, where s is a positive constant share. Note that interest rate u is determined by $u = i + \tau_2$; where i is the domestic real interest rate and $\tau_2 > 0$ is the country-specific risk premium.

Net importers specific debt Eq. (8) describes the change in public debt to income ratio, d_{pub}. Here, fiscal budget, difference between government purchases g and tax revenues t, is offset by required interest payments zd_{pub} and reduced by debt to income ratio growing proportionately to total income, $g_y d_{\text{pub}}$. Consistent with the rest of the debt equations layout, all variables are introduced as proportionate to total GDP rather than as levels. Interest rate is defined as $z = i + \tau_3$, where i is the domestic real interest rate and $\tau_3 > 0$ is the country-specific risk premium. Intuitively the value of τ_3 in the net importer economies will be significantly higher than basic interest rate due to increased country-specific risk (note that if e is defined as foreign currency expressed in domestic currency, foreign currency-denominated income, e.g., would then be expressed as $y^{fx} = (y/e)$).

Further, consider domestic households demand for foreign currency-denominated assets (or equivalently and more realistic in the CIS context) households' demand for foreign currency (denoted as H or $h = (H/y)$ in proportion to total output). Expression (9) reflects evolution of this demand dependant on consumption (C) and wealth (W), in addition to standard interest income and risk premium. Importantly, there is a negative relation between household consumption and h and positive relation to wealth.

Hence, as consumers accumulate extra funds and their consumption needs are satisfied at certain time they invest in foreign currency assets. This is entirely consistent with the evidence from CIS and other transition economies where foreign currency is often the primary store of value. The interest earned and exchange-rate risk premium is captured by the term $\theta = i + \tau_4$, that is, dependant on domestic monetary policy i and the τ_4 premium demanded on foreign currency investments due to currency exchange risk in the CIS (until recently foreign currency deposits promised higher returns than in domestic currency – this has been changing during the current crisis, as Central Banks started implementing new regulatory measures, including interest rates ceilings on foreign currency deposits, to control currency flows in economies).

Finally, Eq. (10) reflects dynamics in the domestic financial institutions' space. Commercial banks and other financial organisations in the CIS have increased their dealings in foreign currencies (e.g. USD 500 billion corporate foreign currency debt in Russia, about a quarter was in the banking sector according to Yershov, 2008). We express effective leverage then as a ratio of loans in foreign currency (or foreign currency on hand, or, which is the same, as foreigners' holdings of domestic financial institutions' bonds) to the present value of the domestic financial institutions' cash flows: $k = (K/V)$. Hence, to stay current on their foreign currency debt repayment and prevent overleveraging, keeping k low, domestic financial institutions must stay profitable (raising V).

Next we draw from research by Caballero and Krishnamurthy (2008) adapting key aspects of their core model to this setup. Evolution of financial institutions foreign currency debt $\dot{K} = (X^f - \zeta K) + \phi K$, where X^f represents returns to foreigners on funds invested in the CIS economy, for example as loans to the financial system (via bonds or other instruments). Here the rate, at which foreign investments in domestic financial institutions are repatriated to foreign investors, is $\zeta = i + \tau_5$. The interest rate on foreign currency debt faced by domestic financial institutions $\phi = i + \tau_6$. Setting $\tau_6 = \tau_1$ for simplicity results in ϕ being essentially the same as the γ rate defined above. Note that τ_5 is defined as $\tau_5 = i - i^f$ the difference between domestic real interest rate and an average one year LIBOR rate. This implies first that domestic real interest rate adjusts in response to some policy measures and second that foreign capital is then repatriated at a higher rate if domestic rates significantly exceed LIBOR rates. This is very relevant to the current crisis situation in the transition economies, as foreign capital exited the CIS economies in a rush, while Central Banks raised the rates to avoid sharp currency devaluation. It was also relevant in the instances of Asian crises and authorities' reactions, as reviewed above (also see discussion in Froot & Thaler, 1990 and Carlson & Osler, 2003 on risk premium calculations).

The financial institutions' wealth is defined as $W = V - K$, hence, the difference between present value of all cash flows and what has to be repaid to foreign creditors in foreign currency. Note also that $V = ((X^d - X^f)/\zeta)$, that is, present value of domestic institutions' cash flows depends on their profitability X^d and negatively related to payouts to foreigners on their investments X^f, discounted at the ζ rate.

With the above characterization of a transition economy and related components, we now look closely into policy specifics. From the central bank's point of view there are three principal targets: the inflation rate, the output gap and precautionary foreign exchange reserves build-up, as discussed earlier. Hence, the monetary instrument that central bank has at its disposal, indirectly affecting three targets in normal times, is the real domestic interest rate. Then central bank's objective is to minimise its loss, defined by the following:

$$\min_i L = \int_0^\infty e^{-rt}\left[\frac{\lambda_1}{2}(\pi - \pi^*)^2 + \frac{\lambda_2}{2}(y - y^*)^2 + \frac{\lambda_3}{2}(R - R^*)^2\right]dt \tag{11}$$

where the new terms are π^*, y^*, R^* and correspond to the target levels of inflation rate, output level and foreign exchange reserves stock. The parameters λ_1, λ_2 and λ_3 measure relative weight of each variable in the objective function. Then using Eqs. (1) and (2) in Eq. (11) the objective function is:

$$\min_i L = \int_0^\infty e^{-rt}\left[\frac{\lambda_1}{2}(\pi^e + \eta(\alpha - \beta(i - \pi^e) + X(e^e) - y^*) - \pi^*)^2 \right. \\ \left. + \frac{\lambda_2}{2}(\alpha - \beta(i - \pi^e) + X(e^e) - y^*)^2 + \frac{\lambda_3}{2}(R - R^*)^2\right]dt \tag{12}$$

subject to Eqs. (3) and (4), and boundary conditions for e^e and R. We add further detailed specification to expression (12) and carry out relevant derivation in the appendix. Solving the model, we obtain first steady-state solution Eq. (A.16).

Incorporating Eq. (A.16) in Eqs. (A.12)–(A.15) and setting $q_1 = q_2 = e^e = R = 0$ and solving for i, e^e, R, q_2, we derive a new set of steady states. We also derive growth conditions for the five debt types in the appendix. That allows us to come up with specific solutions for debt ratios expressed from Eqs. (6)–(10) as the following:

$$b = \frac{m - \varepsilon e^e}{y(g_y - \gamma)} \tag{13}$$

$$d_{\text{prv}} = \frac{\text{inv} - sp}{g_y + su} \tag{14}$$

$$d_{\text{pub}} = \frac{g - t}{g_y - z} \tag{15}$$

$$h = \frac{w - c}{(g_y - \theta)y} \tag{16}$$

$$k = \frac{X^f}{V(g_y + \varsigma - \phi)} \tag{17}$$

Eqs. (13), (17) and (A.16) then allow us derive steady-state values for $b, d_{\text{prv}}, d_{\text{pub}}, h, k$ within the model. Finally, note that in all three cases, among other factors, domestic interest rate i and specific risk premiums $\tau_1, \tau_2, \tau_3, \tau_4, \tau_5, \tau_6$ have a strong effect on the debt ratios, via $\gamma, u, z, \theta, \varsigma, \phi$ as defined earlier. Calibrating the measures in Section 5 helps us analyse some of the specific effects of the above-sketched model.

5. NUMERICAL ANALYSIS AND POSSIBLE POLICY SCENARIOS

5.1. Policy and Effects Without Explicit Reserves Targeting

The model is calibrated for the 12 economies using average macro-indicators for the 2000–2008 period. All actual data are derived from EBRD and IMF tables. Consistent with our approach we run two-country groups analysis: net exporters and net importers. In addition, for each country group we review two distinct cases of the model (a) without foreign exchange reserves (R^*) target level and (b) with explicit foreign exchange reserves (R^*) target level. We begin with the first case of no reserves target. For brevity we review only a few of possible scenarios that may be extrapolated from the model.

To begin with we assume a simple case of no reserves targeting and no risk premium to foreign investor for holding assets in the domestic currency. Hence, we set the relative reserves target weight in the central bank's loss function equal to zero, $\lambda_3 = 0$ and $\sigma_1 = 0$ and $\sigma_2 = 0$, which also means $\rho = 0$. For convenience, we set $m = 0$ and assume expected inflation, π^e, to be a constant. We fine tune parameters for foreign exchange net inflow by setting both $v > 0$ and $\mu > 0$. Following our discussion of Eq. (4), we set both $v > 0$ and $\mu > 0$ with implication that change in the foreign exchange reserves is influenced by exchange-rate and current reserves levels R.

Average parameters for the seven net exporting economies in the simple case of no reserves targeting are shown in Table 2. The table includes averages specific to our extended version of the model with debt Eqs. (6)–(10). Note that net importers' specific parameters (government spending g, tax revenue t and risk premium τ_3) are excluded since they are not relevant to this simulation.

Similarly we run a separate simulation for the net importing economies with the specific parameters as described in Table 3. Here we set non-net importer economies parameters to 'n.a.' accordingly and change values for other relevant variables.

Note that we raise the value of the μ parameter for the net importers case to 100 and lower v to 10. With a lower real foreign interest rate, this allows

Table 2. Net Exporters Parameter Values, No *R* Targeting.

λ_1	λ_2	λ_3	π^*	π^e	y^*	R^*	i^f	r	W	C
1	1	0	0.1	0.1	250	0	0.05	0.05	85	50
α	β	η	σ_1	σ_2	ε	m	v	μ	X^d	X^f
125	25	0.0007	0	0	0.3	0	70	10	200	150
g	t	inv	p	g_y	s	τ_1	τ_2	τ_3	τ_4	g_v
n.a.	n.a.	0.3	0.25	0.09	1	0.1	0.05	n.a.	0.01	0.2

Table 3. Net Importers Parameter Values, No *R* Targeting.

λ_1	λ_2	λ_3	π^*	π^e	y^*	R^*	i^f	r	W	C
1	1	0	0.12	0.16	15	0	0.03	0.05	4	2.5
α	β	η	σ_1	σ_2	ε	m	v	μ	X^d	X^f
5	1.5	0.0009	0	0	−0.01	0	10	100	90	70
g	t	inv	p	g_y	s	τ_1	τ_2	τ_3	τ_4	g_v
0.27	0.13	n.a.	n.a.	0.05	n.a.	0.005	n.a.	0.005	0.012	0.12

us to assign a greater value to the risk of reserves outflow from the smaller and less financially protected economies. We use higher inflation rate but lower output level values to better reflect the specifics of the small five net importer economies. Finally, we adjust the wealth, consumption and profit flow values accordingly. Note that in both net exporters and net importers g_v is exactly half of the output growth rate, g_y.

Given the parameter values in Tables 2 and 3, we derive first steady-state solutions, presented in Tables 4 and 5 for the reserves R, inflation rate π, interest rate i, output y, exchange rate e, external debt to output b, private debt-to-output ratio d_{prv} (net exporters), and public debt-to-output ratio d_{pub} (net importers), household debt-to-output ratio h and effective leverage k. Employing software package *Mathematica*, we computed steady state for the given parameters using Eqs. (13), (A.9)–(A.16).

Clearly there are several steady-state solutions. To preserve economic meaning of our results, we reject solutions with negative exchange rate due to lack of economic rationale. In other words, while mathematical result is accurate it is difficult to imagine a real-life situation with a negative exchange rate. In a situation with negative R result, Kato et al. (2008) suggest that there is a need for an external credit line (e.g. IMF).

Then for the net exporters (steady state 1 in Table 4), there is a range for R between 0 and 13,731 pushing currency reserves away from zero level. Such move requires strong exchange-rate depreciation. That then implies potentially sustainable very high external debt-to-output ratio (in this case it is greater than 1). Hence, large reserves build-up would be required to sustain very large b as the group over-borrows in the international capital markets and has to keep up with the interest payments. Partially this result

Table 4. Net Exporters Steady State, No R Targeting.

Steady State	R	π	i	y	e	b	d_{prv}	h	k
1	13,731	0.1	0.05	250	412.5	8.25	0.26	4.7	1.5
2	185.44	0.016	0.05	130.2	13.11	0.50	0.26	8.9	1.5

Table 5. Net Importers Steady State, No R Targeting.

Steady State	R	π	i	y	e	b	d_{pub}	h	k
1	94.36	0.15	0.03	5.17	2.11	0.27	9.3	36.3	0.9

is confirmed by and relates to the circumstances of Kazakhstan and Ukraine with external debt-to-GDP ratios over 100 percent during the 2000s. Realistically, sustainability of such high debt may not hold in the longer run and as first signs of any instability appear risk of default intensifies. In fact financial market perceives a ratio greater than 1 as risky, indicating country's vulnerability and deterring additional capital flows into the economies.

In the steady state 2 in Table 4 – with the derived equilibrium solutions for reserves, exchange rate and interest rate – net exporting economies' sustainable external debt-to-output ratio is lower at 0.50. On average that is a more reasonable level for the group (see Fig. 3(a) for example). Sustainable private debt-to-income ratio is also at an empirically reasonable level given exogenously defined investment and profit rates. These equilibrium solutions correspond to low inflation and output below its target. One would expect exchange-rate depreciation as indicated by a move from steady state 2 to steady state 1 and output approaches its target level.

Further, it appears that the ratio of foreign currency holdings (either as debt or cash) to output by the households h is lower in the case of growing reserves and exchange-rate depreciation (i.e. steady state 1). As the exchange-rate depreciates, the h falls. This can be explained by households' expectations of domestic currency's loss of value via depreciation and by extension rising costs (including opportunity costs) of investing in foreign currency. Coupled with increasing prices of imported goods (e.g. see increase in inflation) leads to an increase in households consumption rate over time – a situation very characteristic of the CIS.

Note that effective leverage k does not really change between steady states 1 and 2, most likely due to longer term commitments in the financial sector. High effective leverage means that financial institutions are compelled to borrow increased amounts relative to their profits to meet their current outstanding debt payments, a situation of escalating overleveraging.

There is only one meaningful net importers' equilibrium solution (steady state 1 in Table 5). This corresponds to a situation of high inflation and significantly lower, compared to the net exporters', R and b values. This is reasonable reflecting smaller economies' limited presence in the international capital markets. However, results also indicate sustainable public debt-to-GDP ratio d_{pub} greater than one. Clearly, this is the case of government over-borrowing. Sustaining such high debt may not be feasible in the longer run with higher probability risks of governmental insolvency.

Characteristically estimated value of h is much higher than in the net exporters case. This indicates that there is more widespread distrust to domestic currency in the net importers among households. The result is also indicative of the switch to foreign currency assets as store of value in case of exchange-rate depreciation. Lower (than net exporters') k is in fact indicative of lower exposure of the net importers' economies to international capital markets coupled with slower growth of present value cash flows.

Analytically (see Eq. (13)) in case of existent structural issues that may be restricting primary surplus improvement, large public debt sustainability also requires a pickup in economic growth. Then despite high levels of g allocating funds in revenue-generating economic activity helps deal with domestic debt sustainability, expand tax base and feed into economic growth. While exact causality varies by country, the relationship cannot be denied.

In the next test, we preserve the same parameters as above with only one change. We set $\sigma_1 = 2$ for the net exporters and $\sigma_1 = 0.5$ for the net importers. This introduces a risk premium to foreign investor due to low levels of currency reserves (so that $\rho > 0$). Introduction of the risk premium also implies greater degree of openness of the economies to the international capital markets and ability by domestic agents to borrow from abroad. We obtain multiple steady-state solutions presented in Tables 6 and 7.

Results in Tables 6 and 7 reflect only non-negative exchange rate e steady-state solutions. For the net exporters, the upper steady state 1, corresponding to the highest reserves level, also implies strong deflation, while real interest rates are out of bound. This equilibrium solution is achieved at a negative output level. Due to that we exclude this steady state from a reasonable solutions set.

Table 6. Net Exporters Steady State, no R Targeting, $\sigma_1 = 2$, Non-Negative e.

Steady State	R	π	i	y	e	b	d_{prv}	h	k
1	13,732	−0.75	48.73	−967.1	412.5	−0.003	−0.010	0.0007	5.99
2	219.3	0.02	0.06	130.3	14.19	0.47	0.25	12.8	1.87

Table 7. Net Importers Steady State, No R Targeting, $\sigma_1 = 0.5$, Non-Negative e.

Steady State	R	π	i	y	e	b	d_{pub}	h	k
1	93.48	0.15	0.04	5.16	2.10	0.42	14.5	109	1.18
2	3.49	0.15	0.17	4.97	0.70	−0.01	−1.1	−2.23	4.28

Accordingly, the steady-state solution 2 in Table 6, with increasing risk $\rho > 0$ targeting predetermined levels of output and inflation for the net exporters, implies an increase in required reserves levels, while exchange rate continues to depreciate (vs. comparable results in Table 4). In terms of debt sustainability, both external b and private debt d_{prv} ratios are lower than earlier results. Hence, positive low currency reserves risk translates in reduced levels of sustainable debt for the net exporters. The result is intuitive if we recall that reserves are accumulated in various-purposes funds that can be tapped into to provide emergency liquidity to the market, which is exactly what has been happening over late 2008–early 2009 crisis. Therefore, higher foreign reserves accumulation is perceived as a safety cushion signalling possibility of increased borrowing. Yet, explicit country risk acts as a premium lowering sustainable debt levels.

At the same time, this also implies increased effective leveraging of the financial institutions, as it grows from 1.5 to almost 1.9 in net exporter economies (vs. Table 4 positions). Finally, in this situation h increases as economies open up and demand for foreign currency grows. Note that this result is achieved even at depreciating exchange rate but still greater value for reserves of $R = 219.3$.

Table 7 presents two steady-state solutions for the net importers. First steady-state results for the R, π, i, y and e are similar to the case in Table 5. The state variable i is increasing and there is a slight decline in reserves level. These solutions correspond to increased levels of sustainable external and public debts. Vulnerable situation of over-borrowing regarding $d_{\text{pub}} > 1$ applies again: to guarantee debt sustainability fiscal authorities must generate large primary surplus and foster economic growth. Otherwise with output and inflation targets and given primary account continued public borrowing is not feasible in the medium run. Therefore, this result is treated with caution.

Further, increase in b refers to higher sustainable levels of foreign debt. This seems to be only reasonable if the net importers' economies start with high initial net foreign assets value or expect capital inflows from elsewhere that could be used as a guarantee in the net importers' capital market access. For example, these economies may be receiving high foreign aid transfers or negotiate external funding from the IMF or World Bank (alternatively, in the CIS, the largest creditor is Russia). Hence, even with the added perceived risk of low currency reserves there is a possibility for equilibrium with higher sustainable external debt position for the net importer economies.

Steady state 1 in Table 7 also reports significantly higher levels of h and k. As described above, with wider access to foreign markets, foreign currency remains to be the store of wealth in the small transition economies where households view high depreciation as continuous and shift to foreign currency holdings. Financial institutions rely heavily on foreign currency borrowing while still not able to raise the present value of their cash flows, mostly due to higher risk premium τ_5, which contributes to faster foreign investments repatriation rate from domestic economies.

The steady state 2 in Table 7 reports very low reserves level, output close to the target and non-depreciating exchange rate. In fact the value of $e = 0.7$ is strong appreciation, which could be due to sudden large inflows of foreign currency in the economies. At the same time, real interest rate is high and negative ratios of external and private debt to income suggest the country group is a net lender (starting off with initial net assets position) in both external and domestic capital markets. This puts the economy in stringent conditions. Analytically what may help define this initial position are high (relative to output) transfer levels of foreign aid and foreign currency-denominated remittances from labour migrants abroad (between 20 and 40% of GDP) leading to domestic currency strong appreciation (e.g. Gevorkyan & Gevorkyan, 2010 or Gevorkyan, 2008). Still, it is unlikely that these debt solutions would hold in the near-term.

Similar logic applies to the negative result on the households' demand for foreign currency to output ratio (comparing to steady state 1). We interpret this as a temporary, near-term, position confirmed by brief period of net importers consumers markets over-satiation with foreign currency in hand, largely due to remittances transfers. Finally, steady state 2 in Table 7 also shows an increase in effective leverage of financial institutions as the banks (now with greater access to foreign capital) continue to borrow abroad. But if the public holds too much foreign currency in cash, financial institutions are constrained in their activities to invest in competitive profitable projects. This results in lower returns on own capital in relation to foreign investments and is also confirmed in reduction of economic activity via lower output, y, level solution.

It is, however, reasonable to conclude that steady state 2 in Table 7 cannot be a stable value for the economy and there is an upward pressure with exchange-rate depreciation and increase in output and reserves levels. Another way to interpret the negative signs on the debt ratios is to argue that this reflects a tendency that financially less protected economies may be curtailing their sustainable borrowing either due to inability to access financial markets or due to lacking solid macroeconomic performance (see Gevorkyan, 2008 for discussion on international capital markets access) or both. Hence, one might perceive of currency reserves as offering an extra safety cushion motivating economy's borrowing. In terms of public debt, two key factors: primary surplus and economic growth remain vital to ensure sustainability. In the next steps, we analyse the case of explicit reserves targeting by the central bank.

5.2. Policy and Effects with Explicit Reserves Targeting

Following the above analysis we construct parameters in Table 8 for the net exporting economies and in Table 9 for the net importing economies with explicit R target in each case. For net exporters we set $R^* = 100$ and for the smaller net importer economies $R^* = 10$ to accentuate difference in response between two-country groups. In addition, in both groups we set $\lambda_3 = 10$, which represents a strong central bank's reaction to R's deviation from its target.

Here, introduction of new parameters results in multiplicity of steady states for the reserves R, inflation rate π, interest rate i, output y, exchange rate e, external debt to output b, private debt-to-output ratio d_{prv} (net exporters), and public debt-to-output ratio d_{pub} (net importers), household debt-to-output ratio h and effective leverage k. Consistent with our earlier analysis we calibrate the model for two possible scenarios with a risk premium to foreign investors due to low levels of currency reserves (so that $\rho > 0$) and without that (so that $\rho = 0$). We interpret results for economic meaning and report only unique and economically significant outcomes in Tables 10 and 11.

Table 8. Net Exporters Parameter Values, with R Targeting, $\sigma_1 = 2$.

λ_1	λ_2	λ_3	π^*	π^e	y^*	R^*	i^f	r	W	C
1	1	10	0.1	0.1	250	100	0.05	0.05	85	50
α	β	η	σ_1	σ_2	ε	m	v	μ	X^d	X^f
125	25	0.0007	2	0	0.3	0	70	10	200	150
g	t	inv	p	g_y	s	τ_1	τ_2	τ_3	τ_4	g_v
n.a.	n.a.	0.3	0.25	0.09	1	0.1	0.05	n.a.	0.01	0.2

Table 9. Net Importers Parameter Values, with R Targeting, $\sigma_1 = 0.5$.

λ_1	λ_2	λ_3	π^*	π^e	y^*	R^*	i^f	r	W	C
1	1	10	0.12	0.16	15	10	0.03	0.05	4	2.5
α	β	η	σ_1	σ_2	ε	m	v	μ	X^d	X^f
5	1.5	0.0009	0.5	0	−0.01	0	10	100	90	70
g	t	inv	p	g_y	s	τ_1	τ_2	τ_3	τ_4	g_v
0.27	0.13	n.a.	n.a.	0.05	n.a.	0.005	n.a.	0.005	0.012	0.12

Table 10. Net Exporters Steady State, with R Targeting, $\sigma_1 = 0.0$.

Steady State	R	π	i	y	e	b	d_{prv}	h	k
1	100.05	0.015	0.05	129.25	10.01	0.38	0.26	14.2	1.5

Table 11. Net Importers Steady State, with R Targeting, $\sigma_1 = 0.0$.

Steady State	R	π	i	y	e	b	d_{pub}	h	k
1	9.97	0.15	0.03	5.18	0.99	0.13	9.3	36.2	0.9
2	0.002	0.15	0.03	5.19	0.055	0.007	9.3	36.1	0.9

Calibration results for the above parameters and $\rho = 0.0$ for the net exporters and net importers are in Tables 10 and 11. For the net exporters steady-state reserves level R is slightly above the $R^* = 100$ target, with associated exchange-rate depreciation, real interest rate $i = 0.05$, while output is significantly below target level (vs. results reported in Table 4). Given these equilibrium solutions, net exporters' sustainable debt-to-income ratio decreases to $b = 0.38$, down from the pre-R-target level of $b = 0.5$ (as in Table 4). Two aspects are important here: (1) the new conditions allow for any potential accumulation of R above the R^* level to be channelled into the economy, hence reducing the actual required external debt and (2) having the required R^* target pushes economy's resources in the direction of compensating that level, hence decreasing the real economy's potential to sustain high debt-to-income ratio. Which of the two takes precedence will vary based on country specifics. There are no changes to sustainable private debt-to-income ratio (vs. Table 4): initial explanation remains and there is no effect on private debt in the short run.

There is a shift towards higher household foreign currency demand to output ratio $h = 14.2$, which can be explained by still high dollarization of the transition economies, despite announced R target. Still, macroeconomic stability implied by the R^* eventually translates higher households' activity in the domestic and foreign currency credit markets. Finally, financial institutions' effective leverage remains stable, $k = 1.5$. Despite the R^* target as a stability factor, limited access to capital markets keeps effective leverage of domestic financial institutions low consistent with lower economic activity (via below target y) result.

Net importers' results with $R^* = 10$ and $\sigma_1 = 0.0$ are given in Table 11. There are two steady-state solutions. In terms of reserves the lower limit is at

$R = 0.002$, while the upper is closer to the announced R^* level. Achieving that higher steady implies exchange-rate depreciation (from 0.055 to 0.99), while inflation and real interest rate stay the same. In terms of debt: b increases from 0.007 to 0.13 moving from lower to the upper steady-state solution. However, when compared to the results without R^* target (in Table 5) the upper steady state $b = 0.13$ there is a decrease in the sustainable external debt-to-output ratio. This is the same dynamic as in the net exporters. Clearly both country groups face similar constraints but the crucial difference is in the levels (net exporters' sustainable b is significantly higher than net importers value), which in real economy helps buy time and procure strategic financing. Note that there is no change in net importers public debt-to-output ratio. This raises high debt sustainability concern and risk of domestic default intensifies. There is also no significant change in net importers h and k between targeted reserves and no reserves target cases.

Next we introduce home country risk with an explicit reserves target. As mentioned earlier values of $\sigma_1 > 0$ indicate, among others, broader access to capital markets, with foreign investors able to price their risk premiums with greater accuracy. Using the same parameter values as in Tables 8 and 9, we set $\sigma_1 = 2$ for net exporters and $\sigma_1 = 0.5$ for net importers. Unique steady-state solutions are reported in Tables 12 and 13.

In both net exporters and net importers cases reaching their respective target levels of R^* is accompanied by a higher real domestic interest rate, which helps control exchange-rate depreciation setting it at the equilibrium levels same as before (compared to results reported in Tables 10 and 11). However, solutions for sustainable debt-to-output ratios, effective leverage and household debt (foreign currency demand) in both country groups change.

Table 12. Net Exporters Steady State, with R Targeting, $\sigma_1 = 2$.

Steady State	R	π	i	y	e	b	d_{prv}	h	k
1	100.11	0.015	0.069	128.75	10.00	0.29	0.24	27.12	2.25

Table 13. Net Importers Steady State, with R Targeting, $\sigma_1 = 0.5$.

Steady State	R	π	i	y	e	b	d_{pub}	h	k
1	9.97	0.15	0.08	5.11	0.99	−0.055	−3.98	−6.9	2.7

Net exporters' sustainable foreign debt-to-output ratio falls to $b = 0.29$ and sustainable private debt-to-output ratio declines slightly to $d_{\text{prv}} = 0.24$ (when compared to equilibrium solutions with and without R^*). Decreases in the sustainable debt ratios in net exporting economies may be explained similarly to the earlier case of $R^* = 100$ but $\sigma_1 = 0.0$: (a) reserves accumulated above target level substituting external borrowing or (b) keeping up with the target reserves requirement, economy cannot afford to borrow beyond the steady state determined level of b in the international markets. The new result in Table 12 adds the increased perceived risk and hence market instability transmitting negative signals to investors, dropping the ratio further down. Also, with $\sigma_1 > 0$ there is added pressure to account for the risk premium $\sigma_1 = 2$ restricting sovereign borrowing (in the case of external debt B). Private debt-to-output ratio d_{prv} is clearly affected by the changes in the interest rate. Hence an increase in i corresponds to a reduction in sustainable levels of d_{prv}. This result is manifested in recent (early 2009) monetary tightening such as in Russia that raises fears over potential collapse across the banking system and curtailing of corporate lending (see FT, 2009b for insightful discussion).

At the same time, effective leverage rises above earlier levels ($k = 2.27$ now vs. $k = 1.87$ before) largely due to introduction of the risk premium, higher interest rate, access to foreign capital markets and hence low domestic financial institutions' asset value compared to capital borrowed. In the conditions of output performing below the targeted value and higher interest rates (yet, again the situation that applies to current conditions on the ground), investment is lagging and private firms borrow less (manifested in lower sustainable d_{prv} levels), dragging banks' profit rates further down. Increase in households' demand for foreign currency (and households' foreign currency debt-to-output ratio) is a function of low output and higher interest rates.

The case of net importers (Table 13) suggests similar dynamics. The difference is mainly in scale. In economic terms this difference translates in being a natural advantage to net exporters in terms of time and economy's financial manoeuvre with a benefit of a potential medium run balance, while net importers must be wary of immediate short-term results. The rationale for the change in negative debt ratios under explicit reserves target and added risk premium is the same as has already been provided in discussion to Table 7 results. It matters whether the countries enter financial markets with an initially high level of net wealth, which can potentially turn them into net lenders (negative b value). It can be extrapolated from the results that there is a general tendency for the sustainable external and public debt-to-output ratios to decline in net importer economies as the central bank chooses a reserves target too high, given positive risk premium.

Solutions for h and k are similar to steady state 2 in Table 7 results. Negative households' foreign currency demand-to-output ratio is plausible only if this country group is the net foreign currency cash receiver, as all of the CIS net importer economies are. This, however, does not seem to be a result that would hold in the medium term, given general public high dependency on volatile and irregular remittances flows. Higher effective leverage then indicates banks' wider access to international capital markets, but low returns at home.

To help finalise the numerical analysis and shed additional light on the development aspects of the currency reserves targeting with debt implications model we attempt one more simulation. Keeping steady-state solutions for the reserves R, inflation rate π, interest rate i, output y, exchange rate e as in Tables 12 and 13, we change the country's risk premiums and growth rates in each group case to observe changes in debt ratios. This calibration results are in Tables 14 and 15.

For net exporters (Table 14), with $R^* = 100$ and $\sigma_1 = 2$ a reduction in real growth rate to $g_y = 0.075$ lowers the level of the sustainable foreign debt to $b = 0.25$. Sustainable private debt-to-output ratio decreases as the group-specific risk premium increases $\tau_2 = 0.1$. At the same time effective leverage and households' foreign currency to output ratio significantly increase, confirming our concerns about foreign currency treatment as store of value and financial institutions' overleveraging as economy slows down.

For net importers, higher associated country risk $\tau_1 = 0.01$ partially offset by a pickup in real output growth $g_y = 0.088$ produces larger (vs. previous result)

Table 14. Net Exporters Steady State, with R^*, $\sigma_1 = 2$, $g_y = 0.075$, $g_v = 0.15$, $\tau_2 = 0.1$, $\tau_4 = 0.001$.

Steady State	R	π	i	y	e	b	d_{prv}	h	k
1	100.11	0.015	0.069	128.75	10.00	0.25	0.21	67.6	3.85

Table 15. Net Importers Steady State, with R^*, $\sigma_1 = 0.5$, $g_y = 0.088$, $g_v = 0.05$, $\tau_1 = 0.01$, $\tau_3 = 0.002$, $\tau_4 = 0.007$.

Steady State	R	π	i	y	e	b	d_{pub}	h	k
1	9.97	0.15	0.08	5.11	0.99	−0.92	−11.5	329	4.8

negative foreign and public debt-to-output ratios (Table 15). This outcome is only possible, as mentioned earlier, if the net importer economies initially hold net assets. However, this is a very stringent condition and while hypothetically possible may not be a repeated viable outcome in real life. But an exception may apply in the case of the net importer economies receiving large unilateral transfers such as foreign aid. Another example of such transfers is the sustained inflow of foreign currency-denominated remittances from the labour migrants abroad. This then alleviates pressures on the state for some social and public projects outlays. Increasing negative public debt-to-output ratio is also due to a high chosen reserves target relative to GDP and increasing real interest rate, which then curtails borrowing. The general tendency alluded to before is reconfirmed: as the foundational macroeconomic parameters improve (in this case real growth rate) so does the net borrowing position.

Finally, Table 15 also reports dramatic increase in the households' demand for foreign currency (cash or debt) to output ratio and growth in effective leverage of financial institutions. This is a reverse situation of previously reviewed cases, which leads us to believe that a sudden growth in fragile net importing economies leads to a shift to foreign currency debt, as both households and banks perceive it as temporary, hence preparing for possible recession down the road.

5.3. A Possible Currency Crisis Scenario in the CIS

Equipped with the above results and overall analysis we can attempt to derive a general outcome fitted to the ongoing financial crisis and economic slowdown in the CIS economies. Fig. 6 offers a consistent analytical summary.

Fig. 6 represents a hypothetical economy with the demand curve GG (characterised by IS equation similar to the Eq. (1)) and financial markets curve AA. Suppose an economy starts at point E_0 corresponding to natural output level Y_0 and competitive exchange-rate level of e_0 (domestic for foreign currency). With deteriorating external position and as access to credit dries up real output shrinks (a leftward shift on the x-axis) and economy enters a period of recession.

As crisis develops and liquidity leaves the emerging market (as in most CIS economies) and risk premiums on foreign, private and public debts increase (investors demanding higher risk premiums associated with reserves and exchange-rate volatility, $\rho > 0$), as well as worsening effective leverage of

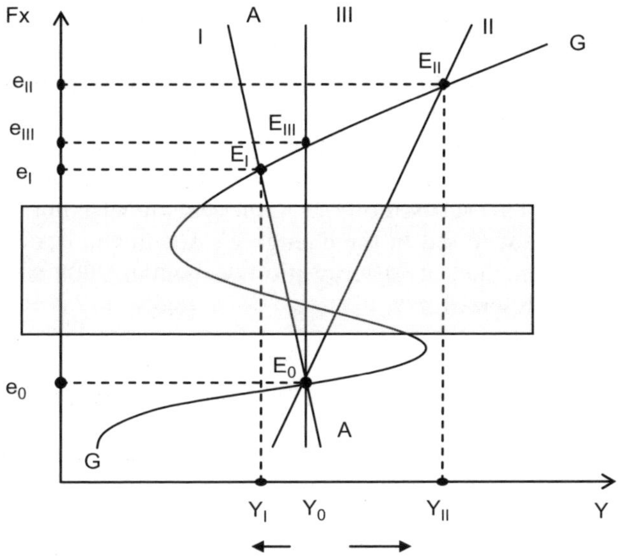

Fig. 6. Possible Currency Crisis Outcome Scenarios in the CIS.

financial institutions, and increased foreign currency demands by the households, there is an imminent pressure on domestic currencies for drastic depreciation. This is accompanied by a drop in net exports and risks of high inflation.

All of the above concerns have been materialized in various forms during the recent 2008–2009 crisis with both systemic and sporadic responses between both country groups. Within each group, each country's individual responses have varied as well. Below we draw some very general conclusions based on these observations. At the same time sustainable levels of foreign, domestic private and public debts decline (consistent with our model's analysis). This then evokes blended fiscal and monetary authorities' decisions: central bank follows extended Taylor-type monetary policy rules as described above, and fiscal authorities watch over sustainable debt (including large semi-private corporations' exposure to debt).

There are two possible approaches to analyse the current situation: (a) countries with large foreign exchange reserves stockpiles rely on the existent reserves capacity to prevent sharp currency depreciation and throw some liquidity in the markets and (b) countries without access to reserves face sharp depreciation, hence request for external funding are practically inevitable. It then does not come as surprise if we report both scenarios playing out in real time in both types of the CIS economies, for example, Russia is providing credit line to the smaller net importer economies, while spending reserves on smoothing the exchange-rate depreciation effects. These trends are indirectly confirmed by the stylised facts discussion above.

We then can hypothesise at least three post-crisis scenarios with three distinct outcomes. This is based on our numerical model calibration exercise conducted earlier, expressed in the changing slope of the AA' curve. In all cases we expect exchange-rate deterioration (Krugman, 2000 refers to this as increased price of reserves):

- *Scenario I*: Following unstable development pattern during the crisis (shaded area) economy ends up at point E_{I} with reduced (or below target) output level Y_{I} and depreciating exchange rate at e_I. This scenario, however, does not guarantee return to the same foreign exchange reserves level.
- *Scenario II*: Following unstable development pattern during the crisis (shaded area) economy ends up at point E_{II} with output growing above the pre-crisis level to Y_{II} and exchange-rate depreciating even further, e_{II}. According to this scenario, there is a chance for an economy to regain not only its productive capacity but also restore and increase its currency reserves stockpiles (e.g. recall exceptionally high steady-state levels for the net exporter economies in the above analysis).
- *Scenario III*: Following unstable development pattern during the crisis (shaded area) economy ends up at point E_{III} with output at the pre-crisis level to Y_0 and exchange rate depreciating to the level e_{III}, which is between Scenarios I and II exchange rate. Accordingly, it is safe to assume that an economy restores its productive capacity and pre-crisis foreign exchange reserves stockpile. This is likely only in the case of explicit reserves target R^*, which, in our model, if set too high given economy's real capacity adversely affects on debt sustainability.

This analytical framework serves as a suitable summary to the model analysed in this chapter. It is still unclear how things are going to play out for the CIS economies. Possible development scenarios must be considered and blending of the monetary and fiscal authorities' decisions factor cannot be excluded from consideration. Fig. 6 clearly identifies the pitfalls of the strategies of pushing out of crisis that focus solely on output increase, for example. For highly indebted CIS economies that almost entirely rely on imported consumer goods, sharp depreciation causes economic vulnerability and social instability. At the same time setting too high reserves targets lowers the sustainable debt-to-output ratios and the value of foreign currency-denominated debt explodes with domestic currency depreciation.

Scenario II then represents a possible best-case scenario considering the circumstances. Provided smooth exchange-rate depreciation, as is currently done in Russia, for example, there is a potential of restoring economy to the pre-crisis output levels. Having clearly identified reserves targets then proves as a beneficial strategy controlling for various aspects of the economy including borrowing. But, as we noted, a lot depends on the relative value of R^* chosen.

Yet, most importantly, and this has to be emphasised with all urgency, there is a need for a critical review of the economic structure across the palette. To sustain medium-term growth and development the fiscal resources freed up in the recent wins over the crisis need to be directed into the real economies to solidify the base for further global financial integration. That comes from macroeconomic and political economy considerations in the CIS. We treat above analysis as directional and results may change if the model is applied to a specific country. We offer some immediate policy implications of this in Section 6.

6. CONCLUSION AND POST-CRISIS POLICY IMPLICATIONS

This chapter offers a policy driven examination of the recent global crisis impacts in the emerging markets of the CIS. The approach is empirical, based on factual data, and theoretical, based on the extended version of the Kato et al. (2008) Taylor-type blended fiscal and monetary policy rules model with possibility of self-fulfilling expectations. Effects on external, domestic private and public debt, as well as effective leverage of domestic financial organisations, and households' holdings of foreign currency cash and debt are derived within the model.

There are at least four crisis propagation channels unique in the two CIS country groups. As a result calibration of the model required country-specific parameters and target values (output, reserves, interest rate etc.). Policy mix is adjusted accordingly and implications for foreign currency dependant economies are immediate. In this the CIS groups are very similar to the emerging markets of Latin America and Southeast Asia.

Working through reasonable equilibrium solutions we observe a tendency for exchange-rate depreciation as steady state settles at each successive higher reserves, R, level. These results are better accentuated with introduction of a currency risk premium ($\sigma_1 > 0$) reflecting vulnerability and risk of low actual currency reserves, increasing the possibility of a crisis. Then given equilibrium solutions for reserves, output, inflation, exchange rate and real interest rate we estimate sustainable debt ratios. For net exporters, there is a reduction in sustainable external debt-to-output ratio and private debt-to-output ratio between $\sigma_1 = 0$ and $\sigma_1 = 2$ steady states, which is intuitive. For net importers sustainable external debt-to-output ratio rises despite added risk premium ($\sigma_1 = 0.5$), possibly due to initially positive net asset position or implicit guarantees, for example via procured financial aid or multilateral loans (e.g. Russia and Kazakhstan's aid to smaller economies in the current conditions). Still, public debt-to-output ratio is greater than 1, indicating significant over-borrowing by the state and the need for generating larger primary account surplus and proactive growth efforts to sustain such high borrowing levels. Otherwise given above equilibrium solutions for the monetary policy targets public borrowing is not feasible in the medium run, creating risks of domestic default in the net importer economies.

With an addition of explicit reserves targets to the model new equilibrium solutions are obtained for each country group. This helps control exchange-rate depreciation and adds stability to the economy, however, at a reserves level. In terms of sustainable debt, we observe continuous decline in net exporters' sustainable foreign debt levels, especially with addition of the currency risk. Also a decline is observed in the net exporters' private debt-to-output ratio. Net importers' results follow similar dynamic, but with the crucial difference in the relative equilibrium levels. In real economy that offers larger economies time for new policy and to procure strategic financing. Extensions suggest a net-lender position based on external debt-to-output and public debt-to-output ratios, indicating a possibility of initially high net asset positions in the net importer economies. Partially then characteristic unilateral transfers, for example, foreign aid and sustained remittances inflows from the labour migrants abroad, may help drive in aggregate net asset holders positions. But a more plausible conclusion is that there is a general tendency for the sustainable external and public debt-to-output ratios in the net importer economies to decline as the central bank chooses a reserves target too high, given positive risk premium. In equilibrium, that drives up the domestic real interest rate, making borrowing costly to sustain at high levels. Finally, given the equilibrium conditions and adjusting real output growth rate and risk premiums for each country group reconfirms the view of basic macroeconomics' primary importance in determining sustainable levels of debt in both net exporters and net importers.

Households' behaviour varies depending on the exact steady-state conditions and ability to borrow from abroad. In all relevant steady-state scenarios, we find households' foreign currency holdings-to-output greater than one. That is an alarming indicator of high dollarization of the CIS economies. The ratio increases as we set explicit reserves targets and introduce country risk (allowing access to the international capital markets) in the net exporters group. In the net importers case the ratio falls to negative levels. If in the first case the result may be due to explicit mistrust for domestic currency by households seeking a secure way to preserve their wealth by investing in foreign currency-denominated assets (or foreign currency cash holdings), in the net importers case the explanation is initially high holdings of foreign currency assets on hand by the households, a quite realistic result given high volumes of migrant workers' remittances.

Finally, effective leverage, low initially, rises with introduction of reserves targets and clearly defined country risk (which allows foreign investors to better price their risk). A possible explanation is the overall macroeconomic stability, implied by the reserves target and the known country risk premium. Linking this result to possible overall macroeconomic stabilisation (a possible scenario under announced reserves accumulation) allows us to suggest increasing speculative borrowing by domestic banks financing their outstanding debt. At the same time higher interest rates suggest higher profits' repatriation by the foreigners, while domestic output is below target levels, investment is low due to high borrowing costs in the private sector (manifested in the net exporters' case in low sustainable private debt-to-output ratios), and consequently economic activity scales down. This, in fact, accurately depicts the economic environment during the 2008–2009 crisis in the CIS. The difference between net exporters and net importers is in scale, while overall tendency is the same.

Based on a schematic summary of the model, we derive three possible scenarios that account for (a) reduction in output below target or natural level, (b) output remaining unchanged and (c) increase in output as a post-crisis situation. There is a different effect on exchange-rate depreciation, level of reserves and implied foreign currency-denominated sustainable debt in each case. Net importers run risks of high inflation, while net exporters tend to over-borrow.

Choice of the foreign exchange reserves target then becomes crucial in the pre-, during-, and post-crisis economy's performance. A too-high reserves level is achieved, as suggested by the model and discussion in the chapter, at a price of high depreciation (inflation stays mainly on target with expected rate, while output reaches its target level only in the net importer economies). It is also clear from the calibration analysis that depreciation could potentially be even higher before economy reaches a steady state in the absence of reserves targets. What helps control exchange-rate depreciation with an explicit reserves target is the increase in real domestic interest rate. But then with the given exogenous determinants, sustainable debt declines, and depreciation might be too high to restore the pre-crisis reserves and output levels.

With the flexibility offered by a reasonable reserves target, lower sustainable debt-to-output may not be an issue, as economy learns to rely on own financing and becomes more financially efficient. Depending on each country's specifics-associated currency depreciation, with an absence of the *J*-curve effect, may result in a competitive exchange rate. Post-crisis outcome also gains from existence of the reserves target that helps alleviate currency pressures and self-propagating expectations.

As with all, this model's calibration results developed in this study must be interpreted with caution. Choice of the *right* reserves target is a complex one and in the CIS it is often a blended policy decision by the monetary and fiscal authorities in the background of vast political economy issues. This in turn shapes the fragile economic and social development context in the region.

The role that blended fiscal and monetary policy plays in the development process and regulation of the crisis-prone foreign currency-denominated transactions, as studied in this chapter, is non-trivial but crucial. Some promising results of this successful blend have been already witnessed in the CIS and other emerging markets. Additional focus must be directed towards analysis of the structure of the emerging markets' economies and transition countries specifically. Our initial separation between net exporters and net importers is critical in that sense, as successful functioning of financial markets must occur in the background of sustainable real economy development. This is the true challenge for the emerging transition economies. Therefore, as the crisis aftershocks propagate through the still recovering economies, additional and multifactor insight into the economic structures and financial markets is required. This chapter is one of such efforts, setting conceptual background for future research.

REFERENCES

Aizenman, J., & Turnovsky, S. J. (2002). The high demand for international reserves in Far East: What is going on? *Journal of the Japanese and International Economies*, *17*, 370–400.

Amsden, A. (2001). *The rise of 'The Rest' challenges to the west from late-industrializing economies*. New York: Oxford University Press.

Asada, T., & Semmler, W. (1995). Growth and finance: An intertemporal model. *Journal of Macroeconomics*, *17*(4), 623–649.
Caballero, R. J., & Krishnamurthy, A. (2008). Global imbalances and financial fragility. *American Economic Review*, *99*(2), 584–588.
Carlson, J. A., & Osler, C. L. (2003). *Currency risk premiums: Theory and evidence*. Seminar Paper, Centre for Economic Performance, LSE, London. Available at http://cep.lse.ac.uk/seminarpapers/13-11-03-OSL.pdf
Central Bank of Russia (CBR). (2010). Statistics database. Available at http://www.cbr.ru
Corsetti, G., Pesenti, P., & Roubini, N. (1999). What caused the Asian currency and financial crises? *Japan and the World Economy*, *11*, 305–373.
Curtis, E., Gardner, R. J., & Waller, C. (2005). Dollarization in the CIS: The case of Ukraine. *Magisterium*, *18*, 4–13.
EBRD. (2009) *Transition Report*. Available at http://www.ebrd.org
Financial Times (FT). (2009a). *Eastern exposure*. Available at http://www.ft.com/cms/s/0/ea19fec8-028e-11de-b58b-000077b07658.html?nclick_check=1
Financial Times (FT). (2009b). *State aid urged for Russian banks*. Available at http://www.ft.com/cms/s/0/5abc63b4-1a4f-11de-9f91-0000779fd2ac.html
Flaschel, P., & Semmler, W. (2003). *Currency crisis, financial crisis, and large output loss*. CEM Bielefeld University Working Paper no. 52. Bielefeld University, Germany.
Froot, K. A., & Thaler, R. H. (1990). Anomalies: Foreign exchange. *Journal of Economic Perspectives*, *4*, 179–192.
Gevorkyan, A. V. (2008). Fiscal policy and alternative sources of public capital in transition economies: The Diaspora bond. *Journal of International Business and Economy*, *9*(2), 33–61.
Gevorkyan, A. V. (2009). *Innovative fiscal policy and economic development in the transition economies*. Unpublished manuscript. New School University, New York.
Gevorkyan, A. V., & Gevorkyan, Ar. V. (2010). Factoring turbulence out: Diaspora Regulatory Mechanism and Migration Development Bank. *International Migration*. doi:10.1111/j.1468-2435.2010.00606.x.
International Monetary Fund (IMF). (2009a). World Economic Outlook. Washington, DC.
International Monetary Fund (IMF). (2009b). International Financial Statistics. Washington, DC.
Kamin, S. B. (1999). The current international financial crisis: How much is new? *Journal of International Money and Finance*, *18*, 501–514.
Kato, M., Proano, C., & Semmler, W. (2008). *Capital flight, nominal exchange rate volatility and optimal international reserves management*. Unpublished paper. The New School University, New York.
Krugman, P. (1979). A model of balance of payment crisis. *Journal of Money Credit and Banking*, *11*(3), 311–325.
Krugman, P. (2000). Crises: The price of globalization? *Federal Reserve Bank of Kansas City Symposium Proceedings: Global Economic Integration: Opportunities and Challenges*. Available at http://www.kc.frb.org/publicat/sympos/2000/sym00prg.htm
Loungani, P., & Sheets, N. (1997). Central Bank independence, inflation, and growth in transition economies. *Journal of Money Credit and Banking*, *29*(3), 381–399.
Mau, V. (2009). Drama 2008 goda: ot ekonomicheskogo chuda k ekonomicheskomu krizisu. *Voprosy Ekonomiki*, *2*, 4–23.
Obstfeld, M. (1984). Balance of payments crises and devaluation. *Journal of Money Credit and Banking*, *16*(2), 208–217.

Semmler, W., Greiner, A., Diallo, B., Rezai, A., & Rajaram, A. (2007). *Fiscal policy, public expenditure composition, and growth*. World Bank Policy Research Paper no. 4405. World Bank, Washington, DC.

Wagner, H. (1999). Central Bank independence and the lessons for transition economies from developed and developing countries. *Comparative Economic Studies*, *4*, 1–22.

Wagner, H. (2000). Controlling inflation in transition economies: The relevance of central bank independence and the right nominal anchor. *Atlantic Economic Journal*, *28*(1), 60–70.

Yershov, M. (2008). Krizis 2008 goda: "moment istiny" dlya global'noj ekonomiki i novye vozmozhnosti dlya Rossii. *Voprosy Ekonomiki*, *12*, 4–26.

APPENDIX

Below we provide solution for the main model defined by Eq. (12). The current value Hamiltonian is:

$$\begin{aligned} H = {} & \frac{\lambda_1}{2}(\pi^e + \eta(\alpha - \beta(i - \pi^e) + X(e^e) - y^*) - \pi^*)^2 \\ & + \frac{\lambda_2}{2}(\alpha - \beta(i - \pi^e) + X(e^e) - y^*)^2 + \frac{\lambda_3}{2}(R - R^*)^2 \\ & + q_1(i - i^f - \rho(i - i^f, R)) + q_2(X(e^e) + F(e^e, R)) \end{aligned} \tag{A.1}$$

The first order conditions of Eq. (A.1) are:

$$\begin{aligned} \frac{\partial H}{\partial i} = {} & -\lambda_1 \beta \eta(\pi^e - \pi^*) - \beta(\lambda_1 \eta^2 + \lambda_2)(\alpha - \beta(i - \pi^e) + X(e^e) - y^*))^2 \\ & + q_1(1 - \rho_{i-i^f}(i - i^f, R)) \end{aligned} \tag{A.2}$$

The differential equation for the first co-state variable is $\dot{q}_1 - rq_1 = -(\partial H/\partial e)$ then,

$$\begin{aligned} \dot{q}_1 = {} & rq_1 - q_2(X'(e^e) - F_{e^e}(e^e, R)) - \lambda_1 \eta X'(e^e)(\pi^e - \pi^*) \\ & - (\lambda_1 \eta + \lambda_2)(\alpha - \beta(i - \pi^e) + X(e^e) - y^*) \end{aligned} \tag{A.3}$$

Similarly then

$$\dot{q}_2 = q_2(r - F_R(e^e, R)) - \lambda_3(R - R^*) + \rho_R(i - i^f, R)q_1 \tag{A.4}$$

Finally, from the model specification we know that

$$\dot{e} = i - i^f - \rho(1 - i^f, R) \tag{A.5}$$

$$\dot{R} = X(e^e) + F(e^e, R) \tag{A.6}$$

Following Kato et al. (2008), and to help us derive concrete solutions, we specify the following functions:

$$\rho(R) = \frac{\sigma_1}{R} + \frac{\sigma_2}{2}(i - i^f)^2 \tag{A.7}$$

where we define the first term on the right-hand side as a currency-run risk and the second term is the exchange-rate risk due to exchange-rate volatility, while σ_1 and σ_2 are constant coefficients.

$$X(e^e) = \varepsilon e^e - m \tag{A.8}$$

where m is an imports level and ε reflects elasticity of net exports to exchange-rate fluctuations. Note that $X(e^e)$ in our model assumes positive value, that is, current account surplus, for net exporting economies and negative value, that is, current account deficit, for the net importers. Finally,

$$F(e^e, R) = ne^e - z(e^e, R) = \frac{v}{e^e} - \frac{\mu}{R} e^{e2} \tag{A.9}$$

with v and μ as constant coefficients.

Replacing the general expressions in Eq. (A.1) and in the first order conditions in Eqs. (A.2)–(A.6) with the specific functions as in Eqs. (A.7)–(A.9), we obtain:

$$\begin{aligned} H = & \frac{\lambda_1}{2}(\pi^e + \eta(\alpha - \beta(i - \pi^e) + ((\varepsilon e^e - m) - y^*) - \pi^*)^2 \\ & + \frac{\lambda_2}{2}(\alpha - \beta(i - \pi^e) + (\varepsilon e^e - m) - y^*)^2 + \frac{\lambda_3}{2}(R - R^*)^2 \\ & + q_1\left(i - i^f - \left(\frac{\sigma_1}{R} + \frac{\sigma_2}{2}(i - i^f)^2\right)\right) + q_2\left((\varepsilon e^e - m) + \left(\frac{v}{e^e} - \frac{\mu}{R} e^{e2}\right)\right) \end{aligned} \tag{A.10}$$

Then First Order Conditions (FOCs) are:

$$\begin{aligned} \frac{\partial H}{\partial i} = & -\lambda_1 \beta \eta (\pi^e - \pi^*) - \beta(\lambda 1 \eta^2 + \lambda_2)(\alpha - \beta(i - \pi^e) + \varepsilon e^e - m - y^*) \\ & + q_1(1 - \sigma_2(i - i^f)) \end{aligned} \tag{A.11}$$

$$\begin{aligned} \dot{q}_1 = & rq_1 - q_2\left(\varepsilon + \frac{v}{e^{e2}} + 2\mu \frac{e^e}{R}\right) - \lambda_1 \eta \varepsilon (\pi^e - \pi^*) - (\lambda_1 \eta + \lambda_2) \\ & \times (\alpha - \beta(i - \pi^e) + \varepsilon e^e - m - y^*) \end{aligned} \tag{A.12}$$

$$\dot{q}_2 = q_2\left[r - \mu\left(\frac{e^e}{R}\right)^2\right] - \lambda_3(R - R^*) - q_1 \frac{\sigma_1}{R^2} \tag{A.13}$$

$$\dot{e}^e = i - i^f - \left(\frac{\sigma_1}{R} + \frac{\sigma_2}{2}(i - i^f)^2\right) \tag{A.14}$$

$$\dot{R} = \varepsilon e^e - m + \frac{v}{e^e} - \frac{\mu}{R} e^{e2} \tag{A.15}$$

From (A.11), we obtain first steady-state solution:

$$q_1 = \frac{\lambda_1 \beta \eta (\pi^e - \pi^*) + \beta(\lambda_1 \eta^2 + \lambda_2)(\alpha - \beta(i - \pi^e) + \varepsilon e^e - m - y^*)}{1 - \sigma_2 (i - i^f)} \tag{A.16}$$

Incorporating (A.16) in (A.12)–(A.15) and setting $\dot{q}_1 = \dot{q}_2 = \dot{e}^e = \dot{R} = 0$ and solving for i, e^e, R, q_2, we derive a new set of steady states. Next, Eqs. (6)–(10) are derived from the following growth definitions (following Asada & Semmler, 1995).

- For both country groups, growth in sovereign debt is $(\dot{b}/b) = (\dot{B}/B) - (\dot{y}/y) = \gamma - (X(e^e)/B) - g_y$, where all terms have been defined above. Then change in debt is exactly as in Eq. (6).
- For net exporters only, growth in private debt is $(\dot{d}_{\text{prv}}/d_{\text{prv}}) = (\dot{D}_{\text{prv}}/D_{\text{prv}}) - (\dot{y}/y) = (I - s(\Pi - uD_{\text{prv}})/D_{\text{prv}}) - g_y$, where all terms have already been defined above and I and Π are the total levels of required investment and total profit, respectively. Then change in private debt is $\dot{d}_{\text{prv}} = [(I - s(\Pi - uD_{\text{prv}})/D_{\text{prv}})]d_{\text{prv}} - g_y d_{\text{prv}} = [(I - s(\Pi - uD_{\text{prv}}))/D_{\text{prv}}](D_{\text{prv}}/y)$ $-g_y d_{\text{prv}}$ simplified and expressed as a ratio to GDP private debt change is $\dot{d}_{\text{prv}} = inv - s(p - ud_{\text{prv}}) - g_y d_{\text{prv}}$, exactly as in Eq. (7).
- Similarly, for net importers only, from public debt growth relationship: $(\dot{d}_{\text{pub}}/d_{\text{pub}}) = (\dot{D}_{\text{pub}}/D_{\text{pub}}) - (\dot{y}/y) = (G - T + zD_{\text{pub}}/D_{\text{pub}}) - g_y$, where the only new terms are G and T are the total levels of government expenditures and tax revenue, respectively. The change in net importers' public debt is then $\dot{d}_{\text{pub}} = [(G - T + zD_{\text{pub}}/D_{\text{pub}})]d_{\text{pub}} - g_y d_{\text{pub}}$, as in Eq. (8).
- Growth rate of $h = (H/Y)$ is given by $(\dot{h}/h) = (\dot{H}/H) - (\dot{Y}/Y) = ((\theta H - C + W)/H) - g_y$ then the change is $\dot{h} = ((\theta H - C + W)/H)h - g_y h = ((\theta H - C + W)/H)(H/Y) - g_y h = \theta h - c + w - g_y h$, where household consumption as a share of GDP $c = (C/Y)$; household wealth as share of GDP $w = (W/Y)$; total holdings of foreign currency-denominated bonds H.
- Growth rate of effective leverage is: $k/k = K/K - V/V = \varphi K + X - \zeta K/K - g_v$ so that the change is defined by: $k = (\varphi K + X^f - \zeta K/K)k - g_v k = \varphi k + X^f/V - \zeta k - g_v k$.

PART II
POLICY IMPLICATIONS OF THE FINANCIAL CRISIS FOR EMERGING MARKETS

BARGAINING GAME AND LDCs' COMMERCIAL BANK DEBT RESTRUCTURING OUTCOMES

Ki C. Han, Sukhun Lee and David Y. Suk

ABSTRACT

When faced with a financial crisis, debtor countries rarely choose to default on their international financial obligations. Instead, they typically choose to renegotiate their debt service obligations. According to a number of economists, the main motivating factor behind borrowers' and creditors' willingness to restructure is the benefit associated with preserving international trade ties. This raises an interesting question: is the benefit associated with maintaining international trade ties shared equally between the borrower and creditor banks? Or is the outcome dependent on a so-called 'bargaining game' between the borrower and creditor banks, and if so, can we identify these variables? According to our analysis, as a borrower's trade ties with developed countries strengthen, the borrower's (and/or creditor's) bargaining power diminishes (strengthens) and it thereafter agrees to restructure at less favourable terms. However, even after controlling for trade ties, we found that major borrowers were able to extract more concessions from the lenders.

Keywords: Emerging markets; debt restructuring; bargaining power.

JEL Code: F34.

The Impact of the Global Financial Crisis on Emerging Financial Markets
Contemporary Studies in Economic and Financial Analysis, Volume 93, 199–229

ISSN: 1569-3759/doi:10.1108/S1569-3759(2011)0000093008

1. INTRODUCTION

The global financial market is currently undergoing one of the worst and perhaps most damaging financial crisis since the Great Depression. The crisis that began in the United States has spread all over the globe. It appears that no country is immune from the current financial malaise, and the focus is now on the sovereign borrowers from the Eurozone, particularly Greece. Unfortunately, such financial crises are not new. Indeed, over the past three decades, the global financial market has witnessed several financial crises involving mainly developing countries from Latin America to East Asia. These past events, however, were not as widespread and severe as the one presently being faced. When faced with a financial crisis, however, debtor countries rarely opt to default on their international financial obligations. Instead, they typically choose to renegotiate their debt obligations (Kletzer & Wright, 2000). This begs the question of why countries choose to renegotiate instead of defaulting on their debt obligations? In the same vein, why do creditors agree to renegotiate instead of allowing debtor countries to default on their debt obligations? That is, what is the motivation behind borrowers' and creditors' willingness to renegotiate and restructure existing debt obligations?

According to a number of economists, the answer to the first part of this question may be that debtors wish to preserve their international trade ties. Otherwise, Bulow and Rogoff (1989) argue that defaulting countries may suffer reduced benefits of international trade. Since international trade accounts for a large percentage of debtor countries' GDP, borrowing countries may choose to renegotiate in order to avoid de facto trade sanctions. (For example, Chile's trade (imports and exports combined) as a percentage of GDP was 80.38% and 84.78% for the Philippines in 2007.) Debtor countries may also choose to renegotiate to preserve their creditworthiness and to secure future access to international capital markets.[1]

What about the creditors? What are their incentives? According to Klimenko (2002) and Rose and Spiegel (2004), outright default is inefficient since the debtor's welfare loss caused by trade sanctions does not accrue as a benefit to the creditors. Instead, creditors prefer a negotiated outcome that allows the debtor country to freely trade in exchange for a share of welfare gains made possible by avoiding default. In addition, if creditor countries have significant economic ties with the borrowing country, it may be in their interest to work with the borrower.

Thus, it appears that both the borrowers and creditors have incentives to avoid outright default by agreeing to restructure existing debt obligations.

This raises an interesting question, namely, how is this surplus – or the welfare gains made possible by avoiding defaults – divided among the participants? Said differently, is the benefit associated with maintaining international trade ties shared equally between the borrower and creditor banks, or is the outcome dependent on the so-called 'bargaining game' between the borrower and creditors' banks? And if so, what determines the bargaining outcome? A review of the current literature sheds some light to these questions. For example, Klimenko (2002) develops a theoretical model that analyzes the effects of a debtor country's pattern of trade with commercial creditors' home countries on the outcome of debt rescheduling negotiations. He states that 'a country's dependency on trade with the rest of the world can weaken its threat point and thereby reduce its static bargaining power in a bilateral relationship with its commercial creditors.' However, it is also possible that a creditor country's dependency on trade with the borrowing country can weaken its threat point and thereby reduce its bargaining power in debt restructuring negotiations. Hence, the main focus of the chapter is to examine the relationship between the bargaining game and debt restructuring outcomes. We will revisit LDC commercial bank debt restructurings of the 1980s and identify any factors that were instrumental in debt restructuring outcomes.

The remainder of the chapter is organized as follows: Section 2 describes the data set; Section 3 evaluates debt restructuring outcomes; Section 4 discusses methodology; Section 5 presents our empirical results; Section 6 performs robustness tests and the last section provides a summary and some concluding remarks.

2. DATA

The data consists of commercial bank debt restructurings from 1980 to 1989.[2] We focus our analysis prior to the introduction of the Brady Plan in 1989 for the following two reasons. First, before the Brady Plan, sovereign debt was mostly held in the form of medium-to-long-term syndicated loans with a limited number of participants. With the introduction of the Brady Plan, syndicated bank claims were converted into securitized debt instruments with potentially numerous and heterogeneous bondholders. In turn, the Brady Plan has effectively altered the dynamics of the bargaining game. Second, with the establishment of the Brady Plan, international financial institutions adopted the policy of 'lending into arrears.' According to Wells (1993), the IMF policy of lending in arrears has a very different effect on the outcome of the bargaining game than a policy of not lending in arrears. Hence, we restrict our analysis to the period of 'no lending in arrears' and to negotiations that took place between a debtor country and a limited number of major creditors' banks.

From 1980 to 1989, there were 97 commercial bank debt restructurings involving 41 countries from five geographical regions. Table 1 provides data on commercial debt restructurings from 1980 to 1989. From Table 1, we make the following observations: (a) the majority of debt restructurings (80%) took place from 1983 to 1988; (b) approximately 45% and 35% of debt restructurings involved countries from Latin America and Africa (South of Sahara), respectively; (c) about 66% of commercial debt restructurings involved 'middle-income' countries and (d) around 61% of debt restructurings involved 'moderately indebted' countries.[3] Hence, the majority of commercial bank debt restructurings in 1980s involved moderately indebted, middle-income countries from Latin America and Africa (South of Sahara).

Of the 97 commercial bank debt restructuring agreements, we were able to obtain complete data on 60 agreements from 28 countries and they are reported in Table 2.[4] The following types of restructuring agreements are included in our sample: restructuring of future payments on medium- and long-term debt, restructuring of future payments on short-term debt, restructuring of past payments on medium- and long-term debt and amendments to earlier restructuring agreements. The majority of commercial bank debt restructuring agreements signed during the 1980s involved restructuring of future payments on medium- and long-term publicly guaranteed debt.

Table 1. Commercial Bank Debt Restructurings during the 1980s.

Restructurings		1980	1981	1982	1983	1984	1985	1986	1987	1988	1989	Total
Number of restructurings		3	5	6	17	13	13	9	14	12	5	97
Geographical region	Latin[a]	2	3	0	9	5	8	4	6	4	3	44
	Africa[b]	1	2	2	5	6	3	3	5	6	1	34
	Others[c]	0	0	4	3	2	2	2	3	2	1	19
Income level	Low	2	3	2	5	7	3	1	3	6	1	33
	Middle	1	2	4	12	6	10	8	11	6	4	64
Level of indebtedness	Severely indebted	2	1	3	7	5	5	3	3	8	1	38
	Moderately indebted	1	4	3	10	8	8	6	11	4	4	59

Sources: World Debt Tables; IMF, International capital markets, various issues.
[a]Includes countries from Latin America, Central America and the Caribbean.
[b]Includes countries from Africa (South of Sahara).
[c]Includes countries from East Asia, Eastern Europe and the Middle East.

Table 2. Restructuring Terms and Debt Restructuring Outcomes (DROs) for Commercial Bank Debt Restructurings during the 1980s.

Year[a]	Country	Restructured Amount (in $ Millions)	Types of Restructuring[b]	Restructuring Terms[c]			DRO[d] (in $ Millions)
				Grace (Yrs)	Maturity (Yrs)	Spread (%)	
1/80	Peru	340	Future, long	2	5	1.25	73.578
12/80	Nicaragua	252	Past, long	5	11	1.385	301.064
4/81	Bolivia	313	Future, long	5 to 7	2 to 3	2.25	192.378
		99	Future, short	2	3.5	2	51.665
6/81	Jamaica	89	Future, long	2	5	2	−8.942
9/81	Madagascar*	147	Past, short	0	3.5	1.5	66.297
12/81	Sudan	383	Past, long	3	7	1.75	25.695
3/82	Turkey	3,105	Amendment	2	7	1.75	562.72
12/82	Romania	1,598	Future, long	3	6.5	1.75	176.041
2/83	Brazil	4,452	Future, long	2.5	8	2	−15.59
3/83	Malawi	57	Future, long	3	6.5	1.875	2.656
6/83	Romania	486	Future, long	3.5	6.5	1.75	67.385
7/83	Chile	2,169	Future, long	4	8	2.063	−14.065
7/83	Peru	380	Future, long	3	8	2.25	30.553
7/83	Nigeria*	1,935	Past, short	1	3	1.438	202.004
7/83	Uruguay	216	Future, long	2	6	2.188	3.833
		359	Future, short	2	6	2.188	6.371
8/83	Mexico	18,800	Future, long	4	8	1.813	1,875.86
9/83	Costa Rica	246	Future, long	3.5	6.5 to 7.5	2.188	7.811
		363	Past, long	3.5	7.5	2.188	11.966
10/83	Ecuador	895	Future, long	1	6	2.188	8.09
12/83	Dominican Republic	500	Past, long	1	5	2.188	4.7
1/84	Brazil	4,846	Future, long	5	9	1.875	−509.85
1/84	Chile	1,160	Future, short	4	8	2.125	−100.791
2/84	Peru	460	Future, long	5	9	1.438	−11.254
2/84	Senegal	78	Future, long	3	7	2	9.741

Table 2. *(Continued)*

Year[a]	Country	Restructured Amount (in $ Millions)	Types of Restructuring[b]	Restructuring Terms[c]			DRO[d] (in $ Millions)
				Grace (Yrs)	Maturity (Yrs)	Spread (%)	
6/84	Jamaica	100	Future, long	2	5	2.5	14.387
10/84	Madagascar	60	Future, long	2.5	8	2	25.8
		18	Past, long	2.5	8	2	7.74
		52	Past, short	2.5	6	1.75	21.343
		65	Future, short	2.5	6	1.75	26.679
3/85	Côte D'Ivoire	221	Future, long	3	8	1.75	−1.951
3/85	Mexico	23,600	Amendment	0	14	1.152	1,056.933
5/85	Costa Rica	440	Future, long	3	10	1.625	19.107
5/85	Philippines	653	Future, long	5	10	1.625	21.238
		1,183	Future, short	5	10	1.625	38.476
5/85	Senegal	20	Future, long	3	7	2	0.667
8/85	Mexico	20,100	Future, long	1	14	1.152	−1,460.473
8/85	Argentina	7,100	Future, long	3	12	1.375	−505.014
		7,100	Past, long	3	10	1.375	−356.331
9/85	Jamaica	195	Future, long	3	10	1.875	−2.991
10/85	Panama	579	Future, long	3.5	12	1.375	−13.594
11/85	Chile	6,007	Future, long	6	12	1.375	−373.254
12/85	Ecuador	2,473	Future, long	3	12	1.375	−67.51
		431	Amendment	2	10	1.438	−1.417
2/86	Dominican Republic	707	Future, long	3	13	1.375	1.915
		80	Past, long	3	13	1.375	0.217
2/86	Morocco	538	Past, long	3	7	1.75	55.963
2/86	Venezuela	20,037	Future, long	0	12.5	1.125	577.63
7/86	Brazil	6,671	Future, long	5	7	1.125	−599.179
7/86	Uruguay	844	Future, long	3	12	1.375	−9.815
		621	Amendment	3	12	1.625	5.99
9/86	Poland	1,970	Amendment	4	4	1.375	8.086

9/86	Romania	800	Amendment	3.5	5	1.375	−258.005
12/86	Côte D'Ivoire	691	Future, long	3	9	1.5	−106.203
4/87	Mexico	43,700	Amendment	7	20	0.813	−1,413.484
5/87	Jamaica	100	Future, long	9	12.5	1.25	0.873
		185	Past, long	1.5	8.5	1.25	3.905
6/87	Chile	1,534	Future, long	5	15.5	1	−36.429
		2,951	Amendment	5	15.5	1	−70.079
8/87	Argentina	4,200	Future, short	5	12	0.813	−270.419
		25,300	Amendment	8	19	0.813	−2,697.853
9/87	Morocco	178	Amendment	4	4	1.75	8.415
11/87	Nigeria	1,725	Future, long	3	9	1.25	64.389
		2,525	Past, short	1	4	1.25	149.589
12/87	Gabon	39	Future, long	4	9	1.375	1.73
3/88	Uruguay	75	Future, long	3	17	0.875	−11.937
		1,695	Amendment	3	17	0.875	−269.784
7/88	Poland	8,301	Future, long	3.5	15	0.813	1,171.86
8/88	Chile	2,951	Amendment	5	15.5	0.813	202.505
9/88	Venezuela	20,338	Amendment	0	13	0.875	915.722
10/88	Malawi	35	Future, long	4	8	1.25	3.577
11/88	Brazil	61,000	Future, long	7	19	0.813	1,278.845
4/89	Nigeria	1,256	Future, long	3	20	0.875	317.066
		1,635	Amendment	3	20	0.875	412.741
9/89	Mexico	6,400	Future, long	7	15	0.813	944.235
11/89	Jordan	580	Future, long	5	11.5	0.813	19.124
12/89	Trinidad & Tobago	446	Future, long	4.5	12.5	0.938	25.511

[a]Refers to the final agreement month and year.
[b]Types of restructurings: future, long: restructuring of future payments on medium- and long-term debt; future, short: restructuring of future payments on short-term debt; past, long: restructuring of past payments on medium- and long-term debt; past, short: restructuring of past payments on short-term debt; amendments: amendments to earlier restructuring agreements.
[c]Grace and maturity periods are rounded to the nearest six months.
[d]DRO = (NPV based on the rescheduling terms)−(NPV based on the average terms on all new loans contracted by the borrower during the debt restructuring agreement year).

3. DEBT RESTRUCTURING OUTCOMES

To examine the outcome of the bargaining game between the borrower and creditor banks, we first construct a measurement for debt restructuring outcome. To assess debt restructuring outcomes, we compute two net present values (NPVs) for each debt restructuring agreement. First, we compute NPV using the terms (i.e. rescheduled amount, grace period, maturity and spread) agreed upon during the debt restructuring negotiation. Next, we compute NPVs using the average terms for all new loans contracted by the borrower during the restructuring agreement year.[5] The terms for these new loans are assumed to be a proxy for market terms that reflect the borrower's creditworthiness at the time of debt renegotiation.[6] That is, in order to determine whether a debtor country received favourable treatment (i.e. received grant elements) in debt restructuring, we need to know what the country would have paid if it had borrowed the rescheduled amount from the market at the prevailing market terms.[7] To compute NPVs, the following assumptions are made:

1. Interest is accrued during the grace period.
2. Grace period and maturity are rounded off to the nearest half year.
3. Payments (interest plus principal) are made at the end of every six-month period.
4. First payment is made six months from the end of the grace period. If there is no grace period, the first payment occurs six months after the loan is made.
5. Rates on 5-, 10- and 30-year T-bonds are used to discount cash flows. Maturities up to 5 years, 5–10 years, and above 10 years are discounted by 5-, 10- and 30-year T-bond rates, respectively.[8]
6. Rescheduling fees and commitment fees are assumed to be approximately equal. Hence, they are not taken into account in the calculation.

Once we have the NPVs, the NPV based on the average terms for all new loans (NPV_{NL}) is subtracted from the NPV obtained using the restructuring terms (NPV_R). We call this difference ($NPV_R - NPV_{NL}$) the debt restructuring outcome (DRO). The DRO measures the size of benefits or costs from debt restructuring. A negative DRO indicates that the borrower was able to restructure her debt service obligation at below the prevailing market terms. Clearly, the smaller the DRO, the greater the benefit that accrues to the borrower. Table 2 presents the DROs. Overall, about two-thirds of the commercial bank debt restructuring agreements included in the sample was restructured at above the prevailing market terms. Further examination of

Table 2 reveals the following three observations. First, the DROs differ across restructuring types. For borrowers who restructured their future debt obligations, 63% of their DROs were positive. For borrowers seeking a rescheduling of past payments, 12 out of 13 restructured at above the prevailing market terms. For borrowers seeking amendments to earlier restructuring efforts, 57% of their DROs were positive. Second, within a given year, there were both positive and negative DROs. Third, 19 out of 28 countries included in the sample restructured more than once during the sample period. For example, Mexico restructured its commercial bank debt four times. What is more, its 1983 debt restructuring resulted in a positive DRO, whereas those restructurings between 1985 and 1987 resulted in negative DROs. As such, not only do we see DRO variation between countries, but also variation within the same debtor country with respect to time.

The above finding raises the main question that this study seeks to address: given that some borrowers restructured at more favourable terms while others did not, can we describe the characteristics of borrowers and lenders that lead to more or less favourable DROs?

4. METHODOLOGY

To isolate and assess the significance of bargaining power on DROs, we include a set of control variables. These variables control for both global economic condition and borrowers' characteristics that may influence DROs. The control variables included in our model were selected from debt restructuring literature. Specifically, we estimate the following logit model:

$$Z_i = \log\left(\frac{P_i}{1 - P_i}\right) = \alpha_0 + \beta_1 \text{GIND} + \beta_2 \text{INTER} + \beta_3 \text{TDGDP}_i + \beta_4 \text{GPGDP}_i + \beta_5 \text{VCPGDP}_i + \delta \text{BP}_i + \varepsilon_i \quad (1)$$

where the variables are defined as follows:[9] $L \equiv 1 - (\text{NPV}_{\text{NL}}/\text{NPV}_{\text{R}})$ is a measure of borrower losses from debt restructuring. A positive L implies that the borrower has agreed to restructure its debt service obligation at above the prevailing market terms.[10] P_i is the probability of a positive L given the explanatory variables. It takes a value of 1 if $L \geq 0$ and 0 otherwise. GIND is the growth rate of industrialized countries' GNP; INTER the interest rate on international lending; TDGDP the ratio of total foreign debt to GDP; GPGDP the growth rate of per capita GDP; VCPGDP the variability of changes in per capita GDP; BP the bargaining power variable and ε_i an error term.

The following proxy variables for bargaining power are selected based on economic theory, empirical findings and intuition:

- Borrower's trade ties
- Major borrowers
- Restructured amount
- Geographical region
- Lenders' trade ties
- Borrower's creditworthiness
- Lenders' coordination
- Alternative sources of funding

Rationale for their inclusion is discussed in the following section.

5. EMPIRICAL RESULTS

From the previous section, we observed that some borrowers were able or allowed to restructure at more favourable terms, while others agreed to restructure at less favourable terms. According to Aizenman (1991), Fernández and Özler (1999), and Klimenko (2002), among others, state that a debtor country with greater bargaining power vis-à-vis banks can improve the terms of debt rescheduling. In this section, we conduct empirical tests to examine the significance of borrower and creditor bargaining power on DROs. The following proxy variables are used to measure bargaining power of parties involved: the borrower's trade ties with creditor countries, borrowers classified as major borrowers by the World Bank, restructured amount, the borrower's geographical location, lender countries' trade ties with the borrowing country, borrower's creditworthiness, lenders' coordination and borrower's alternative sources of funding. First, we will examine the significance of each proxy variable in isolation. Next, we will examine whether there is a subset of proxy variables that were the most influential during debt restructuring negotiations.

5.1. Significance of Bargaining Power Variables in Isolation

5.1.1. Borrower's Trade Ties

Klimenko (2002) develops a theoretical model that analyzes the impact of a debtor country's trade ties with creditors' home countries in terms of debt rescheduling negotiations. He states that 'a country's dependency on trade with the rest of the world can weaken its threat point and thereby reduce its static bargaining power in a bilateral relationship with its commercial creditors.' In addition, Aizenman (1991) argues that trade dependency reduces the borrowing country's bargaining power and results in a greater transfer of resources to creditor countries. We will explore this phenomenon further by actually examining the interplay between a borrower's trade ties with a creditor country and her ability to negotiate DROs. Ideally, we would have identified the major lenders by reviewing prior debt restructuring agreements. Unfortunately, the data was unavailable and so we relied on proxy measures to identify major lenders. Initially, we associated geographical proximity to major sources of funding – for example, if there were at least two developed countries in the same geographical region as the borrower's, we assigned them as major lenders. Hence, for European borrowers, we assigned France, Germany, Italy and the United Kingdom as major lenders. When there were no developed countries in the region – such as in Africa (South of Sahara) – we assigned six developed countries as major lenders. Appendix B lists major lenders for five geographical regions.

The borrower's trade ties variable, TRADE, is added to Eq. (1) and the following equation is estimated:

$$Z_i = \log\left(\frac{P_i}{1 - P_i}\right) = \alpha_0 + \beta_1 \text{GIND} + \beta_2 \text{INTER} + \beta_3 \text{TDGDP}_i + \beta_4 \text{GPGDP}_i + \beta_5 \text{VCPGDP}_i + \delta \text{TRADE}_i + \varepsilon_i \quad (2)$$

where TRADE is defined as

$$\frac{\text{trade(exports + imports) with developed countries in the region}}{\text{borrower's global trade}}$$

The estimation results are presented in the second column in Table 3.

Among the control variables, the GIND is statistically significant at the 10% level. As the growth rate of industrialized countries' economies rises, it seems that the borrower receives less favourable treatment at the renegotiation table. The estimated coefficient of TRADE is positive and statistically significant at the 5% level. The chi-squared statistic for the regression equation is significant at the 10% level. Our result indicates that there is a statistically significant positive relationship between DROs and international trade ties. Thus, it appears that a debtor country's economic ties with major creditor countries in the region do indeed influence DROs. As the borrower's trade ties with developed countries in the region strengthen, the borrower's (and/or creditors') bargaining power diminishes (strengthens)

Table 3. Significance of Borrowers' and Creditors' Bargaining Power on DROs Outcomes.

Variable	Borrower's Trade Ties	Major Borrowers	Restructured Amount	Borrower's Geographical Region	
				Latin	Africa
Constant terms	−2.646 (1.639)	−0.053 (1.666)	−0.31 (1.556)	0.73 (1.633)	−1.051 (1.419)
GIND	0.848 (0.51)*	1.008 (0.544)*	1.121 (0.567)**	0.79 (0.505)	0.992 (0.531)*
INTER	0.202 (0.127)	0.136 (0.148)	0.161 (0.139)	0.247 (0.138)*	0.228 (0.131)*
GPGDP	0.095 (0.163)	0.004 (0.163)	−0.048 (0.157)	0.025 (0.16)	0.112 (0.159)
TDGDP	−1.015 (0.995)	−1.543 (1.04)	−1.074 (0.988)	−1.128 (0.997)	−1.26 (1.012)
VCPGDP	−0.12 (0.159)	−0.107 (0.168)	−0.198 (0.161)	−0.216 (0.163)	−0.246 (0.163)
TRADE[a]	4.426 (2.018)**	–	–	–	–
DMB[b]	–	−2.015 (0.736)***	–	–	–
RATED[c]	–	–	−3.593 (2.215)*	–	–
DLATIN[d]	–	–	–	−1.98 (0.759)***	–
DAFRICA[e]	–	–	–	–	2.407 (1.019)**
Chi-squared	11.974	14.725	9.045	14.834	13.56
Significance	0.063	0.023	0.171	0.022	0.035
Observations	60	60	60	60	60

Notes: The dependent variable measures borrower losses from debt restructuring. Data includes all eligible restructuring cases during the 1980s. Standard errors are reported in parentheses.
*, **, *** Significant at the 10%, 5% and 1% level, respectively.

[a]$\text{TRADE} = \left[\frac{\text{Trade(exports + imports) with developed countries in the region}}{\text{Borrower's global trade}}\right].$

[b]DMB is equal to 1 if the debtor country is classified as a major borrower by the World Bank, and 0 otherwise.

[c]Restructured amount as a percentage of total external debt outstanding.

[d]DLATIN is equal to 1 if the debtor country is from Latin America, and 0 otherwise.

[e]DAFRICA is equal to 1 if the debtor country is from Africa (South of Sahara), and 0 otherwise.

and the borrowing country agrees to restructure at less favourable terms. Our result is therefore consistent with the findings of Klimenko (2002) and Aizenman (1991).

5.1.2. Major Borrowers

Included in our sample are five countries (see Appendix B) classified as major borrowers by the World Bank. These five countries accounted for 18 out of 60 restructuring cases included in the sample. It is possible that since the commitment by lenders is already large, major borrowers are able to exploit lenders' large exposure and demand more favourable restructuring terms. To investigate this possibility, we added a dummy variable, DMB, which takes a value of 1 if the restructuring involved a major borrower, and 0 otherwise. We then re-estimated Eq. (1) including the DMB variable. The results are presented in the third column of Table 3. Among the control variables, the estimated coefficient for the GIND variable is positive and statistically significant at the 10% level. The coefficient of DMB is negative and statistically significant at the 1% level.[11] The chi-squared statistic for the regression equation is significant at the 5% level. Thus, our results suggest that major borrowers take advantage of the lenders' significant exposure as a bargaining tool to extract concessions from them during the restructuring negotiations.

5.1.3. Restructured Amount

The dollar amount of debt restructuring cases included in the sample ranges from \$20 million for Senegal in 1985 to \$61.6 billion for Brazil in 1988. The mean debt restructured amount is roughly \$5.7 billion. Given these figures, one might ask if either side – the borrowers or the creditors – uses the size of the debt restructuring requests to their advantage. More fundamentally, does the size of debt restructuring request influence DROs? To investigate this issue, we added the RATED variable – defined as the restructured amount as a percentage of total external debt outstanding[12] – to Eq. (1). The results are presented in the fourth column of Table 3.

Among the control variables, the estimated coefficient for GIND variable is positive and statistically significant at the 5% level. The estimated coefficient of RATED is negative and statistically significant at the 10% level. Hence, our results suggest that the actual size of debt restructured amount does appear to play a significant role in debt renegotiations. As the size of debt restructuring request increases, the borrower is able to restructure at more favourable terms.

5.1.4. Geographical Region

Our sample includes countries from five different geographical regions of the world. Given that borrowers come from different places, is it possible that the geographical location of the borrower plays a role in DROs? In other words, do creditors view certain parts of the world more favourably than others? On the other side of the token, do borrowers from one region have greater collective bargaining power than those from another? To examine this issue, we inserted two regional dummy variables, DLATIN and DAFRICA, into Eq. (1). DLATIN takes a value of 1 if the restructuring involved a Latin American country, and 0 otherwise. Similarly, DAFRICA takes a value of 1 if the restructuring involved an African country, and 0 otherwise. The last two columns in Table 3 present results for Latin America and Africa.

Among the control variables, the estimated coefficients for GIND and INTER variables are positive and statistically significant at the 10% level. The coefficient of DLATIN is negative and statistically significant at the 1% level, while the estimated coefficient of DAFRICA is positive and statistically significant at the 5% level. Thus, our results suggest that borrowers from Latin America received favourable restructuring terms, whereas borrowers from Africa received less favourable restructuring terms. This is an interesting finding and we will revisit this issue later in the chapter.

5.1.5. Lenders' Trade Ties

As we have discussed earlier, Klimenko (2002) states that 'a country's dependency on trade with the rest of the world can weaken its threat point and thereby reduce its static bargaining power in a bilateral relationship with its commercial creditors.' However, it is also possible that a creditor country's dependency on trade with the borrowing country can weaken its threat point and thereby reduce its bargaining power during the debt restructuring negotiations. To examine the relationship between economic interdependency and DROs, we added three lenders' trade ties variables – CTRADE, CEXP and CIMP – to Eq. (1). CTRADE measures creditor countries' economic dependency and is defined as creditor countries' trade (exports + imports combined) with the borrowing country as a percentage of their GDP.[13] CEXP and CIMP also measure creditor countries' economic dependency and are defined as creditor countries' exports to and imports from the borrowing country, respectively. The results are presented in column two through four in Table 4.

Among the control variables, the estimated coefficient of GIND is positive and statistically significant at the 10% level. Estimated coefficients

Table 4. Significance of Lenders' Trade Ties with the Borrowing Country on DROs Outcomes and Borrower's Creditworthiness on DROs Outcomes.

Variable	Creditor Countries' Trade with a Debtor Country			Borrower's Creditworthiness
	Total trade	Export to	Import from	
Constant terms	−0.747	−0.805	−0.704	2.863
	(1.473)	(1.465)	(1.48)	(2.344)
GIND	0.814	0.811	0.815	0.699
	(0.494)*	(0.494)*	(0.494)*	(0.533)
INTER	0.197	0.200	0.194	0.107
	(0.13)	(0.13)	(0.13)	(0.155)
GPGDP	−0.002	0.001	−0.004	−0.001
	(0.151)	(0.15)	(0.151)	(0.162)
TDGDP	−0.624	−0.589	−0.648	−1.642
	(0.91)	(0.904)	(0.914)	(1.122)
VCPGDP	−0.177	−0.175	−0.178	−0.175
	(0.154)	(0.154)	(0.154)	(0.16)
CTRADE[a]	−1.114	–	–	–
	(1.464)			
CEXP[b]	–	−2.303	–	–
		(3.515)		
CIMP[c]	–	–	−2.068	–
			(2.495)	
CR[d]	–	–	–	−0.097
				(0.041)**
Chi-squared	6.862	6.71	6.976	12.067
Significance	0.334	0.349	0.323	0.06
Observations	60	60	60	57

Notes: The dependent variable measures borrower losses from debt restructuring. Data includes all eligible restructuring cases during the 1980s. Standard errors are reported in parentheses.
*, **, *** Significant at the 10%, 5% and 1% level, respectively.

[a] $\text{CTRADE} = \left[\dfrac{\text{Developed countries' trade(exports + imports)with the debtor country}}{\text{Developed countries' GDP}}\right].$

[b] $\text{CEXP} = \left[\dfrac{\text{Developed countries' exports to the debtor country}}{\text{Developed countries' GDP}}\right].$

[c] $\text{CIMP} = \left[\dfrac{\text{Developed countries' imports from the debtor country}}{\text{Developed countries' GDP}}\right].$

[d] Institutional Investors credit rating.

of the CTRADE, CEXP and CIMP variables are all negative but not statistically significant. Thus, unlike the significant role the borrower's trade dependency plays in DROs, the creditor countries' trade ties with the borrowing country is not a significant factor.

5.1.6. Borrower's Creditworthiness

Starting in September 1979, the Institutional Investor began reporting individual country creditworthiness (Institutional Investors, 1979). A country's credit rating is based on a survey of experts from the economics departments of leading financial institutions around the globe. The rating ranges from 0 to 100 where the higher the rating, the higher the creditworthiness of the country. For countries included in our sample, the credit rating goes from a low of 9.8 for Nicaragua to a high of 71.8 for Mexico in March 1980. In December 1989 (the end of our sample period), Chile had the highest credit rating (33.6) while Nicaragua had the lowest (4.5). During the 1980s, the average credit rating for countries included in our sample declined from 42.3 to 22.3, a 47% decline.[14] With the exception of March and September 1986, the average credit rating declined during the entire sample period. Given the downward trend in the credit rating, did the borrowers or creditors use this development as a bargaining tool during the debt renegotiation? If so, which party benefited from this development? To investigate this issue, we added a credit rating variable (CR) into Eq. (1) and the results are presented in the last column in Table 4.[15]

None of the control variables are statistically significant. The coefficient of CR is negative and statistically significant at the 5% level.[16] The chi-squared statistic for the regression is significant at the 10% level. Thus, it appears that a higher creditworthiness leads to a greater bargaining position which in turn leads to more favourable restructuring terms. Perhaps borrowers are being rewarded for maintaining higher credit ratings.

5.1.7. Lenders' Coordination

According to Fernández and Özler (1999), 'the banks' bargaining power increases with the degree of concentration of a country's debt.' That is, as the country's debt is held by a smaller number of lenders, it may be easier for lenders to coordinate and potentially increase their bargaining power during the debt renegotiations. To examine this issue, we introduced the following proxy variables for degree of concentration: the percentage of outstanding debt provided by the top lending country, TOPL; the percentage of outstanding debt provided by top two lending countries, TOP2L and the percentage of outstanding debt provided by the G-7 country, G-7. The estimation results are provided in columns two through four in Table 5.

Among the control variables, the estimated coefficient of GIND is positive and statistically significant at the 10% level. The estimated coefficients of TOPL and G-7 are positive but not statistically significant. However, the estimated coefficient of TOP2L is positive and statistically

Table 5. Significance of Lenders' Coordination and Alternative Sources of Funding on DROs Outcomes.

Variable	Loans Provided by			Alternative Sources of Funding (ASF)		
	Top lender	Top two lenders	G-7	International reserves	FDI	Total ASF
Constant terms	−2.095	−5.163	−4.069	0.033	−0.877	−0.169
	(1.944)	(2.527)	(4.596)	(1.597)	(1.502)	(1.573)
GIND	0.969	1.304	0.935	1.043	0.941	1.048
	(0.544)*	(0.587)**	(0.541)*	(0.534)**	(0.523)*	(0.539)**
INTER	0.173	0.123	0.192	0.128	0.207	0.149
	(0.133)	(0.138)	(0.126)	(0.139)	(0.138)	(0.139)
GPGDP	−0.022	−0.051	0.008	−0.05	0.014	−0.03
	(0.152)	(0.157)	(0.15)	(0.159)	(0.154)	(0.157)
TDGDP	−0.61	−1.158	−0.527	−1.383	−0.712	−1.238
	(0.904)	(1.004)	(0.893)	(1.056)	(0.91)	(1.019)
VCPGDP	−0.181	−0.194	−0.164	−0.188	−0.175	−0.189
	(0.157)	(0.163)	(0.153)	(0.16)	(0.156)	(0.159)
TOPL[a]	2.279	–	–	–	–	–
	(2.626)					
TOP2L[b]	–	6.324	–	–	–	–
		(3.112)**				
G-7[c]			3.229			
			(4.533)			
IR[d]	–	–	–	−0.0002	–	–
				(0.0001)*		
FDI[e]	–	–	–	–	−0.0006	–
					(0.0004)	
TAFS[f]	–	–	–	–	–	−0.0002
						(0.0001)*
Chi-squared	7.09	11.142	6.798	9.839	8.361	9.618
Significance	0.313	0.084	0.34	0.132	0.213	0.142
Observations	60	60	60	60	60	60

Notes: The dependent variable measures borrower losses from debt restructuring. Data includes all eligible restructuring cases during the 1980s. Standard errors are reported in parentheses.
*, **, *** Significant at the 10%, 5% and 1% level, respectively.

[a]Percentage of the borrower's outstanding debt provided by the top lending country.

[b]Percentage of the borrower's outstanding debt provided by the two top lending countries.

[c]Percentage of the borrowers' outstanding debt provided by the G-7 developed countries.

[d]International reserves $= (IR_{t-1} + IR_t)/2$, where t is the restructuring year.

[e]Foreign direct investment $= (\mathrm{FDI}_{t-1} + IR_t)/2$, where t is the restructuring year.

[f]Total ASF $= (\mathrm{TASE}_{t-1} + \mathrm{TASE}_t)/2$, where t is the restructuring year. Total alternative sources of funding include international reserves, foreign direct investment and remittances.

significant at the 5% level. These results suggest that the top lending country may not have enough exposure to impose a serious threat. In addition, coordinating lenders from all G-7 countries may be too cumbersome and costly. At the same time, a joint effort by top two lending countries may strengthen the lenders' bargaining position and compel the borrowers to restructure at less favourable terms.[17]

5.1.8. Alternative Sources of Funding

Roberts and Sufi (2009) examine 1,000 private credit agreements between U.S. public firms and financial institutions and report that '... (the availability of) a competing sources of funds increases the probability of renegotiations that lead to lower interest rates and more credit for borrowers.' That is, the availability of alternative sources of funds may shift the balance of bargaining power in favour of borrowers as they would no longer be dependent on commercial banks for funding. To investigate this issue, we identified the following three alternative funding sources for a sovereign borrower: international reserves (IR), foreign direct investments (FDI) and remittances.[18] We also defined the total alternative sources of funding (TASF) as the sum of IR, FDI and remittances. These alternative sources of funding variables are added to Eq. (1), one at a time, and the estimated results are presented in the last three columns in Table 5.

Among the control variables, the estimated coefficient of GIND is positive and statistically significant at the 5% level. The estimated coefficient of IR is negative and statistically significant at the 10% level. The estimated coefficient of FDI is also negative but not statistically significant. The estimated coefficient of TASF is negative and statistically significant at the 10% level.[19] Thus, borrowers with greater access to funds outside of commercial lending enhance their bargaining position and are able to extract concessions during debt renegotiations. Our findings confirm the findings of Roberts and Sufi (2009).

5.2. Are There Dominant Bargaining Power Variables?

So far, our results identified the following proxy variables to be statistically significant: borrower's trade ties, major borrowers, restructured amount, geographical region, borrower's creditworthiness, lenders' coordination and alternative sources of funding. Given that the correlation coefficients for some pairs of these variables are high, it is feasible that these variables are proxying for one another. Hence, it would be interesting to investigate whether or not there is a subset of these variables that dominates the others. That is, can we identify a subset of these variables that has the greatest influence in DROs? This issue is examined next.

To begin the process, we added TRADE and DMB to Eq. (1) and estimated the following equation:

$$Z_i = \log\left(\frac{P_i}{1-P_i}\right) = \alpha_0 + \beta_1 \text{GIND} + \beta_2 \text{INTER} + \beta_3 \text{TDGDP}_i + \beta_4 \text{GPGDP}_i + \beta_5 \text{VCPGDP}_i + \delta_1 \text{TRADE}_i + \delta_2 \text{DMB}_i + \varepsilon_i \quad (3)$$

The estimation results are provided in the second column in Table 6.

Among the control variables, the estimated coefficient of GIND is positive and statistically significant at the 5% level, and the estimated coefficient of TDGDP is negative and statistically significant at the 10% level. The estimated coefficient of TRADE is positive and statistically significant at the 5% level, while the estimated coefficient of DMB is negative and statistically significant at the 1% level. The chi-squared statistic for the regression equation is significant at the 1% level. Hence, both the borrower's trade ties and the size of existing exposure significantly influence debt restructuring outcomes, albeit in opposite directions.

Since both the TRADE and DMB variables are statistically significant, we will keep them in Eq. (3) and introduce other proxy variables one at a time. The first variable we will add is restructured amount (RATED). The estimation results are provided in the third column in Table 6. Both the TRADE and DMB variables are statistically significant at the 5% level; however, the estimated coefficient of RATED is not statistically significant. Thus, once we control for the size of the outstanding external debt, the actual debt restructured amount does not appear to play a significant role in debt renegotiations.

Next, we add is DLATIN and DAFRICA, which are dummy variables specific to geographical region. The results are provided in the last two columns in Table 6. The estimated coefficients of TRADE and DMB are statistically significant at the 5% level, whereas the estimated coefficients for DLATIN and DAFRICA are not statistically significant. Since all five countries classified as major borrowers are from Latin America, once we control for the size of exposure, the geographical location of the borrower becomes irrelevant.

Next, the borrower's creditworthiness (CR) is added to Eq. (3). The estimation results are provided in the second column in Table 7.

Table 6. Subset Bargaining Power Variables that had the Greatest Influence on DROs Outcomes.

Variable	Major Borrowers	Restructured Amount	Borrower's Geographical Region	
			Latin	Africa
Constant terms	−1.72	−1.533	−1.068	−1.715
	(1.834)	(1.881)	(1.957)	(1.833)
GIND	1.086	1.264	1.043	1.238
	(0.565)**	(0.644)**	(0.567)*	(0.595)**
INTER	0.114	0.099	0.165	0.133
	(0.14)	(0.145)	(0.146)	(0.139)
GPGDP	0.077	0.049	0.074	0.127
	(0.174)	(0.181)	(0.179)	(0.178)
TDGDP	−2.342	−2.648	−2.419	−2.792
	(1.24)*	(1.354)**	(1.244)**	(1.307)**
VCPGDP	−0.041	−0.059	−0.068	−0.088
	(0.181)	(0.184)	(0.185)	(0.188)
TRADE[a]	4.883	5.064	4.827	4.36
	(2.189)**	(2.26)**	(2.267)**	(2.312)*
DMB[b]	−2.241	−2.026	−1.604	−2.028
	(0.826)***	(0.871)**	(0.914)*	(0.852)**
RATED[c]	–	−1.81	–	–
		(2.683)		
DLATIN[d]	–	–	−1.252	–
			(0.859)	
DAFRICA[e]	–	–	–	1.632
				(1.209)
Chi-squared	20.543	21.002	22.815	22.629
Significance	0.0045	0.0071	0.0036	0.0039
Observations	60	60	60	60

Notes: The dependent variable measures borrower losses from debt restructuring. Data includes all eligible restructuring cases during the 1980s. Standard errors are reported in parentheses. *, **, *** Significant at the 10%, 5% and 1% level, respectively.

[a]$\text{TRADE} = \left[\dfrac{\text{Trade(exports + imports) with developed countries in the region}}{\text{Borrower's global trade}}\right].$

[b]DMB is equal to 1 if the debtor country is classified as a major borrower by the World Bank, and 0 otherwise.

[c]Restructured amount as a percentage of total outstanding external debt.

[d]DLATIN is equal to 1 if the debtor country is from Latin America, and 0 otherwise.

[e]DAFRICA is equal to 1 if the debtor country is from Africa (South of Sahara), and 0 otherwise.

Table 7. Subset Bargaining Power Variables that had the Greatest Influence on DROs Outcomes.

Variable	Borrower's Creditworthiness	Lenders' Coordination	International Reserves	Total ASF
Constant terms	1.42	−4.633	−1.794	−1.678
	(2.592)	(2.90)	(1.90)	(1.84)
GIND	0.971	1.472	1.055	1.164
	(0.605)*	(0.659)**	(0.597)*	(0.623)*
INTER	0.053	0.049	0.122	0.104
	(0.158)	(0.149)	(0.148)	(0.144)
GPGDP	0.073	0.029	0.086	0.065
	(0.179)	(0.179)	(0.185)	(0.179)
TDGDP	−3.166	−2.864	−2.241	−2.565
	(1.484)**	(1.367)**	(1.392)*	(1.455)*
VCPGDP	−0.057	−0.089	−0.034	−0.054
	(0.191)	(0.189)	(0.187)	(0.186)
TRADE[a]	5.307	4.471	4.80	5.268
	(2.298)**	(2.207)**	(2.245)**	(2.54)**
DMB[b]	−1.463	−2.11	−2.399	−1.891
	(0.877)*	(0.83)***	(1.332)*	(1.349)
CR[c]	−0.097	–	–	–
	(0.053)*			
TOP2L[d]	–	4.849	–	–
		(3.764)		
IR[e]	–	–	0.00003	–
			(0.0002)	
TASF[f]	–	–	–	−0.0001
				(0.0002)
Chi-squared	21.938	22.359	20.566	20.646
Significance	0.005	0.0043	0.0084	0.0082
Observations	57	60	60	60

Notes: The dependent variable measures borrower losses from debt restructuring. Data includes all eligible restructuring cases during the 1980s. Standard errors are reported in parentheses. *, **, *** Significant at the 10%, 5% and 1% level, respectively.

[a] $\text{TRADE} = \left[\dfrac{\text{Trade(exports + imports) with developed countries in the region}}{\text{Borrower's global trade}}\right].$

[b] DMB is equal to 1 if the debtor country is classified as a major borrower by the World Bank, and 0 otherwise.

[c] Institutional Investors credit rating.

[d] Percentage of the borrower's outstanding debt provided by the two top lending countries.

[e] International reserves $= (IR_{t-1} + IR_t)/2$, where t is the restructuring year.

[f] Total ASF $= (\text{TASF}_{t-1} + \text{TASF}_t)/2$, where t is the restructuring year. Total alternative sources of funding include international reserves, foreign direct investment and remittances.

The estimated coefficient of TRADE is positive and statistically significant at the 5% level, and the estimated coefficient of DMB is negative and statistically significant at the 10% level. The estimated coefficient of CR is also negative and statistically significant at the 10% level. Therefore, even after controlling for the borrower's trade ties, both major borrowers and countries with higher credit ratings used their bargaining position to influence DROs in their favour.

Next, we add the following three variables, TOP2L, IR and TASF, one at a time to Eq. (3) and the results are presented in columns three through five in Table 7. None of the estimated coefficients for these three variables are statistically significant, while the estimated coefficients of TRADE and DMB are statistically significant.

Based on results presented so far, the most prominent factors affecting commercial debt restructuring outcomes of the 1980s are the borrower's trade ties with the creditor countries and the size of lenders' existing exposure. As the borrower's trade ties with the creditor countries strengthen, the balance of bargaining power shifts to the lenders' side. On the other hand, as the size of the lenders' existing exposure increases, the borrowers use this exposure as a bargaining tool to extract concessions from the lenders.

6. ROBUSTNESS TESTS

In the previous section, we examined a borrower's total trade (exports and imports combined) with developed countries in the region and found it to be a significant factor. In this section, we will examine a borrower's exports to and imports from developed countries separately. In the second and third columns in Table 8, we report estimation results with these new measures of the trade variable.

In the second column, the trade variable Trade 1 measures exports to developed countries in the region as a percentage of the borrower's total trade. In the third column, the trade variable Trade 2 measures imports from developed countries in the region as a percentage of the borrower's total trade. Trade 1 is positive and statistically significant at the 10% level, whereas Trade 2 is positive and statistically significant at the 5% level. Thus, our results suggest that the level of borrower's imports from developed countries has a stronger negative impact on debt restructuring outcomes than the level of borrower's exports to developed countries in the region.

Table 8. Robustness Tests Results.

Variable	Exports to Developed Countries	Imports from Developed Countries	Trade Ties with Industrial Country	Medium- and Long-Term Debt
Constant terms	−1.500	−1.394	−1.938	−0.095
	(1.888)	(1.747)	(1.968)	(2.578)
GIND	1.083	1.082	1.050	0.915
	(0.536)**	(0.573)*	(0.55)*	(0.652)
INTER	0.125	0.112	0.113	−0.06
	(0.144)	(0.139)	(0.143)	(0.177)
GPGDP	0.050	0.079	0.051	0.133
	(0.17)	(0.175)	(0.167)	(0.226)
TDGDP	−1.809	−2.866	−2.237	−3.285
	(1.121)	(1.351)**	(1.224)*	(1.632)**
VCPGDP	−0.044	−0.064	−0.077	−0.092
	(0.18)	(0.179)	(0.176)	(0.226)
TRADE 1[a]	3.035	–	–	–
	(1.775)*			
TRADE 2[b]	–	5.604	–	–
		(2.343)**		
TRADE 3[c]	–	–	3.748	–
			(2.25)*	
TRADE 4[d]				6.646
				(2.877)**
DMB[e]	−2.004	−2.49	−2.601	−3.023
	(0.765)***	(0.885)***	(0.888)***	(1.195)***
Chi-squared	17.901	21.707	17.743	18.468
Significance	0.12	0.003	0.013	0.010
Observations	60	60	60	45

Notes: The dependent variable measures borrower losses from debt restructuring. Data includes all eligible restructuring cases during the 1980s. Standard errors are reported in parentheses. *, **, *** Significant at the 10%, 5% and 1% level, respectively.

[a]$\text{Trade 1} = \left(\frac{\text{Exports to developed countries in the region}}{\text{Borrower's total trade}}\right).$

[b]$\text{Trade 2} = \left(\frac{\text{Imports from developed countries in the region}}{\text{Borrower's total trade}}\right).$

[c]$\text{Trade 3} = \left[\frac{\text{Trade(exports + imports) with industrial countries}}{\text{Borrower's total trade}}\right].$

[d]$\text{Trade 4} = \left[\frac{\text{Trade(exports + imports) with developed countries in the region}}{\text{Borrower's global trade}}\right].$

[e]DMB is equal to 1 if the debtor country is classified as a major borrower by the World Bank, and 0 otherwise.

In the previous section, we associated geographical proximity to major sources of funding. In this section, we introduce two alternative proxy measures for major lenders and re-estimate Eq. (1). First, all industrial countries are considered to be major lenders. Second, G-7 countries are also considered to be major lenders. Since the results are similar, we only report results for all industrial countries. The fourth column in Table 8 presents the estimation results. The trade variable, Trade 3, measures the trade conducted between the borrower and industrial countries as a percentage of the borrower's total trade. The estimated coefficient of the Trade 3 variable is positive and statistically significant at the 10% level. Even though the result is not as statistically significant as before, it still reminds us that the borrower's trade ties with developed countries do matter in DROs.

As we mentioned earlier, the majority of debt restructurings involved restructuring of medium- and long-term publicly guaranteed debt. In our sample, there were 45 such restructuring cases (out of 60). We re-estimate Eq. (1) using only the most common types of debt restructuring cases, and the estimation results are presented in the last column of Table 8. The results are similar to those presented in Table 3.

7. SUMMARY AND CONCLUSIONS

The global financial market is currently in the middle of one of the worst, and perhaps most damaging, financial crises since the Great Depression. This crisis is affecting countries from all over the globe. Worse yet, it appears that no country is immune from the current financial malaise. Unfortunately, such financial crises are not new. Over the past three decades, the global financial market has witnessed several financial crises involving mainly developing countries from Latin America to East Asia. What is common to these crises is that, when faced with a financial crisis, debtor countries choose to renegotiate their debt service obligations instead of defaulting on them. This begs the question of why countries choose to renegotiate instead of defaulting on their debt obligations? In the same vein, why do creditors agree to renegotiate instead of allowing debtor countries to default on their debt obligations? That is, what is the motivation behind borrowers' and creditors' willingness to renegotiate and restructure existing debt obligations?

It appears that both the borrower and creditors have incentives to avoid outright default by agreeing to restructure existing debt obligations. According to a number of economists, the main motivating force behind their willingness to restructure is the benefit associated with maintaining international trade ties. These observations broach the interesting question of whether the benefit associated with maintaining international trade ties is shared equally between borrowers and creditors? Or is the outcome dependent on a bargaining game between the borrower and creditor?

To examine the outcome of the bargaining game between the borrower and creditor banks, we compared the debt restructuring terms against the average terms for all new loans contracted by the borrower during the restructuring agreement year. The terms for these new loans were assumed to be a proxy for market terms that reflect a borrower's creditworthiness at the time of debt renegotiation. Our data set consisted of 60 commercial debt restructuring agreements during the 1980s. For about two-thirds of commercial debt restructuring agreements included in our sample, debtor nations restructured their obligations at above the prevailing market terms. This posed the following two questions: if debt restructurings are conducted on a voluntary basis, why would borrowers agree to reschedule and restructure their loans at less favourable terms? Second, even though the majority of restructurings were more costly to borrowers, they were more costly to creditors for about a third of the agreements. Why, then, do creditors agree to restructure existing debt obligations at terms that are more favourable to the borrowers?

Our results point to a statistically significant relationship between debt restructuring outcomes and international trade ties, that is trade ties between a debtor country and a major creditor country matter in debt restructuring outcomes. According to our data, as the borrower's trade ties with developed countries in the region strengthen, the borrower's (and/or creditors') bargaining power diminishes (strengthens) and it agrees to restructure at less favourable terms. However, even after controlling for trade ties, our analysis showed that major borrowers were able to extract more concessions from the lenders. Since the commitment by lenders is already large, perhaps major borrowers are able to exploit lenders' large exposure and demand more favourable restructuring terms. Our results also reveal that borrowers with higher credit ratings were able to restructure at more favourable terms. However, major borrowers, on average, had higher credit ratings. In the final analysis, it appears that both borrowers and lenders take advantage of their respective bargaining strengths to extract concessions from the other party.

As we conclude the chapter, several countries in the Eurozone are struggling with serious sovereign debt crises. A significant portion of these countries' government bonds are held by the European banks. According to the Bank of International Settlement, at the end of 2009, the European banks had $2.9 trillion at risk in Greece, Italy and Spain. It is feared that a failure to bailout out Greece could trigger contagious effects throughout Europe. Thus, in May 2010, the EU and the IMF came up with a significant rescue package for Greece. Still, even with the rescue package, it is possible that Greece will eventually restructure its sovereign debt. If restructurings were to take place in Greece and perhaps in other Eurozone countries, it will be interesting to study the dynamics of such restructurings, and in particular, the bargaining game played by the sovereign borrower and its lenders. In our study, we found the trade relationship to be a key determinant. Will trade also play a significant role for European countries as well? According to an estimate from the Deutche Bank, a restructuring of Greece's sovereign debt could lead to as much as €75 billion in losses for European banks.[20] The actual outcome, however, may surprise us.

NOTES

1. Armendáriz de Aghion and Armendáriz de Hinestrosa (1995) provide another argument in favour of negotiated debt relief over outright default. According to them, 'negotiated debt relief settlement is likely to dominate as a way for an LDC to achieve higher rates of growth while maintaining price stability.' See Hayri (2000), and Miller and Thomas (2007) for further discussion.
2. Debt restructuring refers to deferment of payments due in a specified interval for repayment on a new schedule, following negotiations between borrower and lenders. Typically, it involves negotiations concerning rescheduling amounts, grace periods (if any), maturity, spread over LIBOR/U.S. prime rate and special features (if any).
3. We used World Bank classifications to classify countries into 'income' and 'indebtedness' groups.
4. Thirty seven restructuring agreements were dropped due to insufficient information on restructuring agreements, lack of data on terms on new loans and/ or due to lack of country data. The 37 dropped cases involved 22 countries; however, the majority of these cases involved countries from Africa (south of Sahara).
5. The average terms for all new loans were obtained from the World Debt tables.
6. It is possible that the rates on new loans may not represent the market terms. Instead, these terms may have a subsidy component to them. If these loans are subsidized, the NPVs will be biased downward.
7. There are other ways of evaluating debt restructuring outcomes. For example, Kozack (2005) and Sturzenegger and Zettelmeyer (2005) compare the NPV of debt

service before and after the debt restructuring. Kozack (2005) also discusses other ways of evaluating debt restructurings.

8. There is no consensus on the appropriate discount rate in the NPV calculation. For our NPV calculations, we applied the same discount rate, risk-free world interest rate across countries. This ensures that any benefit or cost from debt restructuring comes from adjustments in the debt service profile. See Kozack (2005) for a detailed discussion on the choice of an appropriate discount rate for assessing the effectiveness of debt restructurings.

9. Correlations among the explanatory variables included in Eq. (1) are not high. The largest correlation is between INTER and VCPGDP which is equal to −0.32. Appendix A provides a complete description and the sources of the explanatory variables.

10. L, measurement of borrower losses, is conceptually similar to the haircut $H \equiv 1 - [\mathrm{NPV}(\mathrm{new}, r_{\mathrm{new}})/\mathrm{NPV}(\mathrm{old}, r_{\mathrm{new}})]$, a measurement of investor losses as employed by Sturzenegger and Zettelmeyer (2005).

11. We replaced the dummy variable for major borrower with the actual level of external indebtedness, TED, and re-estimated Eq. (1). The estimated coefficient for TED variable is negative and statistically significant at 5%. For the rest of the variables included in the equation, the estimated coefficients are similar to those reported in Table 3.

12. We also used the actual size of debt restructured amount as well as restructured amount as a percentage of GDP and obtained results similar to results presented in the fourth column in Table 3.

13. CTRADE is a GDP weighted average of trade by developed countries in the region with the borrowing country. Developed country's trade with the borrowing country is measured as a percentage of its GDP. We also estimated Eq. (1) with equally weighted CTRADE variable and obtained similar results. This finding also holds true for CEXP and CIMP variables as well.

14. During the 1980s, the global average credit rating declined from 53 to 39, a 26.4% decline. Excluding countries included in our sample, the global average declined from 56.9 to 44.3, a 22% decline. Thus, countries included in our sample experienced a significantly greater deterioration in their creditworthiness compared to the rest of the world.

15. Three observations (Madagascar, 1981, 1984; Peru, 1980) were dropped due to lack of credit rating data.

16. We also investigated whether changes in the credit rating influenced DROs. To examine this issue, we replaced CR variable with PCR – defined as the percentage change in credit rating over the past one year (six months) – variable and re-estimated Eq. (1). The estimated coefficients of PCR are negative but not statistically significant.

17. During the 1980–1989 period, the top lending country provided 45.94% of the borrower's total outstanding debt. The top two lending countries and G-7 countries provided 64.91% and 87.54%, respectively.

18. Alternative sources of funding during the 1980–1989 period for countries included in the sample are provided in Appendix C.

19. We also estimated Eq. (1) with 'remittance' variable added. Its estimated coefficient is −0.00003 with a standard error of 0.0005.

20. Information in the last paragraph in the Summary and Conclusions section are obtained from various recent Wall Street Journal articles.

REFERENCES

Aizenman, Joseph (1991). Trade dependency, bargaining and external debt. *Journal of International Economics*, 31, 101–120.

Armendáriz de Aghion, B., & Armendáriz de Hinestrosa, P. (1995). Debt relief, growth, and price stability in Mexico. *Journal of Development Economics*, *48*, 135–149.

Bulow, J., & Rogoff, K. (1989). A constant recontracting model of sovereign debt. *Journal of Political Economy*, *97*, 155–178.

Fernández, Raquel and Şule, Özler (1999). Debt concentration and bargaining power: large banks, small banks, and secondary market prices. *International Economic Review*, 40–2, 333–355.

Hayri, A. (2000). Debt relief. *Journal of International Economics*, *52*, 137–152.

IMF. *International capital markets*, February 1986, April 1989, April 1990, and May 1991.

Institutional Investors, September 1979 to March 1990.

Kletzer, K., & Wright, B. (2000). Sovereign debt as intertemporal barrier. *American Economic Review*, *90*, 621–639.

Klimenko, M. (2002). Trade interdependence, the international financial institutions, and the recent evolution of sovereign-debt renegotiations. *Journal of International Economics*, *58*, 177–209.

Kozack, J. (2005). *Considerations in the choice of the appropriate discount rate for evaluating sovereign debt restructurings*. IMF Policy Discussion Paper.

Miller, Marcus and Thomas, Dania (2007). Sovereign debt restructuring: the judge, the vultures, and creditor rights. *The World Economy*, 1491–1509.

Roberts, M., & Sufi, A. (2009). Renegotiation of financial contracts: Evidence from private credit agreements. *Journal of Financial Economics*, *93*, 159–184.

Rose, A., & Spiegel, M. (2004). A gravity model of sovereign lending: Trade, default and credit. *IMF Staff Papers*, *51*, 50–63.

Sturzenegger, F., & Zettelmeyer, J. (2005). *Haircuts: Estimating investor losses in sovereign debt restructurings, 1998–2005*. IMF Working Paper 05/137.

Wells, Robin (1993). Tolerance of arrearages: how IMF loan policy can effect debt reduction. *American Economic Review*, *83–3*, 621–633.

APPENDIX A. DEFINITION AND SOURCES OF EXPLANATORY VARIABLES

GIND: The percentage change of industrialized countries' GNP from the previous year. The data on this variable was obtained from the IFS.

INTER: (LIBOR on 6-month U.S. dollar deposit) minus (the US wholesale price increase). Both variables were obtained from the IFS.

TDGDP: The ratio of total public and publicly guaranteed debt (disbursed) only to GDP. TD and GDP were obtained from the World Debt Table and the World Table.

GPGPD: An average of the 7-year annual rates of growth between year $t-6$ and t. To obtain this variable, a regression of the natural logarithm of real per capita GDP on a constant and time was performed for each debtor country. The GPGDP was defined as the coefficient of the time variable.

VCPGDP: Using the time period $t-6$ to t, a regression of the changes in per capita GDP on a constant and time was performed for each country. VCPGDP was defined as the standard error of this regression.

APPENDIX B. GEOGRAPHICAL REGIONS AND THEIR ASSOCIATED DEVELOPED COUNTRIES

Africa	France, Germany, Italy, Japan, the United Kingdom and the United States
Asia	Japan and the United States
Europe	France, Germany, Italy and the United Kingdom
Latin America	Canada and the United States
Middle East	France, Germany, Italy, Japan, the United Kingdom and the United States

Major borrowers according to the World Bank: Argentina, Brazil, Chile, Mexico and Venezuela.

APPENDIX C. ALTERNATIVE SOURCES OF FUNDING DURING THE 1980–1989 PERIOD

Country	Average (in US$ Millions) during the 1980–1989 Period			Alternative Sources of Funding as a Percentage of	
	FDI	IR	Remittances	GDP	Total debt outstanding
Argentina	608.9	4,547.6	34.9[a]	5.54%	10.66%
Bolivia	39.4	515.9	5.7	16.14	13.08
Brazil	1,519.5	7,754.2	64.1	3.37	9.21
Chile	476.9	3,363.3	1.0[b]	16.58	20.95
Costa Rica	66.3	436.4	6.5	10.68	12.51
Côte d'Ivoire	49.2	30.8	32.5	1.31	1.07
Dominican Republic	67.9	254.4	228.6	7.88	17.23
Ecuador	85.1	771.5	2.7	7.70	9.78
Gabon	59.0	149.0	NA[c]	5.66	11.92
Jamaica	7.9	114.8	121.4	7.79	6.68
Jordan	42.8	1,043.2	992.2	40.41	50.34
Madagascar	1.3	96.1	6.0[d]	3.31	4.08
Malawi	1.4	63.3	NA	5.15	6.10
Mexico	2,387.4	6,284.8	1,704.1	5.76	11.41
Morocco	65.3	569.4	1,131.3	10.40	11.17
Nicaragua	0.01	148.1[e]	NA	5.70	2.68
Nigeria	434.0	2,737.4	11.1	8.95	16.13
Panama	−18.3	129.8	86.2	4.02	4.25
Peru	28.9	1,941.3	NA	9.70	14.67
Philippines	214.1	2,073.4	962.8	9.45	12.83
Poland	4.3	1,248.1	NA	1.74	3.68[f]
Romania	0	1,964.8	NA	4.91	27.40
Senegal	3.1	21.7	86.1	3.32	4.22
Sudan	1.0	23.0	248.4	2.18	3.05
Trinidad and Tobago	108.8	1,505.8	3.4[g]	25.92	106.77
Turkey	167.4	3,276.8	2,022.9	72.9	19.35
Uruguay	45.8	1,521.6	NA	20.91	46.87
Venezuela	22.7	11,526.4	1.0[h]	18.73	33.95
Mean	231.8	1,932.6	369.2	9.66	18.09
Standard deviation	523.9	2,713.6	611.4	8.55	21.59

Source: World Bank, Revised Outlook for Remittances Flows, 2009–2011.

[a]Based on 1980–1987 remittances data. Data for 1988 and 1989 were not available.

[b]Based on 1983–1989 remittances data. Data from 1980 to 1982 were not available.
[c]NA stands for 'not available'.
[d]Based on 1984–1989 remittances data. Data from 1980 and 1983 were not available.
[e]Based on 1980–1983 and 1987–1989 international reserves data. Data from 1984 to 1986 were not available.
[f]Calculated as total alternative sources of funding divided by long-term debt.
[g]Remittance data for 1986 is missing.
[h]Based on 1985–1989 remittances data. Data from 1980 to 1984 were not available.

HAS INTERNATIONAL FINANCIAL CO-MOVEMENT CHANGED? EMERGING MARKETS IN THE 2007–2009 FINANCIAL CRISIS☆

John Ammer, Fang Cai and Chiara Scotti

ABSTRACT

Emerging-market (EM) assets have historically been regarded as inherently risky and particularly vulnerable to international shocks that result in a general increase in investor risk perceptions. In this chapter, we assess the ongoing relevance of this view by examining the linkages between EM and non-EM stock and bond markets in the past two decades, with a focus on how these relationships played out during the global financial crisis of 2007–2009. We evaluate how these linkages have evolved over the period 1992–2009, through statistical tests of whether the

☆The authors are staff economists in the Division of International Finance, Board of Governors of the Federal Reserve System, Washington, DC 20551, USA. The views in this paper are solely the responsibility of the authors and should not be interpreted as reflecting the views of the Board of Governors of the Federal Reserve System or of any other person associated with the Federal Reserve System. The authors wish to thank Jane Haltmaier and Nick Klagge for their contributions to an earlier project that this work extends, Daniel Beltran and Steve Kamin for helpful comments, and Michael Gulick and Justin Vitanza for excellent research assistance.

The Impact of the Global Financial Crisis on Emerging Financial Markets
Contemporary Studies in Economic and Financial Analysis, Volume 93, 231–253

ISSN: 1569-3759/doi:10.1108/S1569-3759(2011)0000093009

volatility of EM financial markets changed – either in their response to international shocks originating in advanced-economy markets or in their independent fluctuations.

We find that over a longer period EM, bond and stock prices have on average moved in the same direction as the prices of non-EM risky assets, and this co-movement has persisted. However, these relationships have evolved somewhat over time. Both EM sensitivity to international shocks and EM-specific volatility in EM sovereign-bond spreads appear to have decreased over time, consistent with the greater fundamental stability of EM economies and perhaps a reduced inclination by investors to sell off EM assets in response to a rise in risk perceptions. Somewhat in contrast, while an upward trend in co-variation between EM and non-EM stock prices suggests an increasing degree of global market integration, idiosyncratic volatility has declined, consistent with a diminished level of locally driven risk in these markets.

In addition, the response of EM asset prices to the latest financial crisis appears to be moderate in comparison to historical experience. This evidence may reflect reduced EM vulnerability to external shocks in general, which is consistent with some encouraging improvements in the underlying fundamentals of EM economies over the decade preceding the onset of the crisis.

1. A BRIEF REVIEW OF THE EVENTS

As shown in Fig. 1, emerging-market (EM) stock price indexes followed a relatively volatile path over 1992–2009, and they also have exhibited substantial co-movement with advanced-economy stock markets, as has been documented in a number of prior studies. Similarly, EM sovereign-bond spreads also have fluctuated sharply over time and tended to move quite closely with U.S. high-yield corporate spreads. Against this historical context, the onset of the financial crisis that originated in the United States in the summer of 2007 reverberated promptly in EM financial markets. EM stock prices and bond yields started to deteriorate in July 2007 along with non-EM market prices in response to growing concern about sub-prime mortgage loans. EM financial indicators worsened after a number of adverse news events that followed, such as the August 2007 announcement by French bank BNP Paribas of a suspension of withdrawals from some of its managed

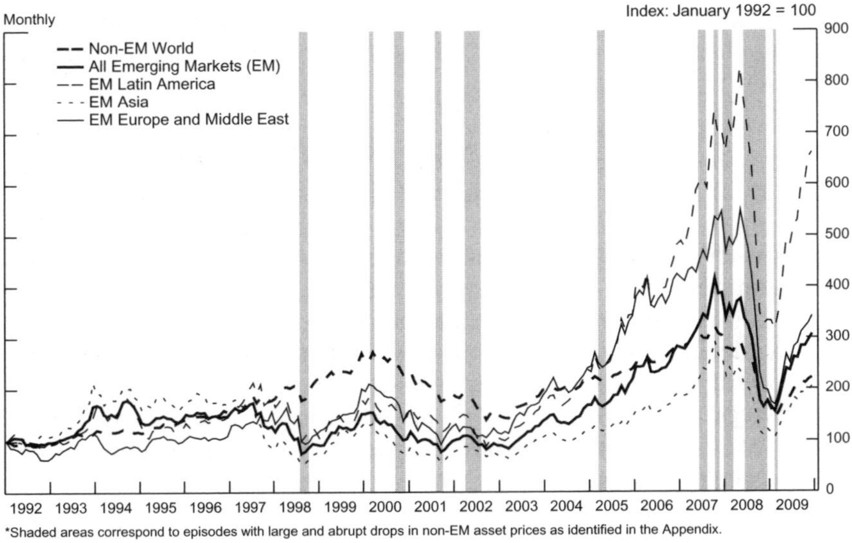

Fig. 1. Emerging-Market Stock Prices.

funds, citing exposure to illiquid sub-prime assets that had become difficult to mark to market value.

Increasing concerns over the strength of the U.S. economy contributed to another downturn in these indicators at the end of October 2007, but in the early stages of the crisis, EM financial markets seemed atypically buoyant, with international spillover to this point relatively muted in magnitude, in comparison to the historical experience, in which EM markets had tended to crash the hardest. It was not until the second half of 2008 and the first quarter of 2009 that EM financial indicators worsened significantly, relative to pre-crisis levels. At this point, stock prices plummeted and bond prices skyrocketed in advanced and EM economies alike, as credit markets froze following Lehman's bankruptcy and amid mounting concerns about the solvency of financial institutions and the global economic outlook. However, EM financial prices generally fared no worse in the darkest days of the crisis than markets elsewhere, and EM markets subsequently rebounded more rapidly and robustly in the last 10 months of 2009 than their advanced-economy counterparts.

The overall picture of EM financial markets through the 2007–2009 financial crisis appears to meaningfully reflect a reduced sensitivity of EM economies to external shocks going into the crisis, in comparison to past dynamics. Accordingly, our analysis is motivated by the question of what has changed over the years for the EM economies and whether their new-found resilience is likely to endure.

2. IMPROVEMENTS IN UNDERLYING FUNDAMENTALS

One point that seems indisputable is that many EM economies appear to have, with help from improved policy choices, become more stable and structurally resilient over the decade preceding the onset of the financial crisis. As documented in the first row of Table 1, the average EM inflation rate dropped from 18.7 percent in 1996 to 5.2 percent in 2006, reflecting an increased policy focus on controlling inflation, in many cases through explicit inflation-targeting regimes. Progress in reducing inflation rates has been particularly dramatic in a number of eastern European and Latin American economies. Fiscal balances have also improved, and were at manageable levels by 2006 in most of the important EM economies. Furthermore, current account surpluses had become the norm across much of emerging Asia and Latin America, and many countries have stockpiled large amounts of foreign exchange reserves. With less need for international financing, the ratio of external debt to GDP generally declined in emerging

Table 1. Mean Emerging Markets (EM) Fundamental Indicators[a].

	All EM		EM Asia		EM Europe, Mid-East and Africa		EM Latin America	
	1996	2006	1996	2006	1996	2006	1996	2006
Consumer price inflation (%)	18.7	5.2	6.7	4.0	23.9	5.9	25.6	5.7
Fiscal balance/GDP (%)	−2.5	−1.2	−1.5	−1.6	−4.5	−2.3	−1.6	0.2
Current account/GDP (%)	−2.4	1.8	−3.8	4.1	−2.3	−1.4	−1.2	2.8
Official reserves/GDP (%)	12.2	21.1	13.9	32.3	11.9	18.8	10.9	12.1
External debt/GDP (%)	40.2	36.7	37.2	29.0	38.6	47.7	44.8	33.5
Domestic credit/GDP (%)	54.4	63.1	83.0	92.2	52.7	59.6	27.5	37.6

[a]Figures given in column "All EM" are means for 27 countries included in the MSCI all-EM stock index and/or the Merrill Lynch indexes of dollar-denominated EM sovereign bonds for which the relevant data were available. Column "EM Asia" includes China, India, Indonesia, Korea, Malaysia, Pakistan, Philippines, Taiwan and Thailand. Column "EM Europe Mid-East and Africa" includes Czech Republic, Egypt, Hungary, Israel, Poland, Russia, South Africa, Turkey and Ukraine. Column "EM Latin America" includes Argentina, Brazil, Chile, Colombia, Ecuador, Mexico, Peru, Uruguay and Venezuela.

Asia and Latin America. In addition, against a background of increasing institutional and macroeconomic stability, domestic sources of credit have tended to expand more rapidly than GDP, further reducing the dependence of EM economies on external capital flows.[1]

It is also worth noting that the crisis in 2007–2009 departed somewhat from past experience in terms of relatively muted EM exchange rate volatility. Most major EM countries now have flexible exchange rate regimes (at least in the downward direction), which means fewer currencies have overvalued and thus been vulnerable to a sharp depreciation. In contrast, some of the EM economies that had seen the largest declines in currency values during past turmoil periods were countries that were financing sizable current account deficits to a large extent through short-term capital inflows.

Given all this, it is not surprising that EM economies would be less vulnerable to abrupt shifts in global risk perceptions than in the past. Probably at least in part as a result of efforts by institutions such as the International Monetary Fund (IMF) and the Bank for International Settlements (BIS) to promote improvements in the quality and consistency of data, transparency also appears to have improved for EM economies. In particular, there is some evidence that investors increasingly have been able to distinguish among different countries on the basis of fundamental factors, with countries that are perceived as more vulnerable (e.g., Greece in 2009–2010) seeing more adverse changes in asset prices during an episode of financial turbulence. Overall, the evidence suggests that investors consider most EM economies to be fairly sound. This theme of increasing stability is apparent in the longer term perspective on EM asset prices that we offer in Section 3.

3. EMERGING-MARKET ASSET PRICE DYNAMICS

EM assets have historically been regarded as inherently risky, with their prices tending to react along with those of other risky assets, such as U.S. high-yield corporate bonds, particularly when international shocks result in a general increase in investor risk perceptions. However, there is some evidence that this relationship has changed. Fig. 2 shows yield spreads for Merrill Lynch indexes of dollar-denominated EM sovereign bonds and U.S. (high-yield) corporate bonds since early 1992. Although EM sovereign spreads were high and quite volatile at times in the 1990s and early 2000s, the exhibit shows a distinct downward trend in both their level and volatility in the past few years, while the corresponding overall trends for U.S. corporate spreads are much less clear. Furthermore, the EM sovereign

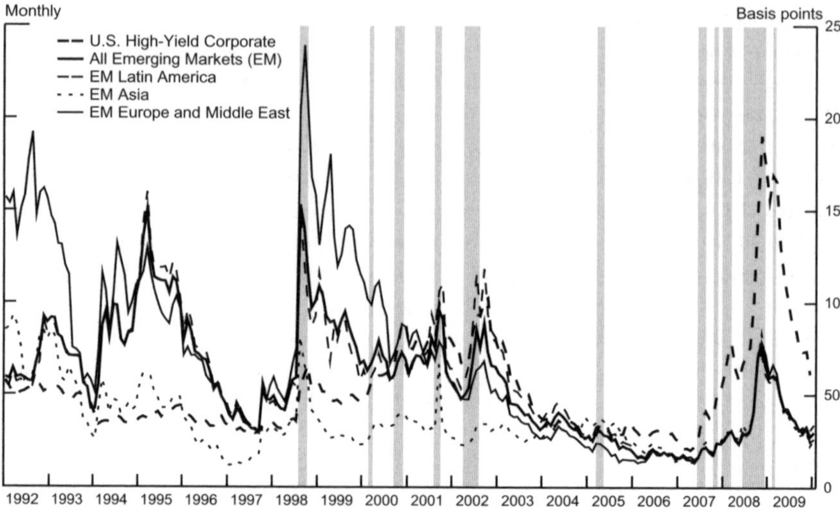

*Shaded areas correspond to episodes with large and abrupt drops in non-EM asset prices as identified in the Appendix.

Fig. 2. Emerging-Market Bond Yield Spreads.

spreads in the exhibit understate the improvement in credit quality because of compositional changes in the series – several countries (including China, Korea and Chile) have been dropped from Merrill Lynch's EM sovereign indexes because credit rating upgrades made them ineligible for the inclusion criteria, while some riskier countries have been added to the indexes following their maiden international bond issues. These facts suggest that investor perceptions of EM credit risk have moderated over the past decade along with the improvement in EM fundamentals documented in Section 2.

The statistical analysis presented below is related to a substantial literature on spillovers and contagion in international capital markets. Many studies, for example, Cheung and Mak (1992), Liu and Pan (1997), Wu and Su (1998) and Cha and Oh (2000) report that the U.S. market is a global factor and the single most influential market in the world, affecting both developed and emerging markets. The identification of channels of shock transmission across countries is, for instance, discussed in Dungey, Fry, González-Hermosillo, & Martin (2005), Dornbusch, Park, and Claessens (2000) and Pericoli and Sbracia (2003). Dungey, Fry, González-Hermosillo, & Martin (2005, 2006), Kaminsky and Reinhart (2003) and

Beirne, Caporale, Schulze-Ghattas, and Spagnolo (2008) examine volatility spillovers from mature to EM countries and test for their changes during crisis periods. In this context, a large body of literature investigates conditional correlations during crisis periods in order to examine any possible breaks in the underlying data. Examples include Forbes and Rigobon (2002), King and Wadhwani (1990), King, Sentana, and Wadhwani (1994), Bekaert, Harvey, and Ng (2005), Caporale, Cippollini, and Spagnolo (2005). Coudert and Gex (2007) conclude that investors' risk appetite can rapidly change during financial crises when seemingly unrelated asset markets feel the impact by seemingly unrelated financial shocks. A closely related study by Frank and Hesse (2009) analyses potential financial linkages between liquidity and bank solvency measures in advanced economies, such as stress in the inter-bank market, market volatility and solvency concerns of large financial institutions with EM stock indexes, bond spreads and CDS measures. Carey, Demarco, Kamin, Lel and Silver (2010) focuses on the crisis of 2007–2009, with an empirical investigation of the macroeconomic determinants of the impact on credit default swap premiums and stock prices, across both EM and non-EM economies, distinguishing between indexes of financial and non-financial firms.

4. LINKAGES BETWEEN EM AND ADVANCED-ECONOMY STOCK AND BOND MARKETS

We begin with the relationship between EM sovereign spreads and U.S. high-yield corporate bond spreads, as indicated by the following equation:

$$(\Delta p_t^{\text{EM sovereign}} - \Delta p_t^{\text{Treasury}}) = \alpha + \beta_0(\Delta p_t^{\text{U.S. corporate}} - \Delta p_t^{\text{Treasury}}) + \varepsilon_t \quad (1)$$

The parenthetical expressions represent the difference between the change in the log price index for a category of risky bonds (EM sovereign or U.S. corporate) and the change in the log price of a U.S. Treasury bond of similar maturity. These relative price change measures essentially capture changes in the yield spread. For the U.S. high-yield corporate bond index, which has an effective duration of about 5 years, a percentage point increase in the relative price change corresponds to a decline in the spread of about 20 basis points.[2] We first examine this relationship over the whole 18-year period (1992–2009); later we will turn to the question of whether it has changed in recent years. It should be noted that this expression represents correlation, but not necessarily causation. Both spreads might react to common shocks, or U.S. spreads might be impacted by events originating in emerging markets. As shown in Table 2, all of the slope coefficients for 1992–2009 are positive and statistically significant. EM sovereign-bond prices moved less than one-for-one with U.S. high-yield corporate bonds over this period.

Next we look at the relationship between EM stock prices and financial markets in advanced countries, which can offer a more direct window into the impact of external shocks on the private sector in these countries than does the relationship between bond yields examined above. The standard approach is to assess the linkage between EM and non-EM stock price indexes, which we do below. However, given that the financial turmoil had its seeds in U.S. debt markets, it is also useful to consider the relationship between EM stock prices and U.S. credit markets. In particular, we use the following regression specification to assess the extent to which EM stock price indexes have co-moved with U.S. high-yield corporate bonds:

$$\Delta p_t^{\text{EM stock}} = \alpha + \beta_0(\Delta p_t^{\text{U.S. corporate}} - \Delta p_t^{\text{Treasury}}) + \varepsilon_t \qquad (2)$$

Table 2. Sensitivity of EM Sovereign Bond Prices to U.S. Corporate Bond Prices (January 1992–December 2009).

$$(\Delta p_t^{\text{EM sovereign}} - \Delta p_t^{\text{Treasury}}) = \alpha + \beta_0(\Delta p_t^{\text{U.S. corporate}} - \Delta p_t^{\text{Treasury}}) + \varepsilon_t$$

EM Sovereign Bond Index	β_0	R^2
All emerging markets	0.772 (0.000)	0.294
Latin America	0.783 (0.000)	0.280
Asia	0.624 (0.000)	0.347
Europe, mid-East and Africa	0.842 (0.000)	0.227

Note(s): These regression estimates are based on month-end data on log changes in bond-price indexes, less the log change in a price index for the 6-year U.S. Treasury bond. Bond indexes are from Merrill Lynch and measured in dollars. The figure in parenthesis below each coefficient estimate is a *P*-value for a two-tailed test for a null hypothesis of a zero coefficient.

Table 3 shows estimates of Eq. (2) for four EM stock price indexes. For every region EM stock prices move more than one-for-one with U.S. corporate bond prices, and the results are statistically significant. Accordingly, we should expect spillovers between these markets to be the rule, rather than the exception.

Returning to the relationship between EM and non-EM equity prices, we estimate the following specification:

$$\Delta p_t^{\text{EM stock}} = \alpha + \beta_0 \cdot \Delta p_t^{\text{non-EM stock}} + \varepsilon_t \qquad (3)$$

Table 4 shows estimates of Eq. (3) for a broad EM stock index and three regional sub-indexes. All four move more than one-for-one with the log change in the MSCI (non-EM) world stock price index. In sum, the estimates reported in Tables 1–3 confirm the notion that, over the past 18 years, EM asset prices have on average moved in the same direction as other risky asset prices and EM stock prices are more volatile than safer assets such as advanced-economy stocks.

Table 3. Sensitivity of EM Stock Indexes to U.S. Corporate Bond Prices (January 1992–December 2009).

$$\Delta p_t^{\text{EM stock}} = \alpha + \beta_0(\Delta p_t^{\text{U.S. corporate}} - \Delta p_t^{\text{Treasury}}) + \varepsilon_t$$

EM Stock-Price Index	β_0	R^2
All emerging markets	1.400 (0.000)	0.368
Latin America	1.612 (0.000)	0.326
Asia	1.282 (0.000)	0.269
Europe, mid-East and Africa	1.481 (0.000)	0.311

Note(s): These regression estimates are based on month-end data on log changes in price indexes. The U.S. Treasury bond-price index is for a 6-year maturity. Bond indexes are from Merrill Lynch and stock indexes are from MSCI, with both measured in dollars. The figure in parenthesis below each coefficient estimate is a *P*-value for a two-tailed test for a null hypothesis of a zero coefficient.

Table 4. Sensitivity of Emerging Market (EM) Stocks to Non-EM World Stock Index (January 1992–December 2009).

$$\Delta p_t^{\text{EM stock}} = \alpha + \beta_0 \cdot \Delta p_t^{\text{non-EM stock}} + \varepsilon_t$$

EM Stock Price Index	β_0	R^2
All emerging markets	1.280 (0.000)	0.608
Latin America	1.424 (0.000)	0.502
Asia	1.201 (0.000)	0.466
Europe, mid-East and Africa	1.303 (0.000)	0.476

Note(s): Data are log changes in month-end stock price indexes from MSCI, measured in dollars. The figure in parenthesis below each coefficient estimate is a *P*-value for a two-tailed test for a null hypothesis of a zero coefficient.

5. HAVE THESE LINKAGES CHANGED OVER TIME?

Next we turn to the question of whether these relationships have changed over time, with EM asset returns becoming either less sensitive to external shocks, less prone to locally driven volatility, or perhaps both. We begin with sovereign-bond prices. The upper panel of Fig. 3 shows estimates of the slope coefficient (β_0) from Eq. (1) (EM sovereign-bond price changes on U.S. corporate bond-price changes) from 25-month rolling regressions. The slope coefficients for the various EM regions vary substantially over time but move closely together. In particular, EM sovereign bonds appeared to be most highly correlated with U.S. high-yield bonds during the 1997 Asian Crisis and 1998 Russian and LTCM Crises. It is difficult to discern any longer term trend in the response of EM spreads to U.S. corporate spreads, although some downward movement may be evident.

The lower panel of Fig. 3 shows the standard errors of the residuals from these regressions. These standard errors may be interpreted as the volatility of EM bond spreads that is not explained by movements in U.S. corporate spreads. Elevated levels around the 1994–1995 Tequila, 1997 Asian, 1998 Russian and LTCM, 2001 Argentina and 2002 Brazil crises are consistent

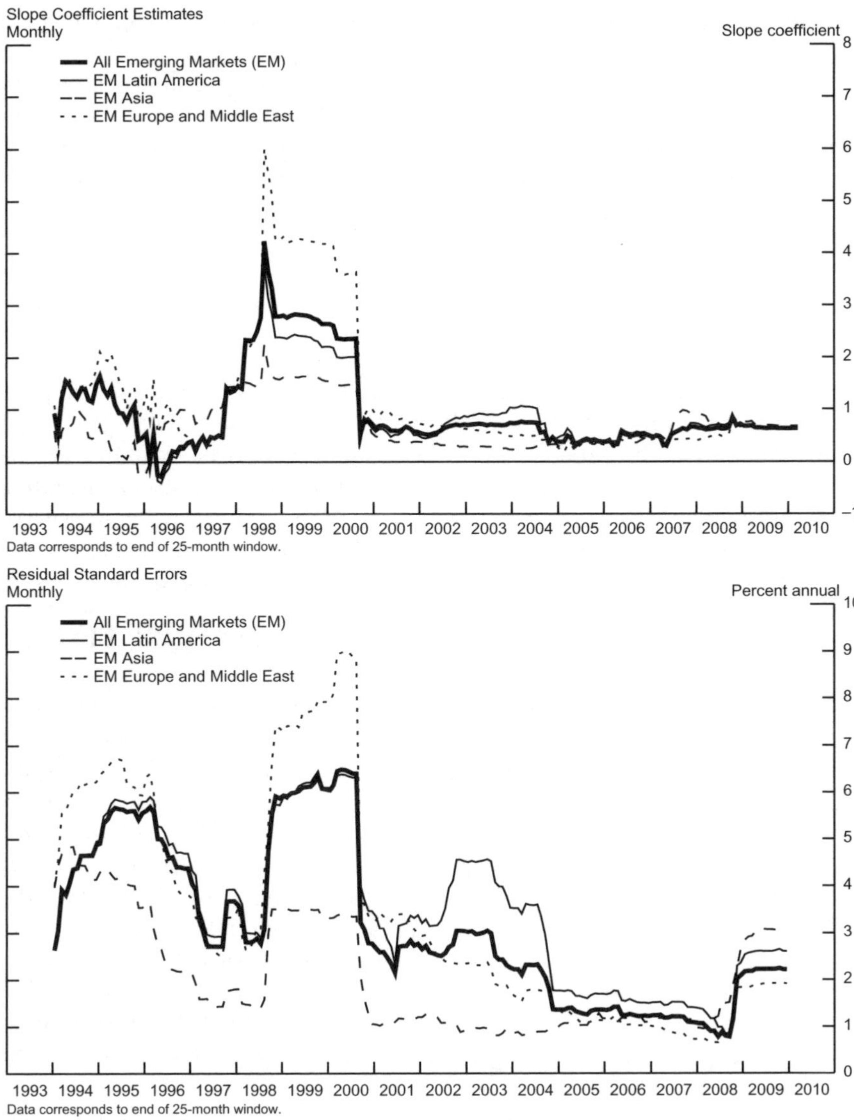

Fig. 3. Regressions of EM Sovereign-Bond Price Changes on U.S. High-Yield Bond Price Changes.

with the EM economies being at least partly the source of their own pain during these events.

There also appears to be a downward trend in idiosyncratic volatility in sovereign-bond prices in all three regions. We assess this trend more formally by augmenting our regression specification Eq. (1) to allow both β and the variance of the residual to trend over time.

$$(\Delta p_t^{\text{EM sovereign}} - \Delta p_t^{\text{Treasury}}) = \alpha + (\beta_0 + \beta_t \cdot t)(\Delta p_t^{\text{U.S. corporate}} - \Delta p_t^{\text{Treasury}}) + \varepsilon_t \quad (4)$$

and

$$E(\varepsilon_t^2) = V_0 + V_t \cdot t \quad (5)$$

An advantage of this framework is that it allows us to decompose a decrease in overall price volatility into reduced sensitivity to global shocks and lower EM-specific volatility. Table 5 reports estimates of the systems (4) and (5). For all four sovereign-bond indexes, our negative point estimates of β_t and V_t suggest both reduced sensitivity to international shocks and a reduction in EM-specific risk. Most of the coefficients are significant at the 5 percent level. These results are consistent with the greater fundamental stability of EM economies and reduced inclination by investors to sell off EM assets in response to a rise in risk perceptions.

A natural question is whether the trends observed in EM bond prices are also evident in EM stock prices. Fig. 4 shows slope coefficients and residual standard errors for rolling regressions of EM stock prices on U.S. corporate bond price changes (Eq. (2)). Both the slope coefficients and residual volatility have trended down from peaks reached during the bout of EM financial crises in the latter half of the 1990s, although the slope estimates turned upward in 2005–2006. We also assess the direction in co-variance and residual risk more systematically by augmenting Eq. (2) to allow trends in the slope coefficient and residual volatility.

$$\Delta p_t^{\text{EM stock}} = \alpha + (\beta_0 + \beta_t t)(\Delta p_t^{\text{U.S. corporate}} - \Delta p_t^{\text{Treasury}}) + \varepsilon_t \quad (6)$$

and

$$E(\varepsilon_t^2) = V_0 + V_t \cdot t \quad (7)$$

Table 6 reports estimates of the systems (6) and (7). Although most of the trend coefficients (β_t and V_t) are not statistically significant, they are

Table 5. Sensitivity of EM Bond Prices to U.S. Corporate Bond Prices over Time (January 1992–December 2009).

$$(\Delta p_t^{\text{EM sovereign}} - \Delta p_t^{\text{Treasury}}) = \alpha + (\beta_0 + \beta_t \cdot t)(\Delta p_t^{\text{U.S. corporate}} - \Delta p_t^{\text{Treasury}}) + \varepsilon_t$$

and

$$E(\varepsilon_t^2) = V_0 + V_t \cdot t$$

EM Sovereign-Bond Index	β_0	β_t	V_0	V_t	R^2
All emerging markets	1.090	−0.062	13.929	−1.421	0.326
	(0.000)	(0.002)	(0.000)	(0.059)	
Latin America	1.097	−0.061	15.247	−1.298	0.309
	(0.000)	(0.003)	(0.000)	(0.020)	
Asia	0.621	0.001	7.420	−0.689	0.347
	(0.000)	(0.971)	(0.000)	(0.014)	
Europe, mid-East and Africa	1.364	−0.102	22.797	−2.431	0.283
	(0.000)	(0.000)	(0.015)	(0.175)	

Note(s): These regression estimates are based on month-end data on log changes in bond-price indexes, less the log change in a price index for the 6-year U.S. Treasury bond. Bond indexes are from Merrill Lynch and measured in dollars. The figure in parenthesis below each coefficient estimate is a *P*-value for a two-tailed test for a null hypothesis of a zero coefficient. The time trend (t) is at an annual frequency and crosses zero in the middle of the sample.

generally negative in sign, which we take to be further evidence of downward trends in EM vulnerability to external credit market shocks and in EM-specific risk.

Fig. 5 addresses trends in international stock market co-movement (Eq. (3)), showing slope coefficients and residual standard errors for rolling regressions of EM stock prices on the world stock index. Interestingly, they go in opposite directions, with EM stock prices showing increasing integration with the rest of the world, but attenuated idiosyncratic volatility.

We obtain similar results from the estimation of a system with trends for the full period, that is,

$$\Delta p_t^{\text{EM stock}} = \alpha + (\beta_0 + \beta_t \cdot t)\Delta p_t^{\text{non-EM stock}} + \varepsilon_t \tag{8}$$

and

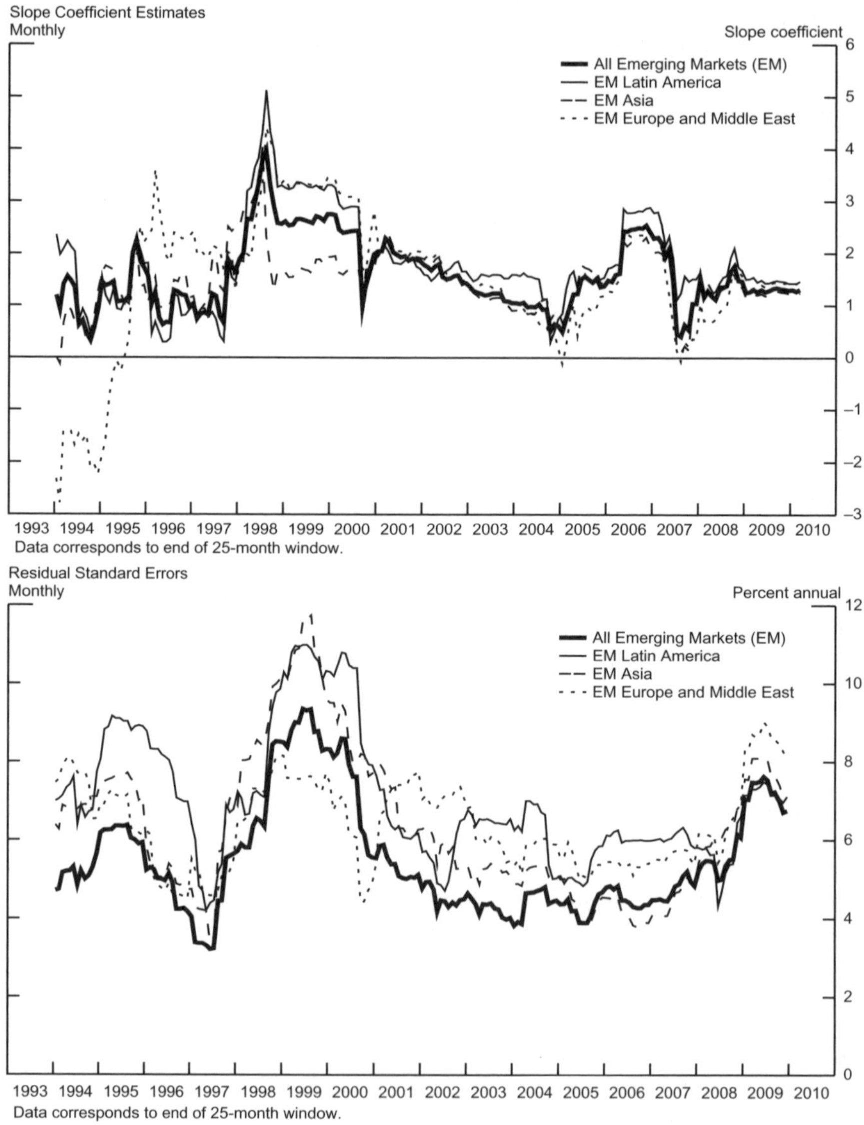

Fig. 4. Regressions of EM Stock Prices Changes on U.S. High-Yield Bond Price Changes.

Table 6. Sensitivity of EM Stock Indexes to U.S. Corporate Bond Prices over Time (January 1992–December 2009).

$$\Delta p_t^{\text{EM stock}} = \alpha + (\beta_0 + \beta_t \cdot t)(\Delta p_t^{\text{U.S. corporate}} - \Delta p_t^{\text{Treasury}}) + \varepsilon_t$$

and

$$E(\varepsilon_t^2) = V_0 + V_t \cdot t$$

EM Stock Price Index	β_0	β_t	V_0	V_t	R^2
All emerging markets	1.661	−0.051	31.971	0.029	0.376
	(0.000)	(0.097)	(0.000)	(0.969)	
Latin America	1.984	−0.072	51.787	−1.605	0.337
	(0.000)	(0.062)	(0.000)	(0.158)	
Asia	1.398	−0.023	43.482	−0.978	0.270
	(0.000)	(0.525)	(0.000)	(0.318)	
Europe, mid-East and Africa	1.655	−0.034	46.883	−0.590	0.314
	(0.000)	(0.358)	(0.000)	(0.574)	

Note(s): These regression estimates are based on month-end data on log changes in price indexes. The U.S. Treasury bond-price index is for a 6-year maturity. Bond indexes are from Merrill Lynch and stock indexes are from MSCI, with both measured in dollars. The figure in parenthesis below each coefficient estimate is a *P*-value for a two-tailed test for a null hypothesis of a zero coefficient. The time trend (t) is at an annual frequency and crosses zero in the middle of the sample.

$$E(\varepsilon_t^2) = V_0 + V_t \cdot t \tag{9}$$

As reported in Table 7, the estimated slope β_t rises over time while the residual variance V_t falls; these results are statistically significant at the 5 percent level in almost all cases.

The striking result that EM stock prices appear to be moving more closely with those of advanced countries while at the same time their volatility has declined is suggestive of an increasing level of maturity in these markets. In other words, EM stocks appear to be becoming more like those of advanced countries, moving in tandem in response to common shocks while at the same time exhibiting greater stability. These results are consistent with the others presented in this section, suggesting that at least on an everyday basis, the perceived riskiness of EM assets appears to be declining. However, the question still remains of what happens when markets are rattled by an unusually large shock, which is the subject of Section 6.

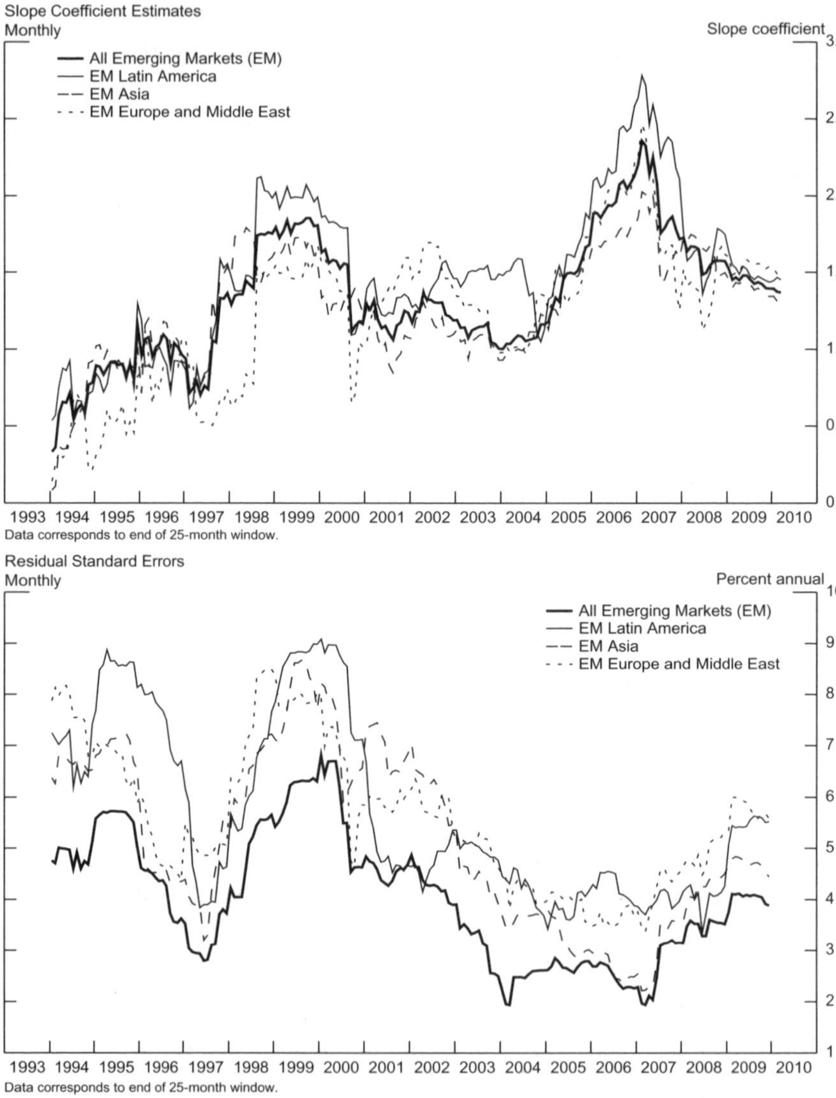

Fig. 5. Regressions of EM Stock Prices Changes on Non-EM World Stock Price Changes.

Table 7. Sensitivity of EM Stock Indexes to Non-EM World Stock Index over Time (January 1992–December 2009).

$$\Delta p_t^{\text{EM stock}} = \alpha + (\beta_0 + \beta_t \cdot t)\Delta p_t^{\text{non-EM stock}} + \varepsilon_t$$

and

$$E(\varepsilon_t^2) = V_0 + V_t \cdot t$$

EM Stock Price Index	β_0	β_t	V_0	V_t	R^2
All emerging markets	1.203	0.030	20.745	−1.150	0.617
	(0.000)	(0.027)	(0.000)	(0.017)	
Latin America	1.356	0.027	39.284	−2.643	0.507
	(0.000)	(0.159)	(0.000)	(0.004)	
Asia	1.116	0.033	31.946	−1.952	0.475
	(0.000)	(0.054)	(0.000)	(0.005)	
Europe, mid-East and Africa	1.173	0.051	35.363	−2.068	0.495
	(0.000)	(0.005)	(0.000)	(0.006)	

Note(s): Data are log changes in month-end stock price indexes from MSCI, measured in dollars. The figure in parenthesis below each coefficient estimate is a *P*-value for a two-tailed test for a null hypothesis of a zero coefficient. The time trend (t) is at an annual frequency and crosses zero in the middle of the sample.

6. HOW DO RECENT EM ASSET PRICE DYNAMICS COMPARE TO PREVIOUS INTERNATIONAL SHOCK EPISODES?

In this section we compare changes in EM sovereign-bond spreads and stock prices in the crisis of 2007–2009 to changes during previous periods when emerging markets suffered in the wake of significant international shocks. We define our comparison periods as those with large and abrupt drops in non-EM asset prices, identifying seven prior credit market episodes since 1992 when the U.S. high-yield corporate bond-price index dropped by at least 5 percentage points, net of the Treasury bond-price index (see appendix for more detail). The identified periods are listed in Table 8; the corresponding increases in U.S. corporate credit spreads (the first column)

Table 8. EM Sovereign-Bond Prices During Large Declines in U.S. Corporate Bond Prices.

Change in Bond Yield Spread over Period (Basis Points)						
Earlier events			Emerging market sovereign indexes			
From	To	U.S. corporate high-yield index	All emerging markets	Latin America	Asia	Europe, mid-East and Africa
7/29/1998	10/16/1998	325	512	416	224	873
2/10/2000	4/4/2000	129	49	67	56	−29
9/11/2000	12/6/2000	256	129	117	81	173
2/15/2001	4/5/2001	127	72	95	4	52
8/7/2001	10/5/2001	243	135	191	30	82
4/1/2002	8/14/2002	441	335	584	51	157
3/11/2005	5/17/2005	176	53	59	75	39
Average of seven periods		242	184	218	74	192
2007–2009 crisis						
6/5/2007	8/16/2007	200	100	107	124	80
10/15/2007	11/26/2007	204	94	98	119	78
12/26/2007	3/17/2008	278	107	110	110	103
6/13/2008	12/16/2008	1434	499	477	457	554
2/9/2009	3/9/2009	283	58	24	61	105
6/5/2007	3/9/2009	1456	459	434	454	511

Note(s): Changes in spreads are adjusted to remove the effect of month-end compositional changes in the Merrill Lynch bond indexes, and thus do not correspond precisely to the figures plotted in Exhibit 7 (which include these structural breaks). The periods chosen are peak-to-trough declines since January 1992 of at least 5 percent in the Merrill Lynch high-yield bond-price index, net of the 6-year Treasury price index, roughly corresponding to a widening in the yield spread of 100 basis points or more (see Appendix for details).

during these episodes range from 127 basis points to 441 basis points. The first episode encompasses the Russian and LTCM crises, but some of the others are more difficult to pin to discrete events. The largest single market movement in the table is for the mid-2002 event, which featured a surge in corporate defaults and bankruptcies, including WorldCom, and concerns about corporate governance and fraud that led to the passage of the Sarbanes–Oxley Act. The last episode, in the spring of 2005, was associated with concerns about the financial viability of two of the world's largest corporate borrowers, Ford and GM.

The crisis of 2007–2009 is identified by our methodology as five distinct events in U.S. credit markets, separated by intervening pauses with partial, but then aborted, recoveries in U.S. credit spreads. The first of these abatements ran from the Federal Reserve's reduction in the discount rate in mid-August 2007 to mid-October 2007 and the second occurred between late November and late December of 2007. We also show price statistics for a period (5 June 2007–9 March 2009) that encompasses all of these sub-periods – this composite period marks the largest increase in U.S. high-yield bond spreads of the past 16 years – 1,456 basis points. They rose nearly as much in the fourth of the five sub-periods and the longest in duration (13 June 2008–16 December 2008), reaching an all-time high at the end of this interval.

The remaining columns of Table 8 show changes in yield spreads for EM sovereign-bond indexes for each period of interest. Interpretation of these figures is sometimes complicated by significant EM-specific developments also occurring during these periods. Nevertheless, only for the 1998 event did our broadest index of EM yield spreads rise more than U.S. corporate spreads. The spread for the broad EM index also increased sharply (more than 300 basis points) during the mid-2002 event. However, a substantial portion of this increase is directly attributable to soaring spreads for Brazil (which has one of the largest country weights in the index), as Socialist candidate and President-to-be Lula began to lead in polls, which triggered concerns that Brazil might fail to honour its external debt if he were elected. More generally, reactions in EM yield spreads to U.S. credit markets during stress periods appear to have decreased over time, consistent with the trend estimates reported in Table 5, and they were relatively muted in the 2007–2009 event periods, with EM sovereign spreads in all regions generally rising by less than half of the increase in U.S. high-yield corporate spreads.

Table 9 reports the results of a similar exercise for percent changes in the EM stock price indexes. Strikingly, the broad EM index was down 15–20 percent in five of the six U.S. credit market events that occurred between 1998 and 2002, with all three of the regional sub-indexes tending to be significantly affected. On average over the seven episodes that precede the crisis of 2007–2009, EM stock prices tended to move more than the broad (all sectors) non-EM World Index, consistent with the slope estimates reported in Tables 4 and 7. However, EM stock price losses were roughly similar to those in other markets during the 2007–2009 price declines, and with the help of a 35-percent rebound between mid-August and mid-October of 2007, the broad EM index declined slightly less than the non-EM World Index over the full June 2007–March 2009 period, as reported in the table. Given the increasing trend in the co-variation between EM and non-EM stock prices that was reported in Table 7, the relative resilience of EM equity markets is consistent with reduced EM vulnerability to external spillovers.

Table 9. Stock Prices during Periods of Large Declines in U.S. Corporate Bond Prices.

Change in Stock Market Index over Period (Percent)							
Earlier events		Non-EM world	Emerging markets				
From	To		All emerging markets	Latin America	Asia	Europe, mid-East and Africa	
7/29/1998	10/16/1998	−7.2	−20.5	−27.2	−6.1	−35.3	
2/10/2000	4/4/2000	3.0	−8.2	−8.8	−8.5	−4.6	
9/11/2000	12/6/2000	−8.1	−17.1	−16.0	−20.3	−12.8	
2/15/2001	4/5/2001	−11.2	−19.0	−12.5	−21.8	−22.4	
8/7/2001	10/5/2001	−11.0	−16.5	−21.4	−15.1	−17.6	
4/1/2002	8/14/2002	−17.5	−15.8	−32.6	−10.7	−11.5	
3/11/2005	5/17/2005	−4.8	−8.5	−7.1	−6.0	−11.5	
Average of seven periods		−8.1	−15.1	−18.0	−12.6	−16.5	
2007–2009 crisis							
6/5/2007	8/16/2007	−9.3	−3.9	−16.0	5.1	3.1	
10/15/2007	11/26/2007	−6.7	−6.5	−9.3	−11.6	−2.0	
12/26/2007	3/17/2008	−13.7	−8.0	−1.5	−12.9	−9.1	
6/13/2008	12/16/2008	−37.2	−51.8	−54.8	−44.5	−60.2	
2/9/2009	3/9/2009	−21.5	−9.4	−8.4	−8.7	−2.5	
6/5/2007	3/9/2009	−57.6	−53.1	−46.5	−51.2	−61.5	

Note(s): The periods chosen are peak-to-trough declines since January 1992 of at least 5 percent in the Merrill Lynch high-yield bond-price index, net of the 6-year Treasury price index, roughly corresponding to a widening in the yield spread of 100 basis points or more. Stock market indexes are from MSCI, including the world index of non-EM countries.

7. CONCLUDING REMARKS

The response of EM asset prices to the crisis of 2007–2009, which was centred on U.S. and European financial intermediaries, was fairly mild in comparison to historical experience. This outcome stands in striking contrast to past periods of financial turbulence, when capital flows typically turned sharply away from EM economies, often resulting in serious economic disruption. Furthermore, the muted response in EM financial markets seems particularly remarkable given that, prior to the onset of this year's turmoil, many EM asset prices had soared during 2002–2007 to unprecedented levels and thus seemed vulnerable to a downward correction.

Notwithstanding, our statistical analysis shows that in the crisis of 2007–2009, the declines in key EM asset values – including sovereign-bonds and stock market indexes – were smaller than in episodes in the past, when investors retreating from risk seemed to sell off EM assets almost indiscriminately. This finding is consistent with econometric evidence that the responsiveness of EM asset prices to movements in U.S. high-yield corporate bond spreads has declined over the past decade. More generally, we are able to document a downward trend in EM asset price volatility – particularly for sovereign bonds – that appears to reflect an increasing resilience of EM economies to external shocks. Signs of increased stability are also apparent in conventional indicators of the vulnerability of EM economies; for example, debt ratios have declined and external balances had strengthened since the 1990s for most of these countries, and with monetary and fiscal policy generally on a steadier course, both inflation and fiscal balances moderated.

Thus, the recent resilience of emerging markets appears to reflect improvements in fundamentals rather than a decoupling from industrial-country markets. In fact, EM markets have become increasingly integrated with the rest of the world, a development that is reflected in stronger international stock price correlations. However, EM-specific stock market volatility has decreased since the 1990s. This apparent decline in risk may be related to one of the most important improvements in EM fundamentals – a shift from fixed exchange rate regimes (once thought to provide an essential nominal anchor) to rates that are flexible at least in the downward direction (although many countries continue to resist appreciation). In the past, investors have often fled EM assets when a currency peg seemed vulnerable, fearing the consequences of a disorderly devaluation. In contrast, EM currency values were relatively resilient in the wake of the financial crisis of 2007–2009, and despite precipitous declines in export volumes in the second half of 2008, real activity in most EM economies recovered fairly quickly. This apparent pay-off from more prudent choices made by EM authorities since the 1990s should also bode well for future commitment to policies that promote stability.

NOTES

1. However, credit growth, when rapid and undisciplined often had been associated with increased risk in earlier crises. Furthermore, in the crisis of 2007–2009, some of the smaller EM economies, notably the Baltic States, experienced heightened turmoil after the collapse of credit booms that had been financed from abroad. In addition, much-wealthier Iceland was rocked by the fallout from a reckless expansion of international intermediation on the part of its banks.

2. The practical advantage of using log changes in bond price indexes as a proxy for changes in spreads – rather than working directly with the yield spread series – is that, unlike the spread, the price index is constructed so that it does not have a jump whenever there is a structural break as a result of a new bond being added to the index. We do not have enough information about the U.S. corporate index to correct for these structural breaks before 1997.

REFERENCES

Beirne, J., Caporale, G. M., Schulze-Ghattas, M., & Spagnolo, N. (2008). *Volatility spillovers and contagion from mature to emerging stock markets*. IMF Working Paper no. 08/286. International Monetary Fund, Washington, USA.

Bekaert, G., Harvey, C. R., & Ng, A. (2005). Market integration and contagion. *Journal of Business*, *78*(1), 39–69.

Caporale, G., Cipollini, A., & Spagnolo, N. (2005). Contagion in East Asia: a conditional correlation analysis approach. *Journal of Empirical Finance*, *12*(3), 476–489.

Carey, M., Demarco, L., Kamin, S., Lel, U., & Silver, D. (2010). *Emerging markets, decoupling, and financial performance during the crisis*, draft manuscript. Board of Governors of the Federal Reserve System (May 10).

Cha, B., & Oh, S. (2000). The relationship between developed equity markets and the Pacific Basin's emerging equity markets. *International Review of Economics and Finance*, *9*, 299–322.

Cheung, Y. L., & Mak, S. C. (1992). The international transmission of stock market fluctuation between the developed markets and the Asian-Pacific markets. *Applied Financial Economics*, *2*, 43–47.

Coudert, V. & Gex, M. (2008). "Does Risk Aversion Drive Financial Crisis? Testing the Predictive Power of Empirical Indicators", *Journal of Empirical Finance*, 15(2), 167–184.

Dornbusch, R., Park, Y. C., & Claessens, S. (2000). Contagion: How it spreads and how it can be stopped. *World Bank Research Observer*, *15*, 177–197.

Dungey, M., Fry, R., González-Hermosillo, B., & Martin, V. (2005). Empirical modeling of contagion: A review of methodologies. *Quantitative Finance*, *5*, 9–24.

Dungey, M., Fry, R., González-Hermosillo, B., & Martin, V. (2006). Contagion in international bond markets during the Russian and LTCM crises. *Journal of Financial Stability*, *2*, 1–27.

Forbes, K., & Rigobon, R. (2002). No contagion, only interdependence: Measuring stock market co-movements. *Journal of Finance*, *57*(5), 2223–2261.

Frank, N., & Hesse, H. (2009). Financial spillovers to emerging markets during the global financial crisis. IMF Working Paper no. WP/09/104. International Monetary Fund.

Kaminsky, G. L., & Reinhart, C. M. (2003). *The center and the periphery: The globalization of financial turmoil*. NBER Working Paper no. 9479. (Cambridge: National Bureau of Economic Research), USA.

King, M., Sentana, E., & Wadhwani, S. (1994). Volatility and links between national stock markets. *Econometrica*, *62*, 901–933.

King, M., & Wadhwani, S. (1990). Transmission of volatility between stock markets. *Review of Financial Studies*, *3*(1), 5–33.

Liu, Y. A., & Pan, M. (1997). Mean and volatility spillover effects in the U.S. and Pacific-basin stock markets. *Multinational Finance Journal*, *1*, 47–62.

Pericoli, M., & Sbracia, M. (2003). A primer on financial contagion. *Journal of Economic Surveys*, *17*, 571–608.
Wu, C., & Su, Y. (1998). Dynamic relations among international stock markets. *International Review of Economics and Finance*, *7*, 63–84.

APPENDIX. IDENTIFYING AND DEFINING LARGE DECLINES IN U.S. CORPORATE BOND MARKETS

- We begin with intervals of at least 20 days in which the ratio of the high-yield bond-price index to the 6-year Treasury bond-price index declines by at least 5 percent.
- We eliminate most of the overlap in candidate periods by choosing only the ones that are 'peak-to-trough'.
- We deem a period of decline to be completed after a 'rebound' of 5 percent from the trough.
- We deem a period of decline to be completed after a 'pause' of 20 or more trading days. A 'pause' means that the ratio of the two indexes never fell below a (virtually flat) trend-line that declines 0.025 percent per day since the proposed trough.
- We excise any interval at the beginning or end of a proposed period of decline for which the rate of decrease is less than 0.025 percent per day from the proposed peak.
- We merge any episodes that are less than 10 days apart.

FINANCIAL SECTOR SURVEILLANCE AND THE IMF

Carlo Gola and Francesco Spadafora

ABSTRACT

The global financial crisis has magnified the role of Financial Sector Surveillance (FSS) in the International Monetary Fund's activities. This chapter surveys the various steps and initiatives through which the Fund has increasingly deepened its involvement in FSS. Overall, this process can be characterised by a preliminary stage and two main phases. The preliminary stage dates back to the 1980s and early 1990s, and was mainly related to the Fund's research and technical assistance activities within the process of monetary and financial deregulation embraced by several member countries. The first 'official' phase of the Fund's involvement in FSS started in the aftermath of the Mexican crisis, and relates to the international call to include financial sector issues among the core areas of Fund surveillance. The second phase focuses on the objectives of bringing the coverage of financial sector issues 'up-to-par' with the coverage of other traditional core areas of surveillance, and of integrating financial analysis into the Fund's analytical macroeconomic framework. By urging the Fund to give greater attention to its member countries' financial systems, the international community's response to the global crisis may mark the beginning of a new phase of FSS. The Fund's financial sector surveillance, particularly on advanced economies, is of

The Impact of the Global Financial Crisis on Emerging Financial Markets
Contemporary Studies in Economic and Financial Analysis, Volume 93, 255–310

ISSN: 1569-3759/doi:10.1108/S1569-3759(2011)0000093010

paramount importance for emerging market and developing countries, as they are vulnerable to spillover effects from crises originated in advanced economies. Emerging market and developing economies, which constitute the majority of the Fund's 187 members, are currently the recipients of over 50 programmes of financial support from the Fund (including those of a precautionary nature), totalling over $250 billion.

Keywords: IMF; surveillance; macro-financial linkages.

JEL Classification: F33.

1. INTRODUCTION

The stability of the international monetary and financial system represents a global public good. In a sound macroeconomic environment, financial stability is a precondition for sustained economic growth. The global financial turmoil that broke out in August 2007 is the most vivid illustration of the fact that financial sector crises, by their very nature, can have disruptive effects on the real economy.

Policies to avoid or lessen the likelihood and severity of financial crises are properly within the purview of the Fund's multilateral and bilateral surveillance. In fact, Article IV of the Fund's Articles of Agreement assigns to the Fund an institutional mandate to promote economic growth and financial stability, as well as to help prevent crises. Surveillance over member countries' policies remains at the core of the institution's mandate, particularly through its focus on the linkages between the safety and soundness of the financial system and macroeconomic performance. Responsible policies on the part of national authorities, and proper practices by the private sector need necessarily to support the Fund's role in crisis prevention.

Although financial sector issues had been the object of the Fund's analysis for some time, the institution's systematic and intensive involvement in Financial Sector Surveillance (FSS) is relatively new. The Mexican and Asian financial crises of the mid-1990s marked a breakthrough in this regard. The role played by financial vulnerabilities in precipitating these crises and the significant economic costs suffered by the affected countries laid the groundwork for an unprecedented effort made by the international community towards the objective of strengthening the so-called "international financial architecture". In a context of growing economic and financial integration among all countries, sustained capital flows and increasingly complex financial products, it became clear that macroeconomic and financial stability would crucially rely also on resilient and well-regulated financial systems.

Given its universal membership and unique comparative advantages, the Fund took centre stage, along with other international fora, in fulfiling the international mandate[1] to develop both the analytical capacity and the operational tools to ensure the stability of financial systems across its membership.

The Mexican and Asian crises had indeed shed light on some weaknesses of the Fund's framework for surveillance, as financial sector issues had generally not received as much coverage as was the case for more traditional macroeconomic issues. The Fund thus became increasingly aware that more and better-focused attention had to be paid by surveillance to monitor a country's financial sector, so as to identify risks and vulnerabilities and, ultimately, prevent financial crises.

Accordingly, reinforcing the Fund's FSS constituted one of the major components of the approach undertaken by the international community to strengthen the international financial architecture.

Overall, the Fund's involvement in FSS can be characterised by a preliminary stage and two main phases. The preliminary stage dates back to the 1980s and early 1990s, and was mainly related to the Fund's research and technical assistance activities that accompanied the process of monetary and financial deregulation embraced by several member countries. Already at this stage, Fund staff underscored the importance of the so-called 'macro-financial linkages', that is, the two-way risk transmission channels between the financial sector and the real economy.

The first 'official' phase of the Fund's involvement in FSS started in the aftermath of the Mexican crisis, and relates to the international mandate to include financial sector issues among the core areas of Fund surveillance. The second phase pertains to the efforts made to bring the coverage of financial sector issues '*up-to-par*' with the coverage of other 'traditional' core areas of surveillance, as well as to integrate financial analysis in the Fund's standard analytical macroeconomic framework.

As a result of the above process, the Fund has over the years significantly strengthened the financial analysis component of its multilateral and bilateral surveillance, including by progressively developing an analytical framework for financial sector assessments, which relies on a wide range of analytical tools and techniques that have been progressively improved and expanded by Fund staff. The Financial Sector Assessment Program (FSAP) is the Fund's flagship instrument for in-depth surveillance of a country's financial sector.[2]

Perhaps the most uncontroversial outcome of the Fund's gradual involvement in FSS is that financial sector issues are now considered among the core areas of Fund surveillance, as was most recently confirmed by the June 2007 *Decision on Bilateral Surveillance over Members' Policies* (IMF, 2007a).

Against this background, the Fund's coverage of financial sector issues is not without controversies: for example, some complain about risks of '*mission creep*' (Truman, 2006, pp. 33–36). But the important role played by the Fund in dealing with such issues is recognised even by those critics of the institution who advocate a narrowing of its mandate.

Notwithstanding the impressive effort put out by the Fund to strengthen the analysis of its member countries' financial systems and monitor global financial stability, the global crisis that has originated in the most sophisticated financial markets in the world has inevitably rekindled the question of why Fund surveillance (but hardly alone) was not fully effective in issuing strong and focused early warnings on the impending turmoil.

Although this outcome owes to a significant extent to serious gaps in the information needed for the assessment of financial system stability (IMF, 2009b, 2009c), which also undermined the role of market discipline, intense discussions are underway within the Fund to understand '*what went wrong*' and devise corrective measures (IMF, 2008c).

As demonstrated in the past by the Mexican and Asian crises, situations of global financial instability have historically been catalysts or accelerators of institutional changes, including for the international financial architecture and the role of the Fund and its surveillance activities. The current episode is no exception in this regard.[3]

The actions taken by the G-20 leaders, starting from their first November 2008 Summit in Washington, constitute an unprecedented effort of international policy cooperation to devise a coordinated approach so as to effectively address the global crisis and enhance the resilience of the international financial system.[4] In the area of coordination of macroeconomic policies, this effort reached its peak with the launch of the *Framework for Strong, Sustainable and Balanced Growth* and the attendant Mutual Assessment Process at the G-20 Summit in Pittsburgh in September 2009 (Group of Twenty, 2009c).

The G-20 leaders' London Declaration of April 2009 may well represent the beginning of a new phase of FSS. The Declaration first reaffirmed the role of surveillance as a core tool underpinning the renewed efforts to strengthen the global financial architecture; it called on the Fund to give "*greater attention to* ... [its member countries'] ... *financial sectors and better integrating the reviews with the joint IMF/World Bank financial sector assessment programs*" (Group of Twenty, 2009a). In the same vein, in its April 2009 Communiqué, the Fund's International Monetary and Financial Committee (IMFC)[5] explicitly underscored the importance of '*embedding financial sector surveillance more effectively as an element of the Article IV consultation* ... [as well as of] ... *integrating its results into the broader macroeconomic surveillance*' (IMF, 2009d). More recently, in April 2010 the IMFC called for '*concrete progress*' on these fronts.

All in all, by underscoring the importance of the linkages and spillovers across markets, sectors and national borders, the global crisis has pushed financial sector issues even more to the centre of Fund surveillance. At the same time, recent events have once again shown that the issuance of warnings on a country's risks and vulnerabilities is a necessary but not sufficient condition for the effectiveness of Fund surveillance. To put it differently, the quality of the Fund's analysis and policy advice (the *output* of surveillance) is something to a large extent separated from the impact (or "traction") of the Fund's warnings and recommendations on the actual policy choices made by policymakers (the *outcome* of surveillance). The full endorsement of the Fund's analysis and a timely follow-up on its advice on the part of country authorities, particularly those systemically important, are essential to ensure the effectiveness of surveillance, and preserve its nature as a public good that fosters economic and financial stability at the global level. At the same time, the crisis has raised the Fund's awareness that, for them to be followed by actual policy action, warnings have to be 'actionable', that is, specific enough about the impending risks and vulnerabilities and effectively communicated to policymakers.[6]

Against the backdrop of a string of new initiatives to enhance the global financial system and the Fund's early warning capabilities, the primary objective of this chapter is to provide a comprehensive survey of the Fund's involvement in the systematic surveillance over its members' financial systems. In order to put into a historical perspective the renewed efforts in this area, the chapter aims at illustrating the various conceptual and operational steps taken by the Fund along the process of placing more and more attention on the analysis of financial systems, including their regulatory and supervisory frameworks. This process culminated in the introduction, in 1999, of the FSAP and the Report on the Observation of Standards and Codes (ROSC).

It is important to underscore that while the focus of the chapter is on *bilateral* surveillance, the analysis of risks and vulnerabilities in the global economic and financial system is the purview of the Fund's *multilateral* surveillance, distiled in its flagship semi-annual publications, the World Economic Outlook (WEO) and the Global Financial Stability Report (GFSR). In this regard, it is imperative to emphasise that in a highly globalised world, bilateral and multilateral surveillance have to be increasingly integrated and conducted in synergy with each other; on the one hand, multilateral surveillance pays attention to potential spillover effects to the global economy arising from the weaknesses in the financial systems of systemically important countries highlighted by bilateral surveillance; on the other hand, risks and vulnerabilities to the global financial system identified by the GFSR help inform FSS at the country level.

This multilateral perspective that bilateral surveillance is increasingly taking on is arguably one of the main innovations in the Fund's FSS in recent years. It recognises that, in many countries, the effectiveness of bilateral FSS is weakened if it fails to take into account the developments in global markets and the related risks of cross-border spillovers. The dramatic evidence brought about by the crisis on the global effects of domestic policies has placed multilateral surveillance at the very centre of the discussions on strengthening the Fund's crisis prevention activities. This is set to represent one of the most lasting and consequential legacies of the crisis.

The rest of the chapter is structured as follows. Section 2 surveys the process of progressive inclusion of financial sector issues among the core areas of Fund surveillance following the Mexican and Asian crises. Section 3 focuses on the effort by the Fund to improve its toolkit for FSS, in the context of the initiatives undertaken by the international community in the late 1990s to strengthen the international financial architecture. Section 4 illustrates the efforts made to bring the coverage of financial sector issues 'up-to-par' with the coverage of other 'traditional' core areas of surveillance, with particular attention to the need for finding a balance between comprehensiveness and depth of such coverage. Section 5 points to the post-global crisis initiatives towards a more rigorous analysis of macro-financial linkages and a better integration between the FSAP and Article IV consultations. Section 6 presents some concluding remarks.

2. ADDING FINANCIAL SECTOR ISSUES TO THE CORE AREAS OF FUND SURVEILLANCE

The preliminary stage of the Fund's involvement in FSS before the Mexican and Asian crises was mainly related to the Fund's research and technical assistance activities within the process of monetary and financial deregulation embraced by several member countries. It was only following the Mexican and Asian crises that the Fund started a process to progressively include financial sectors issues among the core areas of its surveillance.

2.1. Financial Sector Surveillance before the 1994–1995 Mexican Crisis

Ever since the end-1980s and early-1990s, Fund staff had given considerable attention to the analysis of its member countries' financial markets, with special emphasis on the banking sector. However, it is important to note that the analysis of the financial sector, rather than through bilateral surveillance, was mainly carried out by Fund staff in the context of its multilateral surveillance and research activities, in connection with the process of growing integration of international capital markets.

This development had increased the potential for systemic risks and for large spillover effects of domestic macroeconomic policies. In fact, from the mid-1970s all through the 1980s several financial crises, affecting over two-thirds of the Fund's membership, showed that monetary and financial reforms can have potentially destabilising consequences if they are not properly sequenced and, equally important, well supported by an efficient regulatory framework and a sound market infrastructure.

Fund staff started looking systematically at some of these banking crises (Argentina, Chile, Malaysia, the Philippines, Spain, Thailand and Uruguay) with a view to better understand the contributing factors.[7] The methodology followed a case-by-case approach, aimed at identifying the underlying causes in the evolution of a number of macroeconomic and financial variables. The analysis was largely retrospective, focusing on explaining the events rather than on predicting future occurrences.

It is worth noting that such retrospective analysis of banking crises emphasised explicitly the linkages between macroeconomic conditions, financial sector reforms and financial crises. In fact, despite the diversity of the cases, as a crucial common feature of these studies was the early recognition of the importance of the so-called 'macro-financial linkages', that is the two-way relationship between the conditions of the financial sector and macroeconomic stability. A key lesson from these crises was that '*although macroeconomic instability can weaken the portfolio of financial institutions, weaknesses in the financial sector can have feedback effects on the economy, and seriously complicated adjustment and growth policies*' (Sundararajan & Baliño, 1991, p. 1).

The analysis of these important linkages, which are relevant not only for financial stability but also for the evolution of business cycles and long-term economic growth (Claessens, Kose, & Terrones, 2008), would explicitly inform the Fund's policy recommendations on how to strengthen the banking system.

As a result of the Fund's increasing attention to the soundness of its member countries' banking systems, the design of IMF-supported programmes and technical assistance started to progressively place more focus on such issues as banking legislation, regulation, supervision and the framework for crisis resolution (Enoch-Marston-Taylor, 2002).

2.2. Lessons from the Mexican Crisis: The February 1995 Biennial Review of Surveillance

It was only with the 1994–1995 Mexican crisis that the Fund began to draw more systematic attention to financial sector issues. The crisis marked the start of the efforts on the part of the international community towards strengthening the so-called 'international financial architecture'. In fact, over the following years, the Fund's involvement in FSS would result, to a significant degree, from the interactions between the inputs received from the international community, with a leading role played by the Group of Seven (G-7), and the advances made by the institution in analysing and monitoring the stability of financial systems.

The Halifax Summit of the G-7 in June 1995 (Group of Seven, 1995) was a defining moment for the Fund, on account of the decision by the G-7 to expand the scope of surveillance so as to include financial sector issues among its core areas. More generally, the Summit marked a crucial moment as to the contribution of the international community towards the objective of strengthening the international financial architecture. In fact, the Summit represented the beginning of the "*Architecture Exercise*" (Kenen, 2001) and started a new phase of activism by the G-7 in the governance of global finance.[8]

But even before Halifax, the February 1995 Biennial Review of Surveillance (IMF, 1995a) had provided the Fund's Executive Board with a first opportunity to discuss the evolving role of the Fund and the new challenges for surveillance in an environment of increased globalisation of financial markets. Moreover, a further analysis of the relationship between the financial crisis and the conduct of Fund surveillance was carried out a few months after the Biennial Surveillance Review, when the Board discussed an internal confidential document, the Whittome Report (IMF, 1995b), named after its author, Sir Alan Whittome, a former Fund director and counsellor. The objective of the report was to assess how the Fund had dealt with the evolving situation in Mexico, in the context of its surveillance, during the two years preceding the crisis.

While restating the detrimental role played by insufficient data provision, the Board was unanimous in considering that the Fund's relations with Mexico in the period leading up to the crisis illustrated '*some serious weaknesses*' in the way the institution had practiced its surveillance (IMF, 1995c).

The above discussions made the Fund aware that the goal of improving the scope and focus of surveillance would require innovations along two dimensions: countries and issues. On the first one, the Fund would have to be more selective, by concentrating its attention on systematically important countries, as well as those exposed to regional or market spillovers and swings in capital flows.

More importantly for the subject of this chapter, one of the most consequential conclusions of the 1995 review was that Fund surveillance, while giving the highest priority to its core issues, was directed to pay more attention, in a selective way, to capital market and financial sector developments. In particular, staff was asked to allow greater coverage of financial sector issues in Article IV consultations for those members where market issues were especially relevant; it was also encouraged to make better and more regular use, in its internal analyses, of the wide range of financial market data available outside the Fund.

All in all, the discussions on the 1995 Biennial Surveillance Review and the Whittome Report made it clear that surveillance would have to be strengthened if the Fund were to successfully detect financial crises at an early stage. Reaffirming that the globalisation of capital markets and the growth in cross-border flows did carry the potential for a rapid transmission of disturbances across markets and economies, the Board agreed that while the objectives of surveillance would remain unchanged, '*its practice* ... [needed] ... *to evolve so that the Fund can adequately meet new challenges*' (IMF, 1995d, p. 1). This would require a number of key ingredients, including improved procedures for surveillance and efforts to adapt the culture of the Fund to the challenging environment of increasingly globalised capital markets.

2.3. The March 1997 Biennial Review of Surveillance

The March 1997 Surveillance Review (IMF, 1997a, 1997b) provided the first opportunity to assess the progress in the Fund's coverage of financial sector issues against the '*soul searching*' innovations introduced by the previous 1995 Review, as a result of the expanded scope of Fund surveillance to promote sound banking systems.

The review underscored that Article IV reports had made significant efforts in covering a country's financial sector and related policies, with the scope and nature of the coverage differing depending on the state of development of the banking system and the magnitude of the problems. At the same time, the review admitted that some identifiable shortcomings remained, mostly related to the coverage of these issues and the candour of the language.

Firstly, it was pointed out that the coverage of financial sector issues in Article IV consultations appeared, in most cases, to have been of a backward-looking nature, with only rare examples of strong forward-looking judgments made by staff about the state of the financial system and the likelihood of a crisis. This hesitation, which hampered the capacity to detect potential risks at an early stage, was thought of as a reflection of the fact that the full magnitude of banking problems often emerges only with a lag.

Secondly, the language used in the reports made it difficult to infer the extent of the financial risks faced by a country, as staff reports, while in many cases pointing out problems in the financial sector, lacked sufficient differentiation for them to provide clear warnings of a potential crisis.

To remedy the above shortcomings, staff assessments of members' banking systems were directed to be more forward-looking, with a view to detecting emerging tensions at an early stage; besides, the use of a more candid language was deemed as necessary to differentiate country cases according to the relevance of the underlying problems in the financial sector.

Against this background, the gradual increase in the Fund's coverage of financial sector issues as a result of the Mexican crisis becomes clear if one looks at the changes in the content of the 1995 and 1997 Staff Operational Guidance Notes for surveillance. While the previous such notes had made no explicit references to the need of covering financial sector issues, the 1995 Operational Guidance Note (IMF, 1998e) stated that:

> where appropriate, reports will include assessments of financial market developments and their implications for macroeconomic policies and performance. (IMF, 2000a, p. 83)

The 1997 Staff Operational Guidance Note went even further, recommending that:

> reports should include assessments of financial market developments and prospects as well as of problems and policy issues in the banking and financial sector where they are of macroeconomic significance. (IMF, 2000a, p. 86)

2.4. Towards a Framework for Financial Stability

In the aftermath of the Mexican crisis, among the first responses to the calls from the international community and the Interim Committee for strengthening the Fund's FSS, in March 1996 the Board held a topical seminar on the linkages between banking system soundness and macroeconomic policy (IMF, 1996a).

Recognising that "*the condition of the financial sector had elicited little attention at the macroeconomic policy level until recently*" (IMF, 1996a, p. 1), the discussion built on a string of staff papers (Lindgren, Garcia, & Saal, 1996) grounded on the fact that three-fourths of the Fund's member countries, in the past 15 years, had experienced problems in their banking sectors. Apart from provoking negative economic consequences, these crises had displayed an increasingly international nature, with costly spillover effects for the global economy and the international financial systems.

A major difference between these more recent staff papers and those issued in the 1980s (discussed in Section 2.1) is a more forceful emphasis on the two-way linkages between macroeconomic policy and the stability of the banking system.

In particular, while recognising that bank soundness is first an issue for individual banks, it was pointed out that it is more likely to become systemic when unsoundness is due to macroeconomic conditions, because all banks are simultaneously exposed to those same risky conditions (Lindgren et al., 1996, p. 39). Moreover, weaknesses in the banking system can not only have important real effects for the economy, but can also constrain the formulation and effectiveness of macroeconomic policies and policy instruments. In this regard, one of the main conclusions of staff's analyses was that '*the promotion of a sound banking system represents a legitimate policy objective, as well as a* constraint, *in the design of stabilization policies and structural reforms*' (Lindgren et al., 1996, p. 161).

The Board seminar stood out for two reasons: it allowed staff to sketch out for the first time the main elements of a framework for sound banking, and it provided the opportunity of making suggestions on how to integrate banking stability issues into Fund surveillance, the design of Fund-supported programmes and the Fund's technical assistance.

The framework for sound banking outlined by staff was comprised of two main pillars: a supportive institutional environment and a network of control structures.

The institutional environment was defined by the structural characteristics of the banking industry, notably an appropriate degree of competition, and a legal system that facilitates the enforcement of financial contracts.

The network of control structures was meant to consist of three components: the internal governance of individual banks (which staff singled out as the most important ingredient for sound banking), market discipline and the official regulation and supervision at the domestic and international levels. Notably, an appropriate regulatory and supervisory framework was deemed by staff as critical to compensate for failures in internal governance and market discipline (IMF, 1996a, p. 14).

As far as the role of the Fund was concerned, there was an unambiguous awareness that '*the Fund's surveillance role clearly* … [could not] … *be as a banking supervisor, but as an advisor on policy*' (IMF, 1996a, p. 22). Accordingly, along with Fund-supported programmes and technical assistance, surveillance should be used as a vehicle to strengthen banking supervision and the financial systems across the Fund's membership, as well as to promote the adoption, at the international level, of standards and best practices for financial sector reporting, regulation and supervision.[9]

A crucial step in this regard was taken by the Interim Committee at its meeting of September 1996, with the adoption of the Declaration on '*Partnership for Sustainable Global Growth*' (IMF, 1996b). The Declaration acknowledged that Fund surveillance was an integral part of the strategy, and explicitly underscored the role of the Fund in the promotion of sound banking systems and strong prudential regulatory and supervisory frameworks.

2.4.1. A Framework for Financial Stability

While the March 1996 seminar provided a basis for a broader discussion on the role of the Fund in FSS, it was clear that additional work needed to be done '*to develop a set of indicators and an operational framework that*…[would]…*help Fund staff identify and evaluate current and prospective conditions of a banking system and their interface with macroeconomic and structural policy*' (IMF, 1996a, p. 23).

The 1997 Surveillance Review took the discussion one step forward as it pointed out that '*the approach to increased Fund involvement* ... [in financial sector issues] ... *would benefit from clearer specification*' (IMF, 1997a, p. 30).

Fund staff was thus well aware that, in order to effectively enhance the Fund's coverage of financial sector issues, it would be useful to have a framework of general principles, characteristics and best practices of sound and stable financial systems, based on a generally agreed body of knowledge and experience. This framework would help make Fund surveillance as effective, consistent and transparent as possible, and it would also allow staff to effectively discuss appropriate remedial measures with member countries' authorities.

Against this background, it is perhaps no coincidence that on the very same day of the discussion on the 1997 Surveillance Review, the Board also discussed the paper '*Toward a Framework for Sound Banking*', which marked a signpost for the Fund's involvement in financial sector issues.[10]

The starting point of the framework was the recognition that national authorities have the primary responsibility for putting in place the necessary preconditions for a sound financial sector, notably macroeconomic stability and an appropriate regulatory and supervisory framework. At the same time, it was clearly acknowledged that the Fund and the international community also had significant roles to play, since banking crises could have macroeconomic consequences of a systemic nature, and could generate significant regional and international spillovers.

The Fund's actions to support the initiatives of many of its country members to promote the stability and soundness of their banking and financial systems were thus seen as part of a concerted global effort undertaken by international financial institutions and 'standard setters'[11] to complement national initiatives and ultimately reduce systemic risks.

The Executive Board explicitly stated that the Fund's contribution to strengthen its member countries' financial systems should primarily take place '*by enhancing the Fund's surveillance to cover developments in their banking systems, particularly where they exhibit problems with potential for generating serious macroeconomic disturbances*' (IMF, 1998a, p. 5).

In particular, two reasons were deemed to make surveillance a major instrument at the Fund's disposal for promoting financial sector soundness: on the one hand, the continuous nature of surveillance made it well suited to monitor and support the efforts by the member countries' national authorities to improve the stability of their banking systems; on the other hand, the conditionality applied to the use of Fund resources could be used to ensure that weaknesses in these banking systems would be dealt with in a timely and effective fashion.

Overall, the proposed framework for financial stability would provide the Fund's bilateral surveillance with a broad guide for analysing banking systems and identifying key areas of vulnerability. As far as multilateral surveillance was concerned, a consistent application of the framework to systemically important countries could help recognise risks that have a potential for spilling over regionally or internationally. It is also worth mentioning that the availability of a framework for sound banking was explicitly intended to be instrumental in ensuring that macroeconomic risks were adequately reflected in prudential supervision and regulation.

However, two important caveats were in order. Firstly, staff correctly pointed out that '*in the end … Fund surveillance will not be able to certify financial systems as "sound" or even reliably identify all instances in which difficulties in the financial sector may become a major macroeconomic concern*' (IMF, 1998a, p. 4).

Secondly, the proposed framework should clearly not be seen as '*a checklist of issues to be explored in every Article IV consultation, nor is it a diagnostic tool that could allow an assessment of the financial position of individual banking systems*' (IMF, 1998a, p. 4).

Rather, the objectives of the framework were to increase the awareness of vulnerabilities in the financial sector and their potential consequences, as well as to recommend appropriate remedial measures. Ultimately, the framework would provide '*guidance for the direction in which supervisory structures and financial system reforms should progress*' (IMF, 1998a, p. 4).

For its part, the Board set a few conditions for developing and implementing the framework for the Fund's surveillance on the financial sector.

Firstly, the Board cautioned that due regard be paid to the circumstances of individual member countries. Secondly, coverage of financial sector issues in Fund surveillance would need to follow a selective approach, along three dimensions: concentration on the banking system, since banks are usually the dominant type of financial intermediary and are at the core of the domestic payments system; initial focus on countries in which banking sector issues were likely to have significant domestic macroeconomic concerns or systemic implications for the international financial system; and focus on the linkages between the safety and soundness of the banking and financial system and macroeconomic policies and developments.

Finally, the framework to strengthen Fund surveillance of the banking sector should be developed in a cost-effective manner, notably by seeking cooperation with other multilateral institutions and drawing on their expertise. In particular, indispensable input into the formulation of the framework should come from the standard setters, in particular the Basel Committee on Banking Supervision.

These standard setters had been formulating a set of best practices, principles and guidelines that experience had shown to be particularly important for creating an environment and an incentive system conducive to a sound financial system.

As a result, it was clear that one of the major synergies of the Fund's increased focus on banking and financial sector issues would be represented by its contribution to the dissemination of such standards and best practices, their adaptation to the varying circumstances of its wider membership and ultimately to the international harmonisation of financial policies and practices.

2.5. Lessons from the Asian Crisis: The March 1998 Review

Two and a half years after the Mexican crisis, another consequential event shook the international financial community. Following the devaluation of the Thai baht on 2 July 1997, the speed and magnitude with which the Asian crisis spread across the region took virtually all observers by surprise.

At the height of the Asian crisis in March 1998, the Fund carried out a preliminary internal review of its surveillance in the affected countries, in particular Thailand, Indonesia and Korea (IMF, 1998b). This work was conducted using as a benchmark the lessons from the Mexican crisis identified in the 1995 Surveillance Review and the Whittome Report, namely the provision of information and data availability,[12] the continuity, clarity, and candour of surveillance, and its focus.

On continuity, while admitting that more continuous contact in the first half of the 1990s might have improved the staff's ability to understand fully economic developments in the region and enhanced the Fund's effectiveness in alerting the authorities on the potential risks, the Review underscored that by 1995–1996 several Southeast Asian emerging market economies had been the subject of fairly intensive scrutiny by the Fund in both bilateral and multilateral surveillance. Moreover, as staff concerns mounted, the frequency of contacts increased including at the level of management and senior staff.

On focus, the review candidly recognised that '... *with hindsight, it is probably fair to say that in some countries Fund staff might have focused more on financial sector developments in 1993–95*' (IMF, 1998b, p. 32).

This less than intensive coverage of financial sector issues in the first half of the 1990s was attributed to the fact that Fund surveillance over Southeast

Asian economies was mostly concerned about their macroeconomic policy mix, notably the risk of overheating and the extent to which the mounting current account deficits reflected excess demand pressures.

At the same time, the review also emphasised that the post-Mexico expanded scope of Fund surveillance had resulted in an increasingly more intensive coverage of financial sector developments. In fact, the vulnerability of the financial sector and the risks it posed for the economy had increasingly represented the focus of Article IV consultations with some countries hit by the crisis, and the Fund had called for a strengthening of banking supervision and regulation (IMF, 1998b, p. 16).

The review, however, also recognised that '*Fund missions were sometimes not fully aware of the scale of these financial sector problems*' (IMF, 1998b, p. 3). This relatively lower attention to financial sector issues in some Article IV discussions was accounted for by a combination of factors.

Firstly, and again, a lack of full information or unwillingness on the part of some authorities to engage in an open dialogue on the issues '… [hampered] … *financial sector analysis* … [and] … *may have led to an underestimation of the extent of financial sector vulnerability*' (IMF, 1998b, p. 4). This tempered staff's ability to better convey to the authorities the potential risks posed by current policies. Secondly, financial sector issues had grown in complexity in parallel with the rapid expansion of international capital markets, but staff analysis had been weighed down by a shortage of human capital with financial sector expertise on some Fund missions. Finally, Fund surveillance had to cover an increasingly broad spectrum of topics with the authorities, and the intensified focus on financial sector issues had only started in 1995.

Despite the incorporation into surveillance practices of many of the lessons drawn from the Mexican episode, the Asian crisis had revealed several areas in which further efforts were required in order to ensure a fuller integration of financial sector issues into Article IV surveillance. One of the key lessons drawn was the need for '*a closer examination of the functioning of the financial sector* … [in member countries] … *at a much more detailed level than was previously required*' (IMF, 1998b, p. 36).

To this end, the Fund's FSS was explicitly tasked with encouraging the membership to take four key steps: improving prudential regulation and supervision of the banking system; developing domestic capital markets; improving the efficiency of the financial sector (including through the adoption of transparent accounting standards for corporations and efficient domestic bankruptcy codes); and limiting the financial sector safety nets (IMF, 1998b, Box 5, p. 37).

3. FINANCIAL SECTOR SURVEILLANCE IN THE AFTERMATH OF THE ASIAN CRISIS

The role played by financial vulnerabilities in precipitating the Asian crises and the significant economic costs suffered by the affected countries laid the groundwork for an unprecedented effort on the part of the international community to enhance the international financial architecture. The year 1998 set itself apart in that it marked the moment when broad agreement was reached on a number of key aspects of the overall strategy put in place at the international level, and on the supporting role of the Fund.

In this context, it is worth emphasising that Fund surveillance took on a crucial function, as it came to represent the mechanism through which the results of many of the initiatives to reinforce the international financial system would '*come together… and filter*' into the Fund's assessment of individual countries and, more generally, of the global economy (IMF, 2000a).

To intensify surveillance on its member countries' financial sectors, the Fund undertook a two-pronged strategy. On the one hand, it became all the more important to strengthen cooperation with other international organisations, notably the World Bank and various standard setters, to draw on their specific expertise and ensure that each focused on its area of comparative advantage (IMF, 1997c).

On the other hand, it was necessary to develop new instruments and analytical tools to deal more properly with financial sector issues. A first step to this end was the issuance, in June 1998, of the Guidance Note for the Monitoring of Financial Systems under Article IV Surveillance (IMF, 1998e), which explicitly directed staff to focus on the linkages between the safety and soundness of the banking and financial system and macro-economic performance.

Subsequently, in 1999 the Fund and the World Bank jointly launched the Standards and Codes Initiative (Group of Ten, 1997; IMF, 1998d), aimed at assessing the degree of implementation of internationally recognised standards and codes in three areas recognised by the two institutions as relevant to the effective functioning of their members' economic and financial systems: policy transparency, financial sector regulation and supervision, and market integrity.

One of the central ideas underlying the adoption of these standards and codes was that by comparing information on potential borrowers (both public and private) against agreed benchmarks, market participants would be able to better assess and differentiate country risks; in turn, this would lead to better-informed lending and investment decisions, thereby reducing the risk of financial distress and contagion.[13]

The important role played by the Fund in the Initiative, both in setting and assessing standards in the core areas where it has relevant expertise, reflected the awareness on the part of the international community that the mere development of such standards could not be sufficient to improve the stability and efficiency of international capital markets if standards were not reflected in the actual practices (Interim Committee, IMF, 1998c). In other terms, while market incentives could play a major role in encouraging practices that were consistent with international standards, it was clear that the public sector had to play a part in strengthening the incentives to adopt such standards.[14]

The effort to improve the Fund's toolkit to monitor a country's financial system culminated in the introduction of the joint IMF–World Bank FSAP.

3.1. The Financial Sector Assessment Program

The FSAP, introduced in May 1999 and jointly administered with the World Bank, represents the most relevant step towards an in-depth involvement of the Fund in FSS (IMF, 2009f, 2009g; IEO, 2006).

As previously mentioned, the Mexican and Asian crises provided crucial impetus to develop the FSAP, in so far as they contributed to the recognition that despite the increasing attention paid by Article IV missions on financial sector issues, it was '*not feasible to expect them to do the broad and in-depth assessments*' (IMF, 1999b, p. 1) of Fund members' financial systems that were being requested by the international community to improve crisis prevention.

The origin of the FSAP dates back to the G-7 Birmingham Summit of May 1998, where a report from the G-7 finance ministers identified a '*gap*' in the international system with respect to the surveillance of countries' financial supervisory and regulatory systems (Group of Seven, 1998a). On the premise that enhanced surveillance in this area would help encourage national authorities to meet international standards and reduce financial risk, G-7 ministers saw '*an urgent need for a system of multilateral surveillance of national financial, supervisory, and regulatory systems*'.

In the October 1998 Declaration, the G-7 finance ministers and central bank governors took a step forward by establishing '*a process for strengthened financial sector surveillance ... for monitoring and promoting stability in the international financial system*' (Group of Seven, 1998b). This process was explicitly based on the Fund's regular Article IV surveillance.

For its part, the Fund's Executive Board first discussed the launch of the FSAP on a pilot basis in May 1999 (IMF, 1999b). The programme was built heavily on the diagnostic studies of Fund members' financial systems carried out by staff over the previous two decades, in the context of the technical assistance provided by the Monetary and Exchange Affairs Department (MAE), as well as during Article IV consultations, multilateral surveillance and adjustment programmes.

Against this background, the Fund's MAE and the Financial Sector Practice of the World Bank, coordinated by the joint Financial Sector Liaison Committee, developed a format, based on the 1998 Guidance Note, for the Financial Sector Stability Assessment (FSSA), the document that summarises the FSAP findings and is used as input into Article IV consultations.

In its April 2000 Communiqué, the newly renamed International Monetary and Financial Committee (IMFC), the former Interim Committee, provided high-level political commitment and placed the FSAP at the centre of the Fund's surveillance on the financial sector. The IMFC stated that FSAPs would serve '*as the primary basis for enhancing the Fund's monitoring of the financial sector in the context of Article IV surveillance*' (IMF, 2000e).

3.1.1. Objectives and Scope of the Programme

The FSAP aims to strengthen the monitoring and promote the soundness of Fund members' financial system; it rests on the idea that the identification of risks and vulnerabilities in the financial sector, and the implementation of corrective actions at an early stage, will enhance these systems' resilience to a crisis.

In particular, the FSAP provides a coherent and comprehensive framework for pursuing four fundamental objectives: identifying vulnerabilities of financial systems and determining how key sources of risk are being managed; ascertaining the system's developmental and technical assistance needs; assessing the observance and implementation of relevant international standards and codes; and helping develop and prioritise appropriate policy responses.

The FSAP contributes to these objectives by providing the national authorities with a comprehensive and in-depth assessment of their financial systems (the previously mentioned FSSA). To this end, the FSAP builds on a number of complementary analytical tools developed within the Fund in order to improve the quality and effectiveness of its assessments and to ensure consistent treatment among countries.[15]

One of the most significant features of the FSAP is that it is a cooperative international effort, which enhances its legitimacy and provides an important element of 'peer review', especially in the assessments of the observance of international standards and codes of good practices.

Being an ambitious and complex exercise, some features of the FSAP continue to be the object of debate, most notably because they may have prevented the programme from fully delivering its potential. Two such features are the comprehensive nature of the FSAP and its relationship with Article IV surveillance.[16]

3.1.2. The Comprehensive Nature of the Programme

Ever since the pilot phase, a distinctive characteristic of the FSAP has been a sort of tension between its broadly 'one-size-fits-all' nature, on the one side, and the necessary flexibility to adapt the programme to country-specific factors, on the other. This tension is mainly a direct consequence of two opposing forces: the comprehensive nature of the programme, which covers issues related to both the near-term stability of the financial system and its long-term developmental priorities; and the need for greater selectivity and prioritisation in the scope of the assessments, given the intense resource requirements that the exercise places on the Bank and the Fund, as well as on the national authorities.

To mitigate the risk of a 'one-size-fits-all' effect, staff developed '*an approach to financial system assessment that is broadly consistent across countries, while allowing for differences in emphasis to reflect different country circumstances*' (IMF, 1999b, p. 2). To this end, in developing the initial template for FSAP assessments, staff made it clear that '*not every element of the template will be assessed in every case, nor will any of the elements be applied mechanically*' (IMF, 1999b, p. 2).

Despite these guidelines, FSAP assessments during the pilot phase turned out to be generally broad in scope, and resulted in rather long reports covering all the main areas that could be included in a 'full' FSAP assessment.

It soon became clear that this type of assessment would not be practicable in every country. Selectivity and prioritization were thus required for the FSAP process to be cost-effective for all the interested parties. Accordingly, it was understood that the scope of the assessment could vary so as to cover '*those issues and institutional features which are judged to be most important for financial sector stability and development*' (IMF, 2000g, p. 14).

At the same time, however, staff was aware that this selectivity principle should be applied with caution and should not be taken too far so as to preserve the integrity of the exercise. In fact, staff pointed out that '*there will always be a need to maintain a fairly broad scope for* ... [FSAP assessments] ... *to ensure adequate consideration of the particular circumstances of individual countries and to avoid possible 'cherry picking' of the various components of an FSAP assessment that would undermine the quality of the assessment as a whole*' (IMF, 2000g, pp. 14–15).

Progresses towards more selectivity and prioritization of the scope of the FSAP were made on the occasion of the 2003 and 2005 Reviews of the programme (IMF, 2003a, 2005a). In particular, as FSAP '*updates*' (as opposed to '*full*' assessments) began to account for the bulk of the FSAP work, the scope and modalities of such updates have been more clearly defined by mandating that they contain a '*minimum, core element*', namely a stock-taking exercise assessing financial sector developments and progress in implementing FSAP recommendations.

3.1.3. The FSAP as an Input in Article IV Surveillance

Ever since its inception, there was a clear awareness that follow-up work on the FSAP findings and recommendations would be a critical task for the programme to effectively help strengthen a country's financial system. This was clearly underscored by staff in noting that the assessments conducted under the FSAP are '*diagnostic tools, not ends in themselves*' (IMF, 2000g, p. 17).

The results of these assessments were indeed meant to form the basis for the adoption, on the part of national authorities, of measures to re-address the identified vulnerabilities and developmental needs of their financial systems. Follow-ups, largely in the form of technical assistance, were also viewed as essential to maintain the momentum for financial sector reforms and development.

It is important to underline that the issue of the FSAP's follow-up work takes on a dual dimension, being related to both the continuity of the exercise over the years and its role as an input in Article IV surveillance.

On the first dimension, given the voluntary nature of the programme and the limited frequency with which full assessments could be undertaken, Fund staff was aware that in order to ensure continuity and maintain adequate monitoring of financial systems, it would be necessary to develop mechanisms for regularly updating the initial '*baseline*' FSAP assessment. To this end, the Board agreed that '*focused updates*' or '*reassessments*', together with work undertaken during Article IV consultation missions and off-site monitoring of a country's financial sector, would provide '*a framework that can supplement the FSAP effectively, and thus enable more continuous and effective financial sector surveillance*' (IMF, 2003b).

In particular, FSAP updates would cover key issues of systemic relevance identified during previous FSAP work, so as to take into account recent developments and new measures adopted by the authorities.

The second dimension is even more important as it relates to the fact that a crucial objective, perhaps *the* objective, of FSAP reports is to feed into and help strengthen the Fund's Article IV surveillance process, which is mandatory for all member countries.

The role of the FSAP as an input to surveillance has been a crucial feature of the FSAP since its inception. The programme was indeed seen as '*a vehicle to bring the linkages between financial sector soundness and macroeconomic developments to the core of both institutions' work*' (IMF, 2000c, p. 3).

To this end, the FSAP envisaged a procedure, centred on the FSSA, explicitly aimed at including FSAP findings in Article IV consultation discussions. FSSA reports were indeed seen to offer a major analytical advantage to make surveillance more effective, in that they placed the assessment of a financial system's risks and vulnerabilities in a broader macroeconomic and macro-prudential context than had traditionally been the case.

4. FUND SURVEILLANCE UNDER AN EXPANDED SCOPE

The string of initiatives put forward by the international community in the aftermath of the Mexican and Asian crises had resulted not only in the expansion, but also in the increased complexity of the Fund's surveillance mandate.

The growing involvement of the Fund in somewhat uncharted territories associated with the more structured and systematic analysis of financial systems had eventually raised the need to take stock of the ways in which the new activities had been integrated with the institution's more traditional tasks.

To this end, in June 1998 the Board commissioned an evaluation of Fund surveillance under Article IV to a group of independent experts chaired by John Crow, a former Governor of the Bank of Canada.

To a large extent, the Crow Report (IMF, 1999c) marked the start of the second phase of the Fund's involvement in FSS, in that some of its findings contributed to lay the groundwork for the efforts put out by the institution to make progress on two inter-related issues that are being debated still today: how to more closely integrate financial and macroeconomic analyses in bilateral surveillance, and how to bring the coverage of the new areas of surveillance '*up-to-par*' with that of the more traditional ones.

4.1. External Evaluation of Fund Surveillance: The Crow Report

With regard to bilateral surveillance, one of the main findings of the 'Crow Report' was that, although the quality of Fund analysis and advice in areas of core expertise (namely exchange rate policies and the associated macroeconomic framework) was generally highly rated, views were more critical in such areas as FSS and structural issues.

To explain the different opinions on the quality of the Fund's advice, the report pointed to a '*fairly broad sense among interviewees that surveillance had become more difficult to do well, largely because of the expanded mandate to cover capital account and financial sector issues*' (IMF, 1999c, p. 37).

On the Fund's increased involvement in the surveillance of the financial sector, the report found a general agreement that '*having the assessment of financial systems and their vulnerabilities become an integral part of Article IV consultations was highly appropriate*' (IMF, 1999c, p. 39). Importantly, Fund's involvement in FSS was explicitly justified by '*the close linkage – in both directions – between domestic financial sector crises and exchange rate/balance of payments crises*' (IMF, 1999c, p. 67).

More generally, it was acknowledged that the expansion of Fund surveillance into financial sector and capital account issues was inevitable given the increased inter-connectedness between such issues and the Fund's traditional analysis of macroeconomic and external sector issues.

A point worth noting is the Report's recognition that '*improving financial sector surveillance was identified as an important task as long ago as 1995, and the pace of improvement has been slow*' (IMF, 1999c, p. 67).

Similar to the findings of the March 1998 Review, this outcome was in part ascribed to a shortage of expertise in the financial area. In fact, it was clearly emphasised that, up to that point, the expansion of the scope of Fund surveillance to cover financial sector issues had faced difficulties of practical implementation, as '*area departments have tended to treat this remit as another add-on, which they do not have the time and expertise to fulfill in more than a pro forma way, especially if countries drag their heels in providing information*' (IMF, 1999c, p. 40).

Against this background, the Report acknowledged that the FSAP, soon to be undertaken by the Fund, would help improve FSS. To this end, two important conditions were identified: the Fund would need to be able to draw on staff with financial sector expertise; and the financial sector analysis carried out in the context of the FSAP would have to be properly integrated into the Article IV process.

4.2. The Macroeconomic Relevance Test

The discussion on the Crow Report by the Board represented the first occasion to address a question that by that time had become crucial for the effectiveness of Fund surveillance under its expanded scope: how to strike the proper balance between the need for surveillance to cover a wider range of issues, while at the same time ensuring that individual Article IV consultations retain a clear focus on the key concerns in each country: in other terms, a balance between the breadth of coverage and the depth of analysis.

Maintaining a suitable focus of surveillance had come to constitute a challenge for the Fund in light of the string of initiatives undertaken by the international community, in the aftermath of the Mexican and Asian crises, to strengthen the international financial architecture. As a result of such initiatives, the issues identified in Fund surveillance as core had changed over time '*from a narrow focus on exchange rate policy and the balance of payments and attendant monetary and fiscal policies to greater emphasis on capital account, financial sector, nonfinancial structural issues, and cross-country influences*' (IMF, 1999c, p. 4).

Accordingly, the key recommendation of the Report was to focus bilateral surveillance as much as possible on the Fund's core areas, namely exchange-rate policies and the directly associated macroeconomic policies, including financial sector and capital account issues. Analysis outside these core areas should be undertaken '*only if directly relevant to a particular case*' (IMF, 1999c, p. 14).[17]

To address the potential tension between coverage and focus of surveillance, the Crow Report suggested what would soon come to be known as the '*macroeconomic relevance test*': the criterion for addressing non-core issues in Fund surveillance should be '*the extent to which they actively and directly impinge upon the effective conduct of macroeconomic policy*' (IMF, 1999c, p. 63).

In discussing the Crow Report, the Board agreed on the need to revisit the definition of the core areas of surveillance. To sharpen its focus, a number of directors favoured a country-by-country approach whereby '*coverage of issues could differ depending on the circumstances of a particular country, but the staff would be expected to present a clear case for the consideration of any particular set of noncore issues as relevant to the core concerns of the Fund*' (IMF, 1999c, p. 4).

This approach was further refined in the context of the March 2000 and the March 2002 Surveillance Reviews: while falling short of drawing a clearer distinction between core and non-core issues, it was agreed that the twin objectives of comprehensiveness and focus could only be achieved by ensuring that '*selectivity of coverage is moulded to country-specific circumstances*' (IMF, 2002c).

Specifically, the coverage of surveillance should be guided by the following three principles:

- firstly, staff would need to be well informed on the range of issues within the expanded scope of surveillance;
- secondly, within this range of issues, the selection of topics to be covered in discussions with members should derive from the application of the 'macroeconomic relevance test', so that non-core issues would be covered '*only when these have a direct and sizeable influence on macroeconomic developments*' (IMF, 2000b); and
- thirdly, within these selected topics, priority should be given to the matters at the apex of the '*hierarchy of concerns*' relevant for Fund surveillance, namely external sustainability and vulnerability to balance of payments or currency crises; sustainable growth and the policies to achieve it; and for systemically important countries, conditions and policies affecting the global and regional economic outlook.

4.3. Bringing Coverage of Financial Sector Issues 'Up-to-Par' with Coverage of Other Core Areas of Surveillance

To a large extent, the Crow Report marked the beginning of a new phase for the Fund's involvement in FSS. The Report had indeed helped to make it all the more clear that the expansion of surveillance to systematically cover financial sector issues was just a necessary but not sufficient condition to improve its effectiveness. This latter depended more fundamentally on how the expanded scope of surveillance would actually be implemented and translated into effective operational practices during Article IV consultations.

The existence of a sort of '*implementation gap*' was clearly acknowledged in the Crow Report in underlying that FSS still constituted a sort of '*add-on*' to the more traditional macroeconomic analysis that was at the core of Article IV consultations.

In order to close the gap between the strategic expansion of the Fund's surveillance agenda and the actual implementation of such an objective, the Crow Report pointed to the need to address '*something of a disconnect (or at least a very long lag) between the broad policy directions outlined by the Board in review and policy discussions, and actual practice in day-to-day surveillance work, particularly bilateral consultations*' (IMF, 1999b, p. 64).

It was thus no surprise that, for surveillance to become more effective, the Report recommended that the next internal review devote more attention to '*measuring in some detail (by topic and country) the extent to which the specific operational guidance that has been put forward on behalf of the Board is actually followed in Fund consultation reports, and, equally important, if not, why not*' (IMF, 1999b, p. 64).

To this end, the 2000 and 2002 Surveillance Reviews (IMF, 2000a, 2002a, 2002b) looked explicitly and systematically at the coverage of selected core issues in Fund surveillance, with a view to verifying the application of the 'macroeconomic relevance test'. More generally, these reviews assessed the way surveillance was evolving on account of the range of initiatives adopted to strengthen the international financial architecture.

The reviews confirmed that the conduct of surveillance under its broadened framework had presented important implementation challenges for the Fund along three dimensions: the focus of surveillance, the quality and depth of its analysis, and the integration of the framework's different components into an '*overall coherent assessment*' (IMF, 2002a, p. 15) of a country's situation.

With particular reference to FSS, staff emphasised that, by that time, this activity had taken on a more comprehensive nature, since it had been extended to cover the banking sector, non-bank financial institutions, and organised financial markets. Coverage of financial sector issues was found to have deepened considerably, with a clear trend towards greater discussion of such issues as banking sector soundness and the adequacy of a country's prudential and supervisory frameworks. Furthermore, coverage of the linkages between the financial sector and other sectors was recognised as a key development since the Asian crisis.

However, the coverage of financial sector issues was found to show substantial variation across countries (IMF, 2002b, p. 40).

To be sure, it is worth noting that the unevenness in the coverage of financial sector issues was to some extent hardly surprising, and even desirable, as it could partly be attributed to differences in the intensity of concerns about the vulnerabilities of a country's financial sector. Such unevenness was thus just reflecting well-established guidelines mandating that coverage of financial sector issues should naturally vary according to country-specific circumstances, notably the potential interactions between macroeconomic and financial sector developments.

Overall, the 2000 and 2002 Surveillance Reviews were useful to increase the awareness that ensuring a proper focus of surveillance was only one ingredient for it to be effective: in fact, an equally important role had to be played by the ability to maintain satisfactory depth and quality of analysis.

Against this background, two main results of the reviews stood out.

Firstly, while the coverage of financial sector issues had become '*a standard element of Fund surveillance*' (IMF, 2002a, p. 10), the reviews highlighted the important implications in terms of resources and expertise that derived from the broader framework of surveillance. In particular, limited information, expertise or resources had indeed frequently constituted a constraint for an adequate, uniform and in-depth treatment of the new areas of surveillance.

Secondly, a country's participation in the FSAP played a crucial role in accounting for the unevenness in the coverage of financial sector issues (IMF, 2002a, p. 12). The FSAP had proved itself as the tool capable of offering the most extensive coverage of the financial sector, as well as of providing key diagnostics and recommendations. These findings were directly attributed to its explicit focus on the linkages between financial system developments and macroeconomic performance.

4.3.1. Integrating the Elements of the Broader Framework of Surveillance

One of the most relevant outcomes of the 2002 Surveillance Review was its explicit recognition of the operational consequences on the conduct of surveillance arising from the Fund's expanded agenda. In fact, the review proved itself remarkably predictive in stressing the importance of the third component, other than focus and depth, underpinning the effectiveness of surveillance, namely the proper integration of the 'new' elements of the broadened framework for surveillance into the 'traditional' coverage of macroeconomic and structural policies.

The review clearly underscored that the quality of surveillance ultimately depended on the ability to reach such integration: '*covering the various elements of the broadened framework does not automatically amount to a well-integrated assessment of a country's macroeconomic conditions, vulnerabilities and policy challenges. Proper integration of these elements would seem essential if the broadened framework is to strengthen surveillance*' (IMF, 2002b, p. 44).

In other terms, reaching this integration would be key to achieve a '*unified and coherent overall assessment*' of a country's macroeconomic situation, crisis vulnerabilities and the resulting policy challenges.

Against this background, the review underlined that the integration between old and new core areas of surveillance had showed mixed results.

The review recognised that, in many other countries, such integration had not been fully achieved yet. In particular, and in striking similarity to what the Crow Report had found three years earlier, in a significant number of countries, coverage of financial sector issues was still largely considered as an '*add-on to a well integrated macroeconomic analysis*' (IMF, 2002b, p. 44). The main factor to account for such a finding was deemed to be the inadequacy of the information available in the absence of FSAP participation (by the time of the review, FSAPs had been completed for only 14 percent of the Fund's membership).

Overall, the findings of the 2002 Review laid the groundwork for one of the most important lessons drawn by the Fund, namely that '*the quality of Fund surveillance under the broadened framework will primarily depend on the quality of coverage of its elements. Strengthening the coverage of "new" elements will thus likely be critical for the overall effectiveness of surveillance*' (IMF, 2002b, p. 49).

This lesson stands out as it makes clear that the need to ensure an adequate coverage of financial sector issues was not only important in and of itself, but it was also crucial to the objective of reaching a 'unified and coherent overall assessment' of a country's situation. In fact, an inadequate coverage of financial sector issues (as well as of other 'new' issues in Fund surveillance) could carry 'negative externalities', as it could prevent obtaining the targeted integration among all of the individual components of surveillance. Ultimately, it became even clearer that the effectiveness of surveillance would depend not only on the coverage of financial sector issues, but also on the ability to integrate these 'new' issues with the traditional core areas of surveillance.

The 2002 Review had thus made it all the more evident that if FSS were to be treated as part of the core of the Fund's surveillance activities, the quality of treatment would have to measure up to the quality of coverage of other core areas, notably macroeconomic policies and exchange rate issues.

This important finding led the Executive Board to agree on the need to bring the coverage of financial sector issues '*up-to-par*' with coverage of other core areas of surveillance. To this end, the 2002 Operational Guidance Note that followed the Review explicitly underscored that '*the relevant benchmark for the quality of* … [financial sector] … *coverage should be that of other core areas*' (IMF, 2002d).

However, two years later, the 2004 Surveillance Review, while acknowledging some improvements, recognised that, in many cases, financial sector coverage in Article IV reports '*was not yet at par with coverage in other main areas*' (IMF, 2004, p. 16), and had indeed varied substantially across countries.

Against this background, in order to make further progress, the Board took the important step of setting out four '*monitorable strategic priority objectives*' that would function as a guide to staff for the next surveillance review. Enhancing FSS was one such priority objectives.

4.3.2. Operational Consequences of the 2002 and 2004 Reviews

The main results of the 2002 and 2004 Surveillance Reviews were particularly noteworthy as they more forcefully pointed out that the objective of bringing the coverage of financial sector issues up-to-par with that of other core areas of surveillance carried relevant resource and expertise implications. In particular, the unevenness in the coverage of financial sector issues was explicitly recognised as a reflection, inter alia, of '*resources and expertise brought to bear on the analysis of these issues*' (IMF, 2002b, p. 40).

As we have seen throughout the chapter, the availability of adequate financial expertise had been recognised as a crucial precondition for the Fund's successful involvement in FSS ever since the expansion of the scope of surveillance in the aftermath of the Mexican crisis.

Against this background, the 2000 and 2002 Surveillance Reviews made the Fund more aware that a comprehensive analysis of a member country's financial sector was '*rarely achieved without the in-depth analysis afforded by prior participation in the FSAP* … [and indeed was] … *generally not possible solely with the staff resources devoted to regular Article IV consultations*' (IMF, 2002b, p. 47), particularly for non-bank financial institutions and organised financial markets.

Given the constraints on the number of FSAPs that could be concluded in a given year, the Fund engaged in devising alternative means to strengthen FSS in cases where: (i) a member had not participated in an FSAP or (ii) '*significant developments*' had occurred since FSAP participation.

To this end, in April 2002 the Board approved a remedial measure consisting of reinforcing Article IV mission teams from area departments[18] by deploying staff with financial sector expertise from such functional departments as Monetary and Exchange Affairs (renamed Monetary and

Financial Systems Department – MFD since May 2003) or the International Capital Market – ICM.

This measure has subsequently proved itself as the single most effective measure to improve the coverage of financial sector issues in bilateral surveillance. Both the 2004 Review (IMF, 2004) and the more recent 2008 Review of Surveillance (IMF, 2008c) have indeed acknowledged that enhanced quality and depth of coverage of financial sector issues were evident for those Article IV consultations that had benefited from substantial input from financial experts of functional departments. These consultations resulted in richer analyses of financial sector risks, vulnerabilities and transmission channels, which underpinned more specific policy advice.

It is worth noting that the shortage of adequate technical expertise within surveillance teams carries potential negative consequences not only for the quality of the coverage of financial sector issues in Article IV consultations, but also for the usefulness of the FSAP as an input to such consultations.

This risk was well-emphasised by the Fund's Independent Evaluation Office (IEO) in its 2006 review of the FSAP. In fact, the availability of adequate technical expertise within surveillance teams was found to be '*the major constraint on the effectiveness of follow-up work on FSAP recommendations when complex issues were involved*' (IEO, 2006, p. 4). In particular, the IEO warned that in many cases where financial expertise was lacking, the process of tracking the implementation of FSAP recommendations was to some extent compromised, as this process had taken '*a "checklist" approach of enumerating measures rather than appraising whether underlying vulnerabilities have been addressed*' (IEO, 2006, p. 4).

The decision to deploy financial experts from functional departments within Article IV mission teams, and to allow these experts to train staff in area departments, was a further recognition of the important relationship between the quality of FSS and, inter alia, some aspects of the Fund's internal organization, notably the allocation of financial sector expertise among the Fund's departments.

Over the years, the Fund has taken various actions to ensure that the institution develop the necessary expertise to effectively carry out its expanded involvement in financial sector issues and keep pace with the globalisation and sophistication of international finance. In this context, management has even sought the advice of external experts regarding the effectiveness of the Fund's internal organisation of the work on financial sector and capital markets.[19]

More recently, on account of the Fund's tighter budget, financial sector expertise is intended to be used strategically, by following a 'risk-based' approach, centred on the criteria of systemic or regional importance, relevance of vulnerabilities and importance of financial development issues for macroeconomic or external stability (IMF, 2008c).

The initiatives undertaken to further improve FSS as a result of the lessons drawn from the global crisis, including the innovations introduced in the FSAP, have further highlighted the difficult tradeoffs in the allocation of the Fund's financial sector expertise in a constrained budget environment (IMF, 2009e, p. 22, 2009f, p. 42).

5. FINANCIAL SECTOR SURVEILLANCE IN THE AFTERMATH OF THE GLOBAL CRISIS

The importance of further strengthening the Fund's analysis of the financial sector was reiterated in the Strategic Review, launched in mid-2004, and in the subsequent Medium-Term Strategy unveiled in September 2005 (IMF, 2005e, 2006).

Further attention was devoted to two long-standing and interconnected issues that set the stage for the current discussion on how to further improve FSS: the need for effectively following-up on the FSAP findings and recommendations in the context of Article IV consultations; and the fuller integration of financial sector issues into the Fund's traditional macroeconomic framework of surveillance.

The global financial turmoil that broke out in August 2007 has shown, inter alia, that these issues are yet to be fully addressed. They, thus, represent the priorities of the Fund's ongoing work on bilateral FSS and the analysis of macro-financial linkages, which is being informed by the lessons drawn from the crisis.

5.1. Integrating Financial Sector Issues into Macroeconomic Surveillance: The 2007 Financial Sector Task Force

New important initiatives to improve the coverage of financial sector issues and their integration into Article IV consultations were adopted to follow-up on the recommendations by the Review Group set up by the managing director in June 2005 (IMF, 2005b). The ensuing 'McDonough Report' acknowledged the advances made by the Fund in integrating financial and capital market issues into its traditional macro activities, but also noted that several components of the effort remained a work in progress.[20]

The most significant of such initiatives was the establishment of a *Financial Sector Task Force*, explicitly directed at developing a '*broad organising framework*' to facilitate the integration of financial sector issues into the macroeconomic analysis.

It should be noted that Fund staff had already outlined the main features of a framework for financial stability analysis on the occasion of the review of the Financial Soundness Indicators in May 2003. The underlying idea was that a better integration of the different dimensions of FSS would be instrumental in more effectively assessing the impact of shocks to the financial system. In the staff's view (IMF, 2003c), this objective should involve three phases: the identification of the risk of a shock hitting the financial sector, the assessment of the vulnerability of the financial sector to these shocks and their potential impact on capital adequacy, and the analysis of macro-financial linkages to obtain an indication of the effect on macroeconomic conditions and debt sustainability, if the intermediation capacity of the financial sector were impaired. The features of this framework were subsequently expanded by building on the experience developed in the context of the FSAP, and were elaborated in the joint IMF-World Bank *Handbook on Financial Sector Assessment*, published in September 2005 (IMF, 2005d).

The handbook presented an overall analytical framework, consisting of a wide range of tools and techniques, whose primary objective is to achieve an integrated analysis of two topical issues: the stability and the development of the financial system.

Against this background, the work of the *Financial Sector Task Force* set itself apart in underscoring that a closer integration of financial sector analysis into the macroeconomic template that supports Article IV surveillance is not only a matter of content (i.e. better analytical tools), but also of more effective internal processes.

On content, the task force's main contribution was the setting forth of four issues that should be addressed in Article IV surveillance (IMF, 2008d, p. 55): the channels of interaction between the macroeconomy and financial markets, that is macro-financial linkages; the role of the financial sector in initiating, amplifying or muting disturbances to a country's economic system, and the possibility of potential spillovers from systemically important countries to the global economy; the role of the financial sector in facilitating or retarding growth; and a risk assessment of the potential for a financial crisis.

The circulation in April 2009 of an internal FSS Guidance Note (IMF, 2009e, Box 1, p. 7) marked an important progress towards making operational the organising framework for bilateral FSS called for by the 2007 Task Force.

With a view to assess both the likelihood and impact of risks to financial stability, the Note provides specific guidance on how to assess possible sources of risks, describes qualitative and quantitative diagnostic tools to assess various types of risks, and points out possible policy recommendations depending on country circumstances.

On the ways to improve the internal process, the task force emphasised that FSS should be '*a continuous process*' for systemically or regionally important countries, and for countries at risk. To this end, it was emphasised that cooperation and exchange of information among Fund's departments should play a relevant role.

In this regard, the recently announced establishment of an interdepartmental *Financial Surveillance Group* (IMF, 2009e, p. 14) is a further recognition of the importance of inter-departmental cooperation, notably to bridge the various vehicles for surveillance and integrate multilateral and cross-country risk analyses into the bilateral surveillance carried out by area departments.

5.2. The 2008 Triennial Surveillance Review

In October 2008, the Triennial Surveillance Review (TSR) provided the Fund with a timely opportunity for discussing the state of surveillance in the face of the most severe financial crisis since the Great Depression (IMF, 2008c, 2008d). Specific attention was also paid to monitoring the progress towards meeting the four priority objectives set out by the 2004 Surveillance Review.

To this end, the TSR carried out a thorough assessment of bilateral surveillance at the outbreak (August 2007) of what would develop into the global financial crisis. Four countries (the United States, the United Kingdom, Switzerland and Germany) were used as case studies to evaluate the ability of surveillance to identify risks and vulnerabilities.

Such an assessment pointed out that bilateral surveillance had been successful in identifying most vulnerabilities and risks that had subsequently contributed to the above crisis, along with potential spillover channels. Many institutional aspects had also been correctly diagnosed.

However, it was recognised that surveillance made some 'wrong calls', and did not make out the aggregate implications of the individually identified risks. Perhaps more importantly, the Fund, together with most observers, had underestimated or not assessed quantitatively the scale and impact of such risks materializing, and this had hindered the ability to call for remedial policy actions.

These outcomes owed in part to the fact that surveillance had overlooked some specific factors, deemed as 'known unknowns', such as the lack of information on exposures to mortgage-related assets and the complexity of some of these securities. Communication was also at fault, as surveillance had tended to obscure the degree of concerns about the identified risks through reassuring headline messages. Finally, the inter-bank money market freeze, perhaps the hallmark of the financial crisis, was missed as it came as an 'unthinkable' surprise (IMF, 2008d, p. 80).

A crucial point was the clear recognition that the biggest challenges facing surveillance related to the analysis and identification of macro-financial linkages. In fact, both the review of staff reports, and surveys with stakeholders and mission chiefs had confirmed that '*surveillance is significantly better at assessing financial sector vulnerabilities than at analyzing real-financial risk transmission channels*' (IMF, 2008d, p. 42). In particular, it was the assessment of the impact of financial sector events on the real economy that was singled out as the most important test for the Fund.

In this regard, it is important to note that the analysis and identification of macro-financial linkages pose relevant conceptual and empirical challenges, as, for example, many of these linkages can operate in both directions. As a result, designing a uniform framework to monitor and assess these linkages has proven a complex task.[21] The TSR itself acknowledged that the lack of a satisfactory theoretical model and insufficient empirical work had both contributed to make the analysis of macro-financial linkages even more difficult.

One of the main outcomes of the 2008 TSR is that FSS and macro-financial linkages were included among the four areas deserving priority attention by surveillance in the period ahead (along with risk assessment, multilateral perspective and analysis of exchange rates and external stability risks). These areas have thus been included as operational priorities in the first *Statement on Surveillance Priorities* (SSP), adopted by the Board in October 2008 and revised in September 2009.[22]

5.3. The FSAP After 10 Years

The FSAP is by now the Fund's key instrument for in-depth surveillance of a country's financial sector.[23]

Following its inception a decade ago, successive reviews of the FSAP have underscored that the exercise has significantly enhanced the Fund's comprehension of financial sector issues and risks that are essential to surveillance.

In its 2006 review, the Fund's IEO judged the voluntary exercise as '*a distinct improvement in the IMF's ability to conduct financial sector surveillance and in understanding the important interlinkages between financial sector vulnerabilities and macroeconomic stability*' (IEO, 2006, p. 1).[24]

Against this background, the discussion sparked by the global financial crisis on the lessons for Fund surveillance has inevitably involved the FSAP as well. Recognising that the FSAP should continue to be a key element of the strategy for integrating financial sector work into Fund surveillance, the October 2008 IMFC Communiqué (IMF, 2008f) called for '*a reshaped FSAP that is more flexible, better integrated with the Fund's core surveillance mandate, and embraces regional perspectives*'. The commitment of all G-20 members, at the November 2008 Summit, to undertake an FSAP report provided further stimulus to review the programme.[25]

A reassessment of the scope and modalities of the exercise was first necessary in order to overcome some known shortcomings. In fact, despite past efforts to streamline the exercise and better tailor its assessments to country circumstances, the key characteristics of the FSAP represent its limitations as a surveillance instrument: on the one hand, its voluntary nature constrains the scope for prioritization; on the other hand, the requirement that assessments be relatively comprehensive, coupled with tighter resource constraints at the Fund, accounts for the low frequency of FSAP missions.

Furthermore, some dynamics of the global crisis have made it clear that the FSAP needs to be adapted to a more complex financial environment than the one in which the programme was framed. Perhaps more important, it is imperative for the FSAP to properly reflect the relevant lessons drawn from the financial crisis, which point to an expanded coverage of such issues as cross-border aspects of financial markets spillovers, assessment of macro-prudential risks and the financial sector's supervisory and regulatory framework.

5.3.1. Reshaping the FSAP

In September 2009, the Executive Board reviewed the FSAP after 10 years since its inception (IMF, 2009f), with a view to improve the continuity of surveillance and the frequency and focus of FSAP assessments.

The starting point was the recognition that '*the long time gap between FSAP updates is a major handicap for the analysis of financial sector vulnerabilities and macro-financial linkages*' (IMF, 2009f, p. 22).

The Board thus endorsed some major changes to the programme, most notably the introduction of optional 'modular' FSAP updates intended to help '*fill the gap*' between the two ends of the spectrum of bilateral FSS: standard Article IV consultations and full-fledged FSAP assessments.

This option allows the Fund and the Bank to launch, respectively, stand-alone 'stability' and 'developmental' assessment modules that provide distinct, albeit complementary perspectives on a country's financial sector. Importantly, a major objective of the modular option is to '*eliminate the rigidity inherent in the current 'one-size-update-fits-all' approach and allow* ... [the Fund and the Bank] ... *to respond more flexibly to country circumstances*...[and]...*priorities*' (IMF, 2009f, p. 32).

Against the backdrop of the several initiatives aimed at strengthening the crisis prevention capabilities of the FSAP and, more generally, of the Fund's FSS, it is imperative to emphasise once again that the issuance of warnings on a country's risks and vulnerabilities is a necessary, but not sufficient condition for the effectiveness of Fund surveillance.

The 2009 Review itself included a further recognition of this limitation, by making it clear that '*the FSAP's focus on identifying underlying vulnerabilities could not, by itself, address them. Identification of vulnerabilities could only lead to a solution if the country authorities decided to implement the recommendations of the FSAP*' (IMF, 2009f, p. 18).

More broadly, the crisis has also clearly shown that more complex and increasingly interconnected global financial landscapes demand that the FSAP first adapt its assessments in a crucial respect, namely the need to take on a deeper cross-border perspective. In fact, currently the FSAP '*does not assess vulnerabilities associated with problems abroad ... and ... vulnerabilities associated with a global crisis*' (IMF, 2009g, p. 23).

In particular, FSAPs need to focus more squarely on cross-border financial linkages that propagate and amplify the transmission of financial shocks (IMF, 2009f, p. 37).

As a necessary complement to this adaptation effort, FSAPs have to be more systematically informed by the vehicles of the Fund's multilateral surveillance, including the new Early Warning Exercise (EWE) conducted jointly with the newly established Financial Stability Board (FSB)[26] (IMF, 2009l).

5.4. The Joint IMF–FSB Early Warning Exercise

A major lesson of the crisis is that effective surveillance of global stability depends on an enhanced understanding of macro-systemic and financial sector risks and their linkages.

The multifaceted and complex nature of the crisis has required new policy development work in several fields, with contributions from many actors according to their expertise and comparative advantages. To this end, closer collaboration between the Fund and specialised institutions (international bodies and standard setters) is key, and is one of the building blocks of a macro-prudential perspective in Fund surveillance (IMF, 2010f).

A distinctive feature of the international community's response to the crisis is the enhanced cooperation between the Fund and the FSB.[27] This cooperation builds on the complementary roles played by the two institutions and their respective comparative advantages, which improve each institution's ability to achieve its mandate. The Fund complements the FSB's work with its own macro-financial and cross-country perspective. The FSB coordinates and monitors progress in strengthening regulatory and supervisory frameworks.

At the Washington Summit of November 2008, the G-20 leaders called on the Fund and the FSB to jointly conduct EWEs. A characteristic strength of the exercise is that it provides an integrated perspective on risks and vulnerabilities by effectively combining the Fund's economic and macro-financial analysis with the FSB's specialisation on financial system regulatory and supervisory issues.

Crucially, the early warning exercise is meant to be an integral part of Fund surveillance, along many dimensions. Firstly, the findings of the Fund's 'traditional' vehicles of multilateral surveillance, the WEO and GFSR are critical inputs to the EWE.

Furthermore, the exercise is intended to complement these vehicles in a precise way. In fact, the WEO/GFSR analysis incorporates directly those risks to the 'baseline' outlook that are sufficiently probable that they need to be taken into account explicitly in setting policy. In contrast, the EWE, focuses on 'tail' risks, that are low-probability, high-impact risks to the global outlook that may not be relevant for policy-setting at present, but that could become important and would result in policy recommendations different from those generated by the baseline scenarios presented in the WEO and the GFSR (Lipsky, 2010). Finally, the Fund's multilateral and bilateral surveillance is the mechanism to follow-up on the EWE's warnings and policy recommendations (IMF, 2009l).

The EWE aims to identify systemic 'tail' risks by using a broad array of quantitative and qualitative tools and techniques, as well as market information. Moreover, the exercise tries to assess the impact of such risks and vulnerabilities with a view to promote coordinated remedial actions, and evaluates the possible consequences of policy inactions.

5.5. Modernising Financial Sector Surveillance and the Fund's Mandate

The impact of the global crisis on Fund surveillance has been as far-reaching as to encompass the broader role of the Fund in the post-crisis international financial architecture. A major development in this regard was the October 2009 IMFC's call on the Fund, during the Annual Meetings in Istanbul, '*to review its mandate to cover the full range of macroeconomic and financial sector policies that bear on global stability*' (IMF, 2009j).

Accordingly, in February and April 2010, the Executive Board began discussions on how to strengthen the Fund's mandate to better equip the institution to safeguard global stability (IMF, 2010a–c).

The starting point of the discussion was the recognition of the potential systemic impact of domestic economic policies in a world of increased financial interconnectedness among countries. In fact, a key lesson of the crisis is that the larger risks in a globalised world are systemic in nature. This requires the Fund to adopt a more macroprudential perspective that complements the traditional emphasis of surveillance on risks at the country level, notably by paying more attention on cross-border, cross-sector financial interlinkages.

The Fund recognised that in order to reinforce its crisis prevention abilities and identify the risks to the stability of the system as a whole, the multilateral component of surveillance had to be a priority. To this end, in April and September 2010 the Board gave initial consideration to the possibility of a formal Multilateral Surveillance Decision (MSD) adopted by the Executive Board, with a view to '*create clear expectations for both the Fund and each member regarding the conduct of multilateral surveillance, provision of data, analysis of spillovers, and direct engagement with policymakers.*' (IMF, 2010d, p. 5).

The need for a MSD reflects the view that lack of clarity on the scope and modalities of the Fund's multilateral surveillance may have contributed in and of itself to gaps in the coverage and traction of surveillance. The Board will return to this question at the time of this year's Triennial Review of Surveillance and the Review of the 2007 Bilateral Surveillance Decision.

To bridge the gap between multilateral and bilateral surveillance and better analyse the cross-border implications of policies of systemically important countries, in September 2010 the Board approved the introduction, on a trial basis, of 'spillover reports' on five main economies (the United States, Euro Area, China, Japan and the United Kingdom).

Spillover reports intend to achieve a more open and pointed discussion of cross-border effects of domestic policies than has been possible to date in either the bilateral or multilateral context. A key feature of these reports is that they capture the views of both the country originating spillovers and those affected by them. As a result, the most promising quality of such spillover reports lies in their potential to raise the members' awareness of their responsibility towards preserving global financial stability. In so doing, they may increase the traction of surveillance by strengthening the incentives to conduct an effective peer review process.

In this regard, the increased focus of surveillance on the cross-country dimension had been emphasised as a way for the institution to gain traction with country authorities in the recent IEO evaluation on the Fund's interactions with member countries (IEO, 2010, p. 36).

5.6. Integrating FSAP Assessments into Article IV Surveillance

While emphasising the need for a broader cross-country perspective in surveillance in order to capture risks to systemic stability, a common theme of the recent discussions on strengthening the Fund's crisis prevention capabilities is that bilateral surveillance remains a cornerstone of the institution's activities.

Even in the aftermath of the global crisis, the quest for improving FSS bilateral surveillance still relies on embedding financial sector surveillance more effectively in Article IV consultations, and integrating its results into the Fund's broader macroeconomic surveillance.

As noted throughout the chapter, these are long-standing issues, and a brief recollection is thus warranted.

The importance of using bilateral surveillance to follow-up, in the context of a full macroeconomic analysis, on the issues revealed by the FSAP had already been pointed out at the inception of the programme. In fact, given the complementarities between the two vehicles, it was immediately apparent that the success of the FSAP would depend on an effective exploitation of the synergies with the Article IV consultation process.

Fund staff understood that while the FSAP would provide a framework for a comprehensive, in-depth assessment of a country's financial sector, the exercise had limitations as a surveillance instrument, because it is voluntary in nature and low in frequency (updates now take place every six to seven years on average). There was thus awareness that, given its characteristics (and the resource constraints faced by the Fund), the FSAP could not be the only tool for monitoring the financial sector: it had to be necessarily complemented by additional surveillance tools to make this monitoring more continuous and effective.

As a result, it was apparent that Article IV consultations would have to function as the '*primary instrument*' (IMF, 2004, p. 16) of systematic and ongoing bilateral FSS, on account of their mandatory nature and high frequency, taking place usually on an annual basis. In turn, Article IV consultations displayed their own shortcoming, as their coverage of financial sector issues is necessarily more limited than the FSAP, being these issues dealt with only if they are relevant for external stability.

This consequential trade-off made it all the more clear that a closer integration of the FSAP findings and recommendations into the Article IV consultation process was essential in order to deliver on the original objective of making the FSAP '*the preferred vehicle for conducting financial sector assessments as input to Fund surveillance*' (IMF, 2000h).

The importance of ensuring such integration was effectively illustrated by the Fund's IEO in its 2006 review of the programme. Strengthening the links between the FSAP and Fund surveillance was needed not only to assess a country's overall macro-financial stability and potential vulnerabilities, but also to formulate '*policy recommendations that are set in a coherent framework combining macroeconomic and financial sector analysis*' (IEO, 2006, p. 41).

This integration has not been fully achieved yet, notwithstanding the considerable efforts exerted by the Fund. In its review, the IEO considered the FSAP to be at a critical crossroads, and indicated that '*financial stability assessments have not yet been fully 'mainstreamed' as a regular part of IMF surveillance*' (IEO, 2006, p. 1).

Importantly, the IEO underscored that this lack of integration could not only diminish the effectiveness of the FSAP exercise, but also carry negative consequences for the overall quality of FSS. In fact, given that Article IV reports constitute the focus of Board discussions, '*failure to adequately integrate FSAP results into those reports has tended to lower the prominence of financial sector issues, even when the FSSA did spell out the issues*' (IEO, 2006, p. 27).

The IEO evaluation was also noteworthy for having assessed a crucial determinant of the impact of the FSAP, namely the extent of the follow-up work. The main finding was that the quality of the FSAP proved to be crucial in determining the intensity of the follow-up work in ensuing Article IV consultations: in fact, effective follow-ups had proved to be more difficult in cases where the FSAP lacked a clear sense of priorities among the different measures proposed in strengthening a country's financial sector (IEO, 2006, p. 28).

The global financial crisis has provided additional reasons to further advance the integration of FSAP findings into Article IV consultations, and, more generally, to adopt a more risk-based approach to financial sector surveillance.

In a move of '*far-reaching consequence*' (IMF, 2010e), in September 2010 the Board approved the proposal to make stability assessments under the FSAP a regular and mandatory part of Article IV surveillance for a group of 25 members whose financial sectors have been determined to be systemically important on the basis of a methodology based on two criteria (size and interconnectedness).

These assessments cover the 'core elements' of modular stability assessments defined in the 2009 Review of the FSAP (IMF, 2009f), namely: (i) the source, probability and impact of risks to macro-financial stability, (ii) the financial stability framework and (iii) capacity to manage and resolve financial crises.

Mandatory financial stability assessments are expected to help ensure closer integration of financial sector surveillance with the Article IV process through their higher frequency of no more than five years, compared to the current average gap between FSAP updates of six to seven years. As in the past, delivering on this objective is strictly dependant on the ability of effectively following-up in Article IV consultations on the findings of these assessments.

6. CONCLUDING REMARKS

Before the start of the global crisis in July 2007, it was not infrequent to hear distinguished economists, opinion makers and politicians asking whether the huge expansion of private capital markets and the absence of major sovereign crises would greatly diminish the relevance and role of the Fund.

The most severe global crisis since the Great Depression has provided a clear answer to this question. As in previous crisis episodes, the Fund is playing the role of 'firefighter', while the international financial community is involved in an intense debate on how to strengthen the international financial architecture and enhance crisis prevention.

Surveillance is the mainstay of the Fund's crisis prevention activities. The Fund's ability to effectively cover financial sector issues, and to ensure that its findings are fully integrated into the macroeconomic analysis, is critical to the quality, credibility and impact of the institution's policy advice to member countries.

The actual conduct of Fund surveillance by definition develops in parallel with the evolution of financial markets: smooth and tranquil periods are occasionally, and often abruptly, shaken by unexpected financial turbulences that reveal previously unknown (or underestimated) sources of risks and vulnerabilities. These usually lead to reconsider well-established views on how financial markets function and the role of market discipline, and to update regulatory and supervisory practices.

Following the Mexican and Asian crises, where financial factors played a major role, and in response to the calls from the international community, the Fund began undertaking a major effort to deepen its involvement in FSS. The explicit objective was to improve crisis prevention, notably by better understanding the so-called 'macro-financial linkages', the two-way transmission channels between the stability of financial markets and a country's macroeconomic performance.

This chapter analysed comprehensively, and put into a historical perspective, the expansion of the scope of Fund surveillance beyond the traditional macroeconomic areas, as well as the evolution of such process in the face of major financial events.

The Fund's involvement in FSS can be broadly broken down into a preliminary stage and two main phases.

The preliminary stage, dating back to the 1980s and early 1990s, was mainly related to the process of monetary and financial deregulation embraced by several countries, a process that was marked by financial crises affecting over two-thirds of the Fund's membership. In those years, the Fund's coverage of financial sector issues had not so much to do with surveillance, but rather with the institution's research and technical assistance activities.

This preliminary stage was characterised by an increasing awareness that financial liberalisation is generally followed by rapid credit growth and excessive risk-taking if reforms are not tempered by appropriate prudential supervision and regulation. The main lesson learned by the Fund, and by the international community at large, was that financial deregulation needs to be carefully sequenced and supported by appropriate regulatory frameworks and solid market infrastructures.

The first 'official' phase of FSS spans from the Mexican crisis (1994–1995) to the Asian crises (1997–1998) and the crises of the late-1990s (Russia and Brazil). All these events showed in the most dramatic way the unintended consequences of financial globalisation, characterised by swift increases in risk aversion, sudden stops or capital reversals and episodes of 'pure' contagion, that is, the involvement of seemingly unrelated and often sound countries.

The main characteristic of this first phase was the expansion of the scope of Fund surveillance to include financial sector issues among its core areas. This important step took place in parallel with the work done by the institution to follow-up on the calls from the international community to improve several aspects of the global financial architecture, such as transparency, data provision and the adoption of international standards and codes. Given the Fund's unique position as a universal institution and its comparative advantages, surveillance became the vehicle used to engage its membership in the reform process to strengthen the stability of financial systems, culminated in 1999 with the launch of the FSAP, jointly administered with the World Bank.

The second phase of the Fund's involvement in FSS relates to the efforts made to bring the coverage of financial sector issues 'up-to-par' with the coverage of other 'traditional' core areas of surveillance. This phase more clearly highlighted the resource implications of FSS, and was characterised by two main inter-related objectives: improving the coverage of financial sector issues in Article IV consultations and strengthening the links between FSAP findings and the Article IV process.

As a result of the expansion of the scope of Fund surveillance, financial sector issues are now considered among the core areas of surveillance, along with the more traditional monetary, fiscal and exchange-rate policies.

This expansion has often forced Fund staff to rethink a well-established macroeconomic analytical framework, and to extend it towards somewhat less familiar territories; these involve issues such as financial stability, the appropriateness of a country's regulatory and supervisory structure and a more systematic analysis of macro-financial linkages, including their potential for cross-country spillovers.

Fund staff has scored an array of successes in developing such an analytical framework, as well as in enriching it over the years with a wide range of tools and techniques to support FSS.

However, the recent crisis, with its origin in some of the largest and most sophisticated financial markets in the world, its almost unprecedented size and global nature, has demonstrated that despite the long-standing emphasis on the analysis of macro-financial linkages and the advancement made by the institution towards monitoring the stability of the international financial system, the Fund's framework for macro-financial surveillance needs to be further improved (IMF, 2008a).

While many risks and vulnerabilities were identified, often repeatedly, Fund surveillance in the run-up to the global crisis has fallen short of meeting the expectations of the institution's stakeholders; discussions are taking place to understand what inhibited surveillance from being fully effective in its crisis prevention role.

Overall, although information gaps, including on what has come to be known as the 'shadow banking system', seriously undermined the Fund's assessment capacity, a consensus is emerging that the warnings provided before the crisis by official bodies, including the Fund, were generally insufficiently specific to attract the attention of policy makers and, more importantly, to induce them to act (IMF, 2009a, p. 2).

This outcome may owe in part to some features of the Fund's governance structure, as well as to the challenging task of clearly communicating to the public the Fund's assessments of financial risks and vulnerabilities without undermining confidence and triggering adverse market reactions. Moreover, the Fund inherently faces a delicate balancing act between its dual role as both confidential advisor to country authorities and public overseer on economic and financial risks.[28]

Against this background, it seems difficult at first glance to escape a sense of *déjà vu* with regard to the long-standing process of Fund's involvement in FSS.

As we have seen throughout the chapter, macro-financial linkages have been the object of the Fund's analysis as early as the beginning of the 1990s. The FSAP was put in place in 1999 with the explicit goal of bringing the linkages between financial sector soundness and macroeconomic developments to the core of Fund surveillance. The various reviews of the programme soon underscored the need for better integrating the FSAP into the Article IV process in order to ensure that bilateral surveillance follows-up on the programme's recommendations.

And yet, the 2008 TSR has once again included among the areas deserving the highest priority in the period ahead a more rigorous analysis of macro-financial linkages, and a better integration of financial sector surveillance into macroeconomic analysis, including by leveraging FSAP findings in Article IV reports.

Ever since the expansion of the scope of Fund surveillance, in the aftermath of the Mexican crisis, to cover financial sector issues, successive reviews have emphasised both the progresses made in this area and the scope for further improvements. These reviews addressed several recurring themes, with the Board endorsing more focused analyses, more candid assessments by staff of a country's risks and vulnerabilities, a better integration of financial sector analysis, including FSAP recommendations, into the Article IV consultation process and stronger cooperation with other international bodies.

The recurrence of these themes was also noted outside the Fund. One of the main findings of the external evaluation of surveillance (the Crow Report), released back in 1999, was that '*improving financial sector surveillance was identified as an important task as long ago as 1995, and the pace of improvement has been slow*' (IMF, 1999c, p. 67).

Against this background, we believe that our chapter helps reconcile the above-mentioned sense of déjà vu with the significant progresses made by the Fund since the Mexican crisis in covering financial sector issues. Our comprehensive analysis of the various steps taken by the Fund towards this goal demonstrates that this impression captures, to a large extent, only the appearance of things. More fundamentally, this impression overlooks the fact that the expansion of the scope of Fund surveillance to cover financial sector issues has made it an even more complex process, one that poses various types of challenges for the actual conduct of surveillance and its effectiveness.

As shown in the chapter, in the face of a string of initiatives taken by the international community to strengthen the international financial architecture in the aftermath of the Mexican and Asian crises, Fund surveillance took on the crucial function of providing the mechanism through which the results of many of the above initiatives would '*come together ... and filter*' into the Fund's assessments of individual countries and, more generally, of the global economy (IMF, 2000a).

In this context, we believe it is fair to compare the Fund's efforts of improving FSS to a process of targeting an upwards-moving object.[29] In fact, the expansion of the scope of Fund surveillance has taken place against the background of an increasingly complex global financial landscape, continued financial innovations and rapid expansion in cross-border capital flows. These developments have all raised the frontier of FSS.

This has not only required new practices, tools and expertise to cover issues outside of the Fund's traditional focus on macroeconomics, but has also created a need for effectively integrating the various components of surveillance into a consistent and unified summary assessment of a country's economic and financial situation. Staff soon became aware that the expansion of the Fund's coverage of financial sector issues would add a new dimension to surveillance, namely the need to integrate financial analysis into the macroeconomic framework used for Article IV consultations.

This integration has proved to be a major challenge to the efforts of advancing the effectiveness of surveillance, one that has been made more difficult by some characteristics and procedural mechanisms inherent in a complex institution. In this regard, one needs to clearly underscore that the objective of improving FSS is all but just introducing new tools and techniques, as one should not underestimate the necessary institutional, organisational and cultural changes that must complement the above goal, as well as its relevant resource implications. Moreover, FSS suffers from the lack of agreement on a unified theoretical model and analytical framework on how to integrate financial and macroeconomic analyses.

All in all, our study shows that while the recurrence of some surveillance themes may give the impression of a somewhat faltering process, the Fund's operations and policies are actually in a process of '*continuous reform*', much like the Fund's Executive Board is in a 'continuous session'. We are thus sympathetic to the view that the quest for making the Fund a centre of excellence in financial sector analysis is '*more as a marathon than a sprint*' (McDonough Report, IMF, 2005b).

The global crisis, and the ensuing international response to reform many components of the global financial system, is most likely marking the start of a new phase of Fund's involvement in FSS, for a number of reasons.

Firstly, the crisis has made policy makers more aware of old and new forms of systemic risks posed by a build up of financial vulnerabilities, and this has resulted in increased political support for initiatives aimed at safeguarding the stability of financial markets. The G-20 leaders' commitment to undertake an FSAP assessment is a major example in this regard. In the same vein, the members of the FSB, in committing themselves to pursue the maintenance of financial stability, agreed to undergo periodic '*peer reviews*' (Group of Twenty, 2009a).

Secondly, the role played by financial markets and products in triggering a global recession calls for deeper analyses of the adverse dynamics potentially triggered by such markets and products, as well as of their repercussions to the real economy. Macro-financial linkages have thus been placed even more to the centre of Fund surveillance, signalling the need for further expanding the scope of FSS and making it a more continuous process. This awareness has paved the way for reaching consensus on an issue that had proved as very controversial before the crisis: the introduction of mandatory stability assessments under the FSAP for countries with systemically important financial systems, approved by the Executive Board on September 2010.

Thirdly, the fact that a global crisis has been initiated by rising insolvencies in an almost obscure segment of the U.S. housing markets has made it clear that, in an increasingly interconnected and globalised international financial system, surveillance has to pay more attention to the cross-country dimension of domestic policies. This goal has a dual dimension: on the one side, it highlights the importance of deepening the multilateral perspective of *bilateral* surveillance, most notably to take into account the developments in global markets and the risks of cross-border spillovers. Bilateral surveillance is to continue to be one of the mainstays of the Fund's crisis prevention activities, as the ability to detect cross-border spillovers is to a significant extent a by-product of a thorough analysis of risks, vulnerabilities and policies at the domestic level. On the other side, it is undeniable that to better capture the systemic aspects of country policies, a renewed emphasis on *multilateral* surveillance is clearly in order. This latter development is set to become one of the most lasting and consequential legacies of the crisis, whose importance is epitomised by the initial consideration given by the Executive Board to the need for a formal MSD.

Fourthly, the peculiar dynamics of the turmoil and its systemic nature call for the development of crisis prevention instruments that complement and integrate the Fund's macro-prudential analysis with a regulatory and supervisory perspective on risks and vulnerabilities in the financial system. International cooperation is once again crucial to this end. A major development in this regard is the EWE that the Fund has started conducting in cooperation with the FSB, following-up on the calls from the G-20 leaders and the IMFC.

This exercise may help address one of the most relevant lessons drawn from the global crisis, namely that identifying potential risks and vulnerabilities is a necessary but not sufficient condition for surveillance to be effective. In fact, warnings should be issued with appropriate specificity and candour, avoiding overly hedged language, for them to gain traction with national authorities. Early warning exercises can thus contribute to improve Fund surveillance by helping deliver warnings in the form of '*effective, actionable messages*', as well as policy recommendations that are conducive to the timely adoption of remedial measures by country authorities. Fund surveillance will be the mechanism to follow-up on these warnings and policy recommendations; in turn, the findings of surveillance will be an input into the above exercises.

Finally, a discussion on the effectiveness of surveillance in the post-crisis world cannot escape recognition of the political economy dimension of Fund surveillance. This dimension is notably at play in determining the so-called 'traction' of Fund surveillance. As we emphasised in Section 1, surveillance is a cooperative process between management and staff, on the one hand, and country authorities, on the other; its integrity requires mutually supporting actions from both parties. Staff is responsible for the *output* of Fund surveillance (ensuring the quality of its analysis and policy advice, and their candid communication to the interested parties), while country authorities bear the ultimate responsibility for following-up on staff recommendations (the *outcome* of surveillance).

The relationship between the output and outcome of Fund surveillance defines its traction. This concept tries to capture both the extent to which the authorities engage with the Fund on its analysis and recommendations; and the extent to which Fund advice is reflected in policy action (IMF, 2010d).

While cutting-edge analysis and candid advice from the Fund are preconditions for surveillance to gain traction on policymakers, ultimately surveillance is only one of the many complex and intertwined factors that shape a country's economic policies and the extent to which Fund advice triggers policy action.

However, inadequate peer pressures from the international community may represent an important reason contributing to the insufficient traction of Fund surveillance to date, most notably on advanced countries and major emerging markets. In turn, inadequate peer pressures may be due to lack of clarity on (and awareness of) the common risks and threats faced by countries exposed to spillovers originating in other countries.

As a result, a central feature of the post-crisis efforts to improve the traction of Fund surveillance is the focus on achieving better engagement and interaction with country authorities at the highest level in a dialogue on identified risks and vulnerabilities. These efforts are intended to make closer engagement with the Fund more attractive for country authorities, so as to ultimately provide them with incentives to follow-up on the Fund's policy recommendations.

Overall, the Fund, together with other international organisations, is being a key player in shaping the official sector's response to the global turmoil, including the design of exit strategies from extraordinary economic policies. Similar to past episodes, surveillance is set to be the vehicle to disseminate to Fund members the lessons drawn from the crisis and help foster the adoption of corrective measures agreed upon by the international community.

But the consequences of the crisis are as far-reaching as to encompass the broader role of the Fund in the post-crisis international financial architecture. As we underscored in the chapter, two developments, part of the 'Istanbul decision' (IMF, 2009k), stand out in this regard. Firstly, the issue of whether macro-financial stability should be explicitly included as an integral part of the Fund's institutional mandate (IMF, 2009i) has most prominently been recognised by the IMFC, at its October 2009 meeting, through its call on the Fund to '*review its mandate to cover the full range of macroeconomic and financial sector policies that bear on global stability*' (IMF, 2009j).[30]

Furthermore, in launching the '*Framework for Strong, Sustainable, and Balanced Growth*' at their September 2009 Summit in Pittsburgh (Group of Twenty, 2009c), the G-20 leaders called on the Fund to assist the G-20 countries in the new cooperative process of mutual assessment of their policies. This call, endorsed by the IMFC, is set to usher in a new kind of multilateral surveillance for the institution.

Ultimately, a candid, even-handed and independent surveillance is '*vital*' to improve the role and effectiveness of the Fund in supporting stronger cooperation and ensuring a more sustainable global economy and international financial system (Group of Twenty, 2009b).

We believe that a strong, independent and accountable IMF, by following-up through its surveillance activities on the appropriate lessons drawn from the global financial crisis, can provide a crucial contribution to the international effort of restoring and preserving the 'global public good' of macro-financial stability.

NOTES

1. The Fund's institutional mandate on surveillance is defined in the Articles of Agreement, and has not changed since April 1978, when the Second Amendment of the Articles came into effect (see Boughton, 2001, Chapter 2).
2. From a legal viewpoint, FSAPs are a form of technical assistance.
3. '*Strengthening IMF surveillance is probably the most complex issue growing out of the global financial crisis*', Truman (2009, p. 7).
4. See Visco (2009) for a thorough analysis on the impact of the global crisis on international cooperation.
5. Within the Fund's structure of governance, the Board of Governors is the highest decision-making body. It consists of one governor and one alternate governor for each member country. The Board of Governors has delegated most of its powers to the 24-member Executive Board, which takes care of the day-to-day work of the IMF. This work is guided by the *International Monetary and Financial Committee* (formerly the Interim Committee), and supported by the IMF's professional *staff*. The Managing Director is the Head of IMF staff and Chairman of the Executive Board. He is assisted by a First Deputy Managing Director and two Deputy Managing Directors, and together they constitute the Fund's *management*.
6. '*Providing credible intelligence to policymakers that will elicit action requires more than simply identifying risks and vulnerabilities*'. Lipsky (2010).
7. Sundararajan and Baliño (1991).

8. See Saccomanni (2000) for a thorough analysis of the international monetary reforms in the 1990s, culminating in the report of the G-7 finance ministers to the Köln Summit in June 1999. See also, Saccomanni (2008), in particular Chapter 6.

9. The assessment of the observance of standards and codes devised by international standard setters has become an important element of the diagnostics of Fund surveillance. See IMF (1999a) for an initial discussion on the Standards and Code Initiative, jointly launched by the Fund and the World Bank in 1999. See also IMF (2005c) for the latest review of the Standards and Codes Initiative, and IMF (2009h) for the recent introduction of partial, risk-focused updates for financial (regulation and supervision) Reports on the Observance of Standards and Codes.

10. See also Schinasi (2006) for a more recent study on the development of a comprehensive framework for safeguarding financial stability. The author notes that '*the practice of financial-stability analysis is still in its infancy when compared with, for example, the analysis of monetary stability or macroeconomic stability*' (p. 2).

11. Standard setters are fora for international cooperation among regulators, supervisors and industry groupings. The main standard setter in the banking area is the Basel Committee on Banking Supervision (1997) and the IMF (2000d).

12. On account of the role played by information deficiencies for Mexico's external liabilities in determining the 1994–1995 crisis, the latter marked, inter alia, the beginning of a concerted effort on the part of the international community to improve the transparency and disclosure of macroeconomic and financial data. Following-up on the inputs from the Interim Committee and the G-7, in 1996 the Fund undertook the Data Dissemination Initiative. See International Monetary Fund (2008e) for a recent review of the Initiative.

13. It is also worth noting that the role taken on by the Fund in assessing the observance of standards and codes marked a significant development as far as political legitimacy is concerned. In fact, the greater political legitimacy and authority enjoyed by the Fund, as a formal universal international organisation, allow an increased capacity to foster compliance with internationally recognized best practices (Porter, 2000).

14. The assessments of the degree of implementation of these standards and codes are undertaken by member countries on a purely voluntary basis. The results are included in the Report on the Observance of Standards and Codes (ROSC).

15. These tools include: the assessments of standards and codes, the analysis of Financial Soundness Indicators (FSIs) and stress tests.

16. See Section 5 for the most recent discussion on these two issues.

17. In this regard, the report found it important to emphasize that a more central focus on what might be considered the traditional core of surveillance did not mean that important linkages between macroeconomic management and other policies should not be recognized and addressed as part of surveillance.

18. Five 'Area' departments are responsible, across macro-geographical regions, for Article IV consultations. Among 'functional' departments, those most involved in the Fund's work on financial and capital market issues are the Research Department; the Monetary and Financial Markets Department; and the Strategy, Policy, and Review Department.

19. Such external advice (IMF, 2000f) has generally led to follow-up studies carried out by internal task forces that, in turn, have given rise to major organisational changes with the setting-up of new departments and the merging of others. See Bossone (2008, pp. 18–20) for a concise review of such external and internal reports and the ensuing changes in the Fund's organisation.

20. In the same vein, a former director of the IMF's Policy Development and Review Department has recently noticed that '*despite recent efforts, there remains a need for a genuine integration of financial sector issues with the world class macro economic analysis that has been the hallmark of the Fund over its entire history*' (Boorman, 2008).

21. To explicitly address these difficulties, in the spring of 2009 a Macro-Financial Unit was set up within the IMF Research Department (IMF, 2008b).

22. See: *IMF Executive Board Adopts Surveillance Priorities for 2008–2011.* Press release no. 08/238 (8 October 2008). Available at: http://www.imf.org/external/np/sec/pr/2008/pr08238.htm. *IMF Executive Board Revises Surveillance Priorities for 2008-2011.* Press Release No. 09/336 (29 September 2009). Available at: http://www.imf.org/external/np/sec/pr/2009/pr09336.htm

23. As of end-July 2009, the total number of completed, ongoing or formally requested FSAP initial assessments reached 141, corresponding to 80 percent of the Fund's membership (IMF, 2009f). Among the G-20 countries that have not yet undertaken the exercise, China, Indonesia and the United States are scheduled to do so in 2010.

24. See also the last review of the FSAP (IMF, 2009f).

25. Moreover, another recognition of the importance of the programme has come from the decision to use evidence from FSAP reports as input to the periodic '*peer reviews*' agreed upon by the members of the Financial Stability Board (Group of Twenty, 2009a).

26. At the April 2009 G-20 leaders Summit in London, the Financial Stability Forum was re-established as the Financial Stability Board (FSB) with a broadened mandate to promote financial stability, expanded membership, stronger institutional basis and enhanced capacity. At their September 2009 Pittsburgh Summit, the G-20 leaders endorsed the Charter that formally establishes the FSB to coordinate at the international level the work of national financial authorities and international standard setting bodies in order to develop and promote the implementation of effective regulatory, supervisory and other financial sector policies.

27. Joint Letter by the managing director and the chairman of the FSB issued ahead of the G-20 leaders' Summit on Financial Markets and the World Economy in Washington, DC (13 November 2008). Available at http://www.financialstability-board.org/list/fsb_publications/tid_78/index.htm

28. According to the Fund's transparency policy, country authorities retain the right to delete from reports, before publication, information deemed as 'market sensitive'.

29. '*And in other cases, like financial sector surveillance, the goalposts are constantly moving: as the world we analyze is becoming more complex, so is its analysis*'. As a result, it should not come as a surprise if '*future surveillance reviews ...* [will] *... note both that progress was made and that more efforts are needed*' (IMF, 2008c, p. 11).

30. It should be noted that reconsideration of the institution's mandate is part of a broader reform effort underway at the Fund, notably on governance, a key component of the institution's long-term legitimacy and effectiveness.

REFERENCES

Basel Committee on Banking Supervision. (1997). *Core principles for effective banking supervision Basel.*

Boorman, J. (2008). *An agenda for the reform of the International Monetary Fund.* Dialogue on Globalization, Occasional Papers, No. 38. New York.

Bossone, B. (2008). *Integrating macroeconomic and financial sector analyses within IMF Surveillance: A case study on IMF governance.* Independent Evaluation Office Background Paper 08/11.

Boughton, J. M. (2001). *Silent revolution-the International Monetary Fund 1979–1989.* Washington, DC: International Monetary Fund.

Claessens, S., Kose, M. A., & Terrones, M. (2008). *What happens during recessions, crunches, and busts?* IMF Working Paper No. 08/274. International Monetary Fund, Washington, DC.

Enoch, C., Marston, D., & Taylor, M. (2002). *Building strong banks through surveillance and resolution.* Washington, DC: International Monetary Fund.

Group of Seven. (1995). *Review of the International Financial Institutions.* G-7 Halifax Summit.

Group of Seven. (1998a). *Strengthening the architecture of the global financial system.* Report of G-7 Finance Ministers to G-7 Heads of State or Government. G-7 Birmingham Summit.

Group of Seven. (1998b). *Declaration of the G7 Finance Ministers and Central Bank Governors.* Washington, DC.

Group of Ten. (1997). *A strategy for the formulation, adoption and implementation of sound principles and practices to strengthen financial systems.* Report of the Working Party on Financial Stability in Emerging Market Economies.

Group of Twenty. (2009a). *Declaration of the summit on strengthening the financial system.* London.

Group of Twenty. (2009b). *Communiqué of the meeting of finance ministers and central bank governors.* London.

Group of Twenty. (2009c). *Leaders' statement: The Pittsburgh Summit.*

Independent Evaluation Office. (2006). *Financial sector assessment program – Evaluation report.* International Monetary Fund, Washington, DC.

Independent Evaluation Office. (2010). *IMF interaction with member countries.* International Monetary Fund, Washington, DC.

International Monetary Fund. (1995a). *Biennial review of the implementation of the Fund's Surveillance over members' exchange rate policies, and of the 1977 surveillance decision. Summing up by the chairman.* International Monetary Fund, Washington, DC.

International Monetary Fund. (1995b). *Mexico-report on fund surveillance, 1993–94.* International Monetary Fund, Washington, DC.

International Monetary Fund. (1995c). *Mexico-report on fund surveillance, 1993–94. Summing up by the chairman.* International Monetary Fund, Washington, DC.

International Monetary Fund. (1995d). *Report of the executive board to the interim committee on strengthening of fund surveillance.* International Monetary Fund, Washington, DC.

International Monetary Fund. (1996a). *Bank soundness and macroeconomic policy.* International Monetary Fund, Washington, DC.

International Monetary Fund. (1996b). *Communiqué of the Interim Committee of the Board of Governors of the International Monetary Fund.* Press Release No. 96/48. International Monetary Fund, Washington, DC.

International Monetary Fund. (1997a). *Biennial review of the implementation of the fund's surveillance over members' exchange rate policies, and of the 1977 surveillance decision.* International Monetary Fund, Washington, DC.

International Monetary Fund. (1997b). *Biennial review of the implementation of the fund's surveillance over members' exchange rate policies, and of the 1977 surveillance decision. Summing up by the chairman.* International Monetary Fund, Washington, DC.

International Monetary Fund. (1997c). *Toward a framework for sound banking. Summing up by the chairman.* International Monetary Fund, Washington, DC.

International Monetary Fund. (1998a). *Toward a framework for financial stability.* World Economic and Financial Surveys. International Monetary Fund, Washington, DC.

International Monetary Fund. (1998b). *Review of members' policies in the context of surveillance-lessons for surveillance from the Asian crisis.* International Monetary Fund, Washington, DC.

International Monetary Fund. (1998c). *Communiqué of the Interim Committee of the Board of Governors.* Press Release No. 98/14. International Monetary Fund, Washington, DC.

International Monetary Fund. (1998d). *International standard and fund surveillance.* International Monetary Fund, Washington, DC.

International Monetary Fund. (1998e). *Guidance note for the monitoring of financial systems under Article IV surveillance.* International Monetary Fund, Washington, DC.

International Monetary Fund. (1999a). *International standards and fund surveillance-further issues.* International Monetary Fund, Washington, DC.

International Monetary Fund. (1999b). *IMF–World Bank financial sector assessment program.* International Monetary Fund, Washington, DC.

International Monetary Fund. (1999c). *External evaluation of IMF surveillance.* Report by a Group of Independent Expert. International Monetary Fund, Washington, DC.

International Monetary Fund. (2000a). *Biennial review of the implementation of the fund's surveillance over members' exchange rate policies, and of the 1977 surveillance decision.* International Monetary Fund, Washington, DC.

International Monetary Fund. (2000b). *Biennial review of the implementation of the fund's surveillance over members' exchange rate policies, and of the 1977 surveillance decision. Summing Up by the Chairman.* International Monetary Fund, Washington, DC.

International Monetary Fund. (2000c). *Financial sector assessment program-progress report – Lessons from the pilot exercise and next steps*'. International Monetary Fund, Washington, DC.

International Monetary Fund. (2000d). *Experience with basel core principle assessments.* International Monetary Fund, Washington, DC.

International Monetary Fund. (2000e). *Communiqué of the International Monetary and Financial Committee of the Board of Governors of the International Monetary Fund.* Press Release No. 00/31. International Monetary Fund, Washington, DC.

International Monetary Fund. (2000f). News Brief No. 00/93. International Monetary Fund, Washington, DC.

International Monetary Fund. (2000g). *Financial sector assessment program – A review – Lessons from the pilot and issues going forward.* International Monetary Fund, Washington, DC.

International Monetary Fund. (2000h). *Financial sector assessment program – A review – Lessons from the pilot and issues going forward. Summing up by the acting chairman.* International Monetary Fund, Washington, DC.

International Monetary Fund. (2002a). *Biennial review of the implementation of the Fund's surveillance and of the 1977 surveillance decision – Overview.* International Monetary Fund, Washington, DC.

International Monetary Fund. (2002b). *Biennial review of the implementation of the Fund's surveillance and of the 1977 surveillance decision – Framework and conduct of surveillance in 2000–01.* International Monetary Fund, Washington, DC.

International Monetary Fund. (2002c). *Biennial review of the implementation of the Fund's surveillance over members' exchange rate policies, and of the 1977 surveillance decision. Summing up by the chairman.* International Monetary Fund, Washington, DC.

International Monetary Fund. (2002d). *Operational guidance note for staff following the 2002 biennial surveillance review.* International Monetary Fund, Washington, DC.

International Monetary Fund. (2003a). *Financial sector assessment program – Review, lessons, and issues going forward.* International Monetary Fund,Washington, DC.

International Monetary Fund. (2003b). *The acting chair's summing up financial sector assessment program – Review, lessons, and issues going forward.* International Monetary Fund, Washington, DC.

International Monetary Fund. (2003c). *Financial soundness indicators.* International Monetary Fund, Washington, DC.

International Monetary Fund. (2004). *Biennial review of the implementation of the fund's surveillance and of the 1977 surveillance decision-content of surveillance.* International Monetary Fund, Washington, DC.

International Monetary Fund. (2005a). *Financial Sector Assessment Program – Review, lessons, and issues going forward.* International Monetary Fund, Washington, DC.

International Monetary Fund. (2005b). Press Release No. 05/132. International Monetary Fund, Washington, DC.

International Monetary Fund. (2005c). *The standards and codes initiative – Is it effective?* International Monetary Fund, Washington, DC.

International Monetary Fund. (2005d). *Financial sector assessment: A handbook.* International Monetary Fund, Washington, DC.

International Monetary Fund. (2005e). *The managing director's report on the fund's medium-term strategy.* International Monetary Fund, Washington, DC.

International Monetary Fund. (2006). *The managing director's report on the fund's medium-term strategy.* International Monetary Fund, Washington, DC.

International Monetary Fund. (2007a). *Bilateral surveillance over members' policies-executive board decision.* International Monetary Fund, Washington, DC.

International Monetary Fund. (2008a). *The recent financial turmoil – Initial assessment, policy lessons, and implications for fund surveillance.* International Monetary Fund, Washington, DC.

International Monetary Fund. (2008b). *The managing director's statement on the work program of the executive board.* International Monetary Fund, Washington, DC.
International Monetary Fund. (2008c). *2008 Triennial surveillance review – Overview paper.* International Monetary Fund, Washington, DC.
International Monetary Fund. (2008d). *2008 Triennial surveillance review – Thematic findings paper.* International Monetary Fund, Washington, DC.
International Monetary Fund. (2008e). *The data dissemination initiative after 10 years.* In: W. E. Alexander, J. Cady, & J. Gonzalez-Garcia (Eds.). Washington, DC: International Monetary Fund.
International Monetary Fund. (2008f). *Communiqué of the International Monetary and Financial Committee of the Board of Governors of the International Monetary Fund.* Press Release No. 08/240. International Monetary Fund, Washington, DC.
International Monetary Fund. (2009a). *Initial lessons of the crisis for the global architecture and the IMF.* International Monetary Fund, Washington, DC.
International Monetary Fund. (2009b). *Addressing information gaps.* IMF Staff Position Note No. 06. International Monetary Fund, Washington, DC.
International Monetary Fund. (2009c). *Economic and financial statistics in the context of the global financial crisis.* International Monetary Fund, Washington, DC.
International Monetary Fund. (2009d). *Communiqué of the International Monetary and Financial Committee of the Board of Governors of the International Monetary Fund.* Press Release No. 09/139. International Monetary Fund, Washington, DC.
International Monetary Fund. (2009e). *Financial Sector and Bilateral Surveillance – Toward further integration.* International Monetary Fund, Washington, DC.
International Monetary Fund. (2009f). *Financial sector assessment program after ten years – Experience and reforms for the next decade.* International Monetary Fund, Washington, DC.
International Monetary Fund. (2009g). *Financial sector assessment program after ten years – Background material – Experience and reforms for the next decade.* International Monetary Fund, Washington, DC.
International Monetary Fund. (2009h). *Revised approach to financial regulation and supervision standards assessments in FSAP updates.* International Monetary Fund, Washington, DC.
International Monetary Fund. (2009i). *Statement by the managing director to the IMFC on the IMF's post-crisis role.* International Monetary Fund, Washington, DC.
International Monetary Fund. (2009j). *Communiqué of the International Monetary and Financial Committee of the Board of Governors of the International Monetary Fund.* Press Release No. 09/347. International Monetary Fund, Istanbul.
International Monetary Fund. (2009k). *Opening address by the managing director to the 2009 annual meetings of the board of governors of the World Bank Group and the International Monetary Fund*. International Monetary Fund, Istanbul.
International Monetary Fund. (2009l). *IMF-FSB Early Warning Exercise Factsheet.* International Monetary Fund, Washington, DC. Available at http://www.imf.org/external/np/exr/facts/ewe.htm
International Monetary Fund. (2010a). *The Fund's mandate – An overview.* International Monetary Fund, Washington, DC.
International Monetary Fund. (2010b). *Modernizing the surveillance mandate and modalities.* International Monetary Fund, Washington, DC.
International Monetary Fund. (2010c). *Financial sector surveillance and the mandate of the fund.* International Monetary Fund, Washington, DC.

International Monetary Fund. (2010d). *Review of the fund's mandate – Follow-up on modernizing surveillance*. International Monetary Fund, Washington, DC.
International Monetary Fund. (2010e). *Integrating stability assessments under the financial sector assessment program into Article IV surveillance*. International Monetary Fund, Washington, DC.
International Monetary Fund. (2010f). *Executive board report to the IMFC on the Fund's mandate*. International Monetary Fund, Washington, DC.
Kenen, P. B. (2001). *The international financial architecture: What's new? What's missing?* Washington, DC: Peterson Institute for International Economics.
Lindgren, C. J., Garcia, G., & Saal, M. I. (1996). *Bank soundness and macroeconomic policy*. Washington, DC: International Monetary Fund.
Lipsky, J. (2010). *Forewarned is forearmed: How the early warning exercise expands the IMF's Surveillance Toolkit. IMF Direct*. Washington, DC: International Monetary Fund.
Porter, T. (2000). The G-7, the financial stability forum, the G-20, and the politics of international financial regulation. Paper presented at the International Studies Association annual meeting, Los Angeles.
Saccomanni, F. (2000). A new architecture or a new system? A survey of international monetary reform in the 1990s. *Open Economies Review*, *11*(Suppl. 1), 15–41.
Saccomanni, F. (2008). *Managing international financial instability. National tamers versus global tigers*. Cheltenham: Edward Elgar.
Schinasi, G. J. (2006). *Safeguarding financial stability-theory and practice*. Washington, DC: International Monetary Fund.
Sundararajan, V., & Baliño, T. J. T. (1991). *Banking crises: Cases and issues*. Washington, DC: International Monetary Fund.
Truman, E. M. (Ed.), (2006). Reforming the IMF for the 21st century. Peterson Institute for International Economics, Special Report 19. Washington.
Truman, E. M. (Ed.) (2009). *The IMF and the global crisis: Role and reform*. Washington, DC: Peterson Institute for International Economics.
Visco, I. (2009). *Challenges to international cooperation in the wake of the global crisis*. Speech at the Italian Chamber of Commerce and Industry for the UK XXXI Annual Conference 'A New Approach for Global Economic and Social Growth', London.

WHAT CAN THE EAST AND NORTHEAST ASIAN COMMUNITIES LEARN FROM THE EU?

Ali M. El-Agraa

ABSTRACT

Former Japanese Prime Minister Yukio Hatoyama continues to actively promote his party's East Asian Community (EAC), which he had as a centrepiece of his coalition government. This chapter supplements an earlier one where I compare the EAC with that of the late South Korean President Roh Moo-hyun's Northeast Asian Community (NEAC) and examine the impediments that have been the cause of friction in the region, the removal of which is fundamental to the creation of these communities, and show that that they will be around for a very long time. This chapter concentrates on what the EAC can learn from the European Union experience since both Hatoyama and Roh have stated that it is the EU that has been the source of their inspiration. It argues that the basic requirements for a 'customs union', let alone a 'common market' or 'economic community', will not be realised by the EAC in the foreseeable future. This suggests that the best that can be hoped for is a 'preferential trade and investment arrangement', between China, together with Hong Kong and Taiwan, Japan, both the Koreas and the United States,

The Impact of the Global Financial Crisis on Emerging Financial Markets
Contemporary Studies in Economic and Financial Analysis, Volume 93, 311–357

ISSN: 1569-3759/doi:10.1108/S1569-3759(2011)0000093011

otherwise one must wonder why the EAC or NEAC is needed, rather than the ASEAN + 3 and ASEAN + 6 that are presently in the making. The problem is that both Hatoyama and Roh have ruled out the United States as a full member while at the same time they want it to continue to provide security for the region when full membership would enhance that. Nevertheless, the vision is admirable and should be desired by the whole world, not just the parties directly involved, so should receive our full support.

Keywords: East and Northeast Asia; economic integration; six-party talks; China–Korea–Japan relations; the European Union.

JEL classifications: F1; F2; F42; F5; O.

1. INTRODUCTION

Before becoming the prime minister of Japan on 16 September 2009,[1] Yukio Hatoyama published a paper in which he called for the creation of an East Asian Community (EAC).[2] The EAC initiative is however not his own since it is in the Democratic Party of Japan (2005) when the DPJ president was Katsuya Okada, now Japan's foreign minister. Hence, although Hatoyama is no longer the prime minister, the EAC is here to stay. I shall attribute it to him because he has been the most vocal in this respect.

Hatoyama made the EAC a centrepiece of his coalition government, advertising it in all the major international political fora that he has attended, both with individual leaders of concerned nations and generally.[3] Also, the idea continues to be hot news everywhere, especially in the United States, where it is perceived as being aimed at undermining the US–Japan relationship in particular and the US hegemony and its policy towards Asia in general, mainly due to Hatoyama's declaration, during the elections, of his intention to seek an 'equal partnership' with the United States and to his so demonstrating by not being able to reach an agreement with US President Barack Obama on the relocation of the US Marine Corps' Futenma Air Station in Okinawa, which has been in the making for a decade, during his visit to Tokyo on 13–14 November 2009.

The aim of this chapter is to consider the question of what the EAC can learn from the experience of the European Union (EU) since this lies at the very heart of Hatoyama's rationale for the EAC. Obviously, the chapter begins by explaining the nature of the proposed EAC, but does not consider earlier attempts since I have done so elsewhere (El-Agraa, 2009c), demonstrating that the late president of South Korea (Korea) Roh Moo-hyun is the first incumbent Asian leader to seriously initiate it by setting out a clear argument for a close equivalent, the Northeast Asian Community (NEAC) in 2007,[4] also inspired by the EU. Section 3 is then devoted to the relevance of the EU experience for the proposed community and is followed by Section 4 on the feasibility of a preferential trade and investment agreement. Section 5 sets out the main conclusions.

2. HATOYAMA'S EAC

2.1. The Rationale

In his original paper, Hatoyama states that his rationale for an EAC stems from his belief that today's world needs to return to 'fraternity' a la the French slogan 'liberté, égalité, fraternité' so as to lessen the 'danger inherent within freedom' Hatoyama (2009a). He is rather vague on fraternity here, but has since then tried to clarify it:[5] 'my initiative … stems from … "*yu-ai*"[6] [which] … is typically translated as "fraternity" … [within which] people respect the freedom and human dignity of others just as they respect their own … [i.e., it] means not only the independence of people but also their coexistence' (Hatoyama, 2009c).

He adds that fraternity 'can be described as a principle that aims to adjust to the excesses of the current globalized brand of capitalism and accommodate the local economic practices that have been fostered through our traditions'. Citing the problems that have arisen from the perception of the US model as the best, particularly those pertaining to the present financial crisis, he insists that the responsibility of politicians should be 'to focus … attention on those non-economic values that have been thrown aside by the march of globalism'. He stresses that politicians 'must work on policies that regenerate the ties that bring people together, that take greater account of nature and the environment, that rebuild welfare and medical systems, that provide better education and child-rearing support, and that address wealth disparities'. More to the point, he emphasises that fraternity is also behind the EAC, although he is quick to add that the Japan–US security arrangement 'will continue to be the cornerstone of Japanese diplomatic policy', but that simultaneously 'we must not forget our identity as a nation located in Asia'. He believes 'that the East Asian region, which is showing increasing vitality, must be recognized as Japan's basic sphere of being'. He therefore calls for a continuation of efforts to build frameworks for 'stable economic cooperation and security across the region'.

He then tries to be specific:

> The financial crisis has suggested ... that the era of [US] unilateralism may come to an end ... [raising] doubts about the permanence of the dollar as the key global currency. I also feel that as a result of the failure of the Iraq war and the financial crisis, the era of [US]-led globalism is coming to an end and that we are moving toward an era of multipolarity. But *at present no one country is ready to replace the [US] as the dominant country*. Nor is there a currency ready to replace the dollar as the world's key currency. Although the influence of the [US] is declining, it will remain the world's leading military and economic power for the next two to three decades ... [Moreover, ongoing] developments show clearly that [the People's Republic of China (China)] will become one of the world's leading economic nations while also continuing to expand its military power. The size of China's economy will surpass that of Japan in the not-too-distant future. (Hatoyama, 2009a; italics added)

He therefore poses the question: 'How should Japan maintain its political and economic independence and protect its national interest when caught between the [US], which is fighting to retain its position as the world's dominant power, and China, which is seeking ways to become dominant?' He is quick to add that the question also concerns the small and medium-sized Asian nations, but fails to add 'even more so' Hatoyama (2009a). No wonder the United States is up in arms (above), since despite claims to the contrary[7] it is being told to prepare for its future decline, if not its utter demise, which may be true but hurts.

Hatoyama then elaborates on the EAC proposal:

> Unlike Europe, the countries of this region differ in size, development stage and political system, so economic integration cannot be achieved over the short term. However, *we should nonetheless aspire to move toward regional currency integration* as a natural extension of the rapid economic growth begun by Japan, followed by South Korea, Taiwan and Hong Kong, and then achieved by the [ten member nations of the] Association of Southeast Asian Nations (ASEAN[8]) and China. We must spare no effort to build the permanent security frameworks essential to underpinning currency integration ... Establishing a common Asian currency will likely take more than 10 years ... [and for] ... *such a single currency to bring about political integration* [it] will surely take longer still. (Hatoyama, 2009a; italics added)

He adds that ASEAN, Japan, China (including Hong Kong), Korea and Taiwan now account for one-quarter of the world's GDP and that 'the economic power of the East Asian region and the interdependent relationships within ... [it] have grown wider and deeper. So the structures required for the formation of a regional economic bloc are already in place' (Hatoyama, 2009a).

But he is quick to issue a warning which also happens to offer support for an EAC: '*due to historical and cultural conflicts as well as conflicting national security interests*, we must recognize that there are numerous difficult political issues. The problems of increased militarization and territorial disputes cannot be resolved by bilateral negotiations … The more … [they] are discussed bilaterally, the greater the risk that emotions become inflamed and nationalism intensified' (Hatoyama, 2009a; italics added).

He then highlights his enthusiasm for an EAC by adding that:

> Therefore, I would suggest, somewhat paradoxically, that the issues that stand in the way of regional integration can only be truly resolved by moving toward greater integration. *The experience of the [EU] shows us how regional integration can defuse territorial disputes.* (Hatoyama, 2009a; italics added)

He elaborates on the EU experience in his Singapore address:

> Europe had the disastrous experience of two world wars. But Germany and France, once bitter foes, have increased their cooperation dramatically. This started with *the establishment of a common market for coal and steel production*. Then, through further exchanges among people, they succeeded in establishing a *de facto* community. Now, wars against one another are unimaginable. These efforts were initially centered on Germany and France. But, they continued through twists and turns over the years, and they finally resulted in the creation of the [EU]. *The central idea of my [EAC] initiative is based upon reconciliation and cooperation in Europe*. (Hatoyama, 2009c; italics added)

He concludes the article by aptly quoting from Count Richard Coudenhove-Kalergi, founder of the European Movement: 'All great historical ideas started as a utopian dream and ended with reality. Whether a particular idea … [does so would depend] on the number of people who believe in the ideal and their ability to act upon it.'[9] What is intriguing is that Hatoyama does not remind his fellow citizens of the fact that the Count's mother was Japanese.[10] Remind them, because it is due to that affinity that the Count has been written a lot about in Japanese, with several Japanese television programmes based on these writings devoted to him.[11]

2.2. *What's Gone Amiss?*

It should be clear from the above that Hatoyama's EAC does not offer concrete guidelines on a number of pertinent critical issues. First, he is not specific on its exact nature. In his Singapore speech (Hatoyama, 2009c), he suggests that it would be based on 'open regional cooperation', which would lead to 'a multi-layered network of functional communities'; hence, it may not be a single community! For cooperation he chooses anti-piracy patrols, disaster management, nuclear non-proliferation, social security and urban problems, and adds that there may also be 'an opportunity … to discuss possible political cooperation in the future' when he has already stated that that may follow after the single currency (above). Also, nations that had the intention and ability to cooperate in any of the mentioned fields would first take part in that cooperative effort: '[i]t may be possible that countries with the will and the capabilities to cooperate in a particular field may choose to participate in projects initially, and as their efforts bear fruit, other countries could join later' (Hatoyama, 2009c). But this implies that some countries may join only one aspect of it and stay there for good if unable to go further or take a very long time before adopting all facets of the community. In other words, this suggests that different member nations may belong in different ways, resulting in a club with various facets and different affiliations, all of which reinforces the lack of a single community. Maybe because he realises this contradiction that he tries to clarify the situation in his UN speech:

> I look forward to an [EAC] taking shape as an extension of the accumulated cooperation built up step by step among partners who have the capacity to work together, *starting with fields in which we can cooperate* – [FTAs], finance, currency, energy, environment, disaster relief and more. *Of course, Rome was not built in a day, so let us seek to move forward steadily on this, even if at a moderate pace.* (Hatoyama, 2009b)

This indicates that the totality of the member nations would commit simultaneously to the areas agreed at the outset, then progress in a dynamic fashion to include the rest, which would be consistent with a single community that evolves incrementally. But then he returns to confuse when he refers to 'open regionalism' in his Singapore speech (Hatoyama, 2009c), which should come as no surprise at the end of the APEC summit: APEC has always claimed that it stands for open regionalism, one meaning of which is extending all member nations' privileges to non-members.[12] If that were the case, why ask for the EAC: all that would be needed is to simply promote 'global', not regional cooperation.

Second, and as is clear from the above quotation, it does not indicate how long it would take to become a reality. This compounds the previous point leading to an EAC which is open-ended both in terms of its nature and transition period to reality.

Third, it is not categorical on how precisely it relates to the EU experience. It mentions the historical background, the desire for eternal peace and the single currency, but does not depict these within the overall nature of club EU. Since a whole section is devoted to this, I shall return to this point there. However, with regard to the previous point, the EU set a transition period of 12 years, divided into three 4-year stages, for it to achieve its original 1957 aims, and beat the tariff deadlines by 18 months,[13] but as just mentioned Hatoyama has no such clear vision.

Fourth, it is not specific on which particular countries it should comprise. Indeed, pressed on this point at the end of the meeting of the leaders of the countries of the Mekong (Burma – read Myanmar – Cambodia, Laos, Thailand and Vietnam, i.e. 5 of the 10 ASEAN nations), held in Tokyo on 6–7 November 2009, he responded thus:

> I stated earlier my belief that the Mekong region holds the key to the realisation of the [EAC] initiative ... Disparities remain large in the region in an economic sense, and as the countries in the region overcome these differences, their sense of belonging to a community will be strengthened. Also, I believe a sense of mutual trust will increase by undergoing that process. *Now, I am not in a position at this stage to say which countries should be part of, or not part of, the* [*EAC*], but I would like to reiterate that within ASEAN, the Mekong region is indeed a very important one that holds the key to my [EAC] (italics added).[14]

As mentioned above, in his original paper (Hatoyama, 2009a), Hatoyama refers to ASEAN, Japan, China (including Hong Kong), Korea and Taiwan (above), but his statement at the Mekong summit meeting suggests that not all ASEAN member nations would be included. If some ASEAN nations may not qualify, the same problem would naturally arise with regard to the now being negotiated ASEAN + 3, the three being China, Korea and Japan. This would be even more so with the proposed ASEAN + 6, the extra three being Australia, India and New Zealand, which is effectively the so-called 'East Asian Summit', now more or less in the making. That being so, it follows that one should altogether forget about some of the nations of the APEC forum.

Also, and vitally, considering that China will not enter into any negotiations that suggest that Taiwan is not part of it (and that Hong Kong is already integral to it through the one-nation-two-systems set-up, but Hatoyama owns up to this), then China would rule itself out from the start; indeed, all indications suggest that China intends to be the leader in this and other respects and is setting its agenda accordingly.[15] Yet China lies at the very heart of Hatoyama's EAC! And, since common security is of major concern, why is there no mention of the Democratic People's Republic of Korea (DPRK)?

I shall return to some of these important considerations later in the chapter, but what is significant is that some of these issues have already been coherently addressed by the late president of Korea Roh Moo-hyun in 2007, directly in the manner that Hatoyama has set out in his EAC paper and speeches.[16] It is intriguing that Hatoyama does not point this out, especially when it lends support to his dream: if the omission is due to lack of awareness, then his vision would be vacuous; if it is deliberate it would demonstrate either no confidence in the nation that is a pillar of the EAC or in undermining his case with the average Japanese, which would be even worse.

3. LEARNING FROM THE EU EXPERIENCE

3.1. EU Experience

Having established the nature of the EAC, I am now in a position to deal with the question of what it can learn from the EU experience. To answer the question, it is of course necessary to describe what the EU experience is and what the EU stands for today. This is however a well-trodden area, so I need only to highlight the salient and pertinent features very briefly.[17] I should however reiterate that by singling out the path followed by the EU as the benchmark against which to judge the EAC, I am not suggesting that the EU route is the only one available for it: I am doing so simply because it is the benchmark against which Hatoyama, and Roh Moo-hyun before him, has set himself. Indeed, in the light of what is to ensue, it would become increasingly apparent that the EAC should pursue different routes, choosing among alternative possibilities, but I leave this for later.

Also, in order to facilitate easy comparisons, it is important to briefly remind ourselves of where both the EAC and EU stand within the general context of international economic integration (regional integration). Given that this is also a well-trodden area,[18] I can be very brief here too.

Regional integration is concerned with the discriminatory removal of all trade impediments between at least two participating nations and with the establishment of certain elements of cooperation and coordination between them. The elements of cooperation and coordination depend entirely on the actual form that integration takes. Different forms of economic integration can be envisaged (Chart 1) and practically every country in the world belongs to at least one:[19]

(a) FTAs or PTAs where the member nations remove all trade impediments amongst themselves but retain their freedom to determine their own policies vis-à-vis the outside world (the non-participants);

Chart 1. Schematic Presentation of Regional Integration Arrangements.

Scheme	Free Intra-Scheme Trade	Common Commercial Policy	Free Factor Mobility	Common Monetary and Fiscal Policy	One Government
PTA	Yes	No	No	No	No
CU	Yes	Yes	No	No	No
CM	Yes	Yes	Yes	No	No
EcU	Yes	Yes	Yes	Yes	No
PU	Yes	Yes	Yes	Yes	Yes

(b) '*customs unions*' (CUs) which are very similar to PTAs except that member nations must conduct and pursue common commercial policies (CCPs) such as adopting common external tariffs (CETs) on imports from the non-participants;

(c) '*common markets*' (CMs) which are CUs that allow also for free factor mobility across members' frontiers, i.e. capital, labour, technology and enterprise should move unhindered between the participating countries;

(d) '*complete economic unions*' (EcUs) which are CMs that ask for complete unification of monetary and fiscal policies, hence the participants must introduce a common authority to control monetary and fiscal policies and, *arguably*;

(e) '*complete political unions*' (PUs) where the participants become literally one nation as happened in the case of the two Germanys in 1990; this goes beyond regional integration but it is added since it was uppermost in the minds of the fathers of European integration and is suggested by Hatoyama.

One should emphasise that such a schema is meant for only sharpening concentration; it is not intended to represent what is happening in the real world. Indeed, as mentioned, many PTAs now allow for free capital movement to encourage foreign direct investment (FDI) flows; hence, in practice, there is some overlap and in some cases incoherent structures.

Before I embark on my task, however, it is important to make a few points on the European Coal and Steel Community (ECSC)[20] since Hatoyama, and before him Roh Moo-hyun, single it out as the source of inspiration for their communities, with the former doing so categorically[21] and the latter hinting at it by his reference to the foundation of European unity (above) and by so stating after his article was published.[22] Ironically, however, the creation of the ECSC by the Treaty of Paris in 1951 actually marked the parting of ways in post-war Western Europe since it was undertaken without the British (below) and Scandinavians, with particularly the former still being seen as the black sheep of the family since it remains uncommitted to key EU areas.

The immediate factor in the development of the ECSC was the revival of the West German economy. The passage of time, the efforts of the German people and the aid made available by the United States through the Marshall Plan all contributed to this recovery. Indeed, the West German *economic miracle* was then about to unfold. It was recognised that the German economy would have to be allowed to regain its position in the world, and that the *Allied* control of coal and steel under the *International Ruhr Authority* could not last indefinitely. The fundamental question was how the German economy in the sectors of iron, coal and steel, being *the basic materials of a war effort*, could be allowed to regain its former powerful position without endangering the future peace of Europe. The answer was a French plan, elaborated by the now almost household name, Jean Monnet, a French businessman turned adviser, but put forward by Robert Schuman, French minister of foreign affairs, in May 1950. The *Schuman Plan* was essentially political in character. It was brilliant since *it sought to end the historic rivalry of France and Germany by making a war between the two nations not only unthinkable but also materially impossible.* This was to be achieved in a manner that ultimately would have the result of bringing about the European federation which was believed to be indispensable to peace. The answer was not to nationalise or indeed to internationalise the ownership of the means of production in coal, iron and steel, but *to create, by the removal of customs duties, import quota restrictions and similar impediments on trade and factors of production, a CM in these products.* Every participating nation in such a common market would have equal access to the output of these industries wherever they might be located, and, to reinforce this, discrimination on the grounds of nationality was to be forbidden.

The plan had a number of attractive features. First, it provided an excellent basis for solving the 'Saar problem': the handing back of the Saar region to West Germany was more likely to be acceptable to the French if Germany was firmly locked in such a coal and steel community. Second, the plan was extremely attractive to Germany since membership of the community was a passport to international respectability; it was the best way of speeding up the end of occupation and avoiding the imposition of dampers on the expansion of the German economy. Third, the plan was also attractive to the federalists who had found the *Organisation for European Economic Cooperation* (OEEC) far short of their aspirations for the *Council of Europe* (its unanimity rule and that no powers could be delegated to an independent commission or *Commissariat* were extremely frustrating for them), and, in any case, the prospects for the OEEC were not very good since by 1952 the four-year period of the Marshall Plan would be over, and the UK attitude was that thereafter the OEEC budget should be cut and some of its functions passed over to the North Atlantic Treaty Organisation (NATO).

As it turned out, the ECSC was much more to the federalists' taste. That is because its executive body, the *High Authority*, was given substantial direct powers which could be exercised without the prior approval of the *Council of Ministers*, the ECSC's second institution; it also had a *Parliamentary Assembly* and a *Court of Justice*.

The plan received favourable responses from the Six (the BENELUX nations – Belgium, the Netherlands and Luxembourg, who had agreed in 1944 to create a CU, but which became effective in 1948 – France, Italy and West Germany). The United Kingdom was invited to join but it refused. Clement Attlee, the British prime minister at the time, told the House of Commons that *his government was not prepared to accept that the most vital economic forces of the UK should be handed over to 'an authority that is utterly undemocratic and is responsible to nobody*'. The Six were however not to be deterred, and on 18 April 1951 the *Treaty of Paris*, valid for 50 years, was signed. The ECSC was born and it embarked on an experiment in limited economic integration (since iron, coal and steel were but a sector of the economy, albeit a substantial one then, hence Attlee's vehement utterance) on 1 January 1952.

At least three points about the ECSC are of direct vital relevance to the EAC. The first is that it was run by the High Authority which acted independently of the governments of the member nations. In other words, the High Authority was a truly supra-national institution. Given the experience in East and Northeast Asia, is it likely in the foreseeable future that a similar institution can be created? I believe that most serious analysts would respond in the negative. The second is that it is simply misguided to try to justify the EAC on the grounds that the extent of trade between the countries concerned today matches that of intra-Six trade in coal, iron and steel as a proportion of total trade then.[23] This is because in the case of the ECSC not only the location and ownership of production, but also the free movement of labour were of the essence when coal, iron and steel loomed large as the driving locomotive of the economy, hence the devastating wars. But, in the case of China, it is not even possible for Chinese citizens to move freely from one city to another and China, Japan, Korea do not want to have foreign workers in their midst, when especially Japan is in dire need for them to shore up its pensions system.[24] And more to the point is the fact that the ECSC marked the beginning of European integration, but today the EU is a vastly different animal; it is therefore of the essence to go past the ECSC.

There are so many facets to today's EU which the following list does not fully exhaust:[25]

1. It has a CM, allowing free mobility across its member nations' borders for commodities, services,[26] people, capital and enterprises, hence its so-called 'four freedoms', enshrined in its 'single market' (SEM).
2. It has a CCP, entrusted to a single commissioner, that is no single EU member nation can deal with commercial matters by itself.
3. It has a single currency (in the sense that eventually all but the United Kingdom, which has an 'opt-out',[27] will be using it), run by a single central bank, the European Central Bank (ECB), which determines the interest rate for the entire 'eurozone', that is member nations using the euro have no control over their own monetary policy.
4. It has a 'regional policy' and 'structural funds', which help both the poorer regions and the poorer member nations, which have elevated Ireland from the bottom of the EU league of per capita GNI (using PPP data) to the second and galvanising the Spanish economy beyond recognition.[28]
5. It has, since the coming into force of the Lisbon Treaty on 1 December 2009, a single president of the European Council,[29] ex-Belgian Prime Minister Herman Van Rompuy, appointed by the EU national leaders for two and a half years, renewable once.
6. It has, since the coming into force of the Lisbon Treaty on 1 December 2009, a foreign policy chief,[30] called 'foreign policy supremo' by the press, Catherine Margaret Ashton (Baroness Ashton of Upholland) of the United Kingdom, ex-EU trade commissioner, who is appointed for five years, controls a vast diplomatic corps, a third of the senior personnel of which will be provided by the member states, has own budget and is a vice-president of the EU Commission.
7. It has some sort of 'common defence' in that all members belong to NATO.
8. It sets very strict conditions for the joining of the club through the 'Copenhagen criteria'.

In short, the EU is largely a complete economic union (EcU above), exceeding it in some respects, but falling slightly short of it in a few others. Hence, in order to consider what the EAC can or cannot learn from these EU characteristics, it is vital to elaborate on them. I shall however not give them equal weight since three of them are too straightforward to warrant more than a mere statement.

3.1.1. The SEM

Unlike many EU policy areas, the SEM is almost universally positively acknowledged, perhaps because it has been central to EU development.[31] It is an important stepping stone on the route from the CU to a fully-fledged EcU. It is defined in the Single European Act (SEA; European Commission (various years)) as 'an area without internal frontiers in which the free movement of goods, persons, services and capital is ensured'.[32] This means that borders should disappear within the EU: goods, services, capital and people should be able to move between member countries as they move between regions within a country. This requires the removal of customs and passport controls at borders; the elimination of any national barriers to the sale of other EU countries' goods and services and the ending of any national controls on the movement of capital. This is a very extensive agenda that has such wide implications for virtually every EU policy area.

To make the SEM for the EU operate like a national market required the removal of three types of barriers:

(i) Physical barriers were checks at borders for the control of the movement of goods and persons for immigration purposes; customs borders were required due to differences in indirect taxes; animal and plant health was protected by inspections at borders; checks on lorries and drivers were ostensibly for safety reasons and to enforce national restrictions on foreign hauliers. Considerable expense was incurred in preparing the documentation needed and there were delays at borders, further increasing the cost of inter-EU transport.
(ii) Fiscal barriers were needed to check the goods crossing borders because differences in indirect taxes (VAT) and excise duties on alcohol, tobacco etc. were dealt with by remitting these taxes on exports and imposing them on imports.
(iii) Technical barriers cover an enormous range of measures that affect trade. The most pervasive of these are technical regulations and

> standards. *Regulations* are legal requirements which products must satisfy before they can be sold in a particular country; these cover health, safety and environmental requirements. Regulations are also important in relation to services (see below). *Standards* are not legally binding in themselves; they are technical requirements set by private standardisation bodies like DIN in Germany, BSI in the United Kingdom and AFNOR in France. Although they are only voluntary, they often assume a quasi-legal status because they are used in technical regulations and in calls for tendering contracts. They are also important in marketing the product. The existence of different regulations and standards impose additional costs on EU producers who had to make alterations to their products before they could sell them in other member states.

Another technical barrier related to *public procurement*: private sector purchases by governments. Governments frequently discriminated against bids from firms in other member states for a variety of reasons: strategic (e.g. weapons), support of employment, encouragement of emerging high-tech industries, to maintain employment etc. However, such policies imposed costs on both the public authorities (who ended up paying more than they need to) and on firms (because the market available for selling their goods was too limited). One consequence was too many producers, making it difficult to achieve an optimum scale in industries such as defence, electricity-generating and telecommunications equipment.

Technical barriers were the main impediment to trade in *services*. For a range of services from plumbing to legal services, the problems related to the recognition of qualifications and the rights to establish businesses. For *financial services*, trade was limited by government regulatory measures. In banking, there were particular problems with establishing capital adequacy. Insurance could not be sold in most member states unless the insurer had a local permanent establishment. Capital movements were controlled by several member states which interfered with free trade in financial services.

Although problems remain especially in the financial services area, it is widely acknowledged that the EU has made excellent progress with the SEM.[33] Can the EAC really duplicate such an achievement? To do so would require the freedom to move across borders for goods, services, labour, capital and enterprise. Despite some restrictions, goods are not a major problem. However, services remain largely a national domain. With regard to labour, as already mentioned, even Chinese citizens are not allowed to move freely from one city to another, and in the case of China, Japan,

Korea and several countries in this part of the world, foreigners are more or less shut out. As to capital, although several countries, especially Japan, have been investing in China, the bulk of their investment heads to the United States and Europe (below), and China invests mainly in the United States and Europe. Enterprises largely go hand in hand with capital through joint ventures, and hence their movement is similar to that of capital, but especially in the case of China they are asked to sell all their products abroad.[34] It would therefore seem like a wild dream to think that the EAC can emulate the EU in this respect any time soon.

3.1.2. The CCP

The main provisions of the CCP[35] contain the well-known aspiration: 'By establishing a [CU] between themselves member states aim to contribute, in the common interest, to the harmonious development of world trade, the progressive abolition of restrictions on international trade and the lowering of customs barriers' (Article 131). The cornerstone of the CCP is Article 133 which sets out the important rule that: 'the CCP shall be based on uniform principles, particularly in regard to changes in tariff rates, the conclusion of tariff and trade agreements, the achievement of uniformity in measures towards the liberalisation of export policy and in measures to protect trade such as those to be taken in the case of dumping or subsidies'.

Article 133 defines CCP coverage only with an illustrative list: mostly tariffs, anti-dumping or anti-subsidy measures, and trade agreements. Trade in goods, including agriculture, falls unambiguously within the EU's competence. Decision-making concerning trade in goods under the Article is by 'qualified majority voting' (QMV[36]) in the Council. Subject to Council's approval, *the Commission is empowered to conduct negotiations* in consultation with a special committee appointed by the Council for this purpose (the *Article 133 Committee*), and within the framework of such negotiating directives as the Council may issue to it. For example, *the EU Commission negotiates on behalf of the member states in the WTO*. During negotiations, the Commission may sometimes interpret its mandate in a way with which some member states may disagree, which has been a source of tension in the past.

Multilateral trade agreements increasingly cover a wider range of topics including services, intellectual property rights, e-commerce and investment where the EU's competence to negotiate and implement trade policies is much less clear. In 1994, the European Court of Justice (ECJ) was asked to rule on the division of competences with respect to services and intellectual property rights. The *EJC ruled that the EU had exclusive competence with respect to cross-border trade in services but that member states retained joint competence with the EU for trade issues involving commercial presence and factor movements.* As a result, the WTO Agreement was signed by representatives of both the EU Council and of the member states. In 1997, the Amsterdam Treaty modified Article 133 to grant powers to the EU to negotiate agreements on services and intellectual property, but only on the basis of unanimity. The Nice Treaty in 2001 further tilted the balance towards exclusive competence by extending QMV to these areas.[37] But other areas of growing significance, such as investment issues or the traditionally contentious area of export policy, remain under the unanimity rule. Unanimity also continues to prevail in the limited instances where it is required for internal decisions, such as taxation matters; this is called the principle of 'parallelism'. The absence of QMV in these areas could make the conclusion of future trade negotiations cumbersome, where the outcome is presented as a 'single undertaking' because, *de facto*, unanimity is required for the entire agenda.

What this amounts to is that the CCP dictates that in international trade negotiations such as in the on-going WTO's Doha Round, the EU Commission (through its external trade commissioner) is the sole speaker on behalf of all member states. Hence, in this sense, the EU Commission is a supra-national institution. Thus, the pertinent question to ask is: Would the EAC be able to agree to such an arrangement? Again, the answer is in the negative and will remain so for the foreseeable future. It may prove enlightening to see what the other side of the coin looks like by revisiting the 'Poitiers incident'.[38]

For a number of years, the EU (EC then) Commission could not get Japan to accept that it is has sole responsibility for the CCP. This was attributed to the fact that until the mid-1970s, 'Japan found it easier to deal with other nations on the grounds of familiarity, tradition, the emotional factor, and organisational considerations' Hosoya (1979, p. 168). Hence, the need to conclude a comprehensive agreement with the EU as a whole to replace the agreements that had been in force with individual EU member nations created a real dilemma for Japan. The EU commission's efforts to persuade Japan to deal with it as a corporate body were in vain until much later. The success came only after the bizarre Poitiers incident: in 1982, the French government did not know what to do in the face of the 'Japanese invasion' of the French VTR market, so it adopted the tactic of requiring all Japanese VTRs to go through Poitiers for customs inspection. Poitiers was a city almost completely lacking in staff trained in customs inspection procedures; hence a go-slow tactic had been adopted, ensuring that Japanese

VTRs reached the consumer at a much reduced pace. This was a bizarre incident simply because the French knew perfectly well that their tactic was clearly against the rules of GATT (WTO's predecessor), which asked for non-discrimination between its member states, that is, had France asked for VTRs from all other nations to go through Poitiers, there would have been no major problem. This prompted me then to state that 'human ingenuity in the creation of non-tariff trade barriers makes the mind boggle' (El-Agraa, 1988, p. 6). What is of significance is that before that incident, the Japanese government was adamant that it should deal with each EU member nation as a separate entity, but its attempts were shunned by the French. Then, in desperation, the Japanese approached the Commission and asked: 'What can we do in order to solve this problem which is detrimental to our industry?' (Anouil, 1985, p. 5). And here is the moral of the story: If that is what it took Japan to accept the EU's CCP, how likely would be the possibility that it and the major players in the EAC be able to develop one of their own?

3.1.3. The Common Currency

With regard to the single currency, the answers to two pertinent questions are of particular importance. First, why is it used by only 16 of the 27 EU nations? Second, who issues it?

The answer to the first question is that in order to ensure its stability, hence to provide it with the confidence that it needs for its future survival, the EU has set very strict 'convergence criteria' for joining the euro. These criteria are:

(i) *Price stability* – membership requires an inflation rate not exceeding 1.5% of the average for the three EU nations with the lowest rates.
(ii) *Interest rates* – membership requires a long-term rate within two percentage points of the average for the three countries with the lowest inflation rates.
(iii) *Budget deficits* – membership requires a deficit of less than 3% of a member's GDP.
(iv) *Public debt* – membership requires a ratio not exceeding 60% of a member's GDP.
(v) *Currency stability* – membership requires a member nation's currency not to have been devalued in the previous two years and to have been maintained within the 2.25% margin of fluctuation allowed when the 'exchange rate mechanism' (ERM) of the European Monetary System (EMS)[39] was initiated.

One would of course be perfectly justified in asking about the theoretical rationale for these convergence criteria. The answer is simply that there is not one; for example, the inflation criterion is not even based on NAIRUs[40] (i.e. inflation could be convergent simply because the economy is out of internal equilibrium over the examination period), and there is no way to evaluate whether or not a 60% of GDP public debt is better or worse than, say, a 65% of GDP rate. Normally the criterion used for assessing the debt position of a country in rating its debt is 'sustainability', which is subject to a wide range of considerations. There is however a vital 'state of the EU economy' rationalization: 3% of GDP happened to be the average level of public investment at that time, and the member nations deemed this percentage acceptable. Given this, it is often also accepted that investment (provided it has an equivalent financial rate of return) can be sustainably financed by a budget deficit. Calculating this at the steady state of equilibrium and a compound rate of interest of 5% per annum results in a public borrowing of 60% of GDP,[41] which also happened to be the average at the time.

When these criteria were tested at the end of the third and final stage for EMU[42] on 2 May 1998 on the then 15 EU member nations, only Greece failed; Denmark, Sweden and the United Kingdom had decided not to join at that time, with the UK being granted an opt-out. Since then Greece and four of the new members have done so. Thus, the answer is that no member nation can join the euro unless it has passed these criteria.

As to the second question, the euro is controlled by the ECB,[43] which was established on 1 June 1998. *The ECB is given total independence to carry out its mandate*: to ensure price stability in the eurozone; price stability has been defined to be an annual increase in the consumer price index of less than 2%. To achieve this, a so-called two-pillar strategy is followed: the first is the setting of a target for the growth of money supply, defined in the broadest sense, and the second is assessing future price trends and risks to price stability by examining trends in wages, exchange rates, long-term interest rates, various measures of economic activity and the like. The ECB is also responsible for collecting all necessary statistical information, from both the national authorities and economic agents, for example financial institutions, and for following developments in the banking and financial sectors and promoting the exchange of information between the *European System of Central Banks* (ESCB)[44] and banking authorities. In executing its task, *the ECB defines and implements the monetary policy of the eurozone, holds and manages the foreign exchange reserves of the eurozone and conducts foreign exchange operations, issues euro notes and coins and promotes the smooth operation of the payment systems*. These activities are consistent with the necessary conditions set in the early 1970s by specialists in the field for ensuring the sustainability of EMU: explicit harmonisation of member nations' monetary policies, a common pool of foreign exchange reserves and a single central bank or monetary authority.[45]

So the same question has to be reiterated: What is the feasibility of a single currency for the EAC? Again, the previous negative answer has to be repeated since the ECB is a supra-national institution. However, some may object, claiming that Hatoyama's call for a single currency has not come out of the blue, citing in evidence the cooperation developed in the aftermath of the Asian crisis of 1997: the Chiang Mai Initiative (CMI) and the Asian Bond Market Initiative (ABMI). So something on CMI and ABMI is warranted.

The original aim of CMI[46] was the creation of a network of bilateral swap arrangements (BSAs) among the ASEAN + 3 countries to help them manage regional short-term liquidity problems and to facilitate the work of other international financial arrangements and organisations such as the IMF. However, the bilateral CMI framework lacked efficiency and coherence, since a country with excess reserves could not offer assistance to one with liquidity shortage if the two did not have a BSA. Moreover, because no regional surveillance mechanisms were installed, countries that would be in a position to provide liquidity in times of need had no means to regularly assess in normal times the solvency of countries with potential liquidity crises. Accordingly, in order to mitigate the moral hazard risk involved in any 'lender of last resort' activity, liquidity provision was made conditional on the existence of an IMF programme with the particular country recording a liquidity deficit. However, in 2005 it was rightly agreed to make CMI more effective by multilateralising it. Also, in early 2006 it was decided that the agreed total amount of $74 billion was too small to provide a cushion in the case of a severe crisis, so in 2008 it was proposed to raise it to $80 billion and in February 2009 to $120 billion, and in May 2009 it was agreed that China and Japan will contribute 32% each, Korea 16% and the ASEAN nations the remaining 10%.

Although CMI has been active,[47] experience with it does not provide any basis for the introduction of a single currency. The fund is fixed and is issued by countries, not by a single authority. It is for emergencies while a currency is for all daily financial activities. And so on and so forth. Hence, it would be far-fetched to claim that experience with CMI has laid the lawn for a single currency.

The ABMI is a red herring as far as a single currency is concerned. It is a fact that it was endorsed by ASEAN + 3 finance minsters on 7 August 2003, but its aim is to create efficient and liquid bond markets and to contribute to the mitigation of currency and maturity mismatches in financing. Moreover, despite its name, it covers countries in the Middle East like Turkey, some of those belonging to the Commonwealth of Independent States and most of those in APEC. It therefore extends beyond reach for the proposed EAC or NEAC and, vitally, has nothing to do with a single currency.

3.1.4. The Regional Policy and Structural Funds

EU 'regional policy' was introduced in 1975 with the creation of the European Regional Development Fund (ERDF), which the United Kingdom had insisted on during its membership negotiations before joining in 1972. The EU refers to it as an instrument of financial solidarity and a powerful force for cohesion and economic integration.

The policy had a major reform in 1989,[48] specifically designed to accompany the introduction of the 'single market' (above), integrating various EU funds, renaming them the 'structural funds'. These funds comprise the ERDF, the European Social Fund (ESF), the 'guidance' section of the European Agricultural Guidance and Guarantee Fund (EAGGF) and, since 1994, a Financial Instrument for Fisheries Guidance (FIFG). The reforms also included 'match funding' by asking the member states to inject amounts equal to the EU transfers. The Cohesion Fund (CF), also created in 1994 to assist the poorer EU nations prepare for monetary union (EMU), acts in many ways like one of the structural funds. Further reforms were introduced in 1994, designed to accompany steps towards EMU, hence the CF; in 1999, to prepare the way for enlargement to include the former socialist countries in Central and Eastern Europe (the CEECs) and in 2007 to complete the integration of the new member states into regional policy such that the funding for 2007–2013 represented a major shift to the 'east'.

The regional policy which has emerged in the aftermath of the 1989 reforms places great emphasis on four principles. They are the use of a system of *multi-annual programmes* of assistance, the need for a close *partnership* between all of those involved in regional policy, a commitment to *subsidiarity* (the retention at EU level of the minimum necessary powers) and a desire that EU money should be a genuine supplement to regional policy spending by the member states (*additionality*).

In order to ensure that funding is as precisely targeted as possible (called the principle of *concentration*), the structural funds have since 1989 been given the task of attaining specific *priority objectives*. At one time there were no fewer than seven such objectives, but they have been reduced to just three. Objective 1, known since 2007 as the 'convergence' objective, focuses on the most disadvantaged regions in the EU: those whose GDP per capita (at purchasing power parities) is under 75% of the EU average. Hence, all the 12 CEECs benefit from this, receiving about half of total EU regional spending. The objective is designed to help them catch up with the rest of the EU. It is by far the most generously funded of the three, commanding over 80% of total funding, and has less stringent requirements in terms of percentages of investment costs met and matching national funding targets, which are conditional.

Objective 2, known since 2007 as the 'regional competitiveness and employment' objective, focuses on policies to stimulate innovation, the knowledge society, entrepreneurship, the protection of the environment and the enhancement of workers' skills. Areas eligible for funding may[49] comprise all regions other than those under objective 1; hence, it is effectively 'non-regional'. Regions eligible for funding are mainly those suffering from industrial (i.e. manufacturing) decline, certain disadvantaged rural areas, certain urban areas suffering severe economic, social and environmental problems and fishing communities in decline.

Objective 3, named 'territorial cohesion', provides a small percentage of total funding: 2.5% of the 2007–2013 budgetary allocation for regional policy. Its aim is to stimulate cross-border and transnational economic development initiatives.

The EU has always deliberately extended most of its financial assistance to the very poorest areas; in practice those eligible under objective 1. This concentration process has been strengthened for the 2007–2013 period as can easily be seen in Table 1, which sets out the 'indicative' allocations for funding, indicative since the actual expenditures would depend on how the member states and regions actually spend the money during the period: about 82% of the total is objective 1 funding. For a sense of overall perspective, it should be pointed out that EU regional expenditure over the period 2007–2013 is expected to be 36% of the EU general budget, amounting to about €350 billion over the seven-year period.

So what is the moral of the story? As just mentioned, the EU provides substantial assistance to both its poorer regions and member nations. It dictates that the per capita GNI for the poorer countries should be elevated to the average level for the total membership by allocating EU monies for the purpose, that is, the decision regarding allocation is EU-wide, not member country specific. This would be vital if the EAC were to survive and become stable and prosperous. Would this be feasible, given the disparities between the EAC nations, revealed by a glance at the GNI and per capita data, given in Table 2, which includes other nations that I shall refer to in

Table 1. Regional Policy Allocations for 2007–2013 (€ Million; 2004 Prices).

EU Nation	Objective 1	Objective 2	Objective 3	Total
Austria	159	914	228	1,301
Belgium	579	1,268	173	2,019
Bulgaria	5,888	0	159	6,047
Cyprus	194	363	25	581
Czech Rep.	22,979	373	346	23,697
Denmark	0	453	92	545
Estonia	3,011	0	47	3,058
Germany	14,324	8,370	756	23,450
Greece	17,447	584	186	18,217
Finland	0	1,426	107	1,532
France	2,838	9,123	775	12,736
Hungary	20,243	1,865	344	22,452
Ireland	0	681	134	815
Italy	19,255	5,640	752	25,647
Latvia	4,010	0	80	4,090
Lithuania	5,999	0	97	6,097
Luxembourg	0	45	13	58
Malta	747	0	14	761
Netherlands	0	1,477	220	1,696
Poland	59,048	0	650	59,698
Portugal	18,216	843	88	19,147
Romania	16,912	0	404	17,317
Slovakia	9,664	399	202	10,264
Slovenia	3,646	0	93	3,739
Spain	23,411	7,628	497	31,536
Sweden	0	1,446	236	1,682
United Kingdom	2,594	6,232	642	9,468
Total	251,162	49,127	7,750	308,041

Source: European Commission (various years).

the next section? That would be a near-impossibility, especially for China, which despite the size of its GNI not only remains a poor nation in per capita GNI terms, but, pertinently, most of its people live in dire poverty? According to the National Bureau of Statistics of China,[50] the disposable income of urban dwellers was 7,052 yuan while that of rural inhabitants was only 2,111 yuan in the first six months of 2007. Not only that, the annual increase for the former was 14.2% after adjustment for inflation, while that for the latter was only 13.3%; thus, income disparity is on the increase. And, vitally, can a fund be created for the purpose?

Table 2. Population and GNI Indicators for the EAC/NEAC and Related Countries, 2007.

Member Nation	Population (Million)	GNI ($Billion)			Per Capita GNI ($)			
		Market exchange rates	Global rank	PPP	Market exchange rates	Global rank	PPP	Global rank
China	1,318.0	3,126.0	4	7,150.5	2,370	132	5,420	120
DPRK	23.5	40.0			170			
Hong Kong	7.0	218.6	32	304.3	31,560	33	43,940	13
Japan	128.0	4,828.9	2	4,440.2	37,790	26	34,750	29
Korea	48.0	955.8	14	1,203.6	19,730	48	24,840	50
Macau	0.5	14.6			42,386			
Taiwan	22.8	345.2			17,299			
Mongolia	3.0	3.4	156	8.3	1,290	149	3,170	146
Russia	142.0	1,069.8	12	2,036.5	7,530	79	14,330	73
Brunei	0.4	10.2		19.5	26,740		50,200	
Cambodia	14.0	8.0	122	24.9	550	179	1,720	170
Lao PDR	6.0	3.7	151	12.2	630	175	2,080	162
Indonesia	226.0	372.6	23	804.5	1,650	141	3,570	144
Malaysia	27.0	170.5	38	351.2	6,420	81	13,230	77
Myanmar	49.0	18,510.0			249			
Philippines	88.0	142.1	42	326.4	1,620	142	3,710	142
Singapore	5.0	148.4	41	220.0	32,340	31	47,950	10
Thailand	64.0	217.2	33	502.8	3,400	114	7,880	103
Vietnam	85.0	65.4	58	215.4	770	169	2,530	156
Australia	21.0	751.5	15	702.0	35,760	29	33,400	34
India	1,125.0	1,071.0	11	3,082.5	950	159	2,740	153
New Zealand	4.0	114.5	52	107.3	27,080	39	25,380	48
USA	302.0	13,886.4	1	13,827.2	46,040	16	45,840	11
EU	490.0	14,764.0		13,846.0	28,208		25,140	

Source: Selected from the World Bank's World Development Indicators 09.
Notes: Data for DPRK and Taiwan come from own national accounts and those for Macao and Myanmar are from the United Nations Statistical Division. They are therefore not comparable with the rest.

3.1.5. EU President, Foreign Policy Supremo and Security

Here, I can be very brief. The EU president and foreign policy supremo are supra-national appointments, so are subject to the same considerations given to the ECB and EU external commissioner. Hence, the likelihood of the EAC agreeing on similar arrangements is close to zero. This leaves just the common security leg of this dimension.

In the EU, the security leg of the Common Foreign and Security Policy (CFSP)[51] is concerned with stemming the tide of terrorism. Add to it the common defence provided through membership of NATO, the EU has more or less a comprehensive common security system. Of course, the United States is the major contributor to the budget, personnel and logistics of NATO, but it is essentially a partner and in only one leg of the common security. However, it should not be forgotten that the United States made the Marshall Plan conditional on European integration, of course to strengthen its stance against the menacing Soviet Union, asking in return for free access to the European markets for its multinational corporations. It may therefore seem that the EAC and Roh's NEAC are similar to the EU in this respect since they want to be partners with the United States, with the United States providing them with security while they continue to contribute towards the costs. But that relates to only Japan and Korea, not to China, since both want security against all outsiders, including China. However, some may raise objections to this on the grounds that the rationale for the NEAC, hence for the EAC, is the creation of an equivalent to the security facilitated by the Six-Party Talks set-up.[52] But the latter is mainly concerned with the containment of the DPRK, that is, it caters mainly for the claimed threat emanating from only that nation, which was included by the previous US administration of George Bush in its 'axis of evil'. There are also other demands on the Six-Party Talks since especially Japan and to some extent Korea want it to deal with the 'abductions' issue[53] before anything else, but these too are a one-way traffic from the two heading for DPRK. Since China lies at the very heart of the EAC and the Six-Party Talks and, given what has been stated about EAC membership, so does the DPRK. Thus, the creation of the EAC for common security purposes necessarily means that not only should the United States be involved but also in a different way than in the present security arrangements. Would that be possible? I very much doubt it, given the developments mentioned above and China's own hegemonic ambitions, but I shall return to this later.

3.1.6. The Copenhagen Criteria

EU membership is conditional on the meeting of the 'Copenhagen criteria', generally known as the 'accession criteria'. These state that any country seeking EU membership must conform to the conditions set out by Article 49 and the principles laid down in Article 6(1) of the Treaty on European Union.[54] To join the EU, a new member state must meet three conditions:

(i) *Political*: stability of institutions guaranteeing democracy, the rule of law, human rights and respect for and protection of minorities;[55]
(ii) *Economic*: existence of a functioning market economy and the capacity to cope with competitive pressure and market forces within the Union and
(iii) *Acceptance of the Community 'acquis'*: ability to take on the obligations of membership, including adherence to the aims of political, economic and monetary union.

The EU has always dictated that only countries with democratically elected governments would be allowed to join; witness the cases of Greece,[56] Portugal and Spain[57] whose membership was delayed for many years. Can these conditions be seriously contemplated by the EAC? China is certainly adamant that human rights are the concern of individual nations and has repeatedly rebuffed the EU for attempting to act otherwise: witness its confrontations with the EU when the two have a *formal relationship*.[58]

3.2. Lessons from the EU Experience

The EU experience thus indicates that it would be a very tall order for the EAC to emulate the EU experience, since in most of the pertinent areas the EU has recorded its achievements through a supra-national institution. It is doubtful if the ECSC accomplishments would have been possible without the High Authority being granted the freedom to decide by itself. And as mentioned, the ECSC was not about trade, rather about common access to resources and freedom for labour to work anywhere in the member states. In the case of the single currency, it is equally doubtful if it could have become a reality without an independent ECB in charge of inflation control, the issue of the euro, the eurozone foreign exchange reserves and more.

The upshot of all comparisons of the EAC with the EU is therefore that all indications point to the feasibility of only a PTA between Japan and Korea, and the United States if we define the EAC to be the equivalent to the Six-Party Talks. This conclusion is reinforced when the 'unsettled issues' stressed by both Roh and Hatoyama[59] become part of the equation. I shall return to this point in the 'Conclusions', but what needs examination before then is the present situation of the countries concerned regarding the feasibility of a PTA, presented in the following section.

4. HOW FEASIBLE IS A PTA BY THE EAC NATIONS?

Regional integration specialists have for a very long time agreed that for a PTA to be potentially economically beneficial, at least for the partners in question, the member countries should be conducting most of their trade amongst themselves and should have high initial tariffs, but low external tariffs after integration. This is because under such circumstances there is more likelihood that 'trade creation' (TC) would outweigh 'trade diversion' (TD). TC refers to *the replacement of expensive domestic production by cheaper imports from a partner country*; hence, the larger the percentage of trade between the partners relative to their total trade, the more would be the gains from regional integration. TD is about *the replacement of cheaper initial imports from the outside world by more expensive imports from a partner nation*;[60] hence, the lower the percentage of the partners' trade with the non-partners, the less would be the harm from regional integration, and this would be more so the lower the partners' external tariffs. So how does East/Northeast Asia fare in this respect?

As can be seen from the percentages in Table 3, calculated using the data given in the appendix in Table A1, intra-regional trade is almost non-existent. China's exports go mainly to Hong Kong (about 15%; without 'about' hereafter) and Japan (8%), with the EU (20%) and United States (19%) accounting for the bulk of it. The DPRK exports 33% to China and practically nothing to the rest except for 5% to the EU. Hong Kong sends 49% of its exports to China and 14% to each of the United States and EU. Japan fares likewise with 15%, 20% and 15%, respectively, and so does Korea with 22%, 12% and 151%. And Macao almost matches these with 15%, 41% and 20%, respectively, but with 13% going to Hong Kong. Furthermore, Mongolia sends 72% to China, 6% to each of Hong Kong and the EU and 5% to the United States. Russia's exports go mainly to the EU (54%), with only 5% to China and 2% to each of Japan and the United States.

In short, for the countries under consideration, a large percentage of their exports goes to the United States and EU rather than to each other, except in the case of Hong Kong and Mongolia where they mainly head to China. In other words, intra-regional exports are insignificant except in the case of countries which are part of China or almost inseparable from it (Mongolia). Some analysts would insist that these percentages have been improving, but that does not matter much given that the latest percentages are so insignificant; hence, it would be pointless to supply earlier data.

In terms of imports, the percentages in Table 4, calculated using the data given in the appendix in Table A2, reveal a slightly different picture. China's imports come mainly from Japan (14%), the EU (12%), Korea (11%),

Table 3. The Direction of Exports among the EAC/NEAC Countries and Related Nations, 2007 (% of Total Exports).

	China	DPRK	HK	Japan	Korea	Macao	Taiwan	Mongolia	Russia	Brunei	Cambodia	Indonesia
China	0.00	0.11	15.13	8.38	4.61	0.22	1.93	0.06	2.34	0.01	0.07	1.04
DPRK	32.92	0.00	0.00	0.00	0.00	0.00	0.00	1.86	1.86	0.00	0.00	0.00
Hong Kong	48.67	0.00	0.00	4.45	1.97	0.65	1.97	0.00	0.26	0.00	0.17	0.53
Japan	15.30	0.00	5.45	0.00	7.60	0.03	6.28	0.02	1.51	0.02	0.02	1.27
Korea	22.07	0.00	5.02	7.10	0.00	0.01	3.51	0.05	2.18	0.01	0.08	1.55
Macao	14.96	0.00	12.99	1.18	0.00	0.00	0.00	0.00	0.00	0.00	0.79	0.00
Taiwan												
Mongolia	71.86	5.99	0.00	1.20	1.20	0.00	0.00	0.00	2.40	0.00	0.00	0.00
Russia	4.51	0.04	0.10	2.15	1.75	0.00	0.26	0.18	0.00	0.00	0.00	0.07
Brunei	3.17	0.00	0.00	32.85	12.25	0.00	0.00	0.00	0.00	0.00	0.00	24.50
Cambodia	1.23	0.00	0.49	3.19	0.00	0.00	0.00	0.00	0.49	0.00	0.00	0.00
Indonesia	8.48	0.00	1.48	20.71	6.64	0.00	2.28	0.00	0.30	0.04	0.11	0.00
Lao PDR	6.06	0.00	0.00	0.76	4.55	0.00	1.52	0.00	0.00	0.00	0.00	0.00
Malaysia	8.77	0.00	4.63	9.13	3.80	0.01	2.72	0.01	0.36	0.23	0.07	2.93
Myanmar	7.16	1.05	1.47	5.68	1.47	0.00	1.05	0.00	0.00	0.00	0.00	0.63
Philippines	11.40	0.00	11.49	14.47	3.53	0.00	3.90	0.00	0.06	0.00	0.00	1.03
Singapore	9.67	0.02	10.48	4.81	3.55	0.01	3.06	0.01	0.00	0.23	0.75	0.01
Thailand	9.73	0.12	5.70	11.89	1.95	0.01	3.80	0.00	0.37	0.06	0.89	3.13
Vietnam	6.92	0.00	1.19	12.50	2.57	0.00	2.35	0.00	0.95	0.00	2.04	2.29
Australia	14.58	0.00	1.38	22.20	8.20	0.02	3.73	0.01	0.52	0.02	0.02	1.95
India	9.33	0.34	3.43	2.40	3.02	0.00	1.07	0.01	0.78	0.11	0.03	1.33
NZ	5.85	0.00	1.63	8.39	3.20	0.00	1.76	0.00	0.56	0.00	0.00	2.38
USA	5.61	0.00	1.73	5.39	2.98	0.02	2.27	0.00	0.63	0.01	0.01	0.36
EU	1.30	0.35	0.54	1.13	0.64	0.01	0.35	0.00	2.31	0.03	0.00	0.14

Table 3. *(Continued)*

	Lao PDR	Malaysia	Myanmar	Philippines	Singapore	Thailand	Vietnam	Australia	India	NZ	USA	EU
China	0.01	1.45	0.14	0.62	2.44	0.98	0.98	1.48	1.97	0.18	19.14	19.91
DPRK	0.00	0.00	3.11	0.00	0.00	1.86	0.00	0.62	3.73	0.00	0.00	4.97
Hong Kong	0.00	0.94	0.00	0.82	1.88	1.07	0.67	1.29	1.30	0.15	13.72	13.49
Japan	0.01	2.11	0.03	1.33	3.05	3.59	0.80	1.99	0.86	0.35	20.38	14.75
Korea	0.02	1.53	0.08	1.19	3.22	1.21	1.55	1.27	1.78	0.02	12.35	14.81
Macao	0.00	0.00	0.00	0.39	0.00	0.00	0.79	0.39	0.00	0.00	40.55	19.69
Taiwan												
Mongolia	0.00	0.00	0.00	0.00	0.00	0.00	0.00	0.00	0.00	0.00	4.79	5.99
Russia	0.00	0.12	0.01	0.03	0.01	0.09	0.16	0.01	1.14	0.00	2.36	53.74
Brunei	0.00	1.30	0.00	0.00	1.87	1.44	0.00	13.40	0.00	1.87	5.48	1.30
Cambodia	0.00	0.49	0.00	0.00	1.97	1.23	4.42	0.49	0.00	0.00	57.99	20.88
Indonesia	0.00	4.47	0.23	1.62	9.20	2.67	1.19	2.98	4.33	0.32	10.20	11.64
Lao PDR	0.00	2.27	0.00	0.00	0.00	32.58	14.39	0.76	0.00	0.00	1.52	12.12
Malaysia	0.00	0.00	0.12	1.45	14.62	4.95	1.32	3.37	3.34	0.43	15.62	12.80
Myanmar	0.00	2.74	0.00	0.00	1.26	44.42	1.47	0.42	14.53	0.00	0.00	6.95
Philippines	0.00	4.47	0.00	0.00	6.22	2.77	0.87	1.05	0.48	0.22	17.04	17.00
Singapore	0.01	12.91	0.26	2.05	0.00	4.14	2.18	3.74	3.34	0.52	8.90	10.75
Thailand	0.86	5.12	0.63	1.90	0.26	0.00	2.49	3.76	1.74	0.41	12.63	13.80
Vietnam	0.21	2.86	0.04	2.00	4.53	2.12	0.00	7.33	0.37	0.14	20.78	18.49
Australia	0.01	1.84	0.02	0.68	2.89	2.42	0.75	0.00	6.08	4.28	5.54	10.67
India	0.00	1.42	0.10	0.30	3.89	1.17	0.96	0.78	0.00	0.11	12.35	19.89
NZ	0.00	2.25	0.00	1.70	2.02	1.96	0.65	23.15	1.24	0.00	10.12	13.06
USA	0.00	1.00	0.00	0.66	2.26	0.73	0.16	1.65	1.51	0.24	0.00	21.22
EU	0.00	0.30	0.00	0.10	0.53	0.21	0.09	0.59	0.76	0.08	6.78	0.00

Source: Calculated using the selected data given in the appendix in Table A1 from the IMF's *Direction of Trade Statistics Yearbook 2008*.

Table 4. The Direction of Imports among the EAC/NEAC Countries and Related Nations, 2007 (% of Total Imports).

	China	DPRK	HK	Japan	Korea	Macao	Taiwan	Mongolia	Russia	Brunei	Cambodia	Indonesia
China	0.00	0.06	1.34	14.01	10.88	0.03	10.56	0.04	2.05	0.03	0.01	1.29
DPRK	44.35	0.00	0.58	0.29	0.00	0.00	0.58	0.87	4.06	0.00	0.00	0.00
Hong Kong	46.32	0.00	0.00	10.02	4.17	0.10	7.15	0.00	0.10	0.00	0.01	0.56
Japan	20.54	0.0	0.23	0.00	4.39	0.01	3.19	0.00	1.70	0.40	0.02	4.22
Korea	17.66	0.00	0.60	15.76	0.00	0.00	2.79	0.01	1.96	0.26	0.00	2.55
Macao	42.64	0.00	10.06	8.94	1.49	0.00	3.54	0.00	0.00	0.00	0.00	0.56
Taiwan												
Mongolia	31.91	1.70	0.43	7.23	8.09	0.00	1.28	0.00	29.36	0.00	0.00	0.00
Russia	12.24	0.02	0.06	6.38	4.43	0.02	0.45	0.02	0.00	0.00	0.01	0.34
Brunei	3.05	0.00	0.76	3.56	0.76	0.00	0.51	0.00	0.00	0.00	0.00	1.27
Cambodia	15.02	0.00	10.37	1.86	4.80	0.00	7.28	0.00	0.15	0.00	0.00	2.01
Indonesia	11.49	0.00	0.59	8.77	4.30	0.00	2.01	0.00	0.59	2.51	0.00	0.00
Lao PDR	9.48	0.00	0.95	1.90	2.84	0.00	0.00	0.00	0.00	0.00	0.00	0.00
Malaysia	12.87	0.00	2.91	12.99	4.93	0.01	5.68	0.00	0.18	0.07	0.01	4.24
Myanmar	33.70	0.91	0.91	3.44	5.80	0.00	0.00	0.00	0.36	0.00	0.00	5.25
Philippines	7.21	0.00	4.00	12.32	5.91	0.00	5.91	0.00	0.20	0.00	0.00	2.25
Singapore	12.11	0.00	1.47	8.18	4.86	0.01	5.88	0.00	0.28	0.05	0.03	5.57
Thailand	11.59	0.02	1.03	20.28	3.78	0.00	4.10	0.00	1.10	0.08	0.04	1.48
Vietnam	19.94	0.00	3.10	9.86	8.50	0.00	18.14	0.00	0.88	0.00	0.32	2.15
Australia	15.37	0.01	0.63	9.06	2.86	0.01	1.95	0.00	0.27	0.53	0.01	2.28
India	11.00	0.09	2.34	2.75	3.14	0.00	1.05	0.00	1.83	0.09	0.00	2.50
NZ	13.25	0.00	0.41	8.30	2.81	0.00	0.20	0.00	0.15	1.02	0.00	2.54
USA	16.86	0.00	0.36	7.41	2.45	0.06	1.98	0.00	0.00	0.02	0.13	0.77
EU	5.85	0.00	0.28	1.98	0.99	0.01	0.66	0.00	3.52	0.00	0.02	0.32

Table 4. (*Continued*)

	Lao PDR	Malaysia	Myanmar	Philippines	Singapore	Thailand	Vietnam	Australia	ndia	NZ	USA	EU
China	0.01	3.01	0.04	2.42	1.83	2.37	0.34	2.69	1.53	0.16	7.32	11.57
DPRK	0.00	0.00	1.45	0.00	1.74	5.80	0.00	0.00	3.48	0.00	0.00	2.61
Hong Kong	0.00	2.19	0.02	1.66	6.79	2.04	0.20	0.57	1.66	0.10	4.87	7.13
Japan	0.00	2.79	0.05	1.40	1.13	2.94	0.98	4.99	0.67	0.43	11.63	10.42
Korea	0.02	2.37	0.01	0.68	1.92	1.06	0.39	3.71	1.29	0.33	10.48	10.29
Macao	0.00	1.12	0.00	0.00	3.17	1.12	0.19	1.49	0.19	0.19	5.59	15.64
Taiwan												
Mongolia	0.00	0.43	0.00	0.00	1.70	0.00	0.00	0.85	0.00	0.00	1.28	10.64
Russia	0.00	0.74	0.00	0.06	0.23	0.51	0.06	0.33	0.66	0.05	4.76	43.10
Brunei	0.00	11.20	0.00	0.00	19.59	0.25	0.00	0.76	1.53	0.00	3.82	49.36
Cambodia	0.00	2.32	0.00	0.00	7.43	23.22	16.87	0.62	0.46	0.00	2.32	3.56
Indonesia	0.00	8.61	0.00	0.48	13.21	5.76	1.33	4.03	2.16	0.07	6.45	10.29
Lao PDR	0.00	0.47	0.00	0.00	1.90	68.25	5.69	0.95	0.47	0.00	0.95	3.79
Malaysia	0.03	0.00	0.10	1.94	11.48	5.35	1.25	2.02	1.40	0.33	10.84	11.85
Myanmar	0.00	4.17	0.00	0.00	15.58	19.20	0.36	0.54	3.44	0.00	0.18	4.53
Philippines	0.00	4.11	0.00	0.00	11.21	4.11	1.51	1.30	0.88	0.65	14.12	9.55
Singapore	0.00	13.07	0.02	2.21	0.00	3.23	0.81	1.20	2.23	0.18	12.48	12.27
Thailand	0.34	6.15	1.64	1.53	4.49	0.00	0.79	2.72	1.48	0.30	6.83	8.49
Vietnam	0.34	3.65	0.13	0.65	12.14	5.97	0.00	1.69	2.17	0.40	2.71	8.14
Australia	0.00	4.10	0.01	0.32	6.98	4.49	2.33	0.00	0.80	3.37	12.01	21.01
India	0.00	2.59	0.29	0.07	4.18	1.17	0.14	3.94	0.00	0.13	6.52	16.22
NZ	0.00	4.36	0.00	0.35	4.68	2.75	0.35	18.16	0.67	0.00	9.53	15.82
USA	0.00	1.67	0.00	0.49	0.93	1.18	0.57	0.44	1.24	0.16	0.00	17.97
EU	0.00	0.46	0.01	0.14	0.47	0.42	0.20	0.30	0.66	0.08	4.59	0.00

Source Calculated using the selected data given in the appendix in Table A2 from the IMF's *Direction of Trade Statistics Yearbook 2008*.

Taiwan (11%) and the United States (7%). Most of the DPRKs come from China (44%), followed by Thailand (6%), Russia (4%) and the EU (3%). Those of Hong Kong also come mainly from China (46%), Japan (10%), Taiwan (7%), the EU (7%), Singapore (7%), the United States (5%) and Korea (4%), with 2% from each of Malaysia, the Philippines and Thailand. As to Japan, they originate mainly in China (21%), the United States (12%) and EU (10%). For Korea, they come mainly from China (18%), Japan (16%), the EU (11%) and United States (11%), followed by Taiwan (3%) and Russia (2%). For Macao, the picture is very different from that of exports: the imports are mainly from China (43%), the EU (16%), Hong Kong (10%), Japan (9%), the United States (6%), Taiwan (4%), Singapore (3%) and Korea (2%). Mongolia receives 32% from China, 30% from Russia, 11% from the EU, 8% from Korea, 7% from Japan, 2% from the DPRK and from Singapore, 1% from each of Taiwan and the United States. And Russia gets most of its imports from the UK (43%), China (12%), Japan (6%), the United States (5%) and Korea (4%).

As to tariffs, Table 5 provides them for the latest years available. It can be seen that their total weighted average is zero for Hong Kong and Macao; about 2% for Japan, Taiwan and the United States and about 5% for China and Mongolia. They are therefore not far different from those of the EU at 3%. What is interesting is that except for Singapore, with 0%, they are in the range of 3.6–12.7% in ASEAN, the only established regional integration scheme in the area. Note that Russia is on 11.8% while New Zealand is on 3.5%, Australia on 5.5% and India on 8%. Also, except in the case of India and Australia, they are lower for the non-agricultural products and higher for all the agricultural products, with China on 16%, Taiwan on 11.4%, Japan on 10.1%, Korea on 91.6%, Russia on 24.2% and India on 41.9%. It would therefore seem that regional integration may provide economic benefits in mainly agricultural products, but they are practically excluded in all the RTAs in this area on 'sensitivity' grounds, and their liberalisation is a taboo subject in the countries concerned for reasons that require a chapter on its own right, but it suffices to say that agricultural lobbies are supreme especially in Japan, Korea and the United States.

Considering only total trade, there is therefore only some sort of case for regional integration between only China, together with Hong Kong and Taiwan, Japan, Korea and the United States. Some sort, because the percentages are not that significant across the spectrum since the traffic is heading one way to either China or the United States. Yet neither the EAC nor NEAC includes the United States as a full member; thus, less economic gains should be expected. And as just indicated, any arrangement will have

Table 5. Latest Tariffs in the EAC/NEAC and Related Countries.

NEAC Member Nation	Simple Average Final Bound			Simple Average MNF Applied[a]			Total Weighted Average[b]			Binding Coverage	
	Total	Agriculture	Non-Agriculture	Total	Agriculture	Non-Agriculture	Total	Agriculture	Non-Agriculture	Total	Non-Agriculture
China	10.0	15.8	9.1	9.9	15.8	9.0	5.0	16.0	4.6	100.0	100.0
DPRK											
Hong Kong	0.0	0.0	0.0	0.0	0.0	0.0	0.0	0.0	0.0	45.8	37.5
Japan	5.1	22.7	2.6	5.1	21.8	1.3	2.0	10.1	1.3	99.6	99.6
Korea	12.2	59.3	10.2	12.2	49.0	6.6	7.0	91.6	3.6	94.6	93.9
Macau	0.0	0.0	0.0	0.0	0.0	0.0	0.0	0.0	0.0	26.8	15.6
Taiwan	6.6	18.4	4.8	6.3	17.5	4.6	2.1	11.4	1.7	100.0	100.0
Mongolia	17.6	18.9	17.3	5.0	5.1	5.0	5.1	6.5	4.9	100.0	100.0
Russia[c]				11.0	14.6	10.5	11.8	24.2	9.4		
Brunei	25.3	30.7	24.3	3.6	7.9	3.0	5.1	7.1	4.8	95.3	95
Cambodia	19.0	28.1	17.7	14.2	18.1	13.6				100.0	100.0
Lao PDR	na	na	na	9.7	19.5	8.2					
Indonesia	37.1	47.0	35.6	6.9	8.6	6.7	4.0	7.2	3.6	96.6	96.1
Malaysia	24.5	76.0	14.9	8.4	11.7	7.9	4.7	15.0	4.1	83.7	81.3
Myanmar	83.0	102.2	21.1	5.6	8.7	5.1	na	na	na	17.4	4.7
Philippines	25.6	34.6	23.4	6.3	9.6	5.8	4.2	12.9	3.3	66.8	61.8
Singapore	12.1	36.5	6.3	0.0	0.1	0.0	0.0	1.1	0.0	69.2	64.5
Thailand	28.1	40.2	25.5	10.0	22.0	8.2	3.6	14.1	3.2	74.7	70.9
Vietnam	11.4	18.5	10.4	16.8	24.2	15.7	12.7	14.5	12.6	100.0	100.0
Australia	9.9	3.3	11.0	3.5	1.3	3.8	5.5	2.8	5.6	97.0	96.5
India	50.2	114.2	36.2	14.5	34.4	11.5	8.0	41.9	6.5	73.8	69.8
New Zealand	9.9		10.6	3.0	1.7	3.2	3.5	2.5	3.6	99.9	99.9
USA	3.5	5.0	3.3	3.5	5.5	3.2	2.1	5.3	2.0	100.0	100.0
EU[d]	5.4	15.1	3.9	5.2	15.0	3.8	3.0	11.8	2.4	100.0	100.0

Source: Complied from the World Trade Organisation's World Tariff Profiles 2008. The world Banks' World Development Indicators 2009 also contains data but it does not provide it for all the countries in this table and the differences are, for our purposes, on the whole minor.

[a]The tariffs are for 2007, but 2006 for Thailand.

[b]The Tariffs are for 2006, but 2005 for Indonesia, Macao and Vietnam.

[c]Since Russia is not yet a WTO member, there are no 'bindings'.

to include agriculture if it were to bring economic benefits to the region, yet agriculture remains a taboo subject.

Before leaving this section, one may ask about FDI flows, given that it is now widely accepted that PTAs also allow for their freedom (above). So how do these countries fare in terms of FDI? As can be seen from Table 6,[61]

Table 6. Direction of FDI for the NEAC and European Union, 2003–2004, and FDI Stock, 2006.

	Direction of FDI (% of Total)							FDI Stocks	
	China	HK	Japan	Korea	Russia	USA	EU	$ Million	% of GDP
China									
Inward		44.0	6.1	3.9		9.2	4.9	292,559	11.1
Outward		39.3			2.6	8.8	4.4	73,330	2.8
Hong Kong									
Inward	35.1		2.6			4.8	8.6	769,029	405.7
Outward	40.2		1.2			0.6	1.2	688,974	363.5
Japan									
Inward	0.0	0.1		0.6		65.1	18.0	107,633	2.5
Outward	12.8	1.8		2.4		13.2	36.5	449,567	10.3
Korea									
Inward	3.7	1.3	9.3			22.3	41.2	70,974	8.0
Outward	25.6	5.8			1.1	16.7	9.8	46,780	5.3
Russia									
Inward	0.0	0.3				3.5	44.2	197,682	20.2
Outward	4.7					8.1	54.4	156,824	16.0
USA									
Inward	19.6		11.1	0.6			62.2	1,789,087	13.5
Outward	1.0	1.7	3.6	1.0			49.3	2,384,004	18.0
EU									
Inward	0.0	8.0	6.0	1.0	0.0	37.0		2,278,500	16.5
Outward	10.0	10.0	7.0	1.0	6.0	−2.0		2,964,000	21.5

Source: Selected from, inter alia, *European Union Foreign Direct Investment Yearbook 2006*, Japanese Ministry of Finance's website and UNCTAD's *World Investment Report 2007*; using the latest data is to no avail since FDI flows have been dramatically affected by the crises.
It should be noted that: The data in this table should not be used for analytical purposes since it comes from various sources and for separate years; they are used here to provide only a sense of intra-regional distributional perspective.
EU FDI stocks are in euros and have been converted into US dollars at a rate of $1.5 to a euro.
Means not available or zero.

which naturally does not provide data except for the countries that do have them, the flow is largely a one-way traffic to China from Japan (about 13% of Japan's outward FDI goes to China) and Korea (about 26% of Korea's outward FDI goes to China) and, vitally, from the United States (10% of United States' inward FDI comes from China) and the EU (10% of outward FDI goes to China), not to mention its own Hong Kong (35% and 40% of inward and outward FDI, respectively, comes from and goes to China). This reinforces the conclusion just reached on PTAs, that is, the most feasible would be one involving China, Japan, Korea and the United States.

I should hasten to add that I am not suggesting that they should not try to form a PTA. Indeed, a PTA which includes the United States would have great potential not only in economic benefit terms, but also for common security. The former because of the combined trade and FDI flows between them, relative to all the nations mentioned in this context, the data for which are in the tables. The latter since, with China, together with Hong Kong and Taiwan, and the United States being so involved, security efforts can be limited to dealing with problems emanating from DPRK. Such a PTA should not be seen as undermining ASEAN + 3, ASEAN + 9 or the APEC forum since it simply means that these countries form a club of their own; after all, ASEAN is involved in all three. This may galvanise ASEAN into enhancing its own club and promote progress in all the countries concerned unless one is of the opinion that an 'oligopolistic' structure may lead to indeterminate outcomes. I am therefore not trying to undermine the EAC or NEAC initiative; I am simply trying to stress the problems that have to be seriously faced in order to make it a reality.

5. CONCLUSIONS

Several conclusions arise from the examination of the EAC and what it can learn from the EU. First, the EAC is not well articulated since Hatoyama does not offer concrete guidelines on a number of pertinent critical issues related to it. Indeed, his actions clearly indicate that he is in the process of figuring out what it means: every time he utters something on the EAC, it comes as a surprise. One day it is a 'community', that is, a deeply involved association; the next day it is a cooperative effort in certain fields and then it is 'open regional cooperation'. Also, he does not indicate how long it would take to become a reality except that 'Rome was not built in a day' and that a single currency *may be possible* after a decade. Moreover, he is not even specific on which particular countries it should comprise, except that China, including Hong Kong, and Korea must be in and that the United States must continue to offer security for the region without being a member, with Taiwan never mentioned. Furthermore, he is not categorical on how precisely it relates to the EU experience. He mentions the historical background, the desire for eternal peace and the single currency, but does not depict these within the overall nature of club EU and how it got to its present state.

Second, it does not bode well for the EAC when Hatoyama fails to acknowledge that the idea was not only fully articulated before him by the late President of Korea Roh Moo-hyun, but was also clearly set out in Roh's election manifesto and made a major pillar of his government. If the failure is due to ignorance, then how can he expect to be taken seriously by China and Korea when they lie at the very heart of his community? If the omission is for his belief that his fellow citizens would be offended by such acknowledgement, due to unfavourable sentiment towards the Koreans, then that would be even worse. There is no hope for a 'community', if its initiator cannot publicly demonstrate his confidence in the integrity of those he wants to entice into it.

Third, the true EU achievements relevant to the EAC have all been accomplished through supra-national institutions. The ECSC had a High Authority which was an independent institution, taking its decisions without reference to the governments of the member nations. The EU commissioner in charge of external trade speaks and conducts international negotiations and agreements on behalf of the entire EU. The ECB is alone in charge of the monetary policy for the entire eurozone and for the issuing and conducting all matters concerning the euro. And since the Lisbon Treaty came into effect on 1 December 2009, the EU now has a full-time president serving for at least 30 months which could be extended for another term, and has a foreign policy supremo for five years supported by own staff of about 6,000. Thus, even the ECSC experience is beyond the wildest of EAC dreams. This is reinforced when the other EU supra-national institutions are taken into consideration. Of course, miracles can happen, but they are not within my realm.

Fourth, under present circumstances, the basic requirements for a 'customs union', let alone a 'common market' or 'economic community', will not be realised by the various nations mentioned in the EAC context in the foreseeable future. This is because all the existing arrangements in which they are involved, as well as those presently under discussion, do not even meet the criteria for a mere PTA. For example, ASEAN is still not an FTA and the APEC forum is nowhere near there despite its members' vehement statements after each summit to commit to an FTA. The combination of these factors suggests that the best that can be hoped for is a 'preferential trade and investment arrangement', precisely what Roh Moo-hyun ruled out, and in any case one must wonder why EAC is needed, rather than the ASEAN + 3 that is presently in the making or for that matter ASEAN + 6. This compounds the conclusion regarding what the EAC can learn from the EU.

Fifth, China will not enter the EAC simply because it sees itself as the 'leader' in this region with global ambitions in the not-so-distant future. Indeed, it has been very cool on the idea and has stated that cooperation should be extended to all nations in the region. Since China is at the very heart of the EAC, cooperation is therefore all that can be hoped for.

Nevertheless, and finally, a case can be made for a PTA comprising China, with Hong Kong and Taiwan, the DPRK, Japan, Korea and the United States, but with the United States not only as a full partner, but also as the mainstay of security in the region. This is because the trade and investment interactions between them are the deepest relative to the rest; the United States will not sanction an arrangement which does not include it; both Hatoyama and Roh agree that the United States is indispensable for security purposes; and the DPRK will be utterly delighted to belong to a club including the United States, hence the threats by it will be eliminated. But this is a hope which reality suggests is beyond reach – a hope which I am certain would be shared by all of us not only for the sake of just this region, but also the entire world.

NOTES

1. On 30 August 2009, Democratic Party of Japan (DPJ) transformed Japanese politics by dethroning the DPJ, which, apart from nine months, had ruled Japan uninterruptedly and single-handedly since the end of World War II; from 9 August 1993 to 28 April 1994, the coalition led by Prime Minister Morihiro Hosokawa was the first non-LDP government since 1955. The DPJ captured 308 of the 480 Lower House seats and with its prevailing majority in the Upper House, the less powerful of the two Diet chambers, its leader, Dr Yukio Hatoyama, had no match and was hence duly elected prime minister on 16 September 2009. Kaoto Khan replaced him as prime minster in June 2010, but Hatoyama remains powerful within the DPJ.
2. Hatoyama (2009a). Note that the promotion of voluntary *regional cooperation* in Asia has a longer history, going back to the 1979 Pacific Rim cooperation initiative by Japanese Prime Minister Masayoshi Ohira; see, inter alia, Fukukawa (2009).
3. Hatoyama floated his EAC idea in a meeting with Chinese President Hu Jintao in New York on 21 September 2009 before including it as one of the main pillars of his government in his address to the United Nations on the 24th September

(Hatoyama, 2009b). It was also high on the agenda at the Second Trilateral Summit Meeting with China, Japan and Korea, held in Beijing on 10 October 2009 when Hatoyama met with Chinese Premier Wen Jiabao and Korean President Lee Myung-bak. Moreover, it was mentioned at the 15th ASEAN (see note 8 for list of member nations) summit meeting, held in Cha-am Hua Hin in Thailand on 25 October 2009. He also talked about it in the meeting with the leaders of the countries of the Mekong region, held in Tokyo on 6–7 November 2009. Furthermore, he addressed it after the APEC (see note 7 for list of member nations) Economic Leaders Meeting held in Singapore on 14–15 November 2009 when he delivered a lecture on the subject on 15 November (Hatoyama, 2009c).

4. He also had the NEAC as one of his 12 policy goals in his party's manifesto for 2002.

5. He did so in his address to the UN on 24 September 2009 (Hatoyama, 2009b) and APEC lecture in Singapore on 15 November 2009 (Hatoyama, 2009b). The APEC forum was established in 1989 by the then six ASEAN nations (see note 8 for a list of member nations) plus Australia, Canada, Japan, New Zealand, Korea and the United States. These were joined by China, Hong Kong and Taiwan in 1991. In 1993 President Clinton galvanised it into 18 nations, adding Chile, Mexico and Papua New Guinea. In November 1998, Peru, Russia and Vietnam joined, making for a total membership of 21.

6. '*yu-ai*', pronounced yuu-ai, is a combination of two Chinese characters, called *kanji* in Japanese, with the first meaning 'friend' and the second 'love'.

7. See Sahashi (2009) and Ogoura (2009).

8. The 10 members are Brunei Darussalam, Cambodia, Indonesia, Lao PDR, Malaysia, Union of Myanmar (or Burma), the Philippines, Singapore, Thailand and Vietnam. ASEAN was established on 8 August 1967 in Bangkok, Thailand, with the signing of the *ASEAN Declaration* (Bangkok Declaration) by Indonesia, Malaysia, the Philippines, Singapore and Thailand. Brunei Darussalam joined on 8 January 1984, Vietnam on 28 July 1995, Lao PDR and Myanmar on 23 July 1997 and Cambodia on 30 April 1999.

9. '... my grandfather, Ichiro Hatoyama, translated his book, "The Totalitarian State Against Man," into Japanese' (Hatoyama, 2009a).

10. Count Richard Coudenhove-Kalergi (who in 1923 was the Austrian founder-leader of the *Pan-European Movement*, calling for the formation of a *United States of Europe*, his reason being the successful assertion of Swiss unity in 1848, the forging of the German empire in 1871 and the independence of the United States in 1776) was the second son of Heinrich Coudenhove-Kalergi (1859–1906), an Austro-Hungarian count and diplomat of mixed European origin, and Mitsuko Aoyama (1874–1941), a Japanese descendant of a samurai family. The couple met in Tokyo when the future countess helped the Austro-Hungarian diplomat after his falling off a horse.

11. An explanation for why he has not done so would require an chapter of its own, but a generous gesture would be to state that he simply missed the opportunity to point out that the fraternity with Europe has much deeper roots for the Japanese.

12. See, inter alia, El-Agraa (2007a) for a discussion of this term.

13. The 12 years were to be over by the end of December 1969, but the removal of tariffs on intra-trade and the establishment of the common external tariffs were achieved by 1 July 1968. See El-Agraa (2007a).

14. At the joint press conference by the leaders of Japan and the Mekong region countries following the Mekong–Japan summit meeting on 6–7 November 2009, available at http://www.kantei.go.jp/foreign/hatoyama/statement/200911/07mekong_e.html.

15. See, inter alia, Hirano (2009), and Zongze (2006).

16. See El-Agraa (2009c).

17. See, inter alia, El-Agraa (1999, 2007a) for a detailed specification and discussion.

18. See, inter alia, El-Agraa (1997, 1999, 2007a).

19. See El-Agraa (1997, 2007a) for membership of regional integration schemes worldwide.

20. See El-Agraa (2007a) for a detailed discussion.

21. See El-Agraa (2009c).

22. See, inter alia, Ogoura (2009).

23. See, inter alia, Hirano (2009) and Ogoura (2009).

24. See El-Agraa (2009a, 2009b).

25. See, inter alia, El-Agraa (2007a) for a full specification.

26. Services are yet to be fully free across the entire EU.

27. Today, 16 EU nations are members of the eurozone. Nine members are obliged to join when they meet the 'Maastricht criteria' (on inflation, interest rates, public borrowing, public debt and currency stability). The United Kingdom is the only EU nation that has a treaty opt-out, but Denmark is planning to hold a referendum on whether or not it should ask for one.

28. When Ireland joined the EEC in 1973, it had the lowest per capita GNI amongst the then nine member nations, with its GDP being equal to 64% of the then European Community (EC) average. When Greece (1981), Portugal (1986) and Spain (1986) joined the group, these three were only just behind Ireland. Presently, in the EU of 27, Ireland ranks 4th, Spain 13th, Greece 14th and Portugal 16th.

29. The president's task is to chair the European Council, which represents the 27 EU national governments and 'drive forward its work'; 'facilitate cohesion and consensus' among EU nations; present a report to the European Parliament after each EU summit meeting; and represent the EU on foreign and security policy, but without interfering with the EU's foreign policy supremo (next item in the main list). The president will be assisted by the Council's general secretariat on legal matters, policy issues, protocol, translation services, process office and the like.

30. The official name is the High Representative for the Union for Foreign Affairs and Security Policy (Lisbon Treaty, Article 27(a)). The supremo will conduct the EU's Foreign and Security Policy, serve as EU Commission vice-president, express the EU's position in world organisations and international conferences, control a new diplomatic service in which the member states provide a third of senior personnel and be chosen by the EU national leaders with the agreement of the president of the EU Commission and the approval of the European Parliament.

31. There were provisions for a single market in the 1957 EEC Treaty: Article 3 required not only the removal of all internal tariffs and quotas, but 'of all other measures having equivalent effect', and 'of obstacles to freedom of movement of persons, services and capital'. The procedure to eliminate these non-tariff barriers (NTBs) was harmonisation or the approximation of laws (EEC Treaty, Article 100).

After the successful early completion of the CU (see El-Agraa, 2007a, chaps. 2 and 27), internal factors and external events conspired against the completion of that single market. The EEC economy was under strain in the 1970s: the collapse of the Bretton Woods exchange rate regime, the world recession associated with the oil price shocks of 1973 and 1979, rapid changes in technology, the changing structure of the world economy associated with these changes and the emergence of significant new competitors, first Japan and then the newly industrialising countries of Southeast Asia. With growth being slow or negative and unemployment rising rapidly, national governments tried to protect their economies, but with tariffs fixed by the GATT and the EEC Treaty commitments, only NTBs could be used: the 'New Protectionism'. Barriers went up within as well as without the EU, and these economic strains made countries much less willing to agree to integration initiatives in general and harmonisation in particular.

32. Commission of the European Communities (1987), Article 12.

33. See Ardy and El-Agraa (2007) for a detailed exposition and discussion.

34. See El-Agraa and Liu (2007).

35. These are to be found in Articles 131–134 (ex Articles 110–116) of the Treaty of Rome. See Matthews and Brülhart (2007) for a full coverage of the CCP.

36. EU Council decisions are taken by unanimous, simple or QMV, with QMV being the most common. When QMV is used, each member nation is endowed with a number of votes. The votes are weighted so that at least some of the smaller member nations must assent. See El-Agraa (2007a, chap. 3) for details.

37. With certain exceptions such as agreements that relate to trade in cultural and audiovisual services, education, social and human health services as well as transport services, which remain outside the scope of Article 133.

38. See Hosoya (1979), Anouil (1985) and El-Agraa (1988) for details.

39. See El-Agraa (2002) and Mayes and El-Agraa (2007) for these terms and for a full explanation and discussion.

40. This stands for the technical term 'non accelerating inflation rate of unemployment', i.e. the rate of unemployment consistent with an unchanging inflation rate (Stiglitz, 1997).

41. See Buiter, Corsetti and Roubini (1993).

42. See El-Agraa (2007a, chap. 3) and Mayes and El-Agraa (2007) for a full coverage and discussion.

43. The ECB, located in Frankfurt, had its foundations laid through the European Monetary Institute (EMI), introduced on 1 January 1994, during the second stage of EMU.

44. The ECB and the 16 central banks of the euro nations are known as the *Eurosystem*, which distinguishes them from the *European System of Central Banks* (ESCB) since the latter includes the central banks of all 27 EU nations. The ECB lies at the very heart of the Eurosystem. The head of the ECB is its *executive board*, which is responsible for the daily running of the bank, implementation of its monetary policy and transmitting the necessary instructions to the national central banks. It comprises the president, vice-president and four other members, all six being appointed on the agreement of the heads of state or government of the nations in the eurozone. All six hold non-renewable eight-year terms. The top decision-making body of the ECB is the *governing council*, which comprises the six members of the executive board and the 16

governors of the eurozone banks. The president of the ECB acts as its chairperson. It meets twice a month, during the first of which it normally examines the economic conditions and the position of monetary policy and determines the key interest rate, and in the second concentrates on its other tasks. There is also the *general council* consisting of the president and vice-president of the ECB as well as the governors of the national central banks of all 27 EU nations. Its task is to contribute to the advisory and coordinating work of the bank and to assist with the future enlargement of the eurozone.

45. See El-Agraa (2007a, chap. 10) for a survey of the literature.

46. See Winkler (2009) for a succinct and up-to-date statement.

47. For example, Japan concluded *one-way* BSAs in 2001 with Korea ($/won of up to the equivalent of $2 billion, on 4 July), Thailand ($/baht of up to $3 billion, on 30 July), the Philippines ($/peso of up to $3 billion, on August 27) and Malaysia ($/ringgit of up to $1 billion, on 5 October, on top of an earlier one under the New Miyazawa Initiative of up to $2.5 billion). Japan also concluded ones in 2003 with Indonesia ($/rupiah of up to US$ 3 billion, on 17 February) and Singapore ($/Singapore dollar of up to $1 billion, on 10 November). And on 28 March 2002, it concluded a *two-way* ¥/renminbi BSA with China of up to $3 billion.

Following the May 2005 decision to enhance CMI effectiveness, *two-way* BSAs either replaced these or entered into new ones. That of Japan and Korea BSA was replaced on 24 February 2006 with $/won of up to $10 billion from Japan to Korea and $/¥ of up to $5 billion from Korea to Japan, and on 27 May 2007, they also concluded a ¥/won of up to $3 billion, which on 12 December 2008 they raised to $20 billion valid to the end of April 2009 and on 31 March 2009 extended the period to 30 October 2009. Japan and Thailand concluded $/baht and $/¥ of up to $3 billion, on 7 March 2005, and agreed to have a third, involving $/baht of up to $6 billion from Japan to Thailand and $/¥ of up to $3 billion from Thailand to Japan, on 10 July 2007. Japan and the Philippines concluded $/peso of up to $6 billion from Japan to the Philippines and $/¥ of up to US$ 500 million from the Philippines to Japan, on 4 May 2006. Japan and Indonesia replaced it with $/rupiah of up to $6 billion, on 31 August 2005 and agreed to increase the limit to $12 billion available for Indonesia on 21 February 2009 and signing the agreement on 6 April. Japan and Singapore replaced with a $/Singapore dollar of up to $3 billion from Japan to Singapore $/¥ of up to $1 billion from Singapore to Japan, on 8 November 2005.

48. Reforms were also introduced in 1979 and 1984, but they were minor; see Armstrong (2007) for a full analysis of EU regional policy.

49. The lack of certainty is due to leaving it to the individual member nation to decide where to focus the EU receipts for the purpose.

50. All national statistics of China are easily accessible at their website: http://stat.gov.cn.

51. See, inter alia, El-Agraa (2007a) and the EU website.

52. See El-Agraa (2009c).

53. See El-Agraa (2009c) for this and similar issues.

54. Relevant criteria were established by the Copenhagen European Council in 1993 and strengthened by the Madrid European Council in 1995; see El-Agraa (2007a) and the EU website.

55. On the EU insistence on, hence deep concern with, human and economic rights, see El-Agraa (2007b).

56. Military rule prevented accession before 1981 because the Greek military junta ran the country during 1967–1974 after a *coup d'état* in April 1967. Greece was then known to be ruled by 'The Regime of the Colonels'. Indeed, Greece signed an association treaty with the European Community (EC) on 9 July 1961, but due to the junta's rule, political relations with Greece were 'frozen' although the dismantling of tariffs continued. A second financial protocol to the agreement was signed on 28 February 1977.

57. General Franco's military dictatorship was the culprit; he died in November 1975.

58. See, El-Agraa (2007b, 2008).

59. These relate to the Nanking massacre, the DPRK abductions of Japanese and Koreans, the 'comfort women' issue, history texts distortions, disputed territories etc. See El-Agraa (2009c) for a discussion of these.

60. See, inter alia, El-Agraa (1997, 1999) for a technical exposition and discussion.

61. The table also provides the FDI stocks to give a sense of perspective since the flows continuously change, sometimes negatively. As indicated in the notes to the table, the data should not be used for analytical purposes, due to its coming from different sources and for different years, etc. Note that the website for JETRO (Japan External Trade Organization) provides a lot of data and not just for Japan. Its general website is http://www.jetro.go.jp For FDI flows and stocks for the rest of the world simply add 'world/…/stat…/'. For example, in the case of China, it is http://www.jetro.go.jp/world/asia/cn/stat_06/ for inward flows and http://www.jetro.go.jp/world/asia/cn/stat_08/ for outward flows. Also note that data is not available for the DPRK and Taiwan. For a detailed analysis of Chinese FDI, see, inter alia, El-Agraa and Liu (2006, 2007).

REFERENCES

Anouil, G. (1985). EU–Japan relations at a turning point. *EC Studies in Japan*, *18*(5), 3–12.

Ardy, B., & El-Agraa, A. M. (2007). The economics of the single market. Chapter 7 of El-Agraa (2007a).

Armstrong, H. (2007). Regional policy. In El-Agraa (2007a).

Buiter, W. H., Corsetti, G., & Roubini, N. (1993). Excessive deficits: Sense and nonsense in the Treaty of Maastricht. *Economic Policy*, *16*, 58–100.

Commission of the European Communities. (1987). The Single European Act. *Official Journal of the European Union*, *OJL* 169, 29 June.

Commission of the European Communities. (2006). *A reformed cohesion policy for a changing Europe: Regions, cities and border areas for growth and jobs*. Brussels: Inforegio Factsheet.

Democratic Party of Japan. (2005). DPJ manifesto for the 2005 House of Representatives election: Nippon Sasshin: Toward a change of government. Available at http://www.dpj.or.jp/english/policy/indexhtml.

El-Agraa, A. M. (1988). *Japan's trade frictions: Realities or misconceptions?* (St. Martin's Press: New York). New York, London: Macmillan.

El-Agraa, A. M. (Ed.) (1997). *Economic integration worldwide*. London: Macmillan, St. Martin's Press: New York) 434 + xix pp. A major revision of the 1988 second edition of *International Economic Integration*.

El-Agraa, A. M. (1999). *Regional integration: Experience, theory and measurement*. London: Macmillan. Barnes & Noble: New York. 460 + xix pp. A major revision of *The Theory and Measurement of International Economic Integration* 1989.

El-Agraa, A. M. (Ed.) (2002). *The euro and Britain: The implications of moving into the EMU*. Hemel Hempstead: Pearson Education, Prentice Hall and Financial Times389 + xix pp.

El-Agraa, A. M. (Ed.) (2007a). *The European Union: Economics and policies*. Cambridge: Cambridge University Press. Eighth edition of *The Economics of the European Community*, a major revision, including new chapters and new and changed contributors, of the seventh edition. 600 + xxiv pp.; the first edition was published in 1980.

El-Agraa, A. M. (2007b). The EU/China relationship: Not seeing eye to eye? *Asia Europe Journal*, *5*(2), 139–159.

El-Agraa, A. M. (2008). Economic and human rights examined within the context of regional integration worldwide. *Asia Europe Journal*, *6*(3/4), 391–399.

El-Agraa, A. M. (2009a). Public pension provision: A comparison of the British and Japanese systems, based on their university arrangements. *Pensions: An International Journal*, *13*(1/2), 25–48.

El-Agraa, A. M. (2009b). The Japanese pensions scandals. *Pensions: An International Journal*, *14*(3), 191–201.

El-Agraa, A. M. (2009c). On the East and Northeast Asian communities. *Journal of Global Issues & Solutions*. Available at www.bwsociety.org/journal/archive/neac.htm

El-Agraa, A. M., & Liu, W. P. (2006). The direction and composition of China's trade: An 'unexpected' composition of exports for a developing nation? *Journal of Far Eastern Business and Economy*, *3*(4), 32–56.

El-Agraa, A. M., & Liu, W. P. (2007). Rationalising the dramatic change in the composition of China's exports. *The Asia Pacific Economic Journal*, *4*(1), 1–28.

European Commission. (various years). *The European Union foreign direct investment yearbook*.

Fukukawa, S. (2009). East Asian Community primer. *The Japan Times*, 2 December.

Hatoyama, Y. (2009a). A new path for Japan. *The New York Times*, Op-ed Contributor, 27 August. Available at http://www.nytimes.com/2009/08/27/opinion/27iht-edhatoyama.html (with the original Japanese version at http://www.nytimes.com/2009/08/27/opinion/27iht-edhatoyama.html).

Hatoyama, Y. (2009b). Address by H.E. Dr. Yukio Hatoyama, prime minister of Japan, at the 64th session of the General Assembly of the United Nations. 24 September. Available at http://www.mofa.go.jp/policy/UN/asembly2009/pm0924-2.html

Hatoyama, Y. (2009c). Japan's new commitments to Asia – Towards the realization of an East Asian Community. Address delivered on 15 November 2009 in Singapore, following the conclusions of the APEC Leaders Summit. Available at http://www.mofa.go.jp/region/asia-paci/address0911.html

Hirano, K. (2009). China wary of Hatoyama's East Asian Community. *The Japan Times*, 3 October.

Hosoya, C. (1979). Relations between the European Communities and Japan. *Journal of Common Market Studies*, *18*(2), 159–178.

Japanese Ministry of Finance website for Japanese FDI http://www.mof.go.jp/english/fdi/2004b_2.htm

Matthews, A., & Brülhart, M. (2007). The EU external trade policy. Chapter 24 of El-Agraa (2007b).

Mayes, D., & El-Agraa. (2007). The development of EU economic and monetary integration. Chapter 11 of El-Agraa (2007b).

Ogoura, K. (2009). Significance of East Asia. *The Japan Times*, 30 October.

Roh, M.-hyun. (2007). On history, nationalism and a Northeast Asian Community. *Global Asia*, April 16, posted in *Japan Focus* on 19 May 2007. Available at http://japanfocus.org/products/topdf/2424 and http://www.japanfocus.org/articles/print_article/2424

Sahashi, R. (2009). Hatoyama's new path and Washington's anxiety. East Asia forum. 6 September. Available at http://www.estasiaforum.org/2009/09/06/hatoyamaa-new-path-and-washingtons-anxiety

Stiglitz, J. (1997). Reflections on the natural rate hypothesis. *Journal of Economic Perspectives*, *11*(1), 3–10.

UNCTAD. (various years). *World Investment Report 2007*.

Winkler, A. (2009). The financial crisis: A wake-up call for strengthening regional monitoring of financial markets and regional coordination of financial sector policies. Paper presented at the Asian Development Bank Institute, Tokyo, 21 July.

Zongze, R. (2006). China's role in a Northeast Asian Community. *Asian Perspective*, *30*(3), 149–157.

APPENDIX. BASIC INTRA-REGIONAL TRADE DATA

Tables A1 and A2

Table A1. The Direction of Exports among the EAC/NEAC Countries and Related Nations, 2007 (US$ Billion).

	China	DPRK	HK	Japan	Korea	Macao	Taiwan	Mongolia	Russia	Brunei	Cambodia	Indonesia	Lao PDR
China		1.39	184.29	102.12	56.13	2.64	23.50	0.68	28.48	0.11	0.88	12.62	3.18
DPRK	0.53		0.00	0.00	0.00	0.00	0.00	0.03	0.03	0.00	0.00	0.00	0.00
Hong Kong	167.79	0.00		15.34	6.80	2.24	6.80	0.00	0.90	0.00	6.80	0.002	0.00
Japan	109.30	0.01	38.91		54.27	0.23	44.87	0.15	10.77	4.25	8.91	9.07	0.04
Korea	81.99	0.00	18.65	26.37		0.03	70.03	6.37	8.09	0.03	0.28	5.77	0.06
Macao	0.38	0.00	0.33	0.03	0.00		0.00	0.00	0.00	0.00	0.02	0.00	0.00
Taiwan													
Mongolia	1.20	0.10	0.00	0.02	0.02	0.00	0.00		0.04	0.00	0.00	0.00	0.00
Russia	15.89	0.13	0.34	7.56	6.16	0.00	0.90	0.63		0.00	0.01	0.25	0.00
Brunei	0.22	0.00	0.00	2.28	0.85	0.00	0.00	0.00	0.00		0.00	1.70	0.00
Cambodia	0.05	0.00	0.02	0.13	0.00	0.00	0.00	0.00	0.02	0.00		0.00	0.00
Indonesia	9.68	0.00	1.69	23.63	7.58	0.00	2.60	0.00	0.34	0.04	0.12		0.00
Lao PDR	0.08	0.00	0.00	0.01	0.06	0.00	0.02	0.00	0.00	0.00	0.00	0.00	
Malaysia	15.45	0.00	8.15	16.09	6.70	0.02	4.80	0.01	0.63	0.40	0.13	5.17	0.00
Myanmar	0.34	0.05	0.07	0.27	0.07	0.00	0.05	0.00	0.00	0.00	0.00	0.03	0.00
Philippines	5.75	0.00	5.80	7.30	1.78	0.00	1.97	0.00	0.03	0.00	0.00	0.52	0.00
Singapore	28.93	0.06	31.34	14.39	10.61	0.04	9.15	0.04	0.00	0.70	0.44	0.03	0.04
Thailand	14.83	0.18	8.69	18.12	2.97	0.02	3.32	0.00	0.57	0.09	1.36	4.77	1.31
Vietnam	3.36	0.00	0.58	6.07	1.25	0.00	1.14	0.00	0.46	0.00	0.99	1.11	0.10
Australia	27.07	0.00	2.56	41.23	15.22	0.04	6.92	0.02	0.96	0.03	0.04	6.92	0.01
India	18.49	0.67	6.80	4.76	5.98	0.60	2.12	0.02	1.55	0.01	0.06	2.64	0.60
NZ	1.79	0.00	0.50	2.57	0.98	0.00	0.54	0.00	0.17	0.00	0.00	0.73	0.00
USA	65.24	0.00	20.12	62.67	34.70	0.03	2326	0.03	7.37	0.14	0.14	4.24	0.01
EU	68.30	18.22	28.59	59.77	33.92	0.29	18.22	8.22	121.57	1.76	0.21	7.45	0.08

	Malaysia	Myanmar	Philippines	Singapore	Thailand	Vietnam	Australia	India	NZ	USA	EU	Total
China	17.70	1.69	7.51	29.68	11.98	11.91	18.00	24.04	2.16	233.18	242.53	1218.00
DPRK	0.00	0.05	0.00	0.00	0.03	0.00	0.01	0.06	0.00	0.00	0.08	1.61
Hong Kong	2.24	0.00	2.81	6.47	3.70	2.31	4.45	4.47	0.52	47.30	46.50	344.74
Japan	15.06	0.18	9.48	21.82	25.61	5.68	14.22	6.17	2.50	145.58	105.33	714.25
Korea	5.70	0.29	4.42	11.95	4.49	5.76	4.70	6.60	0.07	45.88	55.03	371.45
Macao	0.00	0.00	0.01	0.00	0.00	0.02	0.01	0.00	0.00	1.03	0.50	2.54
Taiwan												
Mongolia	0.00	0.00	0.00	0.00	0.00	0.00	0.00	0.00	0.00	0.08	0.10	1.67
Russia	0.44	0.02	0.12	1.09	0.33	0.57	0.05	4.01	0.00	8.31	189.38	352.37
Brunei	0.09	0.00	0.00	0.13	0.10	0.00	0.93	0.00	0.13	0.38	0.09	6.94
Cambodia	0.02	0.00	0.00	0.08	0.05	0.18	0.02	0.00	0.00	2.36	0.85	4.07
Indonesia	3.40	0.26	1.85	10.50	3.05	1.36	3.40	4.94	0.36	11.64	13.28	114.10
Lao PDR	0.03	0.00	0.00	0.00	0.43	0.19	0.01	0.00	0.00	0.02	0.16	1.32
Malaysia		0.21	2.55	25.77	8.73	2.33	5.94	5.89	0.76	27.53	22.55	176.21
Myanmar	0.13		0.00	0.06	2.11	0.07	0.02	0.69	0.00	0.00	0.33	4.75
Philippines	2.51	0.00		0.44	1.40	0.44	0.53	0.24	0.11	8.60	8.58	50.46
Singapore	38.63	0.78	6.13		12.40	6.52	11.19	10.00	1.56	26.64	32.16	299.17
Thailand	2.90	2.46	2.90	9.54		3.80	5.73	2.66	0.62	19.25	21.04	152.46
Vietnam	1.39	0.02	0.97	2.20	1.03		3.56	0.18	0.07	10.09	8.98	48.56
Australia	3.41	0.03	1.27	5.37	0.29	1.40		11.29	7.94	10.29	19.81	185.69
India	2.82	0.60	0.60	1.901	2.31	1.90	1.54		0.21	24.48	39.43	198.27
NZ	0.69	0.00	0.52	0.62	04.0	0.20	7.09	0.38		3.10	4.00	30.62
USA	11.68	0.00	7.71	26.29	8.45	1.90	19.21	17.59	2.81		246.80	1163.00
EU	15.57	0.22	5.42	28.01	10.81	4.92	31.15	40.02	3.99	357.38		5270.30

Source: Selected from the IMF's *Direction of Trade Statistics Yearbook 2008*.

Table A2. The Direction of Imports among the EAC/NEAC Countries and Related Nations, 2007 (US$ Billion).

	China	DPRK	HK	Japan	Korea	Macao	Taiwan	Mongolia	Russia	Brunei	Cambodia	Indonesia	Lao PDR
China		0.58	12.84	133.90	104.05	0.28	100.99	1.32	19.63	0.24	0.05	12.38	0.09
DPRK	1.53		0.02	0.01	0.00	0.00	0.02	0.03	0.14	0.00	0.00	0.00	0.00
Hong Kong	170.56	0.00		36.89	15.34	0.38	26.32	0.00	0.38	0.00	0.02	2.08	0.00
Japan	127.76	0.00	1.45		27.30	0.04	19.82	0.02	10.56	2.50	0.14	26.26	0.01
Korea	63.03	0.00	2.14	56.25		0.00	9.97	0.02	6.98	0.94	0.00	9.11	0.07
Macao	2.29	0.00	0.54	0.48	0.08		0.19	0.00	0.00	0.00	0.00	0.03	0.00
Taiwan													
Mongolia	0.75	0.04	0.01	0.17	0.19	0.00	0.03		0.69	0.00	0.00	0.00	0.00
Russia	24.41	0.03	0.11	12.72	8.84	0.00	0.89	0.03		0.00	0.02	0.67	0.00
Brunei	0.12	0.00	0.03	0.14	0.03	0.00	0.02	0.00	0.00		0.00	0.05	0.00
Cambodia	0.97	0.00	0.67	0.12	0.31	0.02	0.47	0.00	0.01	0.00		0.13	0.00
Indonesia	8.56	0.00	0.44	6.53	3.20	0.00	1.50	0.00	0.44	1.87	0.00		0.00
Lao PDR	0.20	0.00	0.02	0.04	0.06	0.00	0.00	0.00	0.00	0.00	0.00	0.00	
Malaysia	18.91	0.00	4.27	19.09	7.25	0.02	8.35	0.00	0.26	0.10	0.02	6.23	0.04
Myanmar	1.86	0.05	0.05	0.19	0.32	0.00	0.00	0.00	0.02	0.00	0.00	0.29	0.00
Philippines	4.00	0.00	2.22	6.84	3.28	0.00	4.06	0.00	0.11	0.00	0.00	1.25	0.00
Singapore	31.89	0.00	3.86	21.54	12.81	0.02	15.49	0.00	0.75	0.14	0.08	14.66	0.00
Thailand	16.38	0.03	1.45	28.67	5.34	0.00	5.79	0.00	1.55	0.11	0.05	2.09	0.48
Vietnam	12.50	0.00	1.94	6.18	5.33	0.00	6.92	0.00	0.55	0.00	0.20	1.35	0.21
Australia	29.49	0.01	1.21	17.39	5.48	0.01	3.74	0.00	0.51	1.02	0.01	4.37	0.00
India	34.67	0.28	7.38	8.68	9.88	0.00	3.31	0.00	5.76	0.28	0.00	7.88	0.00
NZ	4.53	0.00	0.14	2.84	0.96	0.00	0.07	0.00	0.05	0.35	0.00	0.87	0.00
USA	340.12	0.00	7.32	149.42	49.32	1.14	39.85	0.09	20.22	0.42	2.60	15.51	0.02
EU	314.85	0.09	14.82	106.46	53.35	0.68	35.38	0.11	189.68	0.09	0.94	17.42	0.18

	Malaysia	Myanmar	Philippines	Singapore	Thailand	Vietnam	Australia	India	NZ	USA	EU	Total
China	28.74	0.37	23.13	17.52	22.65	3.21	25.76	14.66	1.54	70.00	110.61	956.00
DPRK	0.00	0.05	0.00	0.06	0.20	0.00	0.00	0.12	0.00	0.00	0.09	3.45
Hong Kong	8.06	0.08	6.13	25.01	7.51	0.75	2.10	6.13	0.38	17.95	26.24	368.22
Japan	17.35	0.30	8.69	7.05	18.29	6.09	31.06	4.16	2.68	72.33	64.80	621.87
Korea	8.44	0.02	2.44	6.86	3.77	1.39	13.23	4.62	1.17	37.39	36.72	356.85
Macao	0.06	0.00	0.00	0.17	0.06	0.01	0.08	0.01	0.01	0.30	0.84	5.37
Taiwan												
Mongolia	0.01	0.00	0.00	0.04	0.00	0.00	0.02	0.00	0.00	0.03	0.25	2.35
Russia	1.47	0.030	0.12	0.45	1.01	0.52	0.65	1.32	0.09	9.50	85.96	199.44
Brunei	0.44	0.00	0.00	0.77	0.01	0.00	0.03	0.06	0.00	0.15	1.94	3.93
Cambodia	0.15	0.00	0.00	0.48	1.50	1.09	0.04	0.03	0.00	0.15	0.23	6.46
Indonesia	6.41	0.00	0.36	9.84	4.29	0.99	3.00	1.61	0.05	4.80	7.66	74.47
Lao PDR	0.01	0.00	0.00	0.04	1.44	0.12	0.02	0.01	0.00	0.02	0.08	2.11
Malaysia		0.14	2.85	16.87	7.86	1.84	2.97	2.06	0.49	15.93	17.41	146.98
Myanmar	0.23		0.00	0.86	1.06	0.02	0.03	0.19	0.00	0.01	0.25	5.52
Philippines	2.28	0.00		6.22	2.28	0.84	0.72	0.49	0.36	7.84	5.30	55.51
Singapore	34.42	0.06	5.81		8.50	2.14	3.17	5.87	0.47	32.87	32.30	263.33
Thailand	8.70	2.32	2.16	6.34		1.12	3.84	2.09	0.42	9.66	12.00	141.35
Vietnam	2.29	0.08	0.41	7.61	3.74		1.06	1.36	0.25	1.70	5.10	62.68
Australia	7.86	0.02	0.61	13.39	8.61	4.47		1.54	6.47	23.04	40.32	191.92
India	8.16	0.92	0.21	13.16	3.69	0.43	12.42		0.42	20.53	51.12	315.09
NZ	1.49	0.00	0.12	1.60	0.94	0.12	6.21	0.23		3.26	5.41	34.20
USA	33.70	0.00	9.81	18.69	23.79	11.43	8.97	25.11	3.32		362.51	2017.00
EU	24.57	0.36	7.70	25.09	22.62	10.68	15.92	35.52	4.15	247.31		5386.50

Source: Selected from the IMF's *Direction of Trade Statistics Yearbook 2008*.

PART III
REGIONAL STUDIES

HAS THE INTERNATIONAL BANKING AND FINANCIAL CRISIS DAMAGED EMERGING MARKET MNCs?

Jenny Berrill and Colm Kearney

ABSTRACT

We examine how the international financial crisis of 2007–2010 has impacted on the performance of emerging market MNCs relative to their developed market counterparts. We present our multinational classification system and categorise the world's largest firms, the Global Fortune 500 *(*GF500*), according to their degree of multinationality. We show that the number of* GF500 *firms from emerging markets has increased significantly over the past decade, and that the international financial crisis of 2007–2010 has further enhanced this trend. We compare the relative risk-adjusted performance of emerging and developed markets before and since the international financial crisis. We show that although the* GF500 *firms from developed markets tend to be more multinational than the* GF500 *firms from emerging markets, the latter have outperformed the former over the past decade – both before and after the recent international financial crisis.*

The Impact of the Global Financial Crisis on Emerging Financial Markets
Contemporary Studies in Economic and Financial Analysis, Volume 93, 361–377

ISSN: 1569-3759/doi:10.1108/S1569-3759(2011)0000093012

Keywords: Classification of firms; emerging market MNCs.

JEL Classifications: F23; G11.

1. INTRODUCTION

The pace of globalisation over the past quarter century is reflected in the degree to which trade has outpaced world growth since the 1980s (OECD, 2007), the increasingly global production networks and supply chains (De Bakker & Yamano, 2007) and the acceleration in foreign direct investment (FDI) since the 1990s (UNCTAD, 2010). Although the trends towards enhanced international integration are widely recognised, the theoretical and operational definitions of terms such as the multinational corporation (MNC) and globalisation differ across studies (Hettne, Inotai, & Sunkel, 1999; Marchand, Boas, & Shaw, 1999). This has led to considerable confusion amongst analysts, researchers and commentators about the role of MNCs in the international economic and financial systems. It has spawned debate about the extent to which the world's largest MNCs have become truly global (Ghemawat, 2001; Yip, 2002; Rugman & Verbeke, 2003, 2004; Hejazi, 2007; Govindarajan & Gupta, 2008; Rugman & Collinson, 2008). Most importantly, the focus of most researchers on MNCs from the advanced and developed countries within the so-called 'triad' of North America, Europe and Asia (Ohmae, 1985) has led to relative neglect of research on the behaviour, operations and performance of developing and emerging market MNCs.

The past two decades has witnessed spectacular growth in the number of MNCs from developing and emerging markets amongst the world's largest firms. International business, economic and financial analysts are now increasingly aware of firms such as Petrobras, Vale and TBS in Brazil; Sinopec, State Grid, Dongfeng Motor, the Noble Group and Sinosteel in China; Indian Oil and Tata Motors in India; Pemex and Reliance Industries in Mexico; PKN Orlen in Poland; Gazprom, Lukoil, Sberbank and Sistema in Russia; Sabil in Saudi Arabia; and PDVSA in Venezuela. The hitherto relative paucity of research on emerging market MNCs is now being increasingly addressed. Guillen and Garcia-Canal (2009) describe recent work on the 'new', 'emerging' and 'latecomer' MNEs from emerging, upper-middle-income and oil-rich countries, and how their operations and strategise are different to the more traditional MNEs. These 'new' MNEs have to deal with the liability of being 'latecomers' in addition to the liability of foreignness, but this is offset by their specific skills such as project execution, networking and dealing with institutional weakness and political instability (Aulakh, 2007; Goldstein, 2007; Cuervo-Cazurra & Genc, 2008).

In this chapter, we examine how the international financial crisis of 2007–2010 has impacted on the performance of emerging market MNCs relative to their developed market counterparts. This is an interesting and important exercise because it complements the many analyses that are based on more aggregative industry-level, market-level or country-level data. Kali and Reyes (2007) have shown that although the global trading system is hierarchical with a core–periphery structure, smaller countries and those with emerging markets have enhanced their participation in recent decades. Given the increasing influence of emerging market MNCs and the globalisation of world markets, the 'triad' region of Ohmae (1985), along with other previous geographical groupings based on political and economic characteristics (such as EFTA and COMECON) have become increasingly irrelevant. Segregating the world into various regional groupings is not the ultimate answer, even though it is common practice in emerging market studies. Examples include CHINDIA (China and India), BRIC (Brazil, Russia, India and China), VISTA (Vietnam, Indonesia, South Africa, Turkey and Argentina) and Next Eleven (Bangladesh, Egypt, Indonesia, Iran, Mexico, Nigeria, Pakistan, Philippines, South Korea, Turkey and Vietnam). While these regional groupings may seem appropriate at specific times and for specific research questions, their relevance will inevitably decline as globalisation intensifies. This is particularly true for emerging countries that are by definition, on a transformation path. While these countries share similar characteristics at one point in time, their evolution and development will likely follow different paths in the future.

The remainder of the chapter is structured as follows. In Section 2, we describe our classification system that can categorise all firms from every country in the world according to their degree of multinationality. We then apply our system to the world's largest firms, the *Global Fortune 500* (henceforth *GF500*). In Section 3, we show that the number of *GF500* firms from emerging markets has increased significantly over the past decade, and that the international financial crisis of 2007–2010 has further enhanced this trend. Our dataset for this analysis comprises all firms on the *GF500* list over the decade from 2000 to 2009. In Section 4, we compare the relative risk-adjusted performance of emerging and developed markets before and since the international financial crisis. We show that although the *GF500* firms from developed markets tend to be more multinational than the *GF500* firms from emerging markets, the latter have outperformed the former over the past decade – both before and after the recent international financial crisis. Section 5 summarizes our findings and presents our concluding comments.

2. CLASSIFYING MNCS FROM DEVELOPED AND EMERGING MARKETS

We can think of classifying the world's firms on the basis of any number of characteristics, but we suggest that the following six high-level categories are of particular interest:

1. type (public, private listed, private unlisted),
2. industry (NAICS or SIC codes),
3. age (years, based on the date of incorporation),
4. size (assets, employees, revenue, sales; micro, small, medium, large),
5. location (country of headquarters) and
6. multinationality (operations across countries and regions).

Each of these high-level categories contains sub-categories that can be specified in alternate ways. Category 1, for example, can be decomposed into ownership (public, private listed and unlisted), but it could also include other features such as main objective (for profit and non-profit). Category 3 may contain, for example, 'very old' (more than 100 years), 'old' (50–100 years), 'middle-aged' (10–49 years), 'young' (4–9 years) and 'new' (0–3 years). We focus on category 6 – multinationality.

We define the degree of multinationality of any firm's operations along two dimensions: *breadth* and *depth*. To implement the *breadth* dimension, we use four categories of multinationality – domestic, regional, trans-regional and global – and we divide the world into six regions based on the inhabited continents: Africa, Asia, Europe, North and Central America, Oceania and South America. Most countries fit easily into one of these regions, but there are some areas where arbitrary decisions are necessary, such as when countries transcend continents as sometimes defined. Table 1 lists where each country is placed within our system. An activity (such as sales, joint ventures or direct investments) that takes place entirely within the home country is referred to as domestic (*D*), and an activity conducted in the region in which the firm is headquartered it is referred to as regional (*R*). An activity associated with a firm that takes place in more than one region (but not fully global) is defined as trans-regional (*T*), and an activity that takes place in all six regions of the world is classified as 'global' (*G*). For example,

Table 1. Country Constituents by Region.

Africa (53):
Algeria, Angola, Benin, Botswana, Burkina, Burundi, Cameroon, Cape, Verde, Central African Republic, Chad, Comoros, Congo, Congo (Dem. Rep.), Djibouti, Egypt, Equatorial Guinea, Eritrea, Ethiopia, Gabon, Gambia, Ghana, Guinea, Guinea-Bissau, Ivory, Coast, Kenya, Lesotho, Liberia, Libya, Madagascar, Malawi, Mali, Mauritania, Mauritius, Morocco, Mozambique, Namibia, Niger, Nigeria, Rwanda, Sao, Tome and Principe, Senegal, Seychelles, Sierra Leone, Somalia, South Africa, Sudan, Swaziland, Tanzania, Togo, Tunisia, Uganda, Zambia, Zimbabwe.

Asia (44):
Afghanistan, Bahrain, Bangladesh, Bhutan, Brunei, Burma, Cambodia, China, East, Timor, India, Indonesia, Iran, Iraq, Israel, Japan, Jordan, Kazakhstan, Korea, (north), Korea, (south), Kuwait, Kyrgyzstan, Laos, Lebanon, Malaysia, Maldives, Mongolia, Nepal, Oman, Pakistan, Philippines, Qatar, Russian Federation, Saudi Arabia, Singapore, Sri Lanka, Syria, Tajikistan, Thailand, Turkey, Turkmenistan, United Arab Emirates, Uzbekistan, Vietnam, Yemen.

Europe (47):
Albania, Andorra, Armenia, Austria, Azerbaijan, Belarus, Belgium, Bosnia and Herzegovina, Bulgaria, Croatia, Cyprus, Czech Republic, Denmark, Estonia, Finland, France, Georgia, Germany, Greece, Hungary, Iceland, Ireland, Italy, Latvia, Liechtenstein, Lithuania, Luxembourg, Macedonia, Malta, Moldova, Monaco, Montenegro, Netherlands, Norway, Poland, Portugal, Romania, San Marino, Serbia, Slovakia, Slovenia, Spain, Sweden, Switzerland, Ukraine, United Kingdom, Vatican City.

North and Central America (23):
Antigua, Barbuda, Bahamas, Barbados, Belize, Canada, Costa Rica, Cuba, Dominica, Dominican Rep., El Salvador, Grenada, Guatemala, Haiti, Honduras, Jamaica, Mexico, Nicaragua, Panama, St. Kitts & Nevis, St. Lucia, St. Vincent & the Grenadines, Trinidad & Tobago, United States.

Oceania (14):
Australia, Fiji, Kiribati, Marshall Islands, Micronesia, Nauru, New Zealand, Palau, Papua, New, Guinea, Samoa, Solomon Islands, Tonga, Tuvalu, Vanuatu.

South America (12):
Argentina, Bolivia, Brazil, Chile, Colombia, Ecuador, Guyana, Paraguay, Peru, Suriname, Uruguay, Venezuela.

Notes: This table places 193 countries throughout the world into six inclusive regions delineated as the inhabited continents. The list includes all countries that are recognised by the United Nations, excluding dependencies and/or territories.

an Indian firm that has sales only in Asia would be classified as regional, if it also has sales in Europe and the United States, it would be classified as trans-regional.

To shed more light on the extent of a firm's operations within its region, we can further delineate *R* into three categories: *R*1 (penetrating less than one-third of the countries in the region), *R*2 (between one-third and two-thirds of the countries) and *R*3 (more than two-thirds). For example, a Brazilian firm headquartered in Sao Paulo that sells its products in one or two countries in South America would be classified as *R*1 in sales, but if it exports throughout South America (but not elsewhere), it would be classified as *R*3. The trans-regional category *T* is also further subdivided: a firm is classified as *T*2 if it conducts a particular activity in two regions of the world, *T*3 denotes three regions and *T*4 and *T*5 denote four and five regions, respectively.

The *depth* of market engagement is measured by the contractual arrangements that firms engage in as they internationalise. Depth ranges from the 'shallow' engagement in foreign markets associated with exports and imports to the 'deep' commitment of FDI. The three broad categories of depth are *trading*, *alliances* and *investments*. Trading (*T*) involves sales and purchases made by the firm. Alliances (*A*), such as licensing and franchising, are associated with greater asset specificity and resource commitments to foreign markets. Investments (*I*), such as joint ventures and subsidiaries, entail a deep engagement with and exposure to the business and political risks in foreign markets. Further details of this classification methodology are provided in Aggarwal, Berrill, Hutson, and Kearney (2010) and Berrill and Kearney (2010). For ease of exposition, a simplified version of the taxonomy is presented here. It contains the four broad dimensions of the breadth of multinationality: domestic (*D*), regional (*R*), trans-regional (*T*) and global (*G*), and two of the three depth measures of market engagement: trading (*T*) and investments (*I*). We combine the *breadth* and *depth* dimensions to form our matrix of multinationality below.

Matrix of multinationality

Depth of Engagement	Breadth of Geographical Spread			
	Domestic	Regional	Trans-regional	Global
Trading (sales)	TD	TR	TT	TG
Investments (subsidiaries)	ID	IR	IT	IG

The 'triad' analysis used by Ohmae (1985), Rugman and Verbeke (2003, 2004) and others is often justified on the grounds that it includes the world's largest and most developed markets and most of the world's largest MNCs.

Although this is true, many emerging economies are excluded from the 'triad' analysis – including the whole continent of Africa! In fact, the 'triad' analysis excludes 155 countries, and these are mainly emerging economies in Asia, Eastern Europe, the Middle East, South America and Africa. The IMF's and the World Bank's list of the 20 largest economies measured by GDP in 2008 includes Brazil, China, India and Russia (the so-called BRICs) along with Indonesia and Mexico. These countries are all outside the 'triad', as are many of the world's largest 50 countries in Africa, Eastern Europe, Latin America and the Middle East. Also, patterns of international business evolve over time in ways that are not captured within the 'triad' analysis. The emergence of Eastern Europe in the early 1990s, the rise of China and India during the last two decades and the more recent rise of South American economies all point to the importance of including all countries in the world and allowing for evolving patterns of country-, industry- and firm-level production, investment and sales. Our system provides an alternative to the 'triad' system. It has the advantage that it includes the entire geography of the world and is, therefore, more inclusive than the 'triad' regions.

The *GF500* ranks the world's largest firms according to their sales each year. Table 2 presents our data on the geographical distribution of these firms in 2006 using six variables – five accounting variables (sales, income, assets, capital expenditure and depreciation) and one non-accounting variable (subsidiaries). This table also classifies the firms as emanating

Table 2. The *GF500* List in 2006.

Average	Size ($m)	Age	Sales	Income	Assets	CapExp	Depr	Subs
Developed markets	38,818	87	5.91	4.98	5.67	4.98	3.87	6.60
Emerging markets	28,390	46	3.33	2.88	3.00	2.60	2.23	3.33
Difference	10,428	41	2.58	2.1	2.67	2.38	1.64	3.27
Advanced emerging	27,077	64	5.80	6.00	6.33	9.00	7.00	4.38
Secondary emerging	28,853	40	2.56	1.92	2.33	2.14	1.36	3.06

Notes: The table categorises the *GF500* firms in 2006 as being from developed, emerging, advanced emerging and secondary emerging markets. It shows the average size (using sales) and age (using date of incorporation) of firms in each category. It also details the average measure of firm-level multinationality on a scale ranging from 1 to 9 with *D* (domestic)=1; *R*1 (regional across 1/3 of the countries in the firm's home region)=2; *R*2 (across between 1/3 and 2/3 of the countries in its home region)=3; *R*3 (regional across more than 2/3 of the countries in its home region)=4; *T*2 (trans-regional in one region additional to its home region)=5; *T*3=6; *T*4=7; *T*5=8; and *G* (global)=9. This scale is derived from the matrix of multinationality derived in Section 2. Age is calculated as 2010 less the date of incorporation.

from either *developed* or *emerging* markets using the *FTSE* and *MSCI* classification criteria. In both cases, 12 countries with *GF500* firms are classified as *emerging* – Brazil, China, Hungary, India, Malaysia, Mexico, Poland, Russia, South Africa, Taiwan, Thailand and Turkey. The *FTSE* classification further categorises countries as *advanced emerging* and *secondary emerging*. The former includes the upper-middle-income gross national income (GNI) countries with advanced market infrastructures or high-income GNI countries with lesser developed market infrastructures (Brazil, Hungary, Mexico, Poland, South Africa and Taiwan have *GF500* firms). The latter include upper-middle, lower-middle and low-income GNI countries with reasonable market infrastructures and significant size, and upper-middle-income GNI countries with lesser developed market infrastructures (China, India, Malaysia, Russia, Thailand and Turkey have *GF500* firms). We measure size using sales figures for 2006 and age using 2010 less the date of incorporation. Firms from *emerging* markets tend to be smaller and younger than firms from *developed* markets. We assign a number from 1 to 9 representing our scale of multinationality from domestic to global for each variable (*D*, *R*1, *R*2, *R*3, *T*2, *T*3, *T*4, *T*5 and *G*). Using all six variables, firms from developed markets are more multinational than firms from emerging markets. For example, firms from *developed* markets, on average, had sales with a multinationality score of 5.91 in 2006, compared to 3.33 for firms from *emerging* markets. The difference between firms from *developed* and *emerging* markets is greatest using subsidiary data and smallest using depreciation data. When we compare firms from *advanced emerging* and *secondary emerging* countries, we find that they tend to be similar in size. They differ significantly, however, in that firms from *advanced emerging* countries tend to be older and more multinational than firms from *secondary emerging* countries using all six of our measures of multinationality.

Firms use a variety of geographical groupings to categorise their accounting variables, such as the Commonwealth of Independent States (CIS), Europe, Middle East and Africa (EMEA), Asia-Pacific, Latin America, Pacific Basin and 'Far East and Other'. These areas are often ambiguously defined making classification difficult.[1] Most firms also create a category 'Other' or 'Rest of the World' to include all remaining items after the most significant areas have been detailed in the accounts. In our analysis, 228 out of the 374 firms for which sales data are available use the category 'Other' or 'Rest of the World' – the amounts in this category range from 0 (Unicredito Italiano) to 84 percent (Lukoil) of total sales, with an average of 12 percent. This creates ambiguity when using only accounting data, and suggests the importance of using subsidiary data also, as we do in our system.[2]

Table 3 applies our matrix of multinationality to classify the *GF500* firms into categories of multinationality ranging from domestic to global for our six variables. Our results show that most firms have the same multinationality classification for all reported accounting variables. Although relative percentages may change, the elimination or addition of a further geographical region seldom occurs, and is unlikely to occur if firms are using a standardised geographical analysis in their accounts. In 2006, 325 *GF500* firms provided information on more than one of the five accounting variables. Only 44 (13 percent) of these do not classify all variables within the same category. In other words, if a firm's sales are classified as *T*4, the other accounting variables will also be classified as *T*4. This implies that the accounting detail used by firms significantly impacts on its classification, and using further accounting variables in addition to sales data will likely add little to the analysis.

Some interesting patterns emerge. The number of global firms is largest using the subsidiary data, which probably reflects the limitations of using accounting variables to capture the breadth of multinationality. The majority of firms are classified as trans-regional using all variables. Few firms are classified as regional and no variable is classified as *R*2 or *R*3 using

Table 3. The Multinationality of *GF500* Firms.

	D	*R*1	*T*2	*T*3	*T*4	*T*5	*G*	Total
Trading								
Sales	53	8	76	70	78	61	28	374
Investments								
Subsidiaries	47	28	55	72	64	86	103	455
Other accounting data								
Assets	53	7	62	58	62	47	16	305
Income	64	6	62	20	38	31	11	232
Capital Expenditure	49	5	18	20	21	19	13	145
Depreciation	49	1	10	8	8	10	5	91

Notes: The table shows the number of *GF500* firms in 2006 classified at each level of multinationality using several variables. The totals on the right hand side show the number of firms for which data are available for each variable. No variables are classified as *R*2 or *R*3 as no firm in our sample has operations across more than 33 percent of the countries in its home region.

any of the accounting or other metrics. This indicates that the world's largest firms prefer to internationalise across other regions rather than completely within their home regions. This is an interesting finding that could be studied further.

3. EMERGING MARKET *GF500* FIRMS DURING 2000–2009

Has the representation of developing and emerging market MNCs in the *GF500* list increased or decreased during the decade 2000–2009? To conduct our analysis of how emerging market MNCs have performed relative to developed market MNCs before and since the international financial crisis, we first identified the *GF500* firms from each year during the decade from 2000 to 2009. Table 4 presents these details. There is a clear trend for more countries to be represented – *GF500* firms came from 28 countries in 2000 and from 39 countries in 2009. In all years, the largest number of firms comes from the United States, although this number has declined from 185 in 2000 to 140 in 2009. Japan, which has the second largest number of firms, has also seen a fall from 104 firms in 2000 to 68 firms in 2009. Other countries, most notably China and India, have seen their numbers of *GF500* firms increase over the time period.

Panel A of Table 5 shows that the number of *GF500* firms from *emerging* markets has increased dramatically over the past decade – 22 of the world's largest firms (4 percent) were from emerging markets in 2000, and this increased to 73 (15 percent) in 2009. The number of *GF500* firms from both *advanced emerging* and *secondary emerging* countries has tripled in the last 10 years. Panel B of Table 5 shows that the number of *GF500* firms in the 'triad' regions has been falling steadily over the last decade – from 462 firms in 2000 to 437 in 2009. These patterns of increasing numbers of firms from *emerging* markets and decreasing number of firms from the 'triad' regions are clearly visible both before and after the global financial crisis. In fact, the trend appears to become stronger post-crisis. In the first 5 years of our analysis, the number of *GF500* firms from *emerging* markets increased from 22 in 2000 to 34 in 2005, but it has more than doubled from 34 in 2005 to 73 in 2009. The greatest increase was from 2008 to 2009. Furthermore, this has been accompanied by a decrease in the number of firms from the 'triad' regions. These results are consistent with the view that *emerging* markets have an increasingly significant role to play in international trading and

Table 4. *GF500* Firms by Country, 2000–2009.

	2009	2008	2007	2006	2005	2004	2003	2002	2001	2000
Australia	9	8	8	8	9	9	7	6	6	7
Austria	2	2	1	1						
Belgium	5	5	5	4	3	3	3	3	3	3
Belgium/Netherlands		1	1	1	1	2	1	1	1	1
Brazil	6	5	5	4	3	3	3	4	4	3
Britain	26	34	33	38	35	35	35	34	33	33
Britain/Netherlands	1	1	1	1	2	2	2	2	2	2
Canada	14	14	16	14	13	13	13	14	16	15
China	37	29	24	20	16	16	15	11	11	12
Denmark	2	2	2	2	2	2	2		1	
Finland	2	2	3	2	3	4	4	3	2	2
France	40	39	38	38	39	39	37	40	37	37
Germany	39	37	37	35	37	36	34	35	35	34
Hungary	1									
India	7	7	6	6	5	4	4	1	1	1
Ireland	1	2	2	1	1	1	1			
Israel	1									
Italy	10	10	10	10	8	8	8	9	8	8
Japan	68	64	67	70	81	82	82	88	88	104
Luxembourg	1	1		1	1	1	1	1	2	1
Malaysia	1	1	1	1	1	1	1	1	1	1
Mexico	4	5	5	5	2	1	1	2	2	2
Netherlands	12	13	14	14	14	12	12	11	9	9
Norway	1	2	2	2	2	2	2	2	2	2
Poland	1	1	1							
Portugal	2	1								
Russia	8	5	4	5	3	3	3	3	2	2
Saudi Arabia	1	1	1	1	1					
Singapore	2	1	1	1	1	1	1	1	1	1
South Africa										1
South Korea	14	15	14	12	11	11	11	13	12	11
Spain	12	11	9	9	8	7	7	5	5	6
Sweden	6	6	6	6	7	6	6	6	5	5
Switzerland	15	14	13	12	11	12	12	11	11	11
Taiwan	6	6	6	3	2	1	1	1	2	
Thailand	1	1	1	1	1	1	1			
Turkey	1	1	1	1	1					
US	140	153	162	170	176	181	189	192	197	185
Venezuela	1			1		1	1		1	1
Total	500	500	500	500	500	500	500	500	500	500

Notes: The table lists the *GF500* firms by country for each year from 2000 to 2009. Blanks indicate no firms.

Table 5. Developed and Emerging Market *GF500* Firms.

Year	2009	2008	2007	2006	2005	2004	2003	2002	2001	2000
Panel A: *GF500* firms from developed and emerging markets										
Developed markets	427	439	446	454	466	470	471	477	477	478
Emerging markets	73	61	54	46	34	30	29	23	23	22
Total	500	500	500	500	500	500	500	500	500	500
Advanced emerging	18	17	17	12	7	5	5	7	8	6
Secondary emerging	55	44	37	34	27	25	24	16	15	16
Total	73	61	54	46	34	30	29	23	23	22
Panel B: *GF500* firms from 'triad' and non-triad regions										
Triad	437	443	446	451	457	458	460	460	460	462
Non-triad	63	57	54	49	43	42	40	40	40	38
Total	500	500	500	500	500	500	500	500	500	500

Notes: Panel A lists the number of *GF500* firms from developed and emerging markets each year from 2000 to 2009. It further segregates the emerging market firms into 'Advanced Emerging' and 'Secondary Emerging' markets as defined by *FTSE*. Panel B shows the number of *GF500* firms from 'triad' and non-triad regions in each year from 2000 to 2009. We use Rugman and Verbeke's (2004) definition of the extended 'triad' regions as NAFTA, the expanded EU (25 countries) and Asia (ASEAN, China, India and Japan).

investing. The 'triad' regions, although still dominant today, will become less dominant in future years to the extent that these trends continue.

4. MEAN VARIANCE ANALYSIS USING MARKET INDICES

We next compare the performance of developed and emerging markets during the last decade. We gather daily, weekly and monthly market-return data from 1 January 2000 to 31 May 2010. We use *MSCI* BRIC, Emerging Market and World indices, *Datastream* developed, emerging and world indices and *FTSE* developed, emerging and world indices. We also calculate an index of 'triad' regions using *MSCI* indices for North America, Europe and Japan. Table 6 shows the returns, standard deviations and return:risk ratios for each index using monthly data.[3] Panel A of Table 6 shows that the

Table 6. Developed, Emerging and World Indices.

Monthly	Mean Return	Standard Deviation	Return:Risk
Panel A: Entire sample			
Datastream emerging	1.1198	7.2114	0.1553
FTSE emerging	0.7828	5.9678	0.1312
MSCI BRIC	1.1022	8.6162	0.1279
MSCI emerging	0.7557	7.3477	0.1028
Datastream world	0.0669	5.3833	0.0124
FTSE world	0.0121	5.3208	0.0023
Datastream Developed	−0.0073	5.4750	−0.0013
FTSE developed	−0.0504	5.1981	−0.0097
MSCI world	−0.0911	5.1823	−0.0176
MSCI triad	−0.1235	4.9937	−0.0247
Panel B: Pre-crisis period			
Datastream emerging	1.5656	5.3945	0.2902
FTSE emerging	1.1382	5.1034	0.2230
MSCI BRIC	1.5953	7.1866	0.2220
MSCI emerging	1.1433	5.8825	0.1944
Datastream developed	0.4217	4.1914	0.1006
Datastream world	0.4030	4.0083	0.1005
FTSE world	0.3372	3.9143	0.0861
FTSE developed	0.2800	3.8564	0.0726
MSCI world	0.2334	3.8476	0.0607
MSCI triad	0.2072	3.8312	0.0541
Panel C: Post-crisis period			
Datastream emerging	−0.1758	10.9235	−0.0161
MSCI BRIC	−0.3308	11.8672	−0.0279
FTSE emerging	−0.2502	7.9801	−0.0313
MSCI emerging	−0.3707	10.5594	−0.0351
Datastream world	−0.9098	8.1801	−0.1112
FTSE world	−0.9328	8.1569	−0.1144
FTSE developed	−1.0105	7.9163	−0.1277
MSCI world	−1.0344	7.8901	−0.1311
MSCI triad	−1.0846	7.4099	−0.1464
Datastream developed	−1.2540	8.0999	−0.1548

Notes: The table shows the mean return, standard deviation and return:risk ratio for 10 indices. Panel A shows results for the entire sample period. Panel B shows results for the pre-crisis period and Panel C shows results for the post-crisis period.

highest return:risk ratios are for emerging market indices using *MSCI*, Datastream and *FTSE* indices. Although emerging markets tend to have high volatility, they also have higher returns, and have outperformed developed and world markets on a risk-adjusted basis over the past decade.

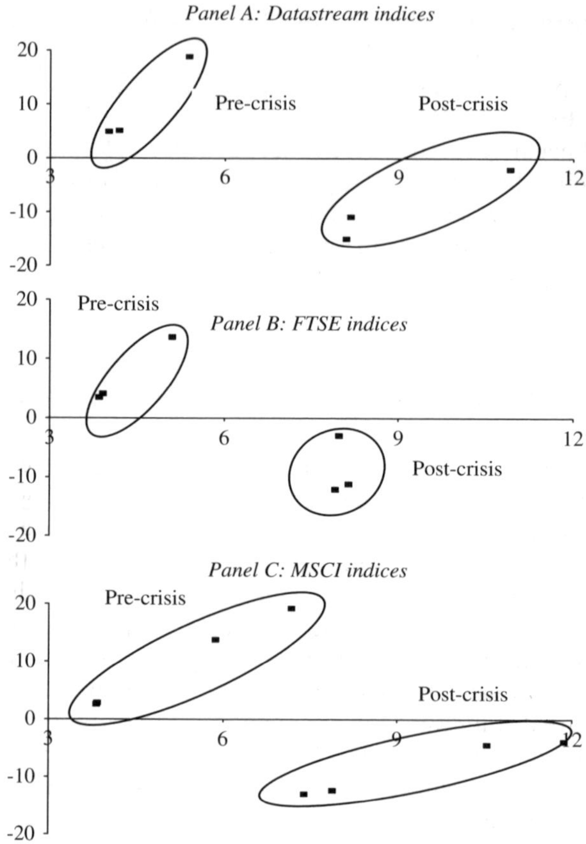

Fig. 1. Emerging, Developed and World Market Indices Pre- and Post- the 2007 International Financial Crisis. *Notes:* This figure shows the risk-return pre-crisis and post-crisis performance of Datastream, *FTSE* and *MSCI* indices of firms from world, developed and emerging markets as presented in Table 6. The pre-crisis period is from 2000 to 2007 and the post-crisis period is from 2007 to 2009. The vertical axis measures the annualised return and the horizontal axes measure the monthly standard deviations.

The 'triad' index is the worst performing of all indices. As a region, it has negative average returns and high volatility. Results show that investing in the 'triad' regions produces inferior results to investing in world, developed or emerging market indices.

We investigate if the global financial crisis has had any impact on these results. We segregate our data into two sub-samples using 15 October 2007 as our cut-off point.[4] Results are presented in Panels B and C of Table 6 and illustrated in Fig. 1. The return:risk ratios are positive for all indices before the crisis and negative for all indices after the crisis. However, the ranking of indices is similar before and after the crisis. Emerging market indices are again the best performers. The 'triad' region is the worst-performing index before the crisis and the second worst after the crisis. These results are confirmed using daily and weekly data.

5. SUMMARY AND CONCLUSIONS

Regional geographical groupings are inappropriate given existing trends towards globalisation. This is particularly true for emerging markets that are, by definition, on a transformation path. We present a classification system for firms that incorporates the entire geography of the world. We classify *GF500* firms in 2006 using our system. We find that developed market MNCs tend to be more multinational than emerging market MNCs. We also show that firms from advanced emerging markets tend to be more multinational than firms from secondary emerging markets.

The literature distinguishes emerging market MNCs and details how they differ from developed market MNCs (Goldstein, 2007; Cuervo-Cazurra & Genc, 2008). Findings generally point to an increasing number of emerging market MNCs. We show that the world's largest firms, the *GF500* firms, are increasingly from emerging markets. The international banking and financial crisis has intensified this trend. Our results also find that emerging markets are performing better than developed markets both before and after the crisis. We conclude that the international banking and financial crisis has emphasised the importance of emerging markets and emerging market MNCs in international investing.

We suggest that future research provide a longitudinal study of firm's breadth and depth of multinationality. Future studies could investigate if the differences between developed and emerging market firms that we find in this study continue to exist over time and if the crisis has had any impact on these findings. Our results show that the crisis has intensified the increasing trend of *GF500* firms from emerging markets but the question for future research is – has the crisis had any impact on the multinationality of emerging market firms? The only robust way to investigate this issue is to clearly define multinationality. Our classification system has a vital role to play in this regard.

NOTES

1. In our system, we classify CIS as European as it contains six European and five Asian countries. The Middle East is ambiguously defined. It traditionally includes Southwest Asia and parts of North Africa. As most definitions include predominantly Asian countries, we classify the Middle East as Asia and divide EMEA figures equally between Europe, Asia and Africa. All classifications in our system are based on the geographical location of the countries involved.
2. Using our system, when a variable has a classification 'Other', we add one area to the original classification. If a firm, for example, has sales in the categories Europe, North America and 'Other', we classify sales as *T*3.
3. Results are broadly similar using daily and weekly data.
4. Andreosso-O'Callaghan and Morales (2009) use a Chow test to identify 15 October 2007 as the initial downturn in American stock markets. We, therefore, use this date as our cut-off point.

REFERENCES

Aggarwal, R., Berrill, J., Hutson, E., & Kearney, C. (2010). What is a multinational company? Classifying the degree of firm-level multinationality. Available at http://papers.ssrn.com/sol3/papers.cfm?abstract_id=900522

Andreosso-O'Callaghan, B., & Morales, L. (2009). 'The Current Global Financial Crisis: do Asian Economies show Contagious or Interdependency Effects?', XVth Euro-Asia International Research Seminar, Pau, 10th–11th September.

Aulakh, P. (2007). Emerging multinationals from developing economies: Motivations, paths and performance. *Journal of International Management*, *13*(3), 235–240.

Berrill, J., & Kearney, C. (2010). Firm-level internationalisation and the home bias puzzle. *Journal of Economics and Business*, *62*(4), 235–256.

Cuervo-Cazurra, A., & Genc, M. (2008). Transforming disadvantages into advantages: Developing-country MNEs in the least developed countries. *Journal of International Business Studies*, *39*(6), 957–979.

De Bakker, K., & Yamano, N. (2007). *The measurement of globalisation using international input-output tables*. STI Working Paper 2007/8, OECD, Paris.

Ghemawat, P. (2001). Distance still matters: The hard reality of global expansion. *Harvard Business Review*, *79*(8), 137–147.

Goldstein, A. (2007). *Multinational companies from emerging economies*. New York: Palgrave Macmillan.

Govindarajan, V., & Gupta, A. (2008). *The quest for global dominance: Transforming global presence into global comparative advantage* (2nd ed.). San Francisco: Jossey-Bass.

Guillen, M. F., & Garcia-Canal, E. (2009). The American model of the multinational firm and the "New" multinationals from emerging economies. *Academy of Management Perspectives, 23*(2), 23–35.

Hejazi, W. (2007). Reconsidering the concentration of US MNE activity: Is it global, regional or national? *Management International Review, 47*(1), 5–27.

Hettne, B., Inotai, A., & Sunkel, O. (Eds). (1999). *Globalism and the new regionalism.* London: Macmillan.

Kali, R., & Reyes, J. (2007). The architecture of globalization: A network approach to international economic integration. *Journal of International Business Studies, 38*(4), 595–620.

Marchand, M. H., Boas, M., & Shaw, T. M. (1999). New regionalisms in the new millennium. *Third World Quarterly, 20*(5), 897–910.

OECD. (2007). *Staying competitive in the global economy: Moving up the value chain.* Paris: OECD.

Ohmae, K. (1985). *Triad power: The coming shape of global competition.* New York: The Free Press.

Rugman, A., & Collinson, S. (2008). The regional nature of Japanese multinational business. *Journal of International Business Studies, 39*(2), 215–231.

Rugman, A., & Verbeke, A. (2003). Regional transnationals and triad strategy. *Transnational Corporation, 13*(3), 1–20.

Rugman, A., & Verbeke, A. (2004). A perspective on regional and global strategies of multinational enterprises. *Journal of International Business Studies, 35*(1), 3–18.

UNCTAD. (2010). *World investment report: Investing in a low carbon economy.* New York: United Nations.

Yip, G. (2002). *Total global strategy II.* NJ: Prentice Hall.

CHANGING CENTRAL BANK TRANSPARENCY IN CENTRAL AND EASTERN EUROPE DURING THE FINANCIAL CRISIS[☆]

Csaba Csavas, Szilard Erhart, Anna Naszodi and Klara Pinter

ABSTRACT

There is ample empirical evidence in the literature for the positive effect of central bank transparency on the economy. The main channel is that transparency reduces the uncertainty regarding future monetary policy and thereby it helps agents to make better investment and saving decisions. In this chapter, we document how the degree of transparency of central banks in Central and Eastern Europe has changed during periods of financial stress, and we argue that during the recent financial crisis central banks became less transparent. We investigate also how these changes affected the uncertainty in these economies, measured by the degree of disagreement across professional forecasters over the future short- and long-term interest rates and also by their forecast accuracy.

[☆] The views expressed in this chapter are those of the authors and do not necessarily reflect the official view of the Magyar Nemzeti Bank.

The Impact of the Global Financial Crisis on Emerging Financial Markets
Contemporary Studies in Economic and Financial Analysis, Volume 93, 379–403

ISSN: 1569-3759/doi:10.1108/S1569-3759(2011)0000093013

Keywords: Central banking; transparency; financial crises; survey expectations; forecasting.

JEL Classifications: E44; E47; E58; G17.

1. INTRODUCTION

Recently, the literature has provided some empirical evidence for the favourable effect of central bank transparency on the economic outcomes. The main channel is that transparency reduces the uncertainty regarding future monetary policy and thereby it helps agents to make better investment, savings and other decisions. By testing the first step of the channel, Swanson (2004), Ehrmann, Eijffinger, and Fratzscher (2010) and Csavas, Erhart, Naszodi, and Pinter (2010) find that the interest rate is forecasted with a higher level of precision by professional analysts when the central bank is more transparent. By testing the effect of transparency directly on macro variables, Chortareas, Stasavage, and Sterne (2002) find that greater transparency about forward looking analysis of central banks is associated with lower inflation rate and unchanged output volatility.

Preceding the recent financial crisis, central banks have become more and more transparent all over the world. They implemented considerable changes in monetary policy communication, and many aspects of the central banks' operational and monetary policy targets and modelling practice became unveiled. The increasing degree of central bank transparency has been clarified by Eijffinger and Geraats (2006) inter alia, who published a transparency index for nine industrial countries covering the period between 1998 and 2002. Dincer and Eichengreen (2007) expanded the number of countries and years covered by Eijffinger and Geraats (2006). By using an even more comprehensive sample of 100 countries for the period between 1998 and 2005, they confirmed that central bank transparency had an increasing tendency even until the mid-2000s.

In this chapter, we examine whether financial stress in 2007, 2008 and 2009 has inclined central banks to become even more transparent. This question has already been investigated in the empirical literature by using the transparency index of Eijffinger and Geraats (2006). Siklos (2010) has updated the index for the period between 2006 and 2009. By studying the updated index, he found the following. First, transparency continued to improve gradually on average even after 2005 although at a slower rate than before. Second, there are some obvious differences across country groups.

The transparency index of developed countries stopped increasing in 2006. From then on, it remained unchanged. In contrast, transparency has risen steadily in the rest of the world with the most impressive developments taking place among the countries in Central and Eastern Europe (CEE). These findings are apparent from Table 1.

The potential explanations for these tendencies are as follows. First, the transparency index is constructed in a way that it has a maximum.[1] Therefore, it cannot increase continuously forever. By the mid-2000s, transparency might have already reached its limit in the developed countries and got close to it in many other countries. Second, the transparency index might have some limitations at measuring the exact degree of transparency and this limitation can be more apparent during periods of financial stress (see Section 3 for the detailed analysis). Third, the global financial crisis of 2007–2009 enforced changes in the monetary policies that might make it impossible for central banks to enhance transparency. Siklos (2010) has left the judgment of these explanations to future research.

We contribute to the literature by analysing the links between central bank transparency and financial system stability in many different ways.

Table 1. The Transparency Index Across Country Groups.

	Level			
	Developed	Developing	Emerging	CEE 4
1998	7.27	2.28	3.81	4.63
1999	7.97	2.37	4.08	5.38
2000	8.20	2.45	4.82	6.00
2001	8.60	2.85	5.19	6.38
2002	8.97	3.15	5.98	7.63
2003	9.17	3.28	6.48	8.00
2004	9.40	3.61	6.71	8.38
2005	9.47	3.75	6.89	9.25
2006	9.63	3.80	7.00	9.38
2007	9.63	3.86	7.11	9.75
2008	9.63	3.88	7.16	9.88
2009	9.63	3.88	7.32	11.00

Note: Source of data: Siklos (2010). The data has been revised and modified by the authors of this chapter (see Section 4.2.2 about the modifications). The categorization of countries into the group of developed, developing and emerging is according to the IMF classification, published in the World Economic Outlook; CEE 4 countries are the Czech Republic, Hungary, Poland and Slovakia.

First, we document that the standard measure of transparency has hardly changed in some CEE countries during periods of financial stress.[2] Second, we review the dimensions of transparency that might have changed during the recent financial crisis but cannot be measured by the standard transparency index. Third, we investigate how the unconventional monetary policy has influenced central bank transparency in the recent years. Finally, we estimate the link between transparency and accuracy of survey forecasts by applying a methodology similar to that of Ehrmann et al. (2010) and Csavas et al. (2010). By using this link, we aim to provide indirect empirical evidence for the hypothesized reduction in transparency during periods of financial stress.

2. STYLIZED FACTS ON FINANCIAL STRESS AND TRANSPARENCY

In this section, we examine how transparency evolved in four CEE countries. The analysed countries are the Czech Republic, Hungary, Poland and Slovakia. This group of countries provides us with a special opportunity to explore the link between transparency and financial stress for two reasons. First, these countries have been hit not only by the global financial crisis but also they had experienced episodes of severe financial stress even before 2005. Second, central bank transparency has not reached its limit by the early 2000s in these countries.

In this analysis, we use the financial stress index (FSI) that has been constructed by Balakrishnan, Danninger, Elekdag, and Tytell (2009). This index is similar to the index of Cardarelli, Elekdag, and Lall (2009) as both consist of the sub-indices measuring the stress in the banking sector, security markets and the foreign exchange market. The main difference between these two indices is that while the index of Cardarelli et al. (2009) has been developed for the advanced economies, the one of Balakrishnan et al. (2009) suits the emerging countries better.[3]

Fig. 1 plots the time series of the FSI together with one of its sub-indices, the stock market volatility index for the analysed four countries. According to the indices, these countries have been hit by as large shocks before 2005 as during the recent global financial crisis. Apparently, Poland's financial stability was as much at risk in 1998 as in 2008. Although the FSI is not available for the other three countries for the year 1998, we know that these countries were affected just as much by the default of Russia on its external

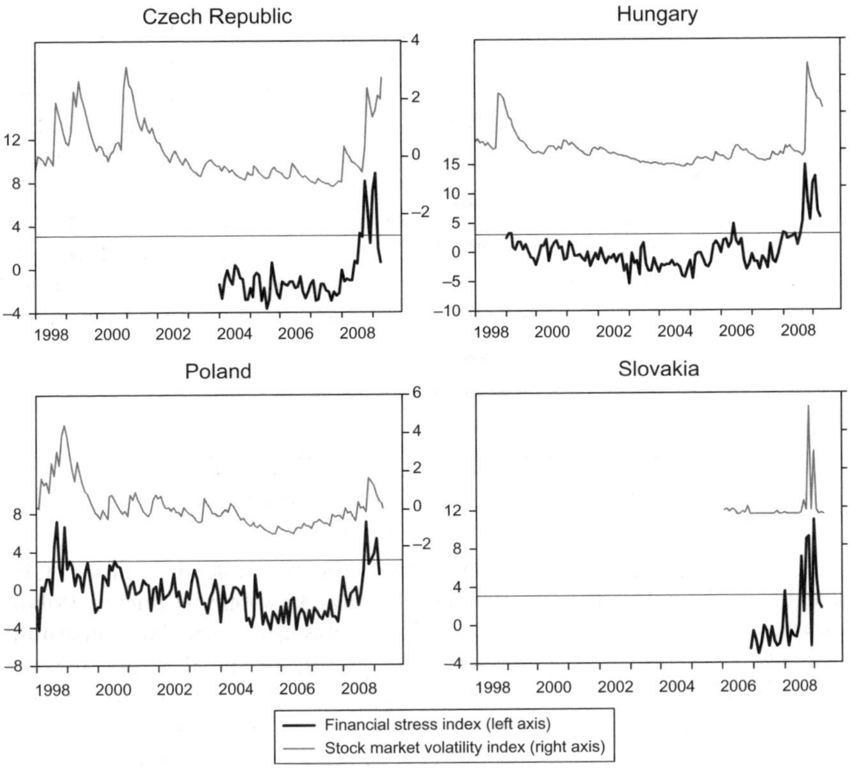

Fig. 1. The Financial Stress Index and the Stock Market Volatility Index Between January 1998 and April 2009. *Note:* The horizontal line is at value 3 of the left axis.

obligations in 1998 and the collapse of Long Term Capital Management (LTCM) in the same year as Poland. This is also reflected by the stock market volatility index in Fig. 1. Another episode of financial stress was the dot-com crash that distressed mostly the Czech market at the end of 2000 and at the beginning of 2001.

In order to get some idea on how transparency changes in periods of financial stress, we plotted the annual changes of the transparency index against the FSI in Fig. 2. It clearly shows that the relationship is non-linear and negative. In relatively calm periods, when the stress index was below 3, central banks either increased the degree of transparency or maintained the

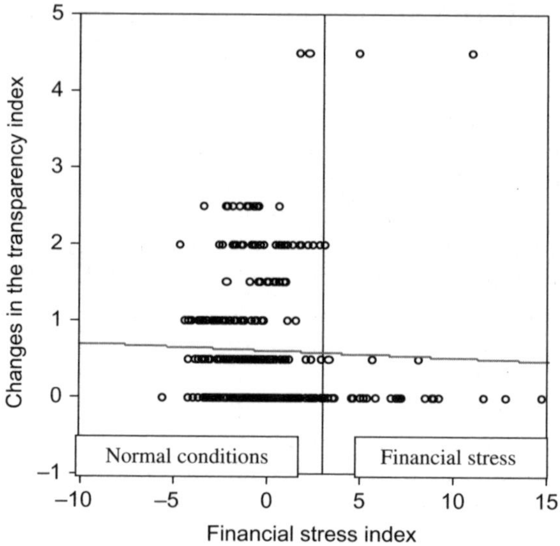

Fig. 2. Annual Changes in the Transparency Index Plotted Against the Financial Stress Index. Sample: January 1998–April 2009, Countries: Czech Republic, Hungary, Poland and Slovakia. *Notes:* Higher values of the transparency and stress indices are associated with a higher degree of transparency and more stress, respectively. The red line is the regression line and the horizontal line is at value 3.

previous level. During periods of financial stress (higher values of the FSI), the transparency of central banks in the CEE region has hardly changed. This finding is not an artificial consequence of the lack of data for the stress index for certain periods and countries. The relationship between financial stress and transparency is qualitatively the same if we measure the stress with the stock market volatility index that is available for almost the entire sample.

Fortunately, our data on the four CEE countries makes it possible to judge some explanations for the lack of changes in the transparency index. Since transparency was not at its peak in the major part of the investigated period, and there were plenty of opportunities for central banks to become more transparent, it would not be fair to blame the transparency index for being bounded. It is more plausible that it is the financial stress that limits transparency.

3. WHAT DIMENSIONS OF TRANSPARENCY HAVE BEEN AFFECTED BY THE FINANCIAL CRISIS?

Geraats (2002) distinguishes five dimensions of transparency that are (1) political transparency, (2) economic transparency, (3) procedural transparency, (4) policy transparency and (5) operational transparency. Each of these dimensions is measured separately by the sub-indices of the transparency index. And the transparency index is the simple sum of the sub-indices. We showed in the previous sections that recent updates of the transparency index reflect almost unchanged circumstances on average. This is also true for the sub-indices because central banks have not made significant changes to their practices that are measured by the index. For instance, they kept on publishing their economic models, strategies and decisions. In this section, we examine how transparency changed in each of its five dimensions. We argue that all aspects of transparency have been affected by the financial crisis, and the impact was unfavourable. Fig. 3 summarizes our arguments.

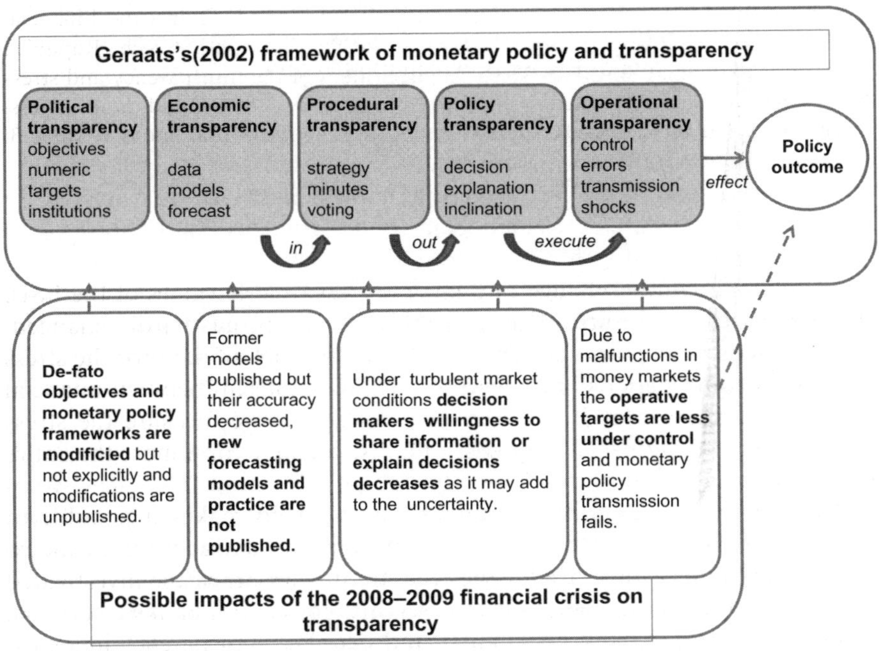

Fig. 3. Components of the Transparency Index and the Possible Impacts of the Financial Crisis.

Political transparency: As the financial crisis highlighted vulnerabilities in the financial systems in many countries, central banks became already formally recognized as an important pillar in the systemic supervisory institutional framework. However, it is in the shroud of opacity how responsibility for financial stability influenced the priority of central bank objectives. For example, Fed Governor Ben Bernanke noted that central bank independence is essential, but it cannot be unconditional. 'We are committed to exploring new ways to enhance the Federal Reserve's transparency without compromising our mandated monetary policy and financial stability objectives'. Borio (2009) claims that stemming from informational gains the financial supervisory role of central banks can lead to synergies with the price stability objective. Nevertheless, the potential conflict of new goals with the price stability can affect transparency negatively.

In addition, central banks have not even had legal mandate to follow the new objectives, while most central banks updated their policy goals in practice. Many central banks have targeted lower interest rates than their announced key policy rates. The European Central Bank (ECB), for example, tolerated that short-term money market rates have been tied to the overnight deposit rate of the ECB, which implies an unannounced monetary loosening.

In a recent study, Geraats (2008) also found that central banks across all monetary policy frameworks had become more transparent during the last decade, although there are significant differences in the degree of information disclosure across monetary policy frameworks. Central banks with inflation targeting have achieved the highest level of transparency, while monetary and exchange rate targeters have exhibited the lowest level in information disclosure. Although in terms of de-jure monetary frameworks central banks have not changed since the financial crisis in 2008, de-facto frameworks altered immensely, implying changes in communication practices, too.

Economic transparency: Most central banks had to realize that old models and economic data no longer apply in the post-financial-crisis 'new world order'. Furthermore, conceptual understanding of the new world will take many years as the data shortage also represents an obstacle for statistical analysis and forecasting. Under these circumstances, central banks publish their usual reports, models and forecasts. So they seem transparent at first sight, while central bank economists and decision-makers have lost their faith in these models and decision-making is influenced more and more by expertise, judgment and gut feelings.

Procedural and policy transparency: While many central banks promptly announce monetary policy decisions, and the explanation of decisions in normal times, most central banks are reluctant to communicate severe systemic distress and extraordinary risks because it may just add to the turmoil and become self-fulfilling.

Operational transparency: Many central banks introduced unconventional monetary policy instruments in order to counteract the adverse effect of increased counterparty risk that led to the lack of liquidity in the markets and jumps in the prices. The markets have been supplied by much fewer information about these new instruments than about conventional instruments before. The next section gives an overview on the unconventional instruments that were applied by the central banks in the CEE region in the crisis, and also on their impact on central bank transparency.

3.1. Transparency and New Monetary Policy Instruments

The Eijffinger–Geraats transparency index was developed in an environment where central banks used almost exclusively the policy rates as an instrument to achieve their objectives, the primary objective being price stability in most cases. However, after the Lehman crisis, many central banks introduced unconventional monetary policy instruments (see a classification of these instruments in Yehoue, Stone, & Ishi, 2009) and objectives other than the price stability gained higher priority. Since the Eijffinger–Geraats index is not able to capture the transparency related to these new instruments, we provide a brief assessment about how the new measures could alter central bank transparency. In this section, we review the practice of the four CEE central banks and that of the ECB.

One of the new central bank measures introduced during the crisis provided liquidity for horizons longer than 1 day. Three CEE central banks in our sample (the Czech Republic, Hungary and Poland) applied these instruments with maturities ranging from 2 weeks to 6 months. In contrast, in Slovakia the domestic interbank market was sufficiently liquid given the imminent euro adoption, thus the National Bank of Slovakia (NBS) did not have to introduce new measures.[4] The ECB introduced long-term liquidity providing operations with maturities up to 1 year (see ECB, 2009).

A common feature of the CEE countries is that their banking systems operate with a liquidity surplus. Therefore, there is no need for the monetary authorities to act as a liquidity provider in normal times. It was the malfunctioning of interbank money markets during the crisis that forced commercial banks to hoard liquid assets and necessitated the active assistance of the central bank.

It is evident from Fig. 4 that the 3-month interbank rates were above the policy rates on the Czech and Polish markets for several months after the Lehman crisis. This wedge has not reflected interest rate hike expectations, but the reluctance of banks to provide credit to each other on the interbank market due to higher counterparty risk.[5] In other words, the wedge was a

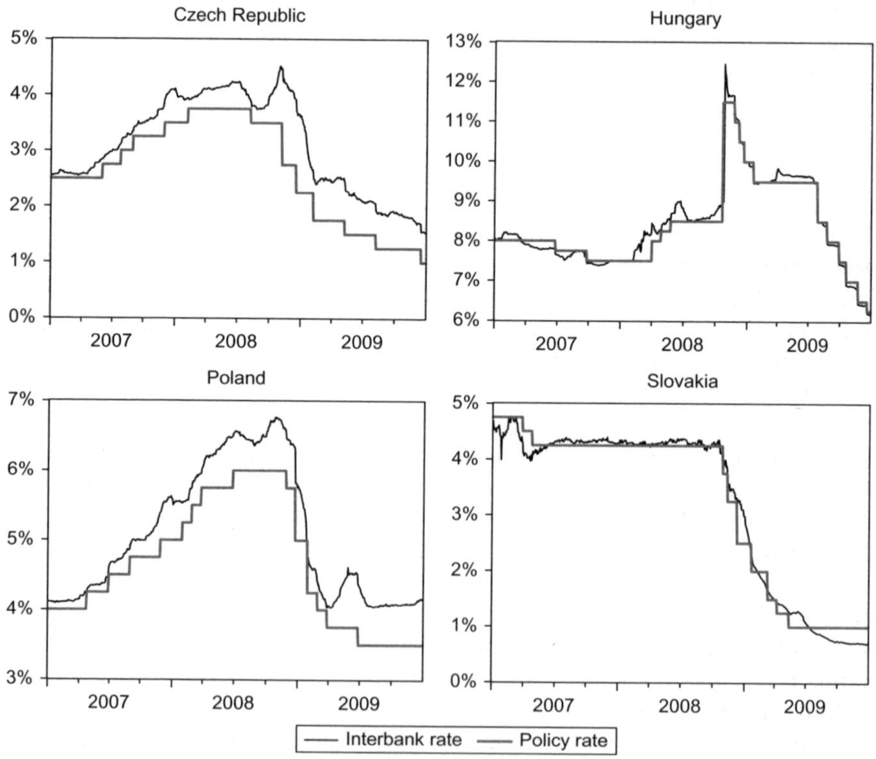

Fig. 4. Central Bank Policy Rates and 3-Month Interbank Money Market Rates Between 2007 and 2009. *Notes:* The interbank rates are the PRIBOR (Czech Republic), the BUBOR (Hungary), the WIBOR (Poland) and the BRIBOR (Slovakia). For Slovakia, the policy rate is replaced by that of the ECB and interbank rate is replaced by the EURIBOR since January 2009.

premium for the extra risk. One of the objectives for liquidity providing measures was to reduce this premium. The premium not only makes loans expensive but also distorts the transmission mechanism as well, that is, the transmission from policy rate to market rates. The Czech National Bank (CNB) explained their measure with the aim of fostering the functioning of the government bond market. Similar considerations prompted Magyar Nemzeti Bank (MNB) to provide liquidity to primary dealers of the Hungarian government bond. The ECB had a further motivation to reduce long-term yield in a situation where the zero bound to the policy rate became effective.

Since central banks shifted from influencing market rates by setting the policy rate to directly intervening on the market, the overall transparency of the central bank can only be assessed by judging how much information has been revealed on these new instruments. Central banks disclosed the pricing and the quantity of these instruments. However, they were less transparent regarding the decision-making about these instruments relative to the transparency of setting the policy rate.[6] It is worth mentioning that even with perfect transparency, the effect of these on money markets would have been uncertain. For market participants to know what will be the market interest rates in the future, it is not enough to have information about the decision-making of the central banks but also about how liquidity situation will be changed in the interbank market.

In both Poland and the Czech Republic, some of the interest rate cuts at the end of 2008 as well as in 2009 were explained by the above-mentioned distortion of the transparency mechanism: the aim was to bring the market interest rates in line with the interest rate which is considered optimal by the central bank.[7] For market participants, this again could make it difficult to understand how exactly the central bank wanted to perform its monetary policy: by using new instruments to reduce market interest rates or by reducing the policy rate which can contribute to lower market interest rates if the premium on this latter remains unchanged. On the other hand, rate cuts were partly explained by arguments related to financial stability in which case it did not necessarily go against the logic of inflation targeting since the risks of undershooting the inflation goals were more pronounced.

The MNB began to purchase government bonds in autumn 2008. The motivation was to restore the smooth functioning of the market and reduce the liquidity premium.[8] Although the purchases were performed in a transparent way, via a tender procedure, the market did not have a clear idea of the level of long-term interest rates that the central bank intended to reach. Possibly, neither could the central bank specify how much of the increase in the government bond yields was due to liquidity premium, and not caused by fundamentals; thus, it was more difficult for market participants to forecast long-term interest rates. The covered bond purchase program of the ECB since June 2009 (ECB, 2009) can be assessed in a similar way; the targeted long-term interest rate was not revealed.

The MNB, the National Bank of Poland (NBP) and the ECB introduced currency swap instruments (Yehoue et al., 2009). The CEE countries supplied EUR and USD against domestic currencies as well as CHF against EUR, while the ECB provided USD and CHF. The aim was to provide foreign currency liquidity to the banking system and also to reduce the stress in financial markets (Moessner & Allen, 2010). Banai, Kiraly, and Varhegyi (2009) describe central banks acting as 'FX lender of last resort'. Regarding swap operations, the market didn't have a clear idea on how decisions about the pricing of these instruments were made. For example, the NBP communicated only that its price (the swap point) would be close to market prices.[9] Nevertheless, the lower transparency of the swap instruments possibly affected the uncertainty related to future interest rates denominated in domestic currency less.

To conclude, the use of unconventional monetary policy instruments in the CEE region possibly lowered the central bank transparency regarding the objectives of the instruments, the explanation of decisions or the achievement of operating goals, which are all important dimensions of transparency.

4. EMPIRICAL ANALYSIS OF THE EFFECT OF TRANSPARENCY ON ECONOMIC UNCERTAINTY

Some theoretical considerations and some stylized facts reviewed in Section 3 suggest that central banks become less transparent during periods of financial stress, and this drop of transparency is not captured by the transparency index. In this section, we use regression analysis to examine both the observed and the unobserved component of transparency and their effect on economic uncertainty. Following the practice of Swanson (2004) and Ehrmann et al. (2010), we measure uncertainty by the forecast accuracy of survey expectations and also by the dispersion of views of survey participants.

4.1. Econometric Model and the Hypotheses to be Tested

Our benchmark econometric model is given by

$$y_{i,t} = \beta_{0,i} + \beta_1 \mathrm{TR}_{i,t} + \beta_2 \mathrm{FSI}_{i,t} + \beta_3 \sigma_{i,t} + \varepsilon_{i,t} \tag{1}$$

where $y_{i,t}$ denotes the dependent variable characterizing the forecasts in country i formed at time t. More precisely, it measures either the degree of disagreement across individual forecasters or the forecast accuracy. On the right-hand side of the equation, $\mathrm{TR}_{i,t}$ and $\mathrm{FSI}_{i,t}$ denote the transparency index and the financial stress index, respectively. The transparency index is either the total index, that is, the sum of the sub-indices measuring different aspects of transparency or one of the sub-indices. The volatility of the variable to be forecasted is $\sigma_{i,t}$, and $\varepsilon_{i,t}$ is the error term.

The *hypothesis* that is usually tested in the literature is that the quality of forecasts depends negatively on central bank transparency ($\beta_1 < 0$), that is, forecasters disagree less and make smaller forecast errors if the central bank is more transparent. As a first step, we also test the above hypothesis; however, our main focus is on the coefficient of the financial stress index $\mathrm{FSI}_{i,t}$. Some theoretical considerations and some stylized facts reviewed in Section 3 suggest that central banks became less transparent during periods of financial stress and this decline in transparency could not be measured by the transparency index. Our aim is to provide empirical evidence for the presence of the unobserved reduction in transparency. The idea is to detect the unobserved component through its effect on the forecasts. The unobserved decline in transparency is likely to have the same effect on the forecasts as the observed component. The latter is that lower degree of transparency is associated with larger forecast errors and higher dispersion of views under our first hypothesis. Suppose that the first hypothesis is true, moreover, financial stress influences the forecasts dominantly through the changing transparency of the central bank. Under these two assumptions, a positive coefficient of the FSI ($\beta_2 > 0$) implies that there is a positive measurement error in the transparency index during financial stress.

It is important to note that the above interpretation depends highly on its assumptions. While we can easily test the first assumption, we cannot test the second one. The reason is that we can hardly distinguish empirically between the direct and the indirect effect of financial stress on the forecasts, where the latter works through the changing transparency of the central bank. Therefore, if the coefficient of the financial stress is positive, then all we can say is that either the unobserved component of transparency declines during periods of financial stress or that financial stress has a direct effect on the forecasts.

We control for the country-fixed effect by $\beta_{0,i}$ that captures some country-specific characteristics. These characteristics are, for instance, the following: how difficult it is in general to forecast the interest rate of the country; what the general level of skills of the forecasters is in the country and also whether the dispersion of views is shaped by the interactions between the forecasters, that is, whether there is a dominant forecaster in the country who is followed by some others.

In addition to the country-fixed effects, we control for the volatility of the variable to be forecasted $\sigma_{i,t}$. We expect that the higher the volatility is, the more difficult the task of forecasting becomes. Hence, both the degree of disagreement and the absolute forecast error ($\beta_3 > 0$) increase.

4.2. Data

In our empirical exercise, we use survey data on forecasts of short interest rates and long interest rates. In addition, we use historical data of these rates, in order to evaluate the performance of these forecasts. Finally, we apply some measures of transparency and an FSI. This section provides a detailed description of these data. Moreover, it discusses how the control variables are constructed.

4.2.1. Data for the Dependent Variable

We use the survey data of the Consensus Economics for both of the dependent variables in Eq. (1), that is, the degree of disagreement across individual forecasters and the forecast accuracy. Consensus Economics surveys the views of a large group of professional forecasters on the future short- and long-term interest rates. It reports forecasts for a broad set of countries, including emerging countries in the CEE region. For the countries we analyse, the forecasted short-term interest rate is the 3-month interbank rate,[10] while the long-term rate is 10-year government bond yield.[11] The forecasts cover both short (3-months) and long (1-year) horizon predictions. The sample is spanned by *January 2003 and December 2009*. The *frequency* is bimonthly prior to May 2007, afterwards it is monthly. Therefore, we have 58 forecast periods in our sample. Consensus Economics started to survey long-term forecasts only in 2006, therefore the sample of these forecasts is shorter. See Table 2 on some summary statistics of our measures of the degree of disagreement and the forecast accuracy.

Table 2. Summary Statistics for the Cross-Sectional Dispersion and the Forecast Accuracy in the Consensus Economics Dataset.

	Number of observations	Mean (%)	Standard deviation (%)	Minimum (%)	Maximum (%)
Standard deviation of the individual forecasts					
Short-term interest rates in 3 months	232	0.29	0.17	0.10	1.10
Short-term interest rates in 12 months	232	0.45	0.22	0.10	1.60
Long-term interest rates in 3 months	160	0.31	0.17	0.10	1.30
Long-term interest rates in 12 months	160	0.42	0.21	0.10	1.40
Absolute forecast error of the consensus forecast					
Short-term interest rates in 3 months	217	0.54	0.62	0.000	3.51
Short-term interest rates in 12 months	187	1.26	1.08	0.010	5.85
Long-term interest rates in 3 months	160	0.55	0.59	0.001	4.45
Long-term interest rates in 12 months	132	0.72	0.84	0.007	5.15

Sample: 2003–2009, countries: Czech Republic, Hungary, Poland and Slovakia.

We measure the *degree of disagreement of the individual forecasters* by the *standard deviation*. Our choice is motivated by the fact that this statistics is readily available for us, as it is reported by the Consensus Economics. An alternative measure would be the inter-quartile range. The latter has the advantage over the standard deviation of not being sensitive to outliers. Ehrmann et al. (2010) used both measures in an empirical exercise similar to ours, and they found all of their results robust to the choice of the dispersion measure. Their finding supports that it is sufficient to use only the standard deviation of the individual forecasts as a measure of cross-sectional dispersion.

We measure the *forecast accuracy* by the *absolute forecast error of the consensus forecast*, where the *consensus forecast* is the cross-sectional mean of the individual forecasts. This statistics, just like the standard deviation, is also reported by the Consensus Economics. In this respect, we deviate again from the methodology of Ehrmann et al., (2010) since they used the *average absolute forecast error* and not the absolute error of the average forecasts. The average absolute forecast error depends not only on the forecast accuracy of the consensus forecast but also on the dispersion of forecasts across individual forecasters. The latter is already captured by our previously introduced measure for the degree of disagreement. Since there is no point to measure the same effect twice, we decided to make our measure for forecast accuracy as much orthogonal to the degree of dispersion as possible. For this reason, the absolute forecast error of the consensus forecast seemed to be a better choice than the average absolute forecast error.

The *historical data* of the end-of-month short- and long-term interest rates are from the Bloomberg. We collected interest rate data not only for the Czech koruna, Hungarian forint, Polish zloty and Slovakian koruna but also for the euro. We used the short-term euro rate as the historical rate for Slovakia from January 2009 on, when Slovakia joined the eurozone.

4.2.2. Measures of Central Bank Transparency

We use the traditional measure of central bank transparency, the so-called transparency index developed by Geraats (2002). It distinguishes five dimensions (political, economic, procedural, policy and operational) described in Section 3. Each of these dimensions is measured separately by 3 sub-indices. All the 15 sub-indices of the transparency index can take the value of 0, ½ or 1 according to the practice of the investigated central bank implying that the total index can take the minimum of 0 and the maximum of 15 (the higher value indicating a more transparent central banking practice).

Central bank communication practices have been surveyed by Eijffinger and Geraats (2006), Dincer and Eichengreen (2007), and Siklos (2010) using the same methodology. In our empirical analysis, we used the latest update by Siklos (2010). We implemented, however, the following minor modifications in his dataset. The Czech National Bank and National Bank of Hungary have been publishing individual voting records since 2008 and 2005, respectively; hence the value of sub-index 3.c is changed to 1 from 0.5 for both countries. Furthermore, Slovakia introduced the euro in January 2009; therefore, we assigned the values of the transparency index of ECB to Slovakia since then.

4.2.3. Measures of Financial Stress

We use the FSI that has been constructed by Balakrishnan et al. (2009).[12] This index is a modified version of the comprehensive index of Cardarelli et al. (2009). Both indices have three subcomponents: (i) banking sector (the slope of the yield curve, TED spread, beta of banking sector stock),

(ii) securities markets (corporate bonds spread, stock market returns and time-varying volatility of stock return) and (iii) exchange rate (time-varying volatility of NEER change). In contrast to the index of Cardarelli et al. (2009), the index of Balakrishnanet al. (2009) has been developed for emerging economies. For instance, it consists of measures for exchange rate pressures and sovereign debt spread that are more relevant for emerging economies than to developed ones.

4.2.4. Volatility of the Variables to be Forecasted

In order to judge how transparency and financial stress affect the quality of forecasts, we control for the overall difficulty of forecasting. In the model specification of Eq. (1), the control variable is the annualized volatility of the variable to be forecasted. It is calculated from the daily interest rate data of 20 days preceding the survey date. The daily historical data are from Bloomberg.

4.3. Estimation Results

This section summarizes the estimation results of Eq. (1). In order to see which aspects of transparency can be the most important in terms of coordinating individual expectations, not only the total index of transparency is used as explanatory variable but also some of the sub-indices measuring different aspects of transparency. In certain dimensions, there is only moderate variation in the data, or the sub-index correlates highly with some other explanatory variables disabling us to run the regression. These dimensions are the political transparency, the policy transparency and the operational transparency. The low variation in the political transparency is because all central banks have already complied with most of the criteria of this aspect of transparency in the sample.

Tables 3 and 4 report the estimates for the forecasted short and long rate, respectively. The left panels of Table 3 show our results on the *dispersion of individual short rate forecasts*. Whenever the parameter of the transparency index or sub-index is significant, it is negative. Therefore, we can say that central bank transparency coordinates survey expectations in the sense of reducing the degree of disagreement over the 3-month-ahead and 1-year-ahead short rates. Moreover, the procedural aspects of transparency seem important as they have parameter estimates significant at 1% for both the short and the long horizon forecasts. Its effect is significant also in economic terms. For instance, if a central bank starts to provide an explicit policy rule

Table 3. The Effect of Central Bank Transparency and Financial Stress on Dispersion of the Individual Forecasts and Forecast Accuracy, where the Forecasted Variable Is the Short Rate.

Transparency Is Measured by Index or Sub-index	2	3	4	5	Total	2	3	4	5	Total
Dependent variable	*Standard deviation* of the individual forecasts for the short-term interest rates with forecast horizon *3 months*					*Absolute forecast error* of the consensus forecast for the short-term interest rates with forecast horizon *3 months*				
Transparency	−0.00	−0.08***	0.15	0.08	−0.02*	−0.31***	−0.4***	–	–	−0.24***
(*t*-stat)	(−0.2)	(−3.44)	(0.86)	(0.86)	(−1.37)	(−5.03)	(−2.94)	–	–	(−4.22)
Financial stress	0.01***	0.02***	0.01***	0.01***	0.02***	0.01	0.04***	–	–	0.03**
(*t*-stat)	(3.01)	(4.72)	(2.91)	(2.91)	(3.4)	(0.44)	(2.63)	–	–	(1.82)
Volatility	3.26***	2.66***	3.26***	3.26***	3.09***	1.28	−0.59	–	–	−0.35
(*t*-stat)	(3.48)	(3.28)	(3.63)	(3.63)	(3.43)	(0.36)	(−0.19)	–	–	(−0.11)
Country-fixed effect	Yes	Yes	Yes	Yes	Yes	Yes	Yes	–	–	Yes
Observations	169	169	169	169	169	162	162	–	–	162
R^2	45.23%	49.28%	45.56%	45.56%	45.92%	21.75%	26.19%	–	–	26.08%
Dependent variable	*Standard deviation* of the individual forecasts for the short-term interest rates with forecast horizon *1 year*					*Absolute forecast error* of the consensus forecast for the short-term interest rates with forecast horizon *1 year*				
Transparency	−0.05**	−0.11***	0.03	0.01	−0.04***	−0.51***	−0.28*	–	–	−0.25***
(*t*-stat)	(−2.33)	(−3.26)	(0.14)	(0.14)	(−2.39)	(−4.13)	(−1.51)	–	–	(−2.8)
Financial stress	0.02***	0.02***	0.01***	0.01***	0.02***	−0.04	−0.02	–	–	−0.02
(*t*-stat)	(2.76)	(3.75)	(2.44)	(2.44)	(3.29)	(−1.17)	(−0.71)	–	–	(−0.62)
Volatility	1.6	0.95	1.82	1.82	1.38	4.79	4.7	–	–	3.76
(*t*-stat)	(0.97)	(0.61)	(1.08)	(1.08)	(0.86)	(0.66)	(0.65)	–	–	(0.53)
Country-fixed effect	Yes	Yes	Yes	Yes	Yes	Yes	Yes	–	–	Yes
Observations	169	169	169	169	169	153	153	–	–	153
R^2	44.61%	48.39%	43.47%	43.47%	45.96%	35.97%	33.39%	–	–	35.28%

Sample: 2003–2009, countries: Czech Republic, Hungary, Poland and Slovakia.
Note: ***, **, * indicate significance at 1%, 5% and 10% respectively.

or strategy that describes its monetary policy framework, then its transparency index increases by 1. Our estimates suggest that this measure decreases the standard deviation of the individual forecasts of the 3-month-ahead short rate by 8 bps given everything else remains unchanged. This effect is not negligible because the standard deviation of these forecasts is between 10 and 110 bps as it is reported in Table 2.

Our results on the *forecast accuracy* reported by the panels on the right-hand side in Table 3 are in line with those on the dispersion of forecasts. Higher transparency is associated with significantly better forecasts. For instance, if the sub-index of the procedural transparency increases by 1, like in our previous example, then the absolute forecast error of the 3-month-ahead short rate decreases by 40 bps ceteris paribus. This effect is comparable in magnitude to the sample mean of the absolute forecast errors, which is 54 bps (see Table 2).

Table 4 reports the estimates for the *long rate*. Surprisingly, central bank transparency has the opposite effect on the long-term rate forecasts than on the short rate forecasts. Higher degree of transparency mostly comes with significantly bigger absolute forecast errors and more disperse views on the future 10-year government bond yields. One potential explanation of this finding is provided by Morris and Shin (2002). They demonstrate that when central banks have noisy private information on the long-term interest rate and market participants rely too much on public information, then higher central bank transparency can lower social welfare and increase uncertainty.

An alternative explanation is that our sample for the long rate forecasts is not representative, and we cannot generalize the results obtained from the period between 2006 and 2009. Obviously, we do a false generalization if the relationship between the transparency index and the forecasts is time varying and atypical during the years of financial stress. Unfortunately, we cannot check the stability of this relationship for the long rate forecasts since these data are available only from 2006 on. However, we can do it for the short rate forecasts. To see whether the relationship between the transparency index and the short rate forecasts is time varying, we re-estimate Eq. (1). However, this time the sample period is the same as that of the long rate forecasts, that is, spanned by 2006 and 2009. Table 5 shows the results for the regressions, whenever estimation is possible. Unlike the estimates for the short rate obtained on the long sample (Table 3), but similar to the estimates for the long rate obtained on the short sample (Table 4), the estimates in Table 5 suggest that higher transparency is associated with higher degree of disagreement and less precise forecasts.

Table 4. The Effect of Central Bank Transparency and Financial Stress on Dispersion of the Individual Forecasts and Forecast Accuracy, where the Forecasted Variable Is the Long Rate.

Transparency Is Measured by Index or Sub-Index	2	3	4	5	Total	2	3	4	5	Total
Dependent variable	*Standard deviation* of the individual forecasts for the long-term interest rates with forecast horizon *3 months*					*Absolute forecast error* of the consensus forecast for the long-term interest rates with forecast horizon *3 months*				
Transparency	0.12***	0.1***	0.35***	0.18***	0.04***	0.28***	−0.01	0.84***	0.42***	0.08**
(*t*-stat)	(4.62)	(2.53)	(4.62)	(4.62)	(4.72)	(2.76)	(−0.11)	(2.76)	(2.76)	(2.23)
Financial stress	0.02***	0.02****	0.02***	0.02***	0.02***	0.05**	0.06**	0.05**	0.05**	0.05**
(*t*-stat)	(6.71)	(5.1)	(6.71)	(6.71)	(5.88)	(1.79)	(1.81)	(1.79)	(1.79)	(1.68)
Volatility	1	1.02	1	1	1.13	4.7	3.99	4.7	4.7	4.77
(*t*-stat)	(1.01)	(0.99)	(1.01)	(1.01)	(1.13)	(0.84)	(0.69)	(0.84)	(0.84)	(0.85)
Country-fixed effect	Yes	Yes	Yes	Yes	Yes	Yes	Yes	Yes	Yes	Yes
Observations	121	121	121	121	121	121	121	121	121	121
R^2	39.86%	38.72%	39.86%	39.86%	40.59%	34.57%	33.43%	34.57%	34.57%	34.26%
Dependent variable	*Standard deviation* of the individual forecasts for the long-term interest rates with forecast horizon *1 year*					*Absolute forecast error* of the consensus forecast for the long-term interest rates with forecast horizon *1 year*				
Transparency	0.09**	−0.05	0.28**	0.14**	0.02*	0.04	0.24**	0.13	0.06	0.04
(*t*-stat)	(2.06)	(−0.89)	(2.06)	(2.06)	(1.37)	(0.46)	(1.78)	(0.46)	(0.46)	(0.94)
Financial stress	0.01**	0.02**	0.01**	0.01**	0.01*	−0.02	−0.03	−0.02	−0.02	−0.03
(*t*-stat)	(1.74)	(1.95)	(1.74)	(1.74)	(1.64)	(−0.8)	(−0.98)	(−0.8)	(−0.8)	(−0.85)
Volatility	0.02	−0.34	0.02	0.02	0.01	−3.47	−2.82	−3.47	−3.47	−3.23
(*t*-stat)	(0.02)	(−0.36)	(0.02)	(0.02)	(0.01)	(−0.49)	(−0.4)	(−0.49)	(−0.49)	(−0.45)
Country-fixed effect	Yes	Yes	Yes	Yes	Yes	Yes	Yes	Yes	Yes	Yes
Observations	121	121	121	121	121	121	121	121	121	121
R^2	55.02%	54.14%	55.02%	55.02%	54.45%	41.81%	42.23%	41.81%	41.81%	41.89%

Sample: 2006–2009, countries: Czech Republic, Hungary, Poland and Slovakia.
Note: ***, **, * indicate significance at 1%, 5% and 10% respectively.

Table 5. The Effect of Central Bank Transparency and Financial Stress on Dispersion of the Individual Forecasts and Forecast Accuracy, where the Forecasted Variable Is the Short Rate.

Transparency Is Measured by Index or Sub-Index	2	3	4	5	Total	2	3	4	5	Total
Dependent variable	*Standard deviation* of the individual forecasts for the short-term interest rates with forecast horizon *3 months*					*Absolute forecast error* of the consensus forecast for the short-term interest rates with forecast horizon *3 months*				
Transparency	0.033	0.04***	0.1	0.05	0.01	–	0.14*	–	–	0.14*
(*t*-stat)	(0.5)	(1.19)	(0.5)	(0.5)	(0.67)	–	(1.35)	–	–	(1.35)
Financial stress	0.02***	0.02***	0.02***	0.02***	0.02***	–	0.04	–	–	0.04
(*t*-stat)	(4.17)	(4.35)	(4.17)	(4.17)	(4.07)	–	(2.87)	–	–	(2.87)
Volatility	3.01***	3.04***	3.01***	3.01***	3.02***	–	−2.42	–	–	−2.42
(*t*-stat)	(3.01)	(3.04)	(3.01)	(3.01)	(3.01)	–	(−0.79)	–	–	(−0.79)
Country-fixed effect	Yes	Yes	Yes	Yes	Yes	–	Yes	–	–	Yes
Observations	121	121	121	121	121	–	114	–	–	114
R^2	52.83%	52.86%	52.83%	52.83%	52.92%	–	20.12%	–	–	20.12%
Dependent variable	*Standard deviation* of the individual forecasts for the short-term interest rates with forecast horizon *1 year*					*Absolute forecast error* of the consensus forecast for the short-term interest rates with forecast horizon *1 year*				
Transparency	−0.02	0.05**	−0.05	−0.02	0	–	1.16***	–	–	1.16***
(*t*-stat)	(−0.23)	(1.23)	(−0.23)	(−0.23)	(0.02)	–	(5.65)	–	–	(5.65)
Financial Stress	0.02*	0.02*	0.02*	0.02*	0.02*	–	−0.02	–	–	−0.02
(*t*-stat)	(3.41)	(3.19)	(3.41)	(3.41)	(3.39)	–	(−0.93)	–	–	(−0.93)
Volatility	1.35	1.39	1.35	1.35	1.35	–	−2.63	–	–	−2.63
(*t*-stat)	(0.64)	(0.66)	(0.64)	(0.64)	(0.64)	–	(−0.88)	–	–	(−0.88)
Country-fixed effect	Yes	Yes	Yes	Yes	Yes	–	Yes	–	–	Yes
Observations	121	121	121	121	121	–	105	–	–	105
R^2	44.50%	44.74%	44.50%	44.50%	44.47%	–	39.10%	–	–	39.10%

Sample: 2006–2009, countries: Czech Republic, Hungary, Poland and Slovakia.
Note: ***, **, * indicate significance at 1%, 5% and 10% respectively.

Although central banks may know less about the long rate than the market, it is unlikely to be true for the short rate given that its most important determinant is the policy rate. Therefore, we think that the explanation of Morris and Shin (2002) has only limited relevance at rationalizing the estimated relationship between transparency and forecasts. However, it is still an open question why the forecasts became relatively less precise in countries with more transparent central banks in the recent years.

Turning to our second hypothesis, the coefficient of the FSI is either insignificant or significantly positive in Tables 3 and 4. The most probable explanation for this is that financial stress has a strong direct effect on the forecasts, and the tenser the situation, the higher is the forecast error and the dispersion of views. However, if we think that all the direct effect of financial stress on uncertainty is controlled by the volatility of the variable to be forecasted, then the FSI accounts only for the effect that works through the central bank transparency. By assuming that in periods of financial stress the unobserved component of transparency declines and affects the forecasts the same way as the observed component, then the parameter of the stress index should have the opposite sign as that of the transparency index. This is true for the estimates for the short rate obtained on the long sample.[13] Therefore, this finding supports the presence of unobserved decline in transparency during the financial turmoil.

Finally, we interpret the estimates for the coefficient of the volatility. The sign of the estimates is in line with our previous expectations. Higher historical volatility of forecasted interest rates is associated with higher forecast error and dispersion of views most of the times. Moreover, the estimates are significantly different from zero when the dependent variable is the standard deviation of the 3-month-ahead short rate forecasts (see the upper left panel in Table 3).

5. CONCLUSIONS

In the past, financial crises have always triggered important changes in the operation of central banks. The recent financial crisis has also played a pivotal role in forming central bank practices; however, recent updates of the transparency index reflect unchanged circumstances. Almost all the measurable aspects of transparency are the same in 2008 as in 2006 since central banks have kept on publishing their economic models, strategies and decisions.

In this chapter, we have argued that during the recent financial crisis central banks indeed had become less transparent as an obvious consequence of applying unconventional measures. This decline in transparency has not been captured by the standard measure of transparency developed by Geraats (2002). In order to provide empirical evidence for the presence of measurement error in the transparency index, we have investigated the effect of transparency on the quality of survey forecasts.

By examining the forecasts for the *short rate* of a sample covering the period between 2003 and 2006 and four CEE countries, we found the following. First, the more transparent the central banks are, the smaller the absolute forecast errors are and the smaller the degree of disagreement across individual forecasters is after controlling for the overall difficulty of forecasting. This finding is in line with the literature (see Swanson, 2004, and Ehrmann et al., 2010). Second, forecasts for the short rate are less precise and more diverse in periods of financial stress even after controlling for the transparency index, the volatility of the variable to be forecasted and some country-specific effects. This second finding can be explained either by the direct or the indirect effect of financial stress on economic uncertainty. If the dominant effect is the indirect one, which works through the central bank transparency, then we can think of the FSI as a proxy for the unobserved component of transparency, and the second finding can be interpreted as an indirect evidence for the measurement error in the transparency index.

ACKNOWLEDGMENT

We are grateful to Pierre Siklos, Nergiz Dincer, Barry Eichengreen and Petra Geraats for providing us with their data on transparency index.

NOTES

1. See Section 4.2.2 about the details on the transparency index.
2. The analysed countries are the CEE-4 countries. Although their transparency indices have increased even in the recent years as it is reported in the last column of Table 1, it can be attributed mostly to one outlier. This is Slovakia that joined the eurozone in 2009 and imported a much higher degree of transparency from the ECB than they had before.
3. See Section 4.2.3 about the details of the financial stress index.
4. Available at http://www.nbs.sk/_img/Documents/ZAKLNBS/PUBLIK/SFS/SFS2008A.pdf

5. See the minutes of the CNB and NBP in the period between 2008 and 2009. Available at http://www.cnb.cz/en/monetary_policy/bank_board_minutes/; http://www.nbp.pl/homen.aspx?f=/en/onbp/organizacja/minutes.html

6. For example, the ECB disclosed the following information related to the pricing of its long-term instrument: 'In subsequent longer-term refinancing operations the interest rate applied may include a spread in addition to the rate on the main refinancing operations, depending on the circumstances at the time'.

7. For example, according to the minutes of the CNB on 17 December 2008, '... the imperfect transmission of monetary policy rates had to be compensated for by making larger changes to monetary policy rates'. Available at http://www.cnb.cz/en/monetary_policy/bank_board_minutes/2008/amom_081217.html

8. Available at http://english.mnb.hu/engine.aspx?page=mnben_pressreleases_2008&ContentID=11643

9. Available at http://www.nbp.pl/Homen.aspx?f=/en/aktualnosci/2009/swa-p270409en.html

10. The only exception is Hungary, where the forecasted short rate is the 3-month Treasury Bill rate.

11. The interest rate is measured in percentage and so is its standard error and the forecast error.

12. The series of the financial stress index can be downloaded from http://www.imf.org/external/pubs/cat/longres.cfm?sk=23039.0

13. In contrast to the estimates for the short rate forecasts obtained on the long sample, the estimates obtained on the short sample are such that the parameter of the stress index has the same sign as that of the transparency index in most of the cases (see Tables 4 and 5). Given that the short sample is not representative, we cannot rely much on these results.

REFERENCES

Balakrishnan, R., Danninger, S., Elekdag, S., & Tytell, I. (2009). The *transmission of financial stress from advanced to emerging economies*. IMF Working Paper no. 09/133. Available at http://www.imf.org/external/pubs/cat/longres.cfm?sk=23039.0

Banai, A., Kiraly, J., & Varhegyi, E. (2009). A special aspect of the past 20 years: Dominance of foreign banks in emerging Europe with special regard to Hungary. CICM Conference paper, London. Available at http://www.londonmet.ac.uk/lmbs/research/cicm/cicm-conference/cicm-conference-2009—conference-papers.cfm

Borio, C. (2009). Implementing the macroprudential approach to financial regulation and supervision. *Banque de France Financial Stability Review*, *13*, 31–41.

Cardarelli, R., Elekdag, S., & Lall, S. (2009). *Financial stress, downturns, and recoveries*. IMF Working Paper no. 09/100. Available at http://www.imf.org/external/pubs/cat/longres.cfm?sk=22923.0

Chortareas, G., Stasavage, D., & Sterne, G. (2002). Does it pay to be transparent? International evidence from central bank forecasts. *Federal Reserve Bank of St. Louis Review*, *84*(4), 99–117(July/August).

Csavas, Cs., Erhart, Sz., Naszodi, A., & Pinter, K. (2010). Central Bank Transparency and Professional Forecasts mimeo. Budapest, Hungary: National Bank of Hungary.

Dincer, N. N., & Eichengreen, B. (2007). *Central bank transparency: Where, why, and with what effects?* NBER Working Paper no. 13003. National Bureau of Economic Research, Inc., Cambridge, Massachusets, USA.

ECB. (2009). Governing council decisions on non-standard measures. *ECB Monthly Bulletin*, June 2009, European Central Bank.

Ehrmann, M., Eijffinger, S., & Fratzscher, M. (2010). *The role of central bank transparency for guiding private sector forecasts*. ECB Working Paper no. 1146. European Central Bank, Frankfurt am Main, German.

Eijffinger, S., & Geraats, P. (2006). How transparent are central banks? *European Journal of Political Economy*, *22*(1), 1–21 March.

Geraats, P. (2002). Central bank transparency. *Economic Journal*, *112*(483), F532–F565-November.

Geraats, P. (2008). Trends in monetary policy transparency. Paper presented at the Bank of Canada Conference International Experience with the Conduct of Monetary Policy under Inflation Targeting. July 2008. Ottawa, Ontario Canada.

Moessner, R., & Allen, W. A. (2010). *Central bank co-operation and international liquidity in the financial crisis of 2008–2009*. BIS Working Paper no. 310. Bank for International Settlements, Basel, Switzerland.

Morris, S., & Shin, H. S. (2002). Social value of public information. *American Economic Review*, *92*(5), 1521–1534.

Siklos, P. L. (2010). Central bank transparency: An other look. Available at http://papers.ssrn.com/sol3/papers.cfm?abstract_id = 1668213

Swanson, E. T. (2004). Federal reserve transparency and financial market forecasts of short-term interest rates. Federal Reserve Board Finance and Economics Discussion Series 2004–6 (February). Federal Reserve Board, Federal Reserve Bank, Washington, USA.

Yehoue, E. B., Stone, M., & Ishi, K. (2009). *Unconventional central bank measures for emerging economies*. IMF Working Paper no. 09/226. International Monetary Fund, Washington DC, USA.

RETURN SEASONALITY IN EMERGING MARKETS: EVIDENCE FROM LATIN AMERICA

Josep García Blandón

ABSTRACT

This chapter simultaneously investigates the most important calendar anomalies in stock returns: day of the week, turn of the month, turn of the year and holiday periods, in four of the most important Latin American stock markets: Argentina, Brazil, Mexico and Chile. Previous evidence available for these countries is very limited. Our results indicate that the three markets show a rather similar pattern regarding return seasonality. A day of the week effect, consisting in negative returns on Mondays, is reported for all the stock markets but the Mexican. The turn of the year effect is observed only in Argentina, and moderate holiday and turn of the month effects are reported in the Brazilian and the Mexican markets, respectively. In addition, significant levels of first-order return auto-correlation are reported for the four stock markets. The contemporary financial crisis has dramatically affected the behaviour of stock prices worldwide, causing, among other effects, a huge increase in price volatility and probably changing the behaviour of participants in financial markets. We have also investigated to what extent our results have been affected by the current abnormal situation.

The Impact of the Global Financial Crisis on Emerging Financial Markets
Contemporary Studies in Economic and Financial Analysis, Volume 93, 405–422

ISSN: 1569-3759/doi:10.1108/S1569-3759(2011)0000093014

Keywords: Calendar anomalies; Garch models; Latin American markets; financial crisis.

JEL Classification: G10.

1. INTRODUCTION

During the last decades, numerous studies have revealed the existence of empirical regularities in daily returns of stocks and market indices in markets around the world. Among these anomalies, abnormal returns associated with the calendar, depending for example, on the day of the week, turn of the month, turn of the year and holiday periods are the most important.

Despite the time elapsed since the initial investigations and the number of papers published on the issue, the seasonality of stock returns is still attracting the interest of researchers nowadays. Some examples of recent research include: Lim, Mun Ho, and Dollery (2010) investigating some calendar anomalies in the Malaysian stock market, McConnel and Xu (2008) addressing the turn of the month effect in the U.S. stock market, or García (2008) investigating the autocorrelation of stock returns depending on the day of the week. Papers investigating calendar anomalies typically focus on a single anomaly. Nevertheless, the simultaneous consideration of the most important calendar anomalies will provide more robust results in relation to those obtained by considering each of them individually. If, for example, returns are exceptionally high during the first days of January, but this is not the case for the first days of the remaining months of the year, those papers analyzing the turn of the year effect will report empirical evidence supporting this anomaly. However, it is also possible that papers investigating the turn of the month effect will report abnormal returns around the change of month. Obviously, this would occur because the turn of the year also includes a change of month. Nevertheless, papers exclusively investigating the turn of the month effect will wrongly support the existence of this anomaly. By contrast, if we jointly investigate the turn of the year and the turn of the month effects, our results will support the former anomaly but not the latter. Similar situations could also occur regarding other anomalies. To avoid this problem, this chapter jointly investigates the most important calendar anomalies: day of the week, turn of the month, turn of the year and holiday periods.

Although most investigations are focused on the United States and European stock markets, a growing number of papers have investigated emerging countries. Since calendar anomalies are often examined in the framework of the market-efficient hypothesis, we would expect to report stronger anomalies in emerging markets compared with developed and, in theory, more efficient ones. Brooks and Persand (2001) investigate the day of the week effect in five Southeast Asian stock markets: Taiwan, South Korea, Philippines, Malaysia and Thailand, for the period 1989–1996. They report a peculiar day of the week effect in Malaysia, Thailand and Taiwan, consisting in negative average Monday returns in the former, and on negative Wednesday returns in the latter. More recently, the results by Lim, Mun Ho, and Dollery (2010) investigating the Malaysian stock market support negative and statistically significant Monday returns followed by positive and significant Wednesday returns. Al-Saad and Moosa (2005) report a July effect, instead of a January effect, in Kuwait since returns were higher in July compared with the others months of the year. Ajayi, Mehdian, and Perry (2004) investigate Eastern European stock markets, reporting negative and significant Monday returns only in 2 of the 12 markets investigated. It is somehow surprising that, in spite of the numerous papers investigating calendar anomalies in stock markets around the world, the issue has received a very limited attention regarding Latin American stock markets. The main aim of this chapter is to address this gap in the international literature about calendar anomalies, by investigating the issue in four of the most important Latin American regional stock markets: Argentina, Brazil, Mexico and Chile. Instead of focusing on a single anomaly, we have followed a more comprehensive approach consisting in a simultaneous investigation of the principal calendar anomalies. The advantage of this approach over the one most widely used, which focus on a single anomaly, has already been discussed in this section. This chapter also contributes to reduce data mining problems concerning empirical investigations of stock returns. The problem was clearly posed by Lakonishok and Smidt (1988, p. 405), 'Data snooping (…) is also a collective sin. One hundred researchers using the same data contrasted a hundred different scenarios. The eleventh cent theory derives from the above results and contrasts using more or less the same data.' More recently, Lucey and Whelan (2001) suggest two possible solutions to this problem: waiting for time to provide new data for checking the validity of the hypothesis, or preferably finding a new relatively independent database, preferably one that has not been used in the past, and contrasting its assumptions. From this perspective, the fact that there are no previous investigations using our specific dataset, jointly with the scarce attention paid to calendar anomalies in Latin American stock markets, make this chapter interesting in terms of its contribution to overcoming data mining problems.

The current financial crisis starting in early 2008 shows specific characteristics that make it unique. One of them is the first-time occurrence of a coordinated international response, with an extraordinarily strong government leadership. Since the crisis is not still over, it is, however, too early to conclude about its potential implications for market efficiency, and more specifically for calendar anomalies. Nevertheless, we should be aware of how this abnormal situation may affect our results. As an example, LeBaron (1992) shows that the level of autocorrelations of daily stock returns changes with the variance of returns. In order to check the robustness of our results to the international financial crisis, our proposed model has been estimated twice: the first time with all the available dataset, and the second one shortening the period of investigation to exclude the observations affected by the financial crisis. Therefore, we intend to shed some light on the effects of the contemporary financial crisis on calendar anomalies.

The structure of the chapter is as follows. In the next section, we discuss the principal calendar anomalies, with particular attention to those papers investigating Latin American markets. Section 3 presents the methodology we propose to comprehensively investigate calendar anomalies in the Argentinean, Brazilian, Mexican and Chilean stock markets, and the dataset used in the investigation. Then, we report the results of estimating our model in the context of previous investigations. Finally, in Section 5 we present our main conclusions.

2. CALENDAR ANOMALIES

This chapter investigates return seasonality associated with the day of the week, turn of the month, turn of the year and holiday periods. In addition, we have also investigated a variation of the classical day of the week effect, consisting of different levels of autocorrelation in daily returns, depending on the day of the week. Next, we are going to discuss previous findings focusing on those papers dealing with emerging markets and, particularly, with the stock markets under study: Argentina, Brazil, Mexico and Chile. This is the first investigation that attempts a comprehensive investigation of calendar anomalies with a Latin American focus, since previous research has limited to a single market or included some of them within a big range of worldwide stock markets, without any specific regional focus.

The so-called day of the week effect was initially revealed by French (1980) who reported lower returns on Mondays, compared with other days of the week. This finding was quite surprising, because if returns were generated during physical time, Monday returns should be about three times higher compared with other days of the week. This anomaly is usually attributed to factors related to the microstructure of financial markets, such as dividend payments, mostly taking place on Mondays, or the dissemination of bad news about firms occurring preferably during the weekend. Regarding emerging stock markets, this anomaly has been reported in many countries, among others, India (Raj & Kumari, 2006), Thailand (Holden, Thompson, & Ruangrit, 2005) and Estonia and Lithuania (Ajayi, Mehdian, & Perry, 2004). Surprisingly, empirical evidence about Latin American stock markets is relatively small. Basher and Sadorsky (2006) include Argentina, Brazil, Mexico and Chile in their comprehensive paper investigating the day of the week effect in 21 countries for the period 1992–2003. The authors do not observe a day of the week effect in any of the four Latin American markets. On the contrary, most of the empirical evidence available for the Brazilian stock market supports negative Monday returns (e.g. Aggarwal & Leal, 1996; Agrawal & Tandon, 1994; Madureira & Leal, 2001). However, according to Fajardo and Pereira (2008) the Monday effect would have disappeared in Brazil after the year 2002. The fact that the Brazilian stock market is one of the leading emerging markets has favoured a relatively stronger attention by researchers, if compared with the other national stock markets. Supporting Basher and Sadorsky's findings, Agrawal and Tandon (1994) do not report negative Monday returns for the Mexican stock market. Recently, Yalcin and Yucel (2006) include Mexico and Chile in their investigation of the day of the week anomaly in 20 emerging stock markets for the period 1999–2005. The authors do not report evidence of this anomaly in any of the two stock markets.

Ariel (1987) was the first to report the existence of abnormally high returns during the first days of the month. This anomaly is usually attributed to the restructuring of portfolios that would occur mainly at the beginning of the month. McConnel and Xu (2008) investigate the turn of the month effect in 35 countries, including Argentina, Mexico and Chile, but not in Brazil. The authors report positive abnormal returns associated to the turn of the month in the three stock markets. Agrawal and Tandon (1994) investigate the most usual calendar anomalies in 18 national stock markets, including Brazil and Mexico. Their results support a turn of the month effect in most of the countries investigated, including Brazil and Mexico, for the period 1971–1987. Later on, Kunkel, Compton, & Beyer (2003) review the turn of the month effect in 19 national stock markets for the period 1988–2000, including both developed and emerging countries, including Brazil and Mexico. The authors report a turn of the month effect in 16 of the 19 countries investigated, among them Mexico but not Brazil. More recently, Giovanis (2009) reports a turn of the month effect in Argentina, Brazil and Mexico, but not in Chile.

The turn of the year effect was initially revealed by Rozeff and Kinney (1976) reporting significantly positive returns during the first days of the year associated to small-capitalization stocks. A similar behaviour, not only affecting small-capitalization companies, has been observed in different countries worldwide. The most accepted explanation for this anomaly is based on the realization of losses by investors for tax purposes. An alternative explanation, similar to the one used to explain the turn of the month effect, blames institutional investors who would restructure their investment portfolios at the beginning of each year. Evidence about emerging markets support a turn of the year effect in Hong Kong and Korea (Chui & Wei, 1998), Greece (Coutts, Kaplanidis, & Roberts, 2000) and Singapore (Tan & Tat, 1998). Regarding our countries of interest, Agrawal and Tandon (1994) observe higher returns in January compared with the rest of the year in Brazil and Mexico. Fountas and Segredakis (2002) investigate the turn of the year effect in 18 emerging stock markets, including Argentina, Mexico and Chile. They report evidence of this anomaly only for five of the markets investigated, among them Chile, but not Argentina or Mexico. Most papers, however, tend to conclude about the weakening of this anomaly through time. Also involving the change of year, there is a widespread belief among investors that stock prices tend to experience a rally as the end of the year approaches. However, we have not found any empirical evidence supporting this anomaly. In fact, if the January effect had its origin in the acquisition in January of those assets sold in December for tax purposes, for the same reason one would expect negative returns during the last days of the year. Nevertheless, we have not found any empirical investigation dealing with this anomaly in our sample of countries.

Lakonishok and Smidt (1988) were the first to report abnormal returns around holiday periods. This anomaly, which involves abnormally high returns on the days before (pre-holiday effect) and after the holidays (post-holiday effect), as well as high levels of autocorrelation for the first trading day after the holiday period, is usually attributed to the preferences shown by different groups of investors to make investments before the start of holiday periods. Empirical evidence available for emerging markets has reported a pre-holiday effect in Greece (Mills, Siriopoulos, Markellos, & Harizanis, 2000) and Hong Kong (McGuinness, 2005). Agrawal and Tandon (1994) observe a pre-holiday effect in Mexico but not in Brazil. More recently, the results by Fajardo and Pereira (2008) investigating the Brazilian market for the period 1995–2007 support Agrawal and Tandon's findings. However, these papers only investigate pre-holiday returns, without considering either post-holiday returns or post-holiday returns autocorrelation. We have not found any empirical article dealing with the holiday anomaly in Argentina or Chile.

Finally, positive first-order autocorrelation in daily returns of stock market indices is a widely known phenomenon. The most accepted explanation, originally proposed by Fisher (1966), relies on the existence of non-synchronous trading. Thus, the delayed reaction of the less liquid stocks of the market index would cause the observed return autocorrelation. Keim and Stambaugh (1984) point out, however, that the autocorrelation of returns is particularly strong between Mondays and Fridays. Subsequently, Bessembinder and Hertzel (1993) conclude that autocorrelation is particularly intense between days separated by intervals of non-trading periods, including not only weekends but also holiday periods. More recently, García (2008) obtains similar results for the Spanish and French stock markets, highlighting the importance of daily closing periods. We have not found any empirical research about this anomaly in the stock markets covered by this investigation.

3. METHODOLOGY AND DATA

In the next two sub-sections we respectively discuss both the model we propose to test the prevalence of calendar anomalies in Latin American stock markets and our dataset.

3.1. Methodology

Unlike previous research mostly focusing on a single anomaly, the model we propose allows for a simultaneous investigation of all the calendar anomalies discussed in the previous section. We introduce daily returns as the dependent variable of the model and dummy variables accounting for each of the anomalies investigated among the regressors. These dummy variables are: M and F (value of 1 if the day is a Monday or Friday respectively, and 0 otherwise); PRH/PTH (value of 1 the day before the start/after the completion of a holiday period, and 0 otherwise. For the purposes of this investigation, holiday periods have been defined as any continuous period of at least four days of no trading); TM (value of 1 for the first five trading days of each month, and 0 otherwise); D (value of 1 for the last 10 trading days of the year, and 0 otherwise); and J (value of 1 for the first 10 trading days of the year, and zero otherwise). We have also included in the model the dependent variable one period delayed, to account for first-order autocorrelation in index returns, and the dependent variable one period delayed multiplied by each of the two dummy variables indicating the days of the week, to measure different levels of return autocorrelation depending on the day of the week. Finally, we have included the dependent variable one period delayed multiplied by PTH, to capture differential levels of return autocorrelation associated to the first trading day after holiday periods.

Accordingly, the model to be estimated is given by expression (1),

$$R_t = \alpha_0 + \alpha_1 M_t + a_2 F + \alpha_3 R_{t-1} + \alpha_4 M_t * R_{t-1} + \alpha_5 F_t * R_{t-1} + \alpha_6 TM_t + \alpha_7 PRH_t + \alpha_8 PTH_t + \alpha_9 PTH_t * R_{t-1} + \alpha_{10} D_t + \alpha_{11} J_t + \varepsilon_t \quad (1)$$

where, R_t is the return of the corresponding market index on day t, calculated as $\ln(P_{it}/P_{it-1})$, where P_{it} is the closing price of the index on day t.

3.2. Data

The research conducted in this chapter has used the most representative market indices of the Argentinean, Brazilian, Mexican and Chilean stock exchanges: Merval, Bovespa, Ipc and Ipsa, respectively. The period of investigation covers the period from November 1999 to December 2008, which means 2,233, 2,277, 2,266 and 2,266 observations for Merval, Bovespa, Ipc and Ipsa, respectively Graphs 1–4.

Previous empirical studies investigating calendar anomalies in national stock markets have mostly used ordinary least squares (OLS), or some of its variants. Nevertheless, since Mandlebrot (1963), numerous studies have shown that daily returns on financial assets hardly satisfy the conditions of the normal distribution function. Rather, these returns tend to be asymmetric, leptokurtic and often show volatility clusters. In this situation,

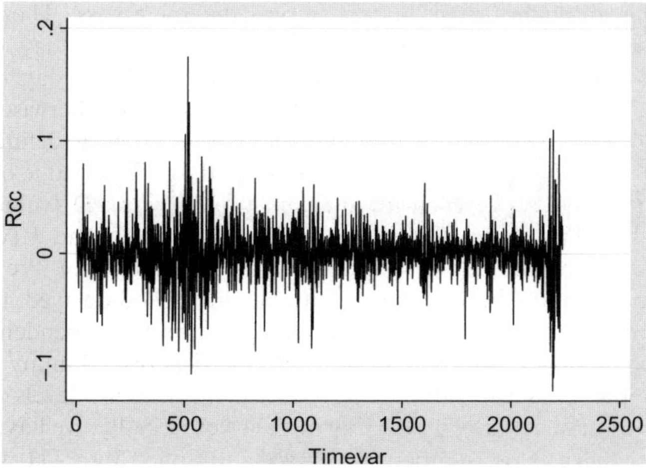

Graph 1. Merval Daily Returns.

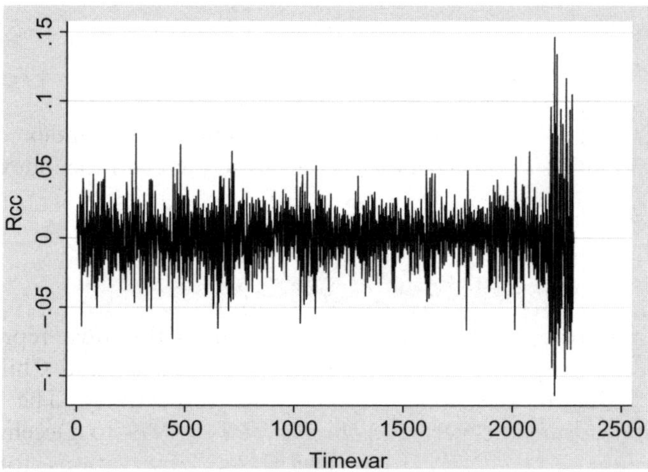

Graph 2. Bovespa Daily Returns.

Connolly (1989) recommends the use of generalized autoregressive conditional heteroskedasticity models (GARCH) in the investigation of anomalies in stock returns, since they allow for the explicit integration of the abnormality of the error term. Since their initial application, numerous

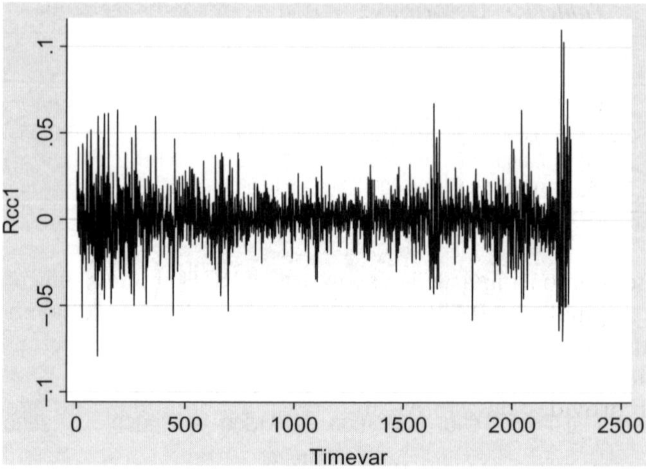

Graph 3. Ipc Daily Returns.

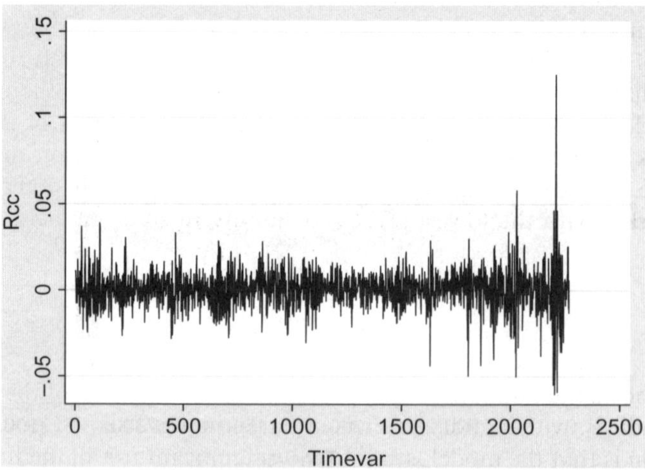

Graph 4. Ipsa Daily Returns.

models within the GARCH family have been proposed. However, following Bollerslev (1986), the initial GARCH (1,1) model including both, one autoregressive and one moving average, lag in the variance of the error term, is appropriate for most financial series. In the same line, Hansen and Lunde

Table 1. Descriptive Statistics of Daily Returns.

Variable	Obs	Mean	Std. Dev.	Min.	Max.	Skewness	Kurtosis
Merval	2,234	0.0006	0.0225	−0.1215	0.1749	0.1957	8.57
Bovespa	2,277	0.0006	0.0212	−0.1139	0.1466	0.1925	7.18
Ipc	2,266	0.0007	0.0153	−0.0793	0.1101	0.2025	7.47
Ipsa	2,266	0.0004	0.0107	−0.0602	0.1253	0.3438	14.11

(2005), after comparing a wide range of GARCH models, find no evidence that the original GARCH model (1.1) has been overtaken by more sophisticated ones. Consequently, this has been the model used in this investigation.

Table 1 provides descriptive information about the four stock market indices.

As expected, Table 1 shows the existence of skewness and kurtosis in daily returns, a common situation in financial series. Accordingly, the skewness and kurtosis test rejects the null hypothesis of normality in daily returns for the four market indices, although, on the basis of skewness, normality is rejected only at a 5% level in the Bovespa index. The graphs show the usual clusters of volatility that tend to characterize daily stock returns. We can also see that the volatility of returns is particularly high for the last part of the period, due to the worldwide financial crisis at the end of 2008 in the four stock markets, but it is especially severe in the Brazilian market. For the whole period investigated, the Chilean market clearly emerges as the stock market with the lowest level or volatility in stock returns.

4. RESULTS

Table 2 shows the estimates of the proposed model for each of the four stock market indices, with standard errors in parentheses. The first point we want to mention is that the model is statistically significant for all the four indices. As it can be seen, the estimates of the GARCH effects are strongly significant in the four markets investigated, supporting our model choice. A general conclusion from the examination of the table is that calendar anomalies do not seem to be particularly strong in none of the markets investigated, and to a certain extent, results are relatively similar across markets.

We are going to discuss our results in the framework of the extant empirical evidence for the stock markets investigated. Nevertheless, the

Table 2. Estimates of the Model.

	Merval	Bovespa	Ipsa	Ipc
M	−0.0018515**	−0.0019154**	−0.0022996***	−0.0006531
	(0.0009075)	(0.0009665)	(0.0004429)	(0.0006431)
F	−0.0000793	0.0005516	0.0006019	−0.0010672
	(0.0010495)	(0.0010181)	(0.000462)	(0.0006758)
R_{t-1}	−0.006572	0.0314942***	0.1738324***	0.0525398*
	(0.0310754)	(0.010516)	(0.0273989)	(0.0274135)
$M*R_{t-1}$	0.2124382***	0.0550929	0.0890357	0.193577***
	(0.059309)	(0.0564138)	(0.0553852)	(0.0614375)
$F*R_{t-1}$	0.0258172	0.0115738	−0.0061653	−0.0194776
	(0.062484)	(0.0546679)	(0.0626553)	(0.0645735)
TM	0.0001068	0.0010987	−0.0003263	0.0010257*
	(0.0008697)	(0.0008667)	(0.0003861)	(0.0005961)
PRH	−0.0009488	0.0050048*	0.0005218	0.0014244
	(0.0023995)	(0.0027172)	(0.0012263)	(0.0018208)
PTH	0.0025427	0.0040006*	−0.0009325	0.0004907
	(0.0018072)	(0.0023354)	(0.0008983)	(0.0018208)
PTH$*R_{t-1}$	−0.0840564	−0.1935079	−0.1419164	0.0159282
	(0.1167651)	(0.1371868)	(0.0008983)	(0.1363801)
D	0.0022703	0.0015162	−0.0001464	0.0010731
	(0.0022426)	(0.019364)	(0.0008295)	(0.0015734)
J	0.0049579***	0.0001806	0.0006009	0.001235
	(0.0013529)	(0.00162)	(0.0007403)	(0.0010692)
CONSTANT	0.0009502*	0.0008759*	0.0010371***	0.0011497***
	(0.000539)	(0.0005212)	(0.0002437)	(0.0003645)
GARCH effects				
C	0.0000118***	9.33e-06***	3.71e-06***	3.08e-06***
	(0.000539)	(2.52e-06)	(8.64e-07)	(6.46e-07)
ARCH(1)	0.1032762***	0.0745744***	0.1616753***	0.0783618***
	(0.00984)	(0.0103294)	(0.0190259)	(0.0083143)
GARCH(1)	0.8715899***	0.9027179***	0.8061217***	0.9090054***
	(0.0115472)	(0.0146188)	(0.0230012)	(0.0088259)
N	2,233	2,277	2,266	2,266
Log likelihood	5,672.613	5,798.574	7,473.129	6,576.84
Sig. level	0.000	0.000	0.000	0.000

*Significant at a 10% level; **significant at a 5% level; ***significant at a 1% level.

different methodological approaches adopted in these papers make results not fully comparable.

We observe the typical Monday effect, consisting of lower returns on Mondays compared with the other days of the week in Argentina, Brazil and Chile, but not in Mexico. The dummy variable accounting for Mondays has a negative associated coefficient statistically significant at a 1% level in the Chilean stock market and at a 5% level in Argentina and Brazil. On the contrary, returns are not significantly different on Fridays than on other days of the week in any of the four stock markets. These findings support most of the previous studies on the Brazilian market: Aggarwal and Leal (1996), Agrawal and Tandon (1994), and Madureira and Leal (2001). Although a recent investigation by Fajardo and Pereira (2008) has concluded that the Monday effect would have disappeared in Brazil in recent periods, in the line suggested by Basher and Sadorsky (2006), our results show that it is still relevant. Evidence reported by Basher and Sadorsky (2006) does not support a Monday effect in Mexico, Chile or Argentina. Similarly, Yalcin and Yucel (2006) do not observe a Monday effect in Chile or Mexico. Unlike them, our findings indicate that the Monday effect is particularly stronger in Chile, compared with Argentina or Brazil, in terms of statistical significance.

As showed by Table 2, we report strong levels of first-order return autocorrelation in the four markets investigated. Nevertheless, the implications of these findings are not the same for all of them. The Brazilian and Chilean stock markets show an identical behaviour in terms of autocorrelation of daily returns. In both markets, the coefficient associated to variable R_{t-1} is positive and statistically significant at a 1% level, while the associated coefficients to $M{*}R_{t-1}$ and $F{*}R_{t-1}$ that account for different levels of autocorrelation for Mondays and Fridays, respectively, compared with the other days of the week, are not significant at the required levels. This result would indicate a strong level of autocorrelation of daily returns, independent of the day of the week. On the contrary, for the Argentinean market, although the associated coefficient to variable R_{t-1} is not statistically significant, this is not the case for variable $M{*}R_{t-1}$ with a positive coefficient statistically significant at a 1% level. This would indicate that in the Argentinean stock market, Monday returns are positively and strongly correlated with Friday returns, but this is not the case for the other days of the week. For example, returns on Wednesdays are not correlated with returns on Tuesdays. Finally, in the Mexican stock market, the associated coefficient to variable R_{t-1} is positive and statistically significant at a 10% level, while the associated coefficient to variable $M{*}R_{t-1}$, also with a positive sign, is significant at a 1% level. This result would indicate a strong level of autocorrelation of stock returns on Mondays and a rather moderate one on the other days of the week.

Regarding the turn of the month effect, with the exception of Mexico and in this case only at a 10% level of significance, we do not observe significant returns associated to the change of month in none of the four stock markets investigated. Therefore, our results support previous evidence regarding the Mexican stock market (Agrawal & Tandon, 1994; Kunkel et al., 2003; McConnel & Xu, 2008), but contradict previous findings for Argentina and Chile (McConnel & Xu, 2008). Regarding the Brazilian market, available evidence was contradictory since Agrawal and Tandon (1994) reported a turn of the month effect but Kunkel et al. (2003) did not.

Our model includes three variables to account for the holiday effect: PRH, PTH and PTH$*R_{t-1}$. The first two will capture abnormal returns the day before and after holidays, while the latter will report for abnormal levels of first-order return autocorrelation the day after a holiday period. None of these variables appears to be statistically significant for any of the four markets investigated at the 5% and 1% levels, although in the Brazilian market, coefficients associated to PRH and PTH are statistically significant at a 10% level. Both coefficients show the expected positive sign. This result will support a moderate holiday effect, only in the Brazilian stock market, as it is usually defined, consisting in higher returns the days before and after holidays. These findings challenges Fajardo and Pereira (2008) who did not report a holiday effect in Brazil either in the whole period of investigation 1995–2007, or in any of the three sub-periods considered.

Regarding the investigation of return behaviour around the turn of the year, a January effect is reported only for the Argentinean stock market. The associated coefficient to variable J is positive and statistically significant at a 1% level for the Merval market index. Previous empirical research supported a January effect in Brazil (Agrawal & Tandon, 1994) and in Argentina and Chile (2002), although pointing out the weakening of this anomaly through time. Regarding the last days of the year, no significant returns are observed in any of the four stock markets investigated, as shown by the significance tests of the associated coefficient to variable D.

The robustness of the results to outliers' values has been checked through a re-estimation of the model after the removal from the dataset of the 0.05% of the observations with the highest estimation errors. The results, not provided, remain largely unchanged.

As discussed in the introductory section, we have re-estimated our model without including the international financial crisis in the estimation period. The results of the estimation for the period November 1999–December 2008 are shown by Table 3. The comparison of Tables 2 and 3 can shed some light on the effects of the financial crisis in stock returns regularities. As observed, the two tables show very similar results, indicating that the effects of the current financial crisis on calendar anomalies has been very limited, at least

Table 3. Estimates of the Model for the Sub-period 1999–2007.

	Merval	Bovespa	Ipsa	Ipc
M	−0.001938**	−0.0021665**	−0.0024179***	−0.0007995
	(0.000975)	(0.0010092)	(0.0004672)	(0.0006835)
F	−1.26e-06	0.000975	0.0005595	−0.0006583
	(0.0011038)	(0.001066)	(0.0004847)	(0.0007091)
R_{t-1}	0.0329783	0.0135495	0.1801135***	0.0544599*
	(0.0310754)	(0.0323004)	(0.0292103)	(0.0295565)
$M{*}R_{t-1}$	0.1716359***	0.103209	0.1048376*	0.2104533***
	(0.0616191)	(0.0673028)	(0.0609806)	(0.0660039)
$F{*}R_{t-1}$	−0.002575	0.0167945	−0.0019519	−0.0255203
	(0.0631995)	(0.0623113)	(0.0652625)	(0.0678725)
TM	0.0004136	0.0016804*	−0.0001353	0.0012876**
	(0.0009362)	(0.0009023)	(0.000399)	(0.0006213)
PRH	−0.0001809	0.0039839	0.0004851	0.0008926
	(0.0025591)	(0.0028145)	(0.0012637)	(0.0021926)
PTH	0.0020458	0.0040005*	−0.0012039	0.0005117
	(0.0019116)	(0.0024241)	(0.0009453)	(0.0018595)
PTH$*R_{t-1}$	0.0147522	−0.1980577	−0.1748797	0.1368559
	(.1323441)	(.1401467)	(.1170906)	(.1464891)
D	0.0020017	0.00189	−0.0001104	0.0009531
	(0.0022496)	(0.0019752)	(0.0008647)	(0.0015978)
J	0.005945***	0.0004562	0.0003443	0.0013244
	(0.0014599)	(0.0016704)	(0.0007945)	(0.0011019)
CONSTANT	0.0010118*	0.0007886*	0.0010481***	0.0011415***
	(0.000569)	(0.0005512)	(0.0002485)	(0.0003774)
N	1,994	1,995	2,009	2,025
Log likelihood	5096.721	5229.199	6751.646	5961.693
Sig. level	0.000	0.000	0.000	0.000

*Significant at a 10% level; **significant at a 5% level; ***significant at a 1% level.

until the end of the year 2008. More specifically, no change at all is observed in the Merval, while small changes are reported for the Bovespa, Ipc and Ipsa. Regarding the Ipc the turn of the month effect changes from 10% in Table 2 to 5% in Table 3. In the Ipsa index the only change is that in Table 2 the coefficient associated to variable $M{*}R_{t-1}$ was not statistically significant, although it was in the limit of significance at a 10% level, while in Table 3 it is significant at a 10% level. Regarding the Bovespa market index, the moderate pre-holiday effect reported by Table 2 disappears in Table 3, while a moderate turn of the month effect, only significant at a 10% level, emerges. More important, however, are the changes observed in the behaviour of return autocorrelation. Results in Table 2 indicate a strong daily return autocorrelation in the Bovespa index that disappears in Table 3. Therefore, we could conclude that in the specific case of the Brazilian stock market, the reported return autocorrelation was caused by the behaviour of stock prices during the year 2008, suggesting that the increase in return volatility during the financial crisis could have caused an increase in return autocorrelation, in the line supported by LeBaron (1992). Nevertheless, this fact should be cautiously interpreted since it has been observed only for the Brazilian market.

5. CONCLUSIONS

Empirical regularities in stock returns have attracted the interest of researchers for many years. Nevertheless, the number of papers investigating the issue in emerging markets is still quite small. If we focus on Latin American stock markets, very limited research on the issue has been carried out so far. This situation makes it somehow difficult to discuss our results in the context of previous investigations. In this chapter, we have investigated the most important calendar anomalies in stock returns, focusing on four of the most important Latin American stock markets. This is, to our knowledge, the first article with a clear regional Latin American focus. The methodology we have proposed is particularly robust in relation to previous research, since we have investigated all the anomalies simultaneously through a single model without assuming normality in daily returns. Our results indicate that the incidence of calendar anomalies in the markets investigated is relatively small. Besides, the four markets show a relatively similar pattern regarding return seasonality. We observe the same day of the week effect in three of the four markets, consisting in lower returns on Mondays compared with other days of the week. In addition, we also report significant levels of daily return autocorrelation in the four stock markets, although the daily autocorrelation pattern is not the same in all of them. We do not observe a holiday effect in Argentina, Chile or Mexico, since returns around holiday periods in these countries do not differ significantly from other days. In addition, return autocorrelation on the first day after holidays is not statistically significant either. Regarding the Brazilian market, we observe a moderate holiday effect, consisting in abnormally high returns the days before and after holidays, but we do not observe significant return autocorrelation after holiday periods. Regarding the turn of the year effect, returns are significantly higher the first days of the year in Argentina but not in Brazil, Chile or Mexico. Finally, our results do not support an end of the year rally in any of the four markets investigated.

Any investigation of the behaviour of stock prices cannot ignore the situation caused by the contemporary financial crisis. Although the effects of the crisis on the behaviour of stock markets participants – and, consequently, on the mechanisms of price formation – are far to be completely understood, our results show that for the period considered, the effects of the financial crisis on calendar anomalies have been very limited. Nevertheless, since the financial crisis is not still over, we cannot yet fully anticipate how it will affect calendar anomalies and the efficiency of financial markets. Papers dealing with this issue would be particularly welcome.

Further research on calendar anomalies would need to expand our proposed model to the rest of Latin American stock markets and focus on the causes behind the observed differences among the stock markets investigated.

REFERENCES

Aggarwal, R., & Leal, R. (1996). Integration and anomalies in the emerging markets of Asia and Latin America. In: J. Doukas & L. Lang (Eds), *Research in international business and finance* (pp. 75–99). Amsterdam: Elsevier.

Agrawal, A., & Tandon, K. (1994). Anomalies or illusions? Evidence from stock markets in eighteen countries. *Journal of International Money and Finance*, *13*(1), 83–106.

Ajayi, R., Mehdian, S., & Perry, M. (2004). The day-of-the-week effect on stock returns. *Emerging Markets Finance and Trade*, *40*(4), 53–62.

Al-Saad, K., & Moosa, I. (2005). Seasonality in stock returns: Evidence from an emerging market. *Applied Financial Economics*, *15*(1), 63–71.

Ariel, R. (1987). A monthly effect in stock returns. *Journal of Financial Economics*, *18*(1), 61–174.

Basher, S., & Sadorsky, P. (2006). Day-of-the-week effects on emerging stock markets. *Applied Economic Letters*, *13*(10), 621–628.

Bessembinder, H., & Hertzel, M. (1993). Return autocorrelations around nontrading days. *Review of Financial Studies*, *6*(1), 155–189.

Bollerslev, T. (1986). Generalized autoregressive conditional heteroskedasticity. *Journal of Econometrics*, *31*(3), 307–327.

Brooks, C., & Persand, G. (2001). Seasonality in Southeast Asian stock markets: Some new evidence on day-of-the-week effects. *Applied Economics Letters*, *8*(3), 155–158.

Chui, A., & Wei, K. (1998). Book-to-market, firm size, and the turn-of-the-year effect: Evidence from Pacific-Basin emerging markets. *Pacific-Basin Finance Journal*, *6*(3–4), 275–293.

Connolly, R. (1989). An examination of the robustness of the weekend effect. *Journal of Financial and Quantitative Analysis*, *24*(2), 133–169.

Coutts, A., Kaplanidis, C., & Roberts, J. (2000). Security price anomalies in an emerging market: The case of the Athens Stock Exchange. *Applied Financial Economics*, *10*(5), 561–571.

Fajardo, J., & Pereira, R. (2008). Efeitos Sazonais no Índice Bovespa. *Brazilian Business Review*, *5*(3), 244–254.

Fisher, L. (1966). Some new stock-market indexes. *Journal of Business*, *39*, 191–225.

Fountas, S., & Segredakis, K. (2002). Emerging stock markets return seasonalities: The January effect and the tax-loss selling hypothesis. *Applied Financial Economics*, *12*(4), 291–299.

French, K. (1980). Stock returns and the weekend effect. *Journal of Financial Economics*, *8*, 55–69.

García, J. (2008). Return autocorrelation anomalies and the importance of non-trading periods: Evidence from Spain, France and Germany. *Quantitative Finance*, *8*(4), 341–350.

Giovanis, E. (2009). Calendar effects in fifty-five stock market indices. *Global Journal of Finance and Management*, *1*(2), 75–98.

Holden, K., Thompson, J., & Ruangrit, Y. (2005). The Asian crisis and calendar effects on stock returns in Thailand. *European Journal of Operational Research*, *163*(1), 242–252.

Hansen, P., & Lunde, A. (2005). A forecast comparison of volatility models: Does anything beat a GARCH(1,1)? *Journal of Applied Econometrics*, *20*(7), 873–889.

Keim, D., & Stambaugh, R. (1984). A further investigation of the weekend effect in stock returns. *Journal of Finance*, *39*(3), 819–835.

Kunkel, R., Compton, W., & Beyer, S. (2003). The turn-of-the-month effect still lives: The international evidence. *International Review of Financial Analysis*, *12*, 207–221.

Lakonishok, J., & Smidt, S. (1988). Are seasonal anomalies real? A ninety-year perspective. *Review of Financial Studies*, *1*, 403–425.

LeBaron, B. (1992). Some relations between volatility and serial correlations in stock market returns. *Journal of Business*, *65*(2), 199–219.

Lim, S., Mun Ho, C., & Dollery, B. (2010). An empirical analysis of calendar anomalies in the Malaysian stock market. *Applied Financial Economics*, *20*(3), 255–264.

Lucey, B., & Whelan, S. (2001). A promising strategy in equity markets. *Journal of the Statistical and Social Inquiry Society of Ireland*, *31*, 74–110.

Madureira, L., & Leal, R. (2001). Elusive anomalies in the Brazilian stock market. *International Review of Financial Analysis*, *10*, 123–134.

Mandlebrot, B. (1963). The variation of certain speculative prices. *Journal of Business*, *36*, 394–419.

McConnel, J., & Xu, W. (2008). Equity returns at the turn of the month. *Financial Analyst Journal*, *64*(2), 49–64.

McGuinness, P. (2005). A re-examination of the holiday effect in stock returns: The case of Hong Kong. *Applied Financial Economics*, *15*(16), 1107–1123.

Mills, T., Siriopoulos, C., Markellos, R., & Harizanis, D. (2000). Seasonality in the Athens Stock Exchange. *Applied Financial Economics*, *10*(2), 137–142.

Raj, M., & Kumari, D. (2006). Day-of-the-week and other market anomalies in the Indian stock market. *International Journal of Emerging Markets*, *1*(3), 235–246.

Rozeff, M., & Kinney, W. (1976). Capital market seasonality: The case of stock returns. *Journal of Financial Economics*, *3*(4), 379–402.

Tan, R., & Tat, W. (1998). The diminishing calendar anomalies in the stock exchange of Singapore. *Applied Financial Economics*, *8*(2), 119–125.

Yalcin, Y., & Yucel, E. (2006). The day-of-the-week effect on stock-market volatility and return: Evidence from emerging markets. *Czech Journal of Economics and Finance*, *56*, 258–279.

HOW LONG MEMORY IN VOLATILITY AFFECTS MARKET RISK ESTIMATION: EVIDENCE FROM EMERGING STOCK MARKETS

Khaled Mokni and Faysal Mansouri

ABSTRACT

In this chapter, we investigate the effect of long memory in volatility on the accuracy of emerging stock markets risk estimation during the period of the recent global financial crisis. For this purpose, we use a short (GJR-GARCH) and long (FIAPARCH) memory volatility models to compute in-sample and out-of-sample one-day-ahead VaR. Using six emerging stock markets index, we show that taking into account the long memory property in volatility modelling generally provides a more accurate VaR estimation and prediction. Therefore, conservative risk managers may adopt long memory models using GARCH-type models to assess the emerging market risks, especially when incorporating crisis periods.

The Impact of the Global Financial Crisis on Emerging Financial Markets
Contemporary Studies in Economic and Financial Analysis, Volume 93, 423–447

ISSN: 1569-3759/doi:10.1108/S1569-3759(2011)0000093015

Keywords: Emerging stock markets; risk management; value-at-risk; volatility; long memory; GARCH models; financial crisis.

JEL Classifications: G10; G15.

1. INTRODUCTION

Emerging stock market volatility is characterized by a complex dynamics, mainly during crises and turbulence periods. Thus, investors need to bring more attention to risk management. Nevertheless, risk management needs to focus primarily on the issue of market risk quantification and prediction. In the literature, several methods of risk estimation are considered. However, value-at-risk (VaR) is the most popular one. Simply defined, VaR is an estimate of the maximum potential portfolio's loss expected over a given period with a fixed probability level.

VaR is frequently used in the literature to estimate market risk, we could refer, among others, to the work of Dowd (1998), Hendricks (1996), Jorion (2001), Hull and White (1998) and Engel and Gizycki (1999). More recent studies estimate market risk using VaR. For instance, we could state the articles of Giot and Laurent (2003b, 2004), Brooks and Persand (2002), Huang and Lin (2004) and Chiu, Lee, and Hung (2005).

So and Yu (2006) estimate the VaR for exchange and stock markets. On the commodity markets, VaR was used by Giot and Laurent (2003a) and Hung, Lee, and Liu (2008). Mokni, Mighri, and Mansouri (2010) estimate stock market risk using VaR technique and investigate the effect of the global financial crisis on the VaR estimation. Marimoutou, Raggad, and Trabelsi (2009) and Aloui and Mabrouk (2010) estimate market risk in the context of energy market using, respectively, extreme value theory and Generalized Autoregressive Conditional Heteroscedastic (GARCH) family models.

As VaR needs an accurate method to be estimated, there are two approaches: parametric and non-parametric. However, a crucial factor for the accuracy of VaR models, based on the parametric approach, is the underlying measure of volatility.

In this context, several methods have attempted to model volatility like GARCH-type models. These models give a crucial tool on volatility modelling because they take into account of volatility-stylized facts as volatility clustering, asymmetry, leverage effects and long memory propriety. In this chapter, we are focusing to use a short and long memory GARCH models to estimate daily VaR for six emerging markets to investigate the effect of long memory propriety on the VaR measure accuracy by incorporating the global financial crisis period in the sample data.

To our knowledge, there are few studies which are interested on the effects of long memory in volatility models in estimating VaR of emerging market indexes. For the short memory models, Mokni et al. (2009) show that the Glosten, Jagannathan and Runkle-GARCH (GJR-GARCH) model, developed by Glosten, Jagannathan, and Runkle (1993), is very successful in volatility modelling and VaR estimation. Moreover, Jondeau and Rockinger (2006) use this model and indicate its importance on volatility modelling. Concerning the long memory volatility models, Degiannakis (2004) checks the capacity of Fractionary Integrated Asymetric Powe Autoregressive Conditional Heteroscedastic (FIAPARCH) model in VaR estimation compared to the other long memory GARCH family models. In addition, Mighri, Mokni, and Mansouri (2010) show that the FIAPARCH model performs better than other long memory volatility models in VaR estimation, mainly for low confidence levels. Thus, in this study, we consider the GJR-GARCH and FIAPARCH models with skewed student error distributions to compute daily in-sample and out-of-sample VaR amounts for long and short trading position.

This chapter is organized as follows: Section 2 introduces the general VaR concept for long and short trading position. In Section 3, we present the models based on VaR such as GJR-GARCH and FIAPARCH models and its estimation methods, and we will show how these two models can be used for VaR estimation. Section 4 presents the empirical results. Finally, Section 5 concludes.

2. VAR FOR LONG AND SHORT TRADING POSITION

Jorion (2001) defines VaR as a statistical method of a portfolio or asset risk estimation. Thus, VaR measures the maximum loss which could be realized during a given time period with a fixed confidence level α. In fact, VaR is a single measure of market risk, which summarizes the exposure of the institution or investor to the risk due to the random prices fluctuations. Since VaR is a loss limit awaited on a given horizon of time with a fixed probability, we could define VaR in long and short trading position.

2.1. VaR for Long Trading Position

Long trading position is defined when the investor preserves the already acquired assets and sells them when prices rise In this case, the risk occurs when the prices of the preserved assets drop.[1] Thus, the investors are interested in risk measurement for the negative returns following the fall of the prices of the preserved assets. The one-day long position VaR of an asset with a confidence level α is defined as follow:

$$\Pr(X_{t-1} - X_t \leq \mathrm{VaR}_{1,\alpha}^{L}) = 1 - \alpha \tag{1}$$

where X_t is the asset price at time t.

The majority of financial studies are based on asset returns series rather than prices. Indeed, we consider returns series defined by

$$R_t = 100(\log(X_t) - \log(X_{t-1}) \tag{2}$$

Under the assumption that asset's returns follow a given distribution, D, the long position one-day-ahead VaR at level α is given by

$$\mathrm{VaR}_{1,\alpha}^{L} = \mu + q_{\alpha}^{D}\sigma_t \tag{3}$$

where μ is the estimated mean of return series, q_{α}^{D} denotes the αth percentile according to the statistical distribution D and σ_t indicates the standard deviation or volatility on day t, which could be obtained via GARCH family models.

2.2. VaR for Short Trading Position

In financial markets, the investment activity is not interested only with the long trading position but also with the short trading position. In this case, the investor sells assets in order to buy it later with lower prices. In fact, the investor waits when asset prices decrease. Thus, the risk occurs when the prices of the sold assets increase. Then, for the short trading position, VaR is defined as follows:

$$\Pr(X_t - X_{t-1} \leq \mathrm{VaR}_{t,1}) = 1 - \alpha \tag{4}$$

Like the long trading position case, we obtain

$$\mathrm{VaR}_{1,\alpha}^{S} = \mu + q_{1-\alpha}^{D}\sigma_t \tag{5}$$

where $q_{1-\alpha}^{D}$ denotes the $(1-\alpha)$th percentile according to the statistical distribution D.

Following Eqs. (3) and (5), we note that VaR depends mainly on the volatility concept which could be modelled via tow GARCH family models in the next section.

3. SHORT AND LONG MEMORY VAR-BASED MODELS

GARCH family models are one of the most interesting methods in VaR estimation and prediction problem. Indeed, these models capture volatility time-varying dynamics and provide efficient variance forecasts (Bollerslev, 1986; Wong & So, 2003; Yu, 2005). To investigate the effect of long memory in VaR estimation, we consider a short memory GARCH model, such as the GJR-GARCH model and the FIAPARCH model, to capture long memory in volatility concept.

It's usually verified in the literature that financial asset distribution could not be normally distributed. The rejection of the normality assumption could be due to the extreme events caused by crisis and crash periods. For this, we model GARCH residual series by the skewed student distribution to take into account the fat-tail property of financial assets distribution.

3.1. Skewed Student GJR-GARCH Model

Glosten et al. (1993) develop the GJR-GARCH model to take account of asymmetry effects on the conditional variance. However, this model is defined according to the error distribution assumption. As in Mokni et al. (2009), the residual series are supposed following skewed student distribution.

The skewed student GJR-GARCH(1,1) model is defined when residual series follow the skewed student distribution. Thus, this model is expressed as follow:

$$R_t = \mu + \varepsilon_t \tag{6}$$

$$\varepsilon_t = \sigma_t z_t \tag{7}$$

$$z_t \sim Skst(\xi, v) \tag{8}$$

$$\sigma_t^2 = w + \alpha_1 \varepsilon_{t-1}^2 + \varphi I_{\varepsilon_{t-1}<0} \varepsilon_{t-1}^2 + \beta_1 \sigma_{t-1}^2 \tag{9}$$

where

$$I_{\varepsilon_t<0} = \begin{cases} 1 & \text{if} \quad \varepsilon_t < 0 \\ 0 & \text{if} \quad \varepsilon_t \geq 0 \end{cases} \tag{10}$$

Eq. (6) indicates that the return of time t is decomposed into a constant mean parameter, μ, and an innovation, ε_t. Eq. (7) defines the innovation as the product between conditional volatility, σ_t, and a residual, z_t. Eq. (8) indicates that innovation series follow the skewed student distribution with asymmetry parameter, ξ, and the tail parameter v. Eq. (9) describes the dynamics of conditional volatility which follows two different processes according to the sign of the error, ε_t. The parameter φ expresses the volatility asymmetry phenomenon.[2] For positivity and stationarity of the volatility process to be guaranteed, parameters are assumed to satisfy the constraints: $w>0$, $\alpha_1>0$, $\beta_1>0$ and $\alpha_1+\beta_1+0.5\,\varphi<1$.

Skst(ξ, v) is the skewed student distribution with parameter asymmetry (skewness), ξ, and tail parameter (degree of freedom or kurtosis), v. In this chapter, we use the Lambert and Laurent's (2001) version of skewed student which could be expressed as follows[3]:

$$f\left(\frac{z_t}{\xi, v}\right) = \begin{cases} \dfrac{2}{\xi + 1/\xi} s \cdot g(\xi(sz_t + m)/v) & \text{if } z_t < -\dfrac{m}{s} \\ \dfrac{2}{\xi + 1/\xi} s \cdot g((sz_t + m)/\xi/v) & \text{if } z_t \geq -\dfrac{m}{s}, \end{cases} \tag{11}$$

where $g(./v)$ is the symmetric (unit variance) Student density. The parameters m and s^2 are, respectively, the mean and the variance of the non-standardized skewed student distribution with

$$m = m(\xi, v) = \frac{r((v-1)/2)\sqrt{v-2}}{\sqrt{\pi}\Gamma(v/2)}\left(\xi - \frac{1}{\xi}\right) \tag{12}$$

and

$$S^2 = \left(\xi^2 + \frac{1}{\xi^2} - 1\right) - m^2 \tag{13}$$

The sign of ln(ξ) indicates the direction of skewness and represents the degree of asymmetry of residual distribution. Hence, if $\ln(\xi)>0$ ($\ln(\xi)<0$), the skewness is positive (negative) and the probability density function is skewed to the right (left). When $\xi = 1$, the skewed student distribution is equal to the standard Student distribution.

The functions $\text{skst}_\alpha(v, \xi)$ and $\text{skst}_{1-\alpha}(v, \xi)$ are, respectively, the left and the right percentile at α according to the skewed student distribution with v degree of freedom and asymmetry coefficient ξ.

The maximum-likelihood method is used to estimate the desired model. Thus, the log-likelihood function is given by

$$\begin{aligned} L(R_t\backslash\theta) = {} & T\left[\ln\Gamma\left(\left(\frac{v+1}{2}\right) - \ln\Gamma\left(\frac{v}{2}\right) - \frac{1}{2}\ln[\pi(v-2)]\right.\right. \\ & \left.\left. + \ln\left(\frac{2}{\xi + (1/\xi)}\right) + \ln(s)\right)\right] \\ & - \frac{1}{2}\sum_{t=1}^{T}\left[\ln(w + \alpha_1\varepsilon_{t-1}^2 + \varphi I_{\varepsilon_{t-1}<0}\varepsilon_{t-1}^2 + \beta_1\sigma_{t-1}^2)\right. \\ & \left. + (1+v)\ln\left[1 + \frac{(sz_t + m)^2}{v-2}\xi^{-2/t}\right]\right] \end{aligned} \tag{14}$$

where

$$I_t = \begin{cases} 1 & \text{if} \quad z_t \geq -m/s \\ -1 & \text{if} \quad z_t < -m/s \end{cases} \tag{15}$$

Hence, the one-day-ahead VaR computed at time t for long and short trading positions are as follows:

$$V\hat{a}R_{1,\alpha}^{L} = \hat{u} + (\hat{w} + \hat{\alpha}_1\varepsilon_{t-1}^2 + \hat{\varphi}I_{\varepsilon_{t-1}<0}\varepsilon_{t-1}^2 + \hat{\beta}_1\sigma_{t-1}^2)^{1/2}\text{Skst}_\alpha(\hat{v}, \hat{\xi})^* \tag{16}$$

$$V\hat{a}R_{1,\alpha}^{s} = \hat{\mu} + (\hat{w} + \hat{\alpha}_1\varepsilon_{t-1}^2 + \hat{\varphi}I_{\varepsilon_{t-1}<0}\varepsilon_{t-1}^2 + \hat{\beta}_1\sigma_{t-1}^2)^{1/2}\text{Skst}_{1-\alpha}(\hat{v}, \hat{\xi})^* \tag{17}$$

with $\text{Skst}_\alpha(\hat{v}, \hat{\xi})^*$ and $\text{Skst}_{1-\alpha}(\hat{v}, \hat{\xi})^*$ denote, respectively, the αth and $(1-\alpha)$th percentile according to the standardized skewed student distribution.

$$\text{Skst}_\alpha(v, \xi)^* = \frac{\text{skst}_\alpha(v, \xi) - m}{s} \tag{18}$$

Lambert and Laurent (2001) show that the quantile function $\text{skst}_\alpha(v, \xi)$ of a non-standardized skewed student density is

$$\text{Skst}_\alpha(v, \xi) = \begin{cases} \frac{1}{\xi}\text{stu}_{a,v}\left(\frac{\alpha}{2}(1+\xi^2); v\right) & \text{if } \alpha < \frac{1}{1+\xi^2} \\ -\xi\ \text{stu}_{\alpha,v}\left(\frac{1-\alpha}{2}(1+\xi^{-2}); v\right) & \text{if } \alpha \geq \frac{1}{1+\xi^2} \end{cases} \quad (19)$$

where $\text{stu}_{\alpha,v}$ is the quantile function of the (unit variance) Student distribution.

3.2. The Skewed Student FIAPARCH Model

It is often indicated in the literature that stock market volatility displays the long memory propriety, in which the autocorrelations of the absolute and squared returns are characterized by very slow decay over long periods, and the spectrum density is infinite at zero frequency. To capture this propriety, many models have been proposed like FIGARCH, Fractionary Exponential GARCH (FIEGARCH) and Hyperbolic GARCH (HYGARCH). In this context, the FIAPARCH model, developed by Tse (1998), is the most important because it considers two volatility-stylized facts at the same time. Indeed, this model combines the long memory property and the asymmetric feature in the conditional volatility.[4] The asymmetries could be explained by the so-called 'leverage effect' (Black, 1976). Like the GJR-GARCH model, the FIAPARCH model can be adjusted by the skewed student residual distribution. Thus, the skewed student FIAPARCH(1,*d*,1) model could be written as follows:

$$R_t = \mu + \varepsilon_t \quad (20)$$

$$\varepsilon_t = \sigma_t z_t \quad (21)$$

$$z_t \sim \text{Skst}(\xi, v) \quad (22)$$

$$\sigma_t^\delta = \omega[1-\beta L]^{-1} + \{1-[1-\beta L]^{-1}(1-\phi L)(1-L)^d\}(|\varepsilon_t| - \gamma\varepsilon_t)^\delta \quad (23)$$

where β, ω, ϕ, γ and d are the parameters to be estimated. d is the factionary integrated parameter such as $0<d<1$. The parameter $\delta(\delta>0)$ plays the role of a Box–Cox transformation of σ_t and represents a coefficient for the power term. The parameter $\gamma(-1<\gamma<1)$ accounts for the volatility asymmetry, in which positive and negative returns of the same magnitude do not generate an equal degree of volatility. It reflects the leverage effect, that is, a positive (negative) value of γ means that past negative (positive) shocks have a deeper impact on current conditional volatility than past positive shocks (Black, 1976; French, Schwert, & Stambaugh, 1987; Pagan & Schwert, 1990). $(1-L)^d$ could be expressed as an infinite summation:

$$(1 - L)^d = \sum_{\xi=0}^{\infty} \frac{\Gamma(k-d)}{\Gamma(k+1)\Gamma(-d)} L^d \tag{24}$$

Following Baillie, Bollerslev, and Mikkelsen (1996), this summation must be truncated in practice to 1000 lags. Then, the truncation order of the infinite $(1-L)^d$ is

$$\begin{aligned}(1 - L)^d &= \sum_{k=0}^{1000} \frac{\Gamma(k-d)}{\Gamma(k+1)\Gamma(-d)} L^d \\ &= 1 - dL - \frac{1}{2}d(1-d)L^2 - \frac{1}{6}d(1-d)(1-d)L^3 - \cdots \\ &= 1 - \sum_{k=1}^{\infty} c_k(d)L^k \end{aligned} \tag{25}$$

where Γ is the gamma function and $c_1(d)=d$, $c_2(d)=1/2d(1-d)$ $c_3(d)=1/6d(1-d)(1-d)L$etc. Furthermore, the persistence of shocks to the conditional variance or the degree of long memory is measured by the fractionally integrated parameter $d(0 \leq d \leq 1)$. For instance, the fractional order of integration allows for an intermediate range of persistence between the covariance stationary process ($d=0$) and the infinite non-stationary process ($d=1$). Therefore, the FIAPARCH model can express some stylized facts of volatility:

- For $0<d<1$, volatility displays the long memory property.
- When $\gamma>0$, negative shocks give rise to higher volatility than positive shocks, and the reverse applies if $\gamma<0$.
- The power term δ of returns for the predictable structure in the volatility pattern should be determined by the database.

Tse (1998) indicates that the FIAPARCH model is more appropriate to others volatility long memory models because it can capture asymmetry and long memory property or long-term dependence in the conditional variance.

This model could be estimated by maximum-likelihood method by maximizing the log-likelihood function:

$$L\left(\tfrac{R_t}{\theta}\right) = T\left[\ln\Gamma\left(\frac{v+1}{2}\right) - \ln\Gamma\left(\frac{v}{2}\right) - \frac{1}{2}\ln[\pi(v-2)] + \ln\left(\frac{2}{\xi+(1/\xi)}\right) + \ln(s)\right]$$
$$-\tfrac{1}{2}\sum_{t=1}^{T}\left[\ln(\omega[1-\beta L]^{-1} + \{1-[1-\beta L]^{-1}(1-\phi L)(1-L)^{d}\}\right.$$
$$\left.(|\varepsilon_t| - \gamma\varepsilon_t)^{2/\delta}) + (1+v)\ln\left[1 + \frac{(sz_t+m)^2}{v-2}\xi^{-2/t}\right]\right] \quad (26)$$

Then, once the parameters are estimated, the VaR can be obtained by

$$\hat{VaR}^{L}_{1,\alpha} = \hat{\mu} + \{\hat{\omega}[1-\hat{\beta}L]^{-1} + \{1-[1-\hat{\beta}L]^{-1}(1-\hat{\phi}L) \times (1-L)^{\hat{d}}\}(|\varepsilon_t| - \hat{\gamma}\varepsilon_t)^{\hat{\delta}}\}^{1/\hat{\delta}}\mathrm{Stu}_{\alpha} \quad (27)$$

$$\hat{VaR}^{S}_{1,\alpha} = \hat{\mu} + \{\hat{\omega}[1-\hat{\beta}L]^{-1} + \{1-[1-\hat{\beta}L]^{-1}(1-\hat{\phi}L) \times (1-L)^{\hat{d}}\}(|\varepsilon_t| - \hat{\gamma}\varepsilon_t)^{\hat{\delta}}\}^{1/\hat{\delta}}\mathrm{Stu}_{1-\alpha} \quad (28)$$

4. EMPIRICAL RESULTS

4.1. Data Description and Preliminary Analysis

In this chapter, we focus on six daily emerging stock markets returns, adjusted from splits and dividends, covering the same period from 2 January 1998 to 30 October 2009. There are Hang Seng Index (HSI) of Hong Kong, IPC of Mexico, Jakarta Composite (JKSE) of Indonesia, KLSE of Malaysia, Seoul Composite (KS11) of Korea and Strait Times (STI) of Singapore. The choice of this time span allows us to include the recent global financial crisis period. Table 1 lists all the return series with descriptive statistics. However, Fig. 1 presents the returns, absolute returns and squared returns of each stock market index considered. Fig. 1 indicates that return series is characterized by volatility clustering in which high (small) returns are followed by height (small) returns.

By consulting Table 1, we remark that both skewness and excess kurtosis statistics show that the return series are fat tailed, and its distribution could not be normally distributed. Likewise, the values of the Jarque–Berra test (J–B) statistic also reject the null hypothesis of normality, at the 1% and 5%

Table 1. Summary Statistics of Return Series for Emerging Stock Markets.

Indices	HSI	IPC	JKSE	KLSE	KS11	STI
Observation	2,941	2,967	2,868	2,919	2,918	2,968
Maximum	13.407	12.154	13.128	20.817	11.284	12.874
Minimum	−13.5820	−10.3410	−12.7320	−24.1530	−12.8050	−9.2155
Mean	0.0241	0.0573	0.0619	0.0253	0.0493	0.0185
Standard deviation	1.8241	1.6569	1.8078	1.5474	2.0959	1.5122
Skewness	0.1569	0.1784	−0.1272	0.4929	−0.1402	0.0016
Excess kurtosis	6.6088	4.3750	6.4273	53.3866	3.3363	6.3679
J–B stat	5364.2**	2370.7**	4944.3**	346765.4**	1362.9**	4989.3**
(*p*-value)	(0.0000)	(0.0000)	(0.0000)	(0.0000)	(0.0000)	(0.0000)
Ljung–Box $Q(10)$	18.0540	37.9590**	65.6470**	63.3620**	16.3320	33.6540**
(*p*-value)	(0.0540)	(0.0000)	(0.0000)	(0.0000)	(0.0910)	(0.0000)
ADF test	−53.6757**	−49.2474**	−46.4897**	−23.5464**	−51.2323**	−50.0812**
PP test	−53.6736**	−49.0946**	−46.5437**	−53.4472**	−51.1740**	−50.1373**
LM(2)	273.7495**	100.5114**	120.0989**	758.5596**	120.6413**	276.2713**
(*p*-value)	(0.0000)	(0.0000)	(0.0000)	(0.0000)	(0.0000)	(0.0000)
LM(5)	472.0932**	305.7508**	221.8723**	804.6759**	257.1457**	343.0097**
(*p*-value)	(0.0000)	(0.0000)	(0.0000)	(0.0000)	(0.0000)	(0.0000)
LM(10)	506.5559**	412.8859**	234.8504**	812.4575**	297.1598**	330.7961**
(*p*-value)	(0.0000)	(0.0000)	(0.0000)	(0.0000)	(0.0000)	(0.0000)

Note: The critical values for ADF and PP tests are −3.437 (1%), −2.864 (5%) and −2.568 (10%), respectively.

* and ** indicate the null hypothesis rejection at the 5% and 1%, respectively.

significance levels, in the distribution of all sample return series. This result indicates that all return series are fat tailed and couldn't be modelled by the normal distribution.

To test the presence of unit roots in return series, we use the ADF (augmented Dickey–Fuller) and PP (Phillips–Perron). Fig. 1 indicates that return series fluctuations vary around zero and the tendency is eliminated. So, the return series are graphically stationary. This result could be verified by the application of unit root tests which indicate that the null hypothesis can be rejected and all return series are stationary.

The ARCH LM test (Engle, 1982) indicates that all return series are volatile and variance is time varying. Indeed, the null hypothesis of homoscedasticity is rejected at 1% significance level by the application of LM test for order 2, 5 and 10 on the squared returns. There is evidence of heteroscedasticity for all return series. In other words, the return series exhibit clustering volatility and that there is a tendency for large (small)

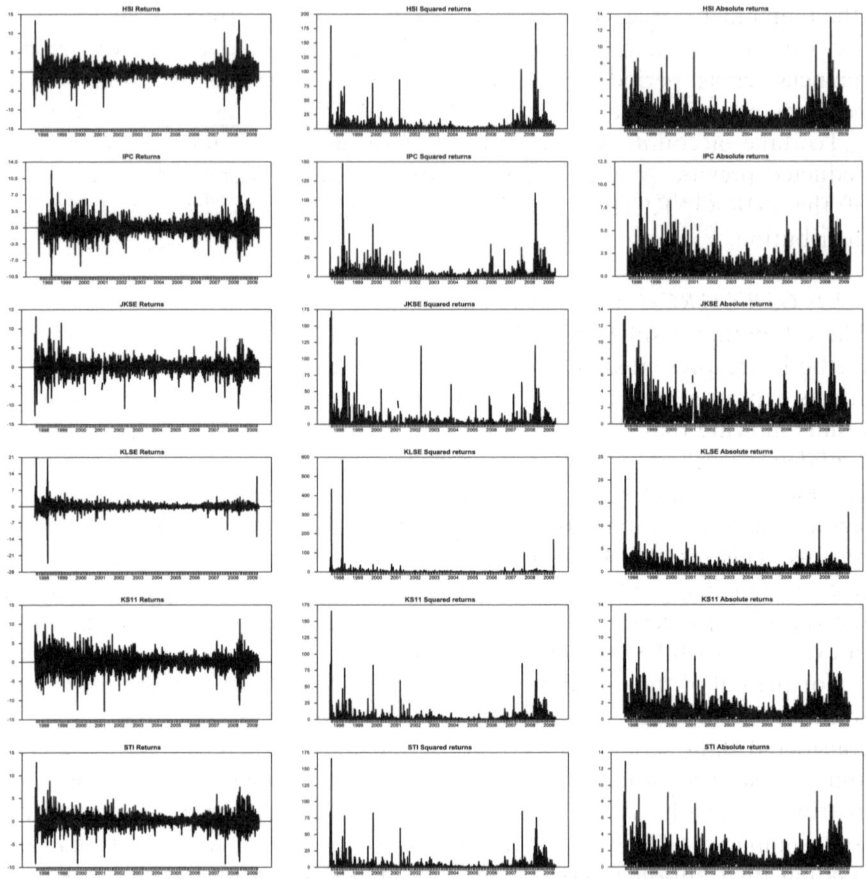

Fig. 1. Stock Returns, Squared and Absolute Returns.

asset price changes to be followed by other large (small) price changes of either sign and tend to be time varying. Thus, GARCH family models could be candidates to model return series.

4.2. Volatility Modelling Results

The whole data set was divided into two parts: the estimation period, or the in-sample period (the first 2,000 observation), which could be used to calculate in-sample VaR amounts and the prediction period, or out-of-sample period (the remainder of the sample), to compute the out-of-sample VaR based on the variance prediction process. The last sub-sample covers the global financial crisis period. Then, we use the two periods to compare the performance of short and long memory models in VaR estimation accuracy.

To take account of presence of ARCH effect and non-normality, deducted previously, we estimate jointly the mean and variance equations of the GJR-GARCH(1,1) and FIAPARCH(1,*d*,1) with skewed student distribution.

4.2.1. GJR-GARCH Model Estimation

The estimation results of the GJR-GARCH(1,1), by maximum-likelihood method, are presented in Table 2. In this model, ARCH and GARCH effects expressed, respectively, by the parameters α_1 and β_1. The estimation results indicate that these two parameters are statistically significant at 1% confidence level, in exception of ARCH effects for HSI. In addition, the parameter φ, expressing the asymmetry phenomenon, is also statistically significant which implies that volatility asymmetry is found for all market returns. This result is frequently found in the literature for financial series (e.g. see Glosten et al., 1993; Mokni et al., 2009). Also, the stationarity of the volatility process ($\alpha_1+\beta_1+0.5\varphi<1$) is guaranteed for all return series, in exception of KLSE index.

For the tail of the distribution expressed by the skewed student degree of freedom parameter, we find that it is statistically significant for all considered data series. This confirms that all return series are fat tailed, and the skewed student distribution is more appropriate than normal distribution to adjust the residual series. However, the asymmetry parameter isn't significant. The sign of this parameter indicates as well as that the residual distribution is skewed in the left for the HIS, JKSE and KLSE ($\ln(\xi)>0$), but skewed in the right for other index ($\ln(\xi)<0$).

4.2.2. The FIAPARCH Model Estimation

The FIAPARCH(1,*d*,1) model with skewed student distribution, estimated by the maximum-likelihood method, is reported in Table 3. By using the FIAPARCH model, we examine the long memory and volatility asymmetry properties for the sample returns. First, the estimates of ARCH and GARCH effects parameters are not significantly different from zero for the majority of the series. Second, the parameter (γ) is positive for all sample returns, in exception of the KS11 index. That is, negative shocks give rise to higher volatility than positive shocks. Also, this parameter is significantly different from zero indicating presence of the leverage effect. Thus, for positive values

Table 2. Estimation Results of the GJR–GARCH(1,1) Model.

Index	HSI	IPC	JKSE	KLSE	KS11	STI
Parameter estimation						
μ	0.0247	0.0940***	0.1037***	0.0142	0.0986**	0.0241**
SE	(0.0272)	(0.0275)	(0.0324)	(0.0188)	(0.0385)	(0.0228)
w	0.0086**	0.0341***	0.1381***	0.0179***	0.0163*	0.0200*
SE	(0.0043)	(0.0117)	(0.0403)	(0.0066)	(0.0093)	(0.0076)
β_1	0.9561***	0.9045***	0.8216***	0.8546***	0.9461***	0.8905***
SE	(0.0094)	(0.0183)	(0.0335)	(0.0233)	(0.0122)	(0.0186)
α_1	0.0091	0.0260**	0.0990***	0.1016***	0.0362***	0.0663***
SE	(0.0072)	(0.0109)	(0.0242)	(0.0238)	(0.0111)	(0.0161)
φ	0.0628***	0.1122***	0.0840**	0.1001***	0.0290**	0.0747**
SE	(0.0144)	(0.0262)	(0.0330)	(0.0294)	(0.0142)	(0.0224)
$\ln(\xi)$	0.0047	−0.0063	0.0432	0.0592*	−0.0493*	−0.0067*
SE	(0.02931)	(0.0316)	(0.0309)	(0.0319)	(0.0289)	(0.0325)
v	7.1731***	8.4758	4.6713***	4.9020***	7.3771***	6.9318***
SE	(1.1665)	(1.4819)***	(0.5020)	(0.5370)	(1.1778)	(0.9666)
Diagnostic						
$Q_s(10)$	9.7467	8.9085	2.6067	9.2187	4.2439	7.7886
(p-value)	(0.2833)	(0.3501)	(0.9566)	(0.3242)	(0.8345)	(0.4544)
ARCH LM	1.1153	0.7860	0.3979	0.9433	0.3333	0.7764
(p-value)	(0.3464)	(0.6425)	(0.9481)	(0.4919)	(0.9723)	(0.6518)
Log-likelihood	−3476.32	−3477.73	−3648.03	−2896.16	−4188.03	−3184.92
AIC	3.4833	3.4847	3.6550	2.9316	4.1950	3.1919

*, ** and *** indicate that parameter is significant at 10%, 5% and 1%, respectively.
$Q_s(10)$: Lejing–Box statistic on squared residual series.
AIC: Akake information criterion.

of γ, the volatility asymmetry will exceed unity.[5] In addition, the power term, δ, for the predictable structure in the volatility pattern is positive and significantly different from zero implying that a squared error term fitted in the conditional variance specification isn't appropriate. Third, the estimated fractionally integrated parameter, d, is significant and $0<d<1$ meaning that volatility displays the long memory property for all series, in exception of the HSI. In addition, the tail's parameter, v, is positive and highly significant indicating a fat-tail phenomenon for all return series. However, the asymmetric coefficient of the skewed student distribution is negative ($\ln(\xi)<0$) for KS11 and positive for the others series, but not significant for all series.

4.2.3. Diagnostic Estimation Results

The diagnostic tests for the short and long memory volatility models are reported in the second parts of Tables 2 and 3. In order to test the remaining

Table 3. Estimation Results of the FIAPARCH(1,d,1) Model.

Index	HSI	IPC	JKSE	KLSE	KS11	STI
Parameter estimation						
μ	0.0267	0.0991***	0.1186***	0.0117	0.0975**	0.0290
SE	(0.0270)	(0.0273)	(0.0324)	(0.0183)	(0.0378)	(0.0224)
w	−0.0556	0.0650	0.2987**	0.0853**	−0.1345	0.0108
SE	(0.0676)	(0.0633)	(0.1370)	(0.0424)	(0.1595)	(0.0507)
d	0.1080	0.2336**	0.3085***	0.2933***	0.2635***	0.2383***
SE	(0.0775)	(0.0940)	(0.0726)	(0.0504)	(0.0663)	(0.0521)
β_1	0.3227**	0.3056	0.1474	−0.1265	0.2757	0.0412
SE	(0.1615	(0.4347)	(0.3057)	(0.3643)	(0.1774)	(0.2149)
α_1	0.2254*	0.1570	0.0356	−0.2440	0.0265	−0.1227
SE	(0.1317)	(0.3787)	(0.2793)	(0.3374)	(0.1327)	(0.1947)
γ	0.9703	0.5990***	0.1706***	0.2301***	0.1788***	0.2949***
SE	(0.7426	(0.1599)	(0.0618)	(0.0649)	(0.0686)	(0.0807)
δ	1.9988***	1.7593***	1.9229***	1.8607***	2.2986***	2.0918***
SE	(0.3457)	(0.2799)	(0.1988)	(0.0951)	(0.1872)	(0.1465)
ln(ξ)	0.0074	0.0024	0.0524*	0.0602*	−0.0569*	0.0017
SE	(0.0297)	(0.0327)	(0.0314)	(0.0327)	(0.0295)	(0.0328)
v	7.1580***	9.9650***	4.9021***	5.3734	7.5921***	7.1077***
SE	(1.1541)	(2.0442)	(0.5595)	(0.6139)	(1.2405)	(0.9929)
Diagnostic						
$Q_s(10)$	22.6880	11.3754	1.8571	10.9546	3.1889	7.5121
(p-value)	(0.0120)	(0.1813)	(0.9851)	(0.2043)	(0.9220)	(0.4825)
ARCH LM	7.8924	0.9654	0.2110	0.2423	0.3582	0.8708
(p-value)	(0.4440)	(0.4717)	(0.9954)	(0.9437)	(0.9641)	(0.5601)
Log-likelihood	−3466.40	−3464.99	−3640.75	−2869.52	−4174.94	−3169.75
AIC	3.4754	3.4740	3.6498	2.8785	4.1839	3.1787

*, ** and *** indicate that parameter is significant at 10%, 5% and 1%, respectively.
$Q_s(10)$: Lejing–Box statistic on squared residual series.
AIC: Akake information criterion.

serial correlation, we compute the Box–Pierce statistics of the squared standardized residuals.[6] If the conditional variance equation is correctly specified, the Box–Pierce statistics should be statistically insignificant. It's clear that the squared residuals series have no correlation because the Box–Pierce is larger than chi-square critical value. In addition, the associated p-values according to this test are greater than 5%, which indicates that the null hypothesis could not be rejected for all index returns data, in the case of both short and long memory models.

The second test focuses on the remaining ARCH effects. From the Engle's (1982) test, we could conclude that the two volatility models indicate no significant ARCH effect in residual series at the 1% confidence level. The third diagnostic concerns the capacity of both models to fit data. We use the Akake information criterion (AIC), for which the best model has the weakest AIC value. By using this criterion, we deduce that the FIAPARCH provides the weakest values of AIC for all return series. Thus, the FIAPARCH model performs the better in volatility modelling.

4.3. VaR Estimation Results and Models Performance Evaluation

The aim of this chapter is to check the performance of the long memory models (FIAPARCH) compared to short memory model (GJR-GARCH) in daily VaR estimation of both long and short trading positions. We use these estimated models to compute the in-sample and out-of-sample VaR amounts for both long and short trading positions. Then, we evaluate, respectively, the estimation and the forecast accuracy of the two estimated models in VaR measure.

4.3.1. Models-Based VaR Evaluation

In the context of market risk measure, the investors wish to obtain VaR estimation providing a *failure rate* ($\hat{\alpha}$) close to the pre-specified VaR confidence level (α). For that, the two models are tested with five VaR level α ranged from 5% to 0.25%, and their performance is, then, cheeked by the LR test for unconditional coverage (Likelihood Ratio Test [LRT]) of Kupiec (1995). Then, we test the null hypothesis that failure rate ($\hat{\alpha}$) is equal to VaR's confidence level (α); that is, we test the hypothesis: $H_0 : \alpha = \hat{\alpha}$ versus $H_1 : \alpha \neq \hat{\alpha}$. Under the null hypothesis, the likelihood-ratio statistic, denoted by LRT, follows the chi-square distribution with one degree of freedom. That is,

$$\mathrm{LRT} = -2\log\left[\frac{\alpha^k(1-\alpha)^{T-k}}{\hat{\alpha}^k(1-\hat{\alpha})^{T-k}}\right] \sim x^2(1) \tag{29}$$

where $\hat{\alpha} = k/T$ is the *failure rate* and T is the total number of observations and $k = \sum_{t=1}^{T} I_t$ denotes the number of exceptions; that is, the number of times returns exceed (in absolute value) the forecasted VaR in the sample, and I_t is a Bernoulli random variable defined by

$$I_t = \begin{cases} 1 & \text{if} \quad r_t < \mathrm{VaR}_t \\ 0 & \text{if} \quad r_t \geq \mathrm{VaR}_t \end{cases} \tag{30}$$

In risk management, the model performs (in VaR estimation) if the null hypothesis doesn't be rejected. That is, if the VaR models are perfectly specified, the failure rates should be equal to the pre-specified VaR level α and the VaR models help investors to forecast correctly their possible trading losses.

4.3.2. VaR Estimation Results

Before assessing the two VaR-based models considered in this study, we use the parameter estimation results reported in Tables 2 and 3 to compute the one-step-ahead VaR for long and short trading position. For the long trading position, the failure rate is equal to the percentage of negative returns smaller than one-step-ahead VaR. However, for short trading positions, failure rate is referred to the percentage of positive returns larger than one-step-ahead VaR.

The Kupiec test results for both in-sample and out-of-sample VaRs computed by the skewed student GJR-GARCH(1,1) and FIAPARCH models are reported in Tables 4 and 5, respectively. These tables contain the values of LRT statistics and its corresponding *p*-values. According to these empirical results, we deduce that both GJR-GARCH and FIAPARCH models perform very successfully for in-sample VaR estimation for the two trading positions. Indeed, the Kupiec test accepts the null hypothesis for all VaR's confidence levels and for all markets. These results show that the two models provide a good performance for the two trading positions and estimate in-sample VaR very accurately for all the markets.

We further evaluate the performance of the two considered models by calculating out-of-sample VaR forecasts (Tables 4 and 5). Following the iterative rolling regression procedure of Mincer and Zarnowitz (1969), used by Tang and Shieh (2006) and Wu and Shieh (2007) in the context of VaR estimation, we could estimate out-of-sample one-day-ahead VaR. Following this procedure, we re-estimate the two considered models every 50 observations, in the out-of-sample period. The out-of-sample VaR implies a one-step-ahead forecast, which signifies the fact that VaR of the $(t+1)$thday is calculated conditionally on the available information on the tth day.

The empirical results show that the LR's Kupiec test rejects the null hypothesis for some cases corresponding, generally to the height and low VaR's confidence levels in the long and short trading position, respectively. But, in almost every case, the Kupiec test does not reject the null hypothesis indicating the good performance of the two models, also, in the out-of-sample analysis. All results allow, as concluding, that we model volatility dynamics very correctly, being given that volatility is an essential component in VaR computation.

Table 4. Kupiec Test for the GJR–GARCH(1,1) Model.

Index	HSI		IPC		JKSE		KLSE		KS11		STI	
	LRT	*p*-value	LRT	*p*-value	LRT	*p*-value	LRT	*p*-value	LRT	*p*-value	LRT	*p*-value
In-sample long position VaR												
5%	0.2591	0.6107	0.1663	0.6834	0.6573	0.4175	0.1706	0.6796	1.7103	0.1909	0.2591	0.6107
2.50%	0.4970	0.4808	0.9624	0.3266	0.0204	0.8865	0.9624	0.3266	0.0810	0.7759	0.497	0.4808
1%	0.0514	0.8207	0.4336	0.5102	0.0497	0.8236	0.1957	0.6582	0.4789	0.4889	0.1957	0.6582
0.50%	0.0000	1.0000	1.4293	0.2319	0.0000	1.0000	0.4317	0.5112	0.1040	0.7471	0.1040	0.7471
0.25%	0.2154	0.6426	0.1884	0.6643	0.1884	0.6643	0.2154	0.6426	0.1884	0.6643	0.2154	0.6426
In-sample short position VaR												
95%	1.7103	0.1909	0.8780	0.3487	0.1706	0.6796	0.6573	0.4175	0.2591	0.6107	0.2674	0.6051
97.50%	0.7691	0.3805	0.0000	1.0000	0.7691	0.3805	0.0206	0.8857	0.0831	0.7731	0.5304	0.4665
99%	1.3822	0.2397	0.2090	0.6475	0.0514	0.8207	0.0514	0.8207	0.4789	0.4889	0.0000	1.0000
99.50%	1.0111	0.3147	0.1040	0.7471	0.1040	0.7471	0.0973	0.7551	1.8781	0.1706	0.3777	0.5388
99.75%	2.3393	0.1261	0.9371	0.3330	2.3393	0.1261	0.9371	0.3330	0.2154	0.6426	1.5246	0.2169
Out-of-sample long position VaR												
5%	5.1687*	0.0230	4.2831*	0.0385	3.5414	0.0599	0.0000	0.9940	4.7608*	0.0291	3.1101	0.0778
2.50%	0.8238	0.3641	0.3264	0.5678	4.3850*	0.0363	0.3921	0.5312	1.0662	0.3018	0.6944	0.4047
1%	1.9666	0.1608	1.7204	0.1896	0.5775	0.4473	0.3388	0.5606	0.0036	0.9522	0.1602	0.6890
0.50%	0.1119	0.7380	0.2620	0.6088	0.0961	0.7565	0.0349	0.8519	0.3967	0.5288	0.0797	0.7777
0.25%	0.9960	0.3183	0.1306	0.7178	0.2841	0.5940	1.0339	0.3092	0.9304	0.3348	0.0398	0.8420
Out-of-sample short position VaR												
95%	1.0337	0.3093	0.0400	0.8414	2.3080	0.1287	0.8058	0.3694	1.5165	0.2181	0.0839	0.7721
97.50%	0.8238	0.3641	0.7850	0.3756	5.2930*	0.0214	0.1780	0.6731	1.1813	0.2771	0.0486	0.8256
99%	0.2248	0.6354	0.0480	0.8266	0.9372	0.3330	5.7050*	0.0169	2.3033	0.1291	0.3427	0.5583
99.50%	0.7130	0.3984	2.1474	0.1428	3.7572	0.0526	NaN	1.0000	0.0797	0.7777	4.1463*	0.0417
99.75%	0.9960	0.3183	0.0768	0.7816	0.7921	0.3735	NaN	1.0000	NaN	1.0000	NaN	1.0000

Note: This table contains the LR statistic of Kupiec (1995) test and its *p*-value.
The * indicates that the null hypothesis is rejected at 5% level.
NaN: not available number.

Table 5. Kupiec Test for the FIAPARCH(1,*d*,1) Model.

Index	HSI		IPC		JKSE		KLSE		KS11		STI	
	LRT	*p*-value	LRT	*p*-value	LRT	*p*-value	LRT	*p*-value	LRT	*p*-value	LRT	*p*-value
In-sample long position VaR												
5%	0.2591	0.6107	0.0000	1.0000	1.9779	0.1596	0.6914	0.4057	0.3720	0.5419	0.2591	0.6107
2.50%	0.3200	0.5716	0.4970	0.4808	0.0204	0.8865	1.5723	0.2099	0.0810	0.7759	0.4970	0.4808
1%	0.0514	0.8207	1.6611	0.1975	0.1957	0.6582	0.0497	0.8236	0.4789	0.4889	0.1957	0.6582
0.50%	0.3777	0.5388	0.8260	0.3634	0.0000	1.0000	0.0000	1.0000	0.4317	0.5112	0.0000	1.0000
0.25%	0.1884	0.6643	0.1884	0.6643	0.1884	0.6643	0.0000	1.0000	0.0000	1.0000	0.0000	1.0000
In-sample short position VaR												
95%	3.2325	0.0722	0.8780	0.3487	0.0956	0.7571	0.1663	0.6834	0.0106	0.9182	0.1706	0.6796
97.50%	1.0543	0.3045	0.0831	0.7731	0.7691	0.3805	1.2496	0.2636	0.0206	0.8857	1.3871	0.2389
99%	2.8244	0.0928	0.0497	0.8236	2.0313	0.1541	0.4336	0.5102	0.4789	0.4889	0.2090	0.6475
99.50%	3.0811	0.0792	0.4317	0.5112	0.4317	0.5112	0.3777	0.5388	1.0111	0.3147	0.3777	0.5388
99.75%	2.3393	0.1261	0.0000	1.0000	2.3393	0.1261	0.9371	0.3330	0.2154	0.6426	1.5246	0.2169
Out-of-sample long position VaR												
5%	4.5659*	0.0326	7.5050*	0.0062	4.6981*	0.0302	0.0949	0.7580	8.9972*	0.0027	4.2510*	0.0392
2.50%	2.8196	0.0931	7.8873*	0.0050	2.9148	0.0878	3.9612	0.0466	5.6051*	0.0179	3.6226	0.0570
1%	6.2490*	0.0124	1.7204	0.1896	1.8839	0.1699	5.3605*	0.0206	0.7979	0.3717	0.1742	0.6765
0.50%	0.9776	0.3228	0.2620	0.6088	1.3807	0.2400	1.0895	0.2966	0.3967	0.5288	0.2595	0.6104
0.25%	0.1643	0.6853	0.1306	0.7178	1.2364	0.2662	1.0339	0.3092	0.1978	0.6565	0.8628	0.3530
Out-of-sample short position VaR												
95%	1.6937	0.1931	0.0586	0.8087	1.8275	0.1764	5.9984*	0.0143	0.3586	0.5493	0.0551	0.8144
97.50%	5.8532*	0.0155	0.0595	0.8073	4.1677*	0.0412	1.0549	0.3044	1.1813	0.2771	0.9192	0.3377
99%	0.2574	0.6119	0.3095	0.5780	7.5403	0.0060	1.2749	0.2589	1.2679	0.2602	0.0494	0.8241
99.50%	0.3294	0.5660	0.8099	0.3682	NaN	1.0000	4.1542*	0.0415	0.0358	0.8500	2.1533	0.1423
99.75%	0.0558	0.8133	0.0768	0.7816	NaN	1.0000	NaN	1.0000	0.1978	0.6565	NaN	1.0000

Note: This table contains the LR statistic of Kupiec (1995) test and its *p*-value.
The * indicates that the null hypothesis is rejected at 5% level.

To investigate the difference between the two model in VaR estimation for the two trading position, we could investigate the effect of long memory in volatility propriety in the context of emerging stock market risk estimation accuracy.

4.4. Long Memory Effects on Market Risk Estimation

In the previous paragraph, we focused on the performance models evaluation. In this part of the chapter, we focus on the performance of long memory model (FIAPARCH) compared to the short memory model (GJR-GARCH) in market risk estimation, when a VaR technique is used. For this, we compute the failure rate corresponding to the two models (Tables 6 and 7).

Table 6. Failure Rate for the GJR–GARCH(1,1) Model.

Index	HSI	IPC	JKSE	KLSE	KS11	STI
In-sample long position VaR						
5%	0.0525	0.0520	0.0540	0.0480	0.0565	0.0525
2.5%	0.0275	0.0285	0.0255	0.0285	0.0260	0.0275
1%	0.0095	0.0115	0.0105	0.0110	0.0085	0.0110
0.5%	0.0050	0.0070	0.0050	0.0040	0.0045	0.0045
0.25%	0.0020	0.0030	0.0030	0.0020	0.0030	0.0020
In-sample short position VaR						
95%	0.9435	0.9545	0.9520	0.9460	0.9475	0.9525
97.5%	0.9780	0.9750	0.9780	0.9755	0.9760	0.9775
99%	0.9925	0.9910	0.9905	0.9905	0.9915	0.9900
99.5%	0.9965	0.9955	0.9955	0.9945	0.9970	0.9940
99.75%	0.9990	0.9985	0.9990	0.9985	0.9980	0.9960
Out-of-sample long position VaR						
5%	0.0670	0.0652	0.0645	0.0501	0.0664	0.0632
2.5%	0.0298	0.0279	0.0369	0.0283	0.0305	0.0294
1%	0.0149	0.0145	0.0127	0.0120	0.0098	0.0087
0.5%	0.0043	0.0062	0.0058	0.0054	0.0065	0.0044
0.25%	0.0011	0.0031	0.0035	0.0044	0.0011	0.0022
Out-of-sample short position VaR						
95%	0.9426	0.9514	0.9608	0.9434	0.9586	0.9521
97.5%	0.9702	0.9793	0.9862	0.9728	0.9804	0.9739
99%	0.9915	0.9907	0.9931	0.9967	0.9946	0.9880
99.5%	0.9968	0.9979	0.9989	1.0000	0.9956	0.9989
99.75%	0.9989	0.9979	0.9989	1.0000	1.0000	1.0000

Table 7. Failure Rate for the FIAPARCH(1,d,1) Model.

Index	HSI	IPC	JKSE	KLSE	KS11	STI
In-sample long position VaR						
5%	0.0525	0.0570	0.0460	0.0530	0.0525	0.0495
2.5%	0.0270	0.0255	0.0295	0.0260	0.0275	0.0275
1%	0.0095	0.0110	0.0105	0.0085	0.0110	0.0080
0.5%	0.0060	0.0050	0.0050	0.0040	0.0050	0.0045
0.25%	0.0030	0.0030	0.0025	0.0025	0.0025	0.0025
In-sample short position VaR						
95%	0.9410	0.9515	0.9480	0.9505	0.9520	0.9555
97.5%	0.9785	0.9780	0.9710	0.9755	0.9790	0.9825
99%	0.9935	0.9930	0.9885	0.9915	0.9910	0.9935
99.5%	0.9975	0.9960	0.9940	0.9965	0.9940	0.9960
99.75%	0.9990	0.9990	0.9985	0.9980	0.9960	0.9970
Out-of-sample long position VaR						
5%	0.0570	0.0668	0.0522	0.0730	0.0651	0.0659
2.5%	0.0255	0.0346	0.0359	0.0381	0.0351	0.0292
1%	0.0110	0.0150	0.0185	0.0131	0.0114	0.0097
0.5%	0.0050	0.0081	0.0076	0.0065	0.0062	0.0054
0.25%	0.0030	0.0046	0.0044	0.0033	0.0041	0.0043
Out-of-sample short position VaR						
95%	0.9515	0.9597	0.9315	0.9543	0.9484	0.9470
97.5%	0.9780	0.9850	0.9695	0.9804	0.9700	0.9762
99%	0.9930	0.9977	0.9935	0.9935	0.9907	0.9860
99.5%	0.9960	1.0000	0.9989	0.9946	0.9979	0.9935
99.75%	0.9990	1.0000	1.0000	0.9967	1.0000	0.9978

To compare the two models based on VaR, we focus on the 'sample coverage' indicator, used by So and Yu (2006). Following this procedure, the best model produces the nearest failure rate to the pre-specified VaR's confidence level. Thus, we focus on comparison between GJR-GARCH and FIAPARCH models on the difference between mean failure rate and pre-specified confidence level. The 'sample coverage' is defined by $|\alpha - \hat{\alpha}|$. In Tables 6 and 7, we compute the mean sample coverage of the six indexes. After this, we compare the results for the two models.

In the case of in-sample VaR in long trading position, the empirical results show that the long memory model (FIAPARCH) is best for almost all confidence levels, especially for the height confidence levels. However, in the short trading position VaR, we note that the FIAPARCH model performs the better only for the 95% and 99.75% VaR's confidence levels. In this case, the short memory (GJR-GARCH) model is generally the better.

Table 8. Performance Comparison of the Two Models in VaR Estimation.

	In-Sample VaR			Out-of-Sample VaR		
	GJR-GARCH	FIAPARCH	L/S	GJR–GARCH	FIAPARCH	L/S
Long position VaR						
5%	0.0026	0.0017	L	0.0127	0.0133	S
2.5%	0.0023	0.0022	L	0.0055	0.0081	S
1%	0.0003	0.0003	L	0.0021	0.0031	S
0.5%	0.0000	0.0001	S	0.0004	0.0015	S
0.25%	0.0000	0.0002	S	0.0000	0.0014	S
Short position VaR						
95%	0.0007	0.0002	L	0.0015	0.0013	L
97.5%	0.0017	0.0024	S	0.0021	0.0015	L
99%	0.0010	0.0018	S	0.0024	0.0024	L
99.5%	0.0005	0.0007	S	0.0030	0.0018	L
99.75%	0.0007	0.0004	L	0.0018	0.0014	L

Note: This table contains the mean sample coverage on the data set for the two models. L/S: long (L) or short (S) memory model is preferred on VaR estimation.

When we interest to the out-of-sample VaR for long trading position, the GJR-GARCH model performs for all confidence levels, while the FIAPARCH model is preferred for the short trading position for all confidence levels. Thus, the long memory model is preferred to compute the in-sample VaR for the long position and the out-of-sample VaR for the short trading position. This result could be explained by the fact that the long memory propriety, as a volatility-stylized fact, should be considered in the risk estimation context. Finally, investors should take account of volatility persistence (long memory) propriety when they interest to the market risk estimation problems (Table 8).

5. CONCLUSION

Recently, the emerging markets have become increasingly volatile and risky mainly during the current global financial crisis. For this reason, risk management against market risk of index prices is extremely important. The VaR is a popular techniques used to estimate emerging markets risk. There are several method to estimate VaR, but the GARCH-type models is the most important method since these models take account of volatility-stylized facts like clustering, asymmetry and persistence.

In this chapter, we use two most important GARCH-type models: GJR-GARCH and FIAPARCH models adjusted by the skewed student distribution. Using emerging stock returns data, the estimation results of one-step-ahead in-sample VaR in long and short trading positions show that both short and long memory models have good performance for the in-sample and out-of-sample VaR estimation and prediction.

If comparing long and short memory models, the estimation results show that the FIAPARCH model performs the better in almost all cases. Finally, this result notes that long memory models could help investors to forecast correctly their possible trading losses better than the short memory models. Overall, the findings of this study imply that long memory models play an important role in VaR estimation and should be considered in risk management. Conservative risk managers may adopt long memory models using GARCH-type models to assess the emerging risks since it provides more accurate VaR estimates.

This work improves our understanding of the periods of crisis. Indeed, during the global financial crisis periods, the VaR amounts were correctly estimated by these two models indicating that long memory GARCH models are a crucial tool in emerging stock market estimation on the stability and crisis periods.

Future research could use the same methodology to assess extreme emerging risks by using other risk measure techniques like the expected shortfall (ES). Also, we could apply the same analysis by using the skewed student distribution with time-varying parameters. On another ground, researchers could investigate period of crisis models characterized by high volatility regime, in a GARCH context, to better estimate the VaR. For this reason, we propose to use the ICSS algorithm for example.

NOTES

1. For more details, see Giot and Laurent (2003b) and Henry (2002).
2. This implies that unexpected negative returns resulted in more volatility than unexpected positive returns of the same magnitude.
3. Lambert and Laurent (2001) re-expressed the Skewed Student density of Fernandez and Steel (1998) in such a way that the innovation process has zero mean and unit variance.

4. See Ding, Granger, and Engle (1993) for the APARCH model and Engle and Ng (1993) for other approaches that may be used to capture an asymmetrical volatility response.

5. The metric used for relative asymmetry captures the extent to which the volatility in response to a 'negative' shock is greater than the volatility in response to a 'positive' shock (see, Jayasuriya, Rossiter, & Shambora, 2009; Brooks, 2007).

6. We choose $Q_S(10)$ as the Box–Pierce statistic of order 10 computed on the squared standardized residuals.

REFERENCES

Aloui, C., & Mabrouk, S. (2010). Value-at-risk estimations of energy commodities via long-memory, asymmetry and fat-tailed GARCH models. *Energy Policy*, *38*, 2326–2339.

Baillie, R. T., Bollerslev, T., & Mikkelsen, H. O. (1996). Fractionally integrated generalized autoregressive conditional heteroskedasticity. *Journal of Econometrics*, *74*, 3–30.

Black F. (1976). Studies of stock price volatility changes. *Proceedings of the 1976 meeting of business and economic statistics section*, American Statistical Association pp. 177–181.

Bollerslev, T. (1986). Generalised autoregressive conditional heteroskedasticity. *Journal of Econometrics*, *31*, 307–327.

Brooks, C., & Persand, G. (2002). Model choice and value-at-risk performance. *Financial Analysts Journal*, *58*(5), 87–97.

Brooks, R. (2007). Power ARCH modelling of the volatility of emerging equity markets. *Emerging Markets Review*, *8*, 124–133.

Chiu, C. L., Lee, M. C., & Hung, J. C. (2005). Estimation of value-at-risk under jump dynamics and asymmetric information. *Applied Financial Economic*, *15*, 1095–1106.

Degiannakis, S. (2004). Volatility forecasting: Evidence from a fractional integrated asymmetric power ARCH skewed-t model. *Applied Financial Economics*, *14*, 1333–1342.

Ding, Z., Granger, C. W. J., & Engle, R. F. (1993). A long memory property of stock market returns and a new model. *Journal of Empirical Finance*, *1*, 83–106.

Dowd, K. (1998). *Beyond value at risk: The new science of risk management*. Wiley.

Engle, R. F. (1982). Autoregressive conditional heteroskedasticity with estimates of the variance of United Kingdom inflation. *Econometrica*, *50*, 987–1006.

Engel, J., & Gizycki, M. (1999). *Conservatism, accuracy and efficiency: Comparing value-at-risk models*. Working Paper Series no. wp0002. Australian Prudential Regulation Authority.

Engle, R. F., & Ng, V. K. (1993). Measuring and testing the impact of news on volatility. *Journal of Finance*, *48*(5), 1749–1778.

Fernandez, C., & Steel, M. (1998). On Bayesian modelling of fat tails and skewness. *Journal of the American Statistical Association*, *93*, 359–371.

French, K. R., Schwert, G. W., & Stambaugh, R. F. (1987). Expected stock returns and volatility. *Journal of Financial Economics*, *19*(1), 3–29.

Giot, P., & Laurent, S. (2003a). Market risk in commodity markets: A VaR approach. *Energy Economics*, *25*(5), 435–457.

Giot, P., & Laurent, S. (2003b). Value-at-risk for long and short trading positions. *Journal of Applied Econometrics*, *18*, 641–664.

Giot, P., & Laurent, S. (2004). Modeling daily value-at-risk using realized volatility and ARCH type models. *Journal of Empirical Finance*, *11*, 379–398.

Glosten, L. R., Jagannathan, R., & Runkle, D. (1993). On the relationship between the expected value and volatility of the nominal excess return on stocks. *Journal of Finance*, *48*, 1779–1801.

Hendricks, D. (1996). Evaluation of value-at-risk models using historical data. *Economic Policy Review*, pp. 39–69, Federal Reserve Bank of New York.

Henry, O. T. (2002). Long memory in stock returns: some international evidence. *Applied Financial Economics*, *12*, 725–729.

Huang, Y. C., & Lin, B. J. (2004). Value-at-risk analysis for Taiwan stock index futures: Fat tails and conditional asymmetries in return innovations. *Review of Quantitative Finance and Accounting*, *22*, 79–95.

Hull, J., & White, A. (1998). Incorporating volatility updating into the historical simulation method for value at risk. *Journal of Risk*, *1*, 1–25.

Hung. J. C, Lee. M. C., & Liu, H. C. (2008). Estimation of value-at-risk for energy commodities via fat-tailed GARCH models. *Energy Economics*, *30*(3), 1173–1191.

Jayasuriya, S. A., Rossiter, R., & Shambora, W. (2009). Asymmetric volatility in emerging and mature markets. *Journal of Emerging Market Finance*, *8*(1), 25–43.

Jondeau, E., & Rockinger, M. (2006). The Copula-GARCH model of conditional dependencies: An international stock market application. *Journal of International Money and Finance*, *25*, 827–853.

Jorion, P. (2001). *Value at risk: The new benchmark for managing financial risk* (2nd ed.). McGraw-Hill.

Kupiec, P. (1995). Techniques for verifying the accuracy of risk measurement models. *Journal of Derivatives 2*, 174–184.

Lambert, P., & Laurent, S. (2001). Modeling financial time series using GARCH-type models and a skewed student density. Mimeo, Université de Liège.

Marimoutou, V., Raggad, B., & Trabelsi, A. (2009). Extreme value theory and value at risk: Application to oil market. *Energy Economics*, *31*, 519–530.

Mighri, Z., Mokni, K., & Mansouri, F. (2010). Empirical analysis of asymmetric long memory volatility models in value-at-risk estimation. *Journal of Risk*, *13*(1), 1–74.

Mincer, J., & Zarnowitz, V. (1969). The evaluation of economic forecasts. In: J. Mincer (Ed.), *Economic forecasts and expectations*. New York: NBER.

Mokni, K., Mighri, Z., & Mansouri, F. (2009). On the effect of subprime crisis on value-at-risk estimation: GARCH family models approach. *International Journal of Economic and Finance*, *1*(2), 88–105.

Pagan, A., & Schwert, G. (1990). Alternative models for conditional stock volatility. *Journal of Econometrics*, *45*, 267–290.

So, M. K. P., & Yu, P. L. H. (2006). Empirical analysis of GARCH models in value at risk estimation. *Journal of International Financial Markets, Institution and Money*, *16*, 180–197.

Tang, T. L., & Shieh, S. J. (2006). Long memory in stock index futures markets: A value-at-risk approach. *Physica A*, *366*, 437–448.

Tse, Y. K. (1998). The conditional heteroscedasticity of the yen-dollar exchange rate. *Journal of Applied Econometrics*, *13*, 49–55.

Wong, C. M., & So, M. K. P. (2003). On conditional moments of GARCH models, with applications to multiple period value at risk estimation. *Statistica Sinica*, *13*, 1015–1104.

Wu, P., & Shieh, S. J. (2007). Value-at-risk analysis for long term interest rate futures: Fat-tail and long memory in return innovations. *Journal of Empirical Finance*, *14*, 248–259.

Yu, J. (2005). On leverage in a stochastic volatility model. *Journal of Econometrics*, *127*, 165–178.

DEPENDENCE AND RETURN DISTRIBUTIONS DURING CRISES: EVIDENCE FROM EMERGING ASIAN ECONOMIES

Craig Ellis and Maike Sundmacher

ABSTRACT

That asset returns are typically neither independent nor normally distributed is a stylised fact of many financial markets. We examine market returns for a number of emerging Asian nations before and during the Asian crisis and global financial crisis periods and consider how well these are described by the assumptions of normality and independence. Specifically we seek to ask how – if at all – these crises impacted upon the time-series properties of stock market returns in the emerging Asian economies. The first part of the chapter examines the comparative fit of the normal distribution to daily stock market returns for each of the economies under observation. The second part of the chapter follows with an examination of dependence relations in emerging Asian market returns around the crises periods.

Keywords: Return distributions; long-term dependence; non-periodic cycles.

The Impact of the Global Financial Crisis on Emerging Financial Markets
Contemporary Studies in Economic and Financial Analysis, Volume 93, 449–471

ISSN: 1569-3759/doi:10.1108/S1569-3759(2011)0000093016

JEL Classifications: G01; G15; C46.

1. INTRODUCTION

The assumption that consecutive price changes are independent and identically distributed (i.i.d.) has particular implications when working with financial asset returns. For investors, knowledge of the distribution is vital to measuring the underlying risk of loss associated with a particular asset or trading strategy. In empirical studies of asset returns, the nature of the distribution also provides information about the return-generating process. Statistical tools for testing model fit and the significance of model parameters are also conditioned on particular types of distribution (Fama, 1965). Finally, and arguably most importantly, general forms of asset pricing models such as the capital asset pricing model (CAPM) and the Black–Scholes option pricing model explicitly require normality of the underlying distribution of asset returns. More general implications for financial asset returns of a stationary normal distribution include the likelihood of a given percentage variation in price remaining constant over time, and the assumption that the probability of price change in either direction (positive or negative) is equal in each period.

This chapter considers the distributional and time-series characteristics of stock market returns for seven emerging Asian nations before and during the Asian crisis and global financial crisis periods. These nations and their respective stock market indices are China (Shanghai A 30), India (S&P CNX 500), Indonesia (Jakarta SE Composite), Korea (KOSPI), Sri Lanka (Colombo SE All), Taiwan (Taiwan SE Weighted) and Thailand (Bangkok S.E.T.).

The first part of this chapter examines the comparative fit of the normal distribution to inter-day returns for each of the markets under observation. Despite their well-known overall poor fit, normal distributions are a critical feature of most financial asset pricing models. The second part of this chapter follows with an examination of dependence relations in these markets and presents evidence of both positive long-term dependence and non-periodic cycles.

The emerging markets' classification adopted in this chapter follows directly from that employed by Standard and Poor's for the construction of the *S&P Emerging Stock Market Indices*. The relevant conditions to be classified as an emerging market according to the S&P standard are that the

Table 1. Indicative Market Size and Value as at January 2010.

	Domestic Market Capitalisation (USD Mil.)	Number of Listed Companies	Average Number of Daily Electronic Book Order Trades (Thousands)
China	2,481,554.8	873	7,958.5
India	1,283,157.8	4,962	7,377.6
Indonesia	224,887.2	398	83.5
Korea	801,029.6	1,794	4,414.7
Sri Lanka	10,215.8	231	10.8
Taiwan	616,849.2	755	1,237.2
Thailand	168,689.0	535	137.3

Source: World Federation of Exchanges (2010).

market meets at least one of the two following general criteria (Standard and Poor's, 2007):

(i) it is located in a low- or middle-income economy as defined by the World Bank and
(ii) the investable market capitalisation is low relative to GDP.

The sample data in this study comprises inter-day returns over the period 1 January 1980 to 31 March 2010.[1] The delineation of emerging Asian stock markets by indicative size, value and liquidity is of interest as it allows us to gauge the potential impact of these measures on the distributional and time-series characteristics of the markets. Figures pertaining to the domestic market capitalisation, number of listed companies and the average number of trades for emerging Asian markets in Table 1 illustrate the significant differences between the markets in the region.

Comparing the relative domestic market capitalisation and the average number of daily electronic book order trades in Table 1, we expect that the distribution of returns for the relatively larger and more liquid markets of China and India should be more likely to be i.i.d. than those of Sri Lanka or Indonesia.

2. RETURN DISTRIBUTIONS OF STOCK MARKETS IN EMERGING ASIAN ECONOMIES

Traditional models of financial asset returns are based on a number of simplifying assumptions. Among these is the primary assumption that consecutive price changes, ε_t, are i.i.d., that is price changes conform to a Wiener process, or Gaussian random walk.[2] The assumption that consecutive price changes are i.i.d. has particular implications for the nature of asset returns. Requiring consecutive price changes to constitute a stable probability distribution, for instance, ensues that the likelihood of a given percentage variation in price will remain constant each period.[3] By nature of symmetry, the additional assumption of normality is also significant in that implies the probability of price increases and decreases is equal in each period as well. When modelling asset returns according to the assumption of normality, the magnitude of price changes may not be known a priori. In most practical applications, the solution to this problem is to assume that ε_t is standard normally distributed such that $\varepsilon_t \sim$ i.i.d. $N(0,1)$. Imposing a standard normal distribution assumes there is a known and finite variance on the magnitude of price changes ε_t. A well-known feature of these processes is that approximately 95% of all price changes are observed to be within ± 2 standard deviations of the mean change in price.

The time-series properties of the natural logarithm of inter-day returns $\ln(P_t/P_{t-1})$ over the whole sample period for the seven emerging Asian stock markets considered herein are presented in Table 2a and for the Asian and global financial crises periods in Tables 2b and 2c respectively. Following from Mitton (2002, p. 223) we define the Asian crisis period as running from 2 July 1997 – corresponding to the devaluation of the Thai baht – to 31 August 1998 – the date after which the Asian stock indices began a sustained upward trend. We similarly defined the dates for the global financial crisis according to the timeline established by the Bank for International Settlements (2009, p. 2) as the start of Q3/2007 through to the end of Q1/2009.

The sample means of inter-day returns for all markets reported in Table 2a are slightly positive, but not significantly different to zero. The Shanghai A 30 (China) recorded the highest mean return over the 1 January 1980 to 31 March 2010 period (0.000637), and the Bangkok S.E.T the lowest mean return (0.000206). The sum of ln returns for a standard Brownian motion process should be approximately zero since long-run gains tend to equal losses. Indicative of the long-run growth in these markets, the sum of ln returns for all the emerging markets in Table 2a is positive however, implying that returns in these markets may be better described by a sub-martingale process with mean expected returns greater than zero.

Non-parametric runs tests are conducted to provide initial indications of the degree of randomness in the inter-day ln returns for each emerging market. For α levels above the critical value, the runs test p-value determines

Table 2a. Whole Sample Period Emerging Markets Descriptive Statistics.

	China	India	Indonesia	Korea	Sri Lanka	Taiwan	Thailand
Start of period	2/01/1991	2/01/1991	4/04/1983	2/01/1980	2/01/1985	2/01/1980	2/01/1980
End of period	31/03/2010	31/03/2010	31/03/2010	31/03/2010	31/03/2010	31/03/2010	31/03/2010
Count	5,030	5,030	7,052	7,901	6,595	7,901	7,901
Mean	6.37E-04	5.01E-04	4.74E-04	3.39E-04	5.64E-04	3.42E-04	2.06E-04
Standard deviation	0.0252	0.0168	0.0156	0.0165	0.0109	0.0178	0.0150
Skewness	5.5421	−0.3497	2.7436	−0.2683	0.9537	0.0264	−0.1392
Kurtosis	145.7111	7.9735	87.2727	6.8851	34.1487	8.7375	9.0155
Maximum	−0.1791	−0.1432	−0.2253	−0.1737	−0.1390	−0.1966	−0.1606
Minimum	0.7192	0.1503	0.4031	0.1128	0.1829	0.1991	0.1135
Sum of ln returns	3.2017	2.5181	3.3424	2.6801	3.7184	2.7027	1.6279
Index points							
Start of period	128.8	353.4	102.0	119.0	96.1	542.7	149.4
End of period	3,109.1	4,313.3	2,777.3	1,692.9	3,724.6	7,920.1	787.9
Index point gain (loss)	2,980.3	3,959.9	2,675.3	1,573.9	3,628.5	7,377.4	638.5
Runs test (*p*-value)	0.000	0.000	0.000	0.000	0.000	0.000	0.000
Anderson–Darling (*p*-value)	<0.005	<0.005	<0.005	<0.005	<0.005	<0.005	<0.005
Ryan–Joiner (*p*-value)	<0.010	<0.010	<0.010	<0.010	<0.010	<0.010	<0.010

Table 2b. Asian Crisis Period Emerging Markets Descriptive Statistics.

	China	India	Indonesia	Korea	Sri Lanka	Taiwan	Thailand
Start of period	2/07/1997	2/07/1997	2/07/1997	2/07/1997	2/07/1997	2/07/1997	2/07/1997
End of period	31/08/1998	31/08/1998	31/08/1998	31/08/1998	31/08/1998	31/08/1998	31/08/1998
Count	305	305	305	305	305	305	305
Mean	−2.73E-04	−8.47E-04	−2.46E-03	−2.87E-03	−1.53E-03	−1.05E-03	−2.95E-03
Standard deviation	0.0160	0.0158	0.0286	0.0319	0.0097	0.0159	0.0264
Skewness	−0.9191	−0.0570	0.1965	0.2264	−0.9776	−0.2473	0.9872
Kurtosis	5.4829	1.6844	3.5965	1.2406	3.1784	2.0907	3.0316
Maximum	−0.0873	−0.0578	−0.1273	−0.1160	−0.0536	−0.0681	−0.1003
Minimum	0.0633	0.0629	0.1313	0.1002	0.0259	0.0555	0.1135
Sum of ln returns	−0.0834	−0.2584	−0.7495	−0.8768	−0.4679	−0.3211	−0.8993
Index points							
Start of period	1,199.1	774.3	730.2	777.3	805.3	8,996.7	568.8
End of period	1,150.2	589.5	342.4	310.2	597.3	6,550.1	214.5
Index point gain (loss)	(48.9)	(184.8)	(387.8)	(467.1)	(208.0)	(2446.6)	(354.3)
Runs test (*p*-value)	0.080	0.014	0.000	0.045	0.000	0.276	0.016
Anderson–Darling (*p*-value)	<0.005	<0.005	<0.005	<0.005	<0.005	<0.005	<0.005
Ryan–Joiner (*p*-value)	<0.010	<0.010	<0.010	<0.010	<0.010	<0.010	<0.010

Table 2c. Global Financial Crisis Period Emerging Markets Descriptive Statistics.

	China	India	Indonesia	Korea	Sri Lanka	Taiwan	Thailand
Start of period	3/09/2007	3/09/2007	3/09/2007	3/09/2007	3/09/2007	3/09/2007	3/09/2007
End of period	31/03/2009	31/03/2009	31/03/2009	31/03/2009	31/03/2009	31/03/2009	31/03/2009
Count	412	412	412	412	412	412	412
Mean	−1.91E-03	−1.17E-03	−1.03E-03	−1.07E-03	−1.05E-03	−1.32E-03	−1.54E-03
Standard deviation	0.0252	0.0241	0.0209	0.0221	0.0110	0.0191	0.0185
Skewness	0.0707	−0.4751	−0.5787	−0.3495	0.0498	−0.2139	−0.7529
Kurtosis	1.2406	2.2079	5.0863	4.6590	6.2429	0.9474	6.6749
Maximum	−0.0804	−0.1159	−0.1095	−0.1117	−0.0511	−0.0674	−0.1109
Minimum	0.0903	0.0680	0.0762	0.1128	0.0534	0.0610	0.0755
Sum of ln returns	−0.7880	−0.4808	−0.4254	−0.4401	−0.4334	−0.5445	−0.6337
Index points							
Start of period	5,321.1	3,746.3	2,213.6	1,881.8	2,525.3	8,979.9	820.2
End of period	2,373.2	2,294.9	1,434.1	1,206.3	1,638.1	5,210.8	431.5
Index point gain (loss)	(2947.9)	(1451.4)	(779.5)	(675.5)	(887.2)	(3769.1)	(388.7)
Runs test (*p*-value)	0.200	0.006	0.013	0.619	0.000	0.517	0.580
Anderson–Darling (*p*-value)	<0.005	<0.005	<0.005	<0.005	<0.005	<0.005	<0.005
Ryan–Joiner (*p*-value)	<0.010	<0.010	<0.010	<0.010	<0.010	<0.010	<0.010

if there is sufficient evidence to conclude that the inter-day returns are not random. The test accepts randomness of inter-day returns for all series at the 0.01 level of confidence.

Inter-day returns in all markets are non-Gaussian for the whole sample period, owing to kurtosis in the return distributions of all markets and significant positive skewness in the Chinese and Indonesian markets in particular. Kurtosis generally implies that a higher level of the observed variance in these markets is due to infrequent extreme deviations from the mean, as opposed to frequent smaller deviations. An intuitive explanation of the observed positive skewness concerns the asymmetric price response to good versus bad news and indicates that participants in these markets may tend to overvalue good news and undervalue bad news. Both the Anderson–Darling and Ryan–Joiner *p*-values reject the null hypothesis of normality for the return distributions in all markets. This result is not surprising since leptokurtic, non-normal distributions are common in financial time series (Pagan, 1996). Taken in conjunction with the results already described, the overall finding is that while the null hypothesis that inter-day emerging market returns for the whole sample period are independent cannot be conclusively rejected, there is overwhelming evidence that the distribution of returns in all markets is highly non-Gaussian.

Compared to findings for the whole sample period just described, findings for both the Asian crisis period and global financial crisis period show the relative impacts of the crises on emerging Asian market returns.

Mean returns and the sum of ln emerging market returns are negative during both the Asian and global financial crisis periods. Relative to the Asian crisis period, return losses are larger (more negative) for China, India and Taiwan during the global financial crisis period. The fact that these markets represent three of the four biggest emerging economies of those under observation highlights the differential impacts of the crises – notably that the Asian crisis was more significant for the smaller less internationally integrated markets in the region and that the global financial crisis was more significant for larger internationally integrated markets. Relative differences in the sum of ln returns across the Asian and global financial crisis periods confirm this result.

Indicative of the findings for the larger emerging Asian markets, Fig. 1a–c graphically demonstrate the varying impacts of the two crises periods on the distribution of Shanghai SE Composite inter-day returns. In Fig. 1a, the positive skewness of the distribution of whole sample period returns is clearly evident, as are the large number of price changes outside of the ± 4 S.D. range. Returns during the Asian crisis period in Fig. 1b are

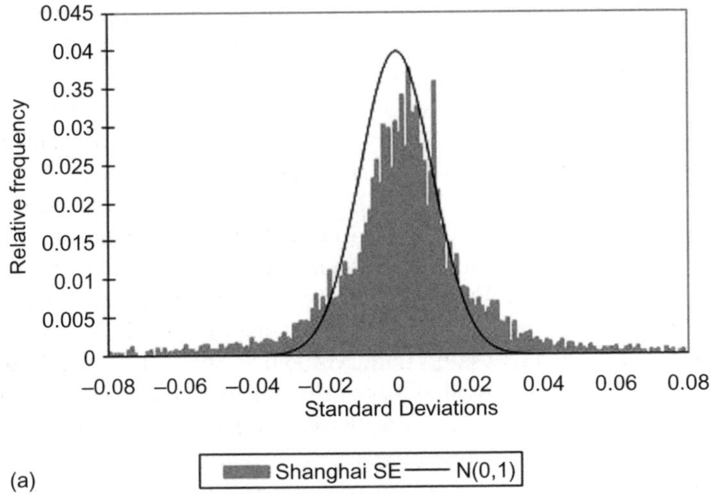

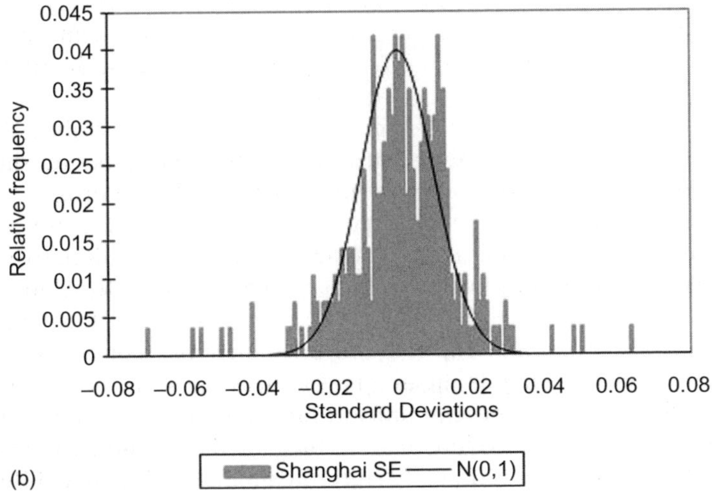

Fig. 1. (Continued)

comparatively more normal than during either the whole sample period or global financial crisis, as shown in Fig. 1c. While returns in Fig. 1b and c are clearly more symmetric than in Fig. 1a for the whole sample period, Shanghai SE Composite inter-day returns during the global financial crisis

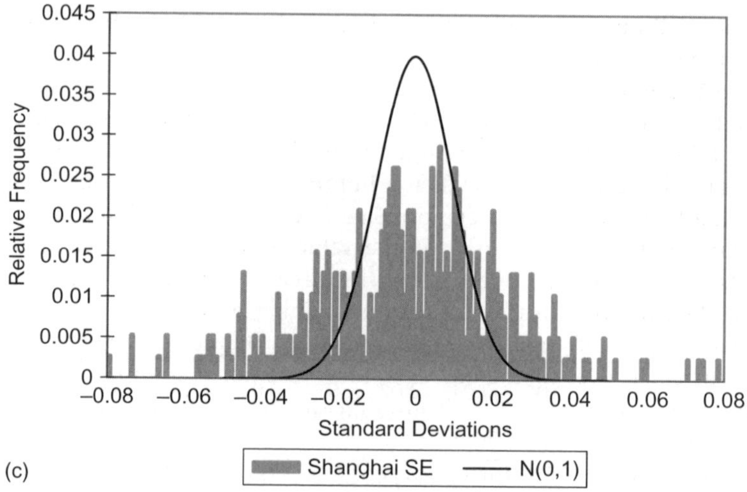

Fig. 1. (a) Distribution of Shanghai SE Whole Sample Period Inter-Day Returns. (b) Distribution of Shanghai SE Asian Crisis Period Inter-Day Returns. (c) Distribution of Shanghai SE Global Financial Crisis Period Inter-Day Returns.

period are more widely dispersed around the mean – indicative of significantly higher volatility during the period.

Non-parametric runs tests reject the independent null at the 0.01 level of confidence for all inter-day returns series except Indonesia and Sri Lanka during the Asian crisis period and India and Sri Lanka during the global financial crisis period.

Consistent with results for the whole sample period, the Anderson–Darling and Ryan–Joiner *p*-values again both reject the null hypothesis of normality for the return distributions in all markets during both the Asian and global financial crisis periods. Excess skewness and kurtosis levels during both periods are however significantly lower for all emerging Asian markets.

An alternate measure of the goodness-of-fit of the normal distribution to emerging Asian market inter-day return is to determine the number of observed versus predicted returns by magnitude. It is well known for instance that approximately 68% of all price changes are observed to be within ± 1 standard deviation of the mean change in price under a normal distributed and approximately 95% within ± 2 standard deviations of the mean. Using this information we can calculate the expected number of price changes at all intervals and compare this to the actual number of observed price changes per interval.

Using Shanghai SE Composite inter-day returns to illustrate this process in detail, Table 3a shows the observed and predicted number of percentage returns $(P_t - P_{t-1})/P_{t-1}$, at each interval in the range 1% to >13% for the whole sample period. The predicted number of returns at each interval is calculated first using the observed mean and standard deviation [$N(\mu,\sigma)$] of inter-day returns in column 3 of the table. Column 4 of the table then predicts the expected number of returns at each level assuming a standard normal distribution with zero mean and unit standard deviation [$N(0,1)$]. The last column of the table gives the ratio of the observed number of returns at each level to the corresponding predicted number of returns in column 3. Ratio values <1 indicate that the observed number of returns is less than the predicted number. Conversely, ratio values >1 indicate that the actual number of returns exceeds the predicted number. Where the predicted number of returns is equal to zero at 30 decimal places, the ratio of observed to predicted returns in the table is indeterminate and is denoted IND.

It can be seen from Table 3a that both of the normal distribution $N(\mu,\sigma)$, and the standard normal distribution $N(0,1)$, are reasonable approximations

Table 3a. Observed versus Predicted Returns by Magnitude: Shanghai SE Composite Whole Sample Period.

±	Observed	$N(\mu,\sigma)$	$N(0,1)$	Observed/$N(\mu,\sigma)$
1%	2870	3168.055	3443.486	0.906
2%	1106	636.068	1370.056	1.739
3%	522	497.579	215.843	1.049
4%	214	342.175	13.296	0.625
5%	124	206.852	0.317	0.599
6%	70	109.924	0.003	0.637
7%	44	51.350	0.000009937815	0.857
8%	27	21.086	0.000000012902	1.280
9%	18	7.611	0.000000000000	2.365
10%	16	2.415	0.000000000000	6.625
11%	8	0.674	0.000000000000	11.877
12%	6	0.165	0.000000000000	36.337
13%	5	0.036	0.000000000000	140.529
>13%	10	0.000000000000	0.000000000000	IND

IND: Normal prediction = 0, therefore cannot be determined.

Table 3b. Observed versus Predicted Returns by Magnitude: Shanghai SE Composite Asian Crisis Period.

±	Observed	$N(\mu,\sigma)$	$N(0,1)$	Observed/$N(\mu,\sigma)$
1%	178	223.343	206.855	0.797
2%	79	48.637	81.404	1.624
3%	32	22.355	12.926	1.431
4%	3	6.964	0.796	0.431
5%	5	1.470	0.019	3.403
6%	3	0.210	0.000172541650	14.292
7%	2	0.020	0.000000595126	98.607
8%	0	0.00132	0.000000000773	0.000000000000
9%	1	0.000058411866	0.000000000000	17119.809
10%	0	0.000001738124	0.000000000000	0.000000000000
11%	0	0.000000034871	0.000000000000	0.000000000000
12%	0	0.000000000471	0.000000000000	0.000000000000
13%	0	0.000000000004	0.000000000000	0.000000000000
>13%	–	–	–	–

for the distribution of Shanghai SE Composite inter-day returns up to ±7% as the ratio of the observed to Gaussian is near 1.[4] The poor fit of the normal distribution is apparent, however, by the fact that over 10% of all percentage price changes are greater than ±3%. The standard normal distribution predicts that only about 2.7% of all price changes should be greater than ±3% for the Shanghai SE Composite.

Analysing the number of observed versus predicted returns by magnitude for the Shanghai SE Composite during the Asian and global financial crisis periods in Tables 3b and 3c respectively, we find that the normal and standard normal distributions – $N(\mu,\sigma)$ and $N(0,1)$ – overestimate the number of very small price changes (in the 1–2% range) and underestimate the number of large price changes (greater than 3%).

The ratio of observed to predicted percentage returns for all emerging Asian stock markets for the whole sample period is provided in Table 4a, using the same method as described for the last column of Tables 3a–3c above. Ratios for these emerging Asian markets during the Asian and global financial crisis periods are provided in Tables 4b and 4c, respectively.

Consistent with findings already described for the Shanghai SE Composite, ratios in Tables 4a–4c demonstrate the overall poor fit of the normal distribution to inter-day percentage price changes in emerging Asian

Table 3c. Observed versus Predicted Returns by Magnitude: Shanghai SE Composite Global Financial Crisis Period.

±	Observed	$N(\mu,\sigma)$	$N(0,1)$	Observed/$N(\mu,\sigma)$
1%	169	278.521	280.585	0.607
2%	90	52.063	110.759	1.729
3%	66	37.239	17.548	1.772
4%	40	22.816	1.080	1.753
5%	23	11.973	0.025	1.921
6%	9	5.382	0.00023	1.672
7%	5	2.072	0.000000807952	2.413
8%	6	0.683	0.000000001049	8.781
9%	1	0.193	0.000000000001	5.182
10%	2	0.047	0.000000000000	42.852
11%	0	0.00967	0.000000000000	0.000000000000
12%	0	0.00171	0.000000000000	0.000000000000
13%	0	0.00026	0.000000000000	0.000000000000
>13%	0	–	–	–

Table 4a. Comparative Fit of the Normal Distribution, N(μ,σ): Emerging Asian Markets Whole Sample Period.

±	1%	2%	3%	4%	5%	6%	7%	8%	9%	10%	>10%
China	0.91	1.74	1.05	0.63	0.60	0.64	0.86	1.28	2.36	6.63	188.74
India	0.84	1.47	1.13	1.18	2.02	5.56	21.62	130.84	555.77	4,087	357,032,445
Indonesia	1.02	1.00	0.67	0.75	1.90	5.20	25.92	316.85	1,195	46,913	3,189,482,285
Korea	0.85	1.38	1.11	1.34	2.81	7.84	35.70	260.80	2,455	7,446	1,456,280,663
Sri Lanka	1.02	0.80	1.00	3.00	28.06	634.75	54,061	8,381,903	658,784,678	IND	IND
Taiwan	0.84	1.43	1.12	1.17	1.89	4.75	21.40	19.69	225.37	2,507	328,253
Thailand	0.90	1.23	1.04	1.45	2.90	12.29	98.06	1,268	34,629	477,867	1,072,040,880

IND: Normal prediction = 0, therefore cannot be determined.

stock markets. For all the emerging markets under observation, we find that the normal and standard normal distributions overestimate the number of very small price changes and underestimate the number of large price changes. Relative to the whole sample period findings, the misestimation is more pronounced during the Asian crisis period for all markets and most pronounced during the global financial crisis period for the larger emerging Asian markets.

Table 4b. Comparative Fit of the Normal Distribution, $N(\mu,\sigma)$: Emerging Asian Markets Asian Crisis Period.

±	1%	2%	3%	4%	5%	6%	7%	8%	9%	10%	>10%
China	0.80	1.62	1.43	0.43	3.40	14.29	98.61	0.00	17,120	0.00	0.00
India	0.72	1.89	1.54	1.73	3.81	10.86	57.04	0.00	0.00	0.00	0.00
Indonesia	0.66	1.74	1.56	1.25	2.07	1.17	2.11	2.50	2.22	13.35	172.62
Korea	0.63	1.54	1.46	1.52	1.74	1.97	2.89	2.42	4.30	0.00	28.27
Sri Lanka	0.86	1.69	4.52	12.06	0.00	66,329	0.00	0.00	IND	IND	IND
Taiwan	0.74	1.76	1.65	1.75	2.30	16.27	56.53	0.00	0.00	0.00	0.00
Thailand	0.58	1.90	1.91	2.12	1.00	2.12	2.87	0.00	10.45	38.96	2451.11

IND: Normal prediction = 0, therefore cannot be determined.

Table 4c. Comparative Fit of the Normal Distribution, $N(\mu,\sigma)$: Emerging Asian Markets Global Financial Crisis Period.

±	1%	2%	3%	4%	5%	6%	7%	8%	9%	10%	>10%
China	0.61	1.73	1.77	1.75	1.92	1.67	2.41	8.78	5.18	42.85	0.00
India	0.65	1.56	1.81	1.73	1.25	2.79	4.27	2.06	0.00	0.00	441.52
Indonesia	0.78	1.74	1.04	0.99	1.81	2.21	7.03	43.97	0.00	0.00	8,630
Korea	0.68	1.97	1.36	1.30	1.37	1.92	4.40	13.91	0.00	151.36	12,324
Sri Lanka	0.95	0.90	1.92	6.49	135.07	3,005	0.00	0.00	0.00	IND	IND
Taiwan	0.70	1.62	1.62	2.18	2.48	4.91	8.50	0.00	0.00	0.00	0.00
Thailand	0.75	1.89	1.12	1.55	1.54	2.29	34.10	54.33	0.00	8,278	158,414

IND: Normal prediction = 0, therefore cannot be determined.

3. DEPENDENCE AND NONLINEAR CYCLES IN EMERGING ASIAN STOCK MARKET RETURNS

Summarising some of the commonly observed behaviours in statistical finance, Bouchaud (2002, p. 239) notes the following 'stylised facts' about financial time-series data:

- return distributions are highly non-normal and
- although small degrees of autocorrelation may be observed over a period of a few days, consecutive intra-day price changes are generally independent beyond about 10 minutes in liquid markets.

Having already dealt with the distributional characteristics of emerging Asian stock market returns in the previous section, a further analysis of the independence of inter-day returns will now be considered.

Empirically, many studies find that heavy-tail-distributed financial asset returns also exhibit evidence of long-term dependence (Racheva-Iotova & Samorodnitsky, 2003). Early studies investigating long-term dependence in emerging versus developed Asian markets include Howe, Martin, and Wood (1999) and Di Matteo, Aste, and Dacorogna (2005). More recent studies that find evidence of long-term dependence in emerging Asian stock markets focus largely on the Chinese and Korean exchanges and include Kang and Yoon (2007, 2008), Los and Yu (2008) and Kang, Cheong, and Yoon (2010).

Two commonly employed techniques are employed to investigate the presence of long-term dependence in emerging Asian market inter-day returns: the classical rescaled adjusted range statistic developed by Hurst (1951), and the Lo (1991) modification to eliminate low-order or short-term dependence. First proposed by Hurst (1951) the classical rescaled adjusted range $(R/\sigma)_n$ is calculated as

$$(R/\sigma)n = (1/\sigma_n)\left[\underset{1\leq k\leq n}{\mathrm{Max}}\sum_{j=1}^{k}(X_j - \overline{X_n}) - \underset{1\leq k\leq n}{\mathrm{Min}}\sum_{j=1}^{k}(X_j - \overline{X_n})\right] \tag{1}$$

where σ_n is the series standard deviation

$$\sigma_n = \left[\frac{1}{n}\sum_{j}^{n}(X_j - M_n)^2\right]^{0.5} \tag{2}$$

and M_n is the sample mean $(1/n)\Sigma_j X_j$.

For a given series of length N, empirical estimates of the rescaled adjusted range are derived by firstly dividing the series length into subseries n of length $n \leq N$.

Being non-parametric in nature, one advantage of the classical rescaled adjusted range is that the statistic is robust to time series with significant third and fourth moments (Mandelbrot & Wallis, 1969) and to stochastic processes with infinite variance (Mandelbrot, 1972). It will be remembered that high degrees of either/or/both skewness and kurtosis have been observed in the distributions of the emerging Asian stock market returns under observation herein. Mandelbrot and Wallis (1968) suggest that a further advantage of the classical rescaled adjusted range is the statistic's ability to detect non-periodic cycles of a length longer than the underlying sample length. For time series containing either positive or negative dependence, one estimate of the length of the underlying cycle is the V-statistic:

$$V_n = \frac{(R/\sigma)_n}{n^{0.5}} \tag{3}$$

where $(R/\sigma)_n$ is the classical rescaled range as defined in Eq. (2).

Independent processes will exhibit a horizontal V-statistic plot. For series containing positive long-term dependence, the plot of the V-statistic versus the log of the subseries length, n will be upward sloping. For series anti-persistent (negative long-term dependent) series, the V-statistic plot will be downward sloping. A change in the direction of the slope of the V-statistic is indicative of the end of one cycle, and subsequent commencement of the next cycle.

The classical rescaled adjusted range may be biased, however, by non-stationarity in the underlying returns and structured short-term dependence, the latter of which may be accounted for by the modified rescaled range.[5]

The modified rescaled range Q_n is defined by Lo (1991) as

$$\begin{aligned}
\sigma_n^2(q) &\equiv \frac{1}{n}\sum_{j=1}^{n}(X_j - \bar{X}_n)^2 + \frac{2}{n}\sum_{j=1}^{q} w_j(q)\left\{\sum_{j=1}^{n}(X_j - \bar{X}_n)(X_{i-j} - \bar{X}_n)\right\} \\
&= \sigma_x^2 + 2\sum_{j=1}^{q} w_j(q)H\hat{\gamma}_j \\
w_j(q) &\equiv 1 - \frac{j}{(q+1)}
\end{aligned} \tag{4}$$

for $1 \leq k \leq n$ and $q < n$.

By comparison with Hurst's original specification for the classical rescaled adjusted range, Lo's determination of the modified rescaled range in Eq. (4) may be seen to be equivalent to Eq. (2) except for replacement of the observed sample standard deviation σ_n, with the denominator $\sigma_n(q)$, which represents the variance of the series σ_x^2, plus the weighted autocovariance $w_j(q)\gamma$ for various values of the lag q:

$$V_n(q) \equiv \frac{1}{\sqrt{n}} Q_n \tag{5}$$

Critical values for the statistical significance of $V_n(q)$ are provided by Lo (1991). The 95% critical value of the modified rescaled range is $P(V < v) = 1.747$ for all values of the lag q. Values of $V_n(q)$ greater than

Table 5a. Whole Sample Period Emerging Markets Modified Rescaled Range.

Lag (q)	0	10	12	20	30	60	90	120	180	270	360
China	1.4288	1.2773	1.2758	1.2403	1.2180	1.1754	1.1791	1.1972	1.2209	1.1291	1.1328
India	1.7813*	1.5404	1.5197	1.4352	1.3879	1.3399	1.3360	1.3264	1.3011	1.3245	1.4075
Indonesia	1.7733*	1.4266	1.4153	1.3543	1.2954	1.2403	1.2359	1.2354	1.2162	1.1531	1.1092
Korea	1.4249	1.4125	1.4109	1.3801	1.3399	1.2880	1.2739	1.2559	1.2153	1.1712	1.1858
Sri Lanka	2.6886*	1.9719*	1.9387*	1.8262*	1.7490*	1.6126	1.5427	1.4939	1.4626	1.4443	1.4667
Taiwan	1.7596*	1.5803	1.5563	1.4759	1.4299	1.3589	1.3278	1.3090	1.3159	1.3224	1.3028
Thailand	1.7917*	1.5339	1.5147	1.4373	1.3937	1.3295	1.3014	1.3130	1.3248	1.2823	1.2641

*Significant at the 95% level.

Table 5b. Asian Crisis Period Emerging Markets Modified Rescaled Range.

Lag (q)	0	10	12	20	30	60	90	120	180	270	360
China	1.2837	1.3586	1.3940	1.4555	1.5897	1.5769	1.6341	1.8661*	2.5450*		–
India	1.3244	1.2155	1.1881	1.1556	1.1687	1.2511	1.4830	1.9497*	170.6925*	6.0639*	–
Indonesia	1.5088	1.4572	1.4421	1.3913	1.3560	1.5400	1.7041	1.8528*	3.1702*		–
Korea	1.1782	1.2588	1.2601	1.2268	1.1719	1.2307	1.8059*	9.5627*	5.0022*		–
Sri Lanka	2.0643*	1.3489	1.2997	1.2210	1.1821	1.2157	1.1853	1.2787	1.6304	1.3150	–
Taiwan	1.4019	1.3639	1.3471	1.2832	1.2489	1.3180	1.4862	1.7084	2.2984*	2.6146*	–
Thailand	1.2358	1.0681	1.0386	0.9623	0.9251	0.9635	1.0587	1.2745	1.3636	1.2541	–

*Significant at the 95% level.

the critical value will indicate that the series under observation exhibits long-term dependence.

Modified rescaled range statistics for the emerging Asian stock markets for the whole sample period 1 January 1980 to 31 March 2010 are provided in Table 5a and for the Asian crisis and global financial crisis periods in Tables 5b and 5c, respectively. Values of the modified rescaled range $V_n(q)$ are calculated for lengths of the autocovariance lag $q = 0$, 10, 20, 30, 60, 90, 120, 180, 270 and 360.

Results pertaining to the modified rescaled range statistic in Table 4a provide overall support for the null hypothesis of no long-term dependence during the whole sample period for all the emerging markets under observation except Sri Lanka, which shows significant evidence of dependence up to 30 lags with $V_n(q)$ values in excess of the 0.05 level critical value $P(V < v) = 1.747$. Relative to the whole sample period results,

Table 5c. Global Financial Crisis Period Emerging Markets Modified Rescaled Range.

Lag (q)	0	10	12	20	30	60	90	120	180	270	360
China	1.4985	1.4956	1.5110	1.5305	1.5891	1.5946	1.5096	1.4358	1.5587	2.2350*	
India	1.5939	1.4962	1.4995	1.4356	1.4045	1.4539	1.5499	1.5215	1.7564*	1.8614*	
Indonesia	1.7207	1.5419	1.5995	1.5617	1.4666	1.3940	1.3814	1.4218	1.5906	1.8697*	
Korea	1.2863	1.3056	1.3388	1.4313	1.4672	1.5769	1.7125	1.7986*	2.6279*	3.2379*	
Sri Lanka	1.8129*	1.4535	1.4162	1.3081	1.2332	1.2186	1.3042	1.3822	1.4561	1.5593	1.6984
Taiwan	1.6651	1.6802	1.6886	1.5843	1.4949	1.3950	1.3720	1.4204	1.8853*	3.6458*	
Thailand	1.7529*	1.6646	1.6709	1.5934	1.5728	1.5429	1.5730	1.5584	1.7808*	2.0630*	2.7199*

*Significant at the 95% level.

findings for all emerging markets except Sri Lanka reject the no long-term dependence null at lags greater than $q=90$ during the Asian crisis period and greater than $q=120$ during the global financial crisis period. The findings highlight the impact of the crises periods on the long-run independence of inter-day emerging market returns, which may be seen to be highly (nonlinearly) correlated in the long run.

Evidence of non-periodic cycles in emerging Asian stock market returns will provide additional evidence of long-term dependence in these markets. V-statistics for the whole sample period for each emerging market under observation and corresponding bootstrap values are provided in Table 6a. Bootstrap values of the V-statistic are generated from simulated Gaussian returns and are employed to test the significance of departures of the observed V-statistics from their expected value. Significance is herein determined using a simple z-score type analysis incorporating the observed V-statistic, Gaussian mean V-statistic and the standard deviation of mean V-statistic (not reported). Used in this way the V-statistic may be considered as a proxy measure of the level of local dependence in the underlying series in so far as a change from a run of consecutive significant V-statistic values to a run of insignificant V-statistics should be indicative of the end of the current cycle. The significance test just described is used herein in conjunction with a graphical approach to identify cycle lengths from the V-statistic.

An example of the plot of the V-statistic for the Indian S&P CNX stock index is provided in Fig. 2 where the x-axis corresponds to V-statistic, and the y-axis to the log of the subseries length, n. The approximate cycle for the S&P CNX is shown in Fig. 2 to start at 89 days and run to at least 4,539 days (approximately $n=1.9$ to $n=3.7$ on the log scale), indicating the period in between to be the approximate number of days during which the

Table 6a. Whole Sample Period Emerging Markets V-Statistic.

V-statistic (n)	China	India	Indonesia	Korea	Sri Lanka	Taiwan	Thailand	Gaussian
56	1.2441	1.4134*	1.3837*	1.1497	1.4899*	1.2331	1.3497*	1.1253
63	1.3051*	1.3864*	1.4407*	1.2193	1.4320*	1.2554	1.3528*	1.1318
71	1.3215*	1.3823*	1.4230*	1.1844	1.4661*	1.2538	1.3374*	1.1397
80	1.3480*	1.3009*	1.4696*	1.1779	1.4943*	1.3761*	1.4089*	1.1473
89	1.3495*	1.2704	1.5052*	1.1589	1.5227*	1.3295*	1.3878*	1.1544
100	1.3627*	1.2861	1.4717*	1.1397	1.5851*	1.3062*	1.3715*	1.1579
110	1.3797*	1.3296*	1.4452*	1.1517	1.5627*	1.2814	1.3804*	1.1615
125	1.3811*	1.3778*	1.5227*	1.2149	1.6090*	1.2946	1.3940*	1.1678
142	1.3405*	1.3649*	1.6012*	1.2105	1.6199*	1.2964	1.3389*	1.1719
158	1.3920*	1.4100*	1.5565*	1.2198	1.6755*	1.3053*	1.3307*	1.1753
178	1.4986*	1.4281*	1.5620*	1.1618	1.6994*	1.3381*	1.4184*	1.1778
224	1.4209*	1.4253*	1.6829*	1.2723	1.6482*	1.4110*	1.4800*	1.1860
252	1.4626*	1.4247*	1.7333*	1.2567	1.7304*	1.3607*	1.5093*	1.1892
282	1.5462*	1.4093*	1.7061*	1.2609	1.8384*	1.4142*	1.4664*	1.1932
316	1.5003*	1.4542*	1.7530*	1.2713	1.8603*	1.3711*	1.4781*	1.1969
354	1.4574*	1.5526*	1.6840*	1.2318	1.9631*	1.3522*	1.4531*	1.1991
400	1.2864	1.6281*	1.6486*	1.2491	1.9896*	1.3863*	1.4272*	1.2018
450	1.3145	1.7036*	1.6287*	1.2863	2.0204*	1.4736*	1.5315*	1.2037
500	1.3307	1.7227*	1.7459*	1.3499*	2.2403*	1.5361*	1.6767*	1.2057
563	1.3872*	1.7233*	1.8784*	1.3684*	2.2154*	1.5529*	1.5476*	1.2102
630	1.4599*	1.7493*	1.9092*	1.3591*	2.1715*	1.5454*	1.5394*	1.2137
710	1.4993*	1.7711*	1.8966*	1.3368	2.2530*	1.5144*	1.5734*	1.2158
800	1.5488*	1.7601*	1.9013*	1.3248	2.1746*	1.5508*	1.7240*	1.2175
890	1.5215*	1.7697*	2.0103*	1.3795	2.2130*	1.5270*	1.7298*	1.2192
1,000	1.5323*	1.7658*	2.1203*	1.4084*	2.2484*	1.4930*	1.7764*	1.2213
1,152	1.5177*	1.6807*	2.0160*	1.4399*	2.2272*	1.5317*	1.7072*	1.2229
1,322	1.5052*	1.7234*	1.9926*	1.5289*	2.2289*	1.4740*	1.7753*	1.2268
1,536	1.4942*	1.7771*	1.8858*	1.6594*	2.2624*	1.4697*	1.8062*	1.2305
1,768	1.5304*	1.7513*	1.9128*	1.6447*	2.2814*	1.5341*	1.7667*	1.2321
2,048	1.5564*	1.7610*	1.8519*	1.6547*	2.3976*	1.6132*	1.8624*	1.2363
2,390	1.5322*	1.7373*	1.7910*	1.6313*	2.4758*	1.5943*	1.8506*	1.2385
2,793	1.5559*	1.5761*	1.7425*	1.5977*	2.7048*	1.6109*	1.9158*	1.2438
3,274	1.4666	1.6115*	1.7765*	1.6127*	2.8553*	1.5667*	1.9920*	1.2463
3,850	1.3650	1.8010*	1.7591*	1.6319*	2.9300*	1.5205	2.0353*	1.2485
4,539	1.2709	1.6354*	1.8724*	1.5847*	2.9373*	1.5622	2.0861*	1.2467

*Significant at the 95% level.

series exhibits long-term dependence, after which time it dissipates and a new cycle commences.

V-statistic estimates for the whole sample period and the Gaussian mean values are provided in Table 6a and for the Asian crisis period and global financial crisis period in Tables 6b and 6c, respectively.

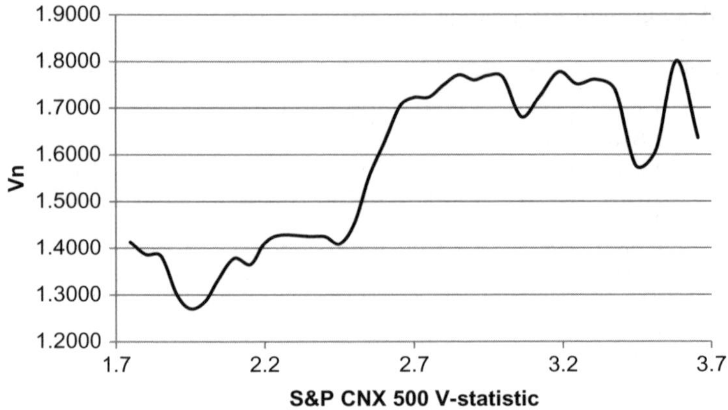

Fig. 2. S&P CNX (India) V-Statistic Plot.

Table 6b. Asian Crisis Period Emerging Markets V-Statistic.

V-statistic (*n*)	China	India	Indonesia	Korea	Sri Lanka	Taiwan	Thailand	Gaussian
56	1.0984	1.3385*	1.3122*	1.0756	1.7321*	1.2687*	1.3150*	1.1253
63	1.1103	1.3701*	1.2441	1.0557	1.7701*	1.2788*	1.3151*	1.1318
71	1.1115	1.3864*	1.2769*	1.0854	1.7295*	1.3864*	1.3602*	1.1397
80	1.0845	1.3707*	1.3246*	1.0900	1.7116*	1.3747*	1.3750*	1.1473
89	1.1620	1.3630*	1.3512*	1.1419	1.7735*	1.3980*	1.4110*	1.1544
100	1.1419	1.3733*	1.3376*	1.2022	1.7874*	1.4106*	1.4733*	1.1579
110	1.1339	1.4444*	1.3010*	1.2436	1.8694*	1.3899*	1.4736*	1.1615
125	1.1279	1.5247*	1.2666	1.3263*	1.9497*	1.4227*	1.4667*	1.1678
142	1.1169	1.4714*	1.2784	1.4255*	2.0033*	1.3886*	1.5548*	1.1719
158	1.0881	1.5180*	1.3036	1.4034*	2.1346*	1.4226*	1.5905*	1.1753
178	1.0569	1.5891*	1.2794	1.3912*	2.2279*	1.4770*	1.5851*	1.1778
224	1.0499*	1.5413*	1.2985	1.3326*	2.3308*	1.4813*	1.4956*	1.1860
252	1.1485	1.4553*	1.2618	1.2787	2.2350*	1.4586*	1.4317*	1.1892
282	1.2056	1.3962*	1.4364*	1.2160	2.1852*	1.4542*	1.3995*	1.1932

*Significant at the 95% level.

Analysis of the significance of the V-statistics in Table 6a for the whole sample period from 1 January 1980 to 31 March 2010 reveals evidence of non-periodic cycles in all the emerging markets under observation. For the Indonesian, Sri Lankan and Thai markets in particular, the length of these cycles is seen to be at least as long as the sample period given the V-statistic

Table 6c. Global Financial Crisis Period Emerging Markets V-Statistic.

V-statistic (n)	China	India	Indonesia	Korea	Sri Lanka	Taiwan	Thailand	Gaussian
56	1.1226	1.1813	1.2143	1.1515	1.2511	1.0779	1.2258	1.1253
63	1.0724	1.1496	1.2414	1.1276*	1.3040	1.0926	1.2782*	1.1318
71	1.0983	1.1995	1.2583	1.1724	1.2660	1.0967	1.2814*	1.1397
80	1.0406	1.2665	1.2466	1.1584*	1.2988	1.1187	1.2539	1.1473
89	1.0357	1.2946*	1.2843*	1.1729*	1.3504	1.1605	1.3146*	1.1544
100	0.9991*	1.2637	1.2402	1.1481*	1.3990	1.1403	1.3352*	1.1579
110	1.0137*	1.3270*	1.2646	1.1681*	1.5030	1.1821	1.3753*	1.1615
125	0.9861*	1.2738	1.3156*	1.1835*	1.5364	1.2130	1.4271*	1.1678
142	0.9993*	1.2694	1.3063	1.2023*	1.5478	1.2550	1.4443*	1.1719
158	1.0309*	1.2694	1.3503*	1.2921*	1.5676	1.3051	1.4486*	1.1753
178	1.0038*	1.2581	1.3405*	1.2534*	1.5931*	1.3303*	1.4890*	1.1778
224	0.9735*	1.2825	1.3610*	1.2328*	1.6244*	1.4523*	1.5061*	1.1860
252	0.9932*	1.2553	1.4274*	1.2655*	1.6986*	1.5085*	1.5598*	1.1892
282	1.0324*	1.1851	1.4643*	1.2276*	1.7615*	1.5095*	1.6445*	1.1932
316	1.1595	1.2185	1.5078*	1.2472*	1.8123*	1.5350*	1.6908*	1.1969
354	1.2500	1.3045	1.5358*	1.2361*	1.8184*	1.5069*	1.6934*	1.1991
400	1.4374*	1.5275*	1.6761*	1.2831*	1.7764*	1.6581*	1.7535*	1.2018

*Significant at the 95% level.

is significant for all subseries lengths n. The Chinese, Indian and Taiwanese markets all show evidence of multiple cycles during the whole sample period. Compared to Howe, Martin and Wood (1999) who find cycle lengths of 114 and 1,292 trading days for Taiwan for the period 1981–1994, we find cycles of 80 and 3,274 days duration, respectively. Time-varying dependence, such as that identified by Cajueiro and Tabak (2005) in the volatility of emerging stock market returns – including Taiwan – may be seen to be one explanation for the difference in our findings compared to those previously of Howe, Martin, and Wood. Differences in sample periods for the two studies may also account for the contrary findings.

Relative to the finding just described for the whole sample period, results in Tables 6b and 6c for the Asian and global financial crises periods, respectively, show varying cycle lengths. The emerging markets of India, Sri Lanka, Taiwan and Thailand for instance all show evidence of cycle lengths at least as long as the Asian crisis period in Table 6b and commencing cycles of between 80 and 178 days during the global financial crisis period in Table 6c. As already inferred, either/or/both of the time-varying nature of dependence and the different time and length of the sample periods may account for the differences in these findings. Taken in conjunction, however, with previously discussed findings, the positive evidence of non-periodic cycles presented here confirms the non-Gaussian and non-independent nature of emerging Asian stock market returns. Our findings serve to question the applicability of standardised models of financial asset pricing and risk analysis in emerging markets.

NOTES

1. Owing to data availability, returns data for all the emerging markets is not available for the entire sample period. Specific beginning-of-sample dates and number of observations for each market are provided in Table 2a.

2. Given specific values of the moments of the distribution (μ and σ), the stability of the distribution and independence of successive price changes, the returns generating process may be defined as either a Wiener process, strict random walk, or standard Brownian motion.

3. Detailed facts about stable distributions and their characteristics are discussed in Nolan (2003).

4. While it is known that 0.99999999999 of the area under a normal curve is within ± 7 standard deviations of the mean, the smallest measurable change in price for most financial assets is only 1/100 of one cent, or 0.0001. Henceforth in most practical financial applications, price changes outside of ± 4 standard deviations of the mean (0.9999 of the area under a normal curve) are not usually considered.

5. Dickey–Fuller and augmented Dickey–Fuller tests conducted on the inter-day returns for each market, though not reported here, confirm mean stationarity in each series.

REFERENCES

Bank for International Settlements. (2009). The international financial crisis: Timeline, impact and policy responses in Asia and the Pacific. Available at http://www.bis.org/repofficepubl/arpresearch200908.2.htms

Bouchaud, J. (2002). An introduction to statistical finance. *Physica A*, *313*, 238–251.

Cajueiro, D. O., & Tabak, B. M. (2005). Testing for time-varying long-range dependence in volatility for emerging markets. *Physica A*, *346*, 577–588.

Di Matteo, T., Aste, T., & Dacorogna, M. M. (2005). Long-term memories of developed and emerging markets: Using the scaling analysis to characterize their stage of development. *Journal of Banking & Finance*, *29*, 827–851.

Fama, E. F. (1965). The behavior of stock market prices. *Journal of Business*, *38*, 34–105.

Howe, J. S., Martin, D. W., & Wood, B. G., Jr. (1999). Much ado about nothing: Long-term memory in Pacific rim equity markets. *International Review of Financial Analysis*, *8*, 139–151.

Hurst, H. E. (1951). Long term storage capacity of reservoirs. *Transactions of the American Society of Civil Engineers*, *116*, 770–799.

Kang, S. H., Cheong, C., & Yoon, S. (2010). Long memory volatility in Chinese stock markets. *Physica A*, *389*, 1425–1433.

Kang, S. H., & Yoon, S. (2007). Long memory properties in return and volatility: Evidence from the Korean stock market. *Physica A*, *385*, 591–600.

Kang, S. H., & Yoon, S. (2008). Long memory features in the high frequency data of the Korean stock market. *Physica A*, *387*, 5189–5196.

Lo, A. W. (1991). Long-term memory in stock market prices. *Econometrica*, *59*, 1279–1313.

Los, C. A., & Yu, B. (2008). Persistence characteristics of the Chinese stock markets. *International Review of Financial Analysis*, *17*, 64–82.

Mandelbrot, B. B. (1972). Statistical methodology for nonperiodic cycles: From the covariance to R/S analysis. *Annals of Economic and Social Measurement*, *1*, 259–290.

Mandelbrot, B. B., & Wallis, J. R. (1968). Noah, Joseph and operational hydrology. *Water Resources Research*, *4*, 909–918.

Mandelbrot, B. B., & Wallis, J. R. (1969). Robustness of the rescaled range R/S in the measurement of noncyclic long-run statistical dependence. *Water Resources Research*, *5*, 967–988.

Mitton, T. (2002). A cross-firm analysis of the impact of corporate governance on the East Asian financial crisis. *Journal of Financial Economics*, *64*, 215–241.

Nolan, J. P. (2003). Modeling financial data with stable distributions. In: S. T. Rachev (Ed.), *Handbook of heavy tailed distributions in finance*. Amsterdam: Elsevier Science Publishing Company.

Pagan, A. (1996). The econometrics of financial markets. *Journal of Empirical Finance*, *3*, 15–102.

Racheva-Iotova, B., & Samorodnitsky, G. (2003). Long range dependence in heavy tailed stochastic processes. In: S. T. Rachev (Ed.), *Handbook of heavy tailed distributions in finance*. Amsterdam: Elsevier Science Publishing Company.

Standard and Poor's. (2007). The S&P emerging market indices. Methodology, definitions, and practices. Available at http://www2.standardandpoors.com/spf/pdf/index/

ELASTICITIES OF STOCK PRICES IN EMERGING MARKETS: A PANEL DATA APPROACH

Luiz Paulo Lopes Fávero and Fernando Barreira Sotelino

ABSTRACT

While differences in stock price behaviours among developed countries have been extensively researched and documented, investigations of this nature for emerging economies are, however, much less comprehensive. We undertake a quantitative analysis that investigates six different types of panel data models to define the best one that explains the stock price behaviour of publicly traded companies in emerging countries. The research is based on a sample from Compustat Global, including 5,167 stocks of companies from 38 emerging countries, covering 119 months (1998–2007), totalling 235,621 observations. This analysis of the elasticities of regressors corresponding to stock transactions in stock markets, through a considerable sample, contributes to a deeper discussion about stock price behaviour in countries with less developed stock markets. The findings demonstrate that stock quantity and total volume traded per month significantly influence closing price behaviour over time, with more efficient estimators for the fixed effect model. Moreover, different elasticities are verified among countries. This chapter

The Impact of the Global Financial Crisis on Emerging Financial Markets
Contemporary Studies in Economic and Financial Analysis, Volume 93, 473–493

ISSN: 1569-3759/doi:10.1108/S1569-3759(2011)0000093017

does not take into account the macroeconomic reasons why the differences among countries occur. Further, the consideration of developed countries, such as United States, United Kingdom, France or Australia, could bring the possibility of comparison of stock prices among countries in a broader perspective. Overall this analysis can help governments and private initiative for the formulation and implementation of strategic actions, in order to constantly improve the quality of their stock markets and, consequently, to increase the entry of resources destined to the development of nations.

Keywords: Elasticity; stock prices; emerging markets; panel data.

JEL Classification: C5; C58; E44; F3; G15.

1. INTRODUCTION

Many authors (King & Levine, 1993; Levine, 1997; Rajan & Zingales, 1998, 2003; Roe & Siegel, 2009) have suggested that a sound domestic financial system is critical for a country's sustainable economic development.

Adjasi and Biekpe (2009) go further to propose that stock market development is a fundamental pillar of financial development in emerging economies as it provides for, both, a most important signalling system for efficient capital allocation and source of permanent capital for investment by the firms.

Differences in stock price behaviours among developed countries have been extensively researched and documented (Bondt, 2008). Investigations of this nature for emerging economies are, however, much less comprehensive. Important works include Islam (1995), Kwon, Shin and Bacon (1997), Lee (1997), Tsoukalas (2003), Karim and Guan (2004), Al-Khazali and Pyun (2004), Ziramba (2007), Benetti and Fávero (2008), Makina (2008), Valadkhani and Chancharat (2008), Al-Khazali (2008), Rutledge, Zhang, and Karim (2008), Valadkhani, Chancharat, and Havie (2009) and Huang, Liu, and Lin (2009). Table A.1 summarizes the main contributions of each of these studies.

This study makes use of a panel data approach to investigate how stock quantities and trade volumes influence monthly closing prices in stock exchanges of emerging economies. Data models with different estimators are utilized to attempt to answer the following two questions: (i) how do the stock prices of publicly traded companies in emerging countries react to stock quantity and to volume traded each month? and (ii) is there a 'country effect' on stock price elasticities? For this purpose, a *Compustat Global* sample from 38 countries was statistically examined from a temporal perspective, through a period of 119 months (1998–2007).

Section 1 presents a diagnosis of the stock price evolution of companies in these 38 emerging countries, focusing on variations over time or within variations, as well as on between variations. Section 2 presents a review of the on-panel data monitoring and its estimators. Sections 3 and 4 address sampling, variable definition, variance decomposition for each regressor and the proposed model. Section 5 presents and discusses the empirical results. Conceptual inferences and suggestions for further empirical work are presented in the last section.

2. MONTHLY EVOLUTION IN STOCK PRICES OF PUBLICLY TRADED COMPANIES LISTED ON STOCK EXCHANGES IN EMERGING COUNTRIES

Initially, it is specified that the performance variable adopted in this research refers to the natural logarithm of the stock's monthly closing price (in dollars), which belongs to the most traded class of each of the 5,167 publicly traded companies listed on the stock exchanges of the 38 countries considered as emerging (lnprice). Due to the possibility of considerable variation in original prices among companies, the application of the natural logarithm favours a distribution with a stronger trend towards normality during the study period, as shown in Graphs 1, 2 and 3.

In the period 1998–2007, many companies presented expressive growth rates in stock prices during one or more months. However, as Graph 1 reveals, the logarithm of these companies' stock prices reveals similar behaviour over time, despite occasional differences in means and inclinations among individual series.

Each point in Graph 1 represents a stock–month pair. This behaviour suggests the elaboration of longitudinal models and, according to Cameron and Trivedi (2009), many of these microeconometric methods emphasize the existence of correlation over time for individual data, with mutual independence. However, in different cases, like models that consider data from companies active in the same countries, correlations can occur between

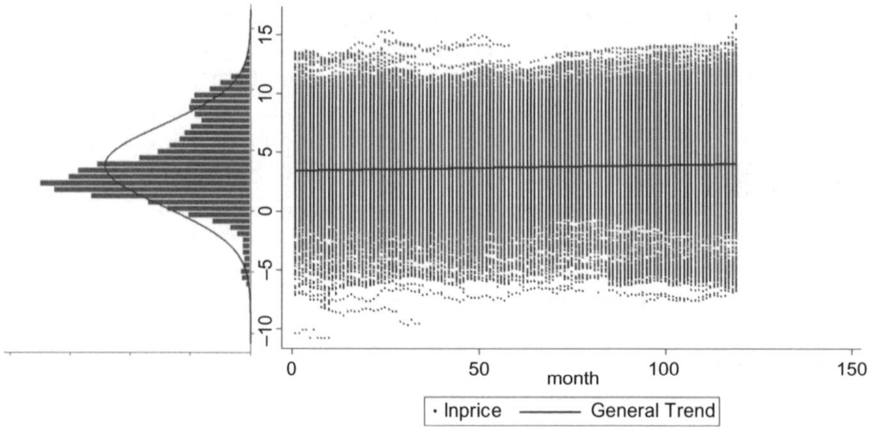

Graph 1. Evolution in Natural Logarithm of Stock Prices of Companies Active in Emerging Countries.

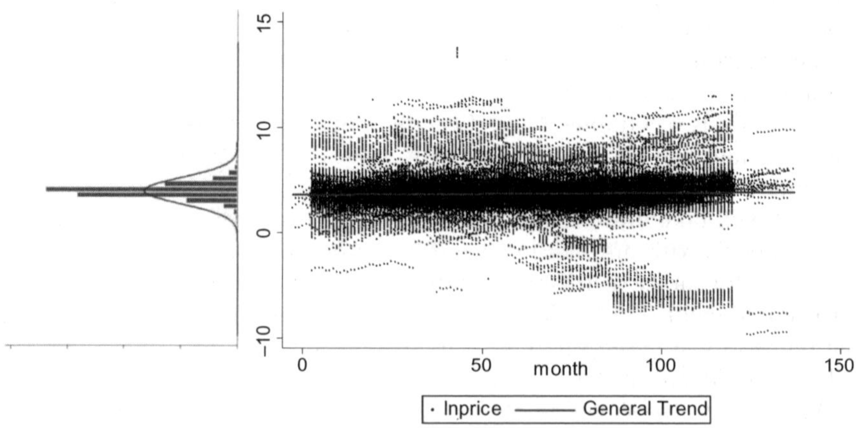

Graph 2. Within Variation in Natural Logarithm of Stock Prices over Time.

companies, as shown in Graph 2. Hence, it is usually necessary to elaborate corrections in the models' standard errors through the application of more consistent panel data estimators.

The justification to adopt panel data models in this research is also related to the fact that part of stock price behaviour can be invariable over time, while another part, as an occasional general trend, can be invariable among

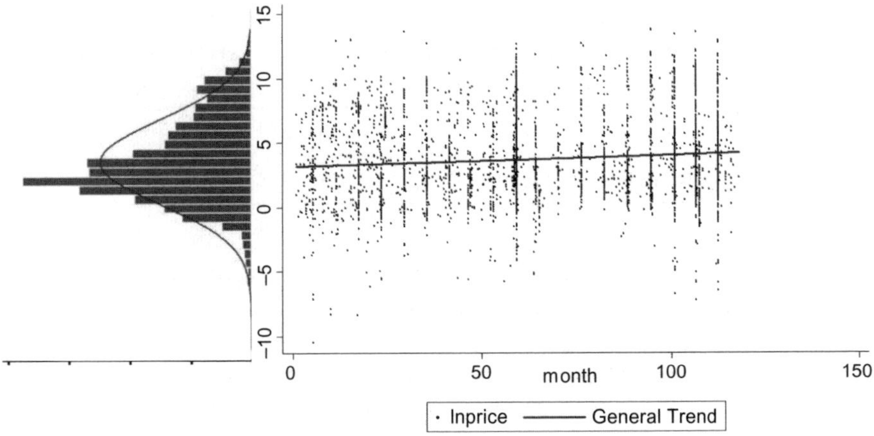

Graph 3. Between Variation in Natural Logarithm of Stock Prices.

companies. A representative part of price behaviour, though, can vary among companies and over time. While Graph 2 shows the within variation in the logarithm of stock prices over time, Graph 3 presents the between variation of these indicators.

The analysis of Graphs 2 and 3 suggests that the effects of time for each company and for each country influence stock prices differently. Section 4 presents the within and between variations of each of the regressors this research will take into account. As discussed further ahead and considered in the models with different types of estimators, the panel data models can permit endogenous regressors, due to the existence of correlation with an error component that is invariable over time (fixed effects), or assume that the regressors are completely exogenous (random effects). Both estimators will be considered in this chapter.

With a view to providing more solid foundations to propose the model adopted in this research, initially, tests for *k* independent samples (Kruskal–Wallis test) are elaborated in order to assess whether stock price distributions over time are equal among companies from the 38 countries. As the premises for the elaboration of a one-way ANOVA are violated for the distributions of each country's indices over time, the use of the Kruskal–Wallis test is justified. Table 1 shows the result of this test.

The results presented in Table 1 reveal differences among the stock price logarithm distributions of companies in this research, which justifies the use of panel data models to investigate the influences of variables related to the

Table 1. Diagnosis to Check for Equality of Natural Logarithm Distributions of Stock Prices among Companies from Different Countries.

Comparison	Chi-square (χ^2)	df	Sig.
Among companies from different countries	1.53×10^5	37	0.000

stock quantities and total volume traded on this behaviour. In other words, there is no propensity towards the existence of idiosyncratic tendencies in the sample, which could result from stock prices' systematic behaviours among countries over time. Therefore, the existence of different price elasticities is expected for stock prices of companies from different countries over time.

3. PANEL DATA MODELS

Many different models can be used for panel data. According to Greene (2007), the basic distinction is the existence of fixed or random effects. The term 'fixed effects' gives a mistaken idea of the model as, for both cases, the individual- (in this case the company) level effects are random. Hence, according to Cameron and Trivedi (2009), the fixed effects models present the additional complication that the regressors are correlated with the effects of the individual-level effects and, therefore, a consistent estimate of the model parameters demands the elimination or control of fixed effects. Hence, a model that takes into account the individual's specific effects for a dependent variable y_{it} specifies that:

$$y_{\text{it}} = \beta_{0i} + x'_{\text{it}}\beta_1 + \varepsilon_{\text{it}} \tag{1}$$

in which x_{it} are regressors, β_{0i} the individual specific random effects and ε_{it} the idiosyncratic error.

Two different models can derive from Eq. (1). In the fixed effects model, the β_{0i} terms can be correlated with the regressors x_{it}, which permits a limited form of endogeneity. Making the error term $\mu_{\text{it}} = \beta_{0i} + \varepsilon_{\text{it}}$ and allowing x_{it} to be correlated with the error term invariable over time (β_{0i}), it is assumed that x_{it} is not correlated with the idiosyncratic error ε_{it}. The fixed effects model implies that $E(y_{\text{it}}|\beta_{0i}, x_{\text{it}}) = \beta_{0i} + x'_{\text{it}}\beta_1$, assuming that $E(\varepsilon_{\text{it}}|\beta_{0i}, x_{\text{it}}) = 0$, so that $\beta_j = \partial E(y_{\text{it}}|\beta_{0i}, x_{\text{it}})/\partial x_{j,\text{it}}$. The advantage of the fixed effects model is that a consistent estimator of the marginal effect of the

jth regressor of $E(y_{it}|\beta_{0i}, x_{it})$ can be obtained, given that $x_{j,it}$ varies over time, even if the regressors were endogenous (with a limited form of endogeneity).

In the random effects model, on the other hand, it is assumed that β_{0i} is purely random, that is it is not correlated with the regressors. Therefore, the estimation is elaborated with a feasible generalized least squares (FGLS) estimator. The advantage of the random effects model is that it estimates all coefficients, even of regressors that do not vary over time and, hence, the marginal effects. Moreover, $E(y_{it}|x_{it})$ can be estimated. The main advantage, however, is that these estimators are inconsistent if the fixed effects model is more appropriate.

As discussed, the dependent variable and the regressors can vary simultaneously over time and among individuals. While the variation over time or for a given individual is known as within variance, the variation between individuals is called between variance. According to Wooldridge (2002), in the fixed effects model, the coefficient of a regressor with low within variance will be estimated imprecisely and will not be identified if there is no within variance whatsoever. Hence, distinguishing between these variances is of fundamental importance to define the best panel data model.

Overall variance (around the general mean $\bar{x} = 1/\sum_i T_i \sum_i \sum_t x_{it}$) can be decomposed into within variance over time for each individual (around the individual mean $\bar{x} = 1/T \sum_t x_{it}$) and between variance among individuals (for $\bar{x}$ around $\bar{x}_i$). According to Cameron and Trivedi (2009), the decomposition of this variance is as follows:

Within variance: $s_W^2 = \frac{1}{\sum_i T-1} \sum_i \sum_t (x_{it} - \bar{x}_i)^2 = \frac{1}{\sum_i T-1} \sum_i \sum_t (x_{it} - \bar{x}_i + \bar{x})^2$

Between variance: $s_B^2 = \frac{1}{N-1} \sum_i (\bar{x}_i - \bar{x})^2$

Overall variance: $s_O^2 = \frac{1}{\sum_i T-1} \sum_i \sum_t (x_{it} - \bar{x})^2$

where N and $\sum_i T$ correspond, respectively, to the number of individuals and the total number of individual-time observations. In Section 4, the variances in each of the regressors to be considered in the research models are presented and discussed. The graphs shown in Section 1 express the overall (Graph 1), within (Graph 2) and between (Graph 3) variances.

Also according to Cameron and Trivedi (2009), the estimators of the β_1 parameters of a fixed effects model for Eq. (1) eliminate the fixed effects β_{0i}, that is a transformation within is elaborated through the distinction among means. Thus, a within estimation elaborates an ordinary least squares (OLS) model with data distinguished around the mean and, as the observations of an invariable regressor over time with differentiation around the mean are zero, the coefficient of a regressor that does not vary over time cannot be estimated. On the other hand, as a within estimator offers a consistent estimate for the fixed effects model, it is frequently called fixed effects estimator.

Hence, the fixed effects β_{0i} in Eq. (1) can be eliminated by subtracting the means of each individual $\bar{y}_i = \bar{x}'_i\beta_1 + \bar{\varepsilon}_i$ in the corresponding model, resulting either in the within model or the model of differences of means:

$$(y_{\text{it}} - \bar{y}_i) = (x_{\text{it}} - \bar{x}_i)'\beta_1 + (\varepsilon_{\text{it}} - \bar{\varepsilon}_i) \tag{2}$$

where $\bar{x}_i = T_i^{-1}\sum_{t=1}^{T_i} x_{\text{it}}$ and the within estimator is the OLS estimator of this model. According to Cameron and Trivedi (2009), due to the fact that β_{0i} has been eliminated, the OLS estimator offers consistent estimates of β_1, even if β_{0i} is correlated with x_{it}, like in the case of the fixed effects model.

The between estimator uses only cross-section variation and is the OLS estimator of a regression of $\bar{y}_i$ in function of $\bar{x}_i$, presented next (Eq. 3). Due to considering only cross-section data variations, the coefficients of any regressor invariable among individuals cannot be identified.

$$\bar{y}_i = \beta_0 + \bar{x}_i'\beta_1 + (\beta_{0i} - \beta_0 + \bar{\varepsilon}_i) \tag{3}$$

The consistency of this estimator requires no correlation between the error term $(\beta_{0i} - \beta_0 + \bar{\varepsilon}_i)$ and x_{it}, which occurs when β_{0i} is a random effect, but not when it is a fixed effect. According to Hsiao (2003), this estimator is rarely used, as the estimators of random effects end up being more consistent.

The random effects estimator, on the other hand, is an FGLS estimator in Eq. (1), based on the hypothesis that the random effect β_{0i} and the idiosyncratic error ε_{it} are independent and identically distributed (i.i.d.). Hence, the random effects model is the individual effects model:

$$y_{\text{it}} = x_{\text{it}}'\beta_1 + (\beta_{0i} + \varepsilon_{\text{it}}) \tag{4}$$

with $\beta_{0i} \sim (\beta_0, \sigma_\alpha^2)$ and $\varepsilon_{\text{it}} \sim (0, \sigma_\mu^2)$. Thus, the error term $\mu_{\text{it}} = \beta_{0i} + \varepsilon_{\text{it}}$ is correlated over time t, for a given observation i, with correlation:

$$\text{corr}(\mu_{\text{it}}, \mu_{\text{is}}) = \frac{\sigma_\alpha^2}{(\sigma_\alpha^2 + \sigma_\varepsilon^2)}, \quad \text{for any } s \neq t \tag{5}$$

The random effects estimator is the FGLS estimator of β_1 in Eq. (4), given the error correlations in Eq. (5).

According to Cameron and Trivedi (2009), in models with heteroscedastic errors and AR(1), the FGLS estimator can be calculated as an OLS estimator in a transformed model, so as to obtain non-correlated homoscedastic errors. Hence, the random effects estimator can be obtained through the OLS estimation of the following transformed model:

$$(y_{\text{it}} - \hat{\theta}_i \bar{y}_i) = (1 - \hat{\theta}_i)\beta_0 + (x_{\text{it}} - \hat{\theta}_i \bar{x}_i)'\beta_1 + \{(1 - \hat{\theta}_i)\beta_{0i} + (\varepsilon_{\text{it}} - \hat{\theta}_i \bar{\varepsilon}_i)\} \quad (6)$$

in which $\hat{\theta}_i$ is a consistent estimate of

$$\theta_i = 1 - \sqrt{\frac{\sigma_\varepsilon^2}{(T_i \sigma_\alpha^2 + \sigma_\varepsilon^2)}}$$

The random effects estimator uses within and between variances for the data model, in which within estimation is a special case when $\hat{\theta}_i = 1$. This estimator will be consistent and completely efficient if the random effects model is appropriate, but will be inconsistent if the fixed effects model is appropriate, as the correlation between x_{it} and β_{0i} results in a correlation between the regressors and the error term in Eq. (6).

Likewise, according to Cameron and Trivedi (2009), if there are no fixed effects but the errors demonstrate correlation inside the panel, then the random effects estimator will be consistent but inefficient and, therefore, an estimate with robust clusterized standard errors will have to be obtained. Hence, for a short panel, like in this research ($t = 119$ months and $n = 5{,}167$ companies, that is, $t < n$), an estimate can be obtained with robust clusterized standard errors by adopting the premise that errors are independent between individuals and that $N \rightarrow \infty$, that is, that $E(\varepsilon_{\text{it}}, \varepsilon_{\text{js}}) = 0$ for $i \neq j$, that $E(\varepsilon_{\text{it}}, \varepsilon_{\text{is}})$ is unrestricted and that ε_{it} is heteroscedastic.

According to Cameron and Trivedi (2009), a starting point for the panel data model is the application of the pooled ordinary least squares (POLS) model, which assumes that regressors are exogenous and that the error is μ_{it}, instead of the decomposition $\alpha_i + \varepsilon_{\text{it}}$. Hence:

$$y_{\text{it}} = \beta_0 + x'_{\text{it}}\beta_1 + \mu_{\text{it}} \quad (7)$$

This model's parameters are estimated through OLS, but the inference requires control of error μ_{it}'s within correlation for a given individual, to be elaborated by using robust standard errors grouped at individual level.

After presenting the panel data model, it is specified that this research will apply six different types of models to obtain a better understanding of the different types of estimators, and also to present the best model to explain the stock price behaviour of publicly traded companies in emerging countries from a longitudinal perspective, in function of the monthly stock transaction characteristics in the respective stock markets. Table A.2 presents the models that will be elaborated.

4. SAMPLING AND VARIABLE DEFINITION

The stock prices of publicly traded companies in each emerging country, as well as the stock quantities and monthly trade volumes, were collected from the *Compustat Global* database. Initially, data were extracted for all sets of companies available in the database, covering the period from 1998 to 2007. The original base included 235,621 observations.

Due to the characteristic of the stock market itself, the database offers an unbalanced panel (different periods for each observation). Moreover, the transformation of the dependent variable into the natural logarithm made some observations get lost (because some are too small) when panel data models were applied. Also, observations from companies with any missing data for the regressors or the dependent variable were eliminated. Finally, the criteria attempted to avoid indetermination in the allocation of different effects caused by the presence of less than two cases in each factor, that is only companies that presented two or more periods of the dependent variable were maintained.

The final sample for the panel data models comprised 227,199 observations for 4,111 companies from 38 countries. This treatment offers an advantage when using panel data models, as these permit studying the regressors' effects on the dependent variable for each separate country over time.

The performance variable adopted for the analysis refers to the logarithm of the monthly closing price of the most traded stock (in dollars) for each company in each country. The variables related to the capital market transactions, that is corresponding to the regressors of the panel data models, are shown in Table A.3.

5. VARIANCE DECOMPOSITION AND THE PROPOSED MODEL

The panel data model is based on the existence of overall, within and between variances in each regressor, as discussed earlier. Table 2 displays the variance decomposition for each of the regressors.

Table 2. Panel Statistics and Decomposition of Overall, Within and Between Variance.

Variable	Decomposition	Mean	Standard Deviation	Minimum	Maximum	Observations
Company	Overall					n.t = 227,199;
	Between					n = 4,111
	Within		0.000			
Month	Overall		35.673	1.000	119.000	n.t = 227,199;
	Between		34.279	5.500	119.000	n = 4,111
	Within		26.520	−3.709	164.734	
lnshare	Overall	5.573	2.313	−5.006	15.721	n.t = 225,815;
	Between		2.268	−2.992	15.721	n = 4,109
	Within		0.565	−3.557	13.665	
lnvalue	Overall	5.840	3.955	−9.210	22.121	n.t = 220,053;
	Between		3.760	−6.712	18.444	n = 3,944
	Within		1.591	−9.440	20.466	

Since the company is invariable over time, its within variation is equal to zero. The time variable (month), however, is not invariable among individuals; since this is a strongly unbalanced panel, its between variation is not equal to zero and is higher than the within variation. The between variation of the panel regressors is higher than the within variation, but it cannot be affirmed yet that the within estimate will result in an efficiency loss, as the proportion between the within and between variances of each variable is different and the statistical significances of each of the models are not known yet. Table 2 also offers further foundations to adopt the panel data models and apply different estimators. Columns 'Minimum' and 'Maximum' present, respectively, the minimum and maximum values of x_{it} for the 'overall' line, $\bar{x}_i$ for the 'between' line and $x_{\mathrm{it}} - \bar{x}_i + \bar{x}$ for the 'within' line.

As discussed in Section 2 and summarized in Table A.2, six panel data models will be elaborated, with different considerations about the estimators and error terms. The general model will be as follows:

$$\text{lnprice}_{it} = \beta_{0i} + \beta_1(\text{lnvalue}) + \beta_2(\text{lnvalue}) + \varepsilon_{\mathrm{it}} \tag{8}$$

in which β_1 and β_2 represent the elasticities of the quantity of stocks traded and the amount traded in dollars, respectively, ceteris paribus. This model helps to verify the hypothesis that the monthly stock quantity and value traded explain the variation in the stock prices of publicly traded companies in emerging countries over time.

6. RESULTS

Table 3 shows the results of each of the six proposed panel data models.

As it can be observed, estimated coefficients vary from model to model, which reflects the existence of different results if within or between variations are used.

First, higher standard errors exist in the fixed effects and random effects models with robust clusterized standard errors when compared with the respective models without this consideration. Moreover, the estimated regressors in the POLS and between models result in even higher standard errors, despite significant regressor coefficients for all models (sig. <0.01).

As to the adequacy of the models themselves, statistical significance of the set of variables is observed in all cases (sig. F for POLS, between and fixed effects models and sig. Wald χ^2 for random effects models). As R^2 statistics are considerably high in the obtained models, these are relatively adequate for prediction purposes. One important result, however, is related to the existence of higher R^2 between values in all models where this statistic is calculated. Based on the expressions of each of the R^2 statistics

$$R^2\text{overall}: \; \rho^2\{(y_{\text{it}} - \bar{y}_i), (x'_{\text{it}}\hat{\beta} - \bar{x}'_i\hat{\beta})\}$$

$$R^2 \text{ between}: \; \rho^2(\bar{y}_i, \bar{x}'_i\hat{\beta})$$

$$R^2 \text{ within}: \; \rho^2(y_{\text{it}}, \bar{x}'_{\text{it}}\hat{\beta})$$

in which $\rho^2(x,y)$ represents a squared correlation between x and y. It is observed, as presented in Table 2, that the between variation of the panel regressors is greater than the within variation.

Breusch–Pagan's LM test, applied after random effects modelling, helps to reject the null hypothesis of the POLS model's adequacy in relation to the random effects model, as $\chi^2 = 3.8 \times 10^6$ (sig. $\chi^2 = 0.000$). Next, using Chow's F-test, the null hypothesis about the existence of equal intercepts and inclinations for all companies (POLS) was rejected. Therefore, these parameters differ from cross-section parameters (fixed effects), as $F = 154.93$ (sig. $F = 0.000$). Finally, Hausman's test, applied after fixed and random effects modelling, helps to reject the null hypothesis that the random effects model offers consistent parameter estimates as, in this case, $\chi^2 = 1{,}131.62$ (sig. $\chi^2 = 0.000$).

While the coefficient of the variable related to the total quantity of stocks traded per month shows a negative influence on monthly stock closing

Table 3. Panel Data Models.

Variable	POLS Robust Error	Between Estimator	Fixed Effects	Fixed Effects Robust Error	Random Effects	Random Effects Robust Error
lnshare	−0.90663**	−0.92680**	−0.92604**	−0.92604**	−0.92004**	−0.92004**
	(0.00940)	(0.00893)	(0.00275)	(0.02542)	(0.00263)	(0.00433)
lnvalue	0.70243**	0.71039**	0.53021**	0.53021**	0.53612**	0.53612**
	(0.00584)	(0.00542)	(0.00098)	(0.01962)	(0.00096)	(0.00262)
Constant	4.69922**	4.71937**	5.81443**	5.81443**	5.66093**	5.66093**
	(0.06024)	(0.05379)	(0.01626)	(0.10987)	(0.02475)	(0.02753)
N	219,501	219,501	219,501	219,501	219,501	219,501
R^2	0.819	0.852	0.649	0.649		
R^2 (overall)		0.819	0.788	0.788	0.791	0.791
R^2 (between)		0.852	0.823	0.823	0.826	0.826
R^2 (within)		0.639	0.649	0.649	0.649	0.649
F	10,741.08	11,324.34	199,291.15	672.88		
Sig. F	0.000	0.000	0.000	0.000		
Wald χ^2					417,918.83	59,130.77
Sig. χ^2					0.000	0.000

Note: Standard errors between parentheses.
**Sig. <0.01.

prices, the sign of the coefficient related to the value traded is positive. The estimated elasticities of the number of traded stocks and the value traded in dollars are approximately −0.93 and +0.53, respectively.

Thus, these regressors explain the stock price variation of publicly traded companies in emerging countries, which sustains the initial study hypothesis. Given that the between effect is greater than the within effect, next, it is examined whether differences exist in the elasticities of regressors on countries' stock prices. According to Islam (1995), the main utility of panel data modelling is its ability to permit differences among individuals in each country, leading to results that significantly differ from those obtained through isolated regressions for each country. In Table 4, regression coefficients are shown for each of the emerging countries considered in the study.

Table 4 reveals the existence of different elasticities of each regressor on companies' stock prices in each country. The existence of different coefficients for the regressors and for the values of the constant express the importance of considering panel data and call for further research about the economic reasons why emerging countries present different behaviours of their companies' stock prices over time. Figs. 1 and 2 show these different

Table 4. Regressor Coefficients per Country.

Country	lnshare	lnvalue	Cons.	Country	lnshare	lnvalue	Cons.
Argentina	−0.593	0.404	3.368	Nigeria	0.052	0.258	1.310
Bahrain	−0.776	0.108	3.623	Oman	−0.744	0.168	2.792
Brazil	−1.066	0.388	6.469	Pakistan	−0.032	0.256	2.193
Chile	−0.555	0.221	8.224	Peru	−0.299	0.297	2.167
China	−0.310	0.265	2.351	Philippines	−0.783	0.250	6.296
Colombia	−0.289	0.301	7.303	Poland	−0.376	0.255	4.141
Czech Republic	−0.694	0.136	7.269	Portugal	−0.363	0.894	1.660
Egypt	−0.586	0.241	4.493	Qatar	−1.358	0.125	10.037
Emirates	−1.103	0.140	9.076	Russia	−0.707	0.368	6.557
Greece	−0.758	0.836	3.428	Saudi Arabia	−0.724	0.306	6.065
Hungary	−0.537	0.203	8.134	Slovakia	1.463	0.009	4.443
India	−0.624	0.336	5.923	South Africa	−0.711	0.463	4.699
Indonesia	−0.397	0.222	7.373	South Korea	−0.565	0.407	6.922
Israel	−0.721	0.330	5.233	Sri Lanka	−0.079	0.142	3.457
Jordan	−0.340	0.172	1.901	Taiwan	−0.556	0.369	4.085
Kuwait	−0.848	0.092	4.641	Thailand	−0.622	0.197	5.705
Malaysia	−0.360	0.218	2.472	Turkey	−1.029	0.957	3.237
Mexico	−0.341	0.187	4.090	Venezuela	−0.876	0.157	9.890
Morocco	−0.490	0.231	6.772	Zimbabwe	−0.769	0.849	4.528

Obs. 1: Dependent variable lnprice.

Obs. 2: Fixed effects.

behaviours per region, obtained by applying these models separately for each regressor.

Fig. 1 shows different slopes and linear coefficients among countries overall, among countries within a geographic region, and among regions. Through this figure, one can infer that:

(i) while most countries present a decrease in monthly stock closing prices for each unitary increase (one million) in the number of stocks traded per month, ceteris paribus, five of the countries (Poland, Colombia, Zimbabwe, Nigeria and Pakistan) display stock price increases;
(ii) among countries within each geographic region, significant variation in lnshare mean inclination is observed and
(iii) among geographic regions, significantly lower lnshare mean inclination is observed for Africa.

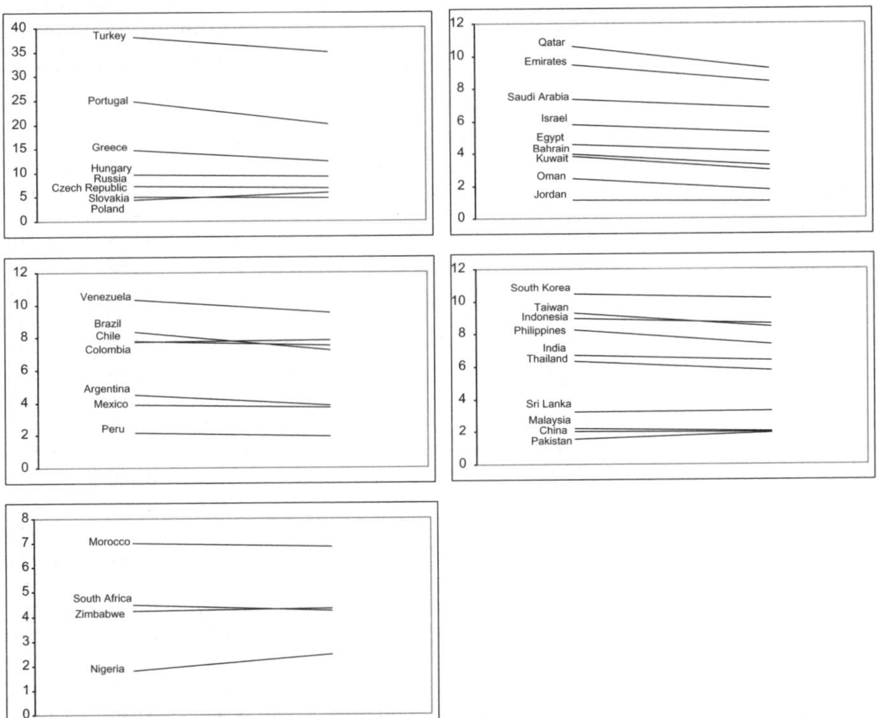

Fig. 1. lnprice (*Y*-axis) Behaviour when Altering One Unit of lnshare (*X*-axis), ceteris paribus, per Country for Each Region.

Fig. 2 reveals that all countries in this study present increases in monthly stock closing prices for each unitary increase (one million dollars) in stocks traded per month, ceteris paribus. As the amount traded results from multiplying the price by the number of stocks traded, a unitary price reduction requires a greater increase in traded quantities, so that the amount in dollars increases.

Conceptual inferences from these findings could be that:

(i) when considered alone, higher number of stocks traded reflects 'sell' tendency in the market, with downward pressure on stock prices;
(ii) higher volume traded (in monetary value) reflects a 'buy' tendency in the market, with an upward pressure on stock prices and

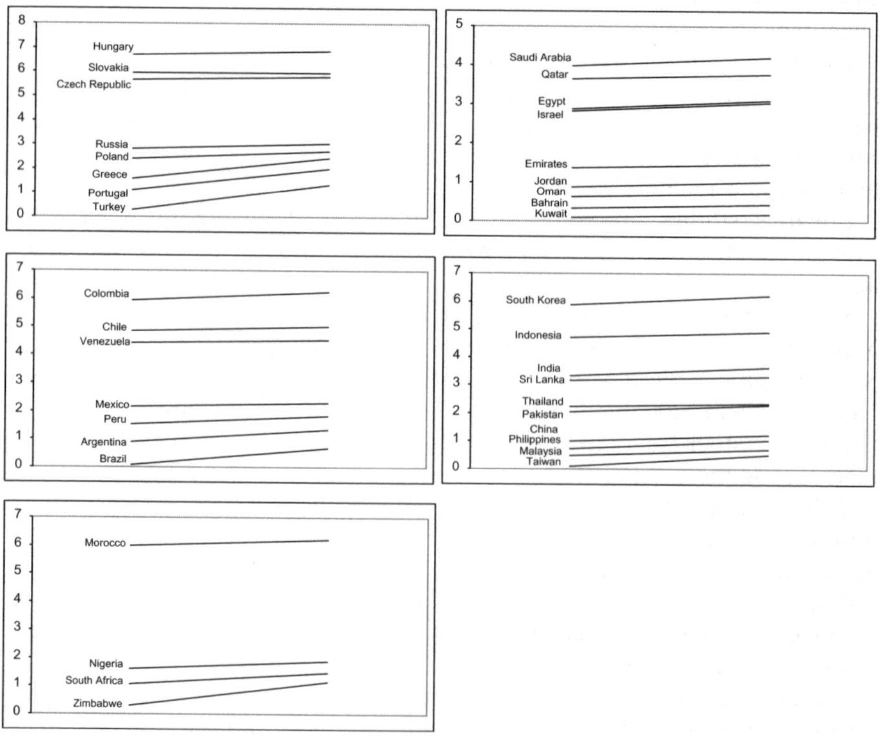

Fig. 2. lnprice (*Y*-axis) when Altering One Unit of lnvalue (*X*-axis), ceteris paribus, per Country for Each Region.

(iii) if greater lnvalue over time could be seen as a proxy for equity capital market development, perhaps as an indicator of market depth, this financial development is, ceteris paribus, a contributor 'per se' to higher stock prices and gains in shareholder wealth.

7. CONCLUSIONS

Econometric techniques are used in many relevant accounting, economics and finance studies whose inferences would have limited validity without them (Barth, Beaver & Landsman, 2001). It is fundamental, however, for the appropriate choice of each statistical technique to be based on an underlying theory and to be in accordance with what one wants to investigate. In this sense, microeconometric tools proliferate in longitudinal studies that aim to create models to explain reality and subject observed phenomena to empirical verification.

Panel data models have been increasingly frequent in the assessment of stock market prices. These models permit one to test the relationship between some performance variable (like the evolution of stock prices) and some predictive variables, allowing the determination of the influences of temporal and regional differences on price evolution.

Previous studies have adopted longitudinal modelling to attempt to explain significant variability in performance variables among companies and countries over time, with empirical researches developed in different areas (Collins, 1990; Mauri & Michaels, 1998; Christmann, Day, & Yip, 1999; Chang & Singh, 2000; Ruefli & Wiggins, 2003; Hawawini, Subramanian, & Verdin, 2004; Makino, Beamish, & Zhao, 2004a; Makino, Isobe, & Chan, 2004b), but it's not common to find longitudinal studies applied to stock markets, considering the differences among them in a macroeconomic perspective.

This research contribution is related to the possible assessment of different estimators when panel data modelling is used, with a view to determining the most adequate model, in function of the characterization of a short panel, and the analysis of the elasticities of regressors corresponding to stock transactions in stock markets arouses a discussion about stock price behaviour in countries with less developed stock markets.

Another contribution refers to estimating the impact of the time variable on stock prices of companies in emerging countries and the comparison of this behaviour among countries. If differences among companies and countries are more significant, then economic and stock market differences should be more focused on the attempt to understand price evolution. If, on the other hand, differences over time explained the largest part of the variance, foreign investors should be less concerned when making decisions about allocating their resources in certain emerging countries instead of others. Since the stock market development is related to the economic situation, the differences among countries can also provide information about the capacity of these economies to maintain the levels of trading, and eventually react, in periods of crisis.

Alternative approaches deserve further study related to stock prices' behaviour over time. Multilevel models with repeated measures can be elaborated, so as to permit investigation of whether differences among countries occur in function of macroeconomic regressors' behaviour. Altering the study period itself can favour a deeper understanding of the mechanisms ruling the performance factors of stock markets in emerging countries. Further, the consideration of developed countries, such as US, UK, France or Australia, could bring one the possibility of comparison of stock prices among countries in a broader perspective.

The subject is really vast and can also be seen as a foundation for governments and private initiative for the formulation and implementation of strategic actions. In this sense, these approaches help one to determine the relative importance of each macroeconomic variable and offer subsidies to the establishment of private initiatives and governmental policies in emerging countries, in order to constantly improve the quality of their stock markets and, consequently, to increase the entry of resources destined to the development of the nations.

REFERENCES

Adjasi, C. K. D., & Biekpe, N. (2009). *Do stock markets matter in investment growth in Africa?*, *43*(1), 109–120.

Al-Khazali, O. M. (2008). The impact of thin trading on day-of-the-week effect. *Review of Accounting and Finance*, *7*(3), 270–284.

Al-Khazali, O. M., & Pyun, C. S. (2004). Stock prices and inflation: New evidence from the Pacific-Basin countries. *Review of Quantitative Finance and Accounting*, *22*(2), 123–140.

Barth, M. E., Beaver, W. H., & Landsman, W. (2001). The relevance of the value-relevance literature for financial accounting standard setting: Another view. *Journal of Accounting and Economics*, *31*(1–3), 77–104.

Benetti, C., & Fávero, L. P. L. (2008). O efeito fim de semana no comportamento dos retornos dos índices de bolsa de valores: uma comparação entre sete países da América Latina e os EUA. *Revista de Economia e Administração*, *7*(3), 268–280.

Bondt, G. J. (2008). Determinants of stock prices: New international evidence. *Journal of Portfolio Management*, *34*(3), 81–92.

Cameron, A. C., & Trivedi, P. K. (2009). *Microeconometrics using stata*. College Station, TX: Stata Press.

Chang, S., & Singh, H. (2000). Corporate and industry effects on business unit competitive position. *Strategic Management Journal*, *21*(7), 739–752.

Christmann, P., Day, D. L., & Yip, G. S. (1999). The relative influence of country conditions, industry structure and business strategy on MNC subsidiary performance. *Journal of International Management*, *5*(4), 241–265.

Collins, J. M. (1990). A market performance comparison of U.S. firms active in domestic, developed, and developing countries. *Journal of International Business Studies*, *21*, 271–288.

Greene, W. H. (2007). *Econometric analysis* (6th ed.). Upper Saddle River, NJ: Prentice Hall.

Hawawini, G., Subramanian, V., & Verdin, P. (2004). The home country in the age of globalization: How much does it matter for firm performance? *Journal of World Business*, *39*(2), 121–135.

Hsiao, C. (2003). *Analysis of panel data* (2nd ed.). Cambridge: Cambridge University Press.

Huang, Y. S., Liu, D. Y., & Lin, F. Y. (2009). Short-sales constraints and stock price behavior: Evidence from the Taiwan stock exchange. *The Business Review*, *13*(1), 93–98.

Islam, N. (1995). Growth empirics: A panel data approach. *The Quarterly Journal of Economics*, *110*(4), 1127–1170.

Karim, M. Z. A., & Guan, T. B. (2004). Stock prices, foreign opportunity cost, and money demand in Malaysia: A cointegration and error correction model approach. *Jurnal Ekonomi Malaysia*, *38*, 29–62.

King, R. G., & Levine, R. (1993). Finance and growth: Schumpeter might be right. *The Quarterly Journal of Economics*, *108*(3), 717–737.

Kwon, C. S., Shin, T. S., & Bacon, F. W. (1997). The effect of macroeconomic variables on stock market returns in developing markets. *Multinational Business Review*, *5*(2), 63–70.

Lee, U. (1997). Stock market and macroeconomic policies: New evidence from Pacific Basin countries. *Multinational Finance Journal*, *1*(4), 273–289.

Levine, R. (1997). Financial development and economic growth: Views and agenda. *Journal of Economic Literature*, *35*(2), 688–726.

Makina, D. (2008). Financial liberalization and time-varying stock price volatility: Firm level evidence from South Africa. *The Business Review*, *11*(1), 309–316.

Makino, S., Beamish, P. W., & Zhao, N. B. (2004a). The characteristics and performance of Japanese FDI in less developed and developed countries. *Journal of World Business*, *39*(4), 377–392.

Makino, S., Isobe, T., & Chan, C. M. (2004b). Does country matter? *Strategic Management Journal*, *25*(10), 1027–1043.

Mauri, A. J., & Michaels, M. P. (1998). Firm and industry effects within strategic management: An empirical examination. *Strategic Management Journal*, *19*(3), 211–219.

Rajan, R. G., & Zingales, L. (1998). Financial dependence and growth. *American Economic Review*, *88*(3), 559–586.

Rajan, R. G., & Zingales, L. (2003). The great reversals: The politics of financial development in the twentieth century. *Journal of Financial Economics*, *69*(1), 5–50.

Roe, M. J., & Siegel, J. I. (2009). Political instability: Its effects on financial development, its roots in the severity of economic inequality. SSRN. Available at http://ssrn.com/abstract=963214. Accessed on 18 September 2009.

Ruefli, T. W., & Wiggins, R. R. (2003). Industry, corporate and segment effects and business performance: A non-parametric approach. *Strategic Management Journal*, *24*(9), 861–879.

Rutledge, R. W., Zhang, Z., & Karim, K. (2008). Is there a size effect in the pricing of stocks in the Chinese stock markets? The case of bull versus bear market. *Asia-Pacific Financial Markets*, *15*(2), 117–133.

Tsoukalas, D. (2003). Macroeconomic factors and stock prices in the emerging Cypriot equity market. *Managerial Finance*, *29*(4), 87–92.

Valadkhani, A., & Chancharat, S. (2008). Dynamic linkages between Thai and international stock markets. *Journal of Economic Studies*, *35*(5), 425–441.

Valadkhani, A., Chancharat, S., & Havie, C. (2009). Analysing the impact of international stock markets and macroeconomic variables on the Thai stock market. *The Business Review*, *12*(2), 50–56.

Wooldridge, J. M. (2002). *Econometric analysis of cross section and panel data*. Cambridge, MA: MIT Press.

Ziramba, E. (2007). Demand for money and expenditure components in South Africa: Assessment from unrestricted error-correction models. *South African Journal of Economics*, *75*(3), 412–424.

APPENDIX

Table A.1. Main Contributions of Some Studies in Emerging Markets.

Studies	Contribution
Islam (1995)	Evolution of growth through a panel data model
Kwon, Shin, and Bacon (1997); Lee (1997); Tsoukalas (2003); Al-Khazali and Pyun (2004); Valadkhani et al. (2009)	Effects of macroeconomic variables on stock markets in developing countries
Karim and Guan (2004); Ziramba (2007)	Relationships among stock prices, opportunity costs and money demand in developing countries
Benetti and Fávero (2008); Al-Khazali (2008)	Day-of-the-week effect on stock prices in emerging countries
Makina (2008)	Relationship between financial liberalization and the evolution of the volatility of stock prices
Valadkhani and Chancharat (2008); Rutledge et al. (2008); Huang et al. (2009); Valadkhani et al. (2009)	General aspects of the stock markets in developing countries and the relationship between these markets and international markets

Table A.2. Panel Data Models for Use.

Model	Description
Fixed effects model	$y_{it} = \beta_{0i} + x'_{it}\beta_1 + \varepsilon_{it}$ β_{0i} terms can be correlated with x_{it} regressors, which permits a limited form of endogeneity. It is assumed that x_{it} is not correlated with the idiosyncratic error ε_{it}.
Fixed effects model with robust clusterized standard errors	$y_{it} = \beta_{0i} + x'_{it}\beta_1 + \varepsilon_{it}$ β_{0i} terms can be correlated with x_{it} regressors, which permit a limited form of endogeneity. It is assumed that errors are independent between individuals and that ε_{it} is heteroscedastic.
Random effects model	$y_{it} = x'_{it}\beta_1 + (\beta_{0i} + \varepsilon_{it})$ The random effect β_{0i} and the idiosyncratic error ε_{it} are i.i.d. The random effects estimator is the estimator FGLS of β_1, given that $\text{corr}(\mu_{it}, \mu_{is}) = \sigma^2_\alpha/(\sigma^2_\alpha + \sigma^2_\varepsilon)$
Random effects model with robust clusterized standard errors	$y_{it} = x'_{it}\beta_1 + (\beta_{0i} + \varepsilon_{it})$ If there are no fixed effects but the errors are present within correlation, the random effects estimator is consistent but inefficient and, therefore, robust clusterized standard errors need to be obtained.
Model with between estimator	$\bar{y}_i = \beta_0 + \bar{x}'_i\beta_1 + (\beta_{0i} - \beta_0 + \bar{\varepsilon}_i)$ The between estimator only uses cross-section variation and is the OLS estimator of a regression of $\bar{y}_i$ in function of $\bar{x}_i$. The consistency of this estimator requires that the error term $(\beta_{0i} - \beta_0 + \bar{\varepsilon}_i)$ is not correlated with x_{it}.
POLS model with robust clusterized standard errors	$y_{it} = \beta_0 + x'_{it}\beta_1 + \mu_{it}$ OLS estimation with control of within correlation of error μ_{it} over time.

Table A.3. Regressors for Panel Data Models.

Variable	Description
lnshare	Natural logarithm of quantity of stocks traded per month in million units
lnvalue	Natural logarithm of amount traded per month in million dollars

FINANCIAL CRISES PROPAGATION: A COMPARISON OF THE RUSSIAN AND TURKISH CRISES

Elvira Sojli and Renée Fry

ABSTRACT

This chapter examines crisis propagation mechanisms to the Southeast European exchange-rate markets during the 1998 Russian crisis and the Turkish crisis of 2001. It focuses on whether and how the crises spread to these markets after interdependencies and common external shocks are accounted for. Results for Albania, Bulgaria and Croatia are presented and compared. Understanding the propagation mechanisms of crises to these countries and the reaction of these markets to such shocks in comparison to trading partners and other countries within Europe is an important issue in the context of their potential accession to the European Monetary Union and the adoption of inflation targeting frameworks. It is found that Albania has relatively isolated financial markets in comparison with the other countries in the sample and is not affected by contagion, while Croatia is mostly affected by the crises directly and indirectly.

The Impact of the Global Financial Crisis on Emerging Financial Markets
Contemporary Studies in Economic and Financial Analysis, Volume 93, 495–522

ISSN: 1569-3759/doi:10.1108/S1569-3759(2011)0000093018

Keywords: Russian crisis; Turkish crisis; emerging markets; southeast Europe; contagion

JEL classifications: F31; F42

1. INTRODUCTION

Both emerging and developed countries are occasionally affected by, or are the source of, financial market crises and contagion. Although these instances are rare, their real effects can be detrimental for developing countries, as the aftermath of the crises of the 1990s demonstrates; Thailand's real gross domestic product (GDP) recovered to its 1996 level six years after the Asian financial crisis. The real effects of such crises for developed countries are usually moderate compared to those in emerging markets. The reasons for this are perhaps partially because fundamentals in developed countries are strong, and partially because developed countries are in a position (either actual or perceived) to mitigate attacks on their financial markets.[1] These observations raise the hypothesis that the level of development of a country appears to exacerbate the impact of contagion during times of crises, and hence emerging markets have an added incentive to develop quickly. That the level of development appears to be an important risk factor for financial crises subsequently has implications for countries making decisions on models for development, including exchange-rate regime choices.

Most work on financial market crises focuses on countries in the middle of the development spectrum. Some papers such as Bae et al. (2003) comment that contagion appears to be confined to emerging rather than developed economies. However, the impact of financial crises on the least developed countries is relatively unexplored, with the exception of Okonjo-Iweala et al. (1999) for the case of Laos and Cambodia during the Asian financial crisis. In this chapter, we examine the impact of the Russian and Turkish crises across several South Eastern European (SEE) exchange-rate markets of various levels of development. The chapter is particularly concerned with measuring the relative importance of contagion in currency markets compared to common and own shocks of Albania, Bulgaria, Croatia, Germany, Russia and Turkey, where contagion is the unanticipated transmission of a shock across national-currency markets during a crisis period.[2]

The chapter focuses predominantly on Albania, Bulgaria and Croatia, given their different levels of development, with some emphasis on Russia and Turkey as well. Germany is included to control for world factors. Albania represents the least developed of the set of countries, in terms of macroeconomic criteria. Bulgaria is an accession country and Croatia is a candidate accession country to the European Union (EU) and the European Monetary Union (EMU), and it is a long-term possibility for Albania and Turkey to follow the same development route. Shock transmission across national borders within Europe is an important issue in the context of this potential accession and the fulfilment of the convergence criteria required during this process.

By comparing the magnitude of the effects of contagion on the set of sample countries, it is possible to glean some understanding about (i) how these countries are affected by systemic shocks such as the Russian shock which affected most countries around the world, and (ii) shocks which are more confined in nature such as the Turkish shock. Comparing the impact of these crises across the sample provides a benchmark on how each of these countries are affected relative to world shocks in tranquil times.

A multivariate model of contagion is specified by using a latent factor framework. We use a generalised method of moments (GMM) estimation and variance decomposition techniques to identify the relative importance of each crisis on the exchange-rate markets in the sample. Examples of modelling contagion in currency markets using latent factor models are: Corsetti et al. (2001), Dungey and Martin (2004), Dungey et al. (2004) for the Asian crisis; Bekaert et al. (2005) for various crises; Dungey et al. (2007) and Rigobon (2003) for the Russian crisis. Kaminsky and Reinhart (2000) use factor analysis in understanding asset market syncronisation during the Russian crisis.[3]

There does not appear to be much written on the subject of contagion from the Turkish crisis in 2000–2001 to other countries within the region. Serwa and Bohl (2005) briefly examine contagion from Turkey to Poland, Hungary and the Czech Republic. They find little evidence of contagion and also find that Eastern European countries do not seem to be as affected by a common factor (as measured by principal components). Others examine causes and implications of the crisis, but don't estimate empirical models of contagion (see for example Özatay and Sak, 2002 and Eichengreen, 2002).

In this chapter, we specifically model the reinforcing contagion transmission effects amongst the sample set of countries. Contagion from Russia that transmits to the SEE countries during the Russian crisis period is important for Bulgaria, Croatia, Turkey and Germany. Albania is the only

SEE economy where contagion from Russia is not important, while Croatia is affected the most from the crisis. Some of the effects of the Russian crisis are propagated to all the SEE countries via Germany and Turkey and there is little spillover between Croatia and Bulgaria.

The results for the Turkish crisis are similar to those of the Russian crisis, in that Albania, apart from a small amount of contagion from Croatia, is predominately unaffected by contagion. In both the pre-crisis and crisis periods, currency returns are driven mainly by country-specific factors rather than world factors. Bulgaria and Croatia seem to be unaffected by Turkey, although there are more important cross-contagion effects between these two countries. Overall, the Russian crisis systemically spills over to most markets in the sample, while the Turkish crisis is much more localised.

That Albania is relatively unaffected by the two crises compared to Bulgaria and Croatia can possibly be explained by two hypotheses. The first hypothesis is that Albania managed the crisis well. The second is that its financial markets are relatively less developed than the other SEE countries in the sample, and hence are driven mainly by idiosyncratic factors. The latter hypothesis is more likely to be the case. However, understanding the impact of such crises on Bulgaria and Croatia is important, as Albania is likely to react to a shock in similar ways as it develops and particularly in light of its potential accession to the European Union and the subsequent integration and development of financial markets that would ensue.

The rest of the chapter proceeds as follows: Section 2 presents the background to the Russian and Turkish crises along with a brief overview of the exchange-rate systems of the sample countries. Section 3 presents the model of contagion and briefly explains the estimation methodology, followed by an overview of the data in Section 4. Section 5 presents the empirical results, while the conclusions are contained in Section 6.

2. BACKGROUND

2.1. The Russian Crisis

Following the collapse of the communist regime in 1989, the newly formed state of the Russian Federation inherited an over-industrialised economy dominated by a highly inefficient heavy industry and endless bureaucracy. The 'give-away' mass privatisation process, between 1992 and 1994, resulted in the accumulation of most of the productive capacity in the hands of previous company managers. They had little incentive or capital to keep the companies running, or to undertake the desperately needed restructuring of the enterprises (Illarionov, 1999).

Table 1 presents some key economic indicators for Russia over the period 1995–1998. GDP growth between 1995 and 1997 was negative; Russia relied heavily on foreign direct investment and activities performed by the state in order to achieve growth. The constant passage of unrealistic laws seriously destabilised budget fulfilment and the government deficit became an unbearable burden for the Russian economy. The growth in state debt led to a rise in spending to service it. Interest expenditures amounted to 8.7% of GDP in the first months of 1998, while 60.9% of tax revenues was needed to cover interest expenditure. These two factors led to a debt crisis which in turn provoked the currency crash and enhanced the banking crisis. 17 August, 1998 marks the beginning of the Russian crisis, as the rouble was devalued and Russia defaulted on its sovereign debt obligations.

Despite measures taken by the Russian government to control the crisis, including the attempt to replace debt instruments denominated in roubles with ones denominated in foreign currency, the currency peg was abandoned on the 17 August 1998.[4] This had repercussions across world financial markets (Committee on the Global Financial System, 1999 and Kharas et al., 2001), because international financial linkages with Russia prior to the onset of the crisis were strong. At the time of the crisis outbreak, the total exposure of non-residents to the Russian economy in the form of debt and equity amounted to $200–250 billion.[5] Many foreign banks were exposed on two fronts, because not only were they directly exposed to the Russian bond market (holding 30% of Russia's total debt), but they had

Table 1. Selected Indicators on the Russian Economy for the Period 1995–1998.

Year	1995	1996	1997	1998
GDP growth (%)	−4.1	−3.5	0.8	−4.8
Unemployment rate (%)	8.8	9.9	11.3	13.3
Inflation (annual average)	66%	32%	13%	22%
Average yield on short-term (3M) Treasury bills	168.04	86.1	23.4	n.a.
Gross forex debt (in billion $)	120.5	125	130.8	149
Trade balance (in billion $)	20.4	26.8	19.8	13.3
Exchange rate (period average)	4.56	5.12	5.78	9.71

Source: International Financial Statistics.

lent to Russian banks through repurchase agreements, taking Russian bonds as collateral. This was particularly true of German banks (Van Rijckeghem and Weder, 2001, 2003).

The Russian crisis severely affected credit risk concerns. The liquidation of positions in Russian assets by international investors became very difficult due to the 90-day moratorium on the repayment of credits received by non-residents of the Russian Federation. The current view is that the abandonment of the Russian currency peg and the default on debt resulted in more conservative behaviour by international investors due to increased risk aversion, and liquidity considerations (Greenspan, 1999; Bank of England, 2002; Dungey et al., 2003a). This led to the unwinding of positions in asset markets outside of Russia especially in Eastern Europe. However, unlike previous financial crises affecting emerging markets such as the Asian financial crisis, the Russian crisis was not just a regional crisis contained within Eastern Europe, but spread dramatically to various industrialised and emerging economies alike (see Dungey et al., 2002; Sojli, 2007). The spread of uncertainty following the Russian default is demonstrated by unusual fluctuations in the currency markets of these countries, as can be seen from Fig. 1.

2.2. The Turkish Crisis

Turkey experienced several crises during the 1990s and early 2000s. In this period, Turkey had high levels of inflation, and as a result, negative real GDP growth (see Table 2). Economic growth in the mid-1990s was mainly driven by government consumption and financed by extensive government deficits (see Fig. 2). Towards the end of 1999, when the public deficit was running at 23% of GDP, short-term debt was larger than reserves and the current account deficit had reached 5% of GDP, partly due to an overvalued currency.

The large current account deficit accumulated by 2000 and the expanding public deficit (domestic and foreign), led to a liquidity crisis in November 2000. Despite the short time span, the crisis had longer term implications for the financial system due to the erosion of the central bank reserves. The IMF intervened by giving Turkey an emergency loan in December 2000, which was a temporary measure. On 22 February, 2001 Turkey had to adopt a free floating exchange-rate policy. Özatay and Sak (2002) argue that the collapse of the lira was a third generation crisis, caused by high public lending from private banks.

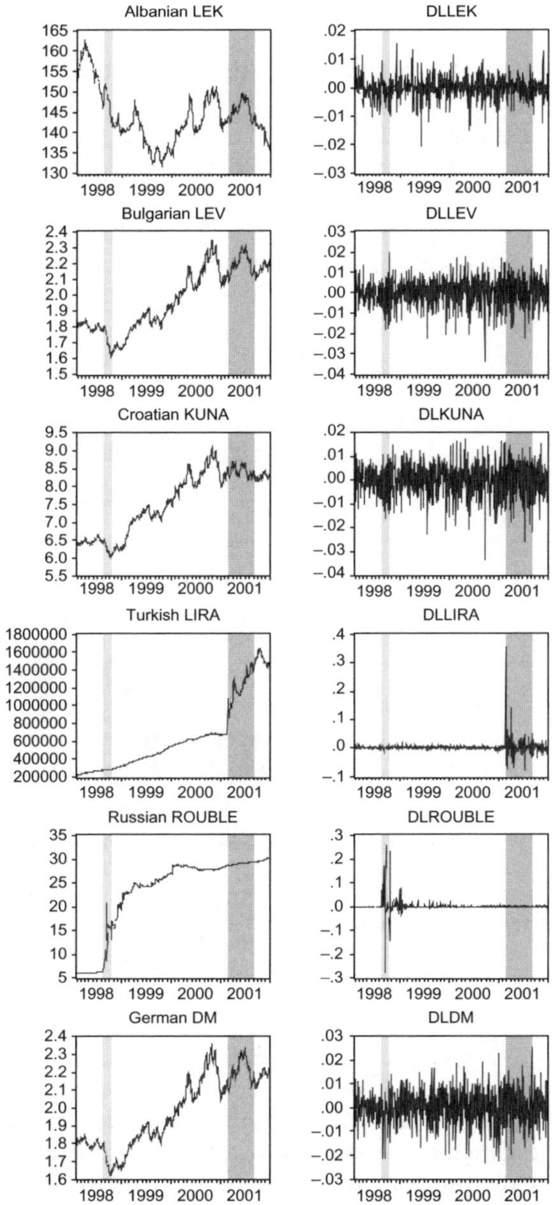

Fig. 1. Exchange rates. Levels and returns (in natural logs) of the exchange rates of the Albanian lek, the Bulgarian lev, the Croatian kuna, the German mark, the Russian rouble and the Turkish lira from January 1998 to September 2001 (the Russian crisis is marked in light shading and the Turkish crisis in dark shading).

Table 2. Turkish Macroeconomic Indicators for the Period 1995–2002.

	1995	1996	1997	1998	1999	2000	2001	2002
Inflation (%)	80	86	85	65	55	54	45	25
Unemployment (%)	6.6	5.8	6.9	6.2	7.3	6.6	8.4	10.3
GDP Growth (%)	90	95	81	48	61	43	55	30

Source: International Financial Statistics.

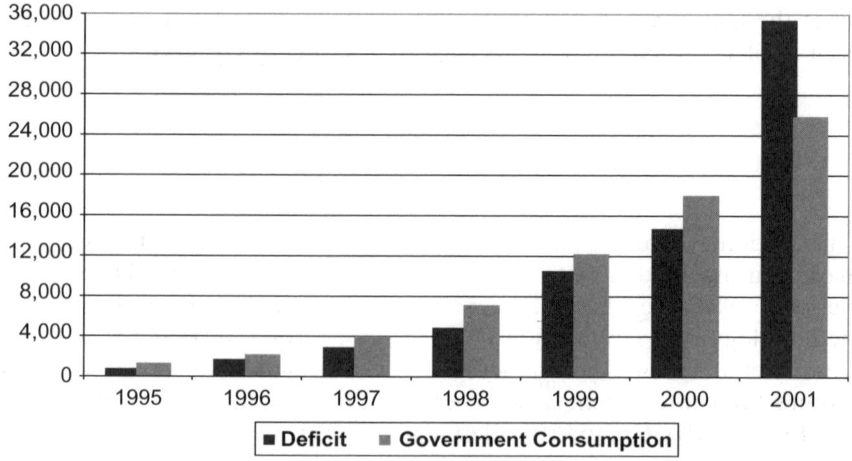

Fig. 2. Turkish macroeconomic variables. Turkish government deficit and expenditure for the period 1995–2002, in trillions of liras.

2.3. Exchange-Rate Regimes

To complete the background information, this section briefly discusses the exchange-rate regimes of Albania, Bulgaria and Croatia in order to put them into context in understanding the empirical results. These countries follow different exchange-rate regimes. The Bank of Albania operates under a 'dirty' floating regime (Edwards & Savastano, 2002), which means that the bank intervenes sporadically in the exchange-rate market. Modes and frequency of intervention vary, but the bank mainly intervenes in periods of significant changes in supply due to the arrival of expatriates that work in Europe, mainly in April, July/August and December.

Since its establishment in 1994, Croatia has operated a managed floating exchange-rate regime where most of the time the exchange-rate against each foreign currency reflects the equilibrium of supply and demand. On certain occasions, the Central Bank intervenes in the exchange-rate market to prevent the occurrence of major fluctuations in terms of both appreciations and depreciations. The Central Bank does not have a predetermined band for the exchange-rate but until now the kuna has fluctuated within a 6% band against the Deutsch mark/euro.

Bulgaria, on the other hand, is different from the other two countries. Since the hyper-inflation of 1996–1997, a currency board arrangement has been in place, where the lev is pegged to a basket of currencies.

3. THE MODEL

This section specifies a model of financial market contagion in currency markets using a latent factor framework (see King et al., 1994; Diebold and Nerlove, 1989; Ng et al., 1992 and Mahieu and Schotman, 1994). This methodology was developed in Dungey and Martin (2004) and extended in Dungey et al. (2004) for currency markets. The model of contagion aims to capture both interdependencies between the financial markets of Albania (A), Bulgaria (B), Croatia (C), Germany (G), Russia (R) and Turkey (T), as well as any contagion effects which transmit across this set of countries during the crises periods. To model these relations, a factor framework commonly used in the finance literature is utilised, where financial market returns are a function of systematic and idiosyncratic risk (Solnik, 1974 and Campbell et al., 1997).

3.1. Pre-Crisis Period Relations

Let $s_{i,t}$ denote the continuously compounded percentage return of the ith asset ($S_{i,t}$) at time t, which is calculated by taking the daily difference of the natural logarithm of the currency data; that is

$$s_{i,t} = 100 \times (\ln(S_{i,t}) - \ln(S_{i,t-1})). \tag{1}$$

The currency returns are then demeaned and denoted $z_{i,t}$, where

$$z_{i,t} = s_{i,t} - \bar{s}_i \tag{2}$$

and $\bar{s}_i$ is the sample mean of the ith currency return.

The model of contagion can be built up by first considering a period in which there is no financial crisis, generally, a pre-crisis period. The data set $z_{i,t}$ can be separated into a set of pre-crisis period observations $x_{i,t}$ containing t_1 observations, and a set of crisis period observations $y_{i,t}$ containing t_2 observations. Returns for each country in the pre-crisis period are specified formally as follows:

$$x_{i,t} = \lambda_i W_t + \theta_0 V_t + \gamma_i C_{i,t} \quad i = \mathrm{A, B, C, G, R, T}, \tag{3}$$

where each return is a linear function of three independent factors. The first factor is a world factor (W_t) which impacts on each series with loadings λ_i. The second factor is a numeraire factor, or fixed factor (V_t) with loading θ_0. The numeraire factor is included in the model for currency returns to capture the impact of expressing currency returns in a common currency, namely, the US dollar. These two common factors capture interdependencies across the six currency markets. These are the factors which capture systematic risk. The third factor for each country is a country-specific factor ($C_{i,t}$) with loading γ_i. This factor captures information that is unique to each countries asset return, and captures the idiosyncratic risk referred to above.

3.2. Crisis Period Relations

Contagion is defined as the unanticipated transmission of a shock across financial markets, over and above those which exist during tranquil times. To formally model such crisis period linkages, the model in Eq. (3) can be augmented by allowing for shocks from a source crisis country to the other countries in the model. Using a simple example to illustrate, consider the impact of contagion from Russia to Albania. Currency returns in the crisis period are denoted as $y_{i,t}$. The returns for Russia follow a similar process to that in Eq. (3), with the addition of a structural break in the country-specific factor, denoted as σ_t which captures the crisis in Russia. That is

$$y_{\mathrm{R},t} = \lambda_\mathrm{R} W_t + \theta_0 V_t + \sigma_\mathrm{R} \gamma_\mathrm{R} C_{\mathrm{R},t}. \tag{4}$$

Contagion from Russia to Albania is modelled by allowing the country specific shock in Russia to impact on the asset returns of Albania during the crisis period. Returns for Albania can be expressed as

$$y_{A,t} = \lambda_A W_t + \theta_0 V_t + \gamma_A C_{A,t} + \delta_A C_{R,t}. \quad (5)$$

The Albanian returns are still a function of the world and country-specific factors, but now, the country-specific factor for Russia ($C_{R,t}$) transmits to Albania with loading δ_A.

The model of contagion can be generalised for all i and augmented to allow for additional contagious linkages, so that the expression above becomes

$$y_{i,t} = \lambda_i W_t + \theta_0 V_t + \gamma_i C_{i,t} + \sum_{i=1}^{j} \delta_{i,j} C_{j,t} \quad i = \mathrm{A, B, C, G, R, T}, \ \forall i \neq j. \quad (6)$$

Finally, all factors are *iid* with zero mean and unit variance.

3.3. Variance Decomposition

An advantage of the assumption that the factors are independent is that the relative importance of the factors in Eqs. (3) and (6) can be determined quite simply by calculating variance decompositions. Using the simple example from above, the expression for the variance in the pre-crisis period is expressed as

$$var(x_{i,t}) = \lambda_i^2 + \theta_0^2 + \gamma_i^2. \quad (7)$$

The variance of the pre-crisis asset returns can be decomposed into its constituent factors, whereby, the contribution of world shocks as a proportion of the total variance can be expressed as

$$\lambda_i^2 / var(x_{i,t}). \quad (8)$$

The contribution of the numeraire factor can be expressed as

$$\theta_0^2 / var(x_{i,t}), \quad (9)$$

and the contribution of the country-specific factor can be expressed as

$$\gamma_i^2 / var(x_{i,t}). \quad (10)$$

A similar decomposition is calculated for the crisis period from Eq. (6), where for all countries except Russia, the total variance is expressed as

$$var(y_{i,t}) = \lambda_i^2 + \theta_0^2 + \gamma_i^2 + \sum_{i=1}^{j} \delta_{i,j}^2 \quad \forall i \neq j, \tag{11}$$

while for Russia the total variance is

$$var(y_{\mathrm{R},t}) = \lambda_{\mathrm{R}}^2 + \theta_0^2 + (\sigma_{\mathrm{R}}\delta_{\mathrm{R}})^2 + \sum_{i=1}^{j} \delta_{\mathrm{R},j}^2 \quad j = \mathrm{A,B,C,G,T}. \tag{12}$$

Following the above formulae, the contribution of contagion to the total variance in the crisis period is

$$\frac{\sum_{i=1}^{j} \delta_{i,j}^2}{var(y_{i,t})} \quad \nabla i \neq j. \tag{13}$$

The analysis of the crisis episodes in Section 5 will be undertaken in the variance decomposition framework in order to quantify the relative importance of contagion compared to world and country-specific factors.

3.4. Estimation Methodology

The model in Eqs. (3) and (6) is estimated by GMM (see Hamilton, 1994, Chapter 14, and Hansen, 1982).[6] The set of unknown parameters in Eqs. (3) and (6) denoted θ are estimated by equating the sample moments with the theoretical moments derived from the model. To estimate the model, moments are calculated for each of the distinct pre-crisis and crisis periods. The variance-covariance matrix from the pre-crisis period is used to estimate the world, numeraire and country-specific factors, while the variance-covariance matrix of the crisis period data is used to estimate the contagion parameters. This means that where there are six asset markets, up to $(6 \times 7)/2 = 21$ unique parameters can be estimated for each of the pre-crisis and crisis periods. The Newey–West optimal weighting matrix is also used to account for possible auto-correlation.

3.5. Russian Crisis Model

As noted above, a possible 21 parameters can be estimated in both the crisis and pre-crisis period. Thus, in order to identify the model, some restrictions must be imposed on the contagious linkages estimated, as the total number of possible combinations of contagious linkages is 30. The pre-crisis period model as presented in Eq. (3) has a total of 13 parameters to be estimated using the pre-crisis period moments. Thus, there are eight over identifying restrictions in the pre-crisis model.

The choice of the restrictions to identify the model in the crisis period is motivated by large versus small economy assumptions, as well as relations based on regional trading partnerships. The first key assumption is that contagion from Russia being the origin of the crisis transmits to all other currency markets during the crisis period. Second, Germany being one of the largest economies in Europe, with high exposure to the Russian and Eastern European markets, is also potentially an important conduit of the crisis as a common financial center through which shocks may transmit (Kaminsky and Reinhart, 2008). Third, Turkey, as a historically major trading partner, transmits contagion to Albania, Bulgaria and Croatia, but does not receive contagion from these countries. Finally, linkages due to contagion between Albania, Bulgaria and Croatia exist, due to the inter-linkages through trading relations and similar levels of development.

Given these relations, the equation for each currency market is formally specified below. However, for ease of reference, Table 3 summarises the direction in which contagion is hypothesised to transmit. For Albania, Bulgaria and Croatia the model of contagion is specified as

$$y_{i,t} = \lambda i W_t + \theta_0 V_t + \gamma_i C_{i,t} + \sum_{i=1}^{j} \delta_{i,j} C_{j,t} \qquad (14)$$
$$i = \mathrm{A, B, C},\ j = \mathrm{A, B, C, G, R, T},\ \forall i \neq j,$$

while for Germany, Russia and Turkey.

Table 3. Summary of Linkages due to Contagion in the Russian Crisis Period.

Contagion From	Contagion To					
	Albania	Bulgaria	Croatia	Germany	Russia	Turkey
Albania	n.a.	yes	yes	no	no	no
Bulgaria	yes	n.a.	yes	no	no	no
Croatia	yes	yes	n.a.	no	no	no
Germany	yes	yes	yes	n.a.	yes	yes
Russia	yes	yes	yes	yes	n.a.	yes
Turkey	yes	yes	yes	no	no	n.a.

$$y_{i,t} = \lambda_i W_t + \theta_0 V_t + \gamma_i C_{i,t} + \sum_{i=1}^{j} \delta_{i,j} C_{j,t}\, i = \mathrm{G,R,T},\ j = \mathrm{G,R,T},\ \forall i \neq j. \tag{15}$$

Note that the structural break defined in Eq. (6) is not included in the specification for Russia. Estimating the structural break for the Russian country-specific factor proved to be explosive. Instead, the country-specific factor across the pre-crisis periods was held constant.

3.6. Turkish Crisis Model

The inclusion of Germany in the Turkish crisis was problematic, potentially due to multicollinearity between the two exchange rates, as Turkey operated a crawling peg to a weighted basket of the US dollar and euro currencies until devaluation. This did not seem to be a problem in the estimation of the Russian crisis model, probably because the euro and Deutsch mark were separate currencies in 1998. Estimation of interdependencies and contagion is thus confined to Albania, Bulgaria, Croatia, Russia and Turkey.

Table 4 summarises the direction of contagion hypothesised to transmit across countries. The formal equation for Albania, Bulgaria and Croatia during the Turkish crisis period is specified as

$$y_{i,t} = \lambda_i W_t + \theta_0 V_t + \gamma_i C_{i,t} + \sum_{i=1}^{j} \delta_{i,j} C_{j,t}\, i = \mathrm{A,B,C},\ j = \mathrm{A,B,C,R,T},\ \forall i \neq j. \tag{16}$$

Russia is included as a control to capture events in Eastern Europe, and is a recipient of contagion, but is not a transmitter. Thus, the equation for Russia during the crisis period is the same as that for the pre-crisis period. Namely

$$y_{\mathrm{R},t} = \lambda_{\mathrm{R}} W_t + \theta_0 V_t + \gamma_{\mathrm{R}} C_{\mathrm{R},t} + \delta_{\mathrm{R}} C_{\mathrm{T},t}. \tag{17}$$

The specification for Turkey includes the structural break in the country-specific factor, but it is assumed that no contagious linkages flow back to Turkey as follows

$$y_{\mathrm{T},t} = \lambda_{\mathrm{T}} W_t + \theta_0 V_t + \sigma_{\mathrm{T}} \gamma_{\mathrm{T}} C_{\mathrm{T},t}. \tag{18}$$

Table 4. Summary of Linkages Due to Contagion in the Turkish Crisis Period.

Contagion From	Contagion To				
	Albania	Bulgaria	Croatia	Russia	Turkey
Albania	n.a.	yes	yes	no	no
Bulgaria	yes	n.a.	yes	no	no
Croatia	yes	yes	n.a.	no	no
Russia	no	no	no	n.a.	no
Turkey	yes	yes	yes	yes	n.a.

4. THE DATA

The data used are daily exchange rates of Albania, Bulgaria, Croatia, Turkey, Russia and Germany versus the US dollar.[7] Missing observations due to weekends and holidays are deleted.

4.1. The Russian Crisis

The sample period for the estimation of the factor model for the Russian crisis is defined as from 30 January 1998 until 14 October 1998. The pre-crisis period extends from 30 January until 13 August 1998, for a total of 127 observations. This period is chosen to avoid the effects of the 1997 pyramid scheme collapse in Albania and ends just prior to the effective sovereign bond default in Russia. The crisis period begins on August 14 (just before the Russian default) until 14 October 1998, for a total of 38 observations. This date is chosen as it is just before the Long Term Capital Management (LTCM) near collapse in the United States. Inclusion of the LTCM period would make it difficult to disentangle the impact of the Russian and LTCM crises on Albania, Bulgaria and Croatia. Given that ultimately this chapter is interested in commenting on the impact of shocks within Europe on these three SEE countries, the LTCM period is excluded.

During the crisis period the mean returns of all the currencies decreased significantly and the spread between the minimum and maximum returns increased significantly. Furthermore, the volatility of returns at least doubled for most of the exchange rates (see Table 5). Inspection of the correlation matrices for the pre-crisis and crisis periods in Table 6 shows a

Table 5. The Russian Pre-Crisis and Crisis Sample Statistics for the Log Returns.

Country	Albania		Bulgaria		Croatia		Germany		Russia		Turkey	
Period	Pre-crisis	Crisis	Pre-crisis	Crisis	Pre-crisis	Crisis	Pre-crisis	Crisis	Pre-crisis	Crisis	Pre-crisis	Crisis
Mean	0.000	−0.001	0.000	−0.002	0.000	−0.001	0.000	−0.002	0.000	0.018	0.002	0.001
Median	0.000	−0.001	−0.001	0.000	0.000	0.001	0.000	−0.001	0.000	0.001	0.001	0.000
Maximum	0.011	0.009	0.014	0.019	0.011	0.011	0.012	0.011	0.001	0.259	0.013	0.013
Minimum	−0.010	−0.009	−0.012	−0.018	−0.012	−0.016	−0.014	−0.022	−0.000	−0.278	−0.009	−0.009
Standard Deviation	0.004	0.004	0.005	0.009	0.005	0.008	0.005	0.007	0.000	0.094	0.004	0.004

Table 6. The Correlation Matrix for the Russian Pre-Crisis and Crisis (in bold) Period.

Pre-Crisis/Crisis	Albania	Bulgaria	Croatia	Germany	Russia	Turkey
Albania		**−0.03**	**0.03**	**0.04**	**0.01**	**−0.01**
Bulgaria	0.11		**0.89**	**0.32**	**0.31**	**0.80**
Croatia	0.03	0.54		**0.43**	**0.33**	**0.72**
Germany	−0.01	0.34	0.52		**0.25**	**0.33**
Russia	−0.02	−0.08	−0.12	−0.12		**0.05**
Turkey	0.15	0.51	0.29	0.25	−0.08	

significant change in the correlations between all the markets. More specifically, there is an increase in the correlations of all the countries with Russia and Turkey. This hints that the investigated markets might have been affected by the crisis and that relations between them changed.

4.2. The Turkish Crisis

The sample period for the Turkish crisis extends from 3 January 2000 to 10 September 2001. The pre-crisis period runs until 21 February 2001, the day before Turkey had to give up its peg. The crisis period is defined as 22 February to 10 September 2001, to avoid capturing any effects from the

Table 7. The Turkish Pre-Crisis and Crisis Sample Statistics for the Log Returns.

Country	Albania		Bulgaria		Croatia		Russia		Turkey	
Period	Pre-Crisis	Crisis	Pre-Crisis	Crisis	Pre-Crisis	Crisis	Pre-Crisis	Crisis	Pre-Crisis	Crisis
Mean	0.000	0.000	0.001	0.000	0.000	0.000	0.000	0.000	0.001	0.005
Median	0.000	0.001	0.001	0.000	0.001	0.000	0.000	0.000	0.001	0.001
Maximum	0.012	0.008	0.018	0.017	0.018	0.015	0.025	0.004	0.015	0.357
Minimum	−0.021	−0.008	−0.034	−0.023	−0.034	−0.026	−0.007	−0.004	−0.012	−0.079
Standard Deviation	0.004	0.003	0.007	0.007	0.007	0.007	0.003	0.001	0.004	0.041

Table 8. The Correlation Matrix for the Turkish Pre-Crisis and Crisis (in bold) Period.

Pre-Crisis/Crisis	Albania	Bulgaria	Croatia	Russia	Turkey
Albania		**−0.01**	**0.02**	**0.12**	**0.11**
Bulgaria	0.05		**0.06**	**0.06**	**−0.05**
Croatia	0.07	−0.00		**−0.18**	**0.08**
Russia	0.04	−0.02	0.06		**−0.09**
Turkey	−0.00	0.16	0.63	−0.04	

financial markets turmoil due to the terrorist attacks on the World Trade Centre.

Table 7 shows that standard deviations and mean returns did not change much over the pre-crisis and crisis periods, except for the Turkish lira, which changed dramatically. This can be taken as initial evidence that the Turkish crisis was not systemic like the Russian crisis. The correlation matrices in Table 8 further reinforce this hypothesis, as there is little change in correlations between the countries in the pre-crisis and crisis period, except Turkey and Croatia.

5. EMPIRICAL RESULTS

Tables 9 and 10 present the volatility decompositions of US dollars exchange rates of the sample of countries for the Russian and Turkish crises respectively. In each table, the first panel presents the decomposition for the pre-crisis period, while the second panel presents the decomposition for the crisis period.

5.1. Pre-Crisis Decompositions

In each pre-crisis period, the country-specific factor is the most important factor for Albania. Over the pre-Russian crisis period 99.87% of Albania's volatility is due to country-specific factors (panel A of Table 9) compared to 90.99% for the pre-Turkish crisis period (panel A of Table 10). This result contrasts with those for Bulgaria and Croatia whose decompositions are remarkably similar prior to the Russian crisis with 77% and 70% of volatility in currency markets explained by world factors, and the remainder by idiosyncratic shocks. The similarity of Albania with Bulgaria and Croatia becomes apparent during the pre-Turkish crisis period, as in this sub-sample, Bulgaria and Croatia are affected predominantly by country-specific factors (90.10% and 95.72%, respectively). This marked difference in results for Bulgaria and Croatia compared to the Russian crisis period is

Table 9. Volatility Decomposition for the Russian Crisis.

Factor	Albania	Bulgaria	Croatia	Germany	Russia	Turkey
Panel A. Pre-crisis period						
World	0.13	77.12	69.79	38.53	0.07	36.17
Country	99.87	22.88	30.21	61.47	99.93	63.83
Numeraire	0.00	0.00	0.00	0.00	0.00	0.00
Total	100.00	100.00	100.00	100.00	100.00	100.00
Panel B. Crisis period						
World	0.10	28.04	26.57	25.59	0.07	24.32
Country	81.66	8.32	11.50	40.84	98.60	42.91
Numeraire	0.00	0.00	0.00	0.00	0.00	0.00
Contagion from						
Albania	–	−0.01	0.04			
Bulgaria	0.00	–	7.13			
Croatia	0.01	3.76	–			
Germany	12.90	28.00	6.64	–		19.00
Russia	0.90	29.93	44.79	33.57	1.33	13.77
Turkey	4.43	1.94	3.33	–	–	
Total	100.00	100.00	100.00	100.00	100.00	100.00

Table 10. Volatility Decomposition for the Turkish Crisis.

Factor	Albania	Bulgaria	Croatia	Russia	Turkey
Panel A. Pre-crisis period					
World	0.80	1.76	1.24	0.09	99.47
Country	98.07	98.10	95.72	94.69	0.01
Numeraire	1.12	0.14	3.04	5.21	0.51
Total	100.00	100.00	100.00	100.00	100.00
Panel B. Crisis period					
World	0.79	1.63	0.94	0.09	0.51
Country	90.98	90.95	72.80	93.14	99.49
Numeraire	1.03	0.12	2.31	5.13	0.00
Contagion from					
Albania	–	0.47	8.31		
Bulgaria	0.53	–	13.95		
Croatia	4.22	6.33	–		
Russia					
Turkey	2.48	0.49	1.69	1.64	–
Total	100.00	100.00	100.00	100.00	100.00

probably explained by the fact that Germany is missing from the Turkish crisis sample due to the multicollinearity issue discussed previously.

Germany and Turkey are quite similar before the Russian crisis with around 60% of their volatility determined from country-specific factors. Turkey on the other hand is driven by world factors before its crisis period, probably because of its success in managing to retain the crawling peg exchange-rate system (against the euro and US dollar) in late 2000. Prior to both crises, Russia is mainly driven by country-specific factors (99% and 94.59%). The numeraire is unimportant for the Russian crisis estimation, but has more of an impact for the Turkish crisis estimation. Again, this is probably due to the omission of Germany from this set of results. The numeraire might be picking up some of the effects that Germany may have had on the set of countries considered.

5.2. Crisis Decompositions

The Russian shock is systemic and spread to all countries excluding Albania (Table 9). Even Germany is severely affected with 33.57% of volatility in the market for Deutsch marks caused by contagion from Russia. It can be noticed that contagion from Russia that spills over to the SEE countries (excluding Albania) is important, accounting for large changes in their exchange-rate markets. Compared to all other countries in the sample, Croatia is most affected by Russia in percentage terms. The Wald tests for joint contagion, in Table A4 of appendix B, indicate that contagion is jointly significant during the Russian crisis, from Russia and overall.

Feedback effects from the Russian shock to the other countries in the sample result in Germany, Turkey and Bulgaria becoming sources of contagion as well. Germany in particular, is also a source of contagion to Bulgaria (28%), Turkey (19%), Albania (12.9%) and Croatia (6.64%). In fact, most of the repercussions for Albania are filtered through Germany and a little through Turkey, while there is very little direct impact from Russia or from the other countries of the region.

The similarities between Bulgaria and Croatia carry through to the Russian crisis period. The currency markets for the lev and the kuna experience a similar amount of volatility from total contagion, albeit from slightly different sources. The combined impact of contagion to Bulgaria is 63.64% of total volatility, compared to 65.89% for Croatia. There is also a degree of spillover between these two markets in the Russian crisis period, particularly from Bulgaria to Croatia.

Overall, contagion is not significant individually in the Turkish crisis, apart from the case of Turkey to Albania and Turkey to Croatia. Inspection of Table 10 reveals that although these linkages are significant, they contribute less than 2.5% to total volatility of returns. The joint tests of contagion in Table A4 show that overall, contagion from Turkey to the other four countries is significant, and contagion to Albania and Bulgaria from Croatia is also significant.

The similarities between Bulgaria and Croatia are not as obvious during the Turkish crisis period (Table 10). Croatia is still the main country where contagion is important with 23.35% of total volatility due to contagion. Surprisingly, contagion from Bulgaria is the largest source of contagion to Croatia, accounting for 13.95% of volatility. There is more cross-market contagion amongst the SEE countries during the Turkish crisis, than in the Russian crisis.

One of the key implications of these results is that the country-specific factors driving the Albanian market appear to make it immune to shocks due to contagion, relative to its regional partners. The currency board system in Bulgaria and the managed float system within the 6% band system of Croatia did not insulate either of these countries from contagion during the crises periods. This may indicate that contagion has a smaller impact on Albania due to its country-specific nature, rather than its choice of exchange-rate regime.

There are two hypotheses that may explain why Albania seems to be unaffected by contagion compared to its partners Bulgaria and Croatia. The first hypothesis is that monetary policy and market intervention in Albania at the time contributed to the aversion of the crisis. This hypothesis is not likely to be the case particularly during the Russian shock, which affected countries such as Germany and the United States, which were presumably more able to fend off such crises. The second hypothesis is that Albania's financial markets are relatively less developed than those of Bulgaria and Croatia, and are not a large part of the emerging market portfolios of international investors and so escaped the 'panic' buying and selling of their national currencies. This level of development of the Albanian financial markets may have acted as a kind of natural capital control. The case of Albania can be compared to that of Cambodia and Laos as well as Chile, which although being geographically right beside Thailand and Mexico, respectively, were relatively unscathed in terms of financial market turmoil by the Asian (Okonjo-Iweala et al., 1999) and Mexican (Edwards, 1998) financial crises. Awareness of the impact of external shocks on Bulgarian and Croatian markets provides insight to potential influences of future shocks on Albania, as its financial markets develop.

6. CONCLUSIONS

This chapter investigated the impact of the Russian and Turkish crises of 1998 and 2001 on the SEE currency markets. Germany, Russia and Turkey were also included in the sample as either a control variable in the case of Germany, or as a control variable and source of the crises in the case of Russia and Turkey. It is important to understand how potential European Union accession countries are affected by shocks from their trading counterparties and key economies within the region. Albania, Bulgaria and Croatia are all connected with each other and the control countries directly and indirectly through trade and financial linkages with both crises countries.

The results from the estimation of Russian and Turkish crises models are quite different. The Russian crisis, being a global shock, was jointly and individually contagious for all the countries in the sample, but to a lesser extent to Albania. Bulgaria and Croatia appear to be quite similar in terms of the driving factors of their currency markets, which were mainly world specific. On the other hand the Turkish crisis appears to be country specific and did not spread through the region; there was little significant contagion in this crisis.

In both crises Albania was relatively unaffected and was repeatedly driven by country-specific factors. This is in stark contrast with the other two SEE countries considered, who were more influenced by global shocks. The main reason behind Albania's resilience to the crises could lie in the low level of development of its asset markets. However, understanding the impact of external shocks on Bulgarian and Croatian markets provides insight to potential influences of future shocks on Albania, as its financial markets develop. These results are consistent with those reached by Dornbusch et al. (2001) that the higher the degree of financial market integration, the more pronounced the contagious effects of shocks will be.

These conclusions appear to hold during the current financial crisis. Despite the large declines in developed stock markets between 2007 and 2008, stock and bond markets in emerging economies have shown resilience and have emerged out of the crisis faster and stronger than the developed markets, which are still struggling. Slightly tighter and more managed economies like China, Brazil, Singapore etc. have fared better than the US or European markets.

NOTES

1. Examples include the successful response of the United States to the LTCM crisis and the successful defence of Hong Kong to the sustained speculative attacks on its currency and equity markets during the Asian crisis.
2. For a review of contagion definitions and estimation methodologies, see Dornbusch et al. (2000), Dungey et al. (2005), Pericoli and Sbracia (2003) and Pesaran and Pick (2007).
3. Other methods of modelling contagion include, but are not limited to the bivariate correlation test of Forbes and Rigobon (2002), the multivariate threshold tests of Bae et al. (2003), Eichengreen et al. (1995, 1996) and Favero and Giavazzi (2002).
4. For a chronology of events please refer to appendix C.
5. Harris and Grant (1998, p. 3).
6. The models are estimated using Gauss 5.0.
7. Data sources and codes are contained in Table A1 of appendix A.

REFERENCES

Bae, K., Karolyi, G., & Stulz, R. (2003). A new approach to measuring financial contagion. *Review of Financial Studies*, *16*(3), 717–764.

Bank of England. (2002). *Financial stability review*. Bank of England, London, England. June

Bekaert, G., Harvey, C., & Ng, A. (2005). Market integration and contagion. *Journal of Business*, *78*(1), 39–70.

Campbell, J., Lo, A., & MacKinley, A. (1997). *The Econometrics of Financial Markets*. New Jersey: Princeton University Press.

Committee on the Global Financial System, 1999. *A review of financial market events in autumn 1998*. Bank for International Settlements, Basel, Switzerland, October.

Corsetti, G., Pericoli, M., & Sbracia, M., 2001. *Correlation analysis of financial contagion: What one should know before running a test*. Economic Growth Center, Yale University Discussion paper No. 822. Available at http://www.econ.yale.edu/growth_pdf/cdp822.pdf.

Diebold, F. X., & Nerlove, M. (1989). The dynamics of exchange rate volatility: A multivariate latent-factor ARCH model. *Journal of Applied Econometrics*, *4*(1), 1–22.

Dornbusch, R., Park, Y. C., & Claessens, S. (2000). Contagion: Understanding how it spreads. *World Bank Research Observer*, *15*, 177–197.

Dungey, M., & Martin, V. L. (2004). A multifactor model of exchange rates with unanticipated shocks: Measuring contagion in the East Asian currency crisis. *Journal of Emerging Market Finance*, *3*(3), 305–330.

Dungey, M., Fry, R. A., & Martin, V. L. (2004). Currency market contagion in the Asia-Pacific region. *Australian Economic chapters*, *43*(4), 379–395.

Dungey, M., Fry, R.A., González-Hermosillo, B., Martin, V.L. (2002). "The transmission of contagion in developed and developing international bond markets", in Risk, Measurement and Systemic Risk, Bank for International Settlements, Basel, Switzerland, October.

Dungey, M., Fry, R. A., González-Hermosillo, B., & Martin, V. L. (2007). Shocks and systemic influences: Contagion in global equity markets in 1998. *The North American Journal of Economics and Finance*, *18*(2), 155–174.

Dungey, M., Fry, R. A., González-Hermosillo, B., & Martin, V. L. (2005). Empirical modelling of contagion: A review of methodologies. *Quantitative Finance*, *5*(1), 9–24.

Edwards, S. (1998). Interest rate volatily, contagion and convergence: An empirical investigation of the cases of Argentina, Chile and México. *Journal of Applied Economics*, *1*(2), 55–86.

Edwards, S., & Savastano, M. A. (2002). Exchange rates in emerging economies: What do we know? What do we need to know? In: A. Krueger (Ed.), *Economic Policy Reform: The Second Stage* (pp. 453–510). Chicago, IL: The University of Chicago Press.

Eichengreen, B., (2002). Crisis prevention and management: Any new lessons from Argentina and Turkey? World Bank Finance Forum 2002: Aligning Financial Sector Knowledge and Operations. Washington, DC.

Eichengreen, B., Rose, A. K., & Wyplosz, C. (1995). Exchange market mayhem: The antecedents and aftermath of speculative attacks. *Economic Policy*, *10*(21), 249–312.

Eichengreen, B., Rose, A. K., & Wyplosz, C. (1996). Contagious currency crises: First tests. *Scandinavian Journal of Economics*, *98*(4), 463–484.

Favero, C. A., & Giavazzi, F. (2002). Is the international propagation of financial shocks non-linear? Evidence from the ERM. *Journal of International Economics*, *57*(1), 231–246.

Forbes, K., & Rigobon, R. (2002). "No Contagion, Only Interdependence: Measuring Stock Market Co-movements". *Journal of Finance*, *57*, 2223–2261.

Greenspan, A. (1999). Risk, liquidity and the economic outlook. *Business Economics*, *34*(January), 20–24.

Hamilton, J. (1994). *Time Series Analysis*. New Jersey: Princeton University Press.

Hansen, L. (1982). Large sample properties of generalised method of moments estimators. *Econometrica*, *50*(4), 1029–1054.

Illarionov, A. (1999). How the Russian crisis was organised. *Problems of Economic Transition*, *41*(11), 7–56.

Kaminsky, G., & Reinhart, C. (2000). On crisis, contagion, and confusion. *Journal of International Economics*, *51*(1), 145–168.

Kaminsky, G., & Reinhart, C. (2008). The centre and the periphery: The globalization of financial turmoil. In: C. Reinhart, C. Végh & A. Velasco (Eds), *Money, Crises, and Transition: Essays in Honor of Guillermo Calvo* (pp. 171–216). Cambridge, MA: The MIT Press.

Kharas, H., Pinto, B., & Ulatov, S. (2001). An analysis of Russia's 1998 meltdown: Fundamentals and market signals. *Brookings Papers on Economic Activity*, *2001*(1), 1–68.

King, M., Sentana, E., & Wadhwani, S. (1994). Volatility and links between national stock markets. *Econometrica*, *62*(4), 901–933.

Mahieu, R., & Schotman, P. (1994). Neglected common factors in exchange rate volatility. *Journal of Empirical Finance*, *1*(3–4), 279–311.

Ng, V. K., Engle, R. F., & Rothschild, M. (1992). A multi-dynamic factor model for stock returns. *Journal of Econometrics*, *52*(1–2), 245–266.

Okonjo-Iweala, N., Kwakwa, V., Beckwith, A., & Ahmed, Z. (1999). Impact of Asia's financial crisis on Cambodia and the Lao PDR. *Finance and Development*, *36*(3), 48–51.

Özatay, F., & Sak, G. (2002). The 2000–2001 financial crisis in Turkey. In: S. Collins & D. Rodrick (Eds), *Brookings Trade Forum 2002, Currency Crises: What Have we Learned?* Washington, DC: Brookings Institution.

Pericoli, M., & Sbracia, M. (2003). A primer on financial contagion. *Journal of Economic Surveys*, *17*(4), 571–608.

Pesaran, H., & Pick, A. (2007). Econometric issues in the analysis of contagion. *Journal of Economic Dynamics and Control*, *31*(4), 1245–1277.

Rigobon, R. (2003). On the Measurement of the International Propagation of Shocks: Is the Transmission Stable?. *Journal of International Economics*, *61*(2), 261–283.

Serwa, D., & Bohl, M. (2005). Financial contagion, vulnerability and resistance. A comparison of European capital markets. *Economic Systems*, *29*(3), 344–362.

Sojli, E. (2007). Contagion in emerging markets: The Russian crisis. *Applied Financial Economics*, *17*(3), 197–213.

Solnik, B. (1974). An equilibrium model of the international capital market. *Journal of Economic Theory*, *8*(4), 500–524.

Van Rijckeghem, C., & Weder, B. (2001). Sources of contagion: Is it finance or trade? *Journal of International Economics*, *54*(2), 293–300.

Van Rijckeghem, C., & Weder, B. (2003). Spillovers through banking centers: A panel data analysis of bank flows. *Journal of International Money and Finance*, *22*(4), 483–509.

APPENDIX A. DATA SOURCES

Table A1. Data Sources and Codes.

Country	Source	Database/Code
Albania	Monetary Operations Department, Bank of Albania	
Bulgaria	Central Bank of Bulgaria Website: 29 January–29 November 1998	BULGLV$
	DataStream for the period 30 November 1998–31 December 1999	CROATK$
Croatia	DataStream	CROATK$
Germany	DataStream	USWGMRK
Russia	DataStream	RSUSDSP
Turkey	Reuters Terminal	TRLUSD

APPENDIX B. PARAMETER ESTIMATES

Table A2. Russian Crisis – Currency Markets. Parameter Estimates (t-Stats in Parentheses).

Factor	Albania	Bulgaria	Croatia	Germany	Russia	Turkey
World	0.011	0.321	0.304	0.273	0.020	0.176
	(0.397)	(10.078)	(8.174)	(6.465)	(0.389)	(5.957)
Country	0.307	0.175	0.200	0.345	0.770	0.234
	(12.385)	(3.816)	(7.163)	(13.198)	(10.511)	(7.883)
Numeraire	0.00	0.00	0.00	0.00	0.00	0.00
	(0.000)	(0.000)	(0.000)	(0.000)	(0.000)	(0.000)
Contagion from						
Albania		0.006	−0.040			
		(0.073)	(−0.214)			
Bulgaria	0.003		−0.900			
	(0.027)		(−0.934)			

Factor	Albania	Bulgaria	Croatia	Germany	Russia	Turkey
Croatia	0.014	0. 588				
	(0.181)	(0.243)				
Germany	0.353	−0.931	−0.441		−0.259	−0.452
	(2.127)	(−2.553)	(−1.775)		(−0.474)	(−3.414)
Russia	0.042	−0.431	−0.513	−0.406		−0.172
	(0.582)	(−2.391)	(−3.790)	(−3.414)		(−2.460)
Turkey	−0.305	0.361	0.459			
	(−1.842)	(0.587)	(1.201)			

Table A3. Turkish Crisis – Currency Markets. Parameter Estimates (*t*-Stats in Parentheses).

Factor	Albania	Bulgaria	Croatia	Russia	Turkey
World	−0.022	0.093	−0.017	0.366	−0.004
	(−1.304)	(2.674)	(−2.237)	(18.603)	(−0.392)
Country	0.246	−0.695	−0.147	0.004	0.112
	(8.146)	(−21.166)	(−15.307)	(0.095)	(10.954)
Numeraire	−0.026	−0.026	−0.026	−0.026	−0.026
	(−1.794)	(−2.522)	(−2.522)	(−2.522)	(−2.522)
Structural break					−1264.139
					(−0.095)
Contagion from					
Albania		0.203	−0.203		
		(0.435)	(−0.600)		
Bulgaria	0.027		0.093		
	(−0.460)		(1.971)		
Croatia	0.359	−1.244			
	(0.570)	(−1.308)			
Turkey	0.008	−0.010	0.004	−0.003	
	(2.327)	(−0.975)	(1.983)	(−1.153)	

Table A4. Wald Test Statistics for Contagion During the Russian and Turkish Crises.

Source	Russian Crisis	Turkish Crisis
Albania	0.194[a]	2.045[a]
Bulgaria	0.846[a]	0.460[a]
Croatia	0.029[a]	7.825[a]**
Germany	8.781[d]	
Russia	22.385[d]**	
Turkey	3.320[b]	104.016[c]**
Joint contagion	91.360[e]**	36.250[f]**

Notes: * denotes significance at the 10% level.
** denotes significance at the 5% level.
[a]Critical value chi-squared 2: 5% = 5.991; 10% = 4.605
[b]Critical value chi-squared 3: 5% = 7.815; 10% = 6.251
[c]Critical value chi-squared 4: 5% = 9.488; 10% = 7.779
[d]Critical value chi-squared 5: 5% = 11.071; 10% = 9.236
[e]Critical value chi-squared 19: 5% = 30.144 10% = 27.204
[f]Critical value chi-squared 10: 5% = 18.307; 10% = 15.987.

APPENDIX C. TIMELINE OF EVENTS

2 July 1997	Bank of Thailand announces a managed float of the baht.
23 October 1997	The Hong Kong stock market loses 23% and overnight interest rates shoot to 250%.
17 November 1997	Korea abandons defence of the won.
14 July 1998	Announcement that Russia will receive $22.6 billion from the IMF and other donors.
20 July 1998	IMF approves additional assistance to Russia of $11.2 billion.
6 August 1998	Russian bond market initial crash.
11 August 1998	Foreign investors seem to be the main driving force behind the market drop.
	Fears of a weaker yen and the prospect of devaluation in China sends shock waves throughout the world.

13 August 1998	Russian shares lose more than 10% on growing fears of a banking liquidity crisis.
17 August 1998	Announcement of the devaluation of the rouble.
20 August 1998	Concerns that Russian banks may fail and Venezuela may devalue.
21 August 1998	Russia's Central Bank states that some Russian banks could go bankrupt.
	In Germany stocks plunge, triggering downfalls in London and Paris.
	LTCM loses $550 million.
26 August 1998	Stocks fall as Russia announces its debt-restructuring plan.
27 August 1998	Russia's government unable to sell its newly restructured GKO bills.
21 September 1998	LTCM loses another $550 million.
20 November 2000	Liquidity crisis in Turkey.
6 December 2000	IMF $10 billion financial package for Turkey.
19 February 2001	Turkish interest rates reach 6,200% overnight due to severe political crisis.
22 February 2001	Abandonment of Turkish lira peg.
11 September 2001	Terrorist attacks on the World Trade Centres.

FINANCIAL CRISES AND STRUCTURAL BREAKS IN AUTOCORRELATION ON THE BRIC'S STOCK MARKETS

Galina Smirnova, Olga Saldakeeva and Sergey Gelman

ABSTRACT

The phenomenon of positive autocorrelation in daily stock index returns is often viewed as a consequence of stable behavioural patterns of certain investor groups (see, e.g., Sentana & Wadhwani, 1992; Koutmos, 1997). However, such patterns may change due to extreme events, that is, financial crises, and thus affect the autocorrelation in returns. Emerging markets and especially BRIC countries have experienced severe crises in the last 20 years and are therefore a suitable object for studying this effect.

The focus of this chapter is on identifying substantial changes in the autocorrelation of BRIC markets' index returns after experiencing upheavals of the financial system. For this purpose, we look for structural breaks in the parameters of an ARMA–GARCH model with the standard endogenous search procedure.

The Impact of the Global Financial Crisis on Emerging Financial Markets
Contemporary Studies in Economic and Financial Analysis, Volume 93, 523–544

ISSN: 1569-3759/doi:10.1108/S1569-3759(2011)0000093019

Our approach yields no statistically significant evidence of the autocorrelation changes due to the crises. Only in India the decline in autocorrelation in 1998 seems to be economically relevant, but is not significant statistically. Significant shifts that we could identify were rather related to microstructural changes, such as abolishment of price change limits by China and the removal of a leading player in India's market in 1992. All in all our results suggest that even though extreme negative events on financial markets may induce changes in feedback trading strategies, their influence on autocorrelation is not pronounced enough. The impact of other factors, in the first place of regulatory changes, seems to be of larger relevance.

Keywords: autocorrelation in stock returns; structural breaks; feedback trading; price limits.

JEL Classifications: G14; C22.

1. INTRODUCTION

There is a plethora of papers devoted to autocorrelation in stock returns. The earliest literature found little evidence for any autocorrelation and concluded that random walk models are good approximations to stock price data, hence supporting the efficient market hypothesis (EMH) (Fama, 1970). Later a number of papers appeared that revealed the presence of autocorrelation in stock returns (e.g. the seminal paper Lo & MacKinlay, 1988). Moreover, autocorrelation seems to vary in time: it has been found to be high and positive in tranquil times – when the volatility of returns is low – and low or even negative in volatile periods. Sentana and Wadhwani (1992) trace these changes in dynamic dependence back to the shifts in behaviour of investors which react only to the price changes – the so-called 'feedback traders'. These traders either 'chase the trend', that is, buy after market rises and sell on declines, and then they are referred to as positive feedback traders, or 'play against the trend' – if they are negative feedback traders. Given that there is also a group of rational investors on the market, actions of positive feedback traders lead to overshooting and thus to negative autocorrelation, whereas negative feedback traders rather stabilize price movements and cause positive autocorrelation. It has been argued that in periods of tranquility the negative type prevails, and under increased volatility most of the feedback traders turn to be 'trend-chasers', thus providing the explanation of changes in autocorrelation. Developing this line Bohl and Siklos (2008) suggest that particularly financial crises should lead to shifts in feedback strategies and autocorrelation decline. Comparing the period from July 1997 to December 1998, which contains both Asian and Russian crises, with the rest of the decade sample 1994–2003, they find supportive evidence for Central and Eastern European (CEE) emerging stock markets. However, it is not clearly evident in how far this result depends on the choice of the countries and definition of the crisis period.

The aim of our chapter is to close this research gap, namely (1) to test the impact of the financial crises on the markets of other emerging countries and, more importantly, (2) endogenously estimate the changing points (i.e. time periods with different autocorrelation), to allow for other factors to cause autocorrelation shifts.

Therefore, this chapter explores autocorrelation patterns in the time series of stock market returns for the four largest emerging countries: Brazil, Russia, India and China. These so-called BRIC countries are of research interest being at the same time global players and emerging economies (whereby only Russia is also analysed by Bohl & Siklos, 2008). The stock markets of these countries experienced strong blows of financial crises in their early years, which supposedly should have led to noticeable changes in investment strategies.

To track the latter down, we use endogenous search for break dates in the parameters of an autoregressive moving average (ARMA)–generalized autoregressive conditional heteroskedasticity (GARCH) model for the stock returns of each of the four markets. Thereby, we test for changes in all model parameters as well as in only crucial ones. To support the feedback hypothesis, significant changes in the autocorrelation in stock returns on BRIC markets should be detected around the dates of financial crises, whereby we consider not only the Asian crisis of 1997 and crisis in Russia in 1998 but also Brazilian crisis in 1999.

Our approach yields no statistically significant evidence for the autocorrelation changes due to the crises. Only in India the decline in autocorrelation in 1998 seems to be economically relevant, but this result does not hold statistically. On the contrary, we are able to detect autocorrelation increases associated with changes in market microstructure, such as the abolishment of price change limits by China and the removal of a leading player in India's market in 1992. All in all our results suggest that even though extreme negative events on financial markets may induce changes in feedback trading strategies, their influence on autocorrelation patterns is not pronounced enough; it could be overcompensated by the impact of other factors, in the first place by the impact of regulatory changes.

The structure of the chapter is organized as follows: Section 2 discusses the theory and methodological issues. Section 3 presents the data used. Section 4 describes the results for modelling the time series of stock returns in BRIC countries and contains empirical results of a test for the existence of structural breaks. Section 5 concludes.

2. THEORY

The fundamental theory of finance, assuming that the EMH holds, argues that stock prices quickly reflect all available information. Particularly, a weak form of EMH claims that the current price of a stock reflects its own past prices, so that agents in the financial markets have no opportunity to find misevaluated stocks. But at the same time there are many investors in the financial markets that make their decisions based on past stock returns.

The phenomenon of return autocorrelation has been thoroughly analysed by previous researchers. Boudoukh, Richardson, and Whitelaw (1994) give an overview of the three schools that provide different explanations of autocorrelation in short-horizon shock: the schools of 'loyalists', 'revisionists' and 'heretics'. According to the first (the 'loyalists'), both the pattern and the magnitude of the correlations are consistent with measurement error in the data (Keim, 1989) (e.g. non-synchronous trading (Atchison, Butler, & Simonds, 1987; Perry, 1985), price discreteness, or bid-ask spreads (Conrad, Gultekin, & Kaul, 1991)), institutional structures (e.g. trading mechanisms such as different market structures or trading/non-trading periods) or microstructure effects (e.g. systematic changes in either inventory holdings or the flow of information). They assume that the market rationally processes information so that market efficiency holds but significant autocorrelation arises from the market frictions. For example, Mech (1993) shows that transaction costs can cause positive autocorrelation in stock returns. Such costs prevent informed investors from reacting quickly to news, thus delaying the incorporation of information into stock prices and giving rise to positive autocorrelation in stock prices. Because of non-synchronous trading of some stocks, the reported prices for these securities do not reflect the news that was released after the last trade in this stock. The prices of such securities respond to the news during trading the following day, thus inducing a positive portfolio autocorrelation. However, Boudoukh et al. (1994) provide evidence that the degree of the daily aggregate return autocorrelation is too large to be completely explained by transaction costs and the non-synchronous trading hypothesis.

The 'revisionists' (e.g. Lo & MacKinlay, 1988; Hameed, 1992) see the origin of stock market return autocorrelation in time-varying risk premium. They also assume efficient markets, but show the possibility of short-term autocorrelation even in a frictionless market due to time variation in expected returns. Changes in past market returns, past size returns, interest rate spreads and other risk factors can cause variations in the risk premium in the short term.

The 'heretics' believe that markets are not fully efficient and that profitable trading strategies do exist. They also emphasize the importance of behavioural factors for pricing securities. Several papers examine the profitability of trading rules for individual securities and portfolios and report supportive evidence (e.g. Jegadeesh & Titman, 1992; Brock, Lakonishok, & LeBaron, 1992). However, Sullivan, Timmermann, and White (1999) show that predictability patterns change and even the trading strategies proven to be profitable in the past would not yield reliable profits in the future.

In this chapter, we follow the behavioural explanation of return autocorrelation and focus on capturing switches in predictability patterns. In line with Sentana and Wadhwani (1992), we assume that the predictability pattern changes together with the behavioural pattern of 'feedback' (or technical) traders. These traders base their strategy on trends in past stock prices and adhere to technical rules, causing a correlation in stock returns. Feedback traders fall into two groups: 'positive' and 'negative' ones. 'Positive' ('negative') feedback traders systematically follow the strategy of buying (selling) after price rises and selling (buying) after price falls. Thus, the strategy of 'positive' feedback traders only reinforces price movements that create trends on the market when prices will continually overshoot the levels suggested by current public information. As the market corrects for this over-reaction in the following trading period, prices tend to move in the opposite direction and so negative autocorrelation is induced. The opposite situation is true for negative feedback traders, who tend to induce positive autocorrelation in stock returns. Hence, different signs and strengths of autocorrelation can be assigned to the dominance of a particular group of investors on the market, depending on whether they are positive or negative feedback traders. A negative (positive) stock return autocorrelation would suggest the dominance of positive (negative) feedback traders on the market for a particular asset. Such trading strategies are thought to deteriorate trends, which may cause overshooting, excess volatility and increased market vulnerability (see Dornbusch & Park, 1995; Choe, Kho, & Stulz, 1999; Kim & Wei, 2002). Following Sentana and Wadhwani (1992), negative feedback traders dominate at low levels of volatility and positive feedback traders dominate on highly volatile markets. Extending this idea, Bohl and Siklos (2008) suggest an increase in positive feedback trading and thus declining (or even negative) autocorrelation during crises. They measure autocorrelation conditional on volatility and find supportive evidence for several developed markets (Germany, UK and US) as well as for some CEE stock markets (Czech Republic, Hungary, Poland and Russia). The autocorrelation decline is more pronounced for their sample of emerging CEE markets. However, since Bohl and Siklos (2008) do not provide confidence bounds for conditional autocorrelation, the question whether crises cause significant shifts in autocorrelation is still open.

We address this question by analysing the sample of the most prominent emerging markets (Brazil, Russia, India and China) and identifying structural breaks in ARMA models, fitted for each market individually.

3. METHODOLOGY

We address the question whether financial crises cause shifts in autocorrelation by identifying structural breaks in ARMA processes of BRIC's stock markets' returns. Finding a structural break in an autocorrelation parameter at a date close to the start of a crisis period would support our hypothesis. In our sample, major financial downturns begin on the following dates: 2 July 1997 (the devaluation of the Thai baht responsible for the start of the Asian crisis); 17 August 1998 (the devaluation of the Russian rouble) and 13 January 1999 (the devaluation of the Brazilian real). The simplest approach would be testing for structural break explicitly on these three points of time. However, this way one would obtain distorted results if further events could have influenced autocorrelation patterns. As possible alternative events, one could consider microstructure changes such as transaction tax increases (following Baltagi, Li, & Li, 2006; Gelman & Burhop, 2008). To isolate the effect of financial crises, we apply an endogenous sequential structural break estimation procedure of Bai and Perron (1998, 2003a), which allows for estimating several break dates and several sets of model parameters.

Our adaptation of the procedure involves several steps.

First, we choose an appropriate specification of an ARMA(p,q)–GARCH(1,1) model for daily index returns on the full sample:

$$\begin{aligned} r_t &= \alpha_0 + \alpha_1 \cdot r_{t-1} + \cdots + \alpha_p \cdot r_{t-p} + e_t + \beta_1 \cdot e_{t-1} + \cdots + \beta_q \cdot e_{t-q} \\ e_t &= v_t \sigma_t \\ \sigma_t^2 &= a_0 + a_1 e_{t-1}^2 + b_1 \sigma_{t-1}^2 \end{aligned} \qquad (1)$$

We include a GARCH model for conditional variance to account for known violation of classical assumptions (such as excess kurtosis and volatility clustering). All potential specifications (whereby the maximum number of lags p,q is constrained to 2) are estimated using maximum likelihood algorithm with t-distribution of shocks v_t. The best specification is chosen based on information criteria and residual autocorrelation.

Second, we test for structural breaks in parameters of the previously chosen model using the sequential sup-LR (likelihood ratio) algorithm suggested by Bai and Perron (2003a). This endogenous algorithm allows testing sequentially for i against $i-1$ structural breaks, starting from the null hypothesis H_0: 'no breaks at all' against the alternative H_1:'one structural break at some date'. The test used is the following:

$$\begin{aligned} &\sup_{\lambda_i \in \Lambda_\varepsilon^i} - \mathrm{LR}_T(\lambda_i) \\ &\mathrm{LR} = 2[(l_1(\lambda_i) + l_2(\lambda_i)) - l_r] \end{aligned} \qquad (2)$$

where l_1, l_2 and l_r are the maximized values of the log-likelihood function in the subsamples before and after a possible break date $T_i = T * \lambda_i$ and for the whole sample with only $i-1$ partitions. $\lambda_i = T_i / T$ is a fraction of the first subsample length of the full sample length. The break date T_i should have a minimum distance ε to the adjacent breaks: $\lambda_{i-1} + \varepsilon < \lambda_i < \lambda_{i+1} - \varepsilon$. We thus ensure that all periods between two adjacent breaks are at least ($T * \varepsilon$) days long. Since we have a rather large sample for all BRIC stock index returns, we use $\varepsilon = 5\%$ (what corresponds to 150–250 days), and so λ_1 belongs to (0.05, 0.95). In this way we treat each possible date and calculate the LR statistics in order to find the most significant one. The largest LR statistic is compared to the 1% critical values provided by Bai and Perron (2003b).[1] If this break is significant, we repeat the procedure for the two subsamples and so on, until no significant breaks can be found in any subsample.

Third, we test explicitly for changes in autoregressive or moving average terms. The procedure suggested by Bai and Perron (2003a) allowed us to identify structural breaks if one or several parameters of either the mean equation or the conditional variance equation significantly change. Because the focus of our chapter is to verify changes in autoregressive terms or moving averages parameters, at this step we perform a Wald test for stability of the coefficients of interest. Thereby, we compare autoregressive parameters (or moving average parameters) for any two adjacent subsamples:

$$W = \frac{(a_{1,1} - a_{1,2})^2}{\sigma^2_{a_{1,1}} + \sigma^2_{a_{1,2}}} \tag{3}$$

where $\sigma^2_{a_{1,1}}$ and $\sigma^2_{a_{1,2}}$ are asymptotic variances of the autoregressive parameter estimates for each of the subsamples. Owing to the presence of a nuisance parameter, the test-statistic is not necessarily $\chi^2(1)$-distributed as in the standard case and it is reasonable to use Bai and Perron's (2003b) critical values here as well.

Fourth, if the Wald test reveals a significant break in at least one of the parameters, we re-run the Bai and Perron (2003a) procedure allowing only for partial break. At this step, we assume stability in the parameters of the conditional variance equation except for the constant term, but allow a break to occur in either the ARMA part or the GARCH constant term. The following equation is estimated (particularly for the AR process):

$$\begin{aligned} r_t &= \alpha_0 + \sum_{i=1}^{n} \gamma_{0i} * d_{it} + \alpha_1 * r_{t-1} \cdots + \alpha_p * r_{t-p} + \sum_{j=1}^{p} r_{t-j} \sum_{i=1}^{n} \gamma_{ji} * d_{it} + e_t, \\ \sigma_t^2 &= \alpha_0 + \sum_{i=1}^{n} \gamma_{2i} * d_{it} + \alpha_1 * e_{t-1}^2 + \beta_1 * \sigma_{t-1}^2 \end{aligned} \tag{4}$$

Here we use dummies to model partial changes, whereby $d_{it} = 0$ for $t \leq T_i$ and $d_{it} = 1$ for $t > T_i$. Aside from the initial assumption, the procedure with dummies is similar to the procedure applied in the second step of the search. We also use Bai and Perron (2003b) critical values at the 1% significance level and run the procedure until no further significant breaks can be found. Having finished the search for partial structural changes, the Wald test is applied to test for changes in individual parameters.

Having implemented the procedure described above, we may come to a conclusion about the significance of change in the autocorrelation. Finally we check whether any of the endogenously estimated break points lie close to the dates related to the start of the targeted financial crises. Therefore, we consider all dates up to 2 months before or after the dates of the breaks and attempt to identify as many events as possible that could be potential causes for the structural break. We choose this time frame following Gelman and

Burhop (2008). If the start of any of the targeted financial crises falls into this confidence interval, then we consider the hypothesis 'Financial crises induce changes in the predictability of the stock market' as confirmed; if not, this hypothesis is rejected and an alternative explanation is due.

4. DATA DESCRIPTION

We use domestic BRIC stock market indexes denoted in the local currency. The BRIC stock indexes are the BOVESPA for Brazil (4,207 observations), the index of the Russian trading system for Russia (3,250 observations), the India Bombay Stock Exchange (BSE) 100 National index for India (5,220 observations) and the Shanghai SE Composite index for China (4,467 observations).

Returns are proxied by the log difference change in the price index:

$$R_t = \log P_t - \log P_{t-1}$$

where R_t is the return at time t, and P_t, P_{t-1} are the values of the stock price index at times t, $t-1$.

The data were sourced from Datastream. All index time series end on 14 February 2008; the beginning of the sample period differs from country to country depending on data availability (in the range from March 1989 to September 1995, see Table 1 for details). News on the stock markets were sourced from Reuters, and Bloomberg was utilized for the identification of an alternative event that may have caused each structural break.

Table 1 provides descriptive statistics of the stock index returns. Brazilian and Russian indices exhibit very high average returns, about 68% and 38% on annualized basis, respectively. Such extraordinary properties are due to

Table 1. Descriptive Statistics of Daily Stock Market Indices.

Country	Index	Period Start	Period End	Number of Observations	Mean	Standard Deviation	Skewness	Kurtosis
Brazil	BOVESPA	1/1/1992	14/2/2008	4207	0.0027	0.0270	0.4530	10.55
Russia	RTS	1/09/1995	14/2/2008	3250	0.0015	0.0307	−0.0514	24.25
India	Indian BSE (100) National	3/17/1989	14/2/2008	4935	0.0005	0.0170	−0.1175	9.65
China	Shanghai Se Composite	2/1/1991	14/2/2008	4467	0.0008	0.0255	5.9925	158.01

the periods of high inflation in those countries, falling into our sample. Chinese index returns are also rather high on average (about 20% annualized), whereby the average return on Indian BSE (100) National with 12.5% p.a. does not differ substantially from values known from developed markets. Daily return standard deviations show that returns are rather volatile and the Indian market seems to be closer to developed markets in this extent, too. Shanghai SE Composite and BOVESPA index returns are positively skewed, whereby the skewness of the former is very pronounced. Russian and Indian index returns are slightly negatively skewed. High kurtosis values indicate heavy tails in return distributions of all four indices. The Jarque–Bera test for joint normal kurtosis and skewness rejects the normality hypothesis, which is a common feature of financial data (not reported in Table 1).

5. RESULTS AND DISCUSSION

In this section, we describe the results obtained in course of the structural break estimation procedure, as outlined in Section 3.

In the first step, where we define the specification of the initial model to be tested for break, our procedure picks first-order ARMA models for all four countries. For the daily returns of the stock markets of Brazil, India and China, these models contain only one autoregressive component of lag one (see Table 2). The best-fit model for the Russian stock market includes one first-order moving average component (see Table 2). All the AR and MA coefficients in the estimated models are positive and significant at the 5% level or higher. Autocorrelation in stock returns in the short period seems to be the norm rather than the exception. The components of the conditional variance equations are all significant for all four markets and indicate high persistence of conditional variance (sum of the slope coefficients exceeds 0.98 in all four cases).

High values of Ljung–Box statistics for lag 20 Q_{20} indicate that residual autocorrelation is still present, and it is significant at the 1% level. This shows that even our best-fit models for all four markets do not pick up all the autocorrelation in the data, which could be a sign of either the presence of 'long memory' or possible structural breaks in the estimated model.

Since we find different dates of breaks for different markets, we discuss the results of procedure steps two to four (full change tests, individual parameter tests and partial change tests) for each country separately.

For Brazil we identify two structural breaks when testing for a change in all model parameters in step two (see Table 3): 1 September 1994 and 17

Table 2. Estimates of ARMA Models.

	Brazil	Russia	India	China
	ARMA(1,0)	ARMA(0,1)	ARMA(1,0)	ARMA(1,0)
α_0	0.002052***	0.002006***	0.000899***	0.000766***
	(0.000285)	(0.000313)	(0.000190)	(0.000182)
α_1	0.035390**		0.150521***	0.063129***
	(0.015740)		(0.013733)	(0.01573)
β_1		0.079282***		
		(0.017979)		
a_0	6.56E-06***	9.84E-06***	6.38E-06***	8.3E-06***
	(1.75E-06)	(1.98E-06)	(1.03E-06)	(1.096E-06)
a_1	0.097710***	0.148207***	0.127766***	0.217559***
	(0.011378)	(0.014515)	(0.011143)	(0.015542)
b_1	0.904073***	0.849787***	0.856405***	0.774548***
	(0.010258)	(0.012345)	(0.010764)	(0.011902)
SBC-value	−4.806734	−4.837755	−5.700250	−5.478706
Q_{20}	60.726***	45.785***	52.401***	86.844***
R^2	0.002559	0.005990	0.008291	0.001557
Adj. R^2	0.001609	0.004765	0.007530	0.000661

Note: Estimates of ARMA models for the BOVESPA, RTS, Indian BSE (100) National, Shanghai SE Composite. Asymptotic standard errors are in parentheses. Each model presents an iteration of the Box–Jenkins procedure. Q-statistics are reported for twenty lags. *** and ** indicate statistical significance at the 1% and 5% level, respectively.

Table 3. Brazil: ARMA(1,0)–GARCH(1,1).

	1/03/1992–9/01/1994	9/02/1994–1/17/1999	1/18/1999–2/14/2008
α_0	0.013567***	0.002140***	0.001426***
	(0.001366)	(0.000547)	(0.000333)
α_1	0.022184	0.054877*	0.007214
	(0.038652)	(0.030567)	(0.020236)
a_0	4.93E-05	1.19E-05**	8.32E-06**
	(4.00E-05)	(4.92E-06)	(3.35E-06)
a_1	0.085073***	0.195772***	0.057714***
	(0.032842)	(0.033507)	(0.013197)
b_1	0.899877***	0.822260***	0.926430***
	(0.040614)	(0.026589)	(0.017075)
R^2	0.000676	0.002942	0.000191
LL	1276.971	2685.525	6222.927
Q_{20}	30.186**	27.375*	24.923

Note: Estimates of ARMA (1,0)-GARCH(1,1) models for the BOVESPA. Asymptotic standard errors are in parentheses. ***, ** and * indicate statistical significance at the 1%, 5% and 10% level, respectively.

January 1999. The second break is estimated only for four calendar days after the devaluation of the local currency, and the change is likely to be caused by the resulting financial turmoil. Thus, we obtain three sets of model estimates for the three subsamples: (1) 1 March 1992–1 September1994, (2) 2 September 1994–17 January 1999 and (3) 18 January 1999–14 February 2008. In all three subsamples, the constant term is significantly positive, what indicates a clear up trend. The autoregressive coefficient is insignificant in the first and the last subsample and is weakly significant in the middle one. All the GARCH parameters but the constant in the first subsample are significant at the 5% level at least. The sum of the slope coefficients in the conditional variance equation indicates high persistency in the first and the last subsample ($a_1 + b_1 \approx 0.985$ in both cases) and possibly explosive variance behaviour in the middle subsample ($a_1 + b_1 \approx 1.015$). Residual autocorrelation up to lag 20 is still significant at the 5% level for the first period, tends to significance in the second subsample and diminishes in the third one (Fig. 1).

In step three, using a Wald test to find significant changes in individual parameters, we can track back the first break identified on 1 September 1994 to the decrease in the constant term in the mean equation from 0.013 to 0.002. All other parameters do not experience statistically significant changes. The second break on 18 January 1999 primarily involves changes in the slope parameters of the variance equation a_1 and b_1 : a_1 drops from 0.196 to 0.058, while b_1 rises from 0.82 to 0.93, whereby both changes are statistically significant according to the Wald test at the 2.5% significance

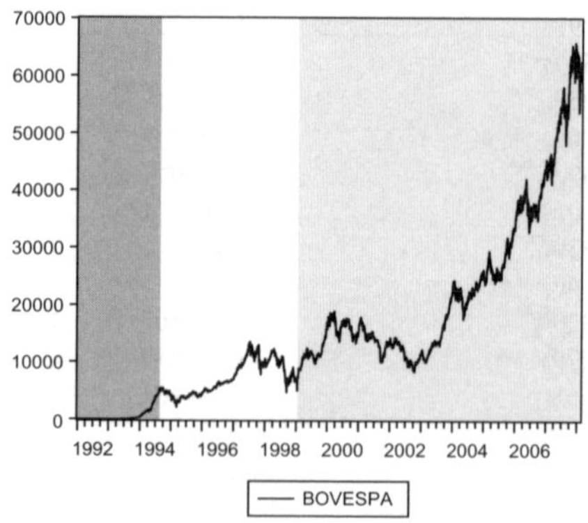

Fig. 1. Brazilian Stock Market Index. *Source:* Datastream. *Note:* A change in colour indicates an identified structural break point.

level. This reflects a decrease in sensitivity of conditional variance to the previous day's shock and an increase in shock persistence in the conditional variance.

In step four, the test for a partial change which constrains the structure of conditional variance to remain unchanged, we find only the first break point, as expected. The change in the autoregressive term remains statistically insignificant.

Thus, we find no significant changes in autocorrelation patterns for Brazilian stock market returns.

As for Russia, in the second step, we identify two structural break points (see Table 4). These dates are 16 June 1996 and 21 July 2002. In all three sets of parameter values, the MA term is positive and significantly different from zero. Positive constant terms indicate significant upward trends in the second and third subsamples (which are also visually distinguishable in Fig. 2). GARCH parameter values indicate high conditional variance persistence in the second and third subperiods ($a_1 + b_1 \approx 0.98$ and 0.95, respectively). The conditional variance equation in the first subsample yields clearly inadequate estimates, with $b_1 < 0$, what is possibly due to the short subsample length (9.5 months). Residual serial correlation remains a highly significant issue in the subsample 17 June 1996–21 July 2002, but is not significant at the 5% level for the rest of the period under study. That could

Table 4. Russia: ARMA(0,1)–GARCH(1,1).

	9/01/1995–6/16/1996	6/17/1996–7/21/2002	7/22/2002–2/14/2008
α_0	0.001798	0.001976***	0.002148***
	(0.001427)	(0.000673)	(0.000362)
β_1	0.116053***	0.086308***	0.059944**
	(0.025165)	(0.025605)	(0.027141)
a_0	0.000393***	3.04E-05***	1.47E-05***
	(7.89E-05)	(8.10E-06)	(4.22E-06)
a_1	0.764339***	0.144099***	0.129506***
	(0.217146)	(0.021722)	(0.025431)
b_1	−0.122329**	0.838466***	0.820298***
	(0.054279)	(0.019981)	(0.032541)
R^2	0.031858	0.004813	0.001999
LL	480.4735	3356.686	4073.196
Q_{20}	28.771*	39.240***	13.195

Note: Estimates of ARMA (0,1)-GARCH(1,1) models for the RTS. Asymptotic standard errors are in parentheses. ***, ** and * indicate statistical significance at the 1%, 5% and 10% level, respectively.

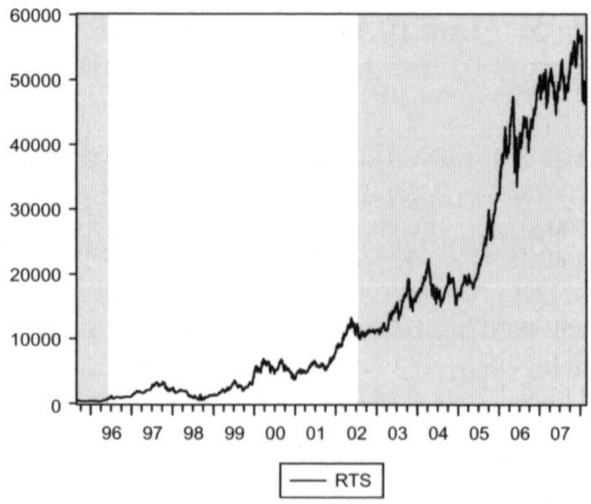

Fig. 2. Russian Stock Market Index. *Source:* Datastream. *Note:* A change in colour indicates an identified structural break point.

possibly indicate further breaks in the middle subsample, which our procedure is unable to identify.

For both identified break points, we perform Wald tests for individual parameter changes. None of the mean equation parameters turn out to experience statistically significant shifts on these dates. Moreover, one can see from Table 4 that the parameters of both the mean equation and the conditional variance equation do not differ by more than two standard errors from subsample to subsample, with the exception of the parameter b_1 in the conditional variance equation for the first break point. Since the Wald tests did not provide evidence for structural changes in the parameters of interest, we skipped the next step.

Overall, for the Russian stock market, we can also conclude that there are no structural breaks in autocorrelation and hence in predictability of returns.

The search for structural breaks in the Indian stock markets yielded five break points and six sets of model parameter values (see Table 5). The break points are 11 June 1992, 10 April 1996, 26 February 1998, 8 November 1998 and 28 April 2003. The autoregressive term is positive for all six regimes and significant at the 5% level at least for all but the fourth subsample. The constant term is significant only for the period 17 March 1989–10 June 1992 and insignificant for the rest of the sample. Coefficients of the variance equation are significant and yield high variance persistence in the first, second, fifth and sixth regimes ($a_1+b_1 \approx 0.97$–0.99). Variance persistence is slightly lower for the period 26 February 1998–8 November 1998

Table 5. India: ARMA(1,0)–GARCH(1,1).

	3/17/1989–6/10/1992	6/11/1992–4/09/1996	4/10/1996–2/25/1998	2/26/1998–11/07/1998	11/08/1998–4/27/2003	4/28/2003–2/14/2008
α_0	0.001177**	−0.000264	6.64E-05	0.000640	0.000236	0.002799
	(0.000464)	(0.000402)	(0.000822)	(0.000811)	(0.000442)	(0.000323)
α_1	0.131704***	0.309846***	0.194667***	0.024567	0.089322***	0.071327**
	(0.032504)	(0.027329)	(0.053172)	(0.047918)	(0.033674)	(0.029794)
a_0	5.54E-06***	2.86E-06***	0.000162***	3.19E-05	7.97E-06***	8.33E-06***
	(1.87E-06)	(8.86E-07)	(4.63E-05)	(3.12E-05)	(3.08E-06)	(2.58E-06)
a_1	0.070611***	0.113994***	0.247096**	0.059308	0.162217***	0.158894***
	(0.016745)	(0.021891)	(0.109027)	(0.037022)	(0.035010)	(0.029005)
b_1	0.899096***	0.875097***	−0.018354	0.856503***	0.831162***	0.818418***
	(0.020997)	(0.019877)	(0.228783)	(0.108622)	(0.031909)	(0.029505)
R^2	0.018437	−0.001724	0.035019	−0.000913	0.009845	0.001852
LL	2407.034	3489.134	1050.407	1150.482	2535.145	3712.267
Q_{20}	23.989	22.532	23.187	26.639	24.443	13.433

Note: Estimates of ARMA (1,0)-GARCH(1,1) models for the Indian BSE (100). Asymptotic standard errors are in parentheses. *** and ** indicate statistical significance at the 1% and 5% level, respectively.

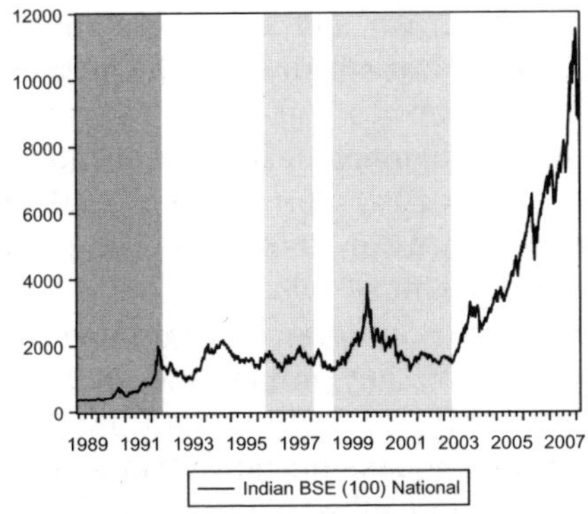

Fig. 3. Indian Stock Market Index. *Source:* Datastream. *Note:* A change in colour indicates an identified structural break point.

($a_1 + b_1 \approx 0.92$), and the conditional variance is strongly mean reverting for the period 10 April 1996–26 February 1998 ($a_1 + b_1 \approx 0.24$). In the latter subsample the b_1 coefficient is insignificant (and of a wrong sign). The Ljung–Box statistics indicate no serial correlation left in the residuals in all of the six subsamples (Fig. 3).

For the first break point on 11 June 1992, the Wald test yields a highly significant increase (at the 1% level) in the autoregressive term. In fact, the AR-coefficient more than doubles from 0.132 to 0.31. This implies an increase in the predictability of the stock market returns by 3.6 times from the first 3.2 years of our observation period to the next 3.8 years. On the basis of the Wald test at the 10% level of significance, we infer that the second and third structural breaks were due to changes in the parameters of the variance equation. For the fourth break on 8 November 1998 and the fifth on 28 April 2003, the parameters of the mean equation do not differ by more than two standard errors from subsample to subsample. For these break points, the Wald test also indicates that the variance equation parameters exhibit no significant changes.

Testing for partial change in the next step reinforces our results of a highly significant change in autoregressive term at the first break point and of no significant changes further on.

However, if we compare the values of the autoregressive parameter during the fourth subsample (0.31; 26 February 1998–8 November 1998) with the one in the second subsample (0.025; 11 June 1992–10 April 1996), we see a more than 12-fold difference, which is significant at all conventional levels. Clearly, even though each of the break points (10 April 1996, 26 February 1998) does not induce a statistically significant drop in autocorrelation, predictability decreases in a statistically significant fashion over this 2-year period.

Summarizing, we find a significant increase in autocorrelation in stock index returns on 11 June 1992 for the Indian market. Furthermore, autocorrelation in index returns in 1998 is significantly lower than in 1992–1996, but this decline is a result of two individually insignificant steps.

Turning to the Chinese stock market, we find four structural break points: 11 June 1992; 23 January 1996; 29 October 1997 and 12 December 2005. The autoregressive term is positive and highly significant (moreover, it is close to unity) in the first subperiod and insignificantly different from zero in the other four subsamples. The constant term of the mean equation alternates signs from subsample to subsample and is significant in the second, third and the last one. This indicates a pronounced downward trend in June 1992–January 1996, as well as pronounced upward trends for January 1996–October 1997 and December 2005–February 2008. The coefficients of the conditional variance equation are significant throughout all five regimes and signal high persistency. In the first subsample, the estimates even imply an explosive behaviour of the conditional variance ($a_1 + b_1 \approx 1.03$). In all five subsamples, serial residual correlation is insignificant at the 5% level (Table 6).

Table 6. China: ARMA(1,0)–GARCH(1,1).

	1/02/1991–6/10/1992	6/11/1992–1/22/1996	1/23/1996–10/28/1997	10/29/1997–12/11/2005	12/12/2005–2/14/2008
α_0	0.004006	−0.002788***	0.003032***	−0.000224	0.003233***
	(0.004226)	(0.000725)	(0.000793)	(0.000228)	(0.000517)
α_1	0.972427***	−0.041015	−0.051977	0.005814	−0.026005
	(0.021140)	(0.035191)	(0.054060)	(0.022747)	(0.040445)
a_0	1.17E-06***	5.51E-05***	7.60E-05***	1.97E-05***	5.70E-06***
	(1.83E-07)	(1.34E-05)	(2.36E-05)	(3.96E-06)	(2.52E-06)
a_1	0.692142***	0.240618***	0.284326***	0.172461***	0.087312
	(0.111256)	(0.040132)	(0.073503)	(0.027093)	(0.021957)
b_1	0.341013***	0.719594***	0.579052***	0.712614***	0.896284**
	(0.039804)	(0.033522)	(0.083547)	(0.039973)	(0.023239)
R^2	−0.666839	−0.006393	−0.002173	−0.000079	−0.001281
LL	1485.422	2010.953	1126.136	6401.757	1560.234
Q_{20}	3.615	24.496	30.010*	29.554*	26.290

Note: Estimates of ARMA (1,0)-GARCH(1,1) models for the Shanghai SE Composite. Asymptotic standard errors are in parentheses. ***, ** and * indicate statistical significance at the 1%, 5% and 10% level, respectively.

For the first identified break, there is a sharp decrease in the autoregressive term from 0.972 to −0.041, which is also highly statistically significant according to the Wald test. In absolute value, the autocorrelation decreases nearly 24 times. The Wald test shows that the first structural change involves, aside from the autocorrelation term, a significant change in the variance equation parameters. The rest of the break points do not involve significant changes in the autoregressive term, but the constant in the mean equation tends to vary significantly over all subsamples. The latter is supported by visibly changing trends in Fig. 4. As for the other countries in the BRIC group, the partial change test only reinforces the results of the previous two steps of our procedure.

Thus, we find for the Chinese stock index returns only one significant change in autocorrelation on 11 June 1992, the same date as for India, but with an opposite impact on autocorrelation.

For India, the rise in autocorrelation is possibly linked to the removal of H. Mehta, the leading player at the Indian stock exchange at that time. In May 1992, it was revealed that he had been illegally funnelling the money of the state bank and corresponding banks into the BSE. Money raised on the interbank loan market was then used by Mehta for speculations on the stock market (Dubey, 1992). With huge amounts of money not known to have

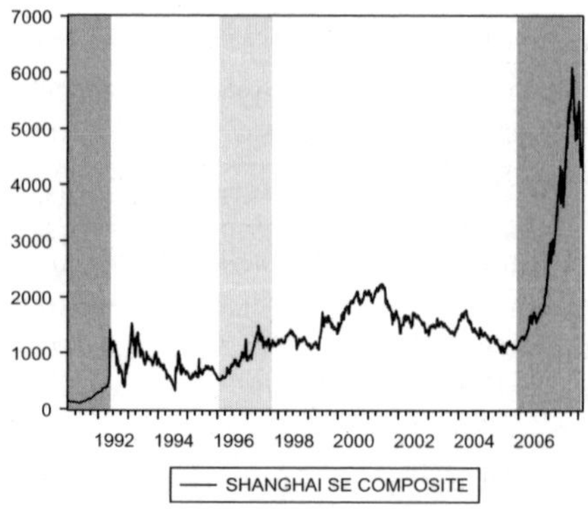

Fig. 4. Chinese Stock Market Index. *Source:* Datastream. *Note:* A change in colour indicates an identified structural break point.

been supplied by banks, Mehta drove the exchange on a long boom (that took off in July 1991).

How could the actions of one person change the autocorrelation in stock returns? The following explanation seems reasonable to us. Being the leader of the market, Mehta was able to sustain liquidity and a high volume of trading. High liquidity and large trading volumes led to lower autocorrelation (Shen & Wang, 1998) and allowed for low bid-ask spreads. These low spreads meant low transaction costs that led to less price adjustment delays and to lower autocorrelation in returns (Mech, 1993). When the player left the market, liquidity dropped, the volume of trading went down and spreads became higher. These high transaction costs caused mispricing by making it unprofitable for investors to trade on minor information. Greater price adjustment delays strengthened the autocorrelation in returns and increased their predictability, making the market less efficient.

The situation on the Chinese market was different: liquidity of the market increased substantially, and serious regulatory hurdles had been removed prior to 11 June 1992. In particular, 36 days before the estimated change point the maximum 1% limit on the daily price fluctuation of 9 out of the 15 shares listed on the Shanghai Securities Exchange was relaxed to 5%. Fifteen days thereafter (21 days prior to the estimated break), the restrictions on any fluctuation of share prices were fully abolished and the market was allowed to float freely. The existence of narrow price limits could explain the tremendously high autoregressive coefficient for the subsample before June 1992. If a market is subject to a price limit regulation, the shock will not be completely felt within a trading day and will be partly manifested over the subsequent trading days (see Chiang & Wei, 1995; Chou, 1997). This means that information shocks are acted on less quickly, and therefore positive autocorrelation may arise. Our findings support the results for the Taiwan stock market, obtained by Shen and Wang (1998), who found that the correlation of the returns is positively affected by price limits.

Thus, the abolishment of the price limits led to a sharp decrease in the predictability of stock returns. Interestingly, we could report this effect only with a lag since the Shanghai SE Composite gained 105.5% over its previous close following the abolition of price limits. This possibly further aggravated our positive autocorrelation estimate. As the rally ended several days later, the demise of predictability became detectable.

It is very interesting that we did not find break points caused by changes in the transaction tax. The Chinese government, for example, increased the stamp tax on stock trading on the Shanghai stock market from 0.3% to 0.5% on 10 May 1997. This tax rate had been changed several times between 1997 and 2008, yet our endogenous search procedure for structural breaks failed to identify any points for which the confidence interval covered these dates. The finding conflicts somewhat with the results published for the Chinese stock market by Baltagi et al. (2006), who found regime switching in the conditional variance equation as a result of the stamp tax rate increase on 10 May 1997. However, they did not control for other potential structural breaks possibly leading to spurious results.

Overall, regulatory actions other than the abolishment of price limits and the removal of a liquidity supplier, such as the establishment of derivative markets, the introduction of electronic trading systems, or the permission of short sales, seemingly did not cause breaks in the autocorrelation in stock indices returns, or at least the algorithm we applied did not reveal any such breaks.

6. CONCLUSION

The purpose of this chapter was, first, to test our hypothesis about whether financial crises (such as the 1997 Asian, 1998 Russian and 1999 Brazilian crises) can lead to structural breaks in the autocorrelation in stock index returns in emerging BRIC markets. Second, we aimed at determining whether possible changes in autocorrelation correspond to reversals of investors' behaviour around extreme events, as proposed in the literature (Koutmos, 1997; Bohl & Siklos, 2008; Sentana & Wadhwani, 1992).

Using the Bai and Perron (2003a) algorithm of sequential endogenous search for full and partial breaks in an ARMA–GARCH model, we arrive at results that are surprising in certain respects. Although the search algorithm identified some dates as break points associated with crises, we find only in one case (India, 26 February 1998–8 November 1998) very weak evidence of lower autocorrelation during the crisis period. For all other cases, we did not detect significant changes in the autocorrelation in the stock index returns. Outcomes are robust as they are supported by the partial change test results. Thus, the initial hypothesis of financial crises being possible causes of changes in the autocorrelation is not supported.

Instead, we identified significant shifts in autocorrelation patterns: for the Indian and Chinese stock market indices, which took place on 11 June 1992, and were both associated with regulatory measures. For the Indian stock market, the break was likely caused by the removal of the leading player, who had been driving the market for 1 year using illegal money. His removal possibly led to deteriorating liquidity and an increase in the autocorrelation in stock returns. For the Chinese stock market, the break possibly occurs as a result of the discontinuation of price limits leading to diminished autocorrelation.

Thus, we find that regulatory changes rather than financial crises are able to change autocorrelation patterns of stock index returns in emerging markets.

NOTE

1. We use a 1% significance level instead of the usual 5% level since Bai and Perron (2003b) critical values have been developed for linear models. Andrews (1993) provides critical values for a single break in a non-linear model, which are slightly above the corresponding values of the first stage of the Bai and Perron (2003b) procedure. Thus, the choice of 1% significance level yields fairly conservative results.

ACKNOWLEDGMENT

We gratefully acknowledge the financial support of the SU-HSE Scientific Fund, grant #08-04-0043.

REFERENCES

Andrews, D. W. K. (1993). Tests for parameter instability and structural change with unknown change point. *Econometrica, 61*(4), 821–856.

Atchison, M., Butler, K., & Simonds, R. (1987). Nonsynchronous security trading and market index autocorrelation. *Journal of Finance* (42), 533–553.

Bai, J., & Perron, P. (1998). Estimating and testing linear models with multiple structural changes. *Econometrica, 66*(1), 47–78.

Bai, J., & Perron, P. (2003a). Computation and analysis of multiple structural change models. *Journal of Applied Econometrics, 18*(1), 1–22.

Bai, J., & Perron, P. (2003b). Critical values for multiple structural change tests. *Econometrics Journal, 6*, 72–78.

Baltagi, B. H., Li, D., & Li, Q. (2006). Transaction tax and stock market behavior: Evidence from an emerging market. *Empirical Economics, 31*, 393–408.

Bohl, M. T., & Siklos, P. L. (2008). Empirical evidence on feedback trading in mature and emerging stock markets. *Applied Financial Economics, 18*, 1379–1389.

Boudoukh, J., Richardson, M., & Whitelaw, R. (1994). A tale of three schools: Insights on autocorrelations of short-horizon stock returns. *Review of Financial Studies* (7), 539–573.

Brock, W., Lakonishok, J., & LeBaron, B. (1992). Simple technical trading rules and the stochastic properties of stock returns. *Journal of Finance* (47), 1731–1764.

Chiang, R., & Wei, K. C. J. (1995). Estimation of volatility under price limits. Technical Report, Working Paper, University of Miami.

Choe, H. C., Kho, B.-C., & Stulz, R. M. (1999). Do foreign investors destabilize stock markets: The Korean experience in 1997. *Journal of Financial Economics* (54), 227–264.

Chou, P.-H. (1997). A Gibbs sampling approach of the estimation of linear regression models under daily price limits. *Pacific Basin Finance Journal, 5*, 39–62.

Conrad, J., Gultekin, M. N., & Kaul, G. (1991). Asymmetric predictability of conditional variances. *The Review of Financial Studies, 4*(4), 597–622.

Dornbusch, R., & Park, Y. (1995). Financial integration in a second-best world: Are we still sure about our classical prejudices? In: R. Dornbusch & Y. Park (Eds), *Financial opening: Policy lessons for Korea*. Seoul, Korea: Korea Institute of Finance.

Dubey, S. (1992). Grindlays, India in talks over scandal. *The Asian Wall Street Journal*, June 11, p. 14.

Fama, E. F. (1970). Efficient capital markets: A review of theory and empirical work. *Journal of Finance, 25*, 383–417.

Gelman, S., & Burhop, C. (2008). Taxation, regulation, and the information efficiency of the Berlin stock exchange, 1892–1913. *European Review of Economic History* (12), 39–66.

Hameed, A. (1992). Time varying factors and cross-autocorrelation in short-horizon stock returns. *The Journal of Financial Research, 20*(4), 435–458.

Jegadeesh, N., & Titman, S. (1992). Overreaction, delayed reaction, and contrarian profits. *The Review of Financial Studies, 8*(4), 973–993.

Kim, W., & Wei, S.-J. (2002). Foreign portfolio investors before and during a crisis. *Journal of International Economics* (56), 77–96.

Keim, D. (1989). Trading patterns, bid-ask spreads, and estimated security returns: The case of common stocks at calendar turning points. *Journal of Financial Economics* (25), 75–98.

Koutmos, G. (1997). Feedback Trading and the Autocorrelation Pattern of Stock Returns: Further Empirical Evidence. *Journal of International Money and Finance, 16*(4), 625–636.

Lo, A. W., & MacKinlay, A. C. (1988). Stock market prices do not follow random walks: evidence from a simple specification test. *Review of Financial Studies*, *1*, 41–66.

Mech, T. (1993). Portfolio return autocorrelation. *Journal of Financial Economics*, *34*, 307–344.

Perry, P. (1985). Portfolio serial correlation and nonsynchronous trading. *Journal of Financial and quantitative Analysis* (20), 517–523.

Sentana, E., & Wadhwani, S. B. (1992). Feedback traders and stock return autocorrelations: Evidence from a century of daily data. *Economic Journal* (102), 415–425.

Shen, C.-H., & Wang, L.-R. (1998). Daily serial correlation, trading volume and price limits: Evidence from the Taiwan stock market. *Pacific-Basin Finance Journal*, *6*, 251–273.

Sullivan, R., Timmermann, A., & White, H. (1999). Data-snooping, technical trading rule performance, and the bootstrap. *Journal of Finance*, *54*, 1647–1691.

PART IV
EMERGING MARKET COUNTRY STUDIES

MACROECONOMIC DYNAMICS AND THE TERM STRUCTURE OF INTEREST RATES IN EMERGING MARKETS: THE CASE OF BRAZIL ☆

Samer Shousha

ABSTRACT

In this chapter I characterize the relationship between macroeconomic variables and the terms structure of interest rates using the recent macro-finance approach adapted to the case of an emerging economy and applying it to Brazil. I find that macro variables help to explain the dynamics of the yield curve in emerging markets, specially in periods of high volatility. Moreover, the notion of great external vulnerability of emerging economies is confirmed by the strong role of the nominal exchange rate change, which explains up to 37% of the variation in yields in Brazil. However, the model does a poor job in forecasting yields during the financial crisis of 2008. This fact seems to be related to the strong fall in international commodity and industrial goods prices (in dollar terms), which limited the passthrough from the strong depreciation of the exchange rate to inflation.

☆This article is based on chapter 3 of my MA Thesis at PUC-Rio.

The Impact of the Global Financial Crisis on Emerging Financial Markets
Contemporary Studies in Economic and Financial Analysis, Volume 93, 547–579

ISSN: 1569-3759/doi:10.1108/S1569-3759(2011)0000093020

Keywords: Interest rates; term structure; affine term structure model; monetary policy; emerging markets; Brazil

JEL classifications: E43; E44; E58; F41; G12; G15

1. INTRODUCTION

As in most industrialized countries, several emerging markets use the short-term interest rate as its monetary policy tool. However, the cost of credit of the agents depends on the rates of different maturities. The term structure represents the relationship between the rates of different maturities at a certain moment in time. Therefore, it is essential to understand its dynamics in order to understand the monetary policy transmission mechanism in a more comprehensive way.

Recent macroeconomic theory demonstrates that the monetary authority determines the short-term rate responding to the different macroeconomic shocks to ensure economic stability. Therefore, the short end of the curve is likely to be strongly influenced by such shocks. Moreover, the long-term rates are determined by the future expectations of the short-term rates, adjusted by the risks of retaining these bonds. Consequently, changes in the expectations regarding the way monetary policy is conducted should also affect long-term rates. Therefore, we would expect the path of macro-economic variables to be relevant to explain the dynamics of the entire yield curve.

This chapter aims to characterize the relationship between the term structure of interest rates and macroeconomic variables in an emerging markets environment. This way, it is related to the growing macro-finance literature. The pioneering work along these lines is that of Ang and Piazzesi (2003), which basically extends the state vector of the standard affine model, including variables related to the real activity and inflation. Other studies, such as those by Rudebusch and Wu (2008) and Bekaert Cho and Moreno (2010), broadened this approach by using new Keynesian structural models together with an affine term structure model. Finally, Liu and Spencer (2010) develop a multi-country macro-finance model to study international economic and financial linkages and find that the standard closed economy specification might not be correct even for the United States.

Despite the different reasons for understanding the joint dynamics of the term structure of interest rates and macroeconomic variables, the papers related to this subject in open economies and specially in emerging markets present a limited approach and are usually focused on sovereign debt. Matsumara and Moreira (2005), for instance, develop a model based on term structure, credit risk and vector autoregressive models to study the relation between macroeconomic variables and the term structure of sovereign spreads of Brazil, while Bonomo and Lowenkron (2008) derive and estimate an affine no-arbitrage model with default risk and macroeconomic state variables to investigate the determinants of the term structure of emerging market external debt for Brazil, Colombia and Mexico. A probable reason for this inceptive aspect is the absence of long-term investments in local markets due to the long-lasting inflationary experience and economic instability. This chapter tries to fill this gap by estimating an affine term structure model for the local yield curve including macroeconomic variables.

The main contribution of the chapter is to evaluate whether macro variables help to explain the dynamics of the yield curve in an emerging economy. Besides that, differently from most of the previous studies, which are focused on developed countries, I include variables related to the external sector to understand their impact on rates in a small open economy. I find that macro variables help to explain the dynamics of the yield curve in emerging markets, specially in periods of high volatility. Variance decompositions show that cyclical variables (output gap, inflation rate and nominal exchange rate change) explain up to 53% of the variation of forecast errors in yields. Moreover, the additional variation, represented by unobservable factors, seems to be related to the variation in international risk aversion and inflation expectations. Finally, the notion of great external vulnerability of emerging economies is confirmed by the strong role of the nominal exchange rate change, which explains up to 37% of the variation in yields.

However, if we extend the forecasting period to include the great financial crisis of 2008, the model does a poor job in forecasting the term structure of interest rates. Although we had a strong depreciation of the Brazilian real, which lead my model to project higher rates,[1] the actual data showed a sharp fall since September 2008. These differences seem to be related to the strong fall in international commodity and industrial goods prices (in dollar terms), which strongly limited the passthrough of the exchange rate depreciation to inflation. This way, the Central Bank could focus on the real activity and reduce sharply the overnight rate. This movement was anticipated by the market and, consequently, longer rates also fell.

The chapter is organized as follows. Section 2 describes the data. Section 3 describes the modeling framework. Section 4 shows the empirical results. Section 5 concludes.

2. DATA

The period chosen to study the Brazilian case was from September 1999 to July 2008,[2] after the consolidation of the inflation targeting regime.[3] To summarize the yield curve, I used monthly averages of the pre-fixed DI swap yields with maturities of 1, 2, 3, 4, 6 and 12 months,[4] provided by the Brazilian Mercantile and Futures Exchange (BM&F). The pre-fixed DI swap is quoted as a zero coupon bond, in terms of a yield for a fixed maturity. In order to summarize the macroeconomic environment, some variables related to the real activity, inflation and the external sector were taken into consideration.[5] A proxy for the output gap was obtained by removing a trend from the industrial production index with seasonal adjustment, supplied by the Brazilian Institute of Geography and Statistics (IBGE), using the HP filter. As for inflation, I used the monthly trimmed mean core inflation rate measured by the extended consumer price index (IPCA), also supplied by the IBGE. Finally, I used the monthly change of the logarithm of the nominal exchange rate in relation to the U.S. dollar (multiplied by 100), supplied by the Central Bank of Brazil (BACEN). Table 1 presents a summary of the statistics related to each of the variables.

The evolution of the core inflation rate and the nominal exchange rate change for the period can be seen in Fig. 1.

Despite a reduction after the end of the fixed exchange rate regime, we can observe that we still have a great volatility in interest rates for different maturities due to the strong volatility of macroeconomic fundamentals, as the monetary authority tries to stabilize the economy and the yields respond

Table 1. Summary Statistics of Data (09/1999–07/2008).

	$i_t^{(1)}$	$i_t^{(2)}$	$i_t^{(3)}$	$i_t^{(4)}$	$i_t^{(6)}$	$i_t^{(12)}$	y	π	Δe
Mean	17.29	17.40	17.53	17.68	17.87	18.37	0.01	0.55	−0.16
Median	17.67	17.69	17.64	17.79	17.67	17.83	0.01	0.51	−0.85
Min	11.09	11.08	11.08	11.08	11.07	10.82	−5.76	0.20	−10.01
Max	26.63	27.00	27.38	27.70	28.23	31.18	5.46	1.36	13.00
Standard deviation	3.74	3.84	3.95	4.09	4.30	4.91	2.04	0.23	3.69
Skewness	0.35	0.31	0.29	0.27	0.32	0.57	−0.12	1.55	0.55
Kurtosis	0.17	−0.01	0.18	−0.37	−0.45	−0.21	0.38	3.25	1.10
Autocorrelations	0.99	0.98	0.98	0.97	0.97	0.96	0.68	0.83	0.35

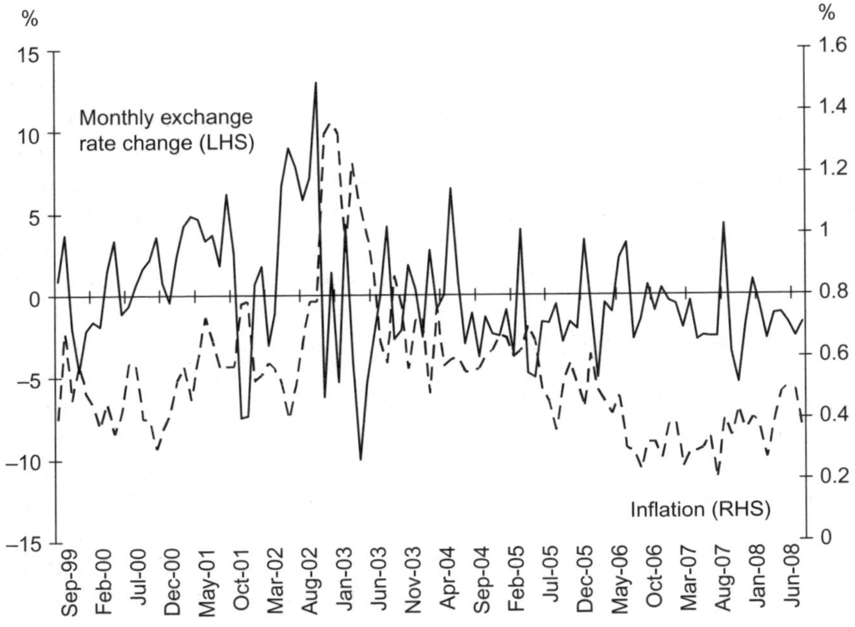

Fig. 1. Monthly Inflation Rate and Nominal Exchange Rate Change.

to the changes in expectations after the shocks. The evolution of rates for different maturities can be observed in Fig. 2.

As we can see in Figs. 1 and 2, the periods of higher volatility for rates are those with greater macroeconomic stability. It is important to note that the period studied was marked by several shocks, especially in 2001 and 2002, when the Central Bank could not keep inflation under the target range limits.[6] In 2001, the monetary authority had to deal with the energy crisis, the terrorist attacks of September 11 and the Argentinean crisis, and in 2002, with the election crisis. The confidence crisis of 2002 was particularly critical, faced with strong exchange rate devaluation caused by uncertainties over the future economic performance, together with an increase in international risk aversion. The presence of such a large number of shocks, in a short period, demonstrates the difficulties in the implementation of monetary policy in emerging economies, extremely prone to external vulnerability. Thus, it seems natural to evaluate the joint dynamics of the term structure of interest rates and the macroeconomic scenario.

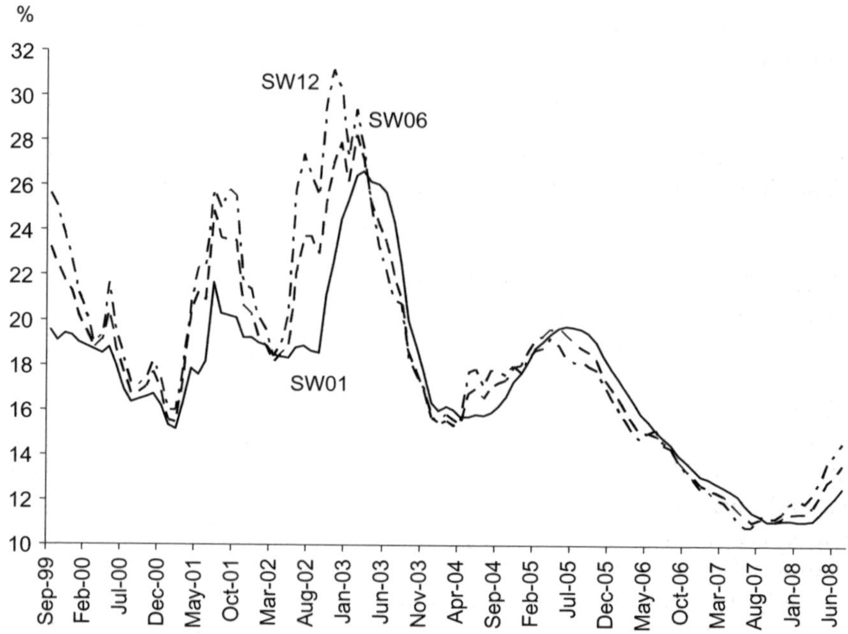

Fig. 2. Monthly Swap Yields.

3. MODEL

3.1. General Structure of the Model

The model selected was an affine model of the term structure of interest rates introduced by Duffie and Kan (1996). Basically, all applications of multifactor models of the yield curve have focused on the special cases of this family, since it "accommodates time-varying means and volatilities of the state variables through affine specifications of the risk-neutral drift and volatility coefficients" (Dai & Singleton, 2000). This model allows us to have a time-varying risk premium with relatively simple specifications of the system dynamics. This characteristic is very important, since there is plenty of evidence that the expectations hypothesis usually does not hold. Furthermore, this class of models provides us with closed solutions, which make its econometric application easier.

In the affine model, the vector of state variables F_t of dimension $n \times 1$ follows a Gaussian process VAR(1):[7]

$$F_t = \Phi_0 + \Phi F_{t-1} + \Sigma \varepsilon_t \tag{1}$$

where $\varepsilon_t \sim N(0, I_n)$, Σ is diagonal and $\Phi_{n \times n}$ is a lower triangular matrix.

The short-term interest rate is defined as a linear function of the variables:

$$i_t = \Delta_0 + \Delta_1' F_t \tag{2}$$

The risk prices associated with the shocks ε_t are defined as a linear function of the state vector:

$$\Lambda_t = \Lambda_0 + \Lambda_1 F_t \tag{3}$$

The state Eq. (1), the short-term rate Eq. (2) and the prices of risk Eq. (3) form an essentially affine Gaussian term structure model in discrete time with the imposition of absence of arbitrage or an $A_0(N)$ model, as defined in Dai and Singleton (2000). This model contains a constant volatility for the yield curve factors, but the risk pricing is state-dependent, which implies conditional heteroscedasticity in the risk premium.

Finally, I would like to relate the interest rates of the bonds to the state variables in such structure. The compound rate $i_t^{(n)}$ of a bond with maturity n is given by

$$i_t^{(n)} = -\frac{\log P_t^{(n)}}{n} \tag{4}$$

Under the hypothesis used, Duffie and Kan (1996) show that the price of a bond with maturity n is given by

$$P_t^{(n)} = \exp(A_n + B_n' F_t) \tag{5}$$

where A_n and B_n are defined recursively by

$$A_{n+1} = A_n + B_n'(\Phi_0 - \Sigma \Lambda_0) + \frac{1}{2} B_n' \Sigma \Sigma' B_n - \Delta_0 \tag{6}$$

$$B_{n+1} = B_n'(\Phi - \Sigma \Lambda_1) - \Delta_1 \tag{7}$$

and the initial values are $A_1 = -\Delta_0$ and $B_1 = -\Delta_1$.

In order to obtain the interest rates, I use Eq. (4) and therefore have

$$i_t^{(n)} = -\frac{A_n}{n} - \frac{B_n}{n} F_t = a_n + b_n F_t \tag{8}$$

where $a_n = -A_n/n$ and $b_n = -B_n/n$.

We can also calculate the implicit term premium present in the term structure. In order to do so, I focus on the one-period excess return (conditional expected excess holding period return), where I compare the return obtained from buying a long-term bond and keeping it for one period to the return obtained from the short-term rate. This way, the one-period excess return can be obtained through the following expression:

$$rx_{t+1}^{(n)} = \log\left(\frac{P_{t+1}^{(n-1)}}{P_t^{(n)}}\right) - i_t = ni_t^{(n)} - (n-1)i_{t+1}^{(n-1)} - i_t^{(1)} \tag{9}$$

The conditional expected excess return is therefore

$$\begin{aligned} E_t(rx_{t+1}^{(n)}) = & -(A_n + B_n' F_t) + A_{n-1} + B_{n-1}' E_t(F_{t+1}) - (\Delta_0 + \Delta_1' F_t) \\ = & -[A_{n-1} + B_{n-1}'(\Phi_0 - \Sigma\Lambda_0) + \frac{1}{2} B_{n-1}' \Sigma\Sigma' B_{n-1} - \Delta_0] \\ & - [B_{n-1}'(\Phi - \Sigma\Lambda_1) - \Delta_1']F_t + A_{n-1} \\ & + B_{n-1}'(\Phi_0 + \Phi F_t) - (\Delta_0 + \Delta_1' F_t) \\ = & B_{n-1}' \Sigma\Lambda_0 + B_{n-1}' \Sigma\Lambda_1 F_t - \frac{1}{2} B_{n-1}' \Sigma\Sigma' B_{n-1} \end{aligned} \tag{10}$$

From this equation, it can be seen that we have a Jensen inequality component, a constant risk premium and a time-varying risk premium. It is easy to see that if $\Lambda_1 = 0$, the expected excess return is constant in time and therefore, the expectations hypothesis is valid. As several studies reject, at least partially, the validity of the expectations hypothesis, I specify $\Lambda_1 \neq 0$.

3.2. Yields Only Model Structure

Having introduced the affine term structure model, I would like first of all to check its applicability to emerging markets using Brazilian data.[8] To do that, I begin by formulating a standard affine model only with latent variables which, despite not providing any economic insights, can function as a benchmark for the Complete Model.

Initially, following Litterman and Scheinkman (1991), I carried out a principal components analysis to identify the number of necessary factors to describe the yield curve dynamics. The principal components analysis consists of the diagonalization of the yield covariance matrix, which represents a risk measure associated with the movement of the yield curve. Through this technique, we obtain a matrix of eigenvectors and a vector of

Table 2. Proportion of Variance Explained by Principal Components Analysis.

	PC1	PC2	PC3	PC4	PC5
Eigenvalue	5.8070	0.1874	0.0048	0.0006	0.0001
Variance explained	0.9678	0.0312	0.0008	0.0001	17E−06
Variance accumulated	0.9678	0.9991	0.9999	1.0000	1.0000

eigenvalues with the matrix of covariances V satisfying the following equation:

$$VA = A\Lambda$$

where A is the eigenvector matrix and Λ is a diagonal matrix with the eigenvalue vector on the main diagonal. By using this relationship and knowing that A is an orthonormal matrix, I can write

$$V = A\Lambda A'$$

The proportion of risk attributed to each factor is obtained through the normalization of the eigenvalues associated with each factor obtained from this decomposition. Table 2 shows the variance explained by each of the factors. We can observe that the first two principal components account for 99.9% of the rate variation. The components obtained have a very clear interpretation, similar to the one suggested by Litterman and Scheinkman (1991) with a component of level and another one of slope. Fig. 3 shows the weights of each component for the different rates.

The first principal component accounts for 96.78% of the rate variation and is clearly a component of level, while the second principal component accounts for 3.12% of the rate variation. This way, we use a Gaussian model with two latent factors and constant volatility, or, as in Dai and Singleton (2000) classification, an $A_0(2)$ model.

3.3. Complete Model Structure

Since Taylor's (1993) seminal work, several studies have been using some variance of Taylor rule to represent how the central bank sets the short-term

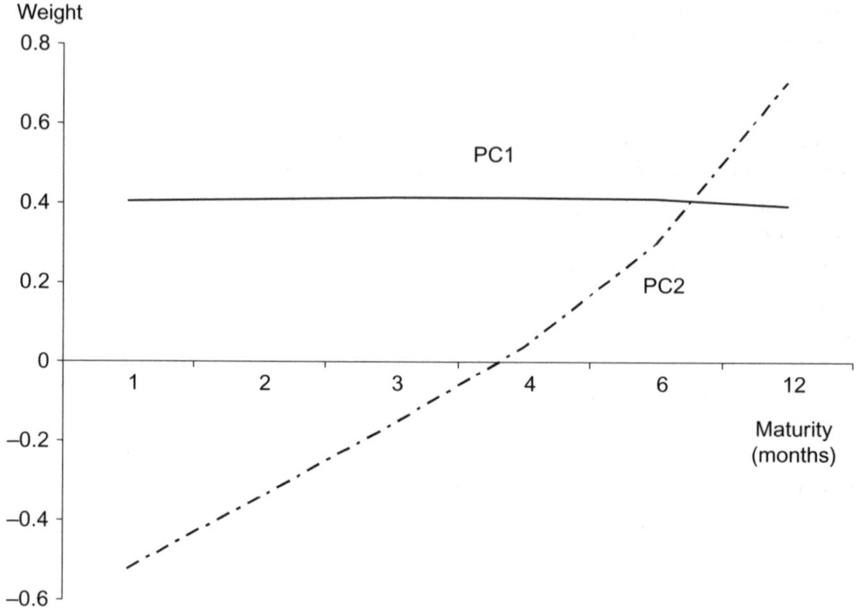

Fig. 3. Principal Components Weights in Each Yield.

rate. In an inflation targeting regime of a small open economy, the reaction function of the central bank can be represented as

$$i_t = r^* + \pi_t^* + \alpha_\pi(E_t\pi_{t+j} - \pi_{t+j}^*) + \alpha_y y_t + \alpha_{\Delta e}\Delta e_t + u_t \tag{11}$$

where i_t is the short-term rate, r^* the neutral real rate (potentially variant in time), $E_t\pi_t$ the inflation expectation, π_t^* the inflation target, y_t the output gap, Δe_t the nominal exchange rate change and u_t the monetary policy shocks. In this case, the monetary authority determines the short-term rate in its long-term value plus the cyclical adjustments related to the deviations in the inflation expectation regarding the target, output gap change and exchange rate movements.[9] Besides, as can be seen in Ang, Dong and Piazzesi (2005), forward-looking Taylor rules like these are compatible with the affine model, since after putting the system under the state space form, the inflation expectations can be obtained as a function of the current variables. On the other hand, in a free floating exchange rate regime, the uncovered interest rate parity characterizes the relationship between the domestic and the international interest rate:

$$i_t = i_t^* + E_t(\Delta e_{t+1}) + x_t$$

where i_t^* is the international interest rate and x_t the risk premium or the country risk. Therefore, the potential variables for the model are π_t^*, π_t, y_t, Δe_t, i_t^* and x_t. However, it is impossible to include more than three endogenous variables in the model without eroding the quality of the estimation, due to the increase in the model dimension and the small sample available. Besides, considering the recent process of credibility construction of the monetary authority in Brazil, the inflation target perceived by agents may be different from the target set by the National Monetary Council (CMN).[10] Finally, the country risk is not directly observable, and is also associated with macroeconomic fundamentals. Therefore, I decided to include the variables responsible for the cyclical adjustment of the short-term rate as macroeconomic variables:

$$X_t^o = (y_t \quad \pi_t \quad \Delta e_t)'$$

In order to understand the variations of the long-term level in the interest rates, the monetary policy shocks and the external factors, I also have to include two latent factors, $X_t^u = (L_t \quad S_t)$.[11] Therefore, the Complete Model consists of three macro factors and two latent factors.

The selection of the number of lags is a delicate issue. Although the inclusion of a greater number of lags is compatible with a more realistic characterization of the monetary policy transmission mechanism, it can reduce the precision in the coefficient estimation, especially in the case of Brazil, where the size of the sample is small. When I estimate a VAR with rates, following Evans and Marshall (1998), the inclusion of two lags seems to better accommodate this trade-off.[12]

Therefore, I specify the state vector $X_t = (X_t^o, X_t^u) = (y_t \quad \pi_t \quad \Delta e_t \quad L_t \quad S_t)'$ as a VAR(2) Gaussian process:

$$X_t = \phi_0 + \phi_1 X_{t-1} + \phi_2 X_{t-2} + \Theta u_t \tag{12}$$

where $u_t \sim IIDN(0, I_5)$.

By defining $F_t = (X_t \quad X_{t-1})$, I can rewrite the dynamics in the compact shape of a first-order Gaussian VAR:

$$F_t = \Phi_0 + \Phi F_{t-1} + \Sigma \varepsilon_t \tag{13}$$

where

$$\Sigma = \begin{bmatrix} \Theta & \mathbf{0}_{5x5} \\ \mathbf{0}_{5x5} & \mathbf{0}_{5x5} \end{bmatrix}$$

$$\Phi_0 = (\phi_0' \quad \mathbf{0}_{1x5})'$$

$$\Phi = \begin{bmatrix} \phi_1 & \phi_2 \\ \mathbf{I}_{5x5} & \mathbf{0}_{5x5} \end{bmatrix}$$

4. EMPIRICAL RESULTS

4.1. Yields Only Model Estimation

I estimate the Yields Only Model using maximum likelihood based on the Kalman filter. For Gaussian models, this strategy is optimum in relation to the class of linear estimators and provides consistent and efficient estimators, as can be seen in Bollersev and Wooldridge (1992).[13] Moreover, I manage to avoid the usual hypothesis that only some randomly selected rates are measured with errors, as in studies based on the strategy introduced by Chen and Scott (1993).[14] Therefore, I can assume that all rates are measured with errors and allow the estimation itself to calculate these measurement errors. Given the parameters of the model, as well as other necessary normalizations, unbiased estimators of the latent variables L_t and S_t, which represent the level and the slope of the yield curve, can be obtained through the Kalman filter.

As explained in the previous section, the state vector $F_t = (L_t, S_t)$ follows a VAR(1) Gaussian process. The state equation is therefore given by

$$F_t = \Phi F_{t-1} + \Sigma \varepsilon_t \tag{14}$$

where $\varepsilon_t \sim IIDN(0, I_2)$, Σ_{2x2} is diagonal and Φ_{2x2} is lower triangular.

The yields used in the estimation are those with maturities of 1, 2, 3, 4, 6 and 12 months. This way, the observable variables can be grouped into the vector $Z_t \equiv [i_t^{(1)} \quad i_t^{(2)} \quad i_t^{(3)} \quad i_t^{(4)} \quad i_t^{(6)} \quad i_t^{(12)}]'$.

Being extracted in an endogenous way, the latent factors are invariant to some affine transformations and, therefore, some normalization is necessary to identify them. We then have (i) zero mean for the factors, that is, $\Phi_0 = 0$; (ii) unit weights over the factors in the short-term rate equation and (iii) Δ_0 fixed on the sample mean of the one-month rate. Therefore, our short-term rate equation is

$$i_t^{(1)} = \Delta_0 + \Delta_1' F_t = 17.6817 + L_t + S_t$$

The measurement equation can then be written as

$$Z_t = G' + H'F_t + v_t \tag{15}$$

where

$$G = [a_1 \quad a_2 \quad a_3 \quad a_4 \quad a_6 \quad a_{12}]$$

$$H' = \begin{bmatrix} b_1^{(1)} & b_2^{(1)} \\ b_1^{(2)} & b_2^{(2)} \\ b_1^{(3)} & b_2^{(3)} \\ b_1^{(4)} & b_2^{(4)} \\ b_1^{(6)} & b_2^{(6)} \\ b_1^{(12)} & b_2^{(12)} \end{bmatrix}$$

where a_n and b_n are given by the recursive equations derived in the previous section. I assume that the measurement errors v_t are i.i.d., with zero-mean multivariate normal distribution and diagonal covariance matrix R, that is, $v_t \sim IIDN(0, R)$.

The optimization is carried out using the MATLAB toolbox E^4, which allows the estimate of different models in the state space form.[15] I used a quasi-Newton algorithm with BFGS updating to optimize the likelihood function. The standard errors are calculated through the inversion of a numerical approximation of the Hessian matrix of the likelihood function.

4.2. Complete Model Estimation

To estimate the Complete Model, I used again maximum likelihood based on the Kalman filter. In addition to the advantages described in the estimation of the Yields Only Model, this approach allows us more flexibility in the model specification compared to Chen and Scott's (1993) traditional approach. Ang and Piazzesi (2003), for example, assume that the macroeconomic dynamics does not depend on the latent variables, while Rudebusch and Wu (2008) define random values of the risk premium as zero. On the other hand, the estimation of large and strongly nonlinear models through the Kalman filter becomes especially sensitive to the initial conditions. This way, I must be very careful to guarantee I am not using a local minimum of the likelihood function.[16]

The rates used to construct the Kalman filter are again the 1-, 2-, 3-, 4-, 6- and 12-month rates. This way, the observable variables can be grouped into the vector

$$Z_t \equiv \begin{bmatrix} i_t^{(1)} \\ i_t^{(2)} \\ i_t^{(3)} \\ i_t^{(4)} \\ i_t^{(6)} \\ i_t^{(12)} \\ y_t \\ \pi_t \\ \Delta e_t \\ y_{t-1} \\ \pi_{t-1} \\ \Delta e_{t-1} \end{bmatrix}$$

The measurement equation can be written again as

$$Z_t = G' + H'F_t + v_t \tag{16}$$

where we now have

$$G = [a_1 \quad a_2 \quad a_3 \quad a_4 \quad a_6 \quad a_{12} \quad 0_{1\times 6}]$$

$$H' = \begin{bmatrix} b_1^{(1)} & b_2^{(1)} & b_3^{(1)} & b_4^{(1)} & b_5^{(1)} & b_6^{(1)} & b_7^{(1)} & b_8^{(1)} & b_9^{(1)} & b_{10}^{(1)} \\ b_1^{(2)} & b_2^{(2)} & b_3^{(2)} & b_4^{(2)} & b_5^{(2)} & b_6^{(2)} & b_7^{(2)} & b_8^{(2)} & b_9^{(2)} & b_{10}^{(2)} \\ b_1^{(3)} & b_2^{(3)} & b_3^{(3)} & b_4^{(3)} & b_5^{(3)} & b_6^{(3)} & b_7^{(3)} & b_8^{(3)} & b_9^{(3)} & b_{10}^{(3)} \\ b_1^{(4)} & b_2^{(4)} & b_3^{(4)} & b_4^{(4)} & b_5^{(4)} & b_6^{(4)} & b_7^{(4)} & b_8^{(4)} & b_9^{(4)} & b_{10}^{(4)} \\ b_1^{(6)} & b_2^{(6)} & b_3^{(6)} & b_4^{(6)} & b_5^{(6)} & b_6^{(6)} & b_7^{(6)} & b_8^{(6)} & b_9^{(6)} & b_{10}^{(6)} \\ b_1^{(12)} & b_2^{(12)} & b_3^{(12)} & b_4^{(12)} & b_5^{(12)} & b_6^{(12)} & b_7^{(12)} & b_8^{(12)} & b_9^{(12)} & b_{10}^{(12)} \\ 1 & 0 & 0 & 0 & 0 & 0 & 0 & 0 & 0 & 0 \\ 0 & 1 & 0 & 0 & 0 & 0 & 0 & 0 & 0 & 0 \\ 0 & 0 & 1 & 0 & 0 & 0 & 0 & 0 & 0 & 0 \\ 0 & 0 & 0 & 0 & 0 & 1 & 0 & 0 & 0 & 0 \\ 0 & 0 & 0 & 0 & 0 & 0 & 1 & 0 & 0 & 0 \\ 0 & 0 & 0 & 0 & 0 & 0 & 0 & 1 & 0 & 0 \end{bmatrix}$$

I assume that the measurement errors v_t are i.i.d., with normal multivariate distribution of zero mean and covariance matrix R. In addition, I assume that the observable state variables do not contain measurement errors, so the last six elements of v_t are zeros and R is equally zero except for the upper left 6×6 submatrix, which represents the covariance matrix of the measurement error of the rates and is a diagonal matrix. By using the same filtering procedure as in the previous section, I can obtain the relevant parameters to describe the system dynamics, the short-term rate and the market prices of risk, together with a time series for the latent factors. In order to make the model more treatable and motivated by unrestricted regressions using the latent factors obtained in the affine model, I restricted A_n and B_n and the prices of risk to depend only upon X_t. Technically, this restriction is obtained by imposing that the short-term rate weights are different from zero only in contemporary variables and that the F_t is a VAR(1) under the risk-neutral measure. Besides, I can, without loss of generality, use state variables with zero mean and, therefore, I have $\Phi_0 = \mathbf{0}$.[17]

I also have to perform some normalization in order to obtain an unbiased estimator of the latent variables L_t and S_t through the Kalman filter. For that, I fix again Δ_0 as the unconditional mean of the one-month rate and use unit weights in the latent factors. I therefore have the following equation as short-term rate:

$$i_t^{(1)} = \Delta_0 + \Delta_1' F_t = 17.6817 + \Delta_y * y_t + \Delta_\pi * \pi_t + \Delta_{\Delta e} * \Delta e + L_t + S_t \quad (17)$$

Moreover, as the Brazilian monetary authority follows an inflation targeting regime with a forward-looking rule during the period, I have to carry out some additional normalization. As shown in Ang et al. (2005), some parameters associated with the forecast horizon are not identified for this type of monetary policy rule. In order to identify them, I have to impose the additional identification hypothesis of absence of conditional correlation between the latent factors and the macroeconomic factors. Finally, following the strategy of the previous subsection, I imposed no correlation among the latent variables.

4.3. Main Results

4.3.1. Basic Estimation

The model was estimated from September 1999 to December 2007, using the period from January 2008 to July 2008 to evaluate its forecast performance outside the sample. Tables 3–5 present the estimation results for each model. The factors L_t and S_t are quite persistent and we can once again interpret the latent factors as a level factor and a slope factor. All parameters are strongly significant.[18] The standard deviations of the measurement errors for the 1-, 2-, 3-, 4-, 6- and 12-month yields are, respectively, 13, 0, 6, 9, 13 and 74 basis points for the Yields Only Model and 16, 0, 8, 10, 0 and 47 basis points for the Complete Model, slightly lower than those obtained in Almeida (2004).

Fig. 4 shows that the impact of the macroeconomic variables is growing in module with maturity. We can interpret these initial responses as the presence of some inertia in the inflation rate, which leads to an increase in long-term rates due to the increase in the expectations of future inflation after inflation shocks. In addition, they represent the lags of the pass-through in the exchange rate changes, which also leads to a bigger increase in the long-term rates. Finally, the increasingly negative relationship with the output gap is related to crisis periods, where we have, at the same time, a widening in the output gap and an increase in the yield curve slope.

The fit of the model inside the sample is very good for all rates, as can be seen in Figs. 5 and 6, with an adjusted R^2 greater than 96% for all yields in

Table 3. Yields Only Model Estimates.

Factors Dynamics (Φ)				
	L_{t-1}	S_{t-1}		
L_t	0.9456 (0.0049)	–		
S_t	0.0508 (0.0058)	0.9496 (0.0069)		
Short-Term Rate Parameters (Δ)				
Δ_0		Δ_L	Δ_S	
17.6817*		10,000*	10,000*	
Prices of Risk(Λ)				
	Λ_0		L_t	S_t
$\Lambda_{L,t}$	−6.2795 (0.4426)		−0.0178 (0.0019)	0.1605 (0.0123)
$\Lambda_{S,t}$	11.0297 (1.4600)		0.0031 (0.0003)	0.0086 (0.0009)
Standard Deviations (Σ)				
$\ln(\Sigma_L)$	0.4136 (0.0795)			
$\ln(\Sigma_S)$	−0.3202 (0.0315)			
Measurement Errors (R)				
$\ln(\Sigma_1^2)$	−4.0513 (0.1784)			
$\ln(\Sigma_2^2)$	−34.9686 (1.6983)			
$\ln(\Sigma_3^2)$	−5.4971 (0.2122)			
$\ln(\Sigma_4^2)$	−4.7114 (0.2121)			
$\ln(\Sigma_6^2)$	−4.0708 (0.3951)			
$\ln(\Sigma_{12}^2)$	−0.6134 (0.1967)			

Note: Standard deviations of estimates in brackets. The parameters with asterisks are fixed.

both models. The accuracy of the Yields Only Model is smaller for longer term rate, essentially in the periods of greater volatility.

As the use of a yield curve model also aims at offering good approximations for other rates, Fig. 7 shows the fit of the model for the nine-month rate, which was not included in the estimation. As we can observe, the model also provides a good estimation inside the sample for this rate, confirming the good performance of the model.

I may compare the forecast performance outside the sample of both models and a random walk for different periods, using the root mean square error (RMSE) metric. Table 6 shows the results of this comparison.

Table 4. Complete Model Estimates: Factor Dynamics.

Factors Dynamics (ϕ_1)

	y_{t-1}	π_{t-1}	Δe_{t-1}	L_{t-1}	S_{t-1}
y_t	0.6555 (0.0149)	−0.7109 (0.0160)	0.0040 (0.0001)	−0.0224 (0.0005)	1.4983 (0.0276)
π_t	0.0130 (0.0003)	0.7580 (0.0168)	0.0009 (0.0000)	0.0289 (0.0007)	0.9833 (0.0208)
Δe_t	−0.3673 (0.0067)	0.2160 (0.0052)	0.3095 (0.0074)	−0.7522 (0.0167)	−6.5701 (0.0409)
L_t	−0.0056 (0.0001)	−0.0157 (0.0004)	0.0008 (0.0002)	1.0043 (0.0141)	1.3189 (0.0254)
S_t	0.0006 (0.0000)	−0.0170 (0.0004)	−0.0254 (0.0006)	−0.0289 (0.0007)	0.8478 (0.0185)

Factors Dynamics (ϕ_2)

	y_{t-2}	π_{t-2}	Δe_{t-2}	L_{t-2}	S_{t-2}
y_t	−0.0515 (0.0013)	−0.0037 (0.0001)	0.0860 (0.0021)	−0.0788 (0.0019)	−1.2368 (0.0245)
π_t	−0.0131 (0.0003)	−0.0299 (0.0007)	0.0298 (0.0007)	−0.0241 (0.0006)	−0.8790 (0.0191)
Δe_t	0.5667 (0.0131)	−0.6718 (0.0152)	−0.0792 (0.0019)	0.7648 (0.0170)	4.7827 (0.0398)
L_t	0.0846 (0.0021)	0.4898 (0.0115)	0.0768 (0.0019)	−0.0674 (0.0016)	−2.3816 (0.0342)
S_t	0.0065 (0.0002)	0.0101 (0.0002)	−0.0006 (0.0000)	0.0331 (0.0008)	−0.1485 (0,0036)

Cholesky Decomposition of the Covariance Matrix (Θ)

	y_t	π_t	Δe_t	L_t	S_t
y_t	0.3668 (0.0087)	0*	0*	0*	0*
π_t	0.0108 (0.0003)	−1.7991 (0.0299)	0*	0*	0*
Δe_t	0.0242 (0.0006)	−0.0969 (0.0024)	0.4324 (0.0097)	0*	0*
L_t	0*	0*	0*	−0.3641 (0.0084)	0*
S_t	0*	0*	0*	0*	−2.8868 (0.0318)

Table 5. Complete Model Estimates: Prices of risk.

Short-Term Rate Parameters (Δ)

Δ_0	Δ_y	Δ_π	$\Delta_{\Delta e}$	Δ_L	Δ_S
17.6817*	−0.0103 (0.0003)	−0.2074 (0.0050)	0.0321 (0.0008)	1.0000*	1.0000*

Risk Matrix (Λ)

	y_t	π_t	Δe_t	L_t	S_t
$\Lambda_{y,t}$	0.4205 (0.0099)	2.8814 (0.0362)	−0.1984 (0.0048)	1.5637 (0.0283)	6.0081 (0.0407)
$\Lambda_{\pi,t}$	0.4994 (0.0117)	0.2081 (0.0050)	0.0315 (0.0008)	1.0460 (0.0218)	4.0553 (0.0389)
$\Lambda_{\Delta e,t}$	0.8299 (0.0179)	−1.3767 (0.0260)	−1.6138 (0.0216)	0.0654 (0.0016)	8.7892 (0.0415)
$\Lambda_{L,t}$	−0.1121 (0.0027)	0.0979 (0.0024)	0.0563 (0.0013)	−0.0400 (0.0010)	4.3843 (0.0391)
$\Lambda_{S,t}$	0.6817 (0.0152)	−0.6569 (0.0149)	−1.2454 (0.0217)	−0.1983 (0.0048)	7.1365 (0.0411)

Prices of Risk (Λ_0)		Measurement Errors (R)	
$\Lambda_{y,t}$	3.0082 (0.0366)	$\ln(\Sigma_1^2)$	−3.6970 (0.0383)
$\Lambda_{\pi,t}$	−15.6197 (0.0421)	$\ln(\Sigma_2^2)$	−20.9160 (0.0422)
$\Lambda_{\Delta e,t}$	0.0022 (0.0001)	$\ln(\Sigma_3^2)$	−4.9310 (0.0399)
$\Lambda_{L,t}$	−1.7093 (0.0297)	$\ln(\Sigma_4^2)$	−4.6679 (0.0397)
$\Lambda_{S,t}$	1.9270 (0.0314)	$\ln(\Sigma_6^2)$	−16.8530 (0.0421)
		$\ln(\Sigma_{12}^2)$	−1.5171 (0.0278)

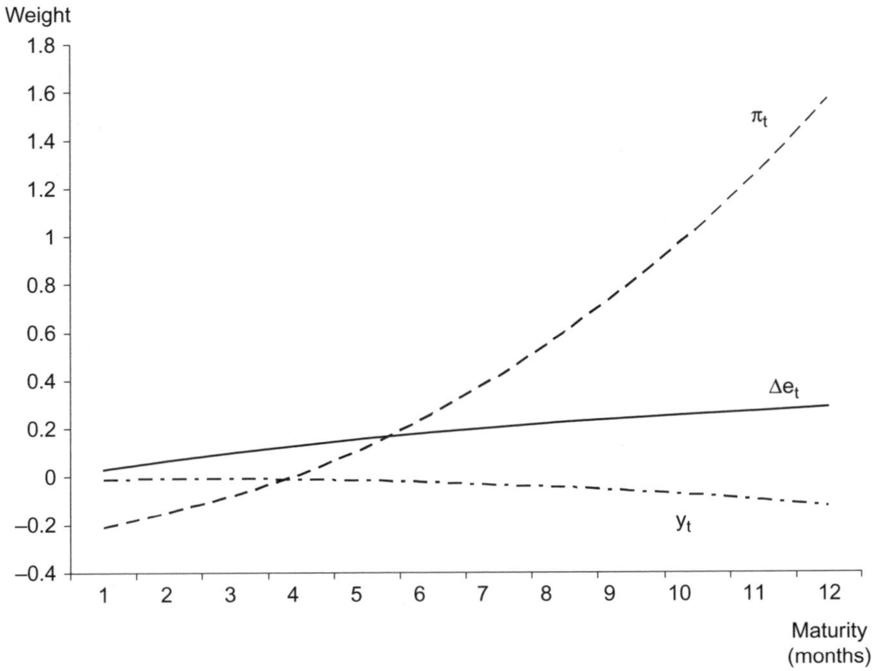

Fig. 4. Macroeconomic Factors Coefficients: Complete Model.

Both models have a good forecast power, but usually worse than a random walk,[19] specially for shorter horizons. The Complete Model has a better performance just for the 12-month rate at short horizons, while the model only with latent variables outperforms the others for the other rates for longer horizons. Therefore, I cannot state that the Complete Model is better for the forecast of the yield curve outside the sample.

I can interpret our model as a Gaussian VAR and therefore compute impulse-response functions and variance decomposition. The results of the impulse responses can be observed in Figs. 8–10, where I present the effect of the macroeconomic shocks on the rates in the Complete Model.[20]

The results obtained regarding the exchange rate and inflation shocks are as expected, with an exchange rate devaluation or an inflation surprise leading to an increase in the rates of all maturities (although we have a small initial reduction in the one month rate). As for the effect of the shock on the output gap, there is a small initial reduction and a later increase in the one-month rate, while the reduction in the 12-month rate is a bit more persistent.

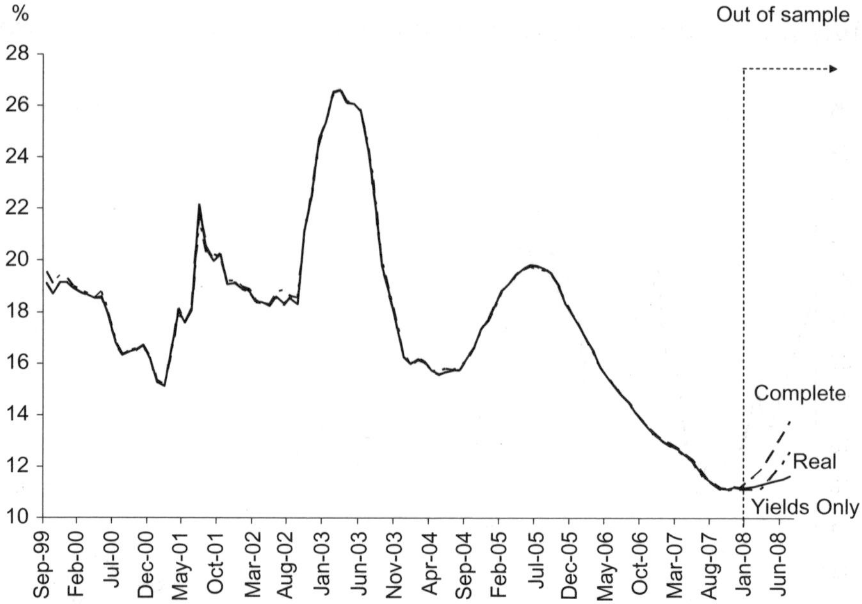

Fig. 5. One Month Swap: Model Comparison.

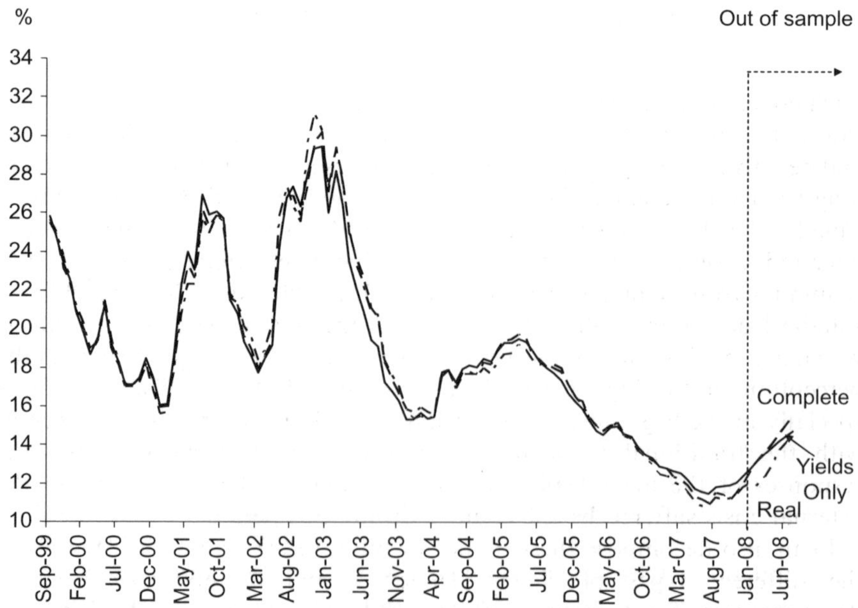

Fig. 6. 12-Month Swap: Model Comparison.

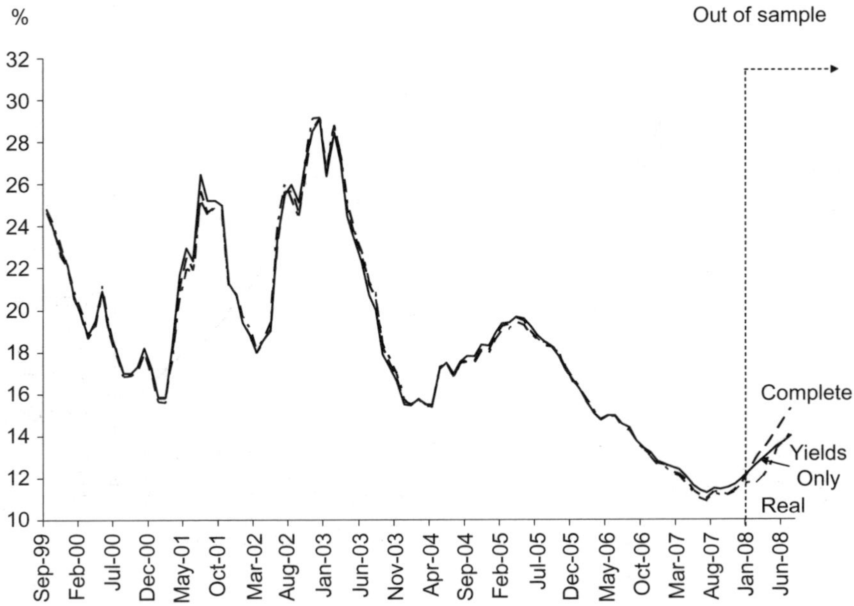

Fig. 7. Nine month Swap: Model Comparison.

Such effect on the 12-month rate stems from the response of the variables to external crisis, where we have, at the same time, exchange rate devaluations and negative output gap, as the economy enters a recession, with increases in long-term rates coming from higher inflation expectations in the future. Finally, the slope presents results as expected, with an initial increase and later reduction after inflation shocks and increases after exchange shocks, stemming from a higher expectation of future inflation. The shock of a standard deviation in the inflation and in the output has absolute effects which are much smaller than the exchange rate shocks, compatible with the perception of the high external vulnerability of the Brazilian economy, specially in the beginning of the period studied. These results are coherent with the traditional monetary policy transmission mechanism and the responses of the macroeconomic variables and of the yield curve to the external crisis suffered by the country during this period.

I can also decompose the variance of the forecast errors that stem from the different types of shock. Tables 7 and 8 show the variance decomposition for forecast horizons of 1, 12 and 60 months for both models.

Table 6. Forecast Comparisons (RMSE).

	Horizon (Months)	RW	Latent	Complete
$i_t^{(1)}$	1	0.01	0.06	0.34
	3	0.02	0.10	0.56
	6	0.74	0.44	1.16
$i_t^{(2)}$	1	0.01	0.08	0.33
	3	0.04	0.16	0.62
	6	0.87	0.41	1.20
$i_t^{(3)}$	1	0.01	0.10	0.39
	3	0.07	0.22	0.71
	6	1.00	0.41	1.28
$i_t^{(4)}$	1	0.01	0.14	0.44
	3	0.11	0.27	0.78
	6	1.12	0.42	1.32
$i_t^{(6)}$	1	0.05	0.25	0.53
	3	0.18	0.43	0.92
	6	1.38	0.48	1.44
$i_t^{(12)}$	1	0.18	0.80	0.63
	3	0.32	1.12	1.08
	6	1.85	1.31	1.47

Several conclusions can be drawn from this decomposition. For the one-month forecast horizon, the macroeconomic variables explain, on average, around 10% of the variance, whereas for longer horizons they explain around 43% on average. In general, the proportion of unconditional variance accounted for by macroeconomic factors is increasing with the maturity of the yields, opposed to what occurs with American rates.[21] This results from the strong role played by the nominal exchange rate change, which may represent both variations in future inflation expectations (stemming from the passthrough of exchange rate devaluations to inflation) and changes in the external risk premium. Besides that, even for the 12-month rates, where I obtain the largest effect, the results are weaker,[22] highlighting the need to use a greater amount of variables in order to characterize the rate dynamics in an emerging economy. Moreover, the proportion of the variance accounted for by the level factor decreases as maturity increases, whilst that explained by the slope factor increases with maturity.

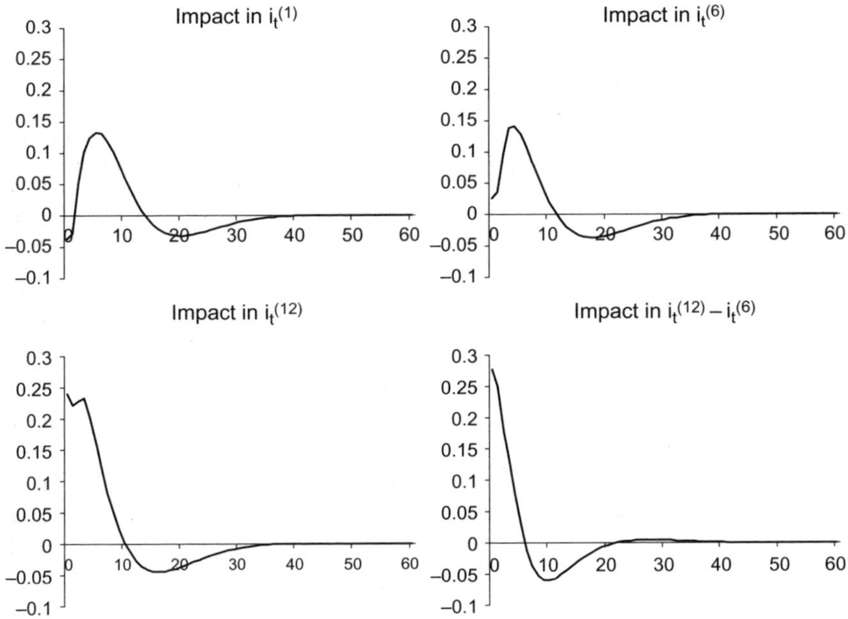

Fig. 8. Impulse-Response Functions for Inflation Shocks: Complete Model.

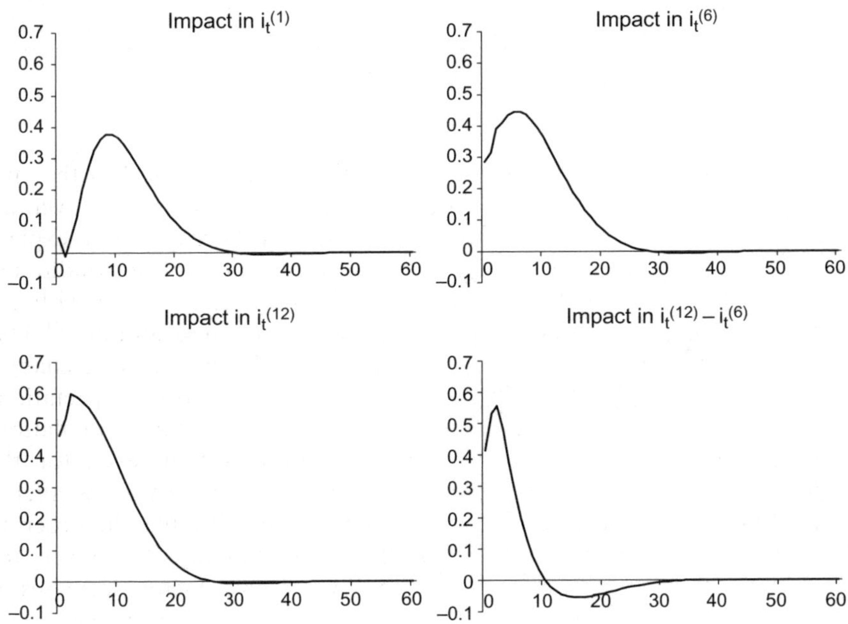

Fig. 9. Impulse-Response Functions for Exchange Rate Shocks: Complete Model.

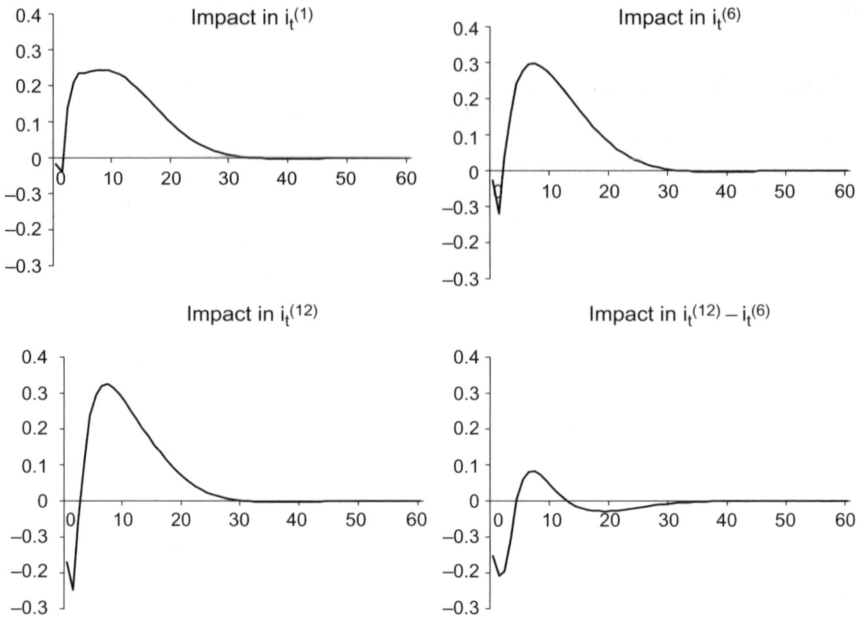

Fig. 10. Impulse-Response Functions for Output Gap Shocks: Complete Model.

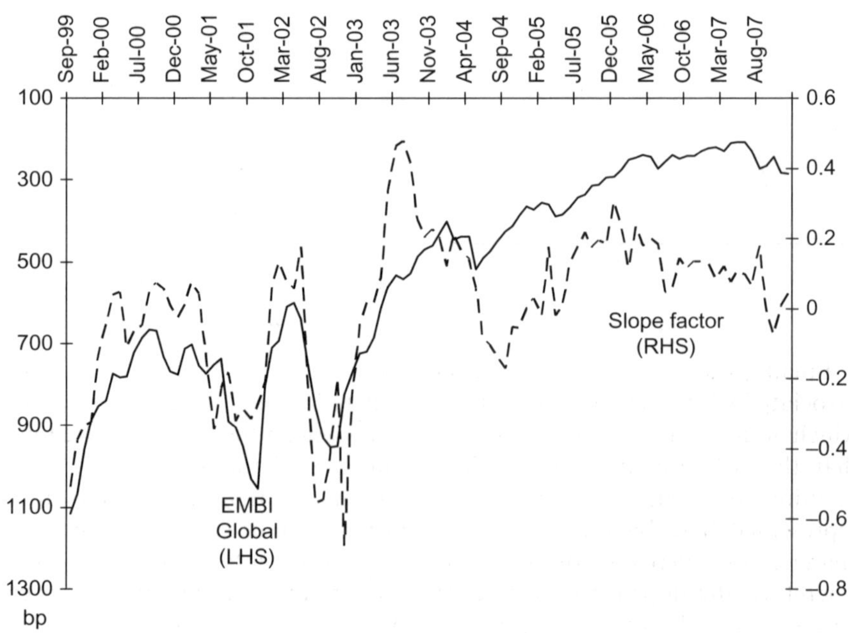

Fig. 11. Slope Factor on the Complete Model and EMBI Global.

Table 7. Variance Decomposition of the Forecast Errors: Yields Only Model.

	Horizon (Months)	*L*	*S*
$i_t^{(1)}$	1	81.97	18.03
	12	86.89	13.11
	60	90.64	9.36
	Infinite	90.74	9.26
$i_t^{(2)}$	1	86.43	13.57
	12	85.73	10.27
	60	92.34	7.66
	Infinite	92.41	7.59
$i_t^{(3)}$	1	90.30	9.70
	12	92.33	7.67
	60	94.01	5.99
	Infinite	94.06	5.94
$i_t^{(4)}$	1	93.54	6.46
	12	94.65	5.35
	60	95.62	4.38
	Infinite	95.64	4.36
$i_t^{(6)}$	1	98.03	1.97
	12	98.21	1.79
	60	98.37	1.63
	Infinite	98.38	1.62
$i_t^{(12)}$	1	96.78	3.22
	12	96.08	3.92
	60	95.33	4.67
	Infinite	95.33	4.67

Finally, due to the fact that a large part of the rate variations is still associated with latent factors in the Complete Model, I would like to verify which additional variables could potentially explain these factors. We know that the risk premium present in the uncovered interest rate parity, in addition to depending on the macroeconomic foundations, which can be represented here by the output gap, current inflation and exchange rate change, also depends on the risk aversion of international investors. Therefore, the slope factor should be related to this variable. Indeed, as can be seen in Fig. 11, the slope factor presents dynamics that are very similar to the EMBI Global index of JP Morgan, which can be used as a proxy for

Table 8. Variance Decompositions of the Forecast Errors: Complete Model.

	Horizon (Months)	y	π	Δe	L	S
$i_t^{(1)}$	1	0.20	0.24	0.28	97.95	1.34
	12	11.36	2.06	20.05	60.26	6.27
	60	13.55	1.96	23.03	53.94	7.52
	Infinite	13.55	1.96	23.03	53.94	7.52
$i_t^{(2)}$	1	0.28	0.14	1.43	98.04	0.11
	12	11.52	1.83	21.85	58.26	6.54
	60	13.59	1.79	24.32	52.65	7.65
	Infinite	13.59	1.79	24.32	52.65	7.65
$i_t^{(3)}$	1	0.45	0.06	3.83	94.41	1.26
	12	11.49	1.64	23.94	55.54	7.38
	60	13.45	1.64	25.92	50.69	8.30
	Infinite	13.45	1.64	25.92	50.69	8.30
$i_t^{(4)}$	1	0.64	0.01	6.82	88.60	3.93
	12	11.35	1.51	26.15	52.38	8.62
	60	13.19	1.54	27.67	48.28	9.32
	Infinite	13.19	1.54	27.67	48.28	9.32
$i_t^{(6)}$	1	1.07	0.13	12.79	75.36	10.64
	12	10.88	1.44	30.33	45.89	11.46
	60	12.51	1.52	31.16	43.01	11.80
	Infinite	12.51	1.52	31.16	43.01	11.80
$i_t^{(12)}$	1	4.19	4.95	22.70	48.28	19.89
	12	10.27	3.73	37.37	32.95	15.68
	60	11.52	3.74	37.48	31.58	15.68
	Infinite	11.52	3.74	37.48	31.58	15.68

global risk aversion,[23] with a correlation of 0.67 for the whole period (0.81 until May 2004).

On the other hand, the level factor is closely related to the average of the rates. Therefore, I can assume that it is absorbing part of the variations in the interest rate related to its long-term level, which is given by the real interest rate and the implicit inflation target perceived by the agents (or to the inflation expectations 12 months ahead). For the period studied, it is reasonable to assume that the dynamics of the long-term level of the interest rate are dominated by the variations in the inflation expectations, since the

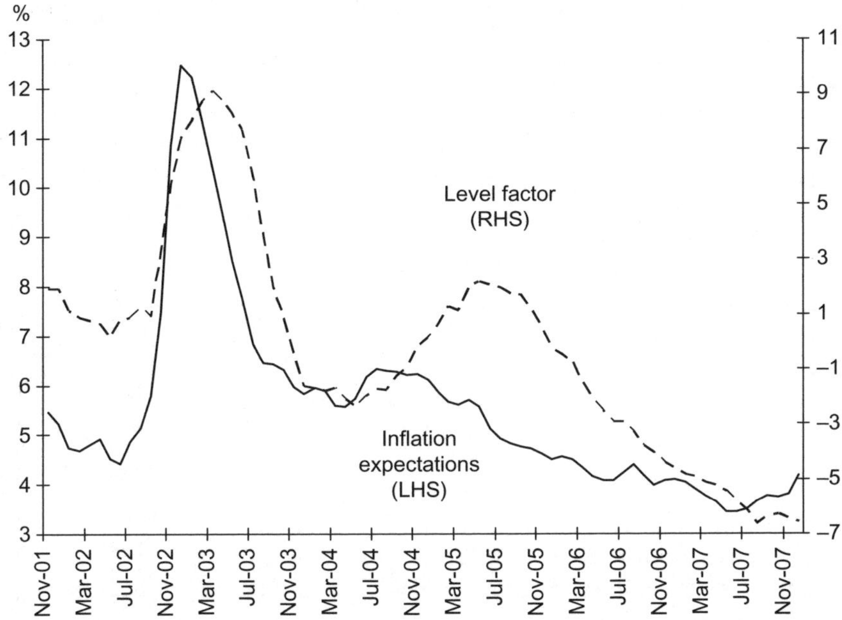

Fig. 12. Level Factor on the Complete Model and Inflation Expectations 12-Months Ahead.

neutral real interest rate may be considered practically constant in short periods of time.[24] In fact, as can be observed in Fig. 12, the level factor dynamics are very much related to the inflation expectations,[25] presenting a 0.82 correlation with them. The most pronounced increase of the level factor between the second half of 2004 and the first half of 2005 stems from the tightening of the monetary policy, as the monetary authority needed to achieve a lower inflation target in the process of inflation convergence in Brazil. This way, it can be explained through the presence of a monetary policy shock.[26]

4.3.2. The Performance of the Model During the Financial Crisis

To discuss the performance of the model during the financial crisis, I extend the forecasting period until June 2009 to include the period after the Lehman Brothers' fall. As can be seen in Fig. 13, which shows the results for

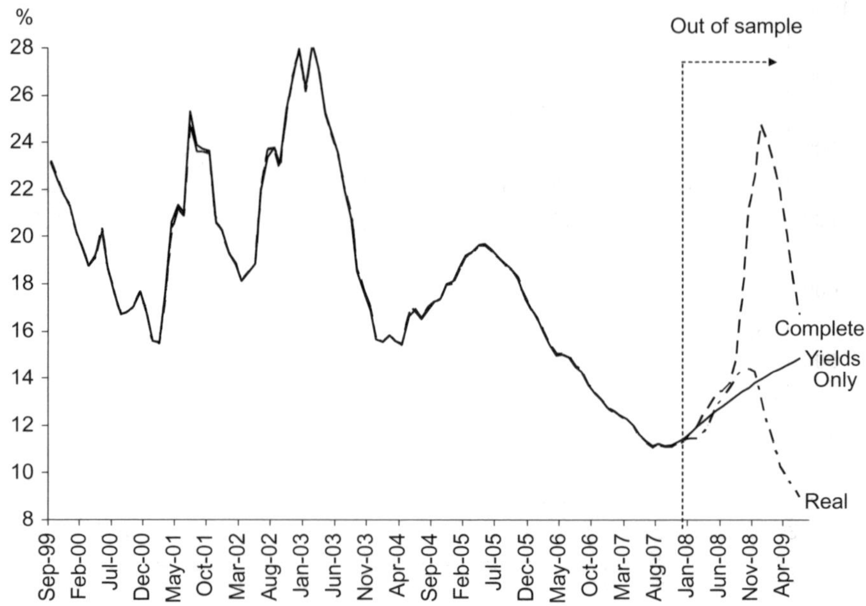

Fig. 13. Six Month Swap: Extended Forecasting Period.

the six month yield, the model performs quite poorly in forecasting the yields.

Due to the strong depreciation of the Brazilian real during this period, the model projects higher rates. However, the actual data has shown a sharp fall since September 2008. The main cause for this disconnect seems to be related to the strong fall in import prices (commodities and industrial goods) in dollar terms, which mitigated the passthrough from the exchange rate depreciation to inflation. We can see this fact in Fig. 14, which shows commodity prices in Brazilian reais. Differently from 2001, 2002 and 2004, commodity prices in local currency were quite stable in 2008. This way, the Central Bank could focus on the sharp deceleration of the real activity and reduce sharply the overnight rate. This movement was anticipated by the market and, consequently, longer rates also fell sharply during the period. This feature suggests that we might need to include also import prices to have a more complete understanding of yield curve dynamics. However, the inclusion of an additional variable would greatly increase the number of parameters to estimate and would not be possible with such a short sample.

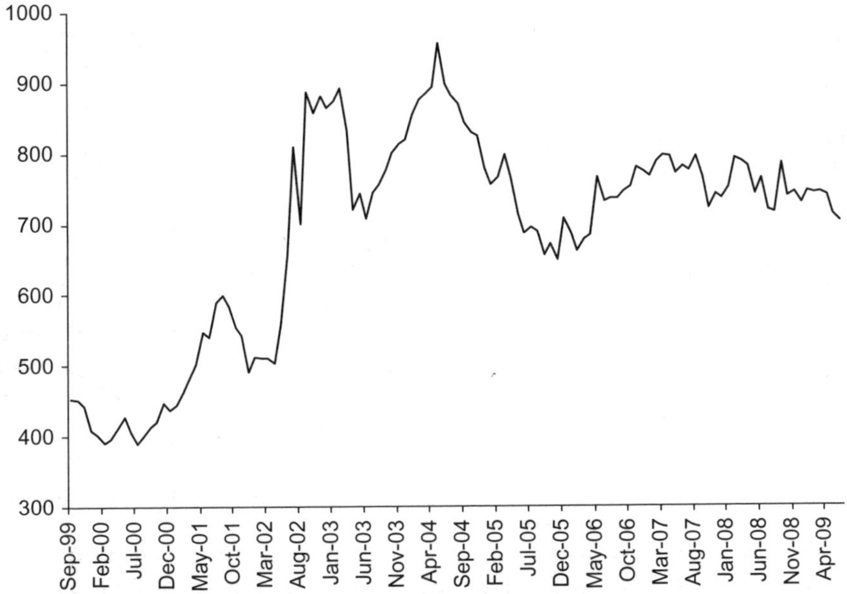

Fig. 14. CRB All Commodities in Brazilian Reais.

Besides that, the selection of an appropriate import prices index is a complex and delicate issue and subject to several types of criticism, as its composition usually changes with time.

5. CONCLUSIONS

The main objective of this chapter was to identify the relationship between the macroeconomic variables and the term structure of the interest rates in emerging markets. Several conclusions can be drawn from it. First of all, it can be concluded that an affine model with two latent factors offers a good approximation for the term structure of interest rates with maturities until one year, except for the periods of great volatility.[27] Moreover, the inclusion of macroeconomic variables is able to solve this problem, which corroborates the intuition that the higher volatility of rates in an emerging economy comes from a greater volatility of macroeconomic fundamentals.

Another important result is that, in a context of an emerging economy, the macroeconomic fundamentals, represented in this case by the output gap, inflation and nominal exchange rate change, explain up to 53% of the forecast errors variation in rates. The notion of great external vulnerability is also confirmed by the relevant role of the nominal exchange rate change, which explains up to 37% of the forecast errors variations in rates. Also, the response of the rates to macroeconomic shocks occurs as expected, with an increase in rates following inflation shocks and nominal exchange rate devaluations. Finally, the latent level and slope factor seem to be related, respectively, to the inflation expectations 12 months ahead and to a measure of international risk aversion.

Although the model had a good performance in forecasting yields until July 2008, the model performs poorly during the financial crisis. It seems that this poor performance is due to the omission of import prices in our set-up, which fell sharply (in dollar terms) during this period. This fact shows the importance of a comprehensive characterization of the external sector in an emerging market context.

Anyway, despite all issues related to the efficacy of the monetary policy transmission mechanism in emerging markets, the yield curve dynamics proved to be closely related to the macroeconomic scenario, both because of the traditional ways of monetary policy transmission and the effect that external crises play upon the variables. This chapter is a first step towards the understanding of this joint dynamics. With the consolidation of a more stable scenario and the consequent strengthening of a longer-term credit market, conditions for studies with longer rates will be created, enabling us to have a much deeper understanding of the relationship between the yield curve and macroeconomic variables in emerging markets, crucial for conducting monetary policy in these countries.

NOTES

1. The exchange rate is the main driver of the yield curve in my model as I will show subsequently.

2. In Section 4.3.2., I extended the forecasting period until July 2009 to study the performance of the model during the great financial crisis.

3. The inflation targeting regime was adopted officially on 21 June 1999, but the analysis started in September 1999, as the implementation of monetary policy in the months of July and August was contaminated by the increases in public tariffs and still suffered the impact of devaluation. In this new regime, the exchange rate anchor is replaced by a nominal anchor for prices, i.e., the inflation target, using the

short-term interest rate as a tool to make inflation head towards the previously set target. For further details about the implementation of monetary policy at the beginning of the inflation targeting regime, see Fachada (2001).

4. Yields of higher maturities could not be used as their time series were very short and their liquidity was quite low until very recently.

5. The selection of macro variables will be detailed in Section 3.

6. For a more detailed analysis of the period, see Minella, Freitas, Goldfajn and Muinhos (2003).

7. The derivation of the model presented here is based on Ang and Piazzesi (2003).

8. Almeida (2004) estimated the affine term structure model for Brazil using daily data.

9. Minella et al. (2003) defend the use of a reaction function for the Central Bank of Brazil, which is very similar to this specification for the period after the adoption of the inflation targeting regime.

10. Several studies showed that, in the election crisis of 2002, the agents were already working with an implicit inflation target different from the one determined by the Central Bank, and this fact was confirmed by the change of the target.

11. I tried a specification with only one latent variable, but the results obtained were not satisfactory.

12. The inclusion of a greater number of lags makes the estimation rather inaccurate, which is confirmed by the great instability of impulse responses.

13. Duffee and Stanton (2001) also defend the use of the Kalman filter as superior to the other approaches.

14. Chen and Scott's (1993) strategy consists in obtaining the latent factors by inverting the rate equations. Therefore, if we have N latent factors, we must have N rates measured without errors.

15. I thank Jaime Terceiro, Jose Manuel Casals, Miguel Jerez, Gregorio R. Serrano and Sonia Sotoca for having provided us with the toolbox for the estimate of the model and especially Miguel Jerez for the help with some technical questions related to the package.

16. Technically, I cannot guarantee I have reached a global minimum. I used a series of different strategies to reduce the risks of having used the results of a local minimum. Among those, at each value found, I tried to re-estimate the model by taking the latent variables as observable and obtaining the estimate of the risk price minimizing the average squared error of the estimated rates. This way, I believe I managed to obtain reliable results.

17. For such, I use the output gap, inflation and nominal exchange rate change without their sampling average.

18. In general, we cannot find very significant risk premia in the literature. A potential reason for the strong significance of risk premium in the Brazilian case could be that interest rates are not stationary in the period studied.

19. In general, it is extremely difficult for a finance model to contain a forecast power which is better than a random walk. Duffee (2002), for example, evaluates the standard affine model for the United States and verifies that its forecast performance is worse than a random walk.

20. The calculation of the impulse-response and the variance decomposition is based on the Cholesky decomposition of the covariance matrix of the innovations regarding the state variables in the order $(y_t \quad \pi_t \quad \Delta e_t \quad L_t \quad S_t)$.

21. As in Ang and Piazzesi (2003).

22. The variance explained by the macroeconomic factors in Ang and Piazzesi (2003) corresponds to 67%, 79% and 78% for the horizons of 1, 12 and 60 months, respectively.

23. In reality, in the chart, the EMBI Global is related to $-1*S$, which does not constitute a problem, since the latent factors may be rotated in any direction.

24. Bianchi, Muntaz and Surico (2009) find a similar result for the term structure of UK interest rates.

25. The inflation expectations used are the ones gathered by the Central Bank from several institutions (financial and non-financial), which started to be released only in November 2001.

26. After the 2002 shock, the target for inflation was adjusted to 8.5% in 2003, 5.5% in 2004, 5.1% in 2005 and 4.5% in 2006, which is the target until today.

27. The inclusion of rates with longer maturity would probably lead to the need of at least one additional factor.

ACKNOWLEDGEMENTS

I am grateful to Ilan Goldfajn for superb supervision and to Caio Ibsen de Almeida and Marco Bonomo for extremely helpful comments. The financial support from CNPq is gratefully acknowledged.

REFERENCES

Almeida, C. (2004). Time-varying risk premia in emerging markets: Explanation by a multi-factor affine term structure. *International Journal of Theoretical and Applied Finance*, *7*, 919–947.

Ang, A., Dong S., & Piazzesi M. (2005). *No-Arbitrage Taylor rules*. University of Chicago Working Paper, Columbia University.

Ang, A., & Piazzesi, M. (2003). A no-arbitrage vector autoregression of term structure dynamics with macroeconomic and latent variables. *Journal of Monetary Economics*, *50*, 745–787.

Bekaert, G., Cho, S., & Moreno, A. (2010). New-Keynesian macroeconomics and the term structure. *Journal of Money, Credit and Banking*, *42*, 33–62.

Bianchi, F., Muntaz, H., & Surico, P. (2009). The great moderation of the term structure of UK interest rates. *Journal of Monetary Economics*, *56*, 856–871.

Bollersev, T., & Wooldridge, J. (1992). Quasi-maximum likelihood estimation and inference in dynamic models with time-varying covariances. *Econometric Review*, *11*, 143–172.

Bonomo, M., & Lowenkron, A. (2008). A term structure model for defaultable bonds with macro and latent variable. Unpublished manuscript.

Chen, R., & Scott, L. (1993). Maximum likelihood estimation for a multifactor equilibrium model of the term structure of interest rates. *Journal of Fixed Income*, *3*, 14–31.

Dai, Q., & Singleton, K. (2000). Specification analysis of affine term structure models. *Journal of Finance*, *55*, 1943–1978.

Duffee, G. (2002). Term premia and interest rate forecasts in affine models. *Journal of Finance*, *57*, 405–443.

Duffie, D., & Kan, R. (1996). A yield factor model of interest rates. *Mathematical Finance*, *6*, 379–406.

Duffee, G., & Stanton, R. (2001). *Estimation of dynamic term structure models*. Haas School of Business Working Paper, UC Berkeley.

Evans, C., & Marshall, D. (1998). Monetary policy and the term structure of nominal interest rates: Evidence and theory. *Carnegie-Rochester Conference Series on Public Policy*, *49*, 53–111.

Fachada, P. (2001). *Inflation targeting in Brazil: Reviewing two years of monetary policy 1999/00*. Central Bank of Brazil Working Paper 25.

Litterman, R., & Scheinkman, J. (1991). Common factors affecting bond returns. *Journal of Fixed Income*, *1*, 54–61.

Liu, Z., & Spencer, P. (2010). An open-economy macro-finance model of international interdependence: The OECD, US and UK. *Journal of Banking and Finance*, *34*, 667–680.

Matsumara, M., & Moreira, A. (2005). *Can macroeconomic variables account for the term structure of sovereign spreads? Studying the Brazilian case*. Discussion Paper IPEA 1106.

Minella, A., Freitas, P., Goldfajn, I., & Muinhos, M. (2003). Inflation targeting in Brazil: Constructing credibility under exchange rate volatility. *Journal of International Money and Finance*, *22*, 1015–1040.

Rudebusch, G., & Wu, T. (2008). A macro-finance model of the term structure, monetary policy and the economy. *Economic Journal*, *118*(530), 906–926.

Taylor, J. (1993). Discretion versus policy rules in practice. *Carnegie-Rochester Conference Series on Public Policy*, *39*, 195–214.

SUBPRIME CRISIS AND ITS IMPACT ON THE BRAZILIAN MUTUAL FUND INDUSTRY

Gyorgy Varga and Maxim Wengert

ABSTRACT

This chapter describes the evolution of the Brazilian investment fund industry and the impact of domestic and international crises on investors, managers and the main types of funds offered in Brazil. In particular, it explores the effect of the subprime crisis and shows that the first wave of this crisis had very little impact, but the second wave with the collapse of Lehman Brothers did have a major impact on risk, returns and flows of the mutual fund industry in Brazil.

Keywords: Mutual funds; Brazilian financial market; hedge funds; emerging markets; risk management; financial crises.

JEL Classifications: G01; G11; G15; G23; G32; G38.

The Impact of the Global Financial Crisis on Emerging Financial Markets
Contemporary Studies in Economic and Financial Analysis, Volume 93, 581–609

ISSN: 1569-3759/doi:10.1108/S1569-3759(2011)0000093021

1. INTRODUCTION

This chapter describes the impact of the crisis originated in the downturn of the US housing market, known as the subprime crisis, on the Brazilian mutual fund industry. This industry is one of the world's largest mutual fund industries with several specific characteristics, such as concentration in fixed income, management by banks and denomination in local currency only. It also offers several different types of funds, some with sophisticated trading strategies. The crisis came in two waves: the first one with subprime loans that culminated with the collapse of Bear Stearns and the second one with the bankruptcy of Lehman Brothers. The first wave did not affect the Brazilian economy and its local mutual fund business, but the second wave had a major impact on global financial markets creating a real global financial crisis, consequently affecting Brazil. The Lehman bankruptcy generated a global liquidity crisis that created the prospect of a global recession. It led to a crash in stock markets and a rapid devaluation of the Brazilian real. The equity mutual funds were hit hard, although not the local fixed-income funds, because they hold local bonds and are sold mostly to local investors. Therefore, only a portion of the business was affected severely by the crisis. Additionally, there was some government intervention, that led to a fast recovery compared to the USA.

This chapter also sheds light on a market with no link to mortgages and little exposure to securitization, but one which did suffer losses due to the generalized market crash in September 2008. The effects of several other recent financial crises on the Brazilian mutual fund industry are also a described and compared to the effects of the subprime crisis.

In the second section, there is a description of the Brazilian mutual fund industry; the third section describes the impact of several recent financial crises on Brazilian financial markets; in the forth section, the impact of the subprime crisis on the mutual fund industry is detailed and the fifth section concludes.

2. THE BRAZILIAN MUTUAL FUND INDUSTRY

The main function of financial markets is the inter-temporal transference of resources, allowing agents to use income earned during their productive lives to reach a better retirement, carry through personal projects and face financial emergencies. Moreover, the financial market facilitates the financing of big projects and the mitigation of financial risks. In order to handle all these tasks, numerous financial instruments have been created, especially in recent years with the diffusion of derivatives. It has led to a huge growth in the size and complexity of financial instruments. Additionally there is the financial markets globalization. All these developments pose great difficulties to individuals taking care of their personal investments directly, making investment services increasingly important in the modern financial market. To this extent, mutual funds offer a great service to modern societies by offering professional money management, higher liquidity, lower transaction costs and access to different markets. These are solid economic reasons that justify the enormous absolute and relative growth of the mutual fund industry around the world. According to Klapper, Sulla, and Vittas (2004), the world's mutual fund industry, in the 1990s, had a spectacular growth, contributing to this the globalization, the internationalization of financial institutions and, the strong positive performance of equities and fixed-income securities. Brazil has followed this trend, with increasing financial market sophistication and relative and absolute growth of the mutual fund industry.

The current Brazilian financial system is based on the law 4,595 from 1964, which created the '*Conselho Monetário Nacional* (CMN)' (National Monetary Council) and the Brazilian Central Bank (BCB), and law 6385 from 1976, which established the '*Comissão de Valores Mobiliários* (CVM)' equivalent to the Securities and Exchange Commission (SEC) in the USA. Since then, few legal changes have been made to the financial system structure. An important article of the last constitution promulgated in 1988, article 192, is yet to be regulated. It deals with the financial system and has the potential to change the current financial system.

The Brazilian financial system is composed of a set of regulatory institutions and a set of financial companies which sell all types of products to individuals, government and private companies. The main regulatory institutions are the BCB which takes care of the monetary control and the banking supervision and the CVM which regulates capital markets. All these government institutions work closely to protect investors and improve savings and investment conditions in Brazil. Financial companies are divided into six groups:

- banking institutions that are allowed to receive demand deposits, thereby having the potential to affect directly the money supply and monetary policy;
- non-banking financial institutions, which can provide loans but cannot receive demand deposits;

- retirement companies, which can be closed pension funds, open pension funds, insurance companies and capitalization companies;
- asset management companies, which manage mutual funds and investment 'clubs';
- custody and settlement companies and
- auxiliary institutions, all others not classified above, such as stock brokers, stock exchanges and investment advisors.

In practice, the main financial companies in Brazil are organized into conglomerates that have national distribution and all types of financial companies, from banks to asset management companies. The banking system is also very concentrated with enormous participation of government banks. The ten biggest banks, as of December 2008, had 83% of the total banking assets, and four government banks (*Banco do Brasil, Caixa Economica Federal, BNDES and NossaCaixa*) had 34% of the total.

2.1. Mutual Funds[1]

The first official document to deal with mutual funds was issued by the Ministry of Finance in 1959. The first mutual fund was created in 1957, and until 1970 only 11 funds existed. The assets under management (AUM) in the funds grew strongly until 1971, in tandem with a rally in the stock markets. However, with the strong fall in stock markets that followed during this decade (the value of stocks fell by 90% from its peak), mutual funds also lost much of their assets, being forgotten until the 1990s. In 1984, BCB created two categories of mutual funds: equity mutual funds, with a minimum of 70% in equities, and fixed-income funds, with a minimum of 60% in fixed-income securities issued by the government, and a maximum of 10% invested in stocks. In 1986, the BCB created the short-term investment funds, aimed at investments with less than 30 days. This was also a period of high inflation, even hyperinflation between 1986 and 1994, when most of the financial system dealt with very short-term investment. Most deals with final investors had a one-day maturity, using repo agreements with government bonds as guarantee, known as 'overnight'.

At the beginning of the 1990s, two economic plans (Collor I and II), aimed to control inflation, had caused major changes in the local financial market and created several types of fixed-income funds. They also transferred the supervision and regulation of equity funds from the BCB to the CVM. Finally in 1994, another economic plan, aimed to tame inflation, was implemented, the Real Plan, that did succeed in controlling the inflation which had devastated the country for over a decade.

The CVM had made several changes in equity mutual fund regulation. Until 1994, these funds were denominated only '*Fundo Mútuo de Ações*'. In 1991 and 1992, the CVM created the '*Fundo Mútuo de Investimento em Ações (FMIA)*', '*Fundo Mútuo de Investimento em Ações – Carteira Livre (FMIA-CL)*' and '*Fundo de Investimento em Cotas de Fundo Mútuo de Investimento em Ações – FICFMIA*'. The first one was a pure equity fund, the second one was allowed to carry more derivatives in their portfolios and the last one was a fund of funds.

After 1994, bonds gained duration and new derivative instruments were launched, increasing the length and depth of the Brazilian financial market. Consequently, the demand for professional money management offered by a mutual fund increased. Moreover, several changes in regulation helped the momentum in the mutual fund industry. Funds that had fewer restrictions on investing in derivatives provided the legal structure to more sophisticated funds with leverage and investments in several asset classes. At this time, new funds were launched with strategies such as inflation and USD indexed, hedge, macro and derivatives. Most of these funds were known as 'derivative funds;' they became quite popular for their leverage and intense use of derivatives contracts, allowing them to play in several asset classes at the same time. This moment marked the beginning of more sophisticated money managers, though not without a little trouble along the way. For instance, '*Linear Investimentos*', run by former BCB president Ibrahim Eris, launched several leveraged funds which at the beginning had great success, but succumbed to the Asian crisis of October 1997.

The several crises that disturbed the mutual fund industry drove the authorities to adopt new regulations to protect investors. In November 1997, BCB enforced financial institutions to separate their asset management activities from the rest of the bank, officially creating the 'Chinese Wall' in Brazil. At the beginning of 1999, BCB issued a norm mandating much more information disclosure by funds and also making sure (in writing) that investors acknowledge the fund risks. The qualified investor was defined as any financial institution, insurance company or pension fund, with assets above BRL 5 million, and individual investors with more than BRL 250 thousand invested in the fund or over BRL 5 million in personal financial assets. The funds were required to send investors quarterly information regarding portfolio holdings and quota value, as well as investment and leverage policies, among other documents. This not only led to more transparency but also to higher maintenance costs for the funds.

In 2004, CVM issued '*Instrução 409*' to establish new rules for the entire funds industry. It better detailed the responsibilities of several participants in this industry; defined and increased the responsibilities of the administrator versus the manager, who became responsible for the investment policy, risks and portfolio concentration limits; defined the distributor responsibility (now responsible for taxes that investors should pay on top of the fund return) and created a presentation standard for fund performance, with 12 months for returns and AUM, fund starting date, administration and incentive fees.

2.2. Comparison with other Assets

In the 1970s and 1980s, the total AUM of the funds was very small compared to other financial investments (e.g. compared to the monetary aggregate M4, it was 1% in 1979). Even with the creation of the fixed-income fund in 1984, the total AUM of the funds continued to be very small (4% of M4 in 1984). In 1990 with Plan Collor I, many financial assets were 'frozen' and the size of the mutual fund industry shrunk to 0.7% of M4 right after the plan, but in 1991 and the following years, possibly due to the end of bearer securities and the creation of new fixed-income funds, the industry size grew again, reaching 18% of M4 by the end of 1993. After the 'Real' plan and the inflation control in 1994, the assets of the mutual fund industry grew to a significant level. Table 1 shows the evolution and a comparison between the fund's AUM and the total assets of savings accounts, federal government bonds, private bonds, stock market capitalization and monetary aggregates M1 and M4, with data starting in 1995. Before this date only sparse data were available.

Fixed-income funds had an annual growth of 15%, between 1995 and 2008. They are competitors for savings accounts and have strongly surpassed the total assets managed by this type of investment. The balance of both types of investments was the same in 1995, but in 2008, the balance of savings accounts was only 29% of the fixed-income funds. Compared to M4, saving accounts also had a strong decrease, from 25% to 12%. Equity funds had an annual asset growth of 28%. The relationship between the equity funds to total equity market capitalization grew from 1% to 8%, suggesting a transfer from direct investment in stocks to indirect investment via funds. In total the funds grew from 26% to 46% of M4, reaching a maximum of 57% in 2007. It should be noted that during the several

Table 1. Total Assets of the Main Types of Investments and Monetary Aggregates.

	1995	1996	1997	1998	1999	2000	2001	2002	2003	2004	2005	2006	2007	2008
M1	29	29	42	42	35	38	36	31	38	48	62	82	131	96
Savings (a)	65	69	87	89	62	57	51	40	50	60	72	88	133	116
Private bonds	82	80	83	79	56	50	51	42	55	77	114	138	176	244
Government bonds	112	170	229	268	232	261	269	176	253	305	419	512	694	546
M4(b)	258	310	352	380	308	334	326	229	332	418	561	729	1.069	956
Fixed-income funds (c)	65	105	100	112	111	139	138	91	162	204	279	372	516	393
Equity mutual funds (d)	2	5	13	11	12	13	11	9	14	18	26	41	94	49
Stock market capitalization (e)	152	217	255	161	229	226	186	124	234	341	482	723	1.399	589
a/b	25%	22%	25%	23%	20%	17%	16%	17%	15%	14%	13%	12%	12%	12%
a/c	101%	66%	87%	80%	56%	41%	37%	43%	31%	29%	26%	24%	26%	29%
d/e	1%	2%	5%	7%	5%	6%	6%	7%	6%	5%	5%	6%	7%	8%
(c + d)/b	26%	35%	32%	32%	40%	45%	46%	44%	53%	53%	54%	57%	57%	46%

Note: In the last four rows, there is a percentage and comparison among them.
Source: BCB monthly bulletin, balance in USD billion, as of December, 1995 to 2008.

financial crises that happened in this period (e.g. the mark to market crisis in 2002 and the subprime crisis in 2008), this percentage decreased.

The number of mutual funds in Brazil is huge: there were 8,266 funds in December of 2008, but only 34% of them were not exclusive for one investor, and among them 49% were funds of funds (they are called FIC in Brazil). Many fund managers created several FICs, all with the same strategy, but with the purpose of charging different administrative fees or to market to different groups of investors. Sometimes one of the funds is the master and the others are only its feeder. Therefore, the number of funds gives a distorted view of the industry size in Brazil; the industry should be tracked by the AUM.

2.3. Comparison with other Countries

In Table 2, there is a comparison of the Brazilian mutual fund industry[2] to the rest of Latin America, BRICs, USA and the rest of the world. The world's annual growth was 14% in this period, in the BRICs[3] this rate was 24%, mostly explained by the entrance of China in this statistic in 2007, and the above average growth coming from Brazil.

Table 2. Mutual Fund Assets Worldwide.

	1996	1999	2002	2005	2007
Brazil	104	118	97	303	615
Latin America	109	148	137	369	723
BRICs	114	117	117	346	1,165
USA	3,526	6,846	6,391	8,905	12,021
Worldwide	6,101	11,416	11,324	17,771	26,199

Source: Mutual Fund Fact Book (2008), balance in USD billion, as of December.

Brazil is responsible for most of Latin America and has grown in relation to the rest of the world. These numbers show the increasing importance of the mutual fund industry in Brazil and the rest of the world. Such volume of resources has great impact on the individual savings and the stock markets of the whole world. According to data of December 2007, 75% of US mutual funds belong to individual investors, and these funds held 23% of the financial assets of the individuals. Those assets correspond to 27% of the capital of the public companies and 10% of the federal government bonds. In Brazil, at the same time, the funds held 42% of the government debt, 23% of debentures and 6% of the stocks.

The numbers indicate that the mutual fund industry has grown strongly and consistently, but in periods of crisis (2002, for example) it loses market share to traditional investments, either due to the loss of value or withdrawals. Possible reasons for this growth are the increasing market sophistication, growth of derivatives and globalization. All of these reasons make it difficult to invest directly, though they are easily done via mutual funds. The changes in regulations have ensured stronger investor protection and information disclosure, but at a cost to the mutual fund companies. The CVM, beyond establishing regulation, has also acted strongly in the supervision and protection of investors. The relative growth of the mutual fund industry can still continue via transference of resources from savings accounts to fixed-income funds and from direct purchase of stocks to equity mutual funds.

2.4. Mutual Fund Industry

The growth of the mutual fund industry and its increasing sophistication contribute to a growing number of money managers. These money managers offer funds that usually are classified according to their asset class, type of investor, taxation or the regulation imposed by the authorities. There is an official classification from CVM and classifications from private companies, such as Quantum,[4] but in general they are very close.

Table 3 shows the total AUM of all types of funds according to the official CVM classification. These totals include fund of funds (FICs) that had USD 244 billion as of December 2008 or 33% of the total. The five largest types of funds are fixed income (42.7%), multimercado (25.2%), referenciado (17.6%), equities (7.1%) and fixed income – short-term (4.1%). In December 2008, they represented 97% of the total AUM.

To better understand the mutual fund industry, only the five largest types of funds (based on AUM) are investigated. The official classification states that

Table 3. AUM by Type of Fund According to the CVM Classification.

CVM Classification	1997	1999	2002	2005	2008
Equities	12.3	8.9	8.4	23.6	52.0
FX linked	1.1	1.5	1.0	1.2	0.6
Fixed income – short term	10.2	6.5	6.7	16.2	30.1
Credit rights	–	–	–	4.9	15.8
Foreign debt	0.2	0.2	0.1	0.9	0.4
Market index	–	–	–	–	0.0
Multimercado	35.9	25.4	31.3	106.0	185.9
Participation	0.8	0.4	0.3	0.6	3.7
Privatization	–	–	1.2	3.7	3.7
Referenciado	21.3	64.1	44.8	114.7	129.9
Fixed income	77.3	79.5	54.0	223.7	314.8
Total	159.1	186.6	147.8	495.5	736.9
Percentage of total					
Equities	7.7	4.8	5.7	4.8	7.1
FX linked	0.7	0.8	0.7	0.2	0.1
Fixed income – short term	6.4	3.5	4.5	3.3	4.1
Credit rights	0.0	0.0	0.0	1.0	2.1
Foreign debt	0.1	0.1	0.1	0.2	0.1
Market index	0.0	0.0	0.0	0.0	0.0
Multimercado	22.6	13.6	21.2	21.4	25.2
Participation	0.5	0.2	0.2	0.1	0.5
Privatization	0.0	0.0	0.8	0.7	0.5
Referenciado	13.4	34.4	30.3	23.1	17.6
Fixed income	48.6	42.6	36.5	45.1	42.7

Source: Quantum, balance in USD billion, as of December, 2009.

- fixed income is the fund where the portfolio has at least 80% invested in fixed-income bonds;
- multimercado is the fund that has an investment policy pursuing diversification in several asset classes;
- referenciado is the fund with a portfolio containing a minimum of 95% of its assets linked to the reference index announced by the fund;
- equities is the fund where the portfolio has at least 65% invested in equities and
- fixed income – short term is a fixed-income fund with all their bonds having a maturity smaller than 375 days and duration lower than 60 days.

There is no official classification for management companies; one possible classification is based on the type of managing company: commercial banks (CBs), investment banks (IBs), independent managers (IMs), pension funds (PFs), insurance companies (ICs) and brokers (B). It can be separated between regular funds (FI) and fund of funds (FICs). Table 4 shows the AUM per type of fund and type of manager for the FIs.

The largest type of money management company in Brazil for all types of funds is the CB with 76.5% of the total. In the case of fixed income – short term, they manage 95% of the assets, but in the case of equities and multimercado, their participation falls to 60.8% and 49.9%, respectively. The IBs have their main action in multimercado, the PFs also in multimercado and insurance companies in fixed income. The PFs and insurance companies do manage funds but they are also important investors in other funds as well, without managing them. The brokers, as expected, have their main participation in equity funds. Finally, the IMs have their main participation in equity and multimercado funds. There are a total of

Table 4. The FIs AUM Distribution per Type of Fund and Type of Manager.

	Dec-2008	CB	IB	PF	IM	I	B
Equities	10.0%	60.8%	4.2%	1.8%	29.8%	0.3%	3.2%
FI – short term	3.4%	95.0%	2.4%	0.0%	2.6%	0.0%	0.0%
Multimercado	22.7%	49.9%	24.4%	6.7%	17.7%	0.5%	0.8%
Referenciado	16.9%	86.2%	6.7%	0.1%	6.8%	0.2%	0.0%
FI	47.0%	88.0%	4.9%	2.6%	2.5%	1.8%	0.3%
Percentage of total		76.5%	9.5%	2.9%	9.4%	1.0%	0.6%

Note: The second column shows the percentage of each type of fund on their total.
Source: Quantum, as of December, 2008.

356 registered money management companies, 40 of which are foreign companies that control approximately 21% of the total AUM.

Table 5 shows a similar analysis for FICs instead of FIs. Regarding the type of fund, there is a smaller participation of multimercados and a larger participation of equities and referenciados. Regarding the manager type, a smaller participation of IMs in equity should be noted as well as a smaller participation of IBs in multimercado, and a larger participation of PFs in multimercado and referenciados.

Another important distinction among funds is the type of investor from which the funds can receive money, which can be exclusive (only from one investor or some sort of restricted public); a qualified investor; an institutional investor and investors in general. Exclusive funds, in general, have external managers to decide on the portfolio allocation, so they are only a vehicle with the objective to diminish transactions costs. The funds aimed at institutional investors usually have a conservative and very constrained investment policy, eventually at a low cost. The funds aimed at qualified investors usually have more sophisticated strategies and charge higher fees.

From the grand total in Table 6, 71% of the funds are exclusive, and these are more concentrated in FIs; institutional ones have 4% of the total, and are more concentrated in FICs; qualified investors have a small share, only 2% of the total and 24% of the funds go for investors in general. Some types of funds were excluded from this table due to their small sizes (FIDC, FMP and others) that comprise 3.4% of the total. Approximately half the number or 72% of AUM of FICs are pure 'feeders' for another FI. Most of the remaining FICs also invest in other funds from the same manager.

Table 5. The FIC's AUM Distribution per Type of Fund and Type of Manager.

FICs	Dec-2008	CB	IB	PF	IM	I	B
Equities	20.8%	90.8%	0.8%	0.0%	8.3%	0.0%	0.1%
FI-short term	5.8%	100.0%	0.0%	0.0%	0.0%	0.0%	0.0%
Multimercado	2.1%	61.3%	0.8%	11.8%	25.9%	0.0%	0.3%
Referenciado	32.5%	53.1%	18.7%	11.0%	14.6%	1.2%	1.3%
FI	38.7%	91.1%	1.3%	4.2%	0.8%	2.5%	0.0%
Percentage of Total		78.6%	6.8%	5.5%	7.4%	1.4%	0.5%

Source: Quantum, as of December 2008.

Table 6. AUM Funds Distribution According to Investor Type.

	FI		FIC		Total	
Exclusive	386	82%	118	48%	504	71%
Institutional investor	9	2%	16	7%	26	4%
Qualified investor	8	2%	3	1%	11	2%
Investors in general	65	14%	106	44%	171	24%
Total	468		244		712	

Note: In the second column are the FIs, in the fourth column the FICs and in the sixth column their total.
Source: Quantum, as of December 2008.

In the USA, there are big companies specialized in fund management and distribution, for instance, Fidelity, Vanguard or American Funds. In Brazil, most of the funds, in terms of AUM, are managed by commercial banks. Recently with increasing sophistication and internationalization of the local financial market, and with the creation of the 'Chinese Wall' in 1997, IMs gained more importance. Since then, the big banks have avoided the management of high-risk funds directly due to the possible negative impact on their image and reputation. More important is the repercussion that a possible loss in a low-risk fund can have on the dozens of other funds they manage. In order to participate in the riskier business, banks have created and distributed funds of funds (FICs) that have been invested in risky funds managed by IMs, reducing their total risk via diversification with many IMs. The growth in the number of IMs is quite impressive: they went from 28 in 1997 to 229 in 2008.

The numbers have shown that IMs are a different type of company: either for their location in terms of fund type or the way they charge their fees. Many IMs are well known for their sophisticated trading strategies and *modus operandi* that resemble international hedge funds, which is why they are locally called hedge funds. Legally they are all treated as mutual funds,[5] and according to the data in Table 4 they deal mainly via multimercado and equity funds. Taking the definition of hedge fund from Fung and Hsieh (1999), as a small organization, one should not confuse multimercado funds with the Brazilian hedge fund because the majority of the multimercado funds are managed by big CBs, although most (58%) of the so-called Brazilian hedge funds (IMs) do use multimercado funds. These managers have strategies with or without leverage and trade in several different markets; their announced strategies are similar to international hedge funds, but they do not always disclose their strategies, in many cases preferring to keep everything secret.

In summary, the mutual fund industry in Brazil shows the strong presence of commercial banks in terms of AUM, but with regard to riskier funds, such as multimercado and equity funds, IMs have grown in the last decade. Those managers are well known for strategies similar to the international hedge funds and the large use of incentive fees as compensation.

2.5. Investors

The Brazilian financial market is relatively closed; only recently were individuals allowed to send money abroad freely. Pension funds still suffer restrictions on investing abroad, and mutual funds only recently were allowed to do so. The distribution of local funds is also very much directed towards local investors, which can be classified as individuals, companies, pension funds and insurance companies. The distribution towards foreign investors is quite recent, although many IM distribute offshore funds that merely mirror their local ones. Nowadays, foreign investors can invest directly in local funds.

The funds distribution can be direct or indirect. In the first case, the manager sells its funds directly to investors, and in the other case it is done indirectly via third parties. Although there are several companies involved in the fund distribution business, it is concentrated in banks. There is very little cross-selling of funds and fund 'supermarket'.

Final investors are individuals, non-financial companies, foreigners and insurance companies. Indirectly, individuals are important investors via pension funds, open retirement plans, wealth managers (WM), private banking (PB) and family offices (FO). Moreover, in Brazil, there is also the personal financial advisor which is regulated by the CVM, although it has little importance in terms of size. Most of the financial advisory job is done directly by banks.

According to data of December 2008, total investments of PFs were USD 190 billion, of which 43% were invested in non-equity funds (including fixed income, multimercado, referenciado and credit rights) and 15% in equity funds. Insurance companies had total reserves of USD 27 billion, with 64% invested in fixed-income funds. Foreign investors had financial investments of USD 123 billion, of which 4 billion was invested in foreign investors special funds. Defining funds with more than 2,000 individual investors as a retail fund, the total AUM of these funds were USD 106 billion. The industry total AUM, excluding FICs, was USD 468 billion, distributed 24% with PFs; 4% insurance companies; 1% foreign investors; 23% retail funds and the rest (49%) with non-financial companies and wealthy investors.

2.6. Explaining the Growth

The Brazilian mutual fund industry has grown in size and complexity, becoming an important financial instrument in the local financial market. The question of why it has grown so much is usually answered by basic economic arguments such as diversification, liquidity, professional management and lower transaction costs provided by these products. These are reasons for greater returns and less market and liquidity risk to investments via funds, vis-a-vis direct investment.

Klapper et al. (2004) have shown many reasons for the mutual fund industry growth relative to GDP. They explain the industry growth by the level of income and wealth, arguing that funds are a luxury good; availability or not of substitutes and complementary products, for instance, bank deposits versus money market funds; well-developed markets for bonds and equities; regulation of the investments of insurance companies and pension funds; return and volatility of alternative instruments; non-neutral tax policy; restrictions on interest payment in bank deposits, as in the USA and transaction costs.

The growth of the mutual fund industry relative to other assets has also been explained by several studies. Khorana, Servaes, and Tufano (2005) show that a better overall legal environment leads to more financial investment but not necessarily via funds; fund regulation and more supervision will give investors higher confidence to invest via funds instead of directly, but excessive regulation can be bad due to costs; taxes should be neutral, funds grow relative to direct investments when benefited by taxes; bearer securities make it easier to avoid taxes via direct investment; barriers to entry into the fund industry such as higher cost to start a fund; industry age is positively correlated with size and growth; investor sophistication and wealthier countries have bigger industries; lower trading costs is associated with a bigger industry and market liquidity and price transparency are associated with a bigger mutual fund industry. Fink (2008) emphasized the role of the general evolution of the financial markets with the creation of new securities, new distribution channels and laws to encourage savings for retirement. He also pinpointed specific situations that pushed up the mutual fund industry, such as the tax advantages of open funds during the thirties,

IRA and others retirement plans during the sixties and eighties, and the money market fund advantages over bank deposits during the seventies. Pozen (1998) describes as key for the past success of the mutual fund industry: high equity returns during the sixties, eighties and nineties; new products such as money market funds; favourable tax treatment for retirement plans during the sixties; diversification effects that held fund values during bear markets; easy access to new markets and low search costs due to fund advertising.

3. THE IMPACT OF THE RECENT FINANCIAL CRISIS

This section investigates extreme situations that occurred in the Brazilian mutual funds industry since 1997, in part due to international crises and in part due to local crises. According to Billio, Getmansky, and Pelizzon (2009) the main recent financial crises were Asian (June 1997–January 1998), Russian and LTCM (August 1998–October 1998), Brazilian (January 1999–February 1999), Internet Crash (March 2000–May 2000), Argentinean (October 2000–December 2000), 11 September 2001, WorldCom (June 2002–October 2002), Subprime (August 2007–January 2008) and the Global Financial Crisis initiated with the Lehman Bankruptcy (September 2008–November 2008).

According to Varga and Wengert (2010), four other domestic crises have affected the mutual fund business: the mark to market (MTM) crisis in May 2002; the two moments in which the BCB increased interest rates in November 2004 and May 2006 and the famous episode of the bankruptcy of Banco Santos without any link to a macroeconomic problem. Certainly the most significant domestic crisis was the MTM in 2002 (see Brito & Taciro, 2003). At this moment a small political crisis arose with the proximity to the presidential election. Some candidates defended the public debt default, which immediately created some difficulty in the financing of the government debt. Interest rates went up, and government bond prices went down, generating losses in funds considered extremely safe. This was the case of the largest type of fixed-income fund, called 'Fundo DI', that were offered without proper mark to market. In May 2002, they were required to correctly mark to market, which uncovered investors' losses, consequently creating a confidence crisis in fixed-income funds that caused a 15% withdrawal in this type of fund.

In the 12 years since 1997, the fund industry has gone through several financial crises, but their effect hasn't lasted too long and has had a small impact on the size of the whole industry. Nonetheless these periods have been characterized by bigger withdrawals from more riskier funds, especially from funds managed by IMs.

Fig. 1 shows the several crises that occurred from December 1996 to July 2010, the evolution of the foreign exchange rate based on USD (FX), Ibovespa (main stock index) and the local interest rates. It shows high interest rate volatility until 1999, a period of fixed exchange rates. Thereafter, the interest rate volatility diminished, the FX volatility increased, and a negative correlation between FX and Ibovespa is notable. In both periods, the interest rates fell and Ibovespa increased. Many crises coincide with or are the starting points of higher interest rates, lower Ibovespa and higher FX.

In Fig. 2, there is the evolution and the flow of the entire industry. The relative size of the industry grew from 19.7% in 1996 to 25% in 2010. The relative size decreased in 1997, 2002, 2004, 2007 and 2009. In 1997 and 2002

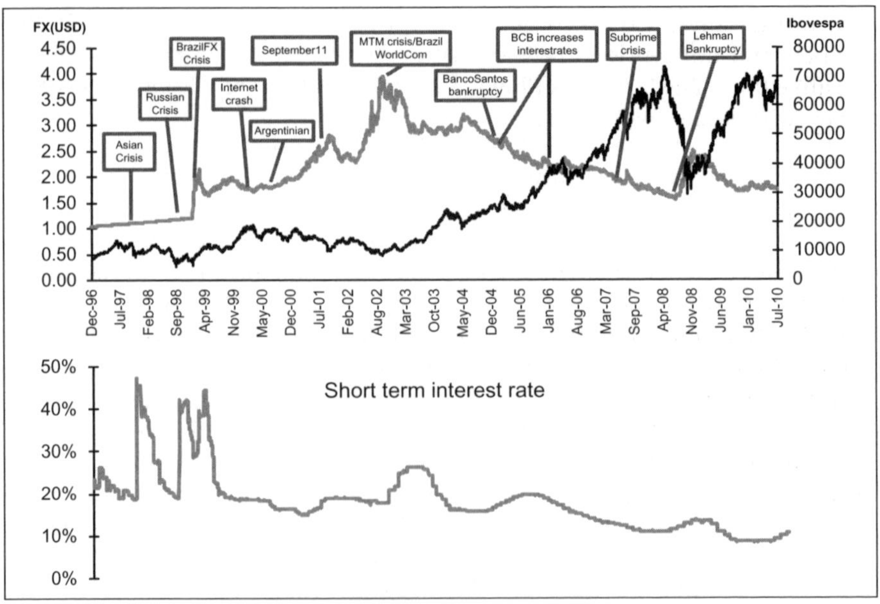

Fig. 1. Evolution of the FX Rates and Ibovespa Index in the First Graph and the Short-Term Interest Rates in the Second Graph. *Note:* Several crises are indicated on the first graph. *Source:* Quantum.

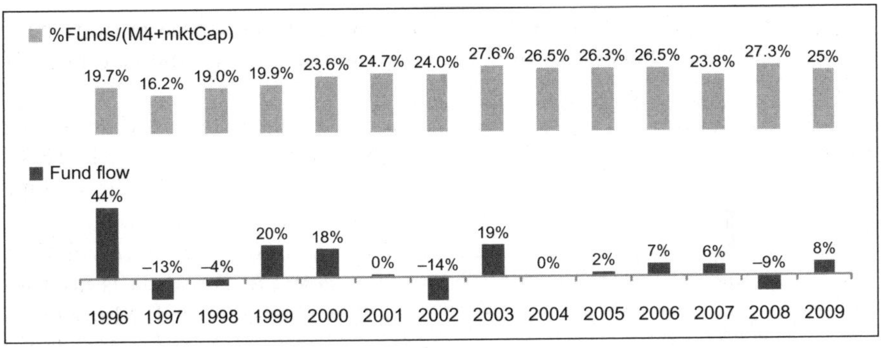

Fig. 2. Relative Growth and Flows of the Mutual Fund Industry. *Note:* The relative value is funds' AUM over monetary aggregate M4 plus stock market capitalization. The fund flow is the total flow of the mutual fund industry in each year. *Source:* Quantum and Brazilian Central Bank.

this move coincided with a large outflow (–13% and –14%, respectively), but in the other years there was an inflow. It happened because the stock market and bond prices increased so much that they compensated for the positive flow. The largest outflows occurred in 1997, 1998, 2002 and 2008, all years with large financial crises.

3.1. Channels of Contagion

The major channels of contagion shown in the financial literature are via external trade and portfolio reallocation. Table 7 shows the results of two simple regressions: the first between foreign investments in financial assets and a dummy for each month with a financial crisis and the second using exports as the dependent variable. The result shows a significant negative portfolio effect but no significant effect for the export side, which suggests that the portfolio channel has been the most important factor to propagate these crises in Brazil.

3.2. Impact on Size and Flows

The same regression is done in Table 8, using as the dependent variable, the relative and the absolute size of the equity and the fixed-income industry.

Table 7. Univariate Regressions that Show the Effect of the International Crises on Foreign Investments and Exports.

	Foreign Investment in Financial assets	Exports
Constant	1.38	1.05
Crises	(1.641)	(0.050)
	(3.55)	(0.48)
R^2	7%	0%

Note: Each column has one regression, the dependent variable is in the first line and the explanatory variable is a dummy for each month with a crisis, below the dummy is the *t*-statistic, and in the last line is the regression R^2. The sample ranges from January 1996 to May 2010, with monthly observations totalling 173 observations; the dependent variables are normalized.

Table 8. Univariate Regressions Explaining the Effect of the International Crises on the Relative and Absolute Sizes of the Equity and Fixed Income Funds.

	Relative Size		Absolute Size	
	Equity/Market capitalization	Fixed-income funds/M4	Equity	Fixed-income funds
Constant	0.08	0.42	57.67	498.82
Crises	0.007*	(0.025)	(6.759)	(87.433)
	2.06	(1.77)	(0.71)	(1.48)
R^2	2.4%	1.8%	0.3%	1.3%

Note: Each column has one regression, the dependent variable is on the first line, the explanatory variable is a dummy for each month with a crisis, below the dummy is the *t*-statistic, and in the last line is the regression R^2. The sample ranges from January 1996 to May 2010, with monthly observations totalling 173 observations, in local currency (BRL); the dependent variables are normalized.
*Indicates significant at 10%.

The relative size of the equity mutual fund industry is measured by total AUM divided by the stock market capitalization (MktCap), and the relative size of the fixed-income industry is divided by the monetary aggregate M4.

The only significant result is a positive effect of the crises on the relative size of equity mutual fund business. It can have two explanations: (1) a higher decrease in the stock prices versus the fund value occurs because the equity fund, in general, has part of the portfolio invested in bonds or close

Table 9. Univariate Regressions Explaining the Effect of International Crises on Fund Flows to Equity Funds, Fixed Income Funds, Banks and Savings Institutions.

	Flows			
	Equity	Fixed income funds	Time deposit	Savings
Constant	0.014	0.008	(0.004)	(0.000)
Crises	(0.005)	(0.021)*	0.011*	0.008*
	(0.47)	(6.31)	2.10	3.49
R^2	0%	19%	3%	7%

Note: Each column has one regression, the dependent variable is in the first line and the explanatory variable is a dummy for each month with a crisis, below the dummy is the *t*-statistic, and in the last line is the regression R^2. The sample ranges from January 1996 to May 2010, with monthly observations totalling 173 observations, in local currency (BRL); the dependent variables are normalized.
*Indicates significant at 10%.

to cash instruments or (2) a transfer of money from direct investment to funds during periods of crisis due to the expertise of professional managers in turbulent times.

In Table 9, the effect of the crises on fund flows is addressed. Now, the effect on equity funds is no longer significant, but it is significant and negative on fixed-income funds and also significant and positive on time deposits and savings accounts. It suggests that investors move money from fixed-income funds to time deposits in banks and savings accounts in periods of crisis.

3.3. Impact on Managers, Investors and Different Types of Funds

The impact of crises can also be evaluated on the volatility, return and flow aggregated by type of manager, investor or fund, which is shown in Table 10. The sample is shorter[6] than the one in Table 9, but it allows a more detailed analysis. The effects of crises are a higher risk on all types of managers[7] for all types of investors, but in two types of funds, fixed income – short term and referenciado this effect is not significant. The effect on returns is negative and significant for most types of funds (except fixed income – short term and referenciado). The effects of crises on fund flows are negative and significant for all types of managers. Only funds directed to

Table 10. Univariate Regressions Explaining the Effect of International Crises on Volatility, Return and Fund Flows per Type of Manager, Investor and Fund.

Full Sample	AUM		Volatility				Return				Fund Flows			
	N	BRL	Constant	Coefficient	*t*	R^2	Constant	Coefficient	*t*	R^2	Constant	Coefficient	*t*	R^2
Manager type														
Commercial banks	3967	1467	0.015	**0.017**	5.38	29%	0.012	**−0.004**	(2.62)	9%	0.004	**−0.009**	(2.14)	6%
Investment banks	2402	210	0.049	**0.036**	5.10	27%	0.015	**−0.010**	(2.99)	11%	0.005	−0.008	(1.62)	4%
Independent managers	1731	116	0.040	**0.043**	4.86	25%	0.014	**−0.012**	(3.51)	15%	0.002	**−0.014**	(2.68)	9%
Target investor														
Exclusive	4025	481	0.020	**0.019**	5.73	32%	0.013	**−0.004**	(2.83)	10%	0.005	**−0.017**	(2.71)	10%
Exclusive to the manager	387	328	0.008	**0.011**	4.64	24%	0.012	**−0.003**	(3.16)	12%	0.001	−0.009	(1.20)	2%
Exclusive for retirement account	1331	540	0.016	**0.017**	5.37	29%	0.012	**−0.004**	(2.85)	10%	0.006	0.002	0.69	1%
Investor in general	1654	363	0.025	**0.029**	4.72	24%	0.012	**−0.007**	(2.96)	11%	0.001	**−0.010**	(2.41)	8%
Institutional investor	169	76	0.007	**0.010**	6.68	39%	0.011	**−0.003**	(3.13)	12%	0.010	−0.017	(1.28)	2%
Qualified investors	809	85	0.034	**0.024**	4.31	21%	0.013	**−0.009**	(3.37)	14%	0.011	**−0.016**	(2.34)	7%
Official classification														
Equities	1290	113	0.209	**0.147**	4.37	21%	0.029	**−0.045**	(2.40)	8%	0.006	0.003	0.56	0%
Fixed income – short term	120	90	0.000	−0.000	(1.31)	2%	0.010	−0.001	(1.23)	2%	0.012	−0.014	(0.61)	1%
Multimercado	4722	491	0.029	**0.025**	5.40	29%	0.014	**−0.006**	(3.01)	11%	0.007	**−0.013**	(2.37)	7%
Referenciado	489	314	0.001	0.000	0.88	1%	0.011	−0.001	(1.45)	3%	−0.003	0.006	1.32	2%
Fixed income	1460	807	0.003	**0.003**	5.61	31%	0.011	**−0.002**	(2.08)	6%	0.004	**−0.014**	(3.01)	11%

Note: Each line shows the regression results for the aggregation of each type of fund. In the first column is the name of the type, the second has the number of funds in that type, the third column has the AUM, the next four columns the regression for the volatility, then the regression for return and the regression for the fund flow. Each regression is done using the aggregated value of that type, not on each fund. One particular fund should have one type of manager, one type of investor and one classification. For each regression, it shows the value of the constant, the value of the dummy for each month with a crisis, below the dummy is the *t*-statistic and in the last column it's R^2. The sample ranges from October 2003 to September 2009, in local currency (BRL), with monthly observations totalling 72 observations. Bold coefficients are significant at 10%.

three types of investors have negative and significant coefficients for crises: funds aimed at retirement accounts; institutional investors and those exclusive to managers who do not have a significant coefficient. Regarding the type of fund, only multimercado and fixed-income funds have negative and significant coefficients for crises.

In general, the results do not differ from what one would expect in periods of crisis. The mutual fund industry shows more volatility, lower returns and outflows.

One interesting feature of the Brazilian mutual fund industry is the huge size of exclusive funds, which account for 72% of the total AUM and 69% of the total number of funds as of September 2009. The investment in this type of fund does not depend on performance and other traditional variables that dictate the investment in mutual funds because it is only a shelter for taxes and transaction costs. Therefore, further investigation should be done without exclusive funds. It is also necessary to exclude funds of funds to avoid double counting. Table 11 shows the same analysis from Table 10 without exclusive and funds of funds.

The results are similar to the results on Table 10 for volatility and returns, but the fund flow results are a bit different. It is no longer significant for the commercial bank manager type but significant for investment banks; it is still negative but no longer significant for all three types of investors.

This simple regression allows the evaluation of the direction and the impact of the crises. The direction is described above; the size of the effect can be calculated by adding the dummy coefficient to the constant. The crises effect on the volatility is bigger for commercial banks than for investment banks or independent managers; bigger for investors in general than institutional or qualified investors and obviously bigger for equity funds than any other type of fund. The effect on return is similar for all types of managers; bigger for investors in general than institutional and qualified investors and much bigger for equity funds than any other type of fund. Regarding the flows, the crisis effects are much bigger for investment banks and independent managers than commercial banks and bigger for the multimercado and fixed-income funds.

4. THE SUBPRIME CRISES

After describing the Brazilian mutual fund industry and the effects of crises in the former sections, this section describes the impact of the subprime crises. This crisis had two waves: the first one in 2007, which originated in

Table 11. Univariate Regressions Explaining the Effect of International Crises on the Volatility, Return and Fund Flows per Type of Manager, Investor and Fund.

No Exclusive Funds and Fund of Funds	AUM		Volatility				Return				Fund Flows			
	N	BRL	Constant	Coefficient	*t*	R^2	Constant	Coefficient	*t*	R^2	Constant	Coefficient	*t*	R^2
Manager type														
Commercial banks	537	129	0.082	**0.074**	4.69	24%	0.015	**−0.014**	(1.94)	5%	0.002	−0.002	(0.42)	0%
Investment banks	367	58	0.061	**0.035**	4.48	22%	0.016	**−0.013**	(2.64)	9%	0.008	**−0.014**	(1.80)	4%
Independent managers	41 6	25	0.065	**0.046**	5.06	27%	0.016	**−0.017**	(3.35)	14%	0.016	**−0.030**	(2.44)	8%
Target investor														
Investor in general	814	119	0.063	**0.060**	4.25	20%	0.015	**−0.015**	(2.62)	9%	0.006	−0.011	(1.67)	4%
Institutional investor	77	26	0.016	**0.027**	6.48	38%	0.013	**−0.007**	(3.51)	15%	0.002	−0.002	(0.12)	0%
Qualified investors	380	47	0.056	**0.029**	3.63	16%	0.013	**−0.010**	(2.34)	7%	0.011	−0.006	(0.54)	0%
Official classification														
Equities	435	55	0.214	**0.143**	4.13	20%	0.028	**−0.043**	(2.26)	7%	0.007	0.003	0.42	0%
Fixed income – short term	18	5	0.000	−0.000	(0.91)	1%	0.011	−0.001	(1.12)	2%	0.019	−0.021	(0.35)	0%
Multimercado	446	45	0.021	**0.012**	4.21	20%	0.013	**−0.004**	(2.77)	10%	0.010	**−0.035**	(2.80)	10%
Referenciado	82	40	0.001	**0.001**	3.03	12%	0.011	−0.001	(1.58)	3%	0.005	0.024	1.44	3%
Fixed income	186	39	0.002	**0.002**	4.84	25%	0.011	**−0.002**	(2.22)	7%	0.000	**−0.027**	(3.02)	12%

Note: Each line shows the regression results for the aggregation of each type of fund. In the first column is the name of the type, the second has the number of funds in that type, the third column has the AUM, the next four columns the regression for the volatility, then the regression for return and the regression for the fund flow. Each regression is done using the aggregated value of that type, not on each fund. One particular fund should have one type of manager, one type of investor and one classification. For each regression, it shows the value of the constant, the value of the dummy for each month with a crisis, below the dummy is the *t*-statistic, and in the last column it's R^2. The sample ranges from October 2003 to September 2009, in local currency (BRL), with monthly observations totalling 72 observations. Bold coefficients are significant at 10%.

mortgages and securitized bonds, and the second one occurred with the collapse of Lehman Brothers on 15 September 2008, causing panic in the entire global financial market. To investigate its impact, at each month of this crisis, we calculate the difference between the average actual volatility, return, fund flow and its expected value in case of no crisis and crisis. This expected value is obtained from the regression in Table 11.

For each type of manager, investor and fund, this difference is presented in Table 12a for the volatility, in Table 12b for the return and in Table 12c for the fund flow.

The average volatility for the first wave of the crisis (August 2007–January 2008) is bigger than the expected volatility in the case of no crisis,

Table 12a. The Effect of the Subprime Crisis on the Volatility, per Type of Manager, Investor and Fund.

	Expected Volatility		August 07–January 08		September 08–November 08	
	No crisis	Crisis	Average	Maximum	Average	Maximum
Manager Type						
Commercial banks	8.22%	15.67%	14.78%	20.17%	28.69%	36.00%
Investment banks	6.12%	9.61%	7.87%	11.06%	16.75%	18.42%
Independent managers	6.51%	11.14%	9.23%	13.59%	19.41%	25.22%
Target investor						
Investor in general	6.30%	12.35%	11.06%	14.33%	24.27%	30.41%
Institutional investor	1.62%	4.36%	4.69%	6.93%	7.09%	9.56%
Qualified investors	5.60%	8.46%	6.41%	8.58%	15.24%	16.85%
Official classification						
Equities	21.37%	35.68%	30.28%	36.95%	66.94%	83.01%
Fixed income-short term	0.01%	0.01%	0.01%	0.01%	0.02%	0.03%
Multimercado	2.14%	3.33%	2.73%	4.08%	4.99%	6.79%
Referenciado	0.05%	0.14%	0.06%	0.10%	0.12%	0.20%
Fixed income	0.18%	0.42%	0.40%	0.89%	0.68%	1.28%

Note: In each line, there is the difference between regression results presented in Table 11 and their actual value for each month. In the first column is the name of the fund type, the second has the expected volatility without crisis and conditional to a crisis, the fourth column has the average and maximum monthly volatility from August 2007 to January 2008 and the next two columns have the average and maximum monthly volatility from September 2008 to November 2008. The sample ranges from October 2003 to September 2009, in local currency (BRL), with monthly observations totalling 72 observations. The sample does not include exclusive funds and FICs.

Table 12b. The Effect of the Subprime Crises on the Returns, per Type of Manager, Investor and Fund.

	Expected Return		August 07–January 08		September 08–November 08	
	No crisis	Crisis	Average	Minimum	Average	Minimum
Manager Type						
Commercial banks	1.51%	0.09%	1.42%	−4.15%	−3.77%	−7.73%
Investment banks	1.61%	0.35%	0.54%	−1.43%	−1.61%	−2.19%
Independent managers	1.60%	−0.11%	0.24%	−2.12%	−2.31%	−5.13%
Target investor						
Investor in general	1.47%	0.00%	0.87%	−2.89%	−3.05%	−6.28%
Institutional investor	1.29%	0.62%	0.69%	−0.83%	−0.14%	−1.30%
Qualified investors	1.33%	0.35%	0.33%	−1.29%	−1.91%	−2.12%
Official classification						
Equities	2.79%	−1.51%	1.21%	−9.35%	−10.33%	−19.78%
Fixed income – short term	1.07%	0.99%	0.82%	0.73%	1.06%	0.98%
Multimercado	1.29%	0.89%	0.59%	0.20%	0.69%	0.30%
Referenciado	1.15%	1.03%	0.88%	0.80%	1.04%	0.98%
Fixed income	1.12%	0.96%	0.81%	0.71%	0.92%	0.75%

Note: In each line there is the difference between regression results presented at Table 11 and their actual value for each month. In the first column is the name of the fund type, the second has the expected return without crisis and conditional to a crisis, the fourth column has the average and minimum monthly returns from August 2007 to January 2008, the next two columns have the average and minimum monthly returns from September 2008 to November 2008. The sample ranges from October 2003 to September 2009, in local currency (BRL), with monthly observations totalling 72 observations. The sample does not include exclusive funds and FICs.

and in most types of funds it is smaller than in the case of the crisis. For the second wave of the crisis (September/2008–November/2008) it is not the case; the average volatility during this period is much higher than the expected volatility in case of a crisis for all types of funds, and in general is twice the expected number. For example, in the case of equity funds, the expected volatility is 21.37% in a no crisis situation, 35.68% in a crisis situation, but during this second wave the volatility reached 66.94% on average and a maximum of 83.01%. In fact, this is the maximum volatility for the whole sample period.

The average return for the first wave of the crisis (August/2007–January/2008) is a bit lower than the expected return in the case of no crisis, and in

Table 12c. The Effect of the Subprime Crises on the Flows, per Type of Manager, Investor and Fund.

	Expected Flow		August 07–January 08		September 08–November 08	
	No crisis	Crisis	Average	Minimum	Average	Minimum
Manager Type						
Commercial banks	0.18%	−0.07%	−0.09%	−3.10%	−2.02%	−2.37%
Investment banks	0.80%	−0.62%	1.32%	−1.78%	−6.32%	−10.72%
Independent managers	1.56%	−1.43%	1.31%	−0.65%	−8.90%	−11.32%
Target investor						
Investor in general	0.57%	−0.57%	0.64%	−1.26%	−5.77%	−8.64%
Institutional investor	0.21%	0.00%	0.48%	−2.86%	−0.05%	−4.71%
Qualified investors	1.13%	0.52%	1.02%	−0.50%	−3.24%	−4.79%
Official classification						
Equities	0.74%	1.05%	2.11%	0.31%	−0.76%	−1.50%
Fixed income – short term	1.92%	−0.19%	5.51%	−20.79%	−13.17%	−19.23%
Multimercado	1.02%	−2.44%	−0.39%	−4.11%	−10.81%	−17.05%
Referenciado	0.45%	2.88%	2.96%	−0.34%	0.71%	−1.23%
Fixed income	0.02%	−2.63%	−2.16%	−9.18%	−7.25%	−12.15%

Note: In each line, there is the difference between regression results presented in Table 11 and their actual value for each month. In the first column is the name of the fund type, the second has the expected flow without crisis and conditional to a crisis, the fourth column has the average and minimum monthly flows from August 2007 to January 2008 and the next two columns have the average and minimum monthly flows from September 2008 to November 2008. The sample ranges from October 2003 to September 2009, in local currency (BRL), with monthly observations totalling 72 observations. The sample does not include exclusive funds and FICs.

most types of funds it is also bigger than in the case of a crisis. For the second wave of the crisis (September/2008–November/2008) this is not the case; the average return during this period is much smaller than the expected return in case of a crisis for all types of funds. For example, in the case of equity funds, the expected return is 2.79% in a no crisis situation, −1.51% in a crisis situation, but during this second wave, the return reached −10.33% on average and a minimum of −19.78%. In fact this is the minimum return for the whole sample period. The commercial banks were the types of managers that suffered the most; the investors in general were the types of investor with the lowest returns, and equity funds had the worst returns. Interestingly, all other types of funds had positive returns, certainly because they held local currency bonds, which were measured in local currency and did not suffer so much during the crisis.

The average flow for the first wave of the crisis (August/2007–January/2008) is a bit lower than the expected flow in the case of no crisis, and in most types of funds it is also bigger than in the case of the crisis. For the second wave of the crisis (September/2008–November/2008) this is not the case; the average negative flow during this period is much worst than the expected flow in cases of crises for all types of funds. For example, in the case of multimercado funds, the expected flow is 1.02% in a no crisis situation, −2.44% in a crisis situation, but during this second wave the flow reached −13.17% on average and a minimum of −19.23%. This was the minimum flow for the whole sample period. The independent managers were the types of managers that suffered the most; the investors in general were the types of investor with the biggest outflow, and fixed income – short-term funds had the biggest outflow. Except for referenciado funds, all other type of fund had negative flows.

These results show that the first wave of the subprime crisis had very little impact on the Brazilian mutual fund industry; it had an impact smaller than the average crisis. The second wave was a totally different story; it was the major crisis to hit this industry during the entire sample period, generating the highest volatility, lowest returns and biggest outflows. It is interesting to note that although they had the lowest returns, it was positive in the case of funds other than equity funds.

The analysis above was done in the Brazilian local currency, the real. If it were done in USD, the results would be stronger because the local currency depreciated during the majority of the crises, especially in the second wave of the subprime crisis.

Several common risk factors like credit risk were less important in the local mutual fund industry than abroad. Problems that contributed to the subprime crisis, such as agency issues, rating agency incentive problems, poor risk management and complexity of financial instruments, were also present in Brazil.

The Brazilian mutual fund industry is dominated by the asset management units of commercial banks. The degree of concentration is extremely high in Brazil, where the top five companies manage approximately 70% of the assets while in USA, for instance, they manage around 18%. The distribution in Brazil is also dominated by banks with very few brokers, financial advisors (except for wealth investors) and fund supermarkets. The fixed-income instruments dominate the business; although credit quality is not a main issue because most of the bonds are issued by the government, the differences in fixed income reside in the type of indexation. Although few banks dominate the business, in more riskier assets or more sophisticated strategies, small managers have gained prominence, via equity and multimercado funds. During the crises they are the ones who suffer the most.

In parallel to this strong development, it is worth mentioning that authorities have established several regulations to protect investors and organize this industry. Moreover, they have supervised the activities of investment management, which may explain the small negative repercussion of financial crises in mutual fund development.

The reason for the subprime crises, the mortgage market, was almost nonexistent in Brazil. The leverage in the banking system is highly controlled by the central bank, so Brazil did not have the same problem as in the USA, even though, the second wave of the crisis strongly affected the local financial markets. The currency devalued, stock markets crashed and several big corporations had financial problems. The risk funds like equities and multimercado suffered quite a lot, but plain vanilla fixed-income funds did not suffer that much at least in local currency terms.

The government did intervene in the financial markets, helping a few corporations via official banks, selling international reserves and increasing

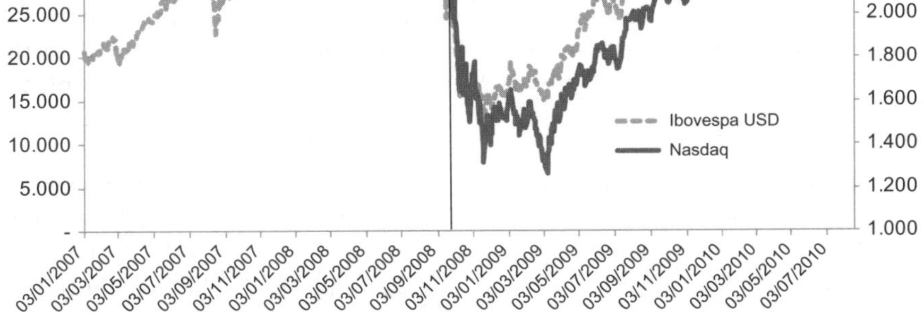

Fig. 3. Stock Index in Brazil and USA (NASDAQ) Around the Lehman Bankruptcy. *Note:* Both indices are in USD. *Source:* Quantum and Brazilian Central Bank.

the credit from official banks. Nevertheless, the crisis did impact severely the local economy and the financial markets. Fig. 3 shows the stock markets index in Brazil and USA, both in USD, suggesting that the crises did hit Brazil as hard as the USA, but recovery was faster in Brazil.

5. CONCLUSIONS

The Brazilian mutual fund industry has grown considerably and become an important instrument in the local financial markets. It has a low integration with the rest of the world, and most of its portfolio comprises local currency bond and stocks traded locally. This fact helps to isolate the local financial market and consequently the mutual fund business from international crises, even though these crises affected the local markets.

In particular, the first wave of the subprime crisis had very little effect, but its second wave with the bankruptcy of Lehman Brothers had a major effect locally. It seems that the local financial market is isolated from small international crises, but any big crises do hit the local market and its mutual fund business. The reasons for that, especially in the case of the subprime crisis, could be the reasons for the crisis; the first wave of subprime crisis was ignited by the mortgage business in USA, and Brazil has no link with business, but the second wave was an international liquidity crisis, and it does affect international portfolios which directly affect the prices of stocks and local bonds.

NOTES

1. Mutual funds are called investment funds in Brazil.
2. The number for Brazil does not include fund of funds, which avoids double counting, but it includes exclusive funds (32%) and funds reserved only for institutional investors (27%). These two types of funds are special vehicles to diminish taxes.
3. Brazil, Russia, India and China.
4. Quantum is a private provider of mutual fund data in Brazil (see www.quantumfundos.com.br).
5. The Brazilian legislation does not distinguish between hedge funds and mutual funds, all funds have the same legal framework, but this regulation is less restrictive than in the USA with regard to leverage and incentive fees charged.
6. The degree of detail obtained in Table 10 is not available before September 2009.
7. For simplicity, the results for managers, brokers, pension funds and insurance companies are not presented.

REFERENCES

Banco Central do Brasil, Monthly Bulletin. Available at www.bcb.gov.br

Billio, M., Getmansky, M., & Pelizzon, L. (2009). *Crises and hedge fund risk*. Mimeo. Available at http://papers.ssrn.com/id=1130742

Brito, N., & Taciro, Jr. A. (2003). Evolução de valor, risco e probabilidade de default na Carteira de LFT's e implicações institucionais: uma síntese. In: A. Duarte Jr. and G. Varga (Eds.), *Gestão de Riscos no Brasil* (Keyword Editora, Brasil, in Portuguese).

Fink, M. (2008). *The rise of mutual funds*. Oxford University Press.

Fung, W., & Hsieh, D. (1999). A primer on hedge funds. *Journal of Empirical Finance*, *6*, 309–331.

Khorana, A., Servaes, H., & Tufano, P. (2005). Explaining the size of the mutual fund industry around the world. *Journal of Financial Economics*, *78*, 145–185.

Klapper, L., Sulla, V., & Vittas, D. (2004). The development of mutual funds around the world. *Emerging Markets Review*, *5*, 1–38.

Mutual Fund Fact Book, Investment Company Institute. Available at www.ici.org

Pozen, R. (1998). *The mutual fund business*. Cambridge, MS: The MIT Press.

Varga, G., & Wengert, M. (2010). The growth and size of the Brazilian mutual fund industry. Mimeo. Available at http://papers.ssrn.com/id=1575510

DETERMINING THE RMB EXCHANGE REGIME

Xiaobing Feng and Ilan Alon

ABSTRACT

Although China has claimed since 2005 that it will move towards a more market-oriented system of managing its foreign exchange, it has remained, in part, a managed economic system. This chapter examines the relative importance of fundamentalist, chartist and currency arrangements in determining the RMB exchange regime using both traditional linear and non-linear artificial intelligence models. We find that the emphasis on the US dollar as a reference currency has declined. Fundamentalist forces are becoming strong determinants of the currency exchange. The genetic programming approach is among the best performing in minimizing forecasting error.

Keywords: China currency; basket regime; market forces; exchange arrangements; artificial neural network.

JEL Classifications: E42; D83; D87.

The Impact of the Global Financial Crisis on Emerging Financial Markets
Contemporary Studies in Economic and Financial Analysis, Volume 93, 611–624

ISSN: 1569-3759/doi:10.1108/S1569-3759(2011)0000093022

1. INTRODUCTION

A currency crisis occurs when the value of a currency deviates from its fundamental equilibrium exchange rate (FEER) and is subjected to speculators' attacks, undermining governments' ability to serve as a stabilizer. The currency, as a result, no longer serves well its original purpose as a medium of exchange or a storage of value. A currency crisis is often related to a real economic crisis, a balance of payment crisis and a regional or global downturn (Alon & Kellerman, 1999).

Given that a currency crisis is defined by some FEER, it is necessary to better understand this concept, originally developed by professor Williamson (1994). Recently Cline and Williamson (2010a, 2010b) updated estimates of FEERs for 30 major economies. They found a few countries that have either overvalued or undervalued their nations' currencies, and China was one of them. Simply put, exchange rates are prices of currency assets determined by their demand and supply. When the actual rates deviate from FEER levels, they are also influenced by non-market forces. A better understanding of China's exchange rate arrangements can also help with forecasting the RMB's future behaviour (Alon & Drtina, 2006). Some emerging research has shown a tendency towards more market forces in the Chinese exchange rate policy (Feng & Alon, 2007).

The Chinese currency, RMB, was effectively pegged to the US dollar from 1997 to 2005, when the government announced a switch from a dollar-fixed regime to a managed floating regime that referenced a basket of currencies. Within the new framework, the exchange rate is determined by considering market forces as the basic principle and the basket arrangement as a reference.

There is ambivalent research that has examined whether the Chinese authority has behaved as it has claimed. Jen (2005), Shah, Zeileis, and Patnaik (2005), Frankel (2006) and Eichengreen (2006) all found that predominant weight was placed on the US dollar and no evidence was found of a downward trend on the weight of the dollar. They concluded that China is still in a dollar-pegged, fixed-rate regime regardless of its announcement. On the contrary, Yamazaki (2006), Xu, Shao, and Tang (2007), Frankel and Wei (2007), Xu and Tang (2008) and Zhou (2009) discovered that the weights had shifted slightly from the US dollar to the euro, yen and other currencies. There is currently no consensus on the issue.

One problem in current research is the emphasis on only one aspect of the regime: the basket arrangements. In this chapter, the role of market forces as well as the basket arrangements will be considered. The flexibility of exchange rate system, the aim of the reform, results from a greater role for market forces in the exchange-rate determination mechanism. Market forces are a much more fundamental factor, and these forces will drive the system towards an eventual free-floating state.

In terms of methodology, previous studies have focused on the estimation of weights in the basket based on a linear model. We believe that the RMB rate is an outcome of complex interactions between and among factors that affect the rate. This study will use three different artificial neural network (ANN) and genetic programming (GP) models to identify the existence of the market force in the exchange-rate determination mechanism. The linear model will then be applied to measure the extent of the market force.

The trade-offs between non-linear and linear models are that the former is able to capture the non-linearity of the system but unable to measure the magnitude of the contribution of each variable in the system. Linear regression models can compare the relative importance of each variable by estimating the coefficient, assuming a much simpler interaction among variables.

2. MODEL SPECIFICATION

2.1. Formulation of Market Forces

Following research by Frankel and Froot (1986) and Frankel (1987), market forces will be determined by transactions of fundamentalists and chartists.

Fundamentalists base their decisions on the difference between the equilibrium exchange rate $\bar{S}_{t-1}$[1] and the actual exchange rate S_{t-1}. α is a positive parameter that reflects the speed of adjustment to the equilibrium rate: $(\Delta S_t)^f = \alpha(\bar{S}_{t-1} - S_{t-1})$.

Chartists base their expectations of future rates by observing asset price movements. The following equation specifies a moving average model with declining coefficients $0<\beta^p<1$, where p is lag length: $(\Delta S_t)^c = \sum_{i=1}^{\infty}\beta^p \Delta S_{t-1}$.[2]

2.2. Formulation of Exchange Arrangements

In a basket regime, the central banker will arrange the exchange rate according to predetermined objectives. $S_t^{\mathrm{rmb}A_i}$ is the exchange-rate arrangement against the US dollar and S_t^i is the exchange rate of currency i against the dollar. All the exchange rates in the following equation are measured in indirect quotations from the US perspective: γ_0 is the weight of the US dollar.

$$\Delta \overset{\text{rmb}}{\underset{t}{S}} = \sum_{i=1}^{\infty} \gamma_i \Delta S_t^i + \gamma_0$$

2.3. *Non-Linear Estimation*

2.3.1. Artificial Neural Network Approach

We chose three types of multivariate ANN models for this study: BP, RBF and GRNN.[3] A single, hidden-layer ANN model can be taken as an extension to non-linear from a linear regression model as follows:

$$\text{RMB}_t = \partial_0 + \sum_{j=1}^{n} \partial_j \log \quad \text{sig}(\sum_{i=1}^{k} \beta_{ij} \text{Var}_i + \beta_{oj})] + \varepsilon_t \qquad (1)$$

where n is the number of the unit in the hidden layer, k is the number of independent variables, log sig is a logistic transfer function, β_{ij} denotes a matrix of parameters from the input to the hidden layer units and ε_t denotes the error term.

We consider three factors as explanatory variables: chartist, fundamentalist and exchange-rate arrangements:

$$\text{RMB}_t = \partial_0 + \sum_{j=1}^{\text{n}} \partial_{\text{j}} \log \quad \text{sig}(\beta_1 F + \beta_2 C + \beta_3 B + \beta_o)] + \varepsilon_t \qquad (2)$$

2.3.2. Genetic Programming Approach

The GP method approaches a solution using evolutionary processes including crossover, mutation, reproduction and deletion. It involves regression models over a series of generation based on the Darwinian principle of nature selection. It starts with solving a problem by creating massive amount of basic parent random functions in a population pool.

The offspring functions are elected by the specified fitness criteria, which can produce the next generation.

2.4. Linear Modelling

Eq. (3) is a simple, linear combination of market forces and exchange-rate arrangements to estimate the rate:

$$\Delta S_t^{\mathrm{rmb}} = \delta_1(\Delta S_t)^f + \delta_2(\Delta S_t)^c + \delta_3 \Delta S_t^{\mathrm{rmb}A_i} \tag{3}$$

3. DATA AND ESTIMATION RESULTS

The daily exchange rates from July 2005 to July 2009 were culled from the Federal Reserve database and from the Central Bank of Russia.[4] The trade data used for weights in the basket rate are from the Ministry of Commerce.[5]

3.1. Non-Linear Modelling: ANN

ANN creates non-linear forms for regression models that automatically handle non-linearities, explanatory variables' interactions, model switching and other complex phenomena. Three non-linear optimization algorithms are applied to implement the models.

Figs. 1 and 2 show estimation and forecasting errors. It is evident that errors from BP are larger[6] than those from RBF and GRNN networks. It is, however, difficult to distinguish between RBF and GRNN as the lines are linked to each other. We therefore rely on the performance evaluation to separate them.

3.2. Performance Evaluation and Economic Implication

Three indicators, mean absolute percentage error (MAPE), mean absolute error (MAE) and root mean square error (RMSE), are applied to evaluate

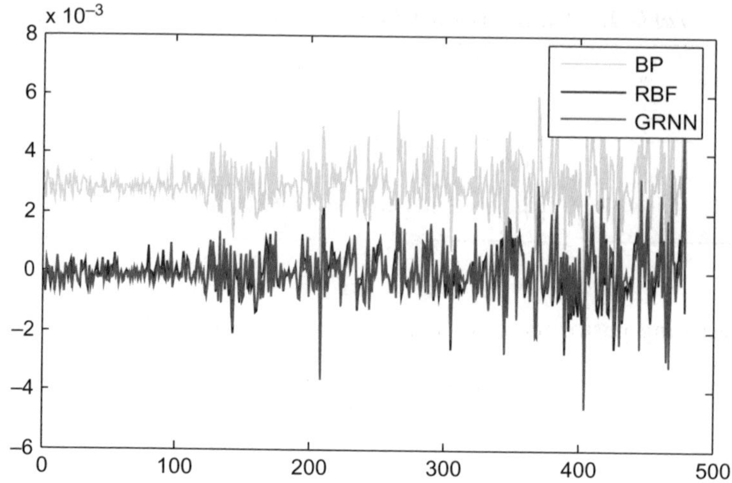

Fig. 1. Comparison of Estimation Errors among BP, RBF and GRNN.

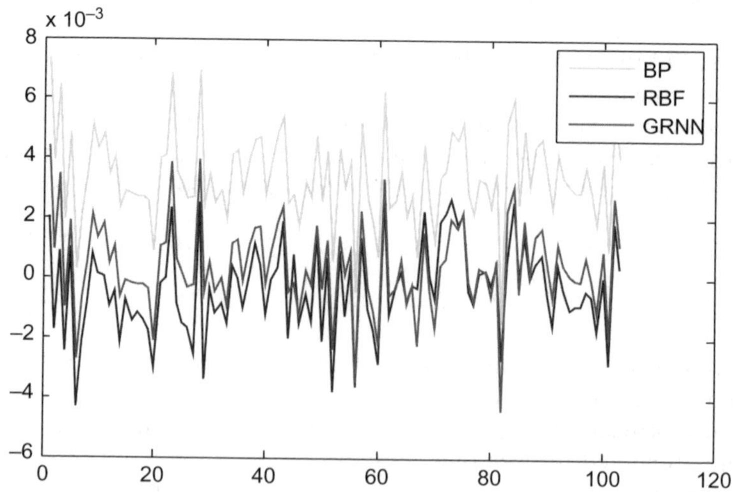

Fig. 2. Comparison of Forecasting Errors among BP, RBF and GRNN.

Table 1. Comparison of Performance across Models.

	Non-Linear ANN		
	BP	RBF	GRNN
MAPE	1.6887	0.6274	0.9431
MAE	0.3581	−0.0355	0.0423
RMSE	0.0034	0.0016	0.0016

the forecasting performance of the non-linear ANN models:

$$\text{MAPE} = \frac{1}{n}\sum_{t \in p}\left|\frac{(x_t - \hat{x}_t)}{x_t}\right| \tag{4}$$

$$\text{MAE} = \frac{1}{n}\sum_{t \in p}(\hat{x}_t - x_t) \tag{5}$$

$$\text{RMSE} = \sqrt{\frac{\sum_{t \in p}(\hat{x}_t - x_t)^2}{n}} \tag{6}$$

where p is the sample size, $\hat{x}_t$ is the forecasted exchange rates and x_t is the real rates. Results, presented in Table 1, show that the RBF model has the lowest MAPE, MAE and RMSE. It is concluded that RBF performs the best among them.

The economic implication of the estimation is that the explanatory variables including fundamentalist, chartist and basket arrangements contain significant power in interpreting the behaviour of the basket rate.

3.3. Non-Linear Modelling: GP

The weakness of an ANN algorithm is that it may converge to local minima instead of global minima. ANN is also considered something of a black box, one which provides no specific functional form for the system. GP[7] is therefore attempted to overcome these problems.

Four input variables including the market force variables are used in this model.[8] Table 2 presents the final results after various experiments. It shows that all the factors – chartist, fundamentalist and currency

Table 2. The Configuration of GP.

Generation	100
Population	200
Algorithm	+, −, *, sin, cos, ln, /
End nodes	{X1 X2 X3 X4}
Fitness criteria (RSS)	0.205609
Depth of the tree	10
Mutation rate	0.01
Stop criteria	GP runs for 100 generations

Note: X1, X2, X3 and X4 are four input variables including fundamentalist, chartist and B4, B11 exchange arrangements.

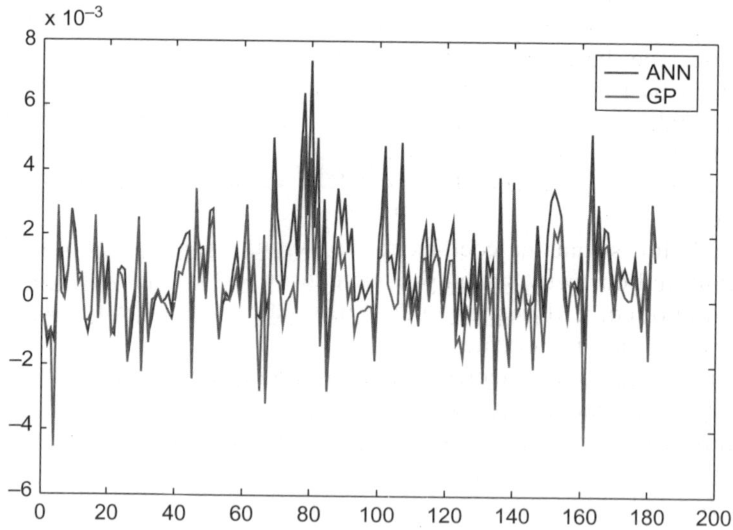

Fig. 3. Estimation Performance Evaluation of ANN and GP.

arrangements – have the power to determine the rate because they all appear in the end nodes.

Based on the function specified by GP, we calculated the forecasting errors using sum square error (SSE). We then compared the results with that from ANN in Fig. 3. Two lines are again mingled with each other; therefore, we calculated the SSE and arrived at 0.001557, 0.001555 for ANN and GP, respectively. Thus, GP outperforms ANN.

3.4. Linear Modelling

The non-linear model shows that market forces as well as the exchange rate arrangements have the explanatory power to interpret the exchange-rate behaviour. Linear modelling is further applied to measure the relative importance of different variables. Eq. (3) is estimated by ordinary least square (OLS), and the estimation results are presented in Table 3.

In the top of Table 3, the estimation results posit that the numeraire is the US dollar; the middle section that the numeraire is the Swiss franc and the bottom section that the numeraire is the special drawing rights (SDR). In each case, the basket is further divided into four types of currency component basket (B4), eleven types of currency component basket (B11) and the single euro case. Frankel (2009) recently found that the weights in the RMB basket had shifted from the US dollar to the EU euro. We therefore add in a separate EU model to see if the same result can be replicated.

Table 3 shows that the coefficients for fundamentalists are in each case significant and correctly signed, but that those for the chartists are neither significant nor correctly signed. The results indicate that the driving force in the market is the fundamentalist.

As for the basket arrangement, when the case of US dollar as numeraire is considered, the coefficients for both types of baskets and the EU are significant and correctly signed. When the numeraire is the Swiss franc, the coefficients for B4 and B11 are significant and correctly signed, but the results do not hold for the EU. When the numeraire is SDR, the coefficient for EU is significant and correctly signed, but the results do not hold for the rest. What we can conclude, therefore, is that variation in basket arrangement also plays a role in the exchange-rate determination. Additionally, we have found that the weight has switched from US dollar to euro.

Comparing the market force and exchange-rate arrangements, it seems that the magnitude of the coefficients of the basket is lower than that of the fundamentalist. This implies that the fundamentalist market rule plays a more critical role in exchange-rate determination, though it is one of several factors.

Table 3. Estimation Results of Eq. (3) Using OLS.

Dollar[a]				
Constant		−0.0034*	−0.0042*	−0.0003*
		(0.0006)	(0.0007)	(0.0001)
Fundamentalist		0.1184*	0.1202*	0.1213*
		(0.0196)	(0.0196)	(0.0197)
Chartist		−0.1135	−0.1158	−0.0867
		(0.5058)	(0.6900)	(0.0497)
Basket	B4		0.0103*	
			(0.0019)	
	B11			0.0114*
				(0.0022)
	EU			0.0262*
				(0.0262)
SWF[b]				
Constant		−0.0006*	0.0001	0.0002
		(0.0003)	(0.0003)	(0.0002)
Fundamentalist		0.08494*	−0.1129*	0.05395*
		(.0196)	(0.0190)	(0.0034)
Chartist		−0.0623	−0.0102	−0.0129
		(0.0913)	(0.909)	(0.0914)
Basket	B4		0.0688*	
			(0.0178)	
	B11			0.0150*
				(0.0112)
	EU			−0.0475
				(0.2615)
SDR[c]				
Constant		−0.0761	−0.0001	−0.0001
		(0.0162)	(0.0011)	(0.0001)
Fundamentalist		0.0761*	0.0766*	0.0788*
		(0.0162)	(0.0162)	(0.0161)
Chartist		−0.0372	−0.0374	−0.0382
		(0.0198)	(0.1885)	(0.0190)
Basket	B4		0.0026	
			(0.0558)	
	B11			−0.0166
				(0.0487)
	EU			0.1701*
				(0.0865)

Note: *Denotes significance level at 5%; **denotes significance level at 10%.

[a]The choice of numeraires: Another interesting observation from this experiment is that the results differ somewhat when different numeraires are used. In the basket exchange literature, researchers have selected various kinds of subjects as numeraire: US dollar, SDR, gold, SWF and oil (Frankel & Wei, 1994; Bénassy-Quéré, 1997; Marquez & Schindler, 2006;

4. CONCLUSIONS

One of the major causes of a currency crisis is the disequilibrium of the exchange rate from its market-determined rate. When the exchange rate is not entirely determined by the market forces, for example, when it is instead influenced by central government arrangements, the rate may be under/overvalued. If the disequilibrium persists, the exchange rate system will become vulnerable to speculative attacks or violent fluctuations that may disrupt normal economic activity.

The long-term aim of China's exchange reform has been to develop a much more flexible exchange-rate system with market forces playing an increasing role. Both the linear model and non-linear estimations show that the market force has contributed to the formulation of the current basket regime. The results from the linear model further indicate that the fundamentalist forecasting rule dominates the chartist rule in the system. It is also evident that the currency arrangement by the central bank plays a role. This shows that China is on its way to a currency system that is changing from the single dollar peg and moving towards a basket peg, which is, in fact, a much more flexible regime. With the existence of exchange-rate arrangements, it nevertheless remains a far cry from a fundamental equilibrium rate. Government involvement in manipulating the currency is still prevalent.

Thorbecke, 2010). Authors sometimes will switch from one type to another in different papers without justification. In this study, we propose that the purpose of a common numeraire is for comparing variations in RMB and other currencies in the baskets. Three different major numeraires selected according to three different principles are used for this study. The first criterion for choosing a proper numeraire is that the candidates will affect the variation in the component currency in the basket more or less uniformly with no significant bias. The choice of US dollar in this research satisfies that criterion. We name this as a dynamic case.

[b]The second principle is to choose a numeraire that is as neutral as possible in relation to all the currencies in the basket. We define 'neutral' as the situation when the corresponding currency has only marginal impact on the variation in the component currencies. The numeraire will always serve as an unbiased ruler to measure the volatility of other currencies. Usually one tends to choose a numeraire with lower the volatility. The choice of the Swiss franc is supposed to serve that purpose. We name this situation as a static case.

[c]In the third case, SDR is selected as a numeraire. SDR can be regarded as a quasi-international currency. It is the most comprehensive and broadest numeraire which implies the variation in US dollar. It is supposed to contain all the possible factors that will cause the variation in a currency using SDR as a numeraire.

NOTES

1. The fundamentalist expectation is the unobserved equilibrium exchange rate, which is estimated by applying the Hodrick–Prescott (HP) filter to the observed exchange rate data.

2. As for chartists, the estimation of geometrically declining distributed lag is used. The choice of the value of the parameter β is 0.8 after various experimentations.

3. Backpropagation (BP), first described by Paul Werbos in 1974 and developed by David E. Rumelhart in 1986, is a supervised learning method. It is implemented using the Delta rule. Radial basis function (RBF) networks, with the RBFs taking on the role of the activation functions, display exponential convergence rates and faster learning speeds than does BP. General regression neural networks (GRNN) have architectures similar to RBF networks but are much faster, are more accurately able to train networks and are less sensitive to outliers. One disadvantage of GRNN models is that the models are larger because there is only one neuron for each training row, causing the model to run more slowly than other networks.

4. We have chosen to collect data from the Federal Reserve, which has about 10% more observations than does the IMF. The Federal Reserve database, however, has no information on the Russian rouble. The transaction and recorded dates in the Federal Reserve database are not exactly the same as those found in data from the Central Bank of Russia. We have used Visual Foxpro 8 to make the dates consistent.

5. We have also collected foreign direct investment data from the Ministry of Commerce except in the cases of Russian and Australia, where we collected data from their respective treasury departments. Predictions were made where data was missing. The missing data accounts for 4.5% of the total. We tried trade-weighted weights and trade-plus-FDI-weighted weights, and the results are consistent. The results from trade-weighted data are reported.

6. For RBF, we tried different values for spread and found that when it takes the value of 1.5, the error reaches the minimum.

7. The white box characteristic is the significant advantage of the GP over black box approach of ANN. The GP model can be the best solver for searching highly non-linear space for global optima via adaptive strategies.

8. We decided on this by trying all possible combinations of one, two, three and four variables. The software by Sara Silva (2008) is used to perform all the GP runs. Available at http://sourceforge.net/mailarchive/forum.php?forum_name=gplab-users.

ACKNOWLEDGMENT

This project is financed by the Interdisciplinary Innovation Project of Education Committee (2009AASH0904). The authors thank Yan Minjian and Wei Lian.

REFERENCES

Alon, I., & Drtina, R. (2006). Chinese currency forecasts and capital budgeting. *Journal of American Academy of Business, Cambridge, 10*(1), 218–226.

Alon, I., & Kellerman, E. (1999). Internal antecedents to the 1997 Asian Economic Crisis. *Multinational Business Review, 7*(2), 1–12.

Bénassy-Quéré, A. (1997). Optimal pegs for Asian currencies, CEPII working paper No. 1997 – 14 (October).

Cline, W., & Williamson, J. (2010a). Notes on equilibrium exchange rates. Policy brief 10-2. Washington: Peterson Institute of International Economics.

Cline, W., & Williamson, J. (2010b). Estimate of fundamental equilibrium exchange rates. Policy brief 10-15. Washington: Peterson Institute of International Economics.

Eichengreen, B. (2006). China's exchange rate regime: The long and short of it. Revision of paper for Columbia University's conference on Chinese money and finance held in New York on February 2–3.

Feng, X. B., & Alon, I. (2007). Chinese RMB exchange rate and local currency stability in ASEAN. *China Economic Review, 18*(4), 417–424.

Frankel, J. (1987). Using survey data to test standard proposition regarding exchange rate expectations. *American Economic Review, 77*, 33–53.

Frankel, J. (2006). On the yuan: The choice between adjustment under a fixed exchange rate and adjustment under a flexible rate. In: G. Illing (Ed.), *Understanding the Chinese economy*. Munich: CESifo Economic Studies. Also in NBER Working Paper No. 11274.

Frankel, J. (2009). *New estimation of China's exchange rate regime*. NBER Working Paper No. 14700.

Frankel, J., & Froot, K. A. (1986). *Short-term and long-term expectations of the yen–dollar exchange rate: Evidence from survey data*. Federal Reserve Board, International Financial Discussion Paper no. 292.

Frankel, J., & Wei, S.-J. (1994). Yen bloc or dollar bloc? Exchange rate policies of the EastAsian economies. In: T. Ito & A. O. Krueger (Eds), *Macroeconomic linkages: Savings exchange rates and capital flows* (pp. 295–329). Chicago: University of Chicago Press.

Frankel, J., & Wei, S. J. (2007). *Assessing China's exchange rate regime*. NBER Working Paper No. 13100.

Jen, S. (2005). Chinese RMB basket still a mystery. Global Economics Forum, Morgan Stanley.

Marquez, J., & Schindler, J. (2006). *Exchange rate effects on China's trade: An interim report*. International Finance Discussion Paper no. 861. Federal Reserve Board, Washington, DC.

Shah, A., Zeileis, A., & Patnaik, I. (2005). *What is the new Chinese currency regime?* Unpublished memo (November). Department of Economics, Monash University.

Thorbecke, W. (2010). How would an appreciation of the RMB and other East Asian currencies affect China's exports? *Review of International Economics, 18*(1), 95–108.

Williamson, J. (1994). Estimates of FEERs. In: J. Williamson (Ed.), *Estimating equilibrium exchange rates* (pp. 177–244). Washington, DC: Institute for International Economics.

Xu, J., Shao, H., & Tang, G. (2007). Empirical study on China basket currency system. *Journal of Shanghai University of Economics and Finance, 66*, 72–76.

Xu, S., & Tang, Q. (2008). An empirical research on China's exchange intervention by referring to currency basket. *Studies of International Finance, 9*, 68–72.

Yamazaki, K. (2006). Inside the currency basket. Columbia University and Mitsubishi UFJ Trust and Banking Corporation working paper.

Zhou, J. (2009). The reference basket for RMB: Composition, stability and commitment. *World Economy*, *3*, 16–22.

GRASS-ROOT STOCK MARKET INVESTMENT AND LONG-TERM COMMONALITY IN LIQUIDITY: EVIDENCE FROM THE SHANGHAI STOCK EXCHANGE

Renaud Beaupain, Lei Meng and Marie Marticou

ABSTRACT

This chapter measures stock market liquidity with three low-frequency liquidity estimators, and investigates the long-term behaviour of commonality in liquidity on the Shanghai Stock Exchange (SSE) through principal component analyses and panel regressions. The findings provide strong evidence of liquidity co-movement on the SSE from its inception to the present. The extent of commonality in liquidity varies significantly over time. Remarkably, it surged in 2007, which corresponds to the onset of the subprime mortgage-triggered financial crisis; however, the subsequent behaviour is divergent among our different liquidity proxies.

Keywords: Commonality in liquidity; low-frequency liquidity estimators; principal component analysis; panel regression.

The Impact of the Global Financial Crisis on Emerging Financial Markets
Contemporary Studies in Economic and Financial Analysis, Volume 93, 625–643

ISSN: 1569-3759/doi:10.1108/S1569-3759(2011)0000093023

JEL Classifications: G10; G12; G19.

1. INTRODUCTION

Commonality in liquidity is an emerging theme in market microstructure studies. Due to its implications for asset pricing, commonality in liquidity has attracted considerable attention from academics and practitioners. If individual liquidity is dictated by a universal common factor, then it becomes a market-wide risk factor for the pricing of that asset class, and there should be a market price for that risk factor. In addition, since the dawn of the subprime mortgage-triggered financial crisis where market-wide illiquidity rampaged, regulators are also making inroads into measures to prevent sudden co-movement into the illiquid extreme (Drahmann & Nikolaou, 2009).

The motivation for investigating liquidity co-movements in the Chinese stock market is as follows. First, although being an emerging market, this market has increasingly grown in importance among the world stock markets. According to WFE (2009) the market capitalization of the Chinese stock market accounted for 5.34% of the world total in 2008, a nearly threefold increase since 2002 (2.02%).[1] Second, the Chinese stock market has a distinct investor basis compared to stock markets from developed economies: the trading volume is dominated by individual investors rather than institutional investors. For example, between 2002 and 2004, the trading volume of individual accounts was 5.76 times that of institutional accounts (Wang & Li, 2007). Due to different investment perspectives, levels of access to information and financial literacy, a market with a majority of individual investors is of interest to investigate. In addition, Yao and Luo (2009) suggest that the unique economic psychology of Chinese individual investors leads to the extreme volatile stock market in China. Third, the evolution of commonality in liquidity during and after the current financial turmoil has by far been under-studied. Finally, the state has profound influence on the performance of the stock market (Yao & Luo, 2009).

This chapter distinguishes from previous studies of commonality in liquidity by using low-frequency liquidity measures (Goyenko, Holden, & Trzcinka, 2009; Hasbrouck, 2009; Korajczyk & Sadka, 2008) for all companies listed on the Shanghai Stock Exchange (SSE) from its inception to the present. Therefore, this chapter not only informs the usefulness of low-frequency liquidity measures in the context of liquidity co-movements, but the empirical findings also provide insights into the evolution of commonality in liquidity in the Chinese stock market and whether this factor should be taken into consideration in equity pricing.

The organization of this chapter is as follows. Section 2 provides background information on the characteristics of the Chinese stock market. Section 3 reviews the literature on liquidity co-movements. Section 4 describes the data and the methodology used in the empirical analyses. Section 5 interprets the empirical results, and Section 6 uses an alternative method to check the robustness of the empirical findings. Section 7 concludes.

2. BACKGROUND

The Chinese stock market mainly consists of A shares, which are quoted in the local currency (RMB), and B shares, which are quoted in US dollars.[2] Both A and B shares are traded either on the SSE or on the Shenzhen Stock Exchange (SZSE). As the summary information on the two stock exchanges reported in Table 1 shows, the SSE is however much larger in terms of the number of companies listed on the exchange, market capitalization and volume. As the table further highlights, the number and turnover in B shares appear only marginal relative to A shares.

The Shanghai and Shenzhen stock exchanges are both pure order-driven markets without designated market makers. Trading is organized as a call auction from 9:15 to 9:25, a continuous trading morning session from 9:30 to 11:30, and a continuous trading afternoon session from 13:00 to 15:00. Price priority and time precedence are used as the primary and secondary order matching rules.

Table 1. 2008 Market Statistics of Shanghai and Shenzhen Stock Exchanges.

	Shanghai		Shenzhen	
	A shares	B shares	A shares	B shares
No. of companies listed	854	54	454	55
Market capitalization (RMB bn)	9,725.2	NA	1,784.5	NA
Trading value (RMB bn)	17,976.2	66.8	6,949.1	55.5

Source: SSE (2009), SZSE (2009).

Table 2. A Selection of Stock Indices of Shanghai Stock Exchange.

Index Name	Description	Launch Date
SSE 50	50 largest stocks of good liquidity and representativeness	02/01/2004
SSE 180	180 largest stocks of good liquidity and representativeness	01/07/2002
SSE Composite	All listed companies	15/07/1991
SSE Dividend	50 largest stocks of good liquidity and high dividend	04/01/2005
SSE Central State-owned Enterprises 50	50 largest and most liquid central state-owned enterprises	30/03/2009
SSE 180 Corporate Governance	100 large stocks of good liquidity and corporate governance from the SSE 180 index	10/09/2008
SSE 180 Financials	Banks, insurance companies, securities companies, trusts, etc. from the SSE 180 index	10/12/20007
SSE Mega-Cap	20 largest and most liquid stocks traded on SSE	23/04/2009
SSE Small-Cap	320 largest stocks by market capitalization after deleting SSE 180 from all the companies listed on SSE	03/07/2009
SSE Large&Mid&Small Cap	The combination of SSE 180 and SSE Small-Cap	03/07/2009
SSE Social Responsibility	Top 100 ranked by social contribution value per share stocks from the SSE Corporate Governance index	05/08/2009
SSE Private-owned Enterprises 50	50 largest, most liquid and representative private-owned companies	25/08/2009

Source: www.sse.com.cn
Note: There are in total 41 indices on SSE; the above are the most popular indices that are included on the front page of SSE's website.

Since the inception of the two stock exchanges, the number of stock indices has increased remarkably. In August 2009, there were 41 stock indices on the SSE (see Table 2). Exchange-traded funds are however only tracking the SSE 50, the SSE 180 and the SSE Dividend.

3. LITERATURE REVIEW

The theory of commonality in liquidity was first proposed by Chordia, Roll and Subrahmanyam (2000). They suggest that co-movements in individual measures of liquidity such as bid-ask spreads and quoted depth are caused by dealers' rebalancing of inventory, which is mainly determined by trading volume, to the optimal level, as well as by the asymmetric information-triggered adverse selection component of transaction costs borne by the uninformed majority when trading with the informed minority. Coughenour and Saad (2004) argue that in markets with designated specialists, specialist's liquidity provision for many stocks can also lead to co-movements in liquidity. Chordia et al. (2000) also show that on the NYSE spreads (quoted and effective) and depth co-move with market and industry liquidity. The effect persists even when allowance is given to firm-specific trading volume, volatility and price level. Hasbrouck and Seppi (2001) use principal component analysis (PCA) to examine commonality in liquidity. They find commonality in order flows and returns across the 30 Dow Jones stocks, and the effect is stronger in small market-capitalization stocks and for stocks traded in specialists markets. Huberman and Halka (2001) also provide evidence of commonality in liquidity in the US stock market. The evidence reported in Beaupain, Giot and Petitjean (2010) further shows the sensitivity of liquidity co-movements on the NYSE to the regime of realized volatility of the market.

The presence of commonality in liquidity is also widely documented around the world. Brockman and Chung (2002) report both market-wide and industry-wide co-movements in spread and quoted depth on the stock exchange of Hong Kong which has an order-driven market structure, though spread-related commonality is more pronounced among medium-sized firms. In addition, they also find commonality in trade frequency, which confirms Chordia et al.'s (2000) hypothesis that the asymmetric information-triggered adverse selection component of transaction cost leads to commonality in liquidity. Fabre and Frino (2004) find a weaker commonality in liquidity on the Australian Stock Exchange compared to the NYSE. Martinez, Nieto, Rubio, and Tapia (2003) find positive evidence that commonality in liquidity exists in the Spanish stock market. Bauer (2004) detected the presence of co-movement in liquidity in the Swiss market. Qin (2007) investigated commonality in liquidity across 19 emerging markets, and suggests that systematic liquidity risk is more significant in emerging markets than in developed markets. Brockman, Chung, and Pérignon (2009) provide a global perspective of the commonality in liquidity by analyzing 47 stock exchanges. They demonstrate that exchange-level commonality in spread and depth is pervasive across the world; however, the cross-sectional variation among exchanges and geographic regions remains large. They also find that liquidity co-movement in individual exchanges is significantly influenced by movements at the global and regional scale. In addition, Brockman and Chung (2008) show that commonality in liquidity on the Stock Exchange of Hong Kong tended to increase with market stress. Naes, Skjeltorp, and Ädegaard (2011) find that in the US and Norway stock markets commonality in liquidity is related to the business cycle.

The accumulation of theories and empirical evidence of commonality in liquidity has led to the argument that commonality in liquidity should be included as a systematic risk factor in asset pricing. Pastor and Stambaugh (2003) suggest that aggregate liquidity be included as a priced state variable, that is investors would require higher expected returns on assets whose returns have higher sensitivities to market-wide liquidity movements. Their empirical analyses provide positive evidence for this.

4. DATA AND METHODOLOGY

4.1. Data

The data used in this study are from Thomson Reuters DataStream. These include daily prices and volumes of all 915 A shares listed on the SSE over the period from March 1991 to August 2009. Our sample is filtered according to the following criteria: (i) we remove any security without volume or price, with an intention to clear and (ii) for any stock, if the daily variation in price exceeds 90% (in absolute value), the trading day is removed for this stock as it is considered as not representative.

4.2. Liquidity Estimators

In this chapter, we rely on low-frequency estimators of the tightness and depth dimensions of market liquidity. All proxies specified below are estimated on a monthly basis.

4.2.1. Tightness Dimension: Roll's Effective Spread

Roll (1984) introduced a way to estimate effective spreads based on the stock return dynamics. He showed that, in an efficient market where price changes are initiated by the side of the last trade (bid or ask) and by no new information arriving in the market, the following formula applies:

$$\mathrm{Cov}(\Delta P_t, \Delta P_{t-1}) = -\frac{1}{4}S^2$$

Or equivalently,

$$S = 2\sqrt{-\mathrm{Cov}(\Delta P_t, \Delta P_{t-1})}$$

where S is the effective spread, ΔP_t the variation in price between time $t-1$ and time t and ΔP_{t-1} the variation in price between time $t-2$ and time $t-1$.

The formula is however undefined for a positive serial covariance. The modified version used in this chapter follows Goyenko et al. (2009) to infer the monthly effective spread (S_m) from the serial covariance of daily price changes (ΔP_d) in the following manner:

$$S_m = \begin{cases} 2\sqrt{-\mathrm{Cov}(\Delta P_d, \Delta P_{d-1})} & \text{if} \quad \mathrm{Cov}(\Delta P_d, \Delta P_{d-1}) < 0 \\ 0 & \text{if} \quad \mathrm{Cov}(\Delta P_d, \Delta P_{d-1}) \geq 0 \end{cases}$$

Since the Roll estimator measures the effective spread, an increase in S indicates an increase in transaction costs, hence making the market less liquid.

4.2.2. Depth Dimension: Amihud's Illiquidity Ratio and Roll's Impact Factor

Amihud (2002) considered liquidity as an elusive concept whereas illiquidity is able to capture the impact of the order flow on the price. He found that across stocks and over time the expected stock return is an increasing function of the expected illiquidity. The Amihud (2002) depth estimator is accordingly defined as the average of the daily ratio of the absolute stock return over the corresponding dollar volume.[3] It can be expressed by the following equation:

$$\mathrm{Illiquidity}_m = \frac{1}{D}\sum_{d=1}^{D}\frac{|r_d|}{V_d}$$

where $\mathrm{Illiquidity}_m$ is the price impact for month m, r_d the stock return between day $d-1$ and day d, and V_d the dollar volume exchanged on day d.

This measure captures the marginal price impact of a unit of dollar volume. The larger the Amihud (2002) measure, the more illiquid the asset.

Goyenko et al. (2009) introduced an alternative depth estimator which is based on the Roll's (1994) estimates of the effective spread:

$$\text{RollIMPACT}_m = \frac{S_m}{(1/D)\sum_{d=1}^{D} V_d}$$

where RollIMPACT_m is the unit-by-unit impact of volume on the effective spread in month m, S_m the Roll's effective spread estimated for month m and V_d the dollar volume exchanged on day d.

The smaller the spread for a given volume or the larger the volume for a given spread, the smaller the Roll price impact estimator, and the more liquid the asset therefore is.

4.3. Principal Component Analysis

Our investigation of liquidity co-movements on the SSE is based on a PCA following the Hasbrouck and Seppi (2001) method. PCA is the standard method for extracting the most important uncorrelated sources of variation in a multivariate data series. In other words, this technique aims to find out the most important latent common component factors among all factors explaining the total observed variability of a set of relative variables. In that way, the first principal component has the greatest explanatory power of the total variability.

This method presents two main advantages. First, it allows reducing the dimensionality of a data set by focusing on a limited number of principal components without losing in computational efficiency. Second, the method provides a tractable pattern from the data set, strengthening the opportunity to explain the sample behaviour. The PCA approach consists in computing the correlation matrix[4] and in determining its eigenvalues and eigenvectors. The principal components are accordingly a linear combination of the variables correlation matrix.

4.3.1. Principal Component Analysis Model

The ith principal component of r is

$$y_i = e'_i r = \sum_{j=1}^{k} e_{ij} r_j \quad \text{for} \quad i = 1, \ldots, k$$

with

$$\mathrm{Var}(y_i) = e'_i \sum_r e_i = \Lambda_i \quad \text{for} \quad i = 1, \ldots, k$$

$$\mathrm{Cov}(y_i, y_j) = e'_j \sum_r e_i = 0 \quad \text{for} \quad i \neq j$$

where

$$\sum_r \text{is the covariance matrix}$$

$$(\Lambda_1, e_1), \ldots, (\Lambda_k, e_k) \text{ are the eigenvalue} - \text{eigenvector pairs of } \sum_r \text{with}(\Lambda_1 > \cdots > \Lambda_k > 0)$$

Numerical results accordingly give the eigenvalues with their proportional contribution in the variance and the corresponding eigenvectors, since the eigenvalues reflect the relative importance of their associated eigenvector. Principal components defined by eigenvalue are ranked by weights, so the first principal component explains the greatest variation part; the second explains the greatest part of the remaining variation and so on. Moreover, principal components are uncorrelated with each other. Therefore, the larger the eigenvalue of the first principal components compared to the remaining components, the more significant the commonality in liquidity. We hypothesize that due to the presence of a large number of individual investors who have homogenous economic psychology in the Chinese stock market, liquidity is driven by a few homogenous factors and therefore should demonstrate significant co-movement. In other words, a small number of principal components should be able to explain most of the variation in the market-wide liquidity. To see the evolution of commonality in liquidity and to analyze its long-term behaviour, we apply PCA for each liquidity estimator on an yearly basis.

5. RESULTS AND INTERPRETATION

For each liquidity estimator, the first eigenvalue ($\lambda 1$) captures the total variation attributable to the first principal component (C1). The second eigenvalue ($\lambda 2$) similarly shows the variability attributable to the second principal component (C2) and so on. In this study, the first three principal components are presented, since in most cases they explain the majority of the variation. Tables 3–5 report the results of the PCA for Roll's effective spread, Amihud's illiquidity ratio and Roll's price impact factor on an yearly basis. Due to the increase in the number of firms listed on the SSE throughout the sample period, using eigenvalues alone is however not informative of the extent of co-movements in liquidity. Therefore, we base our analysis on the percentage of variation explained by each principal component.

In Roll's (1984) effective spread (Table 3), and throughout the whole sample period, the variation in monthly liquidity explained by the first component is, on average, less than one-third. The second and third components explain, on average, 14.68% and 11.60% of the remaining variation in the spread, respectively. The first three components have a cumulative explanatory power of 57.56%. Co-movements in transaction

Table 3. Roll's Effective Spread: Principal Components Analysis.

Year	Eigenvalue $\lambda 1$	Variance Prop. C1	Eigenvalue $\lambda 2$	Variance Prop. C2	Eigenvalue $\lambda 3$	Variance Prop. C3	Cumulative Prop. C1, C2, C3
1991	2.4656	41.09%	1.7179	28.63%	1.1645	19.41%	89.13%
1992	3.2482	40.60%	2.0727	25.91%	1.2610	15.76%	82.27%
1993	13.8995	42.12%	5.2731	15.98%	3.9595	12.00%	70.10%
1994	73.5579	66.27%	10.3706	9.34%	7.3451	6.62%	82.23%
1995	58.2516	35.74%	19.2213	11.79%	16.1521	9.91%	57.44%
1996	57.1571	32.29%	23.1101	13.06%	20.2747	11.45%	56.80%
1997	110.2822	39.81%	27.9316	10.08%	26.1584	9.44%	59.34%
1998	64.8366	18.37%	44.7719	12.68%	38.2819	10.84%	41.90%
1999	151.6820	37.36%	71.5044	17.61%	36.2718	8.93%	63.91%
2000	135.2082	30.18%	57.6643	12.87%	39.3447	8.78%	51.83%
2001	159.3836	30.19%	60.4633	11.45%	54.2923	10.28%	51.92%
2002	159.4450	27.02%	87.2919	14.80%	78.6158	13.32%	55.14%
2003	107.8929	16.18%	80.5864	12.08%	77.5924	11.63%	39.89%
2004	103.2800	14.36%	96.9651	13.49%	76.6137	10.66%	38.51%
2005	167.8265	21.74%	99.2404	12.86%	83.9379	10.87%	45.47%
2006	99.5925	15.51%	84.3765	13.14%	80.5653	12.55%	41.20%
2007	199.9126	28.72%	90.7451	13.04%	71.6621	10.30%	52.06%
2008	225.7913	29.91%	104.1362	13.79%	94.4835	12.51%	56.21%
2009	214.4215	26.80%	130.6292	16.33%	121.2453	15.16%	58.29%
Average		31.28%		14.68%		11.60%	57.56%

Note: $\lambda 1$, $\lambda 2$ and $\lambda 3$ are the eigenvalues for the first, second and third principal components, respectively; C1, C2 and C3 are the corresponding variance proportion of each principal component.

Table 4. Amihud's Illiquidity Ratio: Principal Components Analysis.

Year	Eigenvalue $\lambda 1$	Variance Prop. C1	Eigenvalue $\lambda 2$	Variance Prop. C2	Eigenvalue $\lambda 3$	Variance Prop. C3	Cumulative Prop. C1, C2, C3
1991	2.4515	40.86%	1.4209	23.68%	1.1209	18.68%	83.22%
1992	3.2055	40.07%	2.0045	25.06%	1.1217	14.02%	79.15%
1993	17.4122	52.76%	5.6671	17.17%	3.6881	11.18%	81.11%
1994	79.1023	71.26%	12.3433	11.12%	7.6780	6.92%	89.30%
1995	95.4910	58.58%	45.4151	27.86%	7.8615	4.82%	91.27%
1996	124.2402	70.19%	18.0477	10.20%	11.3720	6.42%	86.81%
1997	151.0674	54.54%	42.7517	15.43%	21.9598	7.93%	77.90%
1998	191.1218	54.14%	51.3629	14.55%	39.4190	11.17%	79.86%
1999	213.9522	52.70%	74.6702	18.39%	42.8670	10.56%	81.65%
2000	203.2342	45.36%	100.1338	22.35%	42.2848	9.44%	77.15%
2001	380.4427	72.05%	39.3096	7.45%	30.1239	5.71%	85.20%
2002	412.7317	69.95%	92.6477	15.70%	21.5778	3.66%	89.31%
2003	343.9657	51.57%	83.0890	12.46%	64.6376	9.69%	73.72%
2004	433.3503	60.19%	74.9089	10.40%	54.2295	7.53%	78.12%
2005	351.5410	45.54%	126.8885	16.44%	70.2037	9.09%	71.07%
2006	238.2263	37.11%	108.3997	16.88%	58.1180	9.05%	63.04%
2007	390.4812	55.86%	93.9633	13.44%	59.6988	8.54%	77.85%
2008	511.4524	67.74%	62.2878	8.25%	46.8179	6.20%	82.19%
2009	606.1906	75.49%	78.5973	9.79%	47.8568	5.96%	91.24%
Average		56.63%		15.61%		8.77%	81.01%

Note: $\lambda 1$, $\lambda 2$ and $\lambda 3$ are the eigenvalues for the first, second and third principal components, respectively; C1, C2 and C3 are the corresponding variance proportion of each principal component.

costs are accordingly mainly driven by three principal components. The first three principal components have an explanatory power of the total variance comprised between 38.51% in 2004 and 89.13% in 1991.

As for Amihud's (2002) illiquidity ratio (Table 4), on average over our sample period, 56.63% of the total monthly variation in price impact can be explained by a single common factor. The second and third principal components explain 15.61% and 8.77% of the remaining variation, respectively. Although the first three components have, on average, a cumulative explanatory power above 81%, they explain between 63.04% in 2006 and 91.27% of the total variation in market depth estimated by this proxy in 1995.

Roll's impact factor (Table 5) supports the above finding regarding the commonality in market depth. The first component alone explains 34.94% of the variation in the price impact proxy, and the second and third explains,

Table 5. Roll's Impact Factor: Principal Components Analysis.

Year	Eigenvalue $\lambda 1$	Variance Prop. C1	Eigenvalue $\lambda 2$	Variance Prop.	Eigenvalue $\lambda 3$	Variance Prop.	Cumulative Prop. C1, C2, C3
1991	1.9511	32.52%	1.6057	26.76%	1.1054	18.42%	77.70%
1992	4.1453	51.82%	1.7120	21.40%	1.4296	17.87%	91.09%
1993	17.7845	53.89%	4.1019	12.43%	3.5198	10.67%	76.99%
1994	31.8467	28.69%	25.1696	22.68%	16.8408	15.17%	66.54%
1995	71.5340	43.89%	38.4655	23.60%	17.2032	10.55%	78.04%
1996	101.6729	57.44%	21.1869	11.97%	17.7709	10.04%	79.45%
1997	94.2836	34.04%	37.4939	13.54%	32.3812	11.69%	59.26%
1998	92.9669	26.34%	53.5728	15.18%	44.2955	12.55%	54.06%
1999	161.4734	39.77%	81.4245	20.06%	32.8498	8.09%	67.92%
2000	107.4133	23.98%	77.2759	17.25%	53.8315	12.02%	53.24%
2001	220.9488	41.85%	75.4574	14.29%	70.6202	13.38%	69.51%
2002	189.9725	32.20%	88.1413	14.94%	65.4562	11.09%	58.23%
2003	112.4741	16.86%	95.6967	14.35%	90.2674	13.53%	44.74%
2004	156.1724	21.72%	106.0377	14.75%	87.2901	12.14%	48.61%
2005	204.4348	26.48%	116.5791	15.10%	92.5165	11.98%	53.57%
2006	115.4099	17.98%	91.9228	14.32%	69.6894	10.86%	43.15%
2007	261.1090	37.46%	122.9504	17.64%	65.4253	9.39%	64.49%
2008	313.3757	41.51%	111.4138	14.76%	71.8139	9.51%	65.78%
2009	282.9471	35.37%	144.2158	18.03%	93.0851	11.64%	65.03%
Average		34.94%		17.00%		12.14%	64.07%

Note: $\lambda 1$, $\lambda 2$ and $\lambda 3$ are the eigenvalues for the first, second and third principal components, respectively; C1, C2 and C3 are the corresponding variance proportion of each principal component.

respectively, 17.00% and 12.14% of the remaining variation. The cumulative variation explained by the first three components fluctuates between 43.15% in 2006 and 91.09% in 1992 and averages 64.07% of the total variation in the depth dimension of market liquidity.

The evidence of strong liquidity co-movements in the tightness and depth dimensions reported above thus confirm the presence of commonality in the liquidity of the SSE between 1991 and 2009.

Figs. 1–3 show that the proportion of variations that can be explained by the first principal component varies markedly year after year. However, it is generally significantly larger than that of the second and the third principal components. The next two principal components have a relatively equal importance in explaining liquidity co-movements, and their influence on market-wide liquidity movements is also relatively stable.

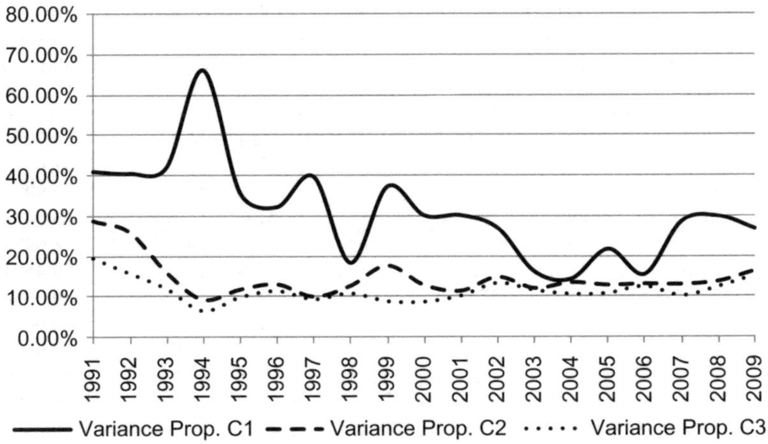

Fig. 1. Roll's Effective Spread: Proportion of Total Variance Explained by the First Three Principal Components.

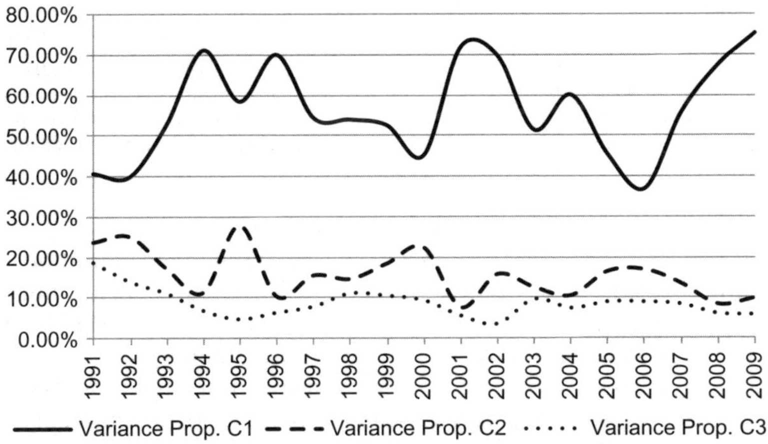

Fig. 2. Amihud's Illiquidity Ratio: Proportion of Total Variance Explained by the First Three Principal Components.

Fig. 4 shows the commonality in liquidity that can be explained by the first three principal components. Overall, co-movements are stronger for depth than spreads. Both Roll's effective spread and Roll's impact factor

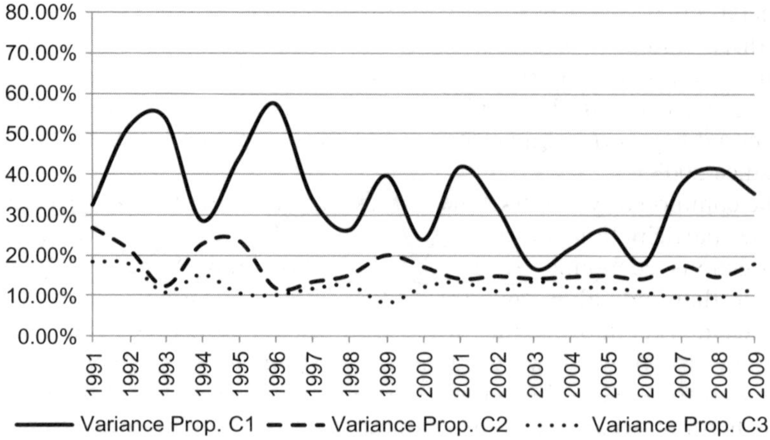

Fig. 3. Roll's Impact Factor: Proportion of Total Variance Explained by the First Three Principal Components.

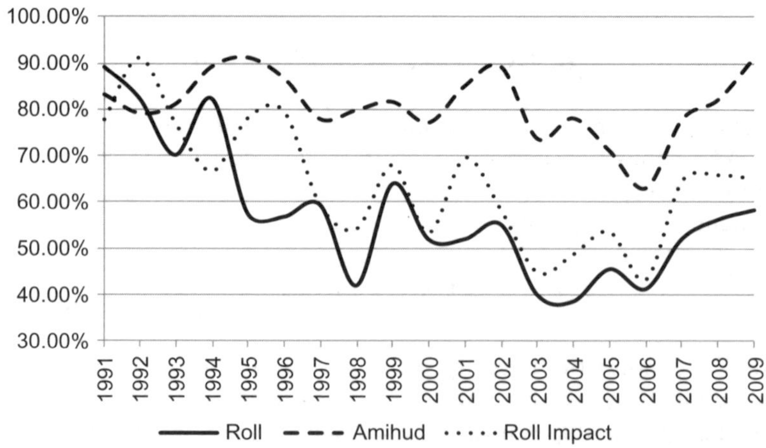

Fig. 4. Roll's Effective Spread, Amihud's Illiquidity Ratio and Roll's Impact Factor: Cumulative Proportion of Total Variance Explained by the First Three Principal Components.

had a downward trend up to 2006, while the trend in Amihud's illiquidity ratio is not pronounced. Co-movements of the tightness and depth dimensions surged in 2007, which corresponds to the subprime mortgage-triggered financial crisis. However, their subsequent behaviour diverges among the three liquidity measures. Whereas commonality in Roll's effective spread continued to rise until 2009, commonality in price impact approximated by Amihud's illiquidity ratio started to subside in 2009 and commonality in price impact proxied by Roll's impact factor has flattened out since 2008.

The commonality in the Chinese stock market liquidity may be attributed to the participation of a large number of individual investors with homogenous economic psychology. Li, Rhee, and Wang (2009) indeed suggest that individual investors, typically less informed, tend to trade towards market movements, while institutional investors have a greater tendency to trade towards the information they receive. Therefore, compared to developed economies where commonality could be attributed to the herding behaviour of institutional investors such as mutual funds (see Hasbrouck & Seppi, 2001), it could be mainly attributed to the herding behaviour of individual investors in the Chinese stock market.

6. ROBUSTNESS CHECK

In Section 5, we have analyzed commonality in liquidity on the SSE by PCA. As a robustness check, we use the following generalized least square random effect panel regression model to confirm the presence of co-movements in the liquidity in this market:

$$Y_{im} = \alpha + \beta \mathrm{CM}_{im} + \gamma \mathrm{RM}_m + v_i + \varepsilon_{im}$$

where Y_{im} denotes the liquidity proxy for stock i in month m, CM_{im} the cross-sectional average liquidity proxy of all companies except company i and RM_m the monthly return of the Shanghai Composite Index in month m.[5] In this model, a significantly positive coefficient for CM would confirm the presence of liquidity co-movements in this market.

Table 6 shows that in 1991 and 1992, liquidity dimensions of the different stocks did not co-move. However, commonality in liquidity is present in all three measures from 1993 to 2009, except that in 2009 there was no significant liquidity commonality in depth measured by Amihud's illiquidity ratio. Overall, this alternative technique therefore supports our previous findings of liquidity co-movements.

Table 6. Panel Regression $Y_{im} = \alpha + \beta CM_{im} + \gamma RM_m + v_i + \varepsilon_{im}$.

Year	Roll's Effective Spread			Amihud's Illiquidity Ratio			Roll Impact Factor		
	α	β	γ	α	β	γ	α	β	γ
1991	0.001**	0.184	0.001	3.752**	−0.306	−7.646	0.077*	−1.113*	−0.020
	(2.34)	(0.74)	(0.35)	(2.35)	(−1.03)	(−0.70)	(4.84)	(−3.22)	(−0.25)
1992	0.027	−2.480*	0.407*	0.119	0.080	0.009	0.006	0.176	0.008
	(1.64)	(−6.03)	(7.20)	(1.36)	(0.30)	(0.06)	(1.57)	(0.70)	(1.30)
1993	0.026	0.178*	−0.004	0.001	0.190*	−0.001	0.006	0.178*	−0.007
	(1.33)	(6.52)	(−0.10)	(1.14)	(8.20)	(−0.31)	(1.23)	(6.49)	(−0.56)
1994	0.004	0.966*	0.008	0.0003	0.981*	−0.0004	0.003	0.873*	0.000
	(0.55)	(18.18)	(0.46)	(0.38)	(24.83)	(−0.19)	(1.06)	(8.50)	(−0.07)
1995	0.003	0.948*	−0.004	0.0005	0.972*	−0.001	0.003	0.925*	−0.017
	(0.73)	(14.41)	(−0.34)	(0.51)	(20.28)	(−0.23)	(0.79)	(11.69)	(−0.62)
1996	0.004	0.911*	0.016	0.001	0.965*	−0.001	0.001	0.965*	−0.001
	(0.95)	(10.55)	(0.78)	(0.49)	(17.90)	(−0.13)	(0.41)	(17.87)	(−0.07)
1997	0.001	0.957*	−0.001	0.0002	0.964*	−0.001	0.001	0.957*	−0.001
	(0.64)	(15.95)	(−0.08)	(0.63)	(17.50)	(−0.43)	(0.64)	(15.95)	(−0.08)
1998	0.006	0.908*	0.026	0.0001	0.976*	−0.001	0.000	0.965*	0.000
	(1.03)	(10.35)	(0.80)	(0.51)	(21.81)	(−0.36)	(0.58)	(17.90)	(0.01)
1999	0.001	0.985*	0.004	0.0001	0.984*	−0.0001	0.000	0.975*	−0.001
	(0.37)	(28.28)	(0.23)	(0.41)	(26.94)	(−0.17)	(0.45)	(21.58)	(−0.21)
2000	0.002	0.981*	0.008	0.001	0.517*	0.002	0.005**	0.544*	0.003
	(0.39)	(24.87)	(0.19)	(1.52)	(2.57)	(0.16)	(1.99)	(2.79)	(0.13)
2001	0.001	0.986*	0.0005	0.00001	0.995*	0.0001	0.0002	0.982	−0.001
	(0.36)	(29.19)	(0.02)	(0.20)	(48.04)	(−0.08)	(0.34)	(25.43)	(−0.12)
2002	0.001	0.990*	0.001	0.0002	0.974*	−0.002	0.0003	0.983*	−0.001
	(0.32)	(33.53)	(0.05)	(0.31)	(21.04)	(−0.21)	(0.39)	(26.02)	(−0.12)
2003	0.003	0.921*	0.013	0.0002	0.962*	−0.001	0.001	0.929*	−0.002
	(0.95)	(11.38)	(0.69)	(0.62)	(17.15)	(−0.19)	(0.86)	(12.10)	(−0.25)
2004	0.002	0.952*	0.001	0.0002	0.970*	−0.001	0.002	0.877*	−0.006
	(0.74)	(15.06)	(0.07)	(0.54)	(19.48)	(−0.19)	(1.07)	(8.66)	(−0.40)
2005	0.001	0.984*	0.0002	0.002	0.735*	−0.007	0.002	0.849*	−0.005
	(0.41)	(26.99)	(0.02)	(1.63)	(4.95)	(−0.68)	(1.15)	(7.56)	(−0.25)
2006	0.002	0.949*	0.003	0.0004	0.867*	−0.0004	0.001	0.832*	−0.002
	(0.73)	(14.52)	(0.25)	(1.20)	(8.22)	(−0.38)	(1.32)	(7.04)	(−0.70)
2007	0.003	0.980*	0.003	0.003	0.980*	0.003	0.0005	0.862*	−0.001
	(0.43)	(23.89)	(0.10)	(0.43)	(23.89)	(0.10)	(1.06)	(8.02)	(−0.27)
2008	0.002	0.988*	−0.004	0.002	0.988*	−0.004	0.0001	0.988*	0.000
	(0.30)	(31.75)	(−0.16)	(0.30)	(31.75)	(−0.16)	(0.27)	(30.99)	(−0.19)
2009	0.002	0.979*	0.003	0.0004**	0.389	−0.0001	0.0002	0.903*	0.000
	(0.38)	(18.98)	(0.15)	(2.01)	(1.41)	(−0.08)	(0.78)	(8.22)	(0.41)

Notes: CM_{im} is the cross-sectional average of all companies except the ith company; RM_m is the monthly return on the Shanghai Composite Index; t-statistics in parentheses.
* and ** denote significance at the 1% and 5% levels, respectively.

7. CONCLUSION

This chapter investigates the long-term behaviour of commonality in liquidity by using low-frequency liquidity estimators for spreads and price impact. We report strong evidence of co-movements in both the tightness and depth dimensions of liquidity on the SSE. The dynamics of the effective spread and the price impact of individual stocks tend to be driven by a single predominant factor. The extent of liquidity co-movement varies significantly from 1991 to 2009. In general the commonality in liquidity tends to decline over time. A significant surge is however observed in 2007, which corresponds to the onset of the subprime mortgage-triggered financial crisis. The subsequent behaviour is divergent among our different liquidity proxies.

This chapter sheds further light on the long-term behaviour of liquidity in the Chinese stock market, and fills the void in the literature on long-term commonality in liquidity. The findings not only inform asset pricing in face of potential systematic liquidity risk, but also provide sight to regulators regarding the liquidity implications of the participation of a large number of individual investors.

Although we have identified the composition of the investor base, in which a large number of individual investors have homogenous economic psychology as a potential cause of commonality in liquidity on the SSE, the lack of information on the dynamics of the investor composition serves as an obstacle for the analysis of the causality between the dominance of individual investors and the co-movement in liquidity. Therefore, the causes of the long-term behaviour of commonality in liquidity would be of interest for future research.

NOTES

1. The Chinese stock market here refers to the Shanghai and Shenzhen stock exchanges.
2. H shares additionally refer to shares issued in Hong Kong or in foreign countries by companies incorporated in China.
3. Dollar volume is adjusted to the local currency; for instance, in the Chinese stock market it should be RMB volume.
4. The PCA could be based on either a covariance or correlation matrix since the correlation matrix is the covariance matrix of the standardized random vector $r^* = D^{-1}r$, where D is the diagonal matrix of the standard deviation of the component of r. This study uses the correlation matrix.
5. The data comes from Thomson Reuters DataStream.

REFERENCES

Amihud, Y. (2002). Illiquidity and stock returns: Cross-section and time-series effects. *Journal of Financial Markets*, *5*, 31–56.

Bauer, W. (2004). *Commonality in liquidity in pure order-driven markets*. Working Paper. The National Centre of Competence in Research: 'Financial Valuation and Risk Management'.

Beaupain, R., Giot, P., & Petitjean, M. (2010). Volatility regimes and liquidity co-movements in cap-based portfolios. *Finance*, *31*(1), 55–79.

Brockman, P., & Chung, D. Y. (2002). Commonality in liquidity: Evidence from an order-driven market structure. *Journal of Financial Research*, *4*, 521–539.

Brockman, P., & Chung, D. Y. (2008). Commonality under stress: Evidence from an order-driven market. *International Review of Economics and Finance*, *17*, 179–196.

Brockman, P., Chung, D. Y., & Pérignon, C. (2009). Commonality in liquidity: A global perspective. *Journal of Finance and Quantitative Analysis*, *44*, 851–882.

Chordia, T., Roll, R., & Subrahmanyam, A. (2000). Commonality in liquidity. *Journal of Financial Economics*, *56*, 3–28.

Coughenour, J. F., & Saad, M. M. (2004). Common market makers and commonality in liquidity. *Journal of Financial Economics*, *73*, 37–69.

Drahmann, M., & Nikolaou, K. (2009). *Funding liquidity risk: Definition and measurement*. Working Paper. European Central Bank.

Fabre, J., & Frino, A. (2004). Commonality in liquidity: Evidence from the Australian stock exchange. *Accounting and Finance*, *44*, 357–368.

Goyenko, R. Y., Holden, C. W., & Trzcinka, C. A. (2009). Do liquidity measures measure liquidity? *Journal of Financial Economics*, *92*, 153–181.

Hasbrouck, J. (2009). Trading costs and returns for US Equities: Estimating effective costs from daily data. *Journal of Finance*, *64*, 1445–1477.

Hasbrouck, J., & Seppi, D. (2001). Common factors in prices, order flows and liquidity. *Journal of Financial Economics*, *59*, 383–411.

Huberman, G., & Halka, D. (2001). Systematic liquidity. *Journal of Financial Research*, *24*, 161–178.

Korajczyk, R. A., & Sadka, R. (2008). Pricing the commonality across alternative measures of liquidity. *Journal of Financial Economics*, *87*, 45–72.

Li, W., Rhee, S. G., & Wang, S. S. (2009). *Differences in herding: Individual vs. institutional investors in China*. SSRN Working Paper series.

Martinez, M. A., Nieto, B., Rubio, G., & Tapia, M. (2003). Asset pricing and systematic liquidity risk: An empirical investigation of the Spanish stock market. *XI Foro de Finanzas*, AEFIN and Universidad de Alicante.

Naes, R, Skjeltorp, J. A., & Ädegaard, B. A. (2011). Stock market liquidity and the business cycle. *Journal of Finance*, *66*(1), 139–176.

Pastor, L., & Stambaugh, R. (2003). Liquidity risk and expected stock returns. *Journal of Political Economy*, *111*, 642–685.

Qin, Y. (2007). *Liquidity and commonality in emerging markets*. Working Paper. Department of Commerce, Massey University.

Roll, R. (1984). A simple implicit measure of the effective bid-ask spread in an efficient market. *Journal of Finance*, *39*, 1127–1139.

Wang, S., & Li, W. (2007). *The dynamics of individual and institutional trading on the Shanghai stock exchange*. Research Paper. Hong Kong Polytechnic University.

WFE. (2009). *WFE annual report and statistics 2008*. Paris: World Federation of Exchanges.

Yao, S., & Luo, D. (2009). The economic psychology of stock market bubbles in China. *World Economy*, *32*, 667–691.

PROPERTIES OF REALIZED CORRELATION: EVIDENCE FROM THE GREEK EQUITY MARKET

Dimitrios I. Vortelinos

ABSTRACT

In this chapter, I examine the properties of four realized correlation estimators and model their jumps. The correlations are between the three main FTSE indices of the Athens Stock Exchange. Using intraday data I first construct four state-of-the-art realized correlation estimators which I then use in testing for normality, long memory, asymmetries and jumps and also in modelling for jumps. Jumps are detected when the realized correlation is higher than 0.99 and lower than 0.01 in absolute values. Then the realized correlation is modelled with the simple heterogeneous autoregressive (HAR) model and the HAR model with jumps (HAR-J). This is the first time, to the best of my knowledge, that the realized correlation between the three indices for the Greek equity market is examined.

Keywords: Athens Stock Exchange; realized correlation; bipower variation; range; optimal sampling; long memory; asymmetry; jumps; heterogeneous autoregressive models.

JEL Codes: G0; G1; C1; C2; C5.

The Impact of the Global Financial Crisis on Emerging Financial Markets
Contemporary Studies in Economic and Financial Analysis, Volume 93, 645–667

ISSN: 1569-3759/doi:10.1108/S1569-3759(2011)0000093024

1. INTRODUCTION

The correlation between asset returns is important in risk management, portfolio optimization, trading strategies, option pricing and structured finance. The non-parametric estimators of volatility can be also applied to the correlation. The use of high-frequency data improves the precision of both volatility and correlation estimation. The realized volatility estimator can be also employed in the computation of covariances and correlations between two assets leading to the analogous concept of realized covariance and realized correlation. The properties of both volatility and correlation are such (e.g. normality, persistence, long memory and jumps) that one has to be quite careful both in modelling and forecasting.

In this chapter, I model the realized correlation between (i) the FTSE and FTSEM indices, (ii) the FTSE and FTSES indices and (iii) the FTSEM and FTSES indices using high-frequency intraday data and four realized volatility estimators. I examine these correlations for normality in their distribution, through descriptive statistics. Then, the long memory (d-values) of these correlations is estimated. There is also an examination of asymmetries. The correlations are then tested for jumps. The realized correlations as well as their jumps series are subsequently modelled using the class of the heterogeneous autoregressive (HAR) models.

For getting the realized correlation, it is assumed that the two assets are sampled simultaneously. The sampling frequency that is mostly used in the literature is to sample every 5 minutes. I choose that frequency because it balances between the advantages of the numerous intraday observations and the bias from the market microstructure noise. I focus on four realized correlation estimators: the realized correlation estimator, the realized bipower variation correlation estimator, the realized Parkinson range-based correlation estimator and the realized optimal correlation estimator. The first estimator is firstly proposed in Andersen, Bollerslev, Diebold, and Labys (1999). The second estimator is a multivariate version of its univariate counterpart, as introduced in Barndorff-Nielsen and Shephard (2002, 2004a, 2004b, 2006, 2007). It is extracted by dividing the realized covariance estimate with the multiplication of the square roots of the realized bipower variation volatility estimators of the two assets. The third estimator is extracted by dividing the realized covariance estimate with the multiplication of the square roots of the realized Parkinson range-based volatility estimators of the two assets. The realized Parkinson range-based covariance and correlation estimators are introduced by Brandt and Diebold (2006), but in a foreign exchange framework. The last estimator is the realized correlation estimator with its sampling frequency chosen optimally, as proposed by Bandi and Russell (2005).

The properties of normality and stationarity for the realized correlations are examined. It has also estimated the long memory (*d*-values) of the realized correlations. Realized correlations are also examined for the presence of asymmetries, like in Thomakos and Wang (2003). Then, the methodology of Andersen, Bollerslev, and Diebold (2007) – ABD (2007) hereafter – is employed in modelling jumps. For an in-depth analysis of the HAR-class of volatility models, see Corsi (2009), Corsi, Pirino, and Reno (2008) and also ABD (2007).

The rest of the chapter is organized as follows. Section 2 presents the methodology for the realized correlation estimators, the jump detection and the modelling of realized correlation and jumps. Section 3 describes the data used in this chapter. Section 4 presents the empirical results and Section 5 summarizes the results.

2. EMPIRICAL METHODOLOGY

2.1. Realized Correlation Estimators

There is an enormous literature on the many available realized volatility estimators. On the other hand, there is only the simple realized volatility estimator used in estimating the realized correlation. Next are presented the estimators that are used in this chapter. There are four estimators of realized correlation: (i) the simple realized correlation estimator, (ii) the simple realized covariance divided by the square roots of the realized bipower variations of the two assets, (iii) the simple realized covariance divided by the square roots of the realized Parkinson estimators of the two assets and (iv) the realized optimal correlation estimator.

To begin with assume that for each day, with time confined in the unit interval [0,1], the observed intraday logarithmic asset prices follow the noise-contaminated process:

$$p_{t_i,m} = p^*_{t_i,m} + u_{t_i} \tag{1}$$

where p denotes the observed logarithmic price, p^* denotes the unobservable equilibrium logarithmic price and u denotes the unobservable market microstructure noise.[1] The time index t_i represents the ith observation in the $m+1$ intraday observations with a sampling frequency equal to $1/m$. Denote by $r_{i,m} = p_{t_i,m} - p_{t_i-1,m}$ and $r^*_{i,m} = p^*_{t_i,m} - p^*_{t_i-1,m}$ the corresponding intraday returns (at the highest frequency of observation) and by $e_{i,m} = u_{t_i} - u_{t_i-1}$ the difference of the noise component and assume that the equilibrium price evolves as a function of a stochastic volatility process as follows:

$$p^*_{t_i} = \int_0^{t_i} \sigma_s dW_s + j_{t_i} \tag{2}$$

where σ_t is a stochastic volatility process and W_t is standard Brownian motion and where j_{t_i} denotes the component that will appear in the price process in the case there are discrete jumps. The integrated volatility over the whole day is then given by

$$V_t = \int_0^1 \sigma_s^2 ds + \lambda_t \tag{3}$$

where $\lambda_t = \sum_{0<s\leq 1} \kappa_s^2$ is the contribution of the jumps into the volatility, with κ_s denoting the size of the discrete jumps.

The covariance matrix for two assets a and b with the generic element $\Sigma_{a,b}$ is

$$C_t = \int_0^1 \sum_{a,b} ds \tag{4}$$

This covariance is latent. As latent, the most appropriate estimator for it is the realized volatility estimator in a multivariate level. Barndorff-Nielsen and Shephard (2004a) introduced the realized covariance and realized correlation estimator. The realized covariance is given by the cross-products of the two 5-minute asset returns series throughout each trading day.

$$\mathrm{RC}_t^{(m)} = \sum_{i=1}^{m/5} r_{a,i,m} r_{b,i,m} \tag{5}$$

The probability limit of the correlation is known by the theory of QV. So, as $m \to \infty$

$$\mathrm{RC}_t^{(m)} \xrightarrow{p} C_t \tag{6}$$

This is also discussed in Andersen, Bollerslev, Diebold, and Labys (2001b). In the absence of noise, $\mathrm{RC}_t^{(m)}$ is a consistent estimator of C_t as the sampling frequency increases. Clearly one cannot recover C_t because of the noise coming from the bid-ask bounce. This observation was used by Bandi and Russell (2006) to construct optimal sampling frequency estimators that is discussed below.

The realized correlation coefficient comes from the $\mathrm{RC}_t^{(m)}$ divided by the square roots of the realized volatility estimators of the two assets ($\mathrm{RV}_{t,a}^{(m)}$ and $\mathrm{RV}_{t,b}^{(m)}$).

$$\mathrm{RC}_t^{(m)} = \frac{\mathrm{RC}_t^{(m)}}{\sqrt{\mathrm{RC}_{t,a}^{(m)}}\sqrt{\mathrm{RC}_{t,b}^{(m)}}} = \frac{\sum_{i=1}^{m} r_{a,i,m} r_{b,i,m}}{\sqrt{\sum_{i=1}^{m} r_{a,i,m}^2}\sqrt{\sum_{i=1}^{m} r_{b,i,m}^2}} \tag{7}$$

Apart from the realized correlation estimator, there are two other estimators ($\mathrm{RC}_t^{(\mathrm{BV})}$ and $\mathrm{RC}_t^{(\mathrm{Par})}$) which have been used in this chapter. These two come from the same realized covariance estimate as the realized correlation. They differ from the realized correlation in the denominator. The realized bipower variation correlation is

$$\begin{aligned} \mathrm{RC}_t^{(\mathrm{BV})} &= \frac{\mathrm{RC}_t^{(m)}}{\sqrt{\mathrm{RC}_{t,a}^{(\mathrm{BV})}}\sqrt{\mathrm{RC}_{t,b}^{(\mathrm{BV})}}} \\ &= \frac{\sum_{i=1}^{m} r_{a,i,m} r_{b,i,m}}{\sqrt{\mu_p^{-2}\sum_{i=2}^{m} |r_{a,i,m}||r_{a,i-1,m}|}\sqrt{\mu_p^{-2}\sum_{i=2}^{m} |r_{b,i,m}||r_{b,i-1,m}|}} \end{aligned} \tag{8}$$

where $\mu_p = E(|Z|^p)$ is the mean of the pth absolute moment of a standard normal distribution. For more detail, concerning the realized bipower variation estimator, see Barndorff-Nielsen and Shephard (2004b). The second estimator is named realized Parkinson range-based correlation estimator

$$\begin{aligned} \mathrm{RC}_t^{(\mathrm{Par})} &= \frac{\mathrm{RC}_t^{(m)}}{\sqrt{\mathrm{RC}_{t,a}^{(\mathrm{Par})}}\sqrt{\mathrm{RC}_{t,b}^{(\mathrm{Par})}}} \\ &= \frac{\sum_{i=1}^{m} r_{a,i,m} r_{b,i,m}}{\sqrt{(1/(4\log(2)))\sum_{i=1}^{m}(h_{a,i,m} - l_{a,i,m})^2}\sqrt{(1/(4\log(2)))\sum_{i=1}^{m}(h_{b,i,m} - l_{b,i,m})^2}} \end{aligned} \tag{9}$$

where $h_{i,m}$ and $l_{i,m}$ are within the ith intraday interval high and low logarithmic prices. Martens and van Dijk (2007) introduced the realized Parkinson range-based volatility estimator – in a univariate level – and Brandt and Diebold (2006) introduced the realized Parkinson range-based covariance and realized correlation estimators. Their realized Parkinson range-based correlation estimator has the same denominator as the realized Parkinson range-based correlation estimator – proposed here – though the nominator in the present case is the realized covariance and in their case is the realized Parkinson range-based covariance. A disadvantage of their estimator is its applicability only to foreign exchange data.

A second realized covariance estimate is the realized optimal covariance estimate, proposed by Bandi and Russell (2006). High sampling frequencies induce accumulation of microstructure noise and, as a consequence, a substantial bias. Low sampling frequencies deliver imprecise estimates. The bias/variance trade-off can be characterized in the form of a conditional, on the underlying covariance (or volatility) paths, mean square error (MSE) for all frequencies. The MSE can be minimized to determine the optimal sampling frequency or, equivalently, the optimal number of equispaced observations $1/m_{\text{opt}}$ to be used to – over any fixed time span – define the realized optimal covariance (or volatility) estimator.

$$m_{\text{opt}} \sim \left(\frac{\hat{Q}_t}{\hat{\sigma}_e^4} \right)^{1/3} \tag{10}$$

where the numerator is the estimated daily quarticity, with $Q_t = \int_0^1 \sigma_s^4 ds$, and the denominator is the square of the estimated noise variance. We have that m_{opt} can be made operational by (a) estimating σ_e^2 using the properties of $\text{RV}_t^{(m)}$, that is, using $\hat{\sigma}_e^2 = m^{-1}\text{RV}_t^{(m)}$ assuming $C=0$ and (b) estimating the daily quarticity using sparse sampling every, for example, 15-minutes as $\hat{Q}_t = (m/3)\sum_{i=1}^{m} r_{i,m}^4$. Once m_{opt} is available, one can estimate the underlying covariance and correlation as:

$$\text{RC}_t^{(m_{\text{opt}})} = \frac{\text{RC}_t^{(m_{\text{opt}})}}{\sqrt{\text{RC}_{t,a}^{(m_{\text{opt}})}}\sqrt{\text{RC}_{t,b}^{(m_{\text{opt}})}}} = \frac{\sum_{i=1}^{m_{\text{opt}}} r_{a,i,m_{\text{opt}}} r_{b,i,m_{\text{opt}}}}{\sqrt{\sum_{i=1}^{m_{\text{opt}}} r_{a,i,m_{\text{opt}}}^2}\sqrt{\sum_{i=1}^{m_{\text{opt}}} r_{b,i,m_{\text{opt}}}^2}} \tag{11}$$

2.2. Asymmetries

The asymmetries between risk and return can be estimated by the asymmetry regression. Bollerslev and Zhou (2006) examine asymmetries in volatilities. Thomakos and Wang (2003) examine asymmetries in correlations also. The relevant equation is

$$\begin{aligned}(1-L)^{d_{\text{RC}}}\text{RC}_t = \alpha + \theta \cdot z_{t-1} + \beta \cdot w_{t-1} + \gamma \cdot w_{t-1} \cdot I_{t-1}^1 \\ + \delta \cdot w_{t-1} \cdot I_{t-1}^2 + u_t\end{aligned} \tag{12}$$

where d_{RC} is the long-memory estimate of the RC_t estimator, $w_{t-1} = r_{t-1,a} + r_{t-1,b}$, $z_{t-1} = (1-L)^{d_{\text{RV}_{t,a}}} \cdot \text{RV}_{t-1,a} + (1-L)^{d_{\text{RV}_{t,b}}} \cdot \text{RV}_{t-1,b}$, $I_{t-1}^1 = I(r_{t-1,a} \cdot$

$r_{t-1,b}>0$) and $I_{t-1}^2 = I(r_{t-1,a}<0, r_{t-1,b}<0)$. $d_{\mathrm{RV}_{t,a}}$ and $d_{\mathrm{RV}_{t,b}}$ are the long-memory estimates of the RV_t estimator for the two assets. $r_{t-1,a}$ and $r_{t-1,b}$ are the lagged returns of the two assets (indices). Lagged logarithmic standard deviations have been used as lagged variables ($\mathrm{RV}_{t-1,a}$ and $\mathrm{RV}_{t-1,b}$) in the long memory estimate, and not lagged volatilities. This specification gives better and more significant estimates for the presence of asymmetries in realized correlations. Logarithmic standard deviations have been also used by Thomakos and Wang (2003). The δ-coefficient gives the degree of asymmetry. A negative δ indicates asymmetric effects of lagged returns on correlations.

2.3. Testing for Jumps

Once a realized correlation estimator is available, we can apply a test for the presence of correlation jumps. The approach used here is similar to the one described in Huang and Tauchen (2005) and Andersen et al. (2007).

The test statistic is given by

$$J_{c,t} = I(\mathrm{RC}_t > c_1)\mathrm{RC}_t + I(\mathrm{RC}_t < c_2)\mathrm{RC}_t \tag{13}$$

with the RC_t being any of the realized correlation estimators ($\mathrm{RC}_t^{(m/5)}$, $\mathrm{RC}_t^{\mathrm{BV}}$, $\mathrm{RC}_t^{\mathrm{Par}}$ and $\mathrm{RC}_t^{m_{\mathrm{opt}}}$). The threshold c can take different values. The values used throughout the chapter are $c_1 = 0.95$ and $c_2 = 0.05$, respectively.

2.4. Modelling Correlation and Jumps

Modelling correlation and jumps is like modelling volatility and jumps. So, when volatility is mentioned, it is like mentioning the correlation and vice versa. There is a class of models that can be used to model the evolution of realized volatility (and correlation alike) while accounting for the possible presence of jumps. This is the class of HAR models, as originally proposed by Corsi (2009), and also used by Corsi et al. (2008) and ABD (2007). This class of models allows one to account for standard features of realized correlation, such as long memory, with a relatively parsimonious, economically coherent model which can be extended to account for jumps. The standard form of a HAR model is given, in regression format, by

$$\mathrm{RC}_t^{(j)} = \mathbf{x}_{t-1}^{\top}\beta + \varepsilon_t \tag{14}$$

where the regression component $\mathbf{x}_{t-1}^{\top}\beta$ is given as a linear function of normalized past correlations as follows:

$$\mathbf{x}_{t-1}^{\top}\beta = \beta_0 + \beta_D \mathrm{RC}_{t-1,t}^{(j)} + \beta_W \mathrm{RC}_{t-5,t}^{(j)} + \beta_M \mathrm{RC}_{t-20,t}^{(j)} \quad (15)$$

with $\mathrm{RC}_{t,t+q}^{(j)} = q^{-1}\sum_{s=1}^{q} \mathrm{RC}_{t+s}^{(j)}$ being the mean q-period lagged volatility. In the terminology used in this context, the explanatory variables are the 'daily (for $q=1$)', 'weekly (for $q=5$)' and 'monthly (for $q=20$)' realized correlations. The regression error term ε_t is allowed to have heteroscedasticity and serial correlation. The implementation of an HAR model in realized correlation is done by Corsi and Audrino (2007). The above model can also be extended in various ways. For example, the jump component can be explicitly included so as to have the HAR-J model with regression function given by

$$\mathbf{x}_{t-1}^{\top}\beta = \beta_0 + \beta_D \mathrm{RC}_{t-1,t}^{(j)} + \beta_W \mathrm{RC}_{t-5,t}^{(j)} + \beta_M \mathrm{RC}_{t-20,t}^{(j)} + \gamma_J J_{c,t-1,t} \quad (16)$$

and the additional significance of its parameter γ_J can be easily tested. In addition, the linear representations can be converted into non-linear ones by a logarithmic or square-root transformation in all variables included.

3. DATA

I consider the FTSE, FTSEM and FTSES of the Athens Stock Exchange (ASE). The FTSE index consists of the 20 Greek companies with the highest capitalization and liquidity in the 'high capitalization' category of the ASE equity market. The FTSEM index includes 40 Greek companies with the highest capitalization and liquidity in the 'median capitalization' category of the ASE. The FTSES index includes 80 Greek companies with the highest capitalization and liquidity in the 'small capitalization' category of the ASE. The data used are intraday, 5-minute transaction prices in standard format (open-high-low-close within the 5-minute interval) and are obtained from the Reuters. The dataset begins on 3 January 2005 and ends on 27 July 2009, for a total of 1,134 trading days. The average number of 5-minute intraday observations is 65 for all three indices.

4. EMPIRICAL RESULTS AND DISCUSSION

4.1. Descriptive Statistics of Daily Returns and Realized Volatility Estimators

Table 1 reports descriptive statistics for the daily returns coming from the dataset just described in Section 3. According to this table, the FTSES has

Table 1. Descriptive Statistics – Returns.

	Mean	SD	Skewness	Kurtosis	LB Test	LB2 Test	*d*-Values
FTSE	−0.023	0.018	−0.27	8.12	50***	1,280***	0.036
FTSEM	0.018	0.016	−1.10	12.44	94***	599***	0.095
FTSES	0.020	0.016	−1.11	11.78	83***	533***	0.055

Note: In rows are reported the descriptive statistics and long-memory estimates (*d*-values) of returns (R_t) for the FTSE, FTSEM and FTSES indices. In the LB and LB2 test columns, the values reported are the statistic values of the tests.
The levels of significance are given as follows: *10%, **5% and ***1%.

the highest average return (2.0%), with the FTSEM second (1.8%) and the FTSE last (−2.3%). It is obvious that the higher the capitalization, the lower are the returns. The standard deviation is low and 1.6% for both FTSEM and FTSES indices and 1.8% for the FTSE. The skewness values are negative but close to zero, with the FTSE having the closer to zero value. The kurtosis values are high enough and higher than the normal 3, ranging from 8 up to 12. This excess kurtosis shows that the tails of the historical distribution of returns are thicker than the ones of the Gaussian distribution.[2] Moreover, it strongly rejected the hypothesis of no-serial autocorrelation (according to the *Q*-values of the Ljung–Box test with 10 lags) in returns, implying stale prices[3] and also strong positive autocorrelation (according to the *Q*-values of the Ljung–Box test with 10 lags) in squared returns, indicating volatility clustering.[4] Volatility clustering in this case means that high returns tend to coincide to high volatility values and low returns tend to coincide to low volatility values. There are no high values for the long-memory (*d*-values) estimates of returns. Values range from 3.6% up to 9.5%. This is something to expect because the long memory is better revealed in the second moment of returns.

Tables 2–4 present the descriptive statistics and the long-memory (*d*-values) estimates of the realized volatility estimators for the three indices. For the FTSE and FTSEM indices (Tables 2 and 3), the $\mathrm{RV}_t^{(m_{\mathrm{opt}})}$ has the highest mean values across levels, square roots and logarithms. The $\mathrm{RV}_t^{\mathrm{BV}}$ has the lowest standard deviations and the highest *d*-values. The $\mathrm{RV}_t^{\mathrm{Par}}$ has the highest skewness and kurtosis values. For the FTSES index, the $\mathrm{RV}_t^{(m_{\mathrm{opt}})}$ has the highest mean, skewness and kurtosis values across levels, square roots and logarithms. The $\mathrm{RV}_t^{\mathrm{Par}}$ has the lowest standard deviation and the highest *d*-values.

For all indices, in both levels and square roots, there are very high skewness and kurtosis values. Only in logarithms, the realized volatility estimators have skewness and kurtosis values near 0 and 3, respectively. Moreover, the *d*-values

Table 2. Descriptive Statistics – FTSE.

	Mean	SD	Skewness	Kurtosis	d-Values
Panel A: Volatilities					
$RV^{(m/5)}$	1.93e-4	4.59e-4	9.18	129.15	0.273
$RV^{(BV)}$	8.91e-5	1.56e-4	4.58	31.44	0.415
$RV^{(Par)}$	9.12e-5	2.43e-4	9.81	129.82	0.299
$RV^{(m_{opt})}$	1.97e-4	4.77e-4	10.16	162.26	0.258
Panel B: Square roots					
$RV^{(m/5)}$	0.011	0.009	2.98	17.46	0.387
$RV^{(BV)}$	0.008	0.005	2.17	9.00	0.476
$RV^{(Par)}$	0.070	0.006	3.70	24.71	0.398
$RV^{(m_{opt})}$	0.011	0.009	3.01	18.29	0.387
Panel C: Logarithmic volatilities					
$RV^{(m/5)}$	−9.450	1.185	0.84	3.18	0.446
$RV^{(BV)}$	−10.147	1.137	0.69	2.83	0.471
$RV^{(Par)}$	−10.189	1.083	1.07	3.88	0.475
$RV^{(m_{opt})}$	−9.446	1.222	0.63	3.21	0.373

Note: In rows are reported the descriptive statistics and long-memory estimates of volatilities, square roots and logarithmic volatilities for the FTSE index.

Table 3. Descriptive Statistics – FTSEM.

	Mean	SD	Skewness	Kurtosis	d-Values
Panel A: Volatilities					
$RV^{(m/5)}$	1.22e-4	2.45e-4	9.16	126.45	0.233
$RV^{(BV)}$	6.04e-5	1.01e-4	9.35	147.72	0.305
$RV^{(Par)}$	6.20e-5	1.52e-4	16.87	398.69	0.204
$RV^{(m_{opt})}$	1.52e-4	3.30e-4	8.52	103.52	0.242
Panel B: Square roots					
$RV^{(m/5)}$	0.009	0.006	3.12	19.72	0.379
$RV^{(BV)}$	0.007	0.004	2.66	16.54	0.465
$RV^{(Par)}$	0.006	0.004	4.25	39.76	0.372
$RV^{(m_{opt})}$	0.001	0.007	3.04	18.39	0.405
Panel C: Logarithmic volatilities					
$RV^{(m/5)}$	−9.612	0.957	0.95	3.59	0.463
$RV^{(BV)}$	−10.215	0.912	0.82	3.20	0.487
$RV^{(Par)}$	−10.376	0.893	1.11	4.15	0.493
$RV^{(m_{opt})}$	−9.532	1.100	0.63	3.34	0.375

Note: In rows are reported the descriptive statistics and long-memory estimates of volatilities, square roots and logarithmic volatilities for the FTSEM index.

Table 4. Descriptive Statistics – FTSES.

	Mean	SD	Skewness	Kurtosis	*d*-Values
Pxanel A: Volatilities					
$RV^{(m/5)}$	1.20e-4	1.94e-4	8.06	115.54	0.456
$RV^{(BV)}$	6.20e-5	9.38e-5	7.27	91.92	0.419
$RV^{(Par)}$	5.41e-5	7.42e-5	7.38	94.48	0.475
$RV^{(m_{opt})}$	1.23e-4	2.37e-4	8.97	120.26	0.350
Panel B: Square roots					
$RV^{(m/5)}$	9.57e-3	5.32e-3	2.71	15.49	0.499
$RV^{(BV)}$	6.96e-3	3.69e-3	2.63	14.66	0.487
$RV^{(Par)}$	6.63e-3	3.18e-3	2.67	15.44	0.499
$RV^{(m_{opt})}$	9.41e-3	5.85e-3	3.03	19.32	0.416
Panel C: Logarithmic volatilities					
$RV^{(m/5)}$	−9.512	0.874	0.89	3.63	0.484
$RV^{(BV)}$	−10.180	0.849	0.85	3.61	0.480
$RV^{(Par)}$	−10.246	0.771	0.87	3.84	0.499
$RV^{(m_{opt})}$	−9.613	1.030	0.13	4.67	0.345

Note: In rows are reported the descriptive statistics and long-memory estimates of volatilities, square roots and logarithmic volatilities for the FTSES index.

are higher in logarithms than in either levels or square roots and are closer to 0.5. Only in square roots series, the mean is higher than standard deviation, across the realized volatility estimators. The *d*-values of the realized volatility estimators for the FTSES index are higher than those for the FTSE index – which is ranked second – and those for the FTSEM index – which comes last – across the levels, square roots and logarithms. The mean values for the FTSE are ranked first, with those for the FTSEM second and those for the FTSES last. The standard deviation values are lower for the FTSES index, with those for the FTSEM index second and those for the FTSE last.

4.2. Realized Correlations

The time series of realized correlation, realized bipower variation correlation, realized Parkinson range-based correlation and realized optimal correlation estimators are estimated for (i) the FTSE and FTSEM indices, (ii) the FTSE and FTSES indices and (iii) the FTSEM and FTSES indices.

According to Table 5, the mean realized correlations are very high between the FTSE and FTSEM indices, ranging from 32% to 67.6%, across the estimators. The mean realized correlations between the FTSE and FTSES indices range from 18.7% up to 38.5%. Between the FTSEM and FTSES indices, correlations range from 20.8% up to 42.1%. The $RC_t^{(m/5)}$ has the lowest standard deviation from the other estimators, across the correlations. The RC_t^{BV} has the highest skewness and kurtosis values. The RC_t^{Par} has the highest mean values and long-memory (*d*-values) estimates. For the FTSE–FTSEM correlation, the mean is higher than the standard deviation in all estimators except for the RC_t^{BV}. For the FTSE–FTSES correlation, the mean is higher than the standard deviation only for the $RC_t^{m_{opt}}$. For the FTSEM–FTSES correlation, the mean is higher than the standard deviation for the $RC_t^{(m/5)}$ and $RC_t^{m_{opt}}$ estimators. The skewness values are always positive but

Table 5. Descriptive Statistics – Correlations.

	Mean	SD	Skewness	Kurtosis	*d*-Values
Panel A: FTSE–FTSEM					
$RC^{(m/5)}$	0.320	0.198	0.29	2.82	0.251
$RC^{(BV)}$	0.655	0.745	1.93	8.97	0.173
$RC^{(Par)}$	0.676	0.512	1.16	5.14	0.267
$RC^{(m_{opt})}$	0.469	0.286	0.15	2.92	0.176
Panel B: FTSE–FTSES					
$RC^{(m/5)}$	0.187	0.190	0.23	2.96	0.204
$RC^{(BV)}$	0.344	0.371	0.89	7.46	0.185
$RC^{(Par)}$	0.385	0.420	0.76	4.26	0.228
$RC^{(m_{opt})}$	0.312	0.284	0.57	5.38	0.106
Panel C: FTSEM–FTSES					
$RC^{(m/5)}$	0.208	0.199	0.35	3.10	0.212
$RC^{(BV)}$	0.385	0.396	1.06	8.07	0.155
$RC^{(Par)}$	0.421	0.443	0.93	4.52	0.248
$RC^{(m_{opt})}$	0.344	0.300	0.20	8.82	0.127

Note: In rows are reported the descriptive statistics and long-memory estimates of volatilities, square roots and logarithmic volatilities for the realized correlation ($RC_t^{(m/5)}$), realized bipower variation correlation ($RC_t^{(BV)}$), realized Parkinson range-based correlation ($RC_t^{(Par)}$) and realized optimal correlation ($RC_t^{(m_{opt})}$). In columns, there are the mean, standard deviation, skewness, kurtosis values and the long-memory estimates for each correlation between the three FTSE indices of the Greek equity market.

not more than 2. Only for the $RC_t^{(m/5)}$, the kurtosis values are near 3. All other estimators have kurtosis values much higher than 3. The FTSE–FTSEM correlation has the highest *d*-values, with the FTSEM–FTSES correlation second and the FTSE–FTSES correlation last, across the estimators. The *d*-values of the realized correlation estimators are lower than those concerning the realized volatility estimators and also not higher than 30%. This result triggers the question whether the ARFIMA models can forecast the realized correlations as accurately as the realized volatilities or not.

In order to compare the four realized correlation estimators (as in Yeh & Kuan, 2007), there is applied the Kolmogorov–Smirnov test (where, the alternative is two-sized). This test aims at testing whether two samples have been drawn from the same population distribution (see Table 6). For all three correlations, there are statistically significant differences across the three estimators in 1% significance level. Only for the FTSE–FTSES and FTSEM–FTSES correlations, the RC_t^{BV} and RC_t^{Par} have significant differences in 10% and 5% significance levels, respectively. These Kolmogorov–Smirnov test results reveal the importance of each realized correlation estimator and the different properties they encounter.

4.3. Asymmetries in Realized Correlations

The response of realized correlations to news is quantified by the asymmetry regression (Table 7A and B). The asymmetries in realized correlations are revealed by (i) the *F*-test of the asymmetry regression (Table 7B, panel B); (ii) the adjusted R^2-values of the asymmetry regression (Table 7B, panel A) and (iii) the value and the significance of δ-coefficient of the asymmetry regression (Table 7A, panel D).

According to Table 7B (panel A), the adjusted R^2-values are not very high. They range from 1.2% up to 4.9%, indicating weak asymmetry effects between lagged returns and correlations. The FTSE–FTSEM correlation has the highest adjusted R^2-values and the FTSE–FTSES correlation the lowest. Moreover, the RC_t^{Par} has the highest R^2-values, across the correlations. According to the *F*-test (Table 7B, panel B), the asymmetry regressions are highly significant for all correlations and estimators.

The importance and the size of the contemporaneous relationship between return and correlation are given by the δ-coefficient. According to Table 7A (panel D), there are significant and negative δ-coefficients for (i) the FTSE–FTSEM correlation for all four estimators; (ii) the FTSE–FTSES correlation for the $RC_t^{m_{opt}}$ estimator and (iii) the FTSEM–FTSES correlation for the

Table 6. Comparison of Realized Correlations – Kolmogorov–Smirnov Test.

	FTSE–FTSEM	FTSE–FTSES	FTSEM–FTSES
Panel A: $RC^{(m/5)}$ vs $RC^{(BV)}$			
K–S statistics	0.376	0.289	0.310
p-values	<2.2e-16***	<2.2e-16***	<2.2e-16***
Panel B: $RC^{(m/5)}$ vs $RC^{(Par)}$			
K–S statistics	0.400	0.303	0.311
p-values	<2.2e-16***	<2.2e-16***	<2.2e-16***
Panel C: $RC^{(BV)}$ vs $RC^{(Par)}$			
K–S statistics	0.105	0.056	0.059
p-values	7.546e-06***	0.054*	0.038**
Panel D: $RC^{(m_{opt})}$ vs $RC^{(m/5)}$			
K–S statistics	0.277	0.249	0.265
p-values	<2.2e-16***	<2.2e-16***	<2.2e-16***
Panel E: $RC^{(m_{opt})}$ vs $RC^{(BV)}$			
K–S statistics	0.145	0.090	0.091
p-values	1.00e-10***	2.07e-4***	1.73e-4***
Panel F: $RC^{(m_{opt})}$ vs $RC^{(Par)}$			
K–S statistics	0.221	0.125	0.113
p-values	<2.2e-16***	3.791e-8***	1.06e-6***

Note: $RC_t^{(m/5)}$ abbreviates for realized correlation, $RC_t^{(BV)}$ for realized bipower variation correlation and $RC_t^{(Par)}$ for realized Parkinson range-based correlation and $RC_t^{(m_{opt})}$ for realized optimal correlation. H0: the two estimators come from the same distribution. There are both statistic- and *p*-values of the Kolmogorov–Smirnov test between the three estimators, for the correlations between the three FTSE indices of the Greek equity market.
The levels of significance are given as follows: *10%, **5% and ***1%. The alternative hypothesis is two-sized.

$RC_t^{(m/5)}$ and $RC_t^{m_{opt}}$ estimators. The highest in absolute-values significant asymmetry effect (δ) is -7.147 (which is for the FTSE–FTSEM correlation and the RC_t^{Par} estimator). The FTSE–FTSEM correlation has the highest asymmetry effect, across the estimators. The RC_t^{Par} estimator has the highest asymmetry effect, across the correlations.

Table 7A. Asymmetries.

	FTSE–FTSEM	FTSE–FTSES	FTSEM–FTSES	FTSE–FTSEM	FTSE–FTSES	FTSEM–FTSES
	Panel A: α-coefficient			Panel C: γ-coefficient		
$RC^{(m/5)}$	0.003	0.012	0.005	0.673	0.615	−1.477
	(0.006)	(0.007)	(0.007)	(1.784)	(1.278)	(1.571)
$RC^{(BV)}$	0.064*	0.026*	0.035*	3.376	2.140	−1.137
	(0.026)	(0.013)	(0.015)	(5.383)	(2.585)	(3.559)
$RC^{(Par)}$	−0.002	0.035	0.016	0.583	0.533	−3.462
	(0.024)	(0.018)	(0.019)	(4.737)	(2.760)	(3.441)
$RC^{(m_{opt})}$	0.014	0.004	0.011	1.883	4.191*	0.822
	(0.007)	(0.007)	(0.007)	(2.531)	(2.087)	(2.261)
	Panel B: β-coefficient			Panel D: δ-coefficient		
$RC^{(m/5)}$	0.505	−0.563	1.782	−2.723*	−0.521	−1.225*
	(1.771)	(1.251)	(1.536)	(0.495)	(0.502)	(0.573)
$RC^{(BV)}$	−0.757	−1.935	1.591	−7.055*	−1.302	−2.067
	(5.347)	(2.446)	(3.529)	(3.127)	(1.494)	(1.267)
$RC^{(Par)}$	1.924	−0.192	3.817	−7.147*	−1.700	−2.701
	(4.632)	(2.664)	(3.355)	(1.676)	(1.235)	(1.464)
$RC^{(m_{opt})}$	−0.724	−3.772	−0.220	−2.728*	−1.677*	−1.860*
	(2.500)	(2.064)	(2.229)	(0.746)	(0.770)	(0.825)

Note: Table entries report standard averages for the corresponding variables in each panel with the Newey–West standard errors in parenthesis.
The * reveals significance in the 5% significance level.

The presence of asymmetries in realized correlations indicates that there is a correlation-return premium which has a reverse connection with correlation. Negative lagged returns imply a stronger negative response of current correlation, when compared to the weaker positive response of current correlation to positive lagged returns. This might be explained as the result of the incremental information captured by the realized correlation estimators.

4.4. HAR-Type Models for Correlation

In this section, there are the results from the estimation of the HAR-type models given in Eqs. (15)–(16). The results concern the levels of the HAR and HAR-J models. The results concern each regression coefficient, across the volatility estimators, in separate tables, plus the values of the *F*-test and

Table 7B. Asymmetries.

	FTSE–FTSEM	FTSE–FTSES	FTSEM–FTSES
Panel A: R^2			
$RC^{(m/5)}$	0.042	0.012	0.016
$RC^{(BV)}$	0.034	0.014	0.022
$RC^{(Par)}$	0.049	0.017	0.022
$RC^{(m_{opt})}$	0.029	0.015	0.015
Panel B: *F*-test			
$RC^{(m/5)}$	12.022***	3.196**	4.452**
	(1.44e-9)	(0.013)	(0.001)
$RC^{(BV)}$	9.687****	3.854***	6.146***
	(1.06e-7)	(0.004)	(6.84e-5)
$RC^{(Par)}$	14.091***	4.623***	6.103***
	(3.23e-11)	(0.001)	(7.40e-5)
$RC^{(m_{opt})}$	8.253***	4.049***	4.081***
	(1.47e-6)	(0.003)	(0.003)

Note: Table entries report the R^2 and the *F*-test of the asymmetric regressions for the corresponding variables in each panel. The *p*-values of the *F*-test there are in parenthesis. The levels of significance are given as follows: * 10%, ** 5% and *** 1%.

R^2 from each regression. The significance of the estimated coefficients is assessed using heteroscedasticity and autocorrelation consistent (Newey–West) standard errors.

4.4.1. HAR Models

Table 8 contains the results of the HAR model. Several interesting observations can be made. First, note that the magnitude of the estimated coefficients declines with the horizon, that is, the daily impact is larger than the weekly impact which, in turn, is larger than the monthly impact. So, there is $\hat{\beta}_D > \hat{\beta}_W > \hat{\beta}_M$. Most estimates are positive and highly significant. These results are also mentioned by Corsi and Audrino (2007). This is an expected sign of strong volatility persistence, as analysed thoroughly by Corsi and Audrino (2007).[5] Also, note that the magnitude of the estimates is quite close across the realized correlation estimators. The overall average daily impact is 0.088, across the correlations and estimators. The overall average weekly impact is 0.248, and the overall average monthly impact is 0.380. Because of the highest impact, there is – in average – a monthly (20-day) persistence (long memory). Corsi and Audrino (2007) result in a

Table 8A. Estimation Results for HAR Model.

	FTSE–FTSEM	FTSE–FTSES	FTSEM–FTSES
Panel A: Estimates of β_D			
$RC^{(m/5)}$	0.153*	0.090	0.070
	(0.035)	(0.036)	(0.037)
$RC^{(BV)}$	0.026	0.094	0.014
	(0.083)	(0.056)	(0.042)
$RC^{(Par)}$	0.175*	0.124*	0.125*
	(0.040)	(0.040)	(0.040)
$RC^{(m_{opt})}$	0.102*	0.006	0.081*
	(0.038)	(0.037)	(0.041)
Panel B: Estimates of β_W			
$RC^{(m/5)}$	0.246*	0.276*	0.346*
	(0.077)	(0.080)	(0.078)
$RC^{(BV)}$	0.182	0.227*	0.277*
	(0.197)	(0.103)	(0.093)
$RC^{(Par)}$	0.257*	0.301*	0.333*
	(0.083)	(0.081)	(0.077)
$RC^{(m_{opt})}$	0.141	0.272*	0.119
	(0.083)	(0.083)	(0.075)
Panel C: Estimates of β_M			
$RC^{(m/5)}$	0.377*	0.414*	0.345*
	(0.083)	(0.088)	(0.084)
$RC^{(BV)}$	0.607*	0.384*	0.383*
	(0.170)	(0.105)	(0.093)
$RC^{(Par)}$	0.360*	0.323*	0.282*
	(0.089)	(0.091)	(0.083)
$RC^{(m_{opt})}$	0.477*	0.229	0.383*
	(0.097)	(0.110)	(0.106)

Note: Table entries report the regression coefficient estimates from the HAR with regression function given by Eq. (15), i.e.

$$\mathbf{x}_{t-1}^{\top}\beta = \beta_0 + \beta_D RV_{t-1,t}^{(j)} + \beta_W \mathrm{RV}_{t-5,t}^{(j)} + \beta_M \mathrm{RV}_{t-20,t}^{(j)}$$

and dependent variable of the corresponding volatility series in the columns of the table. The * indicate significance in a 5% significance level. Heteroscedasticity and autocorrelation consistent (Newey–West) standard errors used in the calculation of the corresponding significance levels are reported in parenthesis.

Table 8B. Estimation Results for HAR Model.

	FTSE–FTSEM	FTSE–FTSES	FTSEM–FTSES
Panel A: R^2			
$RC^{(m/5)}$	0.206	0.190	0.193
$RC^{(BV)}$	0.151	0.118	0.098
$RC^{(Par)}$	0.233	0.184	0.197
$RC^{(m_{opt})}$	0.122	0.042	0.057
Panel B: F-test			
$RC^{(m/5)}$	95.85***	86.98***	88.72***
	(<2.2e-16)	(<2.2e-16)	(<2.2e-16)
$RC^{(BV)}$	65.56***	49.52***	40.01***
	(<2.2e-16)	(<2.2e-16)	(<2.2e-16)
$RC^{(Par)}$	112.28***	83.27***	90.72***
	(<2.2e-16)	(<2.2e-16)	(<2.2e-16)
$RC^{(m_{opt})}$	51.36***	16.35***	22.49***
	(<2.2e-16)	(2.12e-10)	(3.88e-14)

Note: Table entries report the R^2 and the F-test of the HAR regressions for the corresponding variables in each panel.
The * denotes significance in a 1% significance level. The p-values of the F-test are in parenthesis.

weekly (5-day) persistence. Finally, the HAR models are highly significant. This is evident by the F-test and the high adjusted R^2-values. These range from 4.2% up to 23.3%. These results are quite helpful, though Corsi and Audrino (2007) report extremely high R^2-values up to 81%.

4.4.2. HAR-J Models

In Tables 9A and 9B there are the estimation results from the HAR-J models. Here, apart from the daily, weekly and monthly correlations, the jump component enters separately into the regression and their individual and the combined effects can be studied. These results corroborate the previous ones on the HAR models and are quite interesting on their own.

As in the case of the HAR model, also in the HAR-J model (Tables 9A), the magnitude of the estimated coefficients declines with the horizon, that is, the daily impact is larger than the weekly impact which in its turn is larger than the monthly impact. Also, note that only for the weekly and monthly estimates are – in most cases – higher than the jump estimates. The overall average daily impact is 0.089, while the weekly impact is 0.242 and the

Table 9A. Estimation Results for HAR-J Model (with 0.95 and 0.05 Threshold Values).

	FTSE–FTSEM	FTSE–FTSES	FTSEM–FTSES	FTSE–FTSEM	FTSE–FTSES	FTSEM–FTSES
	Panel A: Estimates of β_D			Panel C: Estimates of β_M		
$RC^{(m/5)}$	0.154*	0.089*	0.070	0.377*	0.410*	0.345*
	(0.035)	(0.036)	(0.037)	(0.083)	(0.088)	(0.084)
$RC^{(BV)}$	0.140	0.054	0.007	0.611*	0.393*	0.385*
	(0.088)	(0.050)	(0.049)	(0.169)	(0.104)	(0.092)
$RC^{(Par)}$	0.215*	0.067	0.030	0.361*	0.339*	0.295*
	(0.058)	(0.045)	(0.045)	(0.089)	(0.090)	(0.082)
$RC^{(m_{opt})}$	0.139*	−0.003	0.102*	0.482*	0.235*	0.384*
	(0.039)	(0.044)	(0.037)	(0.097)	(0.111)	(0.105)
	Panel B: Estimates of β_W			Panel D: Estimates of γ_J		
$RC^{(m/5)}$	0.245*	0.277*	0.347*	0.258	−0.463	−0.414
	(0.077)	(0.079)	(0.078)	(0.689)	(0.437)	(0.573)
$RC^{(BV)}$	0.178	0.229*	0.276*	−0.111	0.086	0.012
	(0.194)	(0.103)	(0.093)	(0.079)	(0.078)	(0.052)
$RC^{(Par)}$	0.258*	0.278*	0.310*	−0.038	0.099*	0.140*
	(0.083)	(0.081)	(0.075)	(0.047)	(0.050)	(0.048)
$RC^{(m_{opt})}$	0.126	0.272*	0.113	−0.090*	0.029	−0.062
	(0.082)	(0.083)	(0.075)	(0.046)	(0.052)	(0.068)

Note: Table entries report the regression coefficient estimates from the HAR-J model with regression function given by Eq. (16), i.e.

$$\mathbf{x}_{t-1}^{\top}\beta = \beta_0 + \beta_D \mathrm{RV}_{t-1,t}^{(j)} + \beta_W \mathrm{RV}_{t-5,t}^{(j)} + \beta_M \mathrm{RV}_{t-20,t}^{(j)} + \gamma_J J_{t-1,t}$$

and dependent variable of the corresponding volatility series in the columns of the table. The * denotes significance in a 5% significance level. The heteroscedasticity and autocorrelation consistent (Newey–West) standard errors used in the calculation of the corresponding significance levels are in parenthesis.

monthly impact is 0.385. The jump impact is −0.014 and the overall average combined impact is 0.110, across the correlations and realized correlation estimators. This confirms the relative importance of the daily and jump impacts.

Next, the impact of the jump components is discussed, as presented in panel D of Table 9. First, note that, for most correlations and realized correlation estimators, the estimates of the γ_J-coefficient are insignificant. They are significant when (i) the RC_t^{Par} estimator is used for the FTSE–FTSES and FTSEM–FTSES correlations, and (ii) the $RC_t^{m_{opt}}$ estimator is

Table 9B. Estimation Results for HAR-J Model (with 0.95 and 0.05 Threshold Values).

	FTSE–FTSEM	FTSE–FTSES	FTSEM–FTSES
Panel A: R^2			
$RC^{(m/5)}$	0.206	0.191	0.194
$RC^{(BV)}$	0.153	0.121	0.098
$RC^{(Par)}$	0.233	0.188	0.205
$RC^{(m_{opt})}$	0.126	0.043	0.058
Panel B: F-test			
$RC^{(m/5)}$	71.86*	65.47*	66.64*
	(<2.2e-16)	(<2.2e-16)	(<2.2e-16)
$RC^{(BV)}$	49.91*	38.05*	30.58*
	(<2.2e-16)	(<2.2e-16)	(<2.2e-16)
$RC^{(Par)}$	84.32*	64.02*	71.36*
	(<2.2e-16)	(<2.2e-16)	(<2.2e-16)
$RC^{(m_{opt})}$	39.88*	12.32*	17.21*
	(<2.2e-16)	(8.30e-10)	(1.04e-13)

Note: Table entries report the R^2 and the F-test of the HAR-J regressions for the corresponding variables in each panel.
The * denotes significance in a 1% significance level. The p-values of the F-test are in parenthesis.

used for the FTSE–FTSEM correlation. Half γ_J-estimates are negative. These negative coefficients are in accordance with ABD (2007), where realized volatilities are used. These estimates also indicate that jumps tend to reverse the direction of future correlation and also to temper its persistence. The fact that some jump coefficients are positive suggests that there is a correlation reversal effect in a daily basis, where jumps are present in the sample path of correlation. As in ABD (2007), I compute the combined effect of the daily, weekly and monthly volatilities plus the effect of the jump, that is, $\hat{\beta}_D + \hat{\beta}_W/5 + \hat{\beta}_M/20 + \hat{\gamma}_J$. This combined effect is always positive. Finally, note the adjusted R^2-values from panel A of Table 9B. They range between 4.3% and 23.3%. Looking at the values of the adjusted R^2-values from these regressions (panel A of Table 9B), the R^2-values from the HAR-J model are higher than those values obtained from the HAR model. This further supports the relative importance of the jump component of correlation. The significance of the HAR-J models is also revealed by the highly significant statistics of the F-test.

5. CONCLUDING REMARKS

The daily returns are not distributed normally, with serial autocorrelation in levels and stronger serial autocorrelation in squares, implying volatility clustering. They also have very weak long memory. Daily returns seem to follow a standard geometric Brownian motion. The realized volatility estimators of all three indices are not normally distributed. They have excess skewness, excess kurtosis and strong long memory (persistence). The highest mean correlations occur for the FTSE–FTSEM correlation. All four realized correlations seem to be normally distributed with weak long memory. According to the Kolmogorov–Smirnov test, there are significant differences between the four realized correlation estimators.

The FTSE–FTSEM correlation has the highest long-memory persistence. The highest long-memory persistence is for the RC_t^{Par}. The asymmetry regressions are highly significant, according to the adjusted R^2-values and the statistic values of the F-test. The asymmetry effects (δ-coefficient) are also highly significant with negative value also. The FTSE–FTSEM correlation and the RC_t^{Par} estimator have the highest asymmetry effects, across the estimators and the correlations, respectively.

When correlations are modelled by both the HAR and HAR-J models, the magnitude of the estimated coefficients decreases with the horizon (i.e. from monthly to weekly and then to daily realized correlations). The heterogeneity in realized correlations is highly significant and with meaningful coefficients for all correlations and realized correlation estimators. There are quite enough jumps of correlations above and below the two specific threshold values. Half–jump coefficient estimates are negative, indicating their importance and the reverse connection between correlations and their jumps.

The results revealing the lack of normality and the presence of long memory, asymmetries and jumps in realized correlations direct my research towards forecasting these realized correlations taking into account these properties. The properties and forecasting performance of realized correlation be also examined with other realized correlation estimators that come from the future realized volatility estimation literature.

NOTES

1. The microstructure noise variable is treated under various probabilistic assumptions in the literature, the easiest of which is that it is an i.i.d. sequence.

2. This fact has many consequences in option pricing as it connotes that extreme daily returns occur more often in real financial markets than in the Black–Scholes framework.

3. This means that returns are clustered. In its turn, it further means that the positive mean returns will have had a slightly increasing trend, and the negative mean returns will have had a decreasing trend.

4. This result is important because it shows that the high-frequency intraday characteristics are revealed in the behaviour of their second moment, as evident in the literature. Moreover, volatility clustering in returns is also evident in Andersen et al. (2001, 2005). Also, according to these papers, the standardized returns displayed no evidence of volatility clustering and were close enough to being Gaussian.

5. Remember that the HAR-class of models was designed to actually capture this characteristic of volatility data.

REFERENCES

Andersen, T. G., Bollerslev, T., & Diebold, F. X. (2007). Roughing it up: Including jump components in the measurement, modeling and forecasting of return volatility. *The Review of Economics & Statistics*, *89*, 701–720.

Andersen, T. G., Bollerslev, T., Diebold, F. X., & Labys, P. (1999). *Realized volatility and correlation*. Working Paper. Northwestern University, Duke University, and University of Pennsylvania, USA.

Andersen, T. G., Bollerslev, T., Diebold, F. X., & Labys, P. (2001). The distribution of exchange rate volatility. *Journal of the American Statistical Association*, *96*, 42–55.

Andersen, T. G., Bollerslev, T., Diebold, F. X., & Labys, P. (2005). The distribution of exchange rate volatility. In: N. Shephard (Ed.), *Stochastic volatility: Selected readings* (Chap. 15, pp. 451–479); and In: M. Arellano, G. Imbens, G. E. Mizon, A. Pagan & M. Watson (Eds), *Advanced texts in economics*. Oxford, UK: Oxford University Press.

Bandi, F., & Russell, J. R. (2005). *Realized covariation, realized beta, and microstructure noise*. Working Paper. The University of Chicago, USA.

Bandi, F., & Russell, J. R. (2006). Separating market microstructure noise from volatility. *Journal of Financial Economics*, *79*, 655–692.

Barndorff-Nielsen, O. E., & Shephard, N. (2002). Econometric analysis of realised volatility and its use in estimating stochastic volatility models. *Journal of the Royal Statistical Society B*, *64*, 253–280.

Barndorff-Nielsen, O., & Shephard, N. (2004a). Econometric analysis of realized covariation: High-frequency covariance, regression and correlation in financial economics. *Econometrica*, *72*, 885–925.

Barndorff-Nielsen, O. E., & Shephard, N. (2004b). Power and bipower variation with stochastic volatility and jumps (with discussion). *Journal of Financial Econometrics*, *2*, 1–48.

Barndorff-Nielsen, O. E., & Shephard, N. (2006). Econometrics of testing for jumps in financial economics using bipower variation. *Journal of Financial Econometrics*, *4*, 1–30.

Barndorff-Nielsen, O. E., & Shephard, N. (2007). Variation, jumps, market frictions and high frequency data in financial econometrics. In: R. Blundell, P. Torsten & W. K. Newey (Eds), *Advances in economics and econometrics: Theory and applications. Ninth world congress* (Ch. 10, Vol. 3, pp. 328–372). Cambridge, UK: Cambridge University Press.

Bollerslev, T., & Zhou, H. (2006). Volatility puzzles: A unified framework for gauging return-volatility regressions. *Journal of Econometrics, 131*, 123–150.

Brandt, M. W., & Diebold, F. X. (2006). A no-arbitrage approach to range-based estimation of return covariances and correlations. *Journal of Business, 79*, 1–13.

Corsi, F. (2009). A simple approximate long memory model of realized volatility. *Journal of Financial Econometrics, 7*, 174–196.

Corsi, F., & Audrino, F. (2007). *Realized correlation tick-by-tick*. Working Paper no. 2007-02. University of Lugano and Swiss Finance Institute, Switzerland.

Corsi, F., Pirino, D., & Reno, R. (2008). *Volatility forecasting: The jumps do matter*. Working Paper No. n. 534-Giugno 2008. Available at http://www.econpol.unisi.it/~reno. Università Degli Studi Di Siena, Italy.

Huang, X., & Tauchen, G. (2005). The relative contribution of jumps to total price variance. *Journal of Financial Econometrics, 3*, 456–499.

Martens, M., & van Dijk, D. (2007). Measuring volatility with the realized range. *Journal of Econometrics, 138*, 181–207.

Thomakos, D., & Wang, T. (2003). Realized volatility in the futures markets. *Journal of Empirical Finance, 10*, 321–353.

Yeh, J., & Kuan (2007). *Realized volatility and correlation for non-synchronously traded financial assets*. Working Paper. May 25, Yuan Ze University, Taiwan.

PRICING THE CURRENCY PREMIUM UNDER FLEXIBLE EXCHANGE RATES: EVIDENCE FROM SOUTH AFRICA☆

Martín Grandes, Marcel Peter and Nicolas Pinaud

ABSTRACT

The currency premium is one of the three components of the differential between local and foreign interest rates. Emerging economies such as South Africa typically face positive interest rate differentials, that is, a higher cost of capital than developed economies. In this chapter we aim at identifying the determinants of the South African rand–U.S. dollar currency premium using monthly data over the period 1997–2008. We carry out an empirical analysis using dynamic time series econometric techniques to estimate the determinants of the one-month and one-year currency premia. Our findings show that the currency premia at both horizons are driven by long-run movements in the expected inflation differential between South Africa and the United States, risk aversion as a proxy for the price of rand exchange risk, and the volatility of the rand

☆An earlier version of this study has been published as OECD Working Paper No. 230 under the title "The Currency Premium and Local-Currency Denominated Debt Costs in South Africa."

The Impact of the Global Financial Crisis on Emerging Financial Markets
Contemporary Studies in Economic and Financial Analysis, Volume 93, 669–708

ISSN: 1569-3759/doi:10.1108/S1569-3759(2011)0000093025

exchange rate as an indicator of the quantity of that risk. Misalignments in the real effective or rand–U.S. dollar bilateral exchange rates display mixed results in terms of their impact and statistical significance on both currency premium. Our parameter estimators overall are stable and robust to sample variations. Monetary policy is an important determinant of currency premia at both one-month and one-year horizons, but risk aversion is equally important to determine its time fluctuations.

Keywords: Currency premium; empirical determinants; South Africa.

JEL Classifications: F31; F34; G12; G15.

1. INTRODUCTION

The total interest rate differential is a crucial variable for emerging economies. In general, the lower is the development level of a country, the higher is this differential and, hence, the cost of capital. Moreover, as Schmukler and Servén (2002, p. 367) note, "interest rate differentials for emerging markets vary substantially over time. In particular, they often rise abruptly during periods of local and foreign financial turmoil. Lower differentials typically translate into lower borrowing costs for the public and private sectors and, other things being equal, result in higher growth."

Analytically, the total interest rate differential between local and foreign interest rates can be decomposed into the *currency premium*, the *credit spread*, and the *jurisdiction premium*. When the borrower in question is the government itself, the credit spread is often called *sovereign spread* and reflects mostly *sovereign risk*. The sum of the sovereign spread and the jurisdiction premium is often called *country premium* or simply *country risk*.

While the country premium and the jurisdiction premium have been the subject of extensive empirical research, the currency premium has received less empirical attention, especially in the context of emerging markets. To our knowledge, one of the only studies on the determinants of the currency premium in emerging markets is Schmukler and Servén (2002). Furthermore, as documented in Frankel and Poonawala (2010, p. 586), there is only a recent yet scant literature on foreign exchange efficient markets applied to emerging economies, namely empirical tests of the forward puzzles in these economies (but see Wesso (1999) for evidence on South Africa). The main reason is the lack of forward markets.

Schmukler and Servén, however, study the cases of Hong Kong and Argentina during a relatively short period before the breakdown of the currency board regime in the latter (1998–2001), but little is known about the drivers of the currency premium in an emerging economy with a floating exchange rate regime. In contrast to the scant evidence on the drivers of the currency premium, there is a large empirical literature on the determinants and other characteristics of the country premium.[1] A few papers also investigate the links and interactions between the country and the currency premium.[2] The extent to which the jurisdiction premium equals zero has been used by many studies to assess the degree of international capital mobility.[3] In this context, Obstfeld (1993) has shown that the studies measuring international capital mobility by testing whether the covered interest differential between different countries equals zero are, in fact, equivalent to tests of whether the jurisdiction premium equals zero.[4]

In this chapter, we use dynamic time series techniques to identify the empirical determinants of the currency premium of the South African rand (ZAR) against the US dollar (USD). The analysis is based on monthly data for the period from January 1997 to December 2008, a time span that includes two currency crisis episodes (1998 and 2001) and part of the late global financial crisis (2007–2008) characterized by high (nominal and real) interest rates. We first decompose the ZAR–USD interest rate differential into the currency premium and the country premium and document that the currency premium has indeed been the dominant component over the sample period, especially at the short end of the term structure of the interest rate differential. We then analyze the determinants of the one-month and the one-year ZAR–USD currency premia.

We contribute to the literature on the pricing of currency risk in emerging markets (see Schmukler and Servén (2002) or Frankel and Poonawala (2010)) in at least three ways. First, we offer evidence of how the currency premium is priced in a large emerging economy, which has adopted a flexible exchange rate regime *cum* inflation targeting for most of the period under study and whose currency is traded internationally.[5] South Africa is well suited as a case study because it has a fairly well-developed capital market in its local currency, ZAR, and has for a long time been one among few emerging economies to avoid the so-called "Original Sin" problem, that is, the inability to borrow in local currency at long maturities, at fixed rates, at home and abroad (see Eichengreen and Hausmann (1999) and Hausmann, Panizza, and Stein (2001)). As a result, sufficient data on a broad range of local- and foreign-currency-denominated financial instruments and other capital market-related data are available. Second, we control for the expected inflation differential between South Africa and the United States, an important potential determinant neglected by Schmukler and Servén (2002), perhaps due to the shortness of their sample or the fact that Argentina's and Hong Kong's inflation rates were much aligned with U.S. inflation as a result of the currency board. Third, we are able to empirically separate out the price and quantity effects of foreign exchange risk aversion on the currency premium at both horizons.

The main findings of the chapter are that during 1997–2008, the one-month and one-year ZAR–USD currency premia were driven by long-run movements in the (expected) inflation differential between South Africa and the United States, risk aversion (proxying for the price of rand exchange risk), and the expected volatility of the ZAR–USD exchange rate (measuring the quantity of rand exchange risk). There is mixed evidence of significant effects of misalignments in the real exchange rate on either currency premium depending on the model specification and the measure of the misalignment.

The chapter is organized as follows. Section 2 presents the analytical framework, which defines the currency premium and identifies its most important theoretical determinants. In Section 3, the theoretical determinants are operationalized and their expected impact discussed. Section 4 introduces the econometric methodology, reports the regression output, and discusses the results. Section 5 concludes.

2. ANALYTICAL FRAMEWORK

2.1. Disentangling the Currency Premium from the Total Interest Rate Differential

The total nominal interest differential between an emerging economy and a (default) risk-free benchmark country (typically, the United States) can be disaggregated into the currency premium, the jurisdiction premium, and the credit spread. We work with nominal interest differentials, as for example, Schmukler and Servén (2002) or Domowitz, Glen, and Madhavan (1998), rather than real differentials, as for example, Frankel (1992), because our framework relies on arbitrage arguments and arbitrage arguments work with nominal rather than real returns.[6] Formally, for a local-currency-denominated asset, the interest rate differential over a risk-free asset (typical benchmarks are U.S. treasury securities, denominated in U.S. dollars (USD)) can be broken down as follows:

$$\underbrace{(i_{t,k} - {}^{f}i^{*rf}_{t,k})}_{\substack{\text{Total interest rate}\\\text{differential}}} = \underbrace{(i_{t,k} - i^{*}_{t,k})}_{\substack{\text{Currency}\\\text{premium}}} + \underbrace{\underbrace{\underbrace{(i^{*}_{t,k} - {}^{int}i^{*}_{t,k})}_{\substack{\text{Jurisdiction premium}\\\text{(domestic-international)}}} + \underbrace{({}^{int}i^{*}_{t,k} - {}^{f}i^{*}_{t,k})}_{\substack{\text{Jurisdiction premium}\\\text{(foreign-international)}}}}_{\text{Jurisdiction premium}} + \underbrace{({}^{f}i^{*}_{t,k} - {}^{f}i^{*rf}_{t,k})}_{\text{Credit spread}}}_{\text{Country premium (if the government is the borrower)}}, \quad (1)$$

where

- $i_{t,k} = \ln(1 + R_{t,k})$, where $R_{t,k}$ denotes the annualized yield at time t and maturity k on a local-currency-denominated bond issued by borrower X in the home country;
- $i^{*}_{t,k} = \ln(1 + R^{*}_{t,k})$, where $R^{*}_{t,k}$ denotes the annualized yield at time t and maturity k on a foreign-currency-denominated bond (denoted by the superscript "*") issued by the same borrower X (i.e., having identical default risk) in the home country;
- ${}^{\text{int}}i^{*}_{t,k} = \ln(1 + {}^{\text{int}}R^{*}_{t,k})$, where ${}^{\text{int}}R^{*}_{t,k}$ denotes the annualized yield at time t and maturity k on a foreign-currency-denominated bond issued by borrower X in the international financial market (superscript "*int*"), for example, Luxembourg;
- ${}^{f}i^{*}_{t,k} = \ln(1 + {}^{f}R^{*}_{t,k})$, where ${}^{f}R^{*}_{t,k}$ denotes the annualized yield at time t and maturity k on a foreign-currency-denominated bond issued by borrower X in the financial market of the foreign risk-free borrower (superscript "*f*"), for example, the United States;
- ${}^{f}i^{*rf}_{t,k} = \ln(1 + {}^{f}R^{*rf}_{t,k})$, where ${}^{f}R^{*rf}_{t,k}$ denotes the annualized yield at time t and maturity k on a foreign-currency-denominated bond issued by the benchmark risk-free foreign debtor (superscript "*rf*") – typically the US treasury – in its own financial market.

The *currency premium* reflects expected depreciation or devaluation of the domestic currency, plus a risk premium: the foreign exchange risk premium. Section 2.3 elaborates on the determinants of the currency premium. In the currency premium, we have the same issuer and the same jurisdiction; only the two currencies are different.

Finally, in the literature, the sum of the sovereign default premium and the (entire) jurisdiction premium is often called the *country premium* or simply *country risk* (e.g., Schmukler and Servén (2002), Domowitz et al. (1998), and Frankel (1992)).[7]

2.2. Measuring the Currency Premium: Covered Interest Parity

The currency premium can be measured in essentially two ways. The first is, by definition, through the interest – or yield – differential $(i_{t,k} - i^*_{t,k})$ given in Eq. (1). The second is through the forward premium (or forward discount), which is equal to the currency premium in virtue of covered interest parity (CIP). We choose the second way because ZAR-forward rates are easily available in databases such as Datastream, whereas it would be considerably more difficult to identify the appropriate two interest rates, as explained hereafter.

The CIP condition states that in equilibrium the interest rate differential between two assets that are identical in all respects (i.e., same maturity, same issuer, same jurisdiction, etc.), except their currency of denomination should be equal to the forward premium (or discount) $fd_{t,k}$.[8] Formally, this no-arbitrage condition is

$$(i_{t,k} - i^*_{t,k}) = fd_{t,k} \tag{2}$$

where i and i^* are as defined in Eq. (1), $fd_{t,k} = (1/k)\ln(F_{t,t+k}/S_t)$, $F_{t,t+k}$ is the k-period[9] forward exchange rate at time t, and S_t is the spot exchange rate at identical time, both expressed in number of local currency units per foreign currency unit.

The empirical validity of the CIP condition implies that the forward premium $fd_{t,k}$ is an appropriate measure of the currency premium. Existing empirical evidence suggests that the CIP condition is generally fulfilled if the tests are properly set up.[10] The key challenge for any empirical test is to find two assets that are *identical in all respects except their currency of denomination*, or as Frankel and Levich (1975, p. 337), put it, "empirical deviations from interest parity [...] can be the result of analyzing the wrong pair of [assets] and thus violating the comparability criterion." In light of these difficulties, our strategy is to avoid trying to find the appropriate pair of interest rates (yields) to construct the currency premium $(i_{t,k} - i^*_{t,k})$ and to work with the forward premium $fd_{t,k}$ instead, of which we know – in virtue of the empirically validated CIP condition – that it is the same.

2.3. Identifying the Determinants of the Currency Premium

We derive the empirical determinants of the currency premium from the uncovered interest parity (UIP) condition, which we adjust with a time-varying foreign exchange risk premium. We also assume that relative purchasing power parity (PPP) holds over the longer run, but we allow for deviations from PPP in the short run.

The UIP condition states that in equilibrium and with risk-neutral investors, speculation should ensure that the interest rate differential between two assets that are identical in all respects except their currency of denomination should be equal to the expected depreciation (or appreciation) of the local currency:

$$(i_{t,k} - i^*_{t,k}) = \Delta s^e_{t,k} \tag{3}$$

where i and i^* are as defined in Eq. (1) and $\Delta s^e_{t,k} = (1/k) \cdot \ln[E_t(S_{t+k})/S_t]$.

Extensive empirical research using a variety of methods has however found that UIP does not hold in practice.[11] This finding is the (in)famous forward premium puzzle. According to Isard (2006), the literature offers three different explanations for this puzzle. The first – the existence of a risk premium – rejects the UIP condition but not the rational expectations assumption. The second group of explanations does not require the rejection of either UIP or rational expectations and includes explanations such as the peso problem, simultaneity bias, incomplete information with rational learning, self-fulfilling prophecies or rational "bubbles," and market frictions. The third group of explanations abandons the assumption that market participants are fully rational. Along these lines, recent empirical studies point mainly to heterogeneous expectations in explaining the forward premium puzzle (Sarno & Taylor, 2002, Chaps 2 and 9). Models with heterogeneous expectations combined with a risk premium within a microstructure framework would appear to be the most promising avenue for further research into the forward puzzle.[12]

Although no risk premium model with reasonable measures of risk aversion has yet been able to generate the variability in (ex-post realized) risk premia that are observed in the data, we adopt the risk premium explanation because the presence of a (time-varying) foreign exchange risk premium remains the most intuitive explanation for the failure of UIP. If investors are risk averse, they will require a compensation for the risk of (unexpected) exchange rate changes in order to be indifferent between holding domestic currency-denominated assets and holding foreign currency-denominated assets that are exposed to depreciation risks.[13] This compensation will take the form of a (time-varying) foreign exchange risk premium, $\rho_{t,k}$, which we add to the UIP condition in Eq. (3):

$$(i_{t,k} - i^*_{t,k}) = \Delta s^e_{t,k} + \rho_{t,k} \tag{4}$$

Next, we assume that investors form their expectations of nominal exchange rate changes $\Delta s^e_{t,k}$ on the basis of relative PPP, but also allow for deviations from relative PPP (i.e., changes in the real exchange rate) in the short-to-medium run, similar to Flood and Rose (1999):

$$\Delta s^e_{t,k} = \pi^e_{t,k} - \pi^{*e}_{t,k} + \Delta q^e_{t,k} \tag{5}$$

where $\pi^e_{t,k} = (1/k) \cdot \ln(P_{t+k}/P_t)$ is the expected inflation rate in the home country, $\pi^{*e}_{t,k} = (1/k) \cdot \ln(P^*_{t+k}/P^*_t)$ is the expected inflation rate in the foreign country, and $\Delta q^e_{t,k} = (1/k) \cdot \ln[E_t(q_{t+k})/q_t]$ is the expected deviation of the nominal exchange rate from PPP – that is, the expected change in the real exchange rate – all over the investment horizon k.

The currency premium equation is obtained by substituting Eq. (5) into Eq. (4) and Eq. (4) into Eq. (2):

$$fd_{t,k} = (\pi^e_{t,k} - \pi^{*e}_{t,k}) + \Delta q^e_{t,k} + \rho_{t,k} \tag{6}$$

The currency premium, measured by the forward premium, at time t and with maturity k, is determined by (i) the difference in expected inflation between the home country and the foreign-currency country, (ii) the expected rate of real depreciation (or appreciation) of the domestic currency, and (iii) the exchange risk premium, all over the same horizon k.

3. DATA AND OPERATIONALIZATION OF DETERMINANTS

This section first discusses the choice and main characteristics of the left-hand-side variable in Eq. (6), the currency premium. It then explains how the right-hand side (RHS) of Eq. (6) is operationalized (i.e., how observable counterparts of, or proxies for, the RHS variables are identified). It closes with a brief description of the sample and the data sources. Appendix A provides a detailed description of the data used.

3.1. The currency premium

We will analyze the one-month currency premium (CP1M) and the one-year currency premium (CP1Y) of the ZAR against the USD, for essentially two reasons. The first is data availability. For the reasons explained in Section 2.2, we measure the currency premium with the forward premium. Datastream, our main data source, contains 1-, 2-, 3-, 6-, and 12-month as well as 2- and 5-year rand (ZAR) forward rates against the USD, the British pound (GBP), and the euro (EUR). However, all 2- and 5-year forward rates are only available starting at end-March 2004, and for the EUR the remaining maturities are only available from 1999 on. The longest time series available are the 1-, 2-, 3-, 6-, and 12-months ZAR forward rates against the USD and GBP, starting on December 31, 1996. Comparing the ZAR–USD currency premia at these five horizons with the corresponding ZAR–GBP currency premia, we realize that the USD premia have been more important – about 20 percent higher – than the GBP premia on average during the period December 1996–April 2006. As a result, we decide to investigate the currency premium of the ZAR against the USD, and to do this at the two ends of the 1- to 12-month spectrum.

The second reason to focus on the one-month and the one-year currency premia is their importance at the short end of the term structure of total interest rate differentials (Table 1). Since the start of available data, the currency premium component has been largest at the short end of the term structure of total interest rate differentials. At the one-year (constant) maturity, for instance, it accounted for 86 percent of the total interest rate differential on average.[14] As the maturity lengthens, the importance of the currency premium declines relative to the country premium.

Fig. 1 displays a few additional interesting features of the currency premia at four different maturities. First, they have consistently been positive across all maturities. Second, the one-month and the one-year currency premia were considerably higher on average (813 and 692 basis points on average) than their longer-term peers (410 and 339 basis points for the currency premia with maturity in May 2009 and June 2017, respectively). Third, the one-month and the one-year currency premia appear to have been affected more strongly than the longer-term premia by the two rand crises that occurred in May–August 1998 and September–December 2001.[15] Finally, contrary to what Schmukler and Servén (2002) found for Argentina, the term structure of the South African currency premia was downward sloping most of the time.

Table 1. South Africa: Decomposition of Total Interest Rate Differential (TID) against the United States at Different Maturities (in Basis Points).

	Total interest differential (TID)	Currency premium		Country premium	
At 1-Year Constant Maturity[a]					
			% of TID		% of TID
Average Jan 97–Apr 06	790	683	86	107	14
Average Apr 00–Apr 06	688	615	89	73	11
Average Apr 05–Apr 06	320	271	85	50	15
For Sovereign Bond Maturing in May 2009[b]					
	Total interest differential (TID)	Currency premium[c]		Country premium[d]	
			% of TID		% of TID
Average Jan 97–Apr 06	n.a.	n.a.	n.a.	n.a.	n.a.
Average Apr 00–Apr 06	590	396	67	194	33
Average Apr 05–Apr 06	322	247	77	75	23
For Sovereign Bond Maturing in June 2017[e]					
	Total interest differential (TID)	Currency premium[c]		Country premium[d]	
			% of TID		% of TID
Average Jan 97–Apr 06	n.a.	n.a.	n.a.	n.a.	n.a.
Average Apr 00–Apr 06	518	310	60	208	40
Average Apr 05–Apr 06	320	229	71	91	29

Sources: Thomson Financial Datastream and authors' calculations.

[a]Calculation based on 12-month South African discount house rate, 1-year US Treasury constant maturity rate, and 1-year forward premium.

[b]Calculation based on the yields to maturity of the following bonds: linear interpolation of REP. OF SOUTH AFRICA 1994 9.50% due 15/07/07 (R177) and REP. OF SOUTH AFRICA 1989 13% due 31/08/09-11 (R153), SOUTH AFRICA 1999 9.125% due 19/05/09 (US$ Eurobond), and linear interpolation of US TREASURY NOTE 5.625% due 15/05/08 and US TREASURY NOTE 6% due 15/08/09.

[c]Strictly speaking, this "currency premium" is the sum of the currency premium and the domestic–international jurisdiction premium (see Section 2.1), given the explanations in notes b and d.

[d]Strictly speaking, this "country premium" is the sum of the default premium and the foreign–international jurisdiction premium (see Section 2.1), given the explanations in notes b and d.

[e]Calculation based on the yields to maturity of the following bonds: linear interpolation of REP. OF SOUTH AFRICA 1991 13.5% due 15/09/14-16 (R157) and REP. OF SOUTH AFRICA 1998 10.5% due 21/12/25-27 (R186), SOUTH AFRICA 1997 8.5% due 23/06/17 (Yankee bond), and linear interpolation of US TREASURY BOND 8.75% due 15/05/17 and US TREASURY BOND 8.875% due 15/08/17.

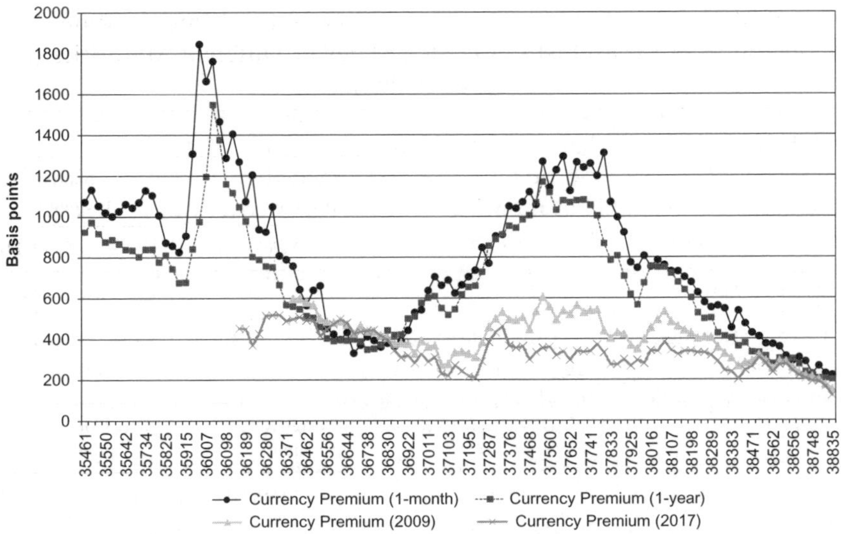

Fig. 1. South Africa: Currency Premia against the US Dollar at Four Different Maturities 1997–2007.

3.2. Operationalization of Determinants

3.2.1. The Expected Inflation Differential

Through the well-known theory of relative PPP, the differential between expected inflation rates in South Africa and the United States should be a determinant of the expected change in the nominal exchange rate between their two currencies and, hence, the currency premium. Moreover, under inflation targeting regimes like in South Africa and the United States, monetary policy rates will be mainly guided by inflation expectations and thereby the impact of the difference between those policy rates on the currency premium will be controlled for by the expected inflation differential over the relevant horizon. We expect a positive sign on the coefficient of the expected inflation differential (INFDIFFCPI) in the two currency premium equations. If relative PPP was to hold over the one-month or one-year horizons analyzed (i.e., if expected real depreciation or appreciation over the horizon was zero), the estimated coefficient of the inflation differential would equal 1.

The next issue to tackle is finding measures for inflation expectations $\pi^{e}_{t,k}$ and $\pi^{*e}_{t,k}$ that are comparable, available at the desired frequency (monthly) and covering the period under investigation. Provided a comparable set of inflation expectation indicators across countries exists, we should construct two measures of the (annualized) expected inflation differential: one for the one-month horizon, and the other for the one-year horizon.

We first search for surveys of inflation expectations in both South Africa and the United States that are released around a similar date. The Consensus Forecasts are one-year-ahead CPI forecasts and available monthly. However, these data are available at monthly frequency and cover our sample period only for the United States but not for South Africa. Unfortunately, other inflation expectations surveys/indexes are not comparable across the two countries.[16]

Given the lack of appropriate comparable indicators of inflation expectations, our strategy is to assume perfect foresight; a second best assumption provided the aforementioned comparability constraints.[17] This assumption seems to be relatively innocuous for inflation, especially under an inflation targeting regime. Arora (2007) documents that the accuracy of private sector inflation forecasts, up to four quarters ahead, has been relatively good in South Africa. Since 2003 the accuracy has even improved markedly. Assuming perfect foresight implies that the rate of inflation expected at time t 12 months ahead will be the actual rate of inflation observed at time $t+12$. Under this assumption, we are able to construct one measure of the expected inflation differential over the year ahead, INFDIFFCPI1Y, which is based on the headline CPI indices. Analogously, we can compute a measure of the annualized inflation rate expected to prevail over the month ahead, INFDIFFCPI1M. As we will see later on though, the time series of INFDIFFCPI1M is too noisy and volatile, so we will use the one-month lead of INFDIFFCPI1Y instead as a proxy for the annualized inflation rate over the month ahead. All data are collected from Datastream. Fig. 2 displays the time series of both inflation differential measures, together with the other potential determinants discussed in the next few sections.

3.2.2. Expected Real Depreciation

We use two different variables to proxy for the expected change in the real exchange rate or, simply, real exchange rate misalignment: (i) the deviation of the real effective exchange rate (REER) or the ZAR–USD real exchange rate (RER$) from their long-run trend and (ii) the first difference of the real effective exchange rate or the ZAR–USD real exchange rate over the relevant horizon (one month and one year), as in Bhundia and Ricci (2005). Note that the implicit weight of the RER$ in REER is about 50% and their

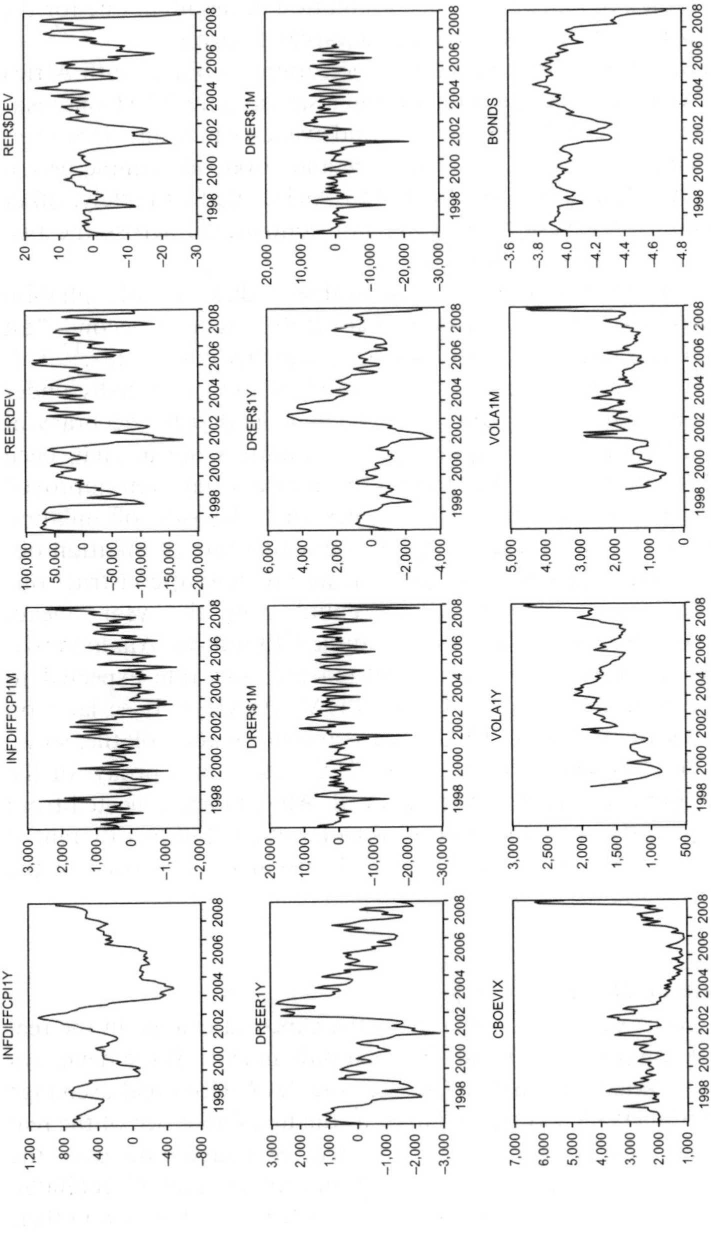

Fig. 2. Potential Determinants of the 1-month and 1-year ZAR/USD Currency Premia 1997–2008.

simple correlation over 1997–2008 is 54%. We use both measures of the real exchange rate in our regressions for the sake of robustness.

The misalignment in the real effective or real rand–dollar bilateral rates from an "equilibrium value" is a well-documented indicator of future exchange rate changes and might therefore be instrumental in shaping expectations of depreciation/appreciation of the currency.

To construct the two measures of real exchange rate misalignment, we first obtain the REER index series from the South African Reserve Bank (SARB, header code KBP5367M). Second, we compute the bilateral ZAR–USD real rate dividing the South African Consumer Price Index (December 1996 = 100) by the multiple of the nominal spot ZAR–USD rate and the U.S. Consumer Price Index (December 1996 = 100). An increase in REER or RER$ means real currency appreciation.

3.2.2.1. Deviation of the Real Effective Exchange Rate from its Long-run Hodrik–Prescott Trend. We compute an approximation of the equilibrium REER and RER$ by applying the Hodrik–Prescott filter on the REER and RER$ series, setting the proper smoothing parameter ($\lambda = 14{,}400$) over the period 1997–2008.[18] The calculated "equilibrium" REER (RER$) is labeled REERHP (RER$HP). The percentage deviation of REER (RER$) from REERHP (RER$HP) is labeled REERDEV (RER$DEV). The higher the REERDEV (RER$DEV) – that is, the more the currency is overvalued in real terms – the higher will be the expected (real) depreciation in the future and, hence, the higher the currency premium. Vice versa, the lower the REERDEV – that is, the more the currency is undervalued in real terms – the higher will be the expected (real) appreciation in the future and, hence, the lower the currency premium. Thus, we expect a positive sign on the REERDEV coefficient in both currency premium equations.

3.2.2.2. First Difference of the Real Effective and ZAR–USD Bilateral Exchange Rates. We take the first difference in the time series of REER (RER$) over a one-month and a one-year horizon. We obtain the series DREER1M (DRER$1M, annualized) and DREER1Y (DRER$1Y), respectively. This way of calculating the degree of REER (RER$) misalignment assumes a flat REER (RER$) trend or, in other words, that REER (RER$) reverts to a constant long-term mean value. In principle, the higher the DREER (DRER$) – that is, the more the currency is overvalued in real terms – the higher will be the expected (real) depreciation in the future and, hence, the higher the currency premium. Vice versa, the lower the DREER (DRER$) – that is, the more the currency is undervalued in real terms – the higher will be the expected (real) appreciation in the future and, hence, the lower the currency premium. Thus, we would expect a positive sign on the DREER and DRER$ coefficients in both currency premium equations. However, a negative sign on both variables cannot be excluded if a short-run momentum effect prevails in foreign exchange markets, that is, if real appreciation in the previous month (or year) leads to further short-term appreciation, contrary to what fundamentals would predict. In conclusion, the impact of DREER and DRER$ on both currency premium could be ambiguous. This statement extends to REERDEV and RER$DEV.

3.2.2.3. Foreign Exchange Risk Premium $\rho_{t,k}$. To proxy for the exchange risk premium, we use a theoretical framework that integrates both the price and quantity components of foreign exchange rate risk. We build on the model by Sarantis (2006), allowing for two major departures: we allow for time-varying risk aversion and separate effects on the currency premium of risk aversion (i.e., price of risk) and the expected volatility of the exchange rate (i.e., quantity of risk).

Assuming the foreign exchange risk premium $\rho_{t,k}$ is time-varying and non-linear, Sarantis (2006, pp. 1171, 1173) shows that it can be expressed as

$$\rho_{t,k} = \gamma V_{t+k}c + \gamma V_{t+k}(b - b^* - s)_{t-1}$$

where γ is a constant embedding the risk aversion coefficient; V_{t+k} is implied volatility of the exchange rate as a measure of expected future variance of the exchange rate; c is a constant; and $(b - b^* - s)$ are relative private holdings of domestic (b) and foreign (b^*) government bonds, expressed in domestic currency at the spot exchange rate (s), at the end of the previous period. Note that the indicator of risk aversion γ is constant here, as in Flood and Marion (2000) or other general equilibrium models of the foreign exchange risk premium (see, for instance, Engel (1999)).

Contrary to Sarantis (2006) and other similar studies, we will assume time-varying risk aversion, that is, γ_t, in line with other empirical studies on emerging market spreads and currency premia (Remolona, Scatigna, & Wu, 2007; García Herrero, & Ortiz, 2005; Schmukler & Servén, 2002). The empirical counterparts of the three variables in the above equation will be:

(1) CBOEVIX as a proxy for risk aversion embedded in γ_t. This is the volatility index (VIX) of the Chicago Board Options Exchange, which

measures the expected stock market volatility over the next 30 days. VIX is often used as a forward-looking indicator of risk aversion. We believe CBOEVIX is a more accurate measure of rand risk aversion than U.S. high-yield and EMBI spreads used by Schmukler and Servén (2002) or Frankel (2007). The reason is that while the latter two indicators are credit spreads and, hence, incorporate both true underlying risk (i.e., the quantity of risk) and risk aversion (i.e., the price of risk), VIX is primarily an indicator of risk aversion.

(2) VOLA1M or VOLA1Y, the one-month and the one-year implied volatilities from ZAR–USD currency options, respectively, reported by Bloomberg, as measures of expectations about future exchange rate volatility, V_{t+k}. Thus, while CBOEVIX is our proxy for the price of rand exchange risk (i.e., rand risk aversion), VOLA1M and VOLA1Y measure the quantity of rand exchange risk.

(3) VOLA1M*BONDS and VOLA1Y*BONDS as proxy for $V_{t+k}(b-b^*-s)$ over horizons $k=1$ month and $k=12$ months, respectively, where BONDS $=(b-b^*-s)=\ln[B/B^*S]$ and S is the ZAR–USD spot rate. B and B^* are the worldwide private holdings of South African and U.S. government bonds, respectively, as reported in the IMF *International Financial Statistics* database. This term captures the non-linearity of the foreign exchange risk premium.

The second departure from the model developed by Sarantis (2006) is that we allow for separate effects of γ_t and V_{t+k} and we drop the term $\gamma_t V_{t+k}(b-b^*-s)$. The reason is that $b-b^*-s$ (i.e., BONDS) displays very little variation relative to $\gamma_t V_{t+k}$ (see Fig. 2), thereby making $\gamma_t V_{t+k}(b-b^*-s)$ redundant (the linear correlation between the two terms $\gamma_t V_{t+k}$ and $\gamma_t V_{t+k}(b-b^*-s)$ is close to 1).

To sum up, we proxy for the foreign exchange risk premium by including γ_t (CBOEVIX), V_{t+k} (VOLA1M or VOLA1Y), and their interaction $\gamma_t V_{t+k}$ (CBOEVIX*VOLA1M/Y) into our regression. In our econometric exercise, we will start by including the separate terms only and later will test whether the interaction term CBOEVIX*VOLA1M/Y and BONDS alone are also significantly related to the currency premia.

If the rand were regarded as riskier than the USD (so that the exchange risk premium is positive), we would expect higher CBOEVIX (lower risk appetite) or higher VOLA to lead to a higher exchange risk premium and, other things equal, to a larger currency premium. From this point of view, we would expect these variables to be positively associated with the currency premium (positive coefficient).

3.3. Sample

We work with monthly data, unlike Schmukler and Servén (2002), who use daily data. Daily currency premium data for a floating exchange regime country like South Africa are very noisy, and it is very difficult (if not impossible) to find daily data for the explanatory variables discussed above. We start with a sample of 144 monthly observations for the period January 1997–December 2008. The lack of (WM/Reuters) forward market data in Datastream prior to 1997 is most likely due to extensive capital account restrictions in place up to 1996.[19] Due to the use of lags (for all variables) and leads (for our proxy of the expected one-year-inflation differential INFDIFFCPI1Y), the avoidance of extreme outliers at end-2008, and the fact that VOLA1M and VOLA1Y start in February 1999 only, the samples for the specifications reported are reduced to 106 observations (November 1999–August 2008) for the one-month currency premium and 114 observations (March 1999–August 2008) for the one-year currency premium.

4. EMPIRICAL METHODOLOGY AND RESULTS

4.1. Econometric Approach

Estimating Eq. (6) might require an empirical specification that allows for some degree of persistence and takes account of possible short-run deviations from the postulated equilibrium relationship in Eq. (6). Thus, using a general-to-specific approach *à la* Hendry, we start from an autoregressive distributed-lag (ARDL) specification of order (*p*,*q*):

$$Y_t = c + \sum_{j=1}^{k}\sum_{\tau=0}^{q} b_{j\tau}X_{j,t-\tau} + \sum_{i=1}^{p} a_i Y_{t-i} + u_t \tag{7}$$

where Y_t is the currency premium and the X_j are the k (=4) explanatory variables described in Section 3.2 (INFDIFFCPI1Y, REERDEV (RER$DEV) or DREER (DRER$), CBOEVIX, and VOLA). After some manipulations, Eq. (7) can be rewritten as an error (or equilibrium) correction model (ECM).[20]

$$\begin{aligned}\Delta Y_t = \sum_{j=1}^{k} b_{j0}\Delta X_j - \sum_{j=1}^{k}\sum_{\tau=1}^{q-1} B_{j\tau}\Delta X_{j,t-\tau} \\ - \sum_{i=1}^{p-1} A_i \Delta Y_{t-i} + \alpha\left[Y_{t-1} - m - \sum_{j=1}^{k}\gamma_j X_{j,t-1}\right] + u_t\end{aligned} \tag{8}$$

where $B_{j\tau} = \sum_{\tau=2}^{q} b_{j\tau}$ for all explanatory variables $j = 1,\ldots, k$ and all their lags $\tau = 1,\ldots q$; $A_i = \sum_{i=2}^{p} a_i$ for all lags of the dependent variable $i = 1,\ldots, p$; $\alpha = (\sum_{t=1}^{p} a_t) - 1, \beta_j = \sum_{\tau=0}^{q} b_{j\tau}$, $m = c/(-\alpha)$, and $\delta_j = \beta_j/(-\alpha)$. The term in brackets represents the deviation of Y in the previous period from its long-run equilibrium value $Y^* = m + \sum_{j=1}^{k} \gamma_j X_{j,t-1}$ and α measures the speed of adjustment of Y toward this equilibrium. For the model to be stable, α needs to be negative.

Eq. (8) can be estimated by ordinary least squares if all RHS variables are $I(0)$ (stationary), or if irrespective of their integration order all of the level variables in brackets have a common long-run trend as demonstrated by Pesaran, Yongcheol, and Smith (2001), or if the latter test is inconclusive and all or some of the level variables in brackets are $I(1)$ (nonstationary), or if these nonstationary variables are cointegrated.[21] As some level variables on the RHS of Eq. (8) are nonstationary,[22] we proceed to test for the presence of a long-run relationship between these variables using the Pesaran et al. (2001) bounds testing procedure. The test is essentially an F-test of joint significance of the level variables, valid if and only if the errors are serially uncorrelated.

Pesaran et al. (2001, pp. 309–314) explain how to proceed in an example of the U.K. earnings equation. The testing procedure has two steps: (1) selection of the appropriate number of lags for the ARDL model and (2) test the null hypothesis (H0): the coefficient on the lagged dependent variable and the coefficients on all lagged regressors are zero (i.e., there exists no long-run relationship between the level variables). This is the well-known F-test. The critical values for this test are different than the usual F-distribution values. Table CI(iii) in Pesaran et al. (2001, p. 300) gives the critical bounds for our specification of the ARDL equation (i.e., unrestricted intercept and no trend) as a function of the number k of RHS variables and the desired level of significance.

Appendix B2 reports the Pesaran et al. (2001) test results for our one-year and one-month currency premium ARDL equations, respectively, and supplies details about the implemented procedure. We use Eviews 6.0. In the specification using first differences of the real exchange rates as a proxy for the expected rate of change in the real exchange rate, we find an optimal lag specification of $p = q = 1$ lags in the one-year equation and $p = q = 2$ lags in the one-month equation. The Pesaran Shin and Smith testing procedure yields F-statistics suggesting we can reject the null hypothesis for both the one-year and the one-month equation. In conclusion, there appears to be a long-run relationship between the level variables in both the one-year and one-month currency premium equations. A similar conclusion is reached when we replace DREER or DRER$ by REERDEV and RER$DEV in the baseline ARDL models. We do not report these results, however, due to space constraints.

Next, following Johnston and Di Nardo (1997) we look for sequential reductions of the estimated one-year ARDL(1,1) equation and the estimated one-month ARDL(2,2) equation to obtain specifications that are as parsimonious as possible.[23] We report White heteroskedasticity-consistent standard errors and covariances.

4.2. Results

Tables 2 and 3 report the OLS regression estimates for the one-year and the one-month currency premium equation resulting from this testing procedure. In both tables, the first three columns (Models 1, 2, and 3) show the full ARDL(p,q) model determined in the first step of the Pesaran et al. (2001) bounds testing procedure over two subsamples (1999–2006, Model 1; 1999–2008, Models 2 and 3) for the sake of testing parameter stability and depending on the measure of the real exchange rate misalignment selected.[24] The last three columns show the final specification resulting from the sequential reduction procedure (Models 4, 5, and 6). To also give some idea of the robustness of these results to a variation in the sample length, the estimates in the Models 4, 5, and 6 are obtained from expanding the sample length to its maximum possible.

In the *one-year currency premium* equation (Table 2), the explanatory power in Eqs. (4)–(6) is relatively high, the adjusted R-squared being between 0.49 and 0.52. The residuals of this model pass a battery of conventional tests: residuals are normally distributed; there is no evidence of serial correlation up to order 12, no evidence of ARCH structure in their

Table 2. The Determinants of the 1-Year Currency Premium in South Africa.

	Full ARDL(1,1) Model 1999(11)–2006(03) Model 1	Full ARDL(1,1) Model 1999(11)–2008(08) Model 2	Full ARDL(1,1) Model using ZAR-USD RER 1999(11)–2008(08) Model 3	Reduced Model 1999(03)–2006(04) Model 4	Reduced Model 1999(03)–2008(08) Model 5	Reduced Model using ZAR-USD RER 1999(03)–2008(08) Model 6
Dependent variable	ΔCP1Y (*t*)	ΔCP1Y (*t*)	ΔCP1Y (*t*)	ΔCP1Y (*t*)	ΔCP1Y (*t*)	ΔCP1Y (*t*)
Long-run coefficients:						
Constant	−177.624***	−133.86***	−143.65***	−188.64***	−142.38***	−148.19***
	(38.896)	(27.29)	(27.68)	(36.559)	(27.99)	(28.23)
CP1Y (*t*−1)	−0.098***	−0.092***	−0.098***	−0.097***	−0.101***	−0.103***
	(0.036)	(0.025)	(0.027)	(0.031)	(0.024)	(0.026)
INFDIFFCPI1Y (*t*+11)	0.043*	0.031**	0.042***	0.060***	0.04***	0.047***
	(0.024)	(0.014)	(0.012)	(0.022)	(0.013)	(0.0118)
DREER1Y (*t*−1)	−0.006	−0.007*		−0.002	−0.0043	
	(0.005)	(0.004)		(0.004)	(0.004)	
DRER$1Y (*t*−1)			−0.002			−0.001
			(0.003)			(0.0028)
CBOEVIX (*t*−1)	0.050***	0.039***	0.041***	0.049***	0.039***	0.04***
	(0.012)	(0.0086)	(0.0089)	(0.012)	(0.009)	(0.009)
VOLA1Y (*t*−1)	0.078***	0.066***	0.0717***	0.083***	0.072***	0.075***
	(0.021)	(0.0156)	(0.016)	(0.019)	(0.0155)	(0.015)
Short-run coefficients:						
ΔINFDIFFCPI1Y (*t*+12)	−0.060	−0.002	−0.0078			
	(0.060)	(0.044)	(0.047)			
ΔDREER1Y (*t*)	−0.020**	−0.0058		−0.019**	−0.0044	
	(0.008)	(0.0089)		(0.008)	(0.0079)	
ΔRER$1Y (*t*)			−0.006			−0.006
			(0.007)			(0.007)
ΔCBOEVIX (*t*)	0.047***	0.0452***	0.047***	0.051***	0.049***	0.05***
	(0.011)	(0.011)	(0.0102)	(0.012)	(0.011)	(0.01)

ΔVOLA1Y (t)	0.090*	0.1078**	0.103**	0.107**	0.127***	0.117***
	(0.048)	(0.0455)	(0.042)	(0.042)	(0.042)	(0.039)
Observations	77	106	106	86	114	114
Adj. R-squared	0.51	0.47	0.47	0.52	0.49	0.49
S.E. of regression	30.95	30.91	31.10	31.15	31.45	31.45
Breusch–Godfrey $\chi^2(4)$ p-value	0.80	0.2067	0.102	0.75	0.15	0.07[1]
Breusch-Godfrey $\chi^2(12)$ p-value	0.30	0.2076	0.145	0.43	0.08	0.053[a]
F-statistic	9.69***	11.63***	11.36***	12.58***	14.85***	14.84***

Omitted Variable Tests Applied in the Reduced Estimated Models: CBOEVIX*VOLA1Y_ and BONDS

Model 5

Omitted variables: CBOEVIX*VOLA1Y(t−1) D(CBOEVIX*VOLA1Y) BONDS(t−1) D(BONDS)

F-statistic	0.885516	Prob. F(4,101)	0.4755
Log likelihood ratio	3.929467	Prob. Chi-square(4)	0.4156

Model 6

Omitted variables: CBOEVIX*VOLA1Y(t−1) D(CBOEVIX*VOLA1Y) BONDS(t−1) D(BONDS)

F-statistic	1.508510	Prob. F(4,101)	0.2053
Log likelihood ratio	6.615011	Prob. chi-square(4)	0.1577

Conclusion: There is no joint significant impact of the interaction term and the variable BONDS. We can safely ignore these variables in the one-year equation

Notes: White heteroskedasticity-consistent standard errors are used in all regressions; standard errors are in parentheses.
***, **, * denote significance at the 1%, 5%, and 10% levels, respectively.
[a]We notice there is some serial correlation of order 1 in Model 6 at the 5% level. When we remedy for the latter by including an AR(1) term in the respective model, the estimated coefficients of the model turn out robust. These results as well as the original Eviews file are available upon request.

Table 3. The Determinants of the 1-Month Currency Premium in South Africa.

	Full ARDL(2,2) Model 1999(11)–2006(06) Model 1	Full ARDL(2,2) Model 1999(11)–2008(08) Model 2	Full ARDL(2,2) Model using USD-ZAR RER 1999(11)–2008(08) Model 3	Reduced Model 1999(04)–2006(06) Model 4	Reduced Model 1999(04)–2008(08) Model 5	Reduced Model using USD-ZAR Bilateral RER 1999(04)–2008(08) Model 6
Dependent variable	ΔCP1M (t)	ΔCP1M (t)	ΔCP1M (t)	ΔCP1M (t)	ΔCP1M (t)	ΔCP1M (t)
Long-run coefficients:						
Constant	−118.82***	−87.36***	−107.45***	−111.84***	−89.40***	−102.92***
	(32.38)	(24.83)	(26.34)	(28.53)	(23.64)	(25.47)
CP1M (t−1)	−0.113***	−0.12***	−0.151	−0.121***	−0.142***	−0.1633***
	(0.032)	(0.027)	(0.031)	(0.029)	(0.027)	(0.030)
INFDIFFCPI1Y (t)	0.040*	0.059***	0.052***	0.047**	0.06***	0.0574***
	(0.024)	(0.017)	(0.018)	(0.021)	(0.016)	(0.0161)
DREER1M (t−1)	0.003	0.000248		0.003	0.0007	
	(0.003)	(0.0017)		(0.002)	(0.0017)	
DRER$1 ($t$−1)			0.003*			0.0026*
			(0.0019)			(0.0015)
CBOEVIX (t−1)	0.048***	0.037***	0.049***	0.044***	0.039***	0.0475***
	(0.015)	(0.001)	(0.011)	(0.013)	(0.009)	(0.0108)
VOLA1M (t−1)	0.051***	0.050***	0.059***	0.053***	0.057***	0.0636***
	(0.017)	(0.0157)	(0.016)	(0.015)	(0.0140)	(0.0147)
Short-run coefficients:						
ΔCP1M (t−1)	0.015	−0.0019	−0.003			
	(0.129)	(0.094)	(0.088)			
ΔINFDIFFCPI1Y (t+1)	0.066	0.133**	0.131			
	(0.087)	(0.067)	(0.066)**			

ΔINFDIFFCPI1Y (*t*)	0.188*	0.021	0.0321	0.204***	0.079	0.08
	(0.096)	(0.056)	(0.053)	(0.063)	(0.053)	(0.051)
ΔDREER1M (*t*)	0.001	−0.0007				
	(0.002)	(0.0009)				
ΔDREER1M (*t*−1)	−0.001	−0.0005		−0.001	−0.001	
	(0.002)	(0.0014)		(0.002)	(0.0014)	
ΔDRER$1 (*t*)			0.0009			
			(0.0012)			
ΔDRER$1 (*t*−1)			−0.0017*			−0.0014*
			(0.0009)			(0.0009)
ΔCBOEVIX (*t*)	0.013	0.019**	0.023**			
	(0.018)	(0.001)	(0.01)			
ΔCBOEVIX (*t*−1)	−0.035	−0.0337**	−0.044***	−0.032	−0.033**	−0.0421***
	(0.022)	(0.015)	(0.015)	(0.020)	(0.0145)	(0.0145)
ΔVOLA1M (*t*)	0.063***	0.027	0.0304	0.065***	0.033	0.0324**
	(0.020)	(0.0227)	(0.0196)	(0.016)	(0.02)	(0.0161)
ΔVOLA1M (*t*−1)	−0.055***	−0.028	−0.037**	−0.049***	−0.030	−0.0364**
	(0.020)	(0.0206)	(0.0178)	(0.017)	(0.0198)	(0.0158)
Observations	80	105	105	87	113	113
Adj. R-squared	0.47	0.36	0.38	0.50	0.38	0.40
S.E. of regression	38.98	39.38	38.63	40.67	40.73	40.27
Breusch–Godfrey $\chi^2(4)$ p-value	0.85	0.84	0.637	0.66	0.90	0.63
Breusch–Godfrey $\chi^2(12)$ p-value	0.23	0.29	0.35	0.79	0.81	0.34
F-statistic	6.02***	5.22***	5.68***	9.46***	8.01***	8.51***

Omitted Variable Tests Applied in the Reduced Estimated Models: CBOEVIX*VOLA_ and BONDS

Model 5

Omitted variables: CBOEVIX*VOLA1M(*t*−1) D(CBOEVIX*VOLA1M) D(CBOEVIX*VOLA1M(−1)) BONDS(*t*−1) D(BONDS) D(BONDSREV(*t*−1))

F-statistic	1.672198	Prob. $F(6,96)$	0.1361
Log likelihood ratio	11.23265	Prob. chi-square(6)	0.0814

Table 3. *(Continued).*

Model 6			
Omitted variables: CBOEVIX*VOLA1M(*t*−1) D(CBOEVIX*VOLA1M) D(CBOEVIX*VOLA1M(−1)) BONDS(*t*−1) D(BONDS) D(BONDS(*t*−1))			
F-statistic	1.929683	Prob. *F*(6,95)	0.0838
Log likelihood ratio	12.88013	Prob. chi-square(6)	0.0450
Conclusion: There is no joint significant impact of the interaction term and the variable BONDS in Model 5 (or borderline acceptance of the null hypothesis). However, we reject the null in Model 6 at the 10% level according to the *F*-test and at the 5% level according to the log likelihood test.			

Notes: White heteroskedasticity-consistent standard errors are used in all regressions; standard errors are in parentheses.
***, **, * denote significance at the 1%, 5%, and 10% levels, respectively.

variances, and estimated parameters appear reasonably stable. In addition, we test for the presence of significant effects of CBOEVIX*VOLA1Y and BONDS ($t-1$) alone (see Section 3.2). We find that these two variables are redundant (results reported below Table 2).[25]

In the *one-month currency premium* equation (Table 3), the explanatory power in Eqs. (4)–(6) is somewhat smaller than that of the one-year currency premium and varies between 0.38 and 0.5 depending on the model specification. The residuals of this model pass the same battery of tests (normality, no serial correlation up to order 12, no ARCH structure in residuals, no parameter instability). In addition, we test for the presence of significant effects of CBOEVIX*VOLA1M and BONDS ($t-1$) alone (see Section 3.2). We conclude that these two variables are redundant in Models 4 and 5 (borderline) but not in Model 6 where the ZAR–USD bilateral real exchange rate is included (results reported below Table 3). An estimated version of Model 6 allowing for those two variables yields robust parameter estimates except for the one associated with INFDIFFCPI1Y ($t-1$). As a result, the one-month currency premium in the reduced model using the misalignment in the rand–dollar real exchange rate depends positively in a nonlinear fashion on CBOEVIX and VOLA1M and negatively on BONDS, that is, a lower stock of South African government debt relative to that of the US drives a lower forward premium.

Overall, the results show that the currency premia at both one-month and one-year horizons are driven by long-run movements in the expected inflation differential between South Africa and the United States, risk aversion (as a proxy for the price of rand exchange rate risk), and the expected volatility of the ZAR–USD exchange rate (quantity of rand exchange risk). There is mixed evidence of significant effects of misalignments in the real effective or ZAR–USD bilateral exchange rates on either currency premium in either way (fundamentals versus short-run momentum effects).

The first main finding is that the expected CPI inflation differential between South Africa and the United States (assuming perfect foresight) has a statistically and economically highly significant and positive long-run impact on both currency premia. We recall that the long-run impacts are equal to $-(\beta_j/\alpha)$ in Eq. (8). We find that a 100 basis point increase in INFDIFFCPI1Y pushes up the one-year premium (CP1Y) by 40–62 basis points and increases the one-month premium (CP1M) by 35–42 basis points depending on the sample size and the real exchange rate selected. Statistically, the long-run impact on the one-year premium (0.62, highest) is not substantially different from 1, while the impact on the one-month premium (0.42) is. In other words, the passthrough of inflation into the currency premium is almost one-to-one at the one-year maturity, but significantly less than one at the one-month maturity. This finding is consistent with relative PPP holding over the medium (and longer) run but not in the short run.

Statistically and economically, the expected volatility of the ZAR–USD exchange rate (VOLA1M/Y) – our measure for the quantity of foreign exchange risk – is an even more significant determinant of both the one-month and one-year currency premia. A 100 basis point increase in VOLA1Y increases the one-year currency premium between 72 and 85 basis points, while a similar change in VOLA1M raises the one-month premium by slightly more than half that amount (39–44 basis points).

Our proxy for foreign exchange risk aversion (CBOEVIX) is the third highly significant determinant of both currency premia. The impact is slightly more important on the one-year premium than on the one-month premium. A 100 basis point increase in CBOEVIX brings about a 40–50 basis point increase in the one-year premium and a 27–37 basis point increase in the one-month premium, again relying on the model specification.

Finally, we do not find a statistically significant long-run effect of our preferred measures of real exchange rate misalignment, DREER and DRER$ on the one-year currency premium. However, we find a negative and significant – at the 5% level – coefficient on the first difference of DREER1Y. As to the one-month equation, while we find a positive and insignificant effect of DREER1M on the one-month currency premium, we get a positive and significant estimate of DRER$1M and a negative and significant – at the 10% level – estimate of its first difference lagged one period. In short, there appears to be evidence supporting both a momentum effect on both currency premium irrespective of the real exchange rate chosen and a weaker but positive (fundamentally driven) impact of the deviation of RER$ from its long-run mean equilibrium on the one-month premium.

The insignificance of DREER1Y (and also REERDEV, not reported here) in the one-year currency premium equation may be a result of high linear correlation (−0.66) between the inflation differential variable INFDIFFCPI1Y at $t+11$ and DREER1Y at $t-1$. One interpretation of this result is that, given the high passthrough of the (expected) inflation differential into (expected) nominal depreciation and the currency premium (almost one-to-one for the one-year premium), there is no additional information to be gained from looking at real exchange rate movements over a one-year horizon.

5. CONCLUSIONS

For many emerging economies, the currency premium tends to be the most important component of the differential between local and foreign interest rates. Using the case of South Africa – an emerging economy with a flexible exchange rate regime and sufficiently long data series available – this chapter first offers a decomposition of the rand–USD interest rate differential into the currency premium and the country premium. It then analyzes the determinants of the one-month and the one-year rand–USD currency premium for the period 1997–2008 (actually 1999–2008 due to some variables constraints and the leads and lags in the econometric equations).

The decomposition of the rand–USD interest rate differential during 1997–2006 reveals that the currency premium has on average been the dominant component over the entire term structure of the interest differential, especially at the short end. At the one-year horizon, for example, it accounted for more than 80% of the total interest differential on average. At the long end (>10 years), it still accounted for about 60%.

Using monthly observations and dynamic time series techniques, we estimate the short-term and long-term impacts of the theoretical determinants on the one-month and one-year currency premia. These determinants are variables related to three factors affecting the currency premium: (i) the expected inflation differential between the home country (South Africa) and the foreign-currency country (United States), (ii) the expected rate of real depreciation (or appreciation) of the domestic currency, and (iii) the exchange risk premium.

We find that the one-month and one-year rand—USD currency premia are both driven by long-run movements in (i) the expected CPI inflation differential between South Africa and the United States, (ii) time-varying risk aversion, our proxy for the price of rand exchange rate risk, and (iii) the implied volatility from rand–USD currency options, proxying for the expected volatility of the future exchange rate, which measures the quantity of rand exchange rate risk. Our measures for the expected change in the real effective or ZAR–USD bilateral exchange rates of the rand yield mixed results since there is evidence favoring the momentum effect of changes in both real exchange rates from their equilibrium values at both horizons, and (weaker) evidence of a level effect of deviations of REER from its long-run trend on the one-year currency premium.

Our results confirm the importance of monetary policy in determining the currency premium and, hence, domestic interest rates in South Africa. They suggest that a monetary policy oriented toward producing low inflation and stable exchange rates can significantly reduce the currency premium component of domestic interest rates. Indeed, as documented in Grandes and Pinaud (2005), the monetary and exchange rate framework was conducive to the squaring off the Oversold Forward Book (higher sales than purchases of USD forward contracts) of the South African Reserve Bank in 2003, the closing out of its Net Open Forward Position (NOFP) in 2004, and subsequent buildup of reserves since. As a result, the currency premium has declined and exchange rate volatility has been less affected by domestic than global factors contrary to the 1990s and until 2001. Alas, the results also show that an emerging market currency like the ZAR can be significantly exposed to the vagaries of risk aversion or investor sentiment toward riskier assets.

NOTES

1. Examples are Edwards (1984), Edwards (1986), Cline and Barnes (1997), Eichengreen and Mody (1998), Kamin and Von Kleist (1999), Arora and Martin (2001), Ferrucci (2003), Durbin and Ng (2005), Diaz Weigel and Gemmil (2006), Uribe and Yue (2006), and Grandes (2007).
2. See Domowitz et al. (1998), Powell and Sturzenegger (2003), and Lowenkron and Garcia (2005).
3. See, for instance, Dooley and Isard (1980) and Obstfeld (1993).
4. See Obstfeld (1993, p. 6). Examples of such empirical investigations are Giavazzi and Pagano (1988), Frankel (1991, 1992), and Kumhof (2001).
5. Calvo and Reinhart (2002) provide evidence that South Africa had not been loath to intervene in order to stabilize its exchange rate, thereby displaying stronger interest rate and foreign exchange reserves volatility than "benchmark" floaters (such as the United States or the eurozone). However, compared to other developing countries under "flexible" regimes, South Africa can be considered as perhaps the closest to a pure float, especially in light of the latest strong (nominal and real) appreciation of the rand (2002–2007). Indeed, the currency has floated without intervention since the adoption of inflation targeting in February 2000, with the exception of purchases of foreign exchange to retire the Central Bank's Net Open Forward Position and then build up reserves.

6. Frankel (1989, p. 13) notes, 'An international investor, when deciding what country's assets to buy, will not compare real interest rates in those countries, i.e., interest rates each expressed in terms of expected purchasing power over those countries' goods. When he/she wishes to evaluate assets in terms of purchasing power, all assets will be evaluated in terms of the *same* consumption basket, namely his/her own. The expected inflation rate then drops out of differentials in expected rates of return among assets.'

7. The studies analyzing the determinants of *emerging market (sovereign credit/bond/debt) spreads* (e.g., Uribe & Yue, 2006; Mauro, Sussman, & Yafeh, 2002; Arora & Martin, 2001; Eichengreen & Mody, 1998; Grandes, 2007) are in fact analyzing the sum of the sovereign spread and the foreign–international jurisdiction premium rather than the sovereign spread alone. The reason is that they use the JP Morgan EMBI spreads or, similarly, calculate the spreads as the difference in yields between emerging economies' Eurobonds and the U.S Treasury yield curve. The use of Eurobonds, issued in the international market, implies that the calculated spreads fail to completely isolate the sovereign (credit) spread.

8. See Frankel and Levich (1975, pp. 325–326).

9. k is expressed in years.

10. See, e.g., Isard (2006), Taylor (1989), Herring and Marson (1976), and Frankel and Levich (1975).

11. For surveys of this literature, see Hodrick (1987), Froot and Thaler (1990), Lewis (1995), and Engel (1996). Specifically for South Africa, see Wesso (1999).

12. Also see, for instance, Carlson, Osler, and Dahl (2008) or Sarantis (2006).

13. In general equilibrium models, for instance, the foreign exchange risk premium arises from the combination of risk aversion and the correlation of the exchange rate with consumption. In flexible price models, this requires correlation of monetary and output supply shocks. In sticky-price models, the correlation arises endogenously because monetary shocks cause output and consumption to change. (see, for instance, Obstfeld & Rogoff (1998) or Engel (1999)).

14. The sample in Table 1 is cut off in April 2006 because data for the South African Eurobond maturing in 2017 were not available to the authors, and the South African Eurobond maturing in 2009 had come to redemption.

15. For an assessment of the potential causes – still subject to some controversy – as well as the differing consequences of these crises in terms of economic performance, see, e.g., Bhundia and Ricci (2005) or Aron and Muellbauer (2006).

16. The other (CPI) inflation expectations survey in the United States is conducted by the University of Michigan and is available historically at a monthly frequency. This is, however, a consumer survey. A third inflation expectation survey, the Philadelphia FED survey, is carried out quizzing financial analysts, economists, and other business people. It is published quarterly. As to South Africa, the SARB used to publish a CPIX (as opposed to a headline CPI) inflation expectations measure named 'Business representatives: One year ahead' (header code KBP7118 M) but this series was discontinued in August 2005. Most importantly, this measure is not comparable with the one produced by the University of Michigan as the latter is based on consumers and quantifies CPI inflation rather than CPIX inflation. Nor it is comparable with the Philadelphia FED survey, as the latter is measured on a quarterly basis. The BER (University of Stellenbosch's think tank) analysts' survey

(quarterly) is the closest to the Philadelphia FED survey (both report analysts' expectations quarterly). The problem is that both surveys are published on a quarterly basis, while we use monthly data. In addition, BER's series starts in 2000, while our sample begins in January 1997.

17. A third best alternative would be to assume 'myopic' expectations, that is, the inflation differential expected over the month ahead (the year ahead) is just assumed to be equal to the inflation differential observed over the previous month (the previous year). But this would be seldom consistent with modern inflation theory and empirical evidence for South Africa (see Arora, 2007).

18. A caveat is in order: The HP filter method for capturing the long run is suspect when a currency is strongly influenced by commodity prices, as is the case in South Africa. For an estimation of the quarterly equilibrium real effective exchange rate in South Africa, see Macdonald and Ricci (2004) or Frankel (2007).

19. See Hviding (2005).

20. An earlier working paper version of this article offers a formal demonstration of this rewriting.

21. See, e.g., Johnston and Di Nardo (1997, pp. 259–265).

22. Philips–Perron (PP) and Augmented Dickey–Fuller (ADF) unit roots tests show that nearly half of the variables in levels are nonstationary (except INFDIFFCPI1Y, VOLA1Y, and REERDEV), while all variables in first-differences are stationary (Appendix B1).

23. See Johnston and Di Nardo (1997, pp. 276–277). We look for groups of possibly redundant short-run effects ($\Delta X_{j,t-\tau}$ and ΔY_{t-i} terms) using the usual F-tests. If (i) the redundant variables test is not rejected, (ii) the adjusted R-squared and (iii) the Akaike criterion move in the 'right' direction, we continue the reduction procedure, otherwise we stop. At each stage of this general-to-specific reduction process, we check that the model is not misspecified, the residuals are well behaved, and the estimated parameters are reasonably stable.

24. Model 1 was the baseline model reported in an earlier working paper of this chapter. It used only the misalignment in the real effective exchange rate (DREER).

25. Model 6 in Table 2 suffers from some significant serial correlation of order 1. When we remedy for the latter by including an AR(1) term in the equation, the estimated parameters turn out robust. These results are available from the authors upon request.

ACKNOWLEDGMENTS

The authors would like to thank Colm Foy, Hans Genberg, Ulrich Hiemenz, John Muellbauer, Helmut Reisen, Luca Ricci, participants in seminars or meetings at the OECD, UN-WIDER, the Bond Exchange of South Africa, the Central Bank of Argentina and the Swiss National Bank for insightful comments and suggestions. They are also grateful to Carla Abbate for efficient editorial assistance.

REFERENCES

Aron, J., & Muellbauer, J. (2006). *Review of monetary policy in South Africa since 1994*. CSAE Working Paper No 7. Centre for the Study of African Economies, Oxford University.

Arora, V. (2007). *Monetary policy transparency and financial market forecasts in South Africa*. IMF Working Paper No. 123. International Monetary Fund, Washington, DC.

Arora, V., & Martin, C. (2001). How does U.S. monetary policy influence sovereign spreads in emerging markets. *IMF Staff Papers*, *48*(3), 474–498.

Bhundia, A. L., & Ricci, L. A. (2005). The rand crises of 1998 and 2001: What have we learned?. In: M. Nowak & L. A. Ricci (Eds), *Post apartheid South Africa: The first ten years* (pp. 156–173). Washington, DC: International Monetary Fund.

Calvo, G., & Reinhart, C. (2002). Fear of Floating. *Quarterly Journal of Economics*, *117*(2), 379–408.

Carlson, J. A., Dahl, C., & Osler, C. L. (2008). *Short-run exchange-rate dynamics: Theory and evidence*. CREATES Research Paper 2008-1. Available at http://ssrn.com/abstract=1148125.

Chicago Board Options Exchange. (2003). VIX® CBOE Volatility Index. White Paper. Available at http://www.cboe.com/micro/vix/vixwhite.pdf.

Cline W. R., & Barnes, J. S. (1997). *Spreads and risk in emerging markets lending*. IIF Research Paper No 1. Institute of International Finance, Washington, DC.

Diaz Weigel, D., & Gemmil, G. (2006). What drives credit risk in emerging markets? The roles of country fundamentals and market co-movements. *Journal of International Money and Finance*, *25*(3), 476–502.

Domowitz, I., Glen, J., & Madhavan, A. (1998). Country and currency risk premia in an emerging market. *Journal of Financial and Quantitative Analysis*, *33*(2), 189–216.

Dooley, M., & Isard, P. (1980). Capital controls, political risk and deviations from interest-rate parity. *Journal of Political Economy*, *88*(2), 370–384.

Durbin, E., & Ng, D. T. (2005). The Sovereign Ceiling and Emerging Market Corporate Bond Spreads. *Journal of International Money and Finance*, *24*(4), 631–649.

Edwards, S. (1984). LDC foreign borrowing and default risk: An empirical investigation, 1976–80. *American Economic Review*, *74*(4), 726–734.

Edwards, S. (1986). The pricing of bonds and bank loans in international markets: An empirical analysis of developing countries' foreign borrowing. *European Economic Review*, *30*, 565–589.

Eichengreen, B., & Hausmann, R. (1999). *Exchange rates and financial fragility*. NBER Working Paper No. 7418. National Bureau of Economic Research, Cambridge, MA.

Eichengreen, B., & Mody, A. (1998). *What explains changing spreads on emerging-market debt? Fundamentals or market sentiment?* NBER Working Paper No. 6408. National Bureau of Economic Research, Cambridge, MA.

Engel, C. (1996). The forward discount anomaly and the risk premium: A survey of recent evidence. *Journal of Empirical Finance*, *3*(2), 123–192.

Engel, C. (1999). On the foreign-exchange risk premium in sticky-price general equilibrium models. In: P. Isard, A. Razin & A. K. Rose (Eds), *International finance and financial crises: Essays in Honor of Robert P. Flood* (pp. 71–85). Washington and Boston: IMF and Kluwer.

Ferrucci, G. (2003). *The empirical determinants of emerging economies' sovereign bond spreads*. Bank of England Working Paper No. 205. Bank of England, London.

Flood, R. P., & Marion, N. P. (2000). Self-fulfilling risk predictions: An application to speculative attacks. *Journal of International Economics*, *50*, 245–268.

Flood, R. P., & Rose, A. K. (1999). Understanding exchange rate volatility without the contrivance of macroeconomics. *Economic Journal*, *109*, F660–F672.

Frankel, J. A. (1989). *Quantifying international capital mobility in the 1980s*. NBER Working Paper No 2856. National Bureau of Economic Research, Cambridge, MA.

Frankel, J. A. (1991). Quantifying international capital mobility in the 1980s. In: B. Douglas Berheim & J. B. Shoven (Eds), *National saving and economic performance* (pp. 227–260). Chicago: University of Chicago Press.

Frankel, J. A. (1992). Measuring international capital mobility: A review. *American Economic Review Papers and Proceedings*, *82*(2), 197–202.

Frankel, J. A. (2007). On the rand: Determinants of the South African exchange rate. *South African Journal of Economics*, *75*(3), 425–441.

Frankel, J. A., & Poonawala, J. (2010). The forward market in emerging currencies: Less biased than in major currencies. *Journal of International Money and Finance*, *29*, 585–598.

Frankel, J. A., & Levich, R. M. (1975). Covered interest arbitrage: Unexploited profits? *Journal of Political Economy*, *83*(2), 325–338.

Froot, K. A., & Thaler, R. H. (1990). Anomalies: Foreign exchange. *Journal of Economic Perspectives*, *4*(3), 179–192.

García Herrero, A., & Ortiz, A. (2005). The role of global risk aversion in explaining Latin American Sovereign Spreads. *International Finance*, March. Banco de España Working Papers, Madrid.

Giavazzi, F., & Pagano, M. (1988). Capital controls and the European Monetary System. In: D. E. Fair & C. de Boisseu (Eds), *International monetary and financial integration: The European dimension*. Dordrecht, The Netherlands: Martinus Nijhoff Publishers.

Grandes, M., & Nicolas, Pinaud (2005). *Reducing Capital Cost in Southern Africa*. OECD Development Centre Studies: Paris.

Grandes, M. (2007). The determinants of sovereign bond spreads: Theory and facts from Latin America. *Cuadernos de Economía*, *44*(130), 151–181.

Hausmann, R., Panizza, U., & Stein, E. (2001). Why do countries float the way they float? *Journal of Development Economics*, *66*(2), 387–414.

Herring, R. J., & Marson, R. C. (1976). In: C. H. Stern, J. H. Makin & D. E. Logue (Eds), *The forward market and interest rates in the eurocurrency and national money markets in eurocurrencies and the international monetary system* (pp. 139–163). Washington: American Enterprise Institute.

Hodrick, R. J. (1987). *The empirical evidence on the efficiency of forward and futures foreign exchange markets*. Chur: Harwood Academic Publishers.

Hviding, K. (2005). Liberalizing trade and capital transactions: An overview. In: M. Nowak & L. A. Ricci (Eds), *Post apartheid South Africa: The first ten years* (pp. 133–141). Washington, DC: International Monetary Fund.

Isard P. (2006). *Uncovered interest parity*. IMF Working Paper No. 96. Washington, DC: International Monetary Fund. Forthcoming in Palgrave Dictionary of Economics.

Johnston, J., & Di Nardo, J. (1997). *Econometric methods* (4th ed). New York: McGraw-Hill.

Kamin, S. B., & Von Kleist, K. (1999). *The evolution and determination of emerging market credit spread in the 1990s*. BIS Working Paper No. 68. Bank for International Settlements, Basel.

Kumhof, M. (2001). International capital mobility in emerging markets: New evidence from daily data. *Review of International Economics*, *9*(4), 626–640.

Lewis, K. (1995). Chapter 37: Puzzles in international financial markets. In: G. Grossman & K. Rogoff (Eds), *Handbook of International Economics* (Vol. III, pp. 1913–1971). North-Holland: Elsevier.
Lowenkron, A., & Garcia, M. G. P. (2005). Cousin risks: The extent and the causes of positive correlation between country and currency risks. Textos para discussão, 507, Department of Economics PUC-Rio.
Macdonald, R., & Ricci, L. A. (2004). Estimation of the equilibrium real exchange rate for South Africa. *South African Journal of Economics*, *72*(2), 282–304.
Mauro, P., Sussman, N., & Yafeh, Y. (2002). Emerging market spreads: Then versus now. *Quarterly Journal of Economics*, *117*(2), 695–733.
Obstfeld, M. (1993). *International capital mobility in the 1990s*. NBER Working Paper No. 4534. National Bureau of Economic Research, Cambridge, MA.
Obstfeld, M., & Rogoff, K. (1998). *Risk and exchange rate*. NBER Working Paper No. 6694. National Bureau of Economic Research, Cambridge, MA.
Pesaran, H., Yongcheol, S., & Smith, R. J. (2001). Bounds testing approaches to the analysis of level relationships. *Journal of Applied Econometrics*, *16* (special issue), 289–326.
Powell, A., & Sturzenegger, F. (2003). Dollarization: The link between devaluation and default risk. In: F. Sturzenegger & E. Levy-Yeyati (Eds), *Dollarization, debates and policy alternatives*. Cambridge: MIT Press.
Remolona, E., Scatigna, M., & Wu, E. (2007). Interpreting sovereign spreads. *BIS Quarterly Review*, March.
Sarantis, N. (2006). Testing the uncovered interest parity using traded volatility, a time-varying risk premium and heterogenous expectations. *Journal of International Money and Finance*, *25*(7), 1168–1186.
Sarno, L., & Taylor, M. P. (2002). *Exchange rate economics*. Cambridge, UK: Cambridge University Press.
Schmukler, S. L., & Servén, L. (2002). Pricing currency risk under currency boards. *Journal of Development Economics*, *69*(2), 367–391.
Taylor, M. P. (1989). Covered interest arbitrage and market turbulence. *Economic Journal*, *99*(396), 376–391.
Uribe, M., & Yue, V. Z. (2006). Country spreads and emerging countries: Who drives whom? *Journal of International Economics*, *69*(1), 6–36.
Wesso, G. (1999). *The forward rate as an optimum predictor of the future spot rate in South Africa: An econometric analysis*. Occasional Paper No. 13, South African Reserve Bank, Pretoria.

APPENDIX A: DATA DESCRIPTION

Table A1.

Variable	Calculation	Subcomponents		Source
		Symbol	Description	
Dependent variables				
CP1M, 1-month ZAR–USD forward premium (annualized, in basis points)	CP1M = 12*[ln(F1M)–ln(S)]*10,000[a]	F1M	South African rand to US$ 1-month forward exchange rate (ZAR–USD), monthly average of daily rates	Datastream (code: USZAR1F)
		S	South African rand to US$ spot exchange rate (ZAR–USD), monthly average of daily rates	Datastream (code: COMRAN$)
CP1Y, 1-year ZAR–USD forward premium (in basis points)	CP1Y = [ln(F1Y)–ln(S)]*10,000[a]	F1Y	South African rand to US$ 1-year forward exchange rate (ZAR–USD), monthly average of daily rates	Datastream (code: USZARYF)
Explanatory variables				
INFDIFFCPI1M, ex-post realized month-on-month inflation differential between South Africa and United States (annualized, in basis points)[b]	INFDIFFCPI1M = 10,000*12*[ln($CPISA_{t+1}$/$CPISA_t$)–ln($CPIUS_{t+1}$/$CPIUS_t$)] 1/	CPISA	South African CPI index, mid-month observations	Datastream (code: SACONPRCF) and OECD
		CPIUS	U.S. CPI index, mid-month observations	Datastream (code: USOCP009F) and OECD
		CPISA, CPIUS	See above	

Table A1. *(Continued).*

Variable	Calculation	Subcomponents: Symbol	Subcomponents: Description	Source
INFDIFFCPI1Y, ex-post realized year-on-year inflation differential between South Africa and United States (in basis points)[b]	INFDIFFCPI1Y = 10,000* [ln($CPISA_{t+12}/CPISA_t$)− ln($CPIUS_{t+12}/CPIUS_t$)][a]			
REERDEV, Real exchange rate deviation from long-run trend (in basis points)	REERDEV = 10,000* [ln(REER)− ln(REERHP)]	REER	Real effective exchange rate index, mid-month observations	South African Reserve Bank website (code KBP5367M)
		REERHP	Hodrik-Prescott filtered REER (with $\lambda = 14{,}400$)	Authors' calculation
DREER1Y, year-on-year change in the real exchange rate (in basis points)	DREER1Y = 10,000* [ln($REER_t$)− ln($REER_{t-12}$)]	REER	Real effective exchange rate index, mid-month observation	South African Reserve Bank website (code KBP5367M)
DREER1M month-on-month change in the real exchange rate (annualized, in basis points)	DREER1M = 12*10,000* [ln($REER_t$)− ln($REER_{t-1}$)]			
REE$DEV, ZAR–USD real exchange rate deviation from long-run trend (in basis points)	RER$DEV = 10,000* [ln(RER$)− ln(RER$HP)]	RER$ = S*CPIUS/ CPISA	ZAR–USD bilateral real exchange rate index, mid-month observations	
See above for S, CPIUS and CPISA	Authors' calculation			
		RER$HP	Hodrik-Prescott filtered RER$ (with $\lambda = 14{,}400$)	Authors' calculation

Table A1. (*Continued*).

Variable	Calculation	Subcomponents		Source
		Symbol	Description	
DRER$1Y, year-on-year change in the real exchange rate (in basis points)	DRER$1Y = 10,000* [ln(RER$$_t$)–ln(RER$$_{t-12}$)]	RER$	ZAR–USD bilateral real exchange rate index, mid-month observations	Authors' calculation
DREE1$M month-on-month change in the real exchange rate (annualized, in basis points)	DRER$1M = 12*10,000* [ln(RER$$_t$)–ln(RER$$_{t-1}$)]	RER$	ZAR–USD bilateral real exchange rate index, mid-month observations	Authors' calculation
CBOEVIX, closing quote of volatility index (VIX) of the Chicago Board Options Exchange (in basis points)	CBOEVIX = 100*VIX	VIX	Expected stock market volatility over the next 30 calendar days, estimated on the basis of weighted prices of out-of-the money options on the S&P 500 stock index, monthly average of daily observations[c]	Chicago Board Options Exchange website (code: SPX VIX close)
VOLA1Y, implied volatility from 1-year ZAR–USD currency options (in basis points)	VOLA1Y = 100* USDZARV1Y	USDZARV1Y	USD-ZAR option implied 1-year volatility, monthly averages of daily observations	Bloomberg
VOLA1M, implied volatility from 1-month ZAR–USD currency options (in basis points)	VOLA1M = 100* USDZARV1M	USDZARV1M	USD-ZAR option implied 1-month volatility, monthly averages of daily observations	Bloomberg

Table A1. *(Continued).*

Variable	Calculation	Subcomponents		Source
		Symbol	Description	
BONDS, worldwide relative private holdings of domestic and foreign government bonds	BONDS = ln(B)−ln(B*)−ln(S)	S	South African rand to US$ spot exchange rate (ZAR–USD), end-month	Datastream (code: COMRAN$)
		B and B*	Total government debt (line 88) minus Monetary authorities' claims on central government (line 12a) for South Africa and the United States, respectively, end-month	IMF, International Financial Statistics

[a]Calculated as implied by formulas in Section 2.3.

[b]A similar differential was calculated on the basis of core CPI indices from Datastream (for United States: CPI all items less food and energy, code: USCPXFDEF; for South Africa: core CPI, code: SACPCORMF).

[c]For details about the calculation of VIX, see Chicago Board Options Exchange (2003).

APPENDIX B: ECONOMETRIC TESTS

B1. Unit Root Tests

Table B1. Philips–Peron and Augmented Dickey–Fuller Unit Root Tests for Variables in Levels and First Differences 01/1997 to 12/2008.

Variable	PP-Test (with Intercept; No Trend)		ADF-Test (with Intercept; No Trend)		
	H0: $\gamma=0$, τ-Value	MacKinnon One-sided p-Value	Optimal Number of Lags (Max. 12 Months) Based on SIC	H0: $\gamma=0$, τ-Value	MacKinnon One-sided p-Value
CP1M	−1.929909	0.3179	1	−1.791330	0.38
CP1Y	−2.315217	0.1686	1	−2.487479	0.1206
INFDIFFCPI1M	−7.497790	0.00***	0	−7.197310	0.00***
INFDIFFCPI1Y	−1.951680	0.3080	1	−0.965941	0.7640
REERDEV	−2.039071	0.2700	1	−2.315115	0.1686
DREER1Y	−2.765583	0.0659*	1	−3.116388	0.0276**
DREER1M	−10.05917	0.00***	1	−9.387873	0.00***
RER$DEV	−3.391893	0.0128**	1	−4.201249	0.0009***
DRER$1Y	−2.273015	0.1822	1	−2.709704	0.0749*
DRER$1M	−8.647449	0.0000***	0	−8.690447	0.0000***
CBOEVIX	−2.105720	0.2428	2	−1.604409	0.4777
VOLA1Y	−1.343084	0.6077	0	−1.100398	0.7141
VOLA1M	−3.533217	0.0087***	0	−3.587199	0.0074***
BONDS	0.335585	0.9794	1	−0.407314	0.9037
Δ CP1M	−8.019219	0.0000***	0	−8.064632	0.0000***
Δ CP1Y	−6.270944	0.0000***	0	−6.239399	0.0000***
Δ INFDIFFCPI1M	−33.16538	0.0001***	1	−13.82722	0.0000***
Δ INFDIFFCPI1Y	−7.232171	0.0000***	11	−6.470757	0.0000***
Δ REERDEV	−10.21413	0.0000***	1	−9.860273	0.0000***
Δ DREER1Y	−9.948411	0.0000***	0	−10.01934	0.0000***
Δ DREER1M	−30.11484	0.0001***	6	−9.659009	0.0000***
Δ RER$DEV	−9.207519	0.0000***	1	−9.444946	0.0000***
Δ DRER$1Y	−7.640903	0.0000***	0	−7.812859	0.0000***
Δ DRER$1M	−42.71372	0.0001***	6	−9.227662	0.0000***
Δ CBOEVIX	−10.31478	0.0000***	1	−10.31193	0.0000***
Δ VOLA1Y	−9.313592	0.0000***	0	−9.395256	0.0000***
Δ VOLA1M	−13.61162	0.0000***	1	−10.12687	0.0000***
Δ BONDS	−8.437490	0.0000***	0	−8.630634	0.0000***

Notes: The equation for the Philips–Peron test is $\Delta Y_t = \alpha + \gamma Y_{t-1} + \varepsilon_t$ and the one for the Augmented Dickey–Fuller test is $\Delta Y_t = \alpha + \gamma Y_{t-1} + \Sigma_j \Delta Y_{t-j} + \varepsilon_t$ for $j = 1,,,p$. For both tests, H0: $\gamma = 0$.
***, **, and * mean statistical significance at the 1%, 5%, and 10% levels, respectively.

B2. Pesaran et al. (2001) Bounds Testing Procedure

Table B2. Bounds Testing Procedure for 1-Year Currency Premium Equation.

$p=q$	Akaike	Schwarz	*F*-stat. of Level Variables	Q(1) *p*-Value	Q(4) *p*-Value	Q(13) *p*-Value	$\chi^2_{SC}(1)$ (*p*-Value)	$\chi^2_{SC}(4)$ (*p*-Value)
1	**9.823071**	**10.12746**	**11.51523**	**0.484**	**0.781**	**0.358**	**0.478296**	**0.796621**
2	9.845177	10.30176	3.984809	0.868	0.851	0.341	0.601817	0.793291
3	9.929763	10.53854	3.239831	0.969	0.867	0.235	0.848206	0.750831
4	10.03681	10.79779	2.166725	0.798	0.971	0.185	0.068449	0.309645
5	9.957688	10.87086	1.951144	0.812	0.926	0.493	0.548132	0.381009
6	9.934255	10.99962	3.029514	0.772	0.723	0.572	0.408728	0.081891
7	10.02225	11.23981	2.784702	0.666	0.865	0.620	0.040536	0.037829
8	9.882372	11.25213	2.82827	0.908	0.945	0.803	0.806735	0.443675
9	9.722394	11.24435	5.063728	0.062	0.271	0.821	0.000088	0.000097

Notes: This table displays Akaike (AIC) and Schwarz (SIC) information criteria, Ljung-Box *Q*-statistics, Breusch–Godfrey LM tests for serial correlation [χ^2_{SC} (p)], and *F*-statistics for H0: $\alpha=\beta_j=0$ for $j=$INFIDIFFCPI1Y, DREER1Y, CBOEVIX, and VOLA1Y for nine ARDL(p,q) specifications of the 1-year currency premium equation. *Step 1*: Given the importance of serially uncorrelated errors for the validity of the bounds test, we base the choice of the appropriate lag length on AIC. As the minimum AIC conditional on the absence of serial correlation is found for $p=q=1$, we chose an ARDL(1,1) specification for the 1-year equation. *Step 2*: For $k=4$, the critical *F*-statistic bounds at the 5% level according to Pesaran et al. (2001) are 2.86 and 4.01, respectively. As the *F*-statistic for ARDL(1,1) equals 11.52 and lies above the upper critical bound, we conclude that there is a long-run relationship among the RHS-level variables.

Table B3. Bounds Testing Procedure for 1-Month Currency Premium Equation.

$p=q$	Akaike	Schwarz	F-Stat. of Level Variables	Q(1) p-Value	Q(4) p-Value	Q(13) p-value	$\chi^2_{SC}(1)$ (p-Value)	$\chi^2_{SC}(4)$ (p-Value)
1	10.41701	10.71476	8.035055	0.887	0.880	0.387	0.884929	0.866702
2	**10.33138**	**10.77801**	**4.567137**	**0.966**	**0.875**	**0.177**	**0.921810**	**0.845916**
3	10.34590	10.94141	3.907133	0.831	0.905	0.148	0.500867	0.820051
4	10.34262	11.08700	2.696664	0.618	0.568	0.116	0.150338	0.095592
5	10.35109	11.24435	2.329949	0.773	0.733	0.507	0.395597	0.067855
6	10.27447	11.31660	3.595673	0.453	0.681	0.112	0.066579	0.142142
7	10.35063	11.54165	3.542922	0.880	0.533	0.170	0.525568	0.021417
8	10.32730	11.66719	4.088105	0.802	0.815	0.308	0.490698	0.059385
9	10.41225	11.90101	2.616771	0.516	0.517	0.189	0.000267	0.000083

Notes: This table displays Akaike (AIC) and Schwarz (SIC) information criteria, Ljung-Box Q-statistics, Breusch–Godfrey LM tests for serial correlation [χ^2_{SC} (p)], and F-statistics for H0: $\alpha=\beta_j=0$ for $j=$INFIDIFFCPI1Y, DREER1M, CBOEVIX, and VOLA1M for nine ARDL(p,q) specifications of the 1-month currency premium equation. *Step 1*: Given the importance of serially uncorrelated errors for the validity of the bounds test, we base the choice of the appropriate lag length on AIC. As the minimum AIC conditional on the absence of serial correlation is found for $p=q=2$, we chose an ARDL(2,2) specification for the 1-month equation. *Step 2*: For $k=4$, the critical F-statistic bounds at the 5% level according to Pesaran et al. (2001) are 2.86 and 4.01, respectively. As the F-statistic for ARDL(2,2) equals 4.57 and lies above the upper critical bound, we conclude that there is a long-run relationship among the RHS-level variables.

DETERMINANTS OF FOREIGN DIRECT INVESTMENT IN THAILAND

Kevin Daly and Chanikarn Teresa Tosompark

ABSTRACT

Before the 1997 Asian Financial Crisis, Thailand had the fastest growing level of foreign direct investment (FDI) inflows amongst Asian economies. The general objective of this research is to evaluate the determinants of FDI investment in Thailand post the 1997 crisis; our empirical investigation of the determinants of Thailand's FDI relates to the period 1998–2008. The end of this period also covers the global financial crisis of 2007–2008; the effects of this crisis on FDI generally may be premature to judge given that most FDI projects have lead times ranging from 12 to 18 months. The chapter also provides an update covering the latest available FDI data by comparing 2008–2009 quarter 1 FDI flows both regionally and for Thailand.

Keywords: Exchange rates; tax; cost of capital; World Bank; ASEAN.

JEL Classifications: G0; F3; F31.

The Impact of the Global Financial Crisis on Emerging Financial Markets
Contemporary Studies in Economic and Financial Analysis, Volume 93, 709–718

ISSN: 1569-3759/doi:10.1108/S1569-3759(2011)0000093026

1. INTRODUCTION

Historically, Thailand has depended heavily on the inflows of foreign direct investment (FDI) from the United States and Japan, which accounted for at least 50% of all FDI inflow. This geographic pattern of FDI changed remarkably from the early 1980s when Japan was looking for production bases abroad to escape appreciating home currencies. The source of Thailand's FDI in recent years is geographically diversified, with new partners including those from ASEAN, EU-151, Australia and New Zealand.

2. FDI FLOWS REGIONAL UPDATE (2008–2009)

South, East, and South-East Asia have not been able to escape the negative impacts of the global financial crisis, and FDI outflows from the region inevitably slowed in 2009, although to a lesser degree than in many other parts of the world. In fact, FDI in the region has already been slowing since the last quarter of 2008. FDI inflows declined by one third in the first quarter of 2009 compared to the same period in 2008. The performance of the major economies in the region in attracting FDI varied significantly, as shown in Table 1.

Among the Asian countries, Singapore was hit the hardest by the global financial crisis, with lower economic growth and FDI inflows declining by a significant 28% and over (2008 Q1–2008 Q4). Heading in the same direction, Thailand and Malaysia saw slight changes in FDI inflows: dropping by 10% and 4%, respectively. On the other hand, countries like South Korea, Indonesia and Vietnam saw an increase in inflows, mostly with credits due to political stability and strong stimulus plan by the government. Outflows from all four Asian new industrialized economies (NIEs) declined: by 2% in Hong Kong (China), by 7% in Taiwan Province of China, by 18% in the Republic of Korea and by a massive 63% in Singapore (with outflows amounting to $60 billion, $10 billion, $13 billion and $9 billion, respectively). This caused their share in total outward FDI from the region to decline from 64% in 2007 to 49% in 2008. The Asian NIEs have been hit particularly hard by the crisis, and their relative significance in the region's outward FDI is continuing to decline, as suggested by the fall in their cross-border M&A purchases in the first half of 2009.

Table 1. South, East and South-East Asia FDI Inflows/Outflows.

Country	FDI Inflows					FDI Outflows				
	2008:Q1	2008:Q2	2008:Q3	2008:Q4	2009:Q1	2008:Q1	2008:Q2	2008:Q3	2008:Q4	2009:Q1
Cambodia	224	272	186	133	87	6	6	6	6	–
China	27 414	24 974	21 986	18 022	21 777	–	–	–	–	–
Hong Kong, China	19 588	14 806	11 097	17 513	11 792	12 381	25 084	6 938	15 518	4 558
India	14 197	11 891	8782	6 684	6 256	–	–	–	–	–
Indonesia	1 460	2 040	1 921	2 498	3511	1730	1 436	1 517	1 217	814
Republic of Korea	−674	−212	1 633	1454	−63	4 116	2 702	3 916	2 061	1 132
Lao People's Democratic Republic	72	37	55	64	58	–	–	–	–	–
Malaysia	1 045	5 342	256	1 410	828	1973	4 448	5 774	1 864	−130
Pakistan	983	2 104	1 117	1234	691	5	36	5	−11	−6
Papua New Guinea	13	−51	6	2	359	–	–	–	–	1
Philippines	266	434	555	265	44	−6	77	102	64	52
Singapore	8 268	3 649	3 561	7 246	3 220	2 656	751	4 012	1509	1 478
Solomon Islands	15	19	18	23	17	3	3	3	3	3
Taiwan Province of China	597	1 107	989	2 739	263	3 165	2 623	2 174	2331	980
Thailand	2 959	2 230	2 545	2 357	2 324	541	1215	186	893	573
Vanuatu	7	9	3	14	5	–	–	–	–	–
Total	76 433	68 651	54 709	61 658	51 169	26570	38381	24 633	25 454	9 456

Source: WIR (2009).

3. THE DETERMINANTS FOR THAILAND'S FDI INFLOWS

Previous studies have investigated (in depth) various factors which influence multinationals' decision to invest in foreign markets. More often these variables include local market demand, cost of local labour and capital endowment, taxes levied, the exchange rate, local economic growth, political and the economic risk and the local infrastructure.

3.1. Market Demand

A large or growing host market is perceived to be a positive sign for profitable investments. In the empirical studies, market size effect is generally measured by gross domestic product (GDP), GDP per capita, gross national product (GNP), GNP capita or the growth rate of these factors. In general, empirical results support market size as a significant and positive influence on inward FDI. The positive relationship between market size and inward FDI is confirmed by Dees (1998) and Zhang (2001).

3.2. Endowment Cost–Labour

The results of the effects of relative factor cost on the FDI inflows are ambiguous. Lower labour costs and higher unemployment are recognized to attract the FDI funds in many studies (Barrell & Pain, 1999; Mody & Srinivasan, 1998a, 1998b). Since labour cost is an important part of total production costs, especially in labour-intensive manufacturing, the lower the labour cost in the host country, the more the foreign investment in the host country. Lower labour costs have obviously an attraction to the foreign multinational investments. One would therefore expect a negative relationship between the labour costs and the inward FDI. However, a positive relationship is also thought to be possible in the literature as wage rate could be regarded as a signal for labour quality. Higher wage rate may indicate the higher skilled labours that foreign investors seek.

3.3. Cost of Capital

FDI is basically financed in the home country. If the cost of borrowing in the home country is lower than in the host country, home country firm can have a cost advantage over host country rivals, and are in a better position considering the cost of capital to enter the host country market via FDI. Thus, the higher the ratio of host country borrowing cost to the home country costs, the higher will be the inward FDI in the host country. However, this relationship has not been supported generally since in reality multinationals can finance their activities from the international capital market besides the local market. In the regression model, we employ interest rate spread (deposit rate less lending rate) relative to US spread as a measure of the relative costs of capital. However, the discussions about the influence of the interest rate on FDI are ambiguous since higher interest rates may indicate a booming local economy which in turn may have a positive effect on the FDI (Liu, Song, Wei, & Romilly, 1997).

3.4. Tax

Several empirical studies have investigated the influence of taxes on FDI; here taxes are measured by the taxes volume, corporate tax rate or average tax rate. Hines and Rice (1999) and de Mooij and Ederveen (2003) research focus on the relationship of tax volume and distribution of FDI, while Bartik (1985) introduced the corporate tax rate into the FDI determinant model. He found that there is a significant impact of the tax rate on business location decisions.

3.5. Exchange Rates

The effects of the exchange rate changes on production are quite ambiguous. If FDI promotes production for re-exports, it is complementary to international trade. In a situation where there is full pass through changes in exchange rates into production costs, an appreciation in the local currency would supposedly reduce FDI inflows since local costs of production have increased. In the opposite situation, a decrease in the relative production costs, caused by a fall in relative wages or real exchange rate deprecation, will attract an increase in foreign investment inflow ceteris paribus. On the other hand, if FDI aims at serving the local market, FDI and trade are substitute for each other. An appreciation in the local currency increases FDI inflows due to higher purchasing power of the local consumers.

Froot and Stein's (1991) empirical study demonstrated that a weakening currency can raise foreign investors' motivation for controlling interests in foreign corporate assets because exchange rate changes have impacts on international wealth, and wealthier buyers find it easier to acquire assets. Blonigen (1997) analysed data on Japanese acquisitions in the United State from 1975 to 1992. His results displayed a strong correlation of a weaker dollar and the higher level of Japanese acquisitions in the United States for industries which involve firm-specific assets. The data revealed that a 10% lower dollar increases Japanese acquisition in high R&D manufacturing sectors by 18–32%. However, this outcome was not repeated in the case of greenfield investments by Japanese multinational enterprise (MNE), where acquisition of firm-specific assets is not involved. If foreign and domestic firms have equal opportunity to purchase firm-specific assets in the domestic market, but different opportunities to generate return on these assets in foreign markets, then currency movements may affect relative values.

Zhang (2001) found the cumulative effect of exchange rate reforms in China led to a substantial real depreciation in the Chinese currency beginning in 1981. The real depreciation in the Chinese currency favoured the foreign firms' purchase of China's asset and allowed foreign investors to take advantage of the relatively cheap labour in China (Liu et al., 1997; Dees, 1998; Wei & Liu, 2001). Therefore, depreciation was expected to be positively associated with FDI inflow. Liu et al. (1997) and Wei and Liu (2001) obtained a positive coefficient for the exchange rate variable in the regression equations designed to test the determinants of FDI on China.

Studies which focused on the effect of exchange rate volatility on the relative prices of intermediate inputs imported from the parent country or final products portray ambiguous results. In general, multinationals may perceive the influence of the exchange rate volatility on trade costs, and choose to produce abroad instead of exporting, if exchange rate volatility is high. As long as TNCs are unable to eliminate exchange rate uncertainty, large swings in exchange rate variability will result in less trade. In studies which examined the long-run responses of trade flows to exchange rate variability; the evidence suggests that a negative relationship exists between trade flows and exchange rate variability.

3.6. Related Variables

Other variables to consider as determinants of FDI inflow include political and economic risk of host country, infrastructure, language, education, legal system and reporting standards. In general, higher economic growth reflects improvement in productivity and development. Along with improvements in the above factors which in turn lower economic and political risks, resulting in a more attractive and stable climate for foreign investors. Improved infrastructure in the host country will influence extra expenditure by multinationals.

4. METHODOLOGY

We can build the following specification due to the discussion in the former literature:

$$\mathrm{FDI}_{it} = f(\mathrm{RWA}_{it},\ \mathrm{RGDP}_{it},\ \mathrm{ER}_{it},\ \mathrm{RX}_{it},\ \mathrm{RM}_{it},\ \mathrm{RIR}_{it}) \tag{1}$$

where FDI is the annual flow of real foreign direct investment inflow Thailand, RWA is real wage average RGDP is real GDP/Capita, ER is the real exchange rate local currency unit (LCU), RX is real Thailand exports, RM is real Thailand imports and RIR is interest rate spread (deposit–lending rate) as a ratio of US spread.

The log-linear form of Eq. (1) is

$$\begin{aligned}\ln \mathrm{FDI}_{it} = {} & \alpha + \beta_1 \mathrm{RWA}_{it} + \beta_2 \ln \mathrm{RGDP}_{it} + \beta_3 \mathrm{ER}_{it} + \beta_4 \ln \mathrm{RX}_{it} \\ & + \beta_5 \ln \mathrm{RM}_{it} + \beta_6 \ln \mathrm{RIR} + \varepsilon_t \end{aligned} \tag{2}$$

We found from the regression results that GDP per capita (constant prices) has a positive effect on FDI inflow. As mentioned in the above review, growing market demand encourages the foreign investment to Thailand. The test results on the trade variables tell us that Thailand's exports have a positive effect on the FDI inflow, while imports appear to be negatively related to FDI inflow. However, neither coefficient is significant. The real average wage has a significant positive effect for FDI inflow into Thailand. This indicates that FDI is attracted by an increasing average real wage as has been ongoing in Thailand for the last decade. The exchange rate measured in constant prices of the LCU has a negative effect on the FDI inflow; however, the coefficient is not significant. In this case, the appreciation in the currency over the period did not significantly reduce the inflows of FDI (Table 2).

The cost of capital in terms of interest rate spread provides us with slightly ambiguous results. The sign appears negative but insignificant indicating that the local interest rate as measured by the spread in deposit to lending rates has a negative influence on FDI inflow. However, in reality multinationals can finance their activities from the international capital

Table 2. OLS Results Determinants of Thailand's FDI Inflows.

Variable	Coefficient	Standard Error	*t*-Statistic	Problem
C	−41.46625	22.58275	−1.836192	0.0893
LEXPORT	1.098142	1.537529	0.714226	0.4877
LGDPP	4.134897	3.196388	1.293616	0.2183
LIMPORT	−1.777745	0.901397	−1.972212	0.0702
LWAGE	6.469245	2.094917	3.088068	0.0086
LEXCHANGE	−1.206502	0.888488	−1.357928	0.1976
LINTERESTE RATE	−0.016698	0.329800	−0.050632	0.9604
R-squared	0.912316	Mean-dependent variable		1.243617
Adjusted *R*-squared	0.871847	Standard Deviation-dependent variable		0.676667
Standard error of regression	0.242237	Akaike info criterion		0.271413
Sum-squared residual	0.762821	Schwarz criterion		0.619920
Log likelihood	4.285867	Hannan–Quinn criterion		0.339445
F-statistic	22.54332	Durbin–Watson statistic		1.928703
Problem (*F*-statistic)	0.000004			

Sources: UNCTAD Handbook of Statistics 2009 and DMFAS (UNCTAD and World Bank).

market besides the local market. What appears to be the case in Thailand's experience over the period is that an increasing interest rate spread indicates increased risk in the credit markets which in turn has placed a negative impact on borrowing from the local market by foreign investors.

4.1. Tax

Given that various forms of reliefs from corporate taxation (in terms of tax free status for limited duration) are employed by Thailand to attract foreign investment, we did not test for the effect of tax on FDI in our regression model. We assume that as in previous studies which have allowed tax to enter as an explanatory variable the impact of tax is an important business location decision in Thailand.

5. THE IMPACT OF RECENT POLITICAL EVENTS ON THAILAND AS A HOST FOR FDI

Although Thailand has long been seen as a strong base for foreign investors, a series of policy reversals and new regulations have led to substantial criticism of recent governments. After taking office, the military government came under criticism from the foreign business community for imposing currency controls (later partially reversed) and introducing a bill that would restrict foreign ownership of Thai companies. The amendment to the law affecting foreign business ownership, stemming from the negative reaction to the sale of Thaksin's family telecommunications company to a Singaporean state-owned enterprise, will reportedly exclude several sectors.

On Transparency International's Corruption Perception Index, Thailand is ranked 80 out of 180 countries, alongside Brazil and Saudi Arabia. This index attempts to measure abuse of public office for private gain. One stated justification for the 2006 military coup was to combat corruption in the Thaksin government.

Amid the chaotic switch of governments, protest groups have caused turmoil in the country over the past two years. Yellow shirts occupied Bangkok's commercial airports in November 2008, only leaving eight days later after the collapse of the government. And then in April 2009, red-shirted anti-government protestors stormed an ASEAN summit in the resort town of Pattaya. The summit had to be abandoned and many delegates evacuated. Violent protests in Bangkok over March to June 2010 resulted in the government declaring a state of emergency and calling in the army to restore order. Thus, one way to improve FDI for Thailand is to resolve its political issues, restore law and order to the country and bring back the investors' confidence. Furthermore, the Department of Commerce's International Trade Administration states that current concerns regarding Thailand are intellectual property rights laws and enforcement, concerns addressed through consultations and technical assistance, improvements in Thai Customs practices, and lack of transparency and efficiency in the customs regime.

6. CONCLUSION

The chapter initially provides an overview of recent evidence in relation to FDI flows both regionally and for Thailand. We found that Thailand was the least affected amongst Asian countries to experience falling levels of FDI inflow over the recent global financial crisis. In terms of accounting for Thailand's FDI experience since the Asian 1997 financial crisis, we found that the determinants in our model performed satisfactorily overall with the diagnostic tests generally indicating a lack of misspecification. The individual results for the variables indicate that growing market size and

Thailand's increasing average real wage, has positive effects on FDI inflow. However, the relationship between the trade variables and FDI inflow, although insignificant, is generally correctly signed. At the national level, FDI has positive relationship with exports. The strengthening exchange rate does appear to be negatively related with FDI but is not highly significant. Regards cost of capital the increasing local spread does indicate a concern with increasing perceived risk, but as discussed the significance of this variables influence on decisions to invest in Thailand can only be revealed on a case-by-case study.

REFERENCES

Barrell, R., & Pain, N. (1999). Trade restraints and Japanese direct investment flows. *European Economic Review*, *43*, 29–45.

Bartik, T. J. (1985). Business location decisions in the United States: Estimates of the effects of unionization, taxes, and other characteristics of states. *Journal of Business & Economic Statistics, American Statistical Association*, *3*(1), 14–22 January.

Blonigen, B. A. (1997). Firm-specific assets and the link between exchange rates and foreign direct investment. *American Economic Review*, *87*(3), 447–465.

De Mooij, R. A., & Ederveen, S. (2003). Taxation and foreign direct investment: A synthesis of empirical research. *International Tax and Public Finance*, *10*(6), 673–693.

Dees, S. (1998). Foreign direct investment in China: Determinants and effects. *Economics of Planning*, *31*(2), 175–194.

Froot, K. A., & Stein, J. C. (1991). Exchange rates and foreign direct investment: An imperfect capital markets approach. *The Quarterly Journal of Economics*, *106*(4), 1191–1217.

Hines, J. R., Jr., & Rice, E. M. (1994). Fiscal paradise: Foreign tax havens and American business. *The Quarterly Journal of Economics*, *109*(1), 149–182.

Liu, X., Song, H., Wei, Y., & Romilly, P. (1997). Country characteristics and foreign direct investment in China: A panel data analysis. *Review of World Economics*, *133*(2), 313–329.

Mody, A., & Srinivasan, K. (1998a). Agglomeration, regional grants and firm location. Working Paper No. 5. Institute for Fiscal Studies.

Mody, A., & Srinivasan, K. (1998b). Japanese and United States firms as foreign investors: Do they march to the same tune? *Canadian Journal of Economics*, *31*(4), 778–799.

Wei, Y., & Liu, X. (2001). Foreign Direct Investment in China: Determinants and Impact. Edward Elgar, UK.

World Investment Report (WIR). (2009). United Nations conference on trade and development (UNCTAD)/world investment report. ISBN: 978-92-1-112775-1.

Zhang, K. H. (2001). How does foreign direct investment affect economic growth in China? *The Economics of Transition*, *9*(3), 679–693.

A COMPARISON OF FINANCIAL ROBUSTNESS IN THE UNITED STATES AND TURKEY DURING 2007–2010

Paul Bennett and Oral Erdogan[1]

ABSTRACT

This study aims to explain that more conservative and supervised but supported banking system can be an advantage during the crises periods. We use the US banking system as the origin of the recent collapse, and the Turkish banking as the more profitable one during the recent crisis years. We have found evidence that, in the context of the specific type of externally initiated yet spreading crisis of confidence and funding that affected world institutions, the structure of the Turkish banks actually turned out to protect the Turkish financial system.

Keywords: Monetary policy; bank capital; financial crisis; United States; Turkey.

JEL Classifications: G21; G28; E52; E61.

The Impact of the Global Financial Crisis on Emerging Financial Markets
Contemporary Studies in Economic and Financial Analysis, Volume 93, 719–732

ISSN: 1569-3759/doi:10.1108/S1569-3759(2011)0000093027

1. INTRODUCTION

Shocks to an economy are typically propagated and not infrequently magnified through their deleterious impacts on banks and financial markets. Bernanke and Gertler (1995) noted that a weakened financial system can significantly magnify negative shocks and affect the ability of a central bank's monetary policy to stabilise an economy. Conversely, a strong financial system can aid economic stability in the face of disruption. This ability to dampen or to accelerate shocks has been well illustrated in the 2007–2010 global crisis, when weakness of financial intermediaries in some cases worsened economic conditions and constrained economic activity, even for otherwise sound businesses and households.

While the slump in asset prices and economic activity was worldwide, not every economy proved equally vulnerable. The US system, in which prominent intermediaries used very high leverage and where there were problematic divisions of responsibility among financial agents, experienced particularly severe financial problems and recession. In contrast, banking systems with less leverage and more traditional lending methods proved more robust. As one prominent observer has noted, '... Emerging economies' financial systems, long regarded as their Achilles heels, have done far better than the Anglo-Saxon model they were once encouraged to emulate'.[2]

One important example of a country whose financial system remained relatively strong while the financial crisis circled the globe is Turkey. Having implemented important economic and financial regulatory reforms after suffering through its own earlier crisis, Turkey was able to avoid some of the types of difficulties that plagued the United States during 2007–2010.

The purpose of this chapter is to compare the performance of the United States and Turkey during the crisis. We find that, although Turkey's real economy was significantly affected by the global economic slump, which cut worldwide final demand for all types of goods and services, the Turkish banking system nevertheless withstood the stress reasonably well, and much better than it had in its 2000–2002 banking and currency crisis. No major Turkish banks failed in 2007–2010. The main reason for today's better performance is that, due to improvements undertaken after its 2000–2002 problems, Turkey implemented reforms that strengthened its banking system and government finances. Entering the prior episode, Turkish banks had avoided extensive domestic credit risk, but were very reliant on high real interest rates for their profitability. This ended unhappily as inflation-related volatility created large losses for the intermediaries.[3] By the outset of the

2007–2010 global crisis, however, Turkish banks were well-capitalised and tightly regulated, and inflation was much better controlled. Moreover, in Turkey, banks for the most part held onto the loans and other credit-risky assets they had originated (i.e. other than government securities). Thus, they avoided the worst of the incentive and information problems that plagued the US originate-to-distribute model.

In contrast, in the United States during the run-up to the recent crisis, banking organisations significantly increased their leverage and the exposure of their capital to risks, subsequently worsening the crisis when it hit. Many banking assets that had been created and securitised in the boom failed to perform, spreading the loss of wealth. The loss of bank capital reduced credit availability broadly in the US economy. The comparison of the Turkish experience with the US crisis supports the view that high levels of financial intermediary capital and related reforms can help make an economy more resilient in the face of economic shocks.

This chapter compares the macroeconomic challenges facing the United States and Turkey at the time of the crisis, highlights important differences in the two financial systems going into the 2007–2010 period and compares how the global turbulence has affected both economies. Our conclusion is that, in comparison to the United States where growing leverage and risky asset securitisation increased systemic vulnerability, Turkey's reformed banking system helped protect its financial system.

2. MACROECONOMIC CONDITIONS

Real growth: Real GDP growth was at first higher in Turkey than in the United States, where the slowdown and recession began (Chart 1). Following the global spread of contraction, however, from the end of 2008 to early 2010, Turkey experienced a V-shaped recession accompanied by strong rebound. In contrast, the US contraction persisted longer, reflecting severe real estate and financial sector problems, as bank credit remained tight during 2008 and 2009.[4,5]

Inflation in Turkey and the United States: In Turkey, a fundamental reform was that very high inflation associated with 2000–2002 was brought under control by 2005 (Chart 2). This in turn reflected improvement in Turkish fiscal balance and central banking policies, epitomised by the adoption of an inflation target. Lira depreciation in 2008 resulted in only a relatively minor acceleration in the Turkish Consumer Price Index (CPI) in 2009. In the United States, consumer prices were controlled. There was a

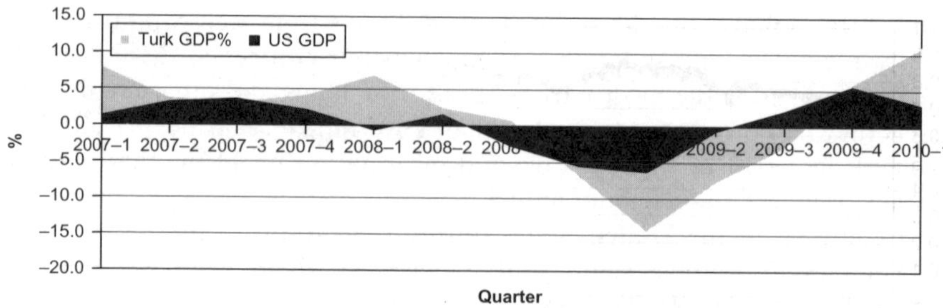

Chart 1. US and Turkish GDP Growth.

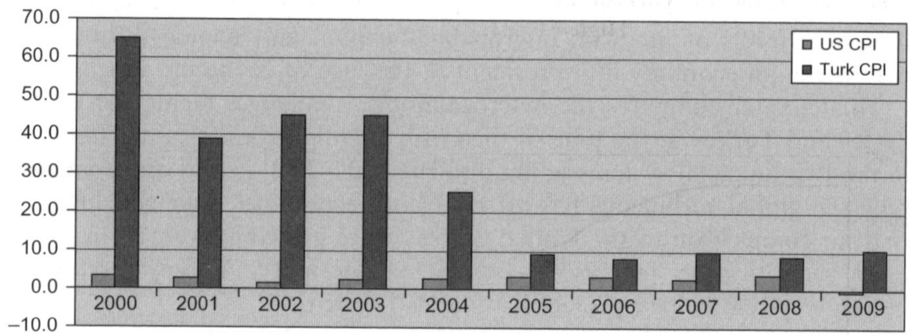

Chart 2. Turkish and US CPI Inflation 2000–2010.

slight acceleration due to higher energy prices in 2007, but then the CPI slowed and fell as the recession cut commodities prices and widened the gap between potential output and aggregate demand.

Exchange rates: The US dollar was subject to countervailing forces, at first pushed down by emerging US economic weakness and later pushed up as investors sought safety in US assets when the recession spread worldwide (Chart 3). The lira stayed strong against the dollar until late 2008, when depreciation occurred. During the more recent European problems in 2010, the lira has generally held its value.

Interest rates: In response to the economic downturn, overnight policy interest rates were lowered by both the Turkish and US central banks. In both countries, falling central bank rates were not fully reflected in market interest rates (Chart 4). In the United States, these widening spreads reflected the weakened and uncertain condition of many borrowers and

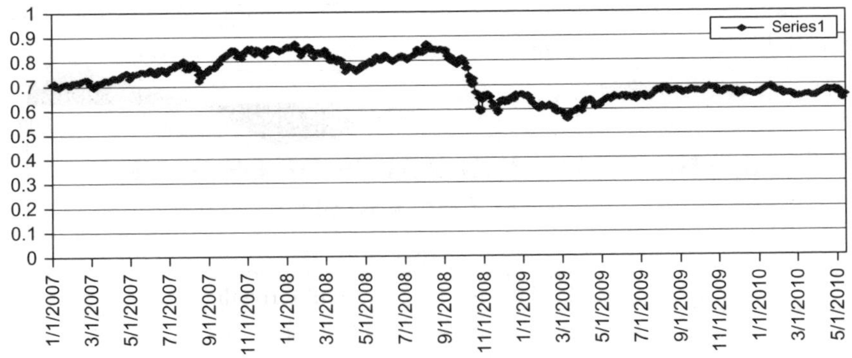

Chart 3. Value of Turkish Lira in US Dollars During 2007–2010 (Intra-Day High = 0.83120; Low = 0.5479).

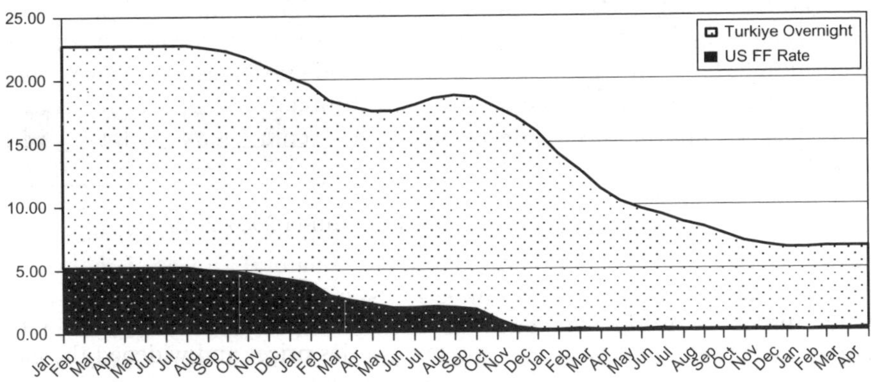

Chart 4. Turkish Overnight Inter-Bank Rate and US Fed Funds Rate (Percent).

distrust of core financial intermediaries. In Turkey, the falling lira put upward pressure on inter-bank rates in late 2008 even as the central bank lowered its policy rate. By 2009, however, the Turkish central bank had pushed the overnight market rate down decisively. The US Federal Reserve (The Fed) became constrained not only by the dysfunction of the inter-bank funding markets but also by the zero interest rate bound at the end of 2008. The Fed then sought to alleviate financial strains by becoming a more direct intermediary, teaming up with the US Treasury to acquire or provide funding for risky bank assets, to inject capital into banks, and to guarantee financial intermediary liabilities, in an attempt to restart credit flows.

3. THE CHANGING ROLES OF US BANKS AND THE CRISIS

The US system was heavily shaped by deregulation of financial markets during the previous decade, as well as by the US property bubble. The Graham Leach Bliley Act had removed 1930s depression era rules separating banking from securities businesses.[6] A key characteristic of the US system prior to the crisis was the division of roles among multiple entities involved in loan origination, distribution and credit risk management. Mortgage bankers had become key loan originators, with the intent to sell the loans as quickly as possible once they were made. Banks and brokers bought the loans and held them on balance sheet in inventory while repackaging them for prompt re-sale or issuance in the form of mortgage securities. Many of these securities were in turn broken down and repackaged yet again, and then sold to institutional investors who, at least in retrospect, appear to have been unable to accurately assess their credit risk.

The bottom line was that the underwriting process in the United States was weakened by two factors. One was the bubble in home prices, which led to overly optimistic assumptions about the collateral values of many US houses. Optimistic assumptions underlay sub-prime lending in particular, where there was reduced reliance on income to meet cash flows and more emphasis on collateral to protect the borrowers. While Turkish home prices in some areas rose significantly, Turkey did not experience a sub-prime mortgage bubble. Most importantly, in Turkey there was little secondary market for mortgages, and Turkish banks, in anticipation of holding the mortgage assets they underwrote, maintained credit standards for borrower incomes.[7]

The crisis in the United States was initiated by the end of a housing bubble combined with severe financial intermediary weakness because of bank exposures to complex instruments.[8] Entering the crisis, US financial markets were not only highly securitised but also had relatively low capital requirements for key intermediaries. The role for traditional, deposit-funded bank credit intermediation had shrunk for several decades, as more and more intermediation was accomplished through securities markets. In the 20

Table 1. Declining Role of Traditional Bank Intermediation in the United States.

All US Depository Institutions	1987	2007
Deposits (billion dollars)	3230.1	8347.5
As % of US GDP	68.0	59.6

Sources: US Flow of Funds (Federal Reserve System) and US National Income and Product Accounts (Bureau of Economic Analysis). Deposits include small and large time and savings deposits plus checkable deposits (FOF Tables L205, and L204 lines 7, 11 and 12). GDP is in current (undeflated) dollars.

years prior to the start of the crisis in 2007, deposits of US bank intermediaries, measured relative to US total GDP, had shrunken very significantly (Table 1).

By the time of the crisis, many of the large banks and other US financial institutions were heavily reliant on non-deposit borrowings in money and short-term securities markets. When the markets contracted, these banks' funding suffered accordingly, and many either failed or were forced to rely on government support. Most large banks and securities firms were the recipients of US Treasury or Federal Reserve support, either via *direct* capital infusions and funding, or *indirectly* via support for their key trading and funding counterparties, whose demise would have caused spreading failures.

4. TURKISH BANKING LEADING UP TO THE CRISIS

In contrast, Turkey entered the crisis with a relatively stable and strongly capitalised banking system. Turkey's banks depend heavily on traditional deposits and rely less than US banks on their ability to continually fund themselves and manage risks in non-deposit securities, derivatives or money markets. In addition, the Turkish banks were very conservative in their exposures to business and household credit risks. The lower inflation trend after 2005 meant that a strategy of holding government securities became less risky; lower inflation and interest rates greatly reduced repricing and refunding risks of their assets and liabilities. Counterparty credit and trading risk within the Turkish financial system also were lower as a result.

In March 2010, the Turkish Banking Regulation and Supervision Agency reported that Turkish bank capital equalled 19.95 percent of assets, and that Turkish banks were highly profitable.[9] While the Turkish economy was hit hard by the global demand contraction, the lower leverage and more tightly managed banking approach helped protect the country's banking system.[10]

When the developed economies were suffering financial crisis because of the banks failure at first in 2007 and 2008, Turkish banks did not have any collapses. In 2009 and in the first half of 2010 while the governments faced severe budget deficits, Turkish government budget was not having a big problem.

The banks in Turkey have not only saved themselves against the contagion effect, but they also increased their profits during crisis quarters. So, why were they profitable? First of all, Turkey applied rigid rules in banking after 2001 when the banks siphoned 40 billion dollars. Turkish Banking Regulatory and Supervision Agency has been very active in Turkey to control and supervise the banks. Rigid rules are based on the prevention of incentive problems too. Defrauding is almost difficult. Not some but all banks are under the supervision of the banking authority. As the system is 'too small to fail', its control was not so difficult.

The entrance to banking market was limited even prohibited after 2003. This also gave a kind of oligopolistic power to a few banks in the system. For instance, 50 percent of all net interest income of the Turkish banking was obtained just by four banks.

Related with the fear after the financial collapse in 2001, the Turkish savers increased their FX deposits in the Turkish banks and the accounts were not even decreased during the crisis. We think they had had a big experience (fear) in the previous crisis in 1994 and 2001. As they did not withdraw, the banks were lucky enough.

Besides, the foreign investors would not prefer to withdraw their capital from Turkey since they believed that they would have not found any carry trade possibility in other countries with respect to their portfolio strategies. Main answer is that relatively higher interest rates in Turkey were very attractive when the other countries capital markets had been living big problems.

The Turkish banks generally preferred to invest in treasury papers instead of giving more credits to real industry firms (one-third of bank assets). As the banks have dominated in capital markets, they somewhat prevented the firms to use capital markets financing. The obvious tool is then credit channels. Mortgage-backed assets was just introduced with a law in March 2007. The banks have not packaged and sold the mortgages yet.

The Turkish banks asked more warranties and mortgages to the companies, who used credits, to sustain the loan to value ratio. They even increased the Libor + 3 to Libor + 10 for instance. Many companies were obliged to accept the new rules by the banks. As many real industry firms wanted not to go into bankruptcy they provided more profit to banks as well. While doing so, those firms also provided new assets as mortgages to make the banks to restructure the credits.

The derivatives instruments are very new in Turkey. The derivatives exchange was just established in 2005. There has been no exchange-traded options yet. The banks that do not have enough experience in domestic derivatives have not entered related 'fancy' contracts abroad too.

Last but not least, the number of banks decreased while the banking volume has increased in Turkey. In addition the banks applied rules of economics of scale perfectly to decrease the unit cost of banking operations.

5. COMPARISON

Table 2 compares the basic differences between the United States and Turkish banking systems going into the crisis. The Turkish banking system has been significantly shaped by reaction to the banking crises of earlier years. Entering the more recent downturn, the Turkish banks had greatly strengthened capital ratios, and credit risk was contained, mainly on balance sheets. The reliance of Turkish banks on overnight money markets (as opposed to more traditional deposits) was limited. While there had been a run-up in housing prices in Turkey, it was not as extreme or widespread as in the United States.

Table 3 compares the amounts of leverage by US and Turkish banks. Exact comparisons are difficult because of technical differences between Turkish and US reporting. For example, the US figures exclude the large Financial Holding Companies such as Lehman Brothers and Bear Stearns, which were particularly highly leveraged and which failed. Because of a US Securities and Exchange Commission (SEC) loophole, those large non-bank intermediaries had been required to hold much less capital relative to assets than the US commercial banks.

Credit risks were increasingly being managed through bilateral OTC market swaps, which were dependent on performance by the major banks and their customers. As property prices fell and losses on badly underwritten home loans mounted, the largest banks took heavy losses and were unable to off-load inventories to newly skeptical secondary market

Table 2. Comparison of Key US and Turkish Banking Practices and System.

	United States	Turkey
Bank assets	Large exposure to housing markets. A large quantity of prime and sub-prime mortgage market assets were held in inventory awaiting resale or repackaging into mortgage derivative instruments for sale.	Much less exposure to rising home prices. There are loan syndications but no secondary market for any bond except government bonds. All other credit is intermediated through the banks. Turkish banks invest heavily in treasury securities and make profits as long as the real interest rate is positive enough.
Bank liabilities	Heavy dependence on 'purchased' funding from short-term money markets, with structural maturity and re-pricing mismatch.	Heavy dependence on traditional deposit liabilities, which provide somewhat stable funding under easy supervision by the authority. There is relatively little liquidity in inter-bank lira markets, except for government securities. Bank regulators have not allowed banks to issue bonds.
	Very large risk exposures, including price, liquidity, credit, operational and counterparty performance risks categories.	Some repricing and mismatching problems persist. There are no mortgage banks and secondary mortgage market yet. The banks cannot sell their mortgages and finance themselves instead by deposits.
Bank capital	According to the US Federal Reserve Flow of Funds, at the end of 2009 US Commercial Banks had total assets of 10,045.6 billion dollars and liabilities of 9,311.6 billion, with assets net of liabilities equal to 734.0 billion, or 7.3% of assets. (Source: US FOF, p. 63, lines 1 and 23). See also Table 3.	Pre-crisis, bank capital was required to be 12% of capital, and was 18.9%, and 18% at the end of 2007 and 2008, respectively. (*Source:* Banking Regulation and Supervision Agency, Turkey, 2009, 2010.)
Off-balance-sheet exposures	Very large relative to capital. As a result, simple capital ratios greatly understate the degree of leverage because they exclude a variety of off-balance sheet exposures.	Comparatively little off-balance-sheet risk. Some forex and interest rate hedging in OTC markets. Recently, increasing amount of forex and stock index futures hedging in the relatively new Turkish Derivatives Exchange

Table 2. (*Continued*)

	United States	Turkey
Regulation	Scattered among multiple federal and state bank, securities, and futures market regulators, and multiple self-regulatory agencies.	Centralized mainly in the Banking Regulation and Supervision Agency (BRSA).
Derivatives use	Widespread use of exchange-traded and OTC derivatives, including credit default swaps, which accentuated the credit crunch as homeowner defaults rose and transmitted systemic risk as counterparties weakened and failed.	Turkey has a relatively new (2005) derivatives exchange, but little or no over-the-counter (OTC) trading of instruments within Turkey.

Table 3. Ratio of Bank Capital to Total Assets.

Turkish Banks	US Banks		
2010	2006	2007	2008
19.95%	8.6%	8.3%	9.0%

Sources: Turkish banks: Banking Regulation and Supervision Agency (2010). US banks: Bank for International Settlements (2009).

investors. Credit availability shrank, and the reliability of existing credit guarantees (including those obtained in the swaps market) were in doubt.

Exacerbating this was a weak system of US regulation in which the largest security firms and financial holding companies avoided the stricter oversight and capital requirements attached to commercial banks. After Bear Stearns and Lehman Brothers failed, and after the credit default swap market was severely damaged by problems at AIG, interbank funding markets froze until the federal government essentially guaranteed the liabilities of financial intermediaries. At the root of the problem was insufficient capital relative to true risks, and ostensibly sophisticated but ultimately weak or even pro-forma credit risk management practices at large banks. In turn, the root of these risk management failures was a lack of incentives to sufficiently control risk taking by profitable centres within banks, by higher management, and even by shareholders, notwithstanding potential systemic spillovers. These incentive problems were magnified by high intermediary leverage, which implicitly spread downside risk to other creditors, counterparties and taxpayers. Government regulators and supervisors permitted significant leverage of risky assets and hence were unable to counterbalance these strongly perverse incentives that existed within the banks and their owners.

In Turkey, the banks originated home mortgages and other assets largely with the intention of keeping them in their own portfolios. This avoided many of the incentive and information problems associated with the originate-to-distribute model. Mortgage-backed assets were not even introduced in Turkey until March 2007, and derivatives markets were still new.

6. LESSONS

While bank regulators worldwide have argued for higher capital, many global banks have pushed back, resisting such requirements as an unnecessary cost. In Turkey, banks have embraced higher capital as a means of strengthening their access of funding. Moreover, unlike the United States, Turkey has avoided the widespread asset problems that are prone to occur when credit origination is separated from subsequent risk bearing. In this chapter, we compared the experiences of the US and the Turkish financial systems during 2008–2009. In the context of the specific type of externally initiated yet spreading crisis of confidence and funding that affected financial institutions worldwide, the structure of the Turkish banks better protected the Turkish economy.

The Turkish economy had its problems, but in Turkey the economic downturn occurred with a lag and in response to external forces. The economic recovery in Turkey was stronger as well. The Turkish banks had been extremely conservative and focused on limiting credit risk. They relied heavily on stable funding sources and did not get into a position of depending on continuous access to the types of short-term money or derivatives markets that dried up in the crisis. Part of this success can be traced to improvements in government finances and central banking inflation targeting, which had been successful in slashing the regime of high inflation and interest rates prevailing early in the decade. No Turkish banks failed, which helped confidence in the financial system and the economy. The conservative behaviour of the Turkish banks, encouraged by their regulator, blunted what otherwise might have turned out to be an even more destructive impact on jobs and output, such as that which had occurred in the United States.

NOTES

1. Paul Bennett was formerly the chief economist of NYSE Euronext during 2001–2008 and is currently a visiting professor of finance and economics, Rutgers Business School, New Jersey, USA. Oral Erdogan is a professor of finance, Istanbul Bilgi University, Turkey, and an economics advisor to the Undersecreteriat of the Maritime Affairs, Turkey.
2. 'Banks in emerging markets, The winners' dilemma,' *The Economist*, 15 May 2010, p. 16.
3. See Akyuz and Boratov (2002).
4. According to the Federal Reserve's Survey of Senior (all data) Loan Officers by the end of 2009 nearly all banks had tightened lending standards, and the availability of credit did not return to neutral until the early 2010. Survey results are posted at http://www.federalreserve.gov/boarddocs/SnloanSurvey.
5. Reinhart and Rogoff (2008) have argued that, historically, financial crises have tended to have long-lived damaging effects on economies. That appears to be the case in the United States, but less so in Turkey (See Karatash, 2010), where the economic downturn appears to have been caused by recessions in the United States and Europe.
6. Financial Services Modernization Act of 1999 (Pub. L. 106-102, 113 Stat. 1338, enacted 12 November 1999) repealed part of the Glass-Steagall Act of 1933, which had prohibited combinations of securities and commercial banking businesses.
7. For a description of the mortgage origination process in the United States leading up to the crisis, please see Dwight Jaffee, Anthony W Lynch, Matthew Richardson and Stijn Van Nieuwerburg, 'Mortgage Origination in the Financial Crisis', in Acharya and Richardson (2009).
8. See Acharya and Richardson (2009). Also see Acharya, Cooley, Richardson, and Walter (2011).
9. Turkish Banking Regulation and Supervision Agency (BRSA) press release, 7 May 2010. According to the release, net profits of Turkish banks rose 21.6 percent in Q1 2010 relative to the same period a year earlier.
10. Arguably, from a longer term perspective, there also may remain important longer run disadvantages in the Turkish approach. A high concentration of government debt in bank portfolios reduces the banks' exposure to domestic credit risk, and also crowds out private credit and potentially retards longer term economic growth (See also Boyd & De Nicoló, 2005 for an analysis of bond holdings in bank asset structure). On balance, however, the Turkish experience holds lessons for US institutions, investors and regulators, particularly in the role of leverage, and in the over-reliance on asset securitization.

ACKNOWLEDGMENT

The authors would like to thank Zekeriya Ozturk from Garanti Bank and Metin Yilmaz from Isbank for very helpful comments.

REFERENCES

Acharya, V. V., & Richardson, M. (Eds). (2009). *Restoring financial stability, how to repair a failed system, NYU Stern*. Wiley.

Acharya, V., Cooley, T., Richardson, M., & Walter, I. (2011). Manufacturing tail risk: A perspective on the financial crisis of 2007–09. *Foundations and Trends in Finance, 4*.

Akyuz, Y., & Boratov, K. (2002). *The making of the Turkish financial crisis*. United Nations Conference on Trade and Development Discussion Papers no. 158.

Bank for International Settlements. (2009). 79th Annual Report, June, Basel. Available at http://www.bis.org/publ/arpdf/ar2009e.pdf.

Banking Regulation and Supervision Agency (BRSA Turkey). (2009). *From crisis to financial stability (Turkey experience)*. Working Paper (revised second edition).

Banking Regulation and Supervision Agency (BRSA Turkey). (2010). General outlook of Turkish banking sector, 2010/4.

Bernanke, B., & Gertler, M. (1995). Inside the black box: The credit channel of monetary policy transmission. *The Journal of Economic Perspectives, 9*(4), 27–48.

Boyd, J. H., & De Nicoló, G. (2005). The theory of bank risk taking and competition revisited. *The Journal of Finance, 60*(3), 1329–1343.

Federal Reserve Survey of Senior Loan Officers (all data). Available at http://www.federalreserve.gov/boarddocs/SnloanSurvey.

Karatash, A. (2010). Greek crisis highlights Turkey's strength. *Bloomberg Businessweek*, April 26.

Reinhart, C. M., & Rogoff, K. S. (2008). Is the 2007 US sub-prime financial crisis so different? An international historical comparison. *American Economic Review: Papers and Proceedings, 98*(2), 1–6.